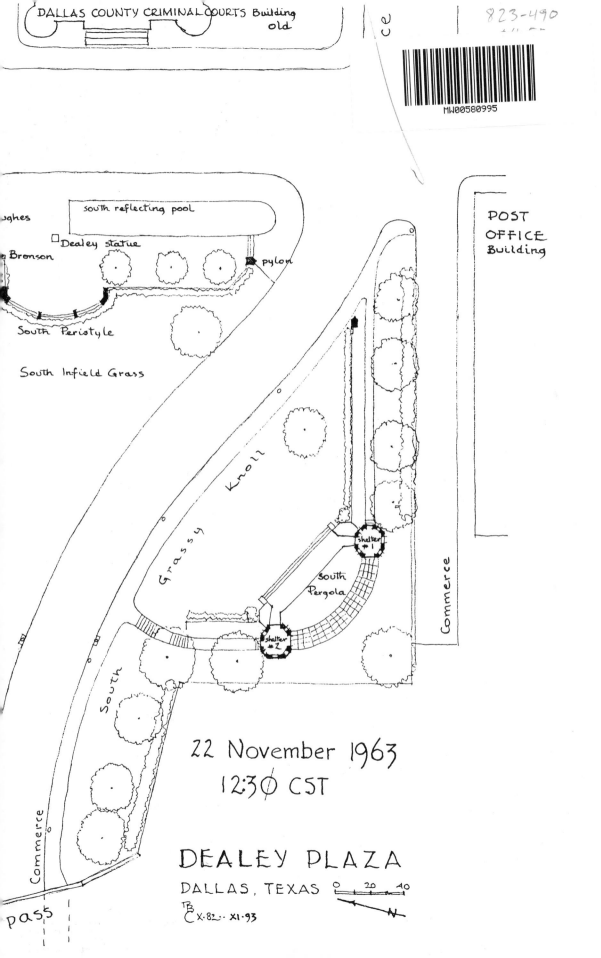

DALLAS COUNTY CRIMINAL COURTS Building
old

823-490

POST
OFFICE
Building

south reflecting pool

Dealey statue

...ughes

Bronson

pylon

South Peristyle

South Infield Grass

Grassy Knoll

Commerce

shelter #1

South Pergola

shelter #2

South

Commerce

22 November 1963
12:30 CST

DEALEY PLAZA

DALLAS, TEXAS

0    20    40

N

TB
C X·82·· X1·93

pass

# PICTURES
## OF THE PAIN

Also by Richard B. Trask

*Salem Village And The Witch Hysteria (1975, revised 1991)*
*As The Century Turned (co-authored, 1989)*
*The Devil Hath Been Raised (1992)*

# PICTURES OF THE PAIN

### PHOTOGRAPHY
### AND THE
### ASSASSINATION OF PRESIDENT KENNEDY

*By*
*Richard B. Trask*

Yeoman Press
Danvers, Massachusetts
1994

Publisher's Cataloguing-in-Publication Data

Trask, Richard Barry, 1947—
        Pictures of the pain:  photography and the assassination of
        President Kennedy/Richard B. Trask.
            639 p.        cm.
        Includes bibliographical references and index.
        1. Kennedy, John F. (John Fitzgerald), 1917-1963—Assassination.
        2. Kennedy, John F. (John Fitzgerald), 1917-1963—Portraits,
                caricatures, etc.
        I. Title.

        Library of Congress Catalogue Card Number:  93-61324
        ISBN 0-9638595-0-1
        E842.9                364.1′524

Printed excerpt credits appear on page *xiv*.
Photograph credits appear on pages 628-629.


Printed in the United States of America

For information, address:
YEOMAN PRESS
35 Centre Street
Danvers, MA  01923

*To Ethel B. Trask*
*with gratitude for all that she has done,*
*and love for all that she is.*

*They say they can't believe it; It's a sacrilegious shame.*
*Now, who would want to hurt such a hero of the game?*
*But you know I predicted it; I knew he had to fall.*
*How did it happen? Hope his suffering was small.*
*Tell me every detail, for I've got to know it all,*
*And do you have a picture of the pain?*

From "The Crucifixion"
By Phil Ochs

CRUCIFIXION
Lyrics and Music by Phil Ochs
©1966 BARRICADE MUSIC, INC. (ASCAP)
All Rights Administered by ALMO MUSIC CORP. (ASCAP)
All Rights Reserved—International Copyright Secured

# Contents

# Acknowledgments

Had I known how long and costly this journey would be, I might not have commenced upon it. Yet at its culmination I am satisfied to have made the effort. Pioneer assassination photo researcher Richard E. Sprague told me in 1984, "You will be drawn further into the puzzle — you can't help it." He was correct. It has been over ten long years of research taking me physically to numerous libraries and sources in Massachusetts, Texas, New York, Washington D.C., Florida, and Pennsylvania. I have attempted to ferret out all the available references to photographs and films made at the time of the assassination of President Kennedy which can be found, including through numerous Freedom of Information Act requests. My telephone has logged countless hours of conversation around the country, and my correspondence files bulge with thousands of letters and documents. One November 22 in the mid-1980s I spent hours with full access to the then empty upper stories of the former Texas School Book Depository Building. Subsequently on various trips I have spent days inspecting almost every yard of Dealey Plaza. During my first visit there I was surprised to see how small and compact the Plaza is and how close Elm Street appears from the sixth floor window of the Book Depository, reality being different from the perceptions of those spaces as seen from photographic sources alone.

I have had the experience of walking and riding, often with photographer-eyewitnesses, throughout Fort Worth, Dallas and Dealey Plaza itself retracing the events of November 22, 1963. The evening of November 21, 1993, I had the unique privilege to listen as one of a threesome at the southeast corner of "The Sixth Floor" exhibit in the old Book Depository as Tom Dillard and Bob Jackson reminisced about what they had seen in this corner 30 years earlier.

Many fine people have shared with me their home hospitality and hours of their time. I have listened to audiotapes and watched videotapes and 8mm and 16mm films by the hour in my own library and at such places as the National Archives and the John F. Kennedy Library. At times the repetition of visual images and the forward and backward drone of sound bytes has taken on a surreal atmosphere. Through the kindness and slowly built trust of persons who were at first reluctant to share their stories or their images, I have been given the opportunity to examine hundreds of film prints and negatives. Through the lens of a magnifying loupe I have looked through closed collections of newspaper negatives and contact sheets. One long day from noon into nightfall, I sat at a desk at the *Dallas Morning News* going through their rich collections, occasionally glancing out of the window in front of me at the former School Book Depository Building, visible and sphinx-like, just a few blocks away.

With notable exceptions, during my research I have attempted to keep from being too familiar with the assassination research network, so as not to jeopardize my independence and credibility. I have often chosen to go it alone and keep my own counsel. Yet, as an observer I have attended several assassination symposia around the country to remain current on new research and possible leads.

My appreciation is offered most cordially to those photographers and others who were at the assassination scene in 1963 and to their families who have been so helpful to me in my research. Though some were less than enthused to have been located and several quite reluctant to talk, I found most extremely generous with their time and effort. Several I am now pleased to consider as friends. A few are now deceased. Among this group of witnesses or family members who have been so helpful are: James W. Altgens; Mr. & Mrs. Charles L. Bronson; Cecil W. and Faith Stoughton; Jim Murray; Thomas Atkins; George E. Smith; Mr. & Mrs. Philip L. Willis; Jim Featherston; Bob Jackson; Mel McIntire; Robert E. Croft, Jr.; Henry D. Burroughs; Bert N. Shipp; F. M. "Mark" Bell; Harry Cabluck; Mrs. Wanda A. Rickerby; W. G. Lumpkin; Thomas J. Craven, Jr.; Frank Cancellare; Kent Biffle; Eddie Barker; Hugh Aynesworth; Gerald Hill; Mrs. Robert J. E. Hughes; David R. Miller; Jean L. Hill; Mrs. Sylvia J. Sara; the family of Wilma Bond; Mrs. R. O. Bothun; William Allen; Hugh W. Betzner, Jr.; Thomas C. Dillard; Tony Record; Jarrold Cabluck; Mrs. Rose A. Cancellare; Tom Alyea; Jimmy Darnell; Denise M. Miller; Charles Brehm; Wilburn G. Davis; Harold Norman; John Shroeder; Darwin Payne; David Taylor; Bill Winfrey; Norman Bradford; Robert E. Miller; Dave Wiegman, Jr.; and Clint Grant.

I would also like to extend my thanks to those persons who are among the loose federation of what the public would term as Kennedy assassination buffs. Many of them have done pioneering work or found or preserved valuable information. Though I heartily disagree with many of them as to their conclusions in this case, on those occasions in which I solicited their help or sources, they were willing to help me in my work. Their assistance in major or minor roles is very much appreciated. Among them are: Robert B. Cutler, Richard E. Sprague, Paul Hoch, Jerry D. Rose, Larry A. Sneed, Martin Shackelford, Mark A. Oakes, Dave Hawkins, Harold Weisberg, Mary M. Ferrell, John R. Woods II, Bernard Fensterwald, Jr., Hal Verb, Howard Upchurch, Andy and Linda Winiarczyk, Gary Mack, Todd Wayne Vaughan, Stephan N. Barber and Stewart C. Yeakel.

For their reference and technical expertise or their assistance in various aspects of this book, I also want to acknowledge the following people and, when applicable, their institutions in the form current at the time of my research: The John Fitzgerald Kennedy Library staff and Allan B. Goodrich, Supervisory Archivist, Audiovisual Archives; Kristin Sandefur, Head Librarian for *The Fort Worth Star-Telegram* and her assistants; Robert H. Selzer, Supervisor, Biomedical Image Processing Group, Jet Propulsion Laboratory; Kathie Burns, Archivist, Western New England College, Springfield, Massachusetts; Staff of the Peabody Institute Library of Danvers, Massachusetts; Billie B. Shaddix, Director of Photographic Services, The White House; John Loengard, Picture Editor, *LIFE* ; Kathryn Chirametti, Senior Collections Librarian, Metropolitan Toronto Reference Library; Dave Powers, Museum Curator, John Fitzgerald Kennedy Library; Ronna Berezin, Polaroid Corporate Archives; C. Ruska, Librarian, Hillcrest High School, Dallas, Texas; Neil Waldman, Director, Archives Development, CBS News; John L. Sigalos, Esq.; Thomas W. Young; Charles J. Ginter, Library Director, Indianola, Iowa, Public Library; R. Orozco, Fort Worth Public Library, Periodicals and Government Documents; Gary Beckworth, P.C.; R. T. Delaney, Itek; James Helminski, Municipal Processor, Myriam Marshall, Manuscript Processor, and Anna T. Zakarija, Research Assistant, The Richard Sprague Papers, Special Collection Division, Georgetown University Library; Barry Kaplan and the Finer Image Photo Lab, Danvers, Massachusetts; Matt Quinn, Reporter, WFAA-TV; Mrs. Reuben H. Adams and Mrs. Clifton Caldwell, Dallas County Historical Foundation; Ms. Conover Hunt, Museum Consultations; Ms. Cheryl Price, Director, Special Services, Dallas County Historical Foundation; David R. Wrone, Department of History, University of Wisconsin; Robert H. Johnson, AP Chief of Bureau, Albuquerque, New Mexico; Sharon Jones and Joan L. Dobson, Dallas Public Library; James K. Hall and Emil P. Moschella, Chief, Freedom of Information-Privacy Acts Section, Justice Department; Yuien Chin, Researcher, NBC News Archives; E. Philip Scott, Audiovisual Archivist, Lyndon Baines Johnson Library; Theresa J. Cartmell, Reference Librarian, Centralia, Illinois, Public Library; Patricia McGraw, Records Analyst, City of Dallas; Edward "Cort" Foley; John K. Lattimer, M.D., Sci.D., College of Physicians and Surgeons of Columbia University; Bryan Woolley, Senior Reporter, *Dallas Morning News* ; Christopher LaPlante, Assistant Director, Texas State Archives; Robert T. Johnson, JFK Assassination Information Center, Dallas, Texas; Marion M. Johnson, Civil Reference Branch, National Archives; Sharyn B. Westmoreland, Administrator, Dallas County Historical Commission; Cindy C. Smolovik, Archivist, Manager, Dallas Municipal Archives and Records Center; Leslie C. Waffen, Motion Picture, Sound and Video Branch, National Archives; Jack Simon, Robert Howard, and Tom Gilbert, Wide World Photos, Inc.; Ms. Eve Pellegrino, The Bettman Archive; Paul Arbor, *LIFE* Picture Sales; Dr. Richard P. Zollo, Boothbay Harbor, Maine; A. L. Morris, West Kennebunk, Maine; Phoenix Publishing and Adrian Paradis, Sugar Hill, New Hampshire; Knowlton and McLeary, Farmington, Maine; R. B. Cutler, Cutler Designs, Manchester-by-the-Sea, Massachusetts; Richard J. Wollensak, Vice President, Program Development, Litton/Itek Optical Systems; Bob Mong, Managing Editor, *The Dallas*

*Morning News*; *The Dallas Morning News* photo department; and those many others (some of whom wish to remain anonymous) to whom I will always be grateful.

I also extend my love and grateful thanks to my supportive family and friends who have encouraged me in this overlong project. As ever, Vartkis and Pauline Boghosian, Mildred Trask, and Elizabeth May Trask have been especially encouraging. My greatest appreciation is given to my wife Ethel, to whom this work is dedicated. She is an equal partner in the project and the foundation of my efforts. Without her this work would never have been accomplished.

Excerpts from *Six Seconds in Dallas,* by Josiah Thompson, Copyright ©1967, reprinted with the permission of the original publisher, Bernard Geis Associates. Excerpts from *Best Evidence*, by David S. Lifton, Copyright ©1980 by David S. Lifton; Foreword Copyright ©1992 by David S. Lifton; Afterword Copyright ©1988 by David S. Lifton; used by permission of Dutton Signet, a division of Penguin Books USA, Inc. Excerpts from *Whitewash II; The FBI—Secret Service Coverup*, Copyright ©1966, by Harold Weisberg, and *Photographic Whitewash: Suppressed Kennedy Assassination Pictures*, Copyright ©1967, 1976, by Harold Weisberg, reprinted by permission of Harold Weisberg. Excerpts from "A Physicist Examines the Kennedy Assassination Film," by Luis W. Alvarez from the September 1976 edition of the *American Journal of Physics*, Copyright ©1976 reprinted by permission of Editor. Excerpts from *The Nix Film Analysis*, by Itek, Copyright ©1967 and *John F. Kennedy Assassination Film Analysis* by Itek, Copyright ©1976, reprinted by permission of Litton/Itek Optical Systems. Excerpts from "JFK's Death, Part II," by Dennis L. Breo from the May 27, 1992 edition of *Journal of the American Medical Association*, v. 267, p. 2806, Copyright ©1992, reprinted by permission of The American Medical Association. Excerpt from *JFK: The Last Dissenting Witness*, by Bill Sloan with Jean Hill, Copyright ©1992, reprinted by permission of Pelican Publishing Company, Inc. Excerpts from *Final Disclosure*, by David W. Belin, Copyright ©1988 by David W. Belin, reprinted with permission of Charles Scribner's Sons, an imprint of Macmillan Publishing Company. Excerpts from "The Shadow of a Gunman," by Maurice W. Schonfeld from the July/August 1975 edition of *Columbia Journalism Review*, Copyright ©1975, reprinted by permission of *Columbia Journalism Review* and Reese Schonfeld. Excerpts from *Kennedy and Lincoln: Medical and Ballistic Comparisons of their Assassinations*, by John K. Lattimer, Copyright ©1980, reprinted by permission of John K. Lattimer. Excerpts from "What Happened Next," by Richard B. Stolley, from the November 1973 edition of *Esquire*, Copyright ©1973, reprinted by permission of Esquire and the Hearst Corporation. Excerpts from *American Grotesque: An Account of the Clay Shaw — Jim Garrison Affair in the City of New Orleans*, by James Kirkwood, Copyright ©1968, 1970 by James Kirkwood, reprinted by permission of International Creative Management, Inc., New York. Excerpts from *Seventy-Six Seconds in Dealey Plaza*, by R. B. Cutler, Copyright ©1978 by R. B. Cutler, reprinted by permission of author. Excerpts from *Eyewitness to History. The Kennedy Assassination: As Seen By Howard Brennan*, by Howard L. Brennan with J. Edward Cherryholmes, Copyright ©1987, reprinted by permission of Texian Press. Excerpts from *The JFK Conspiracy HOAX,* an unpublished manuscript by Tom Alyea and *JFK Facts Update, Preview Edition*, Box 4266, Tulsa OK 74159, a newsletter relating to Mr. Alyea's work, ©Tom Alyea, reprinted by permission.

# Introduction

I was sixteen when he died. Perhaps nothing in my past has so captivated my attention longer than the consequences of those shots fired in Dallas. Other circumstances and events have been personally more traumatic, and during the past 30 years there have been large blocks of time when President John F. Kennedy and his death have all but been abandoned within my mind. Yet inexplicably I am drawn back to this subject.

Like so many of my generation, I found a positive attraction and connection to this man who spoke of ideals to match my own. He had a style, a grace, and a humor which even an adolescent could tell was unusual. As a middle-class Catholic from Massachusetts who possessed great interest in history and was just becoming politically aware, I reveled in the excitement of this native son reaching his way for the presidency. I watched the 1960 Democratic Convention on TV late into the night. During the presidential campaign I exuberantly accumulated a collection of campaign literature, wore on my jacket an embarrassingly large "Kennedy for President" button, voted for him in a school straw poll election, and spent several hours of school time on election day thinking I was quite privileged to be chosen to observe voting at a local precinct. As darkness fell that election evening, I walked down to the local storefront campaign office and obtained a red, white and blue JFK poster. Returning home I watched the TV coverage throughout the night and marked vote tally numbers on a home-made scorecard. And so it was that as a kid, like tens, if not hundreds of thousands of other teenagers, I became enthralled with the excitement and idealism of "The New Frontier." Through television, *LIFE* magazine, and the Boston newspapers, I felt connected with the world. On Inauguration Day, I audiotaped hours of television and from then on I paid attention to news about my President.

Following a mail request, on November 20, 1963, I excitedly received an envelope marked, "The White House." In it was a requested engraved presidential signature card. Two mornings later I remember seeing a political cartoon in a Boston newspaper about the President's visit to Dallas and hearing on the radio an excerpt from his address given the night before. On that crisp, bright Friday afternoon I was in homeroom just prior to the 2:00 weekend dismissal. A wildfire rumor spread from class to class that the President had been shot in Dallas. In my mind's eye I remembered seeing a *You Are There* TV program hosted by Walter Cronkite which portrayed the attempted assassination of former President Teddy Roosevelt. Though wounded, Roosevelt insisted on giving his campaign speech. I could just imagine President Kennedy doing likewise, and thought what a marvelous red badge of courage an assassination attempt would be during the upcoming 1964 re-election campaign. My illusions of youthful bravado and courage were quickly shattered. Except for the death of my father some eight years earlier, no death had up till then ever seemed so sad and wasteful. And now, even after all these intervening years and all the revisionist historians and tabloid press which first attempted to deify Kennedy and now seem to relish trashing all his deeds and motives; and even after personally studying his death in numbing and minute detail, I can still on occasion catch myself feeling a personal hurt of losing a good man, a father figure, and some of my own innocence those decades ago on a street in Dallas.

Like most others, I could not understand how such a seemingly unremarkable nobody as accused assassin Lee Harvey Oswald could have caused such damage to the President's family, our nation, and to me personally. I wanted to know more. When the 26 volumes of the Warren Commission *Hearings* were published, I was able to obtain a set. I wrote to witnesses, many of whom answered. I read almost every book on the subject voraciously. For many years I believed that a large and masterful conspiracy must have been responsible for taking the life of the President. By the late 1970s, I wasn't so sure about an intricate plot, and began to feel manipulated by writers and critics.

Following undergraduate and graduate degrees in history, I became an archivist dealing chiefly with documentation of pre-20th century America. I married, bought a house and had a family. Yet there was always an urge to contribute something constructive in the line of research on the assassination of President Kennedy and to be able to put a personal closure on the subject. I had long ago understood that events and history seldom are composed of easily defined causes and effects, and that one who always wants to find logic or sense from actions in history does not truly understand history. History is often serendipity. Yet the Kennedy assassination continues to attract persons needing to find a logicality to the motive of the killer or killers. A scanning of the shelves of any bookstore will confirm the continued interest in the events of November 22, 1963. Almost every imaginable theory, and indeed some unimaginable ones, have been committed to print supposedly revealing the "Who Done It?" in this, the most famous murder case in modern history. It has been particularly troublesome to see so many of these works so devoid of fundamental scholarship and so exploitatively shallow.

Having both an interest in photography and in the illustrated record of history, I thought that the plentiful, yet generally ignored area of the photographic history of the assassination had been very much under-studied. Historical photography is typically

defined as the use of photographic images capable of supporting the study and interpretation of history.  Photography has limitations for use as historical evidence and
may exhibit only partial truths, biases and distortions of reality.  It can never tell the
whole story of an event.  Yet for all its potential shortcomings, it is closer to being a
trace of reality than any other documentation.  In 1983 I decided to give positive vent
to my interest in the subject of photography and the Kennedy assassination.

My original intention was to gather together research materials and create a
dozen or so copies for distribution within institutional collections.  The more success I
had in finding eyewitnesses not previously interviewed, whose information proved
revealing to the story of the assassination and to the history of photography and media
coverage in the 1960s, the more I was drawn to continue and expand the quest.  Though
I had believed this subject too specific and esoteric to be of trade publication interest,
by five years into my research I finally thought the material worthy enough to test this
assumption.  A resulting condensed version of one of my chapters was accepted and
published in *American Heritage* in November 1988.  A health problem and later com-
mitments to extracurricular work in the field of local history sidetracked my full effort
until last year.  By then my work, which I did not want to submit for publication until
nearing completion, was beyond any hope of finding a publisher willing and able to
commit on such short notice to publish in calendar 1993.  I was vain enough to believe
in the quality of my research and not to want to waste the considerable time and research money previously spent to relegating the text to a few unpublished manuscript
copies.  Thus the decision was made to spend even more money and self-publish a small
but respectable run of books.

I am fortunate to be married to a remarkable and talented woman.  My wife
Ethel, though never interested as a "buff" in the assassination, had always been supportive of my interests.  She never questioned my expensive research, knowing it was important to me, and as a business teacher with a proficiency in personal computers, she
processed my tiny handwriting into readable typescript.

When we together reached the decision to self-publish, we quickly had to
expand our knowledge of book production, layout, permission requests, Library of
Congress book numbers, ISBN request forms, and a myriad of new worries.  To save
money and assure a product that was truly our own, Ethel became the project's typog-
rapher.  With the exception of the actual printing and binding of the volumes, all the rest
has been put together by the two of us.  It has become a very personal work, and we
have striven to make it as attractive and complete as possible.

Self-publication, however, has its drawbacks.  One ends up doing tasks which a
publishing company has a staff of professionals to perform.  Mostly I miss a dedicated
editor who could have critically commented upon the text and assisted in its formulation
and composition.  It also would have been a luxury to have others responsible for
contacting photo sources and, in many cases, paying steep reproduction fees.  Yet for all

the drawbacks associated with self-publishing, the advantages are that the reader has a fuller text than a commercial publisher would have financially been willing to produce. The number of photographs reproduced here are undoubtedly greater than the selection a trade publication would have finally allowed.

This volume does not constitute a new, unified theory of who killed President Kennedy. By this time the answer or answers to that question are so rife with facts, perceived facts, half-truths, innuendoes, self-serving statements, and lies, as to make the truth virtually indistinguishable among the logjam of documents and books. I did not want to add to the cacophony. Rather I decided to keep my focus upon the photographic history of the event centered around Dealey Plaza.

Almost everyone has seen the shocking Abraham Zapruder assassination film, but few realize that in the Dealey Plaza area of Dallas on that mild 1963 fall noon-time, dozens of others had cameras with them. These observers of history recorded in various photographic formats and with differing equipment and skills, the last moments in the life of a United States Chief Executive. They included men, women, and youngsters, top professional photojournalists as well as rank amateurs, who captured on their film in a form truer than any person's eye or memory, brief, relevant and dramatic slices of the reality of the scene. As a result of their camera work, they created objects which can be examined and interpreted as true historical artifacts of the incident itself.

While several of these pictures gained wide publication and notoriety and were the subject of later controversy and scientific study, many of these photos and films would not come to light for years. Scores of them have still not been seen by the public. The history of these photos and films, and the people who created them, makes an intriguing story. It is a story that has never been fully told, for many of the photo witnesses were never interviewed.

The most important area of my research has been to seek out and then interview several dozen of the photographers themselves. White House film maker Tom Atkins, who traveled with the Kennedy entourage and took exceptional color film that day, would in the course of our conversations lament, "I wish this event had never happened, but it did, and if I had to be somewhere in the world that day, I'm glad that I was in Dallas. If only I could have done something — anything to alter the outcome instead of merely recording it." Atkins, like many others, including the Mormon missionary who left Dallas by train within 15 minutes of taking his photos in Dealey Plaza, were at first reluctant to speak with me and chagrined to have been located. They feared I would distort or misuse their recollections. A persistence and care in earning the trust of most of those I located allows me to tell their stories. Among the photographic witnesses I found have been a teenager whose efforts in taking pictures of the motorcade rivaled the best professional photographer, two network cameramen, professional photographers from the White House, Associated Press, UPI, *LIFE* magazine, and various of the local press.

The structure of this volume is in "stand alone" chapters wherein the photographers are introduced as to their backgrounds, circumstances of being at the scene, and camera information. The known printed and written primary source documentation is combined with interviews into a narrative of their activity, eyewitness accounts, and the visual materials created. We see through their eyes the assassination story as they personally experienced it. When appropriate, as with such famous photos as those taken by AP's Jim Altgens and amateurs Mary Moorman and Abraham Zapruder, the story includes how these images were used by the government, media, and critics to explain the assassination or to attempt to discover in this material evidence of an assassination conspiracy. Some probable photographic fakers who have stepped forward in more recent years with their claims are critically examined, while many of the so-called evidences of conspiracy supposedly discovered in certain photos are shown to be merely the imprecise interpretation of photographs made by some of the conspiracy buffs. The sloppiness of the early government investigations as regards photographic evidence is also spotlighted.

In the examination of historical photographs we must be cautious to realize the limits of photography. The medium upon which a photographic image is made also skews our view of the reality of the event being photographed, be it caused by the inferior optics of a cheap box camera or the tonal differences among present-day color film dyes. Visual images must be critically examined, understanding that they can distort, simplify, or misrepresent reality by means of the photographers' including or excluding items (purposefully or accidentally) or pointing the camera in one direction to the exclusion of others. An examination of photographic documentation and the sophisticated image processing methods developed over the last several decades cannot give us "the" truth and reality at Dallas, but rather "a" truth and reality of the event. The story of the photographers at Dallas and their photos and films is a revealing study of the use and abuse of photographic analysis. It captures in rich detail and from a multi-perspective view, what this unique group of eyewitnesses saw and recorded on film during this momentous event.

With regard to several practical textural matters in this book, the notes on sources utilized are included at the end of each chapter. I believe this system to be more useful to those who enjoy frequently referring to them, than if they were included as backnotes. So as not to fill the text and chapter notes with astronomical numbers of references, unless noted, I have essentially bundled references together at the conclusion of a paragraph, rather than numbering each reference. The form of reference is also shortened in the chapter notes to include for published sources an author, title, and page reference. A select bibliography of the published books and articles will be found at the back of the book. When I speak of the assassination and refer to the information within the photos and films themselves, the text is written in the present tense.

I have attempted to acknowledge all sources used and I have sought permission for all published sources directly quoted. When possible, I have tried to use the wordsof the eyewitnesses or the sources writing about the photos, believing primary sources are always better than paraphrasing. I have also attempted to make this volume as inclusive as possible.

It was not my intention to seek, nor my expectation to find, the truth of the question of who killed John Fitzgerald Kennedy. Yet through the accumulating, sorting, and weighing of the documentation and evidence discovered during my lengthy research, I cannot intellectually avoid an opinion within the area of my study. Concentrating specifically on that point of time during and just after the assassination itself in and around Dealey Plaza, and on the testimonies, experiences and resulting photos and films generated by photographer-witnesses, I am convinced that three shots were fired from the sixth floor southeast corner window of the Texas School Book Depository Building. Most likely the second shot hit both President Kennedy and Governor Connally, while the third bullet resulted in the decimating head shot to the President. No convincing or compelling evidence from the photographs or films or from credible witnesses strongly supports the idea that a shot or shots were fired from the grassy knoll area. The known photographs and films, even those to which critics have tied their conspiracy beliefs, do not presently reveal evidence of a conspiracy. In fact, my research helps to debunk a number of such supposed items of evidence. Lee Harvey Oswald appears, from the evidence derived at the scene, to be the likely assassin. The scope of my research did not treat Oswald's background or life, nor did it, other than through the photographic history, look deeply into the death of Oswald or of his killer Jack Ruby's motives and background. From this specifically focused study, I cannot say that others did not conspire with or assist Oswald, or that others absolutely were not present at the scene the day of the assassination. I can say, however, that the evidence of the sixth floor sniper, in all probability Oswald, is compelling.

It will be up to the reader to decide if this introductory statement is justified. The text will attempt to refrain from overbearing editorialization. Rather, each chapter serves as an independent portion of the complex tale, forming a patchwork of stories, of truths and of perspectives never before blended together concerning the events associated with the assassination in Dealey Plaza on November 22, 1963.

*Richard B. Trask*

# PART ONE

## THE WHITE HOUSE PHOTOGRAPHER

President Kennedy delivers his "Alabama Crisis" address to the nation from the Oval Office. Cecil Stoughton (left hand to chin) is there to photograph the June 11, 1963, speech.

President Kennedy greets the 9th Pan American Highway Congress on the White House grounds.
Cecil Stoughton (front row, right with smaller of the two cameras) records the event.

## CHAPTER 1

# "Show Us Where We Are"

It had the feeling of a typical motorcade procession, as typical, that is, as a motorcade can be when you are traveling along with the President of the United States. Cecil Stoughton had been in numerous such processions during the last 35 months. As official White House photographer and a captain in the United States Army, Stoughton had made over 8,000 pictures of events surrounding the activities of President John Fitzgerald Kennedy and the First Family.[1] During the last two days, Stoughton had taken dozens of pictures of the President's much-publicized autumn visit to Texas. He had made exposures of the President and his lovely wife being greeted by numerous dignitaries, special groups, and hordes of common people, many who would hopefully also be Kennedy supporters in the upcoming presidential election of 1964. This was Stoughton's fifth motorcade of the Texas trip, and it seemed not noticeably different from similar receptions the day before at Houston, and San Antonio, and at Fort Worth.

Some of the news people traveling along with the presidential party appeared to want to make more of the fact that this was Dallas — a town possessing a rough right-wing reputation, but Stoughton did not discern anything in the airport reception crowd that indicated hostility towards the President. If anything, the crowd along the route looked larger than in previous motorcades.

It was near the end of the downtown motorcade procession when the open Chevrolet convertible reserved for the still photographers and positioned as the seventh car behind the President's Lincoln, was preparing to make a sharp left turn on a street adjacent to a small park that Stoughton heard three loud reports. Stoughton turned to his left to *LIFE* magazine staff photographer Art Rickerby and exclaimed, "Boy! These Texans know how to welcome a guy, don't they?" In his mind he visualized a Texas cowboy wearing a ten-gallon hat standing on a rooftop and waving a six-shooter while firing it into the sky.[2] Confused reality quickly replaced images of local color. Stoughton, though he could not as yet comprehend it, was for the next few hours not working for his now former President, nor for the United States Army. Rather, beyond any pedantic, immediate, political, or souvenir photographic consideration, he was working, now more than at any time in his career, for the historical record. American presidential history had just taken an oblique turn, not as a result of the ballots of millions of people that Kennedy had been spending so great an effort in wooing, but by the obscene blasts of the barrel of a rifle.

~

Cecil William Stoughton was born in Oskaloosa, Iowa, on January 18, 1920, and at the age of 20 he enlisted in the Army Air Corps seeking a possible photographic career. After war broke out he was sent to a *LIFE* magazine training course, and was assigned to the 13th Air Force, headquartered at Guadalcanal in a unit commanded by one of Hollywood's academy award winning directors, Frank Lloyd. Stoughton worked in both motion picture and still photography in the South Pacific theater of operations during the war, and by 1947 he had determined to make a career of photography in the armed forces. Assigned to Military Air Transport Service, Stoughton served in Hawaii until 1951, when he was reassigned as a motion picture cameraman to the Joint Chiefs of Staff, under the supervision of the Office of the Secretary of Defense. In 1954 he sailed on the shake-down cruise of the first nuclear-powered submarine, the USS *Nautilus*, and in 1957 he traded his Air Force sergeant's stripes for a direct commission as a first lieutenant in the Army Signal Corps as an officer-photographer. In 1958 General Chester V. "Ted" Clifton, Deputy Chief of Information of the Army, needed a photographer for Army Missile Command special assignments, and Stoughton was selected to become photographic officer at Huntsville, Alabama. As part of his assignment Stoughton photographed significant Cape Canaveral launches, including the first successfully launched United States satellite.[3]

By late 1960 Stoughton was working under Major General Clifton at the Pentagon in Washington and was assigned to take pictures of President-elect Kennedy's inauguration. Stoughton had photographed previous presidential inaugurations, and knew where some of the Capitol Building's best vantage points were located. On Inauguration Day, January 20, 1961, Stoughton, using his own initiative, worked his way up to a good spot on the inaugural stand and managed to make a photo of President Kennedy showing a full-face photo using a normal camera lens. General Clifton, who had been appointed military aide to the President, was impressed with Stoughton's photos and showed them to Kennedy, who was also impressed. Clifton suggested to the President that it might be a good idea to have this photographer available to the White House.[4]

Prior to this time, there had never been an "in-house" photographer specifically assigned to the President. Clifton's suggestion of such an inside photographer who would be at the beck and call of the White House, could provide all sorts of souvenir and historical record photographs and, due to the nature of the work would not be competition to the press photographers, seemed an attractive idea. Positive results from such a White House photographer could only add to General Clifton's standing with the President, and if perchance the photographer screwed up, as Stoughton would later wryly comment, "I'd be in Guam tomorrow."[5]

As the weeks passed following Stoughton's new assignment, the White House staff became more familiar with one another. Stoughton's office was right underneath the President's, and he arranged with the President's secretary, Mrs. Evelyn Lincoln, to have a buzzer hooked up to his basement desk, so that when a picture was needed or an opportunity presented itself, Stoughton could be buzzed. The staff also began tipping him off about various developments. After a while, recalls Stoughton, "I became such a part of the scene, that many times I didn't even need a telephoto lens. I was close enough just to take pictures normally. And they expected it."[6]

The value of a presidential photographer from a branch of the military service was not lost on White House Navy Aide, Captain Tazewell Shepard, as later the Navy provided their own photographer, Robert Knudsen, with Thomas Atkins coming aboard in early 1963 to do motion picture work. This inter-service military aide rivalry never bothered the photographers personally, as they got along well, and often found themselves assigned to the same event. Shades of one-upmanship were evident on occasion, however. Stoughton would often cover the visit of an important dignitary, making pictures of the VIP's activities,

White House photographers Cecil Stoughton (right) and Robert Knudsen off Newport, R.I., Sept. 22, 1962

which at the end of the visit would be presented to the dignitary by the State Department in a remembrance album. When Navy cameraman Atkins was assigned to the White House, part of his duty was to make color movies of such visits, presenting an edited film to the departing guest, and on occasion a new projector to go along with the movie film.[7]

Captain Stoughton was on call to make pictures of whatever the President did that required photography for the record or simply as cherished mementoes for a visitor to the Oval Office. Wherever the President went during regular work schedules or on weekend vacations to Hyannis, Massachusetts, or Palm Beach, Florida, the working press would follow, and Stoughton would often go for historical documentation. He recalls that the President and his wife "were good about not using me in times when it was unnecessary. They weren't just frivolous assignments. I'd get a call once or twice at home to come in and do something that hadn't been thought of prior to that, but that was no problem."[8]

Never becoming personally familiar with his Commander-in-Chief, Stoughton nevertheless became a devoted member of the President's team. He often had closer access to the First Family than most of the staff, but he did his work as unobtrusively as possible. He shot his pictures fast, knowing that Kennedy would usually only stand still for a couple of shots, before going off in a different direction. He also quickly learned that the President's nod or a particular glance in Stoughton' direction meant that time was up.[9]

During official presidential sojourns out of the White House, Stoughton did not have 100 percent access to the President or the event. His position during these trips was looked upon as part of the press package. Stoughton would ride with the press in their plane or in a press car within a motorcade. At speeches and other stationary events, Stoughton soon became familiar with and friendly towards many of the Secret Service agents, so that he was recognized as no threat and could be about his job without any fuss. Stoughton remembers many of the agents as his buddies. He often helped out the working photographers by getting the agents to let the photographers come up one at a time and take pictures in what was often a restricted area.[10]

Stoughton's face was often captured in press photos due to the nature of his job. "My job was for the most part to show where the President was, where they were, whom they were with, and what they were doing, not just pictures of their faces. Mrs. Kennedy often said, 'We know what we look like, we don't want pictures of us, show us where we are.' In other words, get behind us. So I'm behind in a lot of pictures."[11]

Stoughton's access to the President was not always consistent. Unlike later assignments with President Johnson, and with the normal procedures of later presidential photographers who are almost constantly near their subject, during tours Stoughton often had to scramble along with other press photographers. "And then when we'd go the weekends to Hyannis, I would have access all day Saturday and Sunday, and my buddies would hire a boat and try to see him with long lenses from a rocking boat. And I'm on the *Honey Fitz* [boat] with him. But they knew that and didn't object because I didn't do anything with the pictures. I didn't give them to AP and UPI."[12]

Stoughton's favorite sequence of presidential pictures taken during his career occurred in October 1962, when the President's children Caroline and John-John made one of their frequent visits to their father in the Oval Office. Recalls Stoughton, "I heard the President clapping and singing out, 'Hey, Here's John-John.'" Stoughton was at the door, and the President signaled for him to come in. Within three minutes Stoughton had squeezed off twelve pictures recording the President playing with his children. After they were processed, Stoughton brought them to Kennedy. The President chose one, and summoning Press Secretary Pierre Salinger told him that particular picture should be released to the press who were always clamoring for such an informal family photo. With that for one rare occasion a Stoughton picture was distributed to the press and was

Captain Stoughton's photo inscribed to him by the President

published around the world.  Later Stoughton requested the President to autograph a copy of this picture, Kennedy inscribing, "For Captain Stoughton, who captured beautifully a happy moment at the White House.  John F. Kennedy."[13]

The mainstay of Stoughton's photographic equipment were two cameras — an Alpha Reflex and a 500 C Hasselblad.  The Alpha Reflex was a 35mm SLR, usually used along with a wide-angle 35mm or a 180mm telephoto lens.  Stoughton's favorite, however, was the Hasselblad.  "The Hasselblad was my tool, an extension of my right arm.  I used it every chance I got.  Hasselblad was a magazine camera with interchangeable magazines.  You would put black-and-white in one, color in one, transparency film in one."  The camera bodies were Army property, although some of his interchangeable lenses were borrowed, including a newly introduced 50mm, which Stoughton obtained from the Hasselblad people in late 1963.  An 80mm and 150mm lens were also used on a regular basis, and Stoughton shot his 120 film into a 12-frame sequence, using the Hasselblad magazine.  Stoughton would use the type of film most appropriate to the occasion. "If it was a colorful event, well, I'd use color. But a lot of times black-and-white was appropriate and adequate."[14]

Although Stoughton was an in-house staff member, neither his photo lab, nor photo archive, was located within the White House. At this time there was no photographic department at the White House, and although most staff understood the concept of photographic documentation for the record, the function was still under the Army or Naval Aide's wing. The immediate use of the photographs was often for the expedient objective of politics, good will, and campaign pictures, without specific forethought of future archival use. As Stoughton remembers, "If there were something somebody wanted or had a need for, I would make a batch of prints and pass them around — give them to the various people." Whereas Stoughton processed his own film for 16 years while in the Air Force, he did less and less while an officer, as the military "didn't like officers running around doing that kind of stuff. They have people who will do it for you." By the end of his stint at the White House in 1965 during the Johnson administration, then Major Stoughton was an exception, actually photographing and going on trips. Back in the early days of the Kennedy administration, however, Stoughton sent his film over to the Pentagon for developing. As time went on and as several of technicians were assigned to Stoughton, they built a darkroom at a location within a former brewery, and later still during the Johnson administration, a color facility on M Street in Georgetown was put together.[15]

Turnaround time for pictures was quite fast. Shots taken in the morning could be proofed by the afternoon with enlargements the next day. Remembering the early operation as "kind of loose," Stoughton recalls that contact sheets were seldom made. "I usually got just a selection of the best — have the guy in the lab select the best pictures technically, sharp and all that, and send them up . . . I wasn't as well prepared for the mechanical type stuff, as I was being busy taking pictures. I let somebody else worry about the details."[16]

All of the Kennedy White House photographic materials are now located and preserved at the John F. Kennedy Library in Boston. What is quite evident is that in the working White House during the Kennedy administration no one was responsible nor concerned about the archival nature of the films other than a vague understanding that they would some day be historically valuable. The chief concern was day-to-day operations. Photographer Robert Knudsen "was told specifically not to make contact prints of his rolls, no one at the White House wanted to bother with them, and instead to print each negative frame in 5" x 7" for the files and for viewing by the White House Staff."[17]

Stoughton's numbering system for his rolls of film was numerical, beginning each calendar year with the first assignment. An assignment could be anywhere from 1 to 95 negatives depending upon the occasion, and included a prefix "C" if it was done in color. As Kennedy Library Audio-visual Archivist Allan Goodrich explained it, "The numbering system with each assignment is simply a numerical listing as the negative was printed and/or identified by Stoughton after his films were processed and printed. No attempt was made by either Stoughton or his lab to keep the film frames in numerical sequence as they had been in the roll, or to keep them serially numbered according to day or time."[18] Stoughton confirms this procedure remarking, "I had a technician at the lab who, after the negatives were processed, would put a number on them so we could find them, and it was rather loose. Whatever roll the person was processing at the time would be the first number."[19]

In 1963 Stoughton was given an additional assignment area. "I started in the movie business in 1963 when the President went to Europe, and Jackie was pregnant and didn't go. She charged me with the responsibility of covering his trip so she could see what he did while he was gone. When I came back I had 3,600 feet of Kodachrome to which I attached sound, and some of his speeches and crowd noise and music. I showed it on the Fourth of July weekend in 1963. I showed it three times. He wanted to see what he did. From then on I did a lot of weekend filming, at the Cape and the last weekend they were together in Virginia in November."[20] Stoughton had made some personal family shots of the First Family at their farm at Wexford in Atoka, Virginia, including a funny sequence of a horse nosing a sitting and relaxed President for a sugar cube. This weekend was the last one the family would spend together.

Twenty years after the events, Stoughton would recount on ABC's *Good Morning America* television show his one-man multi-media process. "I'd have three cameras around my neck on straps and a 16mm movie camera in my hand, and I'd squirt off a few feet of movies and I'd take a couple of stills. So I would have both kinds of records, because we were talking about history. And Mrs. Kennedy would like to have the fact that they were living in the White House recorded. . . ."[21]

In the fall of 1963 Kennedy's approval rating with the American public was, according to a Gallup Poll, at 59%, having fallen due in part to many displeased with his civil rights stance. Kennedy had decided in light of the 1964 presidential election, that he should visit the South in order to boost his image, and the states of Florida and Texas, so crucial during his 1960 campaign, were targeted. Then serving Texas Governor John B. Connally would state 15 years later before the House Select Committee on Assassinations his belief that Kennedy had requested the five-city Texas visit in order to raise campaign money and to enhance his political position in Texas.[22]

Any time the President journeys outside of the Washington area the event initiates scores of hours of pre-planning and dozens of personnel being put to work on logistics. Political advance men would make contacts and arrangements for events, meetings, and speeches, while security, transportation, and communication coordinators would handle their numerous tasks. Like the many other military and governmental employees as well as political aides who would be needed to fulfill various functions in a presidential journey, Cecil Stoughton was informed that he would be making the trip and began to put his professional gear and personal wardrobe together. As was typically the case, Stoughton, like the other assigned White House military photographers, did not wear his uniform on such trips, but like Tom Atkins, who would also be going on the Texas tour, he would wear a civilian suit in order not to draw undue attention and comment. As usual, Stoughton brought with him his favorite camera, the Hasselblad, together with a 35mm Alpha Reflex.

On Wednesday evening, November 20, 1963, Stoughton had been on duty to record the formally attired presidential reception at the White House for the members of the Supreme Court. During the morning of the 21st he had been called in to photograph the President's meeting with U. S. Ambassadors to Upper Volta and Gabon.

At about 11 a.m. on November 21 the President and his entourage left Andrews Air Force Base for Texas, and Stoughton's photo technicians would later log the photographic sequences of the Texas trip as "C420" for the color pictures, and "525" for the black-and-white photo series. During the next 24 hours Stoughton would make a number of pictures of the President's activities including receptions at San Antonio, Brooks Medical Center, Kelly Field, the Rice Hotel in Houston, the LULACS reception, and a testimonial dinner for Congressman Albert Thomas at the Houston Coliseum.

It was just before midnight on November 21 that the Kennedy motorcade arrived at the Hotel Texas in Fort Worth following a 10-hour whirlwind schedule. Overnight arrangements had been made for the trip by the advance team, and as was typical, the military personnel would sleep two to a room. This night Stoughton was assigned room 804 on the same floor as the President, sharing accommodations, as he sometimes did, with Warrant Officer Ira D. Gearhart. Gearhart was required to travel close to the President while being as inconspicuous as possible, all the time carrying a 30-pound metal suitcase. Often known by the popular euphemism as "the bag man," Gearhart kept in his mind the combination to the suitcase. This suitcase contained codes the President could use in case of nuclear attack in order to launch the United States stockpile of missiles. Also included within were documents containing retaliation options and statistics for the President to consider.[23]

The President emerging from Hotel Texas

November 22 dawned drizzly, and Stoughton's first assignment of the day would be to record the speech the President was to make in the parking lot across 8th Street from Hotel Texas to a soggy, but enthusiastic Fort Worth crowd which had been gathering early to get a glimpse of the Kennedys. Cleaning his camera lenses, Stoughton decided the overcast morning would be suitable for black-and-white film, and as his Alpha Reflex was already loaded with fast-speed Tri-X film from yesterday's events, he decided to finish off the 36-exposure roll, 15 exposures already having been used.

Stoughton captures the President's address on film.

Stoughton's 17-exposure sequence of the parking lot speech captures President Kennedy walking out of the hotel main entrance at about 8:50 a.m. with Vice-President Lyndon Johnson, local Congressman Jim Wright, and other dignitaries in tow. A cordon of over a dozen still and motion picture cameramen record on film almost identical views of the political procession for later TV and newspaper coverage.

Greeting the crowd in the parking lot

Kennedy is next seen within the Stoughton sequence wading into the outer edge of the crowd, the closest members of whom are stretching out their hands for a shake or touch. Then Stoughton makes seven side shots of the flat-bed podium as Congressman Wright introduces those standing on it. Stoughton next moves behind the podium and makes two shots from a perch on a step-ladder above the podium. With the back of the President's head and shoulders in the foreground, the pictures show the front of the crowd listening to his words while the photographers in front of them continue to snap away. Coming around to the front, Stoughton takes three additional shots of the President delivering his remarks, two of which center primarily on his face. The series is a fine example of Stoughton's using his access to make a record of what the President was doing, whom he was with, and what he saw.[24]

Following the outside public rally, the President was next scheduled to address a Chamber of Commerce breakfast in the hotel. Stoughton positioned himself in the large hotel ballroom now using his Hasselblad 500C loaded with 120 color film. The negative size allowed Stoughton to squeeze off 12 exposures per roll. Stoughton used the 6 left on this roll from yesterday's take to record Mr. Kennedy's arrival, introductions at the podium by Chamber of Commerce president Raymond Buck, and Mrs. Kennedy's late but grand arrival wearing a pink suit with matching pillbox hat. She had last worn this suit in a public recep-

Mrs. Kennedy and the Vice-President
at the head table

tion at the White House in October 1962 when Algerian Premier Ahmed Ben Bella was welcomed on a state visit.[25]

Stoughton then records Mrs. Kennedy at the head table and then standing with Vice-President Johnson, both beaming large, natural smiles. The last picture on the roll is of the President at the podium being greeted with applause from the standing head table while the photographers down front shoot the scene. This set of pictures, like many of Stoughton's sequences printed in a small uncropped format, has a candid home snapshot quality about it, much like pictures taken at a wedding reception, the only difference being that Stoughton's includes famous faces and the presidential seal. These are work-a-day pictures of real people.

Changing film, Stoughton next at about 10:30 a.m. makes three shots in front of the Hotel Texas in anticipation of the President leaving for Carswell Air Force Base and the short flight to Dallas. The morning sky had transformed from gray and drizzly to a cloudless and blue sky. In front of the hotel Governor John Connally, wearing a white Stetson, is seen conferring with chain smoking Assistant White House Press Secretary Malcolm Kilduff. In another photograph Presidential Aides Larry O'Brien and Dave Powers are on the sidewalk in front of the hotel while a TV crew from Channel 11 awaits to film the President's departure. Finally Mr. & Mrs. Kennedy emerge from the hotel making straight for the white convertible with red interior being used in Fort Worth as the presidential limousine.[26]

The motorcade through downtown Fort Worth is recorded in two Stoughton photos taken from a moving convertible and looking forward at the motorcade to the front and the crowds on the sides. On the Texas trip, as was highly unusual, both the President and the Vice-President rode in the motorcade, though never in the same car. The presidential limousine was trailed by a Secret Service follow-up car, then the Vice-President with his own follow-up vehicle. Directly behind trailed the White House print press, which carried the Press Secretary, AP and UPI reporters, and usually a local press representative.

The motorcade at Fort Worth City Hall

Behind this car would be either the still-picture camera car or the motion picture camera car. During this motorcade Stoughton's still-camera car was directly behind the print press car, and when they arrived in Dallas, their motorcade position would be switched with that of the movie car. Stoughton's shots of the motorcade are made on Main Street, which has been decked out a little early with Christmas decorations featuring Santa Clauses and garland rings spanning the streets. The second shot is taken with a view of the President's limousine five car lengths ahead as it makes a right turn in front of the Fort Worth City Hall.  President Kennedy stands to acknowledge the band playing on the City Hall's steps.[27]

During such motorcades the President would sometimes see a homemade sign, or a small group of people who would strike his eye,  and he would tell the Secret Service driver to stop the car so that he could greet them.  After a few moments amidst the excited crowd, the car would continue on.  During such impromptu stops some cameramen would instinctively jump out of their convertibles to make that potential "good picture," and often they would not reach the action before the motorcade started up again, and would be forced to jump for their ride.  On several occasions while Stoughton was traveling in such motorcades, he would also get caught in the dash for a picture, but unlike his press colleagues, a few times he was able to catch a ride on the foot jump on the rear of the presidential Lincoln holding on to the handles attached to the trunk.  At the next stop he would get off and get back to his own car.  The Secret Service did not object to this occasional foray on the Lincoln, for Stoughton was a safe buffer.  Both the security men and Stoughton, however, were well aware of the President's dislike for anyone to ride too often or too long at this position, which obscured the President from the people and might look too much like over-protection.[28]

Arriving at Carswell Air Force Base, the President and his manifest of guests boarded Air Force One.  Stoughton, as per usual, did not ride in the President's plane, but instead was a passenger in the press plane.  During the 13-minute flight to Dallas's Love Field, the press plane was allowed to arrive first, so that they would be ready to record the arrival of Air Force One.

Stoughton recalls that the press expected a hostile atmosphere in conservative Dallas, but that "it sure didn't spin off into the Love Field crowd.  My pictures show

The Dallas arrival

dozens of flags, hand-painted welcome signs, a lot of warmth. . . . I did not feel nor see any of that, certainly not during the whole time we were there."  Stoughton later recalled the scene as "just a beautiful reception, a bright, warm, sunny day and thousands of people cheering — screaming like they had at Fort Worth, Houston and San Antonio."[29]

Still working with his Hasselblad, Stoughton captures the President and First Lady walking down the gangway off Air Force One, and Mrs. Kennedy being greeted by Mrs. Lyndon Johnson and Mayor and Mrs. Earle Cabell of Dallas, Mrs. Cabell poised to give the First Lady a bouquet of red roses.

A gangway view of the receiving line and the press line with the spectators in the background

Stoughton then scurries up the plane gangway to shoot a view of the reception line with the large and enthusiastic crowd of spectators to its rear behind a chain link fence. Quickly returning to the tarmac, Stoughton captures two shots of the President and Mrs. Kennedy greeting others in the line while cameramen record the scene in the background, including in one frame cameramen Tom Craven of CBS and Dave Wiegman, Jr., of NBC, taking movie film. Mrs. Kennedy then is seen shaking hands with Annie S. Dunbar, who is seated in a wheelchair.[30]

Now out of film, Stoughton reloads the magazine. Seeing the exuberance of the public, the President and First Lady veer into the crowd of obviously friendly supporters located on the opposite side of a chest-high chain-link fence. Stoughton records two frames showing the Kennedys working their way along the fence as they briefly greet and touch the numerous outstretched hands of the delighted spectators. Mrs. Kennedy's security guard, Clint Hill, stands nearby. Stoughton temporarily leaves the fence area

An exuberant crowd greets the President and Mrs. Kennedy

trying to locate a better shooting position, and while on the move, he takes a shot of Aides Dave Powers and Kenny O'Donnell positioned in the jump seat of the Cadillac Secret Service follow-up car. Powers has in his hand a movie camera with which he often took souvenir home movies.[31]

Recollects Stoughton, "I stood upon a cement foundation of a lamp, about two feet high, and that gave me a chance to look down instead of fighting everybody else's head. And they walked right by me, and that was the last time I made a picture of them. They were just an arm's length away. They got into the car within a couple seconds after that and drove into town."[32]

At about 11:55 the President's shiny blue Lincoln convertible began to move out. As was customary, the camera people made a scramble for their vehicles. The pace was hectic, but routine. Stoughton's car was a convertible, and his place was behind the driver, a Texas Department of Public Safety officer. Stoughton positioned himself for a better view, not in the seat, but on top of the boot which contained the convertible top. To his right was Art Rickerby, staff photographer for *LIFE* magazine, with Henry Burroughs of Associated Press next to Rickerby. Frank Cancellare, veteran United Press International photographer was on the right, virtually straddling the front and back seats. A local *Dallas Morning News* photographer, Clint Grant, who could not find room in the third press camera car reserved for local press, had been invited to ride in the front seat next to the driver. The photographers' silver 1964 Chevrolet Impala was eighth in line from the President's car, it now being behind the motion picture car, the positions exchanged from the Fort Worth motorcade.[33]

This being the second motorcade of the day, conversation in Stoughton's car centered on discussions of the size of the crowd, and anticipation of the next stop for a luncheon speech at the Dallas Trade Mart. The crowds began to grow and then to swell with 6 to 8 persons deep as the motorcade traveled into the downtown business district. Having used up half of his film magazine at the airport, Stoughton shot only one picture during the motorcade, figuring to save the remainder of his roll for events at the Trade Mart. The picture he made of the motorcade was taken from his position on the back left of the Impala looking straight down Main Street. Slightly out of focus in the fore-ground are the occupants of the motion picture press convertible [Camera Car 1], including the crew-cut head of CBS's Craven, and the hatted Dave Wiegman, apparently in the process of taking movies of the crowd. A leaning Tom Atkins is just behind Wieg-man. To their front is seen the blue telephone car occupied by the wire service representatives, then Mayor Cabell's car and in front of that the sedan VP follow-up car with a door on the driver's side ajar so that if there was any trouble the agents could quickly exit. In front of this car, but out of view save for seeing Lady Bird Johnson's head looking backwards as seen through the window of the follow-up car, is the Vice-President's vehicle. Agents on the side running board of the President's follow-up car can be seen in shadow as can be police motorcycles flanking the Lincoln. Neither the presidential car nor its occupants are visible. Further down Main Street four of the lead motorcycle policemen are glimpsed, and in the extreme background appear trees which delineate an open area unfamiliar to Stoughton, and known locally as Dealey Plaza.

On Main Street approaching Griffin Street

Thisphotographreveals that Stoughton's car is approaching a cross-street marked "Griffin," and on both sides of the street are large crowds. Red, white, and blue bunting is draped on wires across the street and a clock on a building sign indicates the time as 12:20. The commercial buildings in evidence are unremarkable and include the Hotel Maurice, upon which a painted wall ad indicates it is "fireproof" and available for rates of "$1 up per day." On the opposite side of the street from the hotel a gold star tops the neon sign for the Texas Bank, while still further down Main Street one may spy the conical towers of the old County Court House located on the corner of Main and Houston Street. The sky is cloudless, and the effects of a breeze are evident in the fluttering of the parade bunting. In only a few moments the motorcade will turn right onto Houston Street and into history.[34]

Just after Stoughton's car had made its turn at the old Court House, he heard three very distinct, loud reports which sounded like shots. "I remember at the time when I heard the shots I was sitting on the outside of the car and Art was sitting next to me. I said 'Hey, Art, these Texans really know how to welcome a guy, don't they" In my mind I saw a guy on the roof in a ten-gallon hat with a six-shooter — bang bang! bang bang! That's what I thought. Then we rounded the corner and saw nothing except a lot of hectic police activity. So then the jollity went out of the statement and it seemed like serious business."[35]

After traveling the short distance on Houston Street and making a sharp left onto Elm Street and past the red brick Texas School Book Depository Building, Stoughton recalls, "We realized something was amiss, as the cars ahead of us were gone. As we rolled to a stop just around the corner, Cancellare leaped out of the car and ran to take a picture of a family cowering on the grass. Tom Atkins was already there shooting his 16mm Arriflex, and instead of doing likewise, I slipped on my 150mm lens on the Hasselblad and shot one frame. . . ."[36]

The most obvious focal point in the confusion of the moment was towards the four members of the Newman family. Mr. and Mrs. Bill Newman and their two young sons had been watching the procession; and when the shots sounded, the father had them all drop to the ground. Most of the press people at the scene momentarily gravitated their attention to that dramatic action. Of all the pictures made by photographic witnesses,a viewing of the photo Stoughton made of this scene is perhaps the closest to a visual reality of environmental conditions at that instant. The camera recorded in color the blue sky, green shrubbery, sharp shadows, and bright sunlight. Black-and-white photographs and color film taken by amateur film makers just could not match the reality captured by superior camera optics in the hands of a pro.

The "grassy knoll" from Camera Car 2

Three of the Newmans are visible on the ground, with Mrs. Newman looking towards the street and obscuring her son from Stoughton's lens. Hovering over them in an unnatural pose is Tom Craven  finishing up taking film of the couple. He had followed Wiegman, now out of view, to this spot. Tom Atkins is behind and to the right of Craven's position looking through the viewfinder of his camera, while to his rear can be seen the crouching figure of a woman wearing sunglasses. The original negative of this picture is marked "8" in sequence, and is the last taken in color by Stoughton in Dallas. A full, uncropped view of this print reveals on the extreme left side of the negative and almost obscured by a lamppost shaft on Elm Street, two persons sitting on the concrete steps leading to the wall on the knoll above the street. These are two of the three men who had been standing near the steps at the time of the assassination who are discerned in other photographs. The stockade fence separating the railroad parking area from the Plaza, and a portion of the concrete peristyle and the pedestal from which Abraham Zapruder had moments ago filmed the shooting, are visible in the upper half of the photograph.[37]

After making this quick picture Stoughton had no time to take others of the area. As soon as he realized something had happened and that the President's car was not around, he "wanted to get out of there — get to where it was going." Having to leave Cancellare behind, Stoughton nonetheless wanted to be where the President was. He yelled to the driver, "Let's get the hell out of here!" Leaving the scene Stoughton observed an abandoned police motorcycle, while a cop with pistol in hand was running up the embankment.[38]

The car, now with four photographer-passengers, drove directly to the Trade Mart, its occupants only knowing that something highly unusual had occurred back at the Plaza. Stoughton recollects people yelling towards the car as it drove through the Trade Mart that "He's at Parkland!" This meant nothing to Stoughton, but to Clint Grant, the local photographer on board, it was an obvious reference, and Grant remarked, "God, that's a hospital! Let's take off!" With that the driver rushed the photographers to the hospital.[39]

Stoughton's Parkland Hospital sequence

Stoughton's car arrived near Parkland's emergency entrance at about the same time as the other two camera cars.  Grabbing his 35mm Alpha Reflex camera loaded with a fresh roll of Tri-X film, Stoughton made two quick shots of the emergency entrance.  Press Secretary Kilduff, cigarette in mouth, is there as is film-maker Wiegman.  Stoughton's boss, General Clifton is in one frame, while Dallas motorcycle cops and plainclothes officers have formed a rough cordon around the three-bay "Ambulance Only" entrance.  A number of civilians, including many hospital personnel, mill around the area, and the presidential limousine is head-first in the middle bay, flanked by two parked ambulances.

A bit later Stoughton made two more pictures of the area, but taken from a different angle, showing agents putting the plastic bubble-top and fabric cover on over the convertible.  The trunk is open and a metal bucket is on the ground next to the President's door.  Stoughton recalls that a man was washing the seat "with a cloth, and he had a bucket.  There was blood all over the seat, and flower petals and stuff on the floor."[40]  Stoughton then went into the hospital.  By this time he had learned that the President was seriously wounded.  He remembers that at the appearance of a priest on the scene General Clifton glanced at Stoughton and both men's eyes filled up.[41]

Stoughton would have missed the opportunity to take the most important photographs of his career, had he not happened to be in the hospital at the right moment.  Signal Corpsman Art Bales was attempting to supply communications to the outside world from Parkland Hospital, and according to Stoughton, "He handed me a phone at a critical time when he had just touched base with the White House switchboard in Washington.  He had an open line, and had to go do something else and asked me to hold this phone and talk into it so that the operator would not listen in, find nobody there, and cut them off.  So just as he handed me the receiver I saw Johnson and Lady Bird going out the 'Out' door rather quickly and I said, 'Where's he going' and when [Bales] said, 'The President is going to Washington,' I knew that President Kennedy had expired and I said, 'So am I,' and handed him back his phone."[42]

Stoughton believed it his duty to be with the new President, but he was not quick enough to catch a ride with the small, fast-departing entourage.  Just after Johnson left, however, vice-presidential Secret Service Agent Thomas L. Johns arrived, having also missed the departure.  Johns obtained a police car and driver and together with Stoughton and Johnson Aides Cliff Carter and Jack Valenti, they made for Love Field.[43]  Stoughton remembers the ride as "hairy and fast."  The driver did not know how to get to the plane, and found himself on the opposite side of the tarmac.  Normally in such a situation, the occupants would have laboriously threaded their way around to the other side, but the day was far from normal.  Johns, who had earlier that day been left on Elm Street by his follow-up car when he had jumped from the car upon the first inkling of trouble in order to run to the Johnson car, did not want to be left behind again.  He shouted to the car's occupants that they were on the opposite side and "Let's shoot the runways,"[44] and contrary to airport rules, common sense, and security dictates, they managed to reach their destination.

President Johnson had decided to travel back to Washington on board Air Force One with its more sophisticated communications system rather than on Air Force Two. He did not want to depart, however, until he had taken the oath of office and the deceased President and his widow were also aboard. Back at Parkland, Assistant Press Secretary Kilduff made the public announcement of the death of President Kennedy at 1:30 CST. Dallas undertaker Vernon O'Neal was notified to bring over a casket, and he arrived with a 400-pound bronze Elgin Brittania model in which the wrapped President's body was placed. Following an ugly confrontation between members of the entourage and Medical Examiner Dr. Earl Rose over removal of the body from the Dallas jurisdiction, at about 2:05 the casket left the hospital in an O'Neal ambulance-hearse.

Stoughton had not taken any photographs of the confused and devastated staff inside Parkland's corridors due to his own shock. Aboard Air Force One, however, he observed the ambulance arriving, and from the forward port-side door of the Boeing 707 he made a series of 11 shots with his 35mm Alpha, finishing off the black-and-white roll he had begun at Parkland's emergency entrance.

The sixth frame taken by Stoughton in the sequence of
President Kennedy's casket being brought aboard Air Force One

The series begins with the ambulance arriving near the rear gangway of Air Force One. Driven by S.A. Andy Berger, Agent Stewart G. Stout, Jr., is in the middle front seat and Agent-in-Charge Roy Kellerman on the passenger side. Hidden from

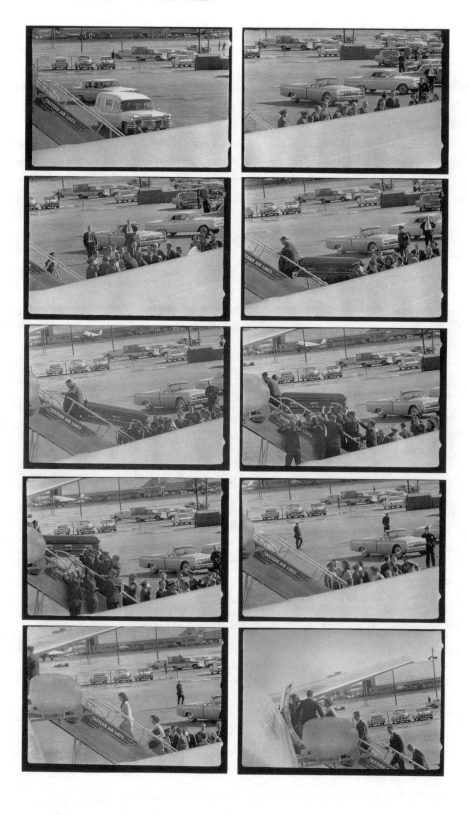

view are Mrs. Kennedy, presidential physician Dr. George Burkley, and Agent Clint Hill, riding in the rear of the ambulance with the coffin. Behind the ambulance follows a light colored sedan with Aides Larry O'Brien, Dave Powers, and Ken O'Donnell, keeping close by their fallen chief. Two uniformed airmen are at the bottom of the gangway, while in the background three Dallas policemen are among those providing security for the plane.

In the second photograph Stoughton has panned slightly to the right. Several other vehicles are seen, including a Mercury Comet convertible with its top up and marked with a number "1" on the windshield. Less than two hours ago this was the vehicle carrying Mayor Cabell and his wife in the motorcade. More uniformed police are in view, including Police Chief Jesse Curry in civilian clothes. Curry had earlier driven President Johnson from Parkland to the airplane. Also seen are various Secret Service agents and members of President Kennedy's staff, including his secretary, Evelyn Lincoln. In the next six photographs, Stoughton captures the carrying of the casket up the gangway, as agents seem to struggle with the almost 600-pound load on the narrow metal stairs. Numerous hands attempt to help with the burden, while on the tarmac below Military Aides Clifton and Godfrey McHugh, Mrs. Kennedy, and members of the President's loyal "Irish Mafia" watch with what looks to be shock and confusion. A uniformed Dallas police officer a few paces behind the melancholy gathering is seen in three subsequent frames, taking off his hat and, in a poignant and private salute, holding it to his heart until the casket is aboard. The final three frames in the sequence follow the former First Lady walking up the steps looking forlorn and disheveled with blood spatters on her skirt and stocking. Behind follow O'Brien and O'Donnell, followed by Powers, whose downcast look reflects more than simply watching his foothold.

This sad sequence, more than any description, conveys the feelings of confusion and haphazardness following the events of the last hours, and seems an obscene twist of fate compared to the elegant and stately arrival of the President and his wife as they walked down this same gangway an era ago.[45]

Stoughton reloaded his Alpha with Tri-X 400 ASA film and put in a roll of 120 black-and-white film in his Hasselblad, as he wanted fast film if he were called upon to make pictures of the swearing-in. Kilduff confirmed to him that the President wanted to record the ceremony, and about 15 minutes after President Kennedy's body was aboard, Federal Judge Sarah T. Hughes arrived to administer the oath. Stoughton suggested to Kilduff that they use the airplane dictograph to record the swearing in so there would be both a photographic and audio record of the event.[46] The ceremony would take place in the state room, which had the largest open space in the cabin, unencumbered by seating, save for two built-in tables, a sofa, and chair. The approximately 16-foot square space, however, was still much too small to accommodate everyone on the plane. Looking over the area, Stoughton stepped up on the sofa and had to "flatten himself against the rear bulkhead of the compartment," in order to get the best view of the proceedings.[47]

Dean UPI White House Reporter Merriman Smith, who had been in Georgia 18 years earlier to file stories on the death of Franklin D. Roosevelt, wrote concerning this scene he was now witnessing, "The compartment became hotter and hotter. Johnson was worried that some of the Kennedy staff might not be able to get inside. He urged people to press forward, but a signal corps photographer, Capt. Cecil Stoughton, standing in the corner on a chair, said if Johnson moved any closer, it would be virtually impossible to make a truly historic photograph."[48]

Stoughton's physical position was uncomfortable enough, and in the ever stuffier compartment, his body felt sticky and clammy. He also felt the professional pressure of not muffing this assignment, the most important of his career. Johnson asked Stoughton how he wanted them, and the photographer replied that he would place Judge Hughes so that the camera view would be over her shoulder. Upon learning that Mrs. Kennedy would be present, he suggested that she should be on one side of the President with Mrs. Johnson on the other.[49] Stoughton began his picture series using his Alpha with available cabin light. The first six pictures show Johnson as the focal point of the camera's lens with others awkwardly waiting. Among those seen in various of these pictures are Judge Hughes, Lady Bird Johnson, Congressmen Brooks, Thornberry, and Thomas, General Clifton, Larry O'Brien, Ken O'Donnell, *Newsweek* correspondent Charles Roberts, Police Chief Curry, Press Secretary Kilduff, Bill Moyers, Jack Valenti, Pilot Jim Swindal, Agents Jerry Kivett, and Lem Johns, Evelyn Lincoln, Mary Gallagher, and Pam Turnure.[50]

Stoughton's first Hasselblad photo of the cabin

Switching to his Hasselblad, Stoughton began to take another photo with his favorite camera with an attached flash unit. For a moment he felt a sinking sensation through his body. As he recalls, "The first time I pushed the button, it didn't work and I about died. I had a little connector that was just loose because of all the bustling around, and I just pushed it with my finger and number 2 went off on schedule. I sprayed the cabin so I could get a picture of everybody there." Prints of the first two Hasselblad photos Stoughton made cover a larger area than the 35mm prints and are much crisper in detail. Unlike the 35mm prints taken with available light, these flash shots fill in the scene with light and show mirror reflections from the overhead lighting rather than white light. Judge

Contact prints of the 35mm photos shot on the plane. The original negative to the next to the last photo is missing and this reproduced frame is from a copy negative made of an original print.

Hughes can be seen holding a Catholic Missal, believed at the time to be a Bible, for the swearing-in ceremony, together with a sheet of paper imprinted with the President's Seal and the words "Aboard Air Force One" with the typed-out oath of office beginning with "I do solemnly swear (or affirm)."[51]

Everyone was awaiting the arrival of Mrs. Kennedy, who moments after the eighth Stoughton picture is taken, enters the room with Ken O'Donnell. Following a few remarks of sympathy awkwardly, but sincerely expressed by some present, the former First Lady moves, with O'Donnell and Powers nearby, to the President's left side. Stoughton had already seen the sickening blood stains on Mrs. Kennedy's dress, and knew that photographing them in these soon-to-be-famous pictures would be terribly inappropriate. He made sure the lens would not reveal them.

One of eight frames made during the swearing-in, this one made with the Hasselblad camera

In the now very cramped quarters in which Merriman Smith, Dave Powers, Dr. Burkley, Liz Carpenter, and Agent Roy Kellerman are now also in partial view of Stoughton's camera lens, Judge Hughes is given the nod to begin the oath. It is 2:38 CST and Kilduff holds up the microphone and depresses the button while Stoughton quickly clicks off four shots with the Hasselblad and four with the Alpha. Except for the words of the oath, everyone was quiet, and Stoughton realized that the only other sound in the cabin was the clicking of the shutter and the clunking of his equipment.

All faces are somber. The hulking form of President Johnson is surrounded by a triangle of three women. His large right hand raised and held seemingly uncomfortably tight to his body, Johnson rests his left palm on the missal, Judge Hughes's thumb in contact with his hand. Lady Bird, as ever, stands next to her husband. Her sad eyes stare towards the judge whose words are confirming a new and heavy burden upon her husband and family. The body of Jacqueline Kennedy is present, giving a manifestation of continuity and grace, yet her soul and mind are elsewhere in a personal hell.[52]

The ceremony was over within half a minute. Congratulations mixed with expressions of sympathy were exchanged by many, and Stoughton finished off his take with five pictures as Johnson turns away. Stoughton's full series of photographs inside the state room included thirteen frames of 35mm and eight of 120 film.

Johnson then ordered Air Force One back to Washington, and quickly those remaining in Dallas scurried off the plane. Stoughton was among those staying behind. He would have his unprocessed film developed and sent out via the wire services as a reassurance that the government continued. Kilduff handed Stoughton the dictabelt recording of the oath of office, and never before had the captain been singularly more responsible for history's remembrance of a momentous event.

Here was the photographer who, through his camera work at the 1961 Kennedy inauguration had been brought to the attention of the President and had obtained the position of White House Photographer. That earlier inauguration had been so full of ceremony, positive expectation, and chilling cold weather. Now Stoughton was there at the end of the cycle, or rather the beginning of a new one. Absent was all that makes inaugurations special, save for the transfer of power. The oath was the same, but joy and pomp had been replaced with sorrow and uncertainty, and the ceremony was conducted in a stuffy, tube-like space. Yet the visible continuity of the republic, no matter how erratically it had been carried out, had in fact been accomplished. The government continued. And Stoughton was carrying that proof.

No one was allowed to enter or leave the air strip until Air Force One took off, and just about the time the plane became airborne at 2:48 CST, a press bus from Parkland arrived on the scene. Pool reporter Sid Davis, who had been aboard during the swearing-in, told of the events to the other reporters who quickly gathered around him. Stoughton was met by his car companions Cancellare and Burroughs, veteran cameramen whom Stoughton greatly respected.

What to do about the undeveloped pictures? A nickel was flipped to see which bureau would accommodate developing of these historic pictures, and Burroughs's AP office won the toss. The three dashed down to the Dallas Morning News Building, where the AP bureau was located, and the film was given over to a technician. Stoughton "went into the darkroom with him, even though there was nothing I could do. I just wanted to be there when it came out. And when he held it up to the light, I could see some images and then I breathed. I was turning blue up to that point."[53]

One of the four Hasselblad prints of the oath-taking was chosen as the picture to send over the wire, and through mutual agreement the picture would not be sent out on the AP drum until a duplicate copy was delivered to UPI for their distribution. In their caption material sent along with the photograph both wire services gave Captain Cecil Stoughton photo credit, and soon his photograph would be reproduced around the world in newspapers under headlines such as "Lyndon Johnson takes helm after Kennedy assassinated." Even before being reproduced in newspapers, wirephoto copies of the picture were flashed on network television, NBC telecasting it at about 5:40 Eastern Standard Time.[54]

Later that day Stoughton received a phone call from Kenny O'Donnell, who had been reading Merriman Smith's wire story concerning the swearing-in of Johnson. Stoughton remembers, "O'Donnell was reading the stories about Jackie being covered in blood, and me taking pictures all in the same breath. He visualized that I was taking pictures of her covered with blood. So he got in touch with me at the laboratory there at the AP office, and said what the hell do I mean putting out pictures like that? I said, 'Kenny, you haven't seen the pictures.' So he said, 'You get your ass back here.'" Stoughton, Cancellare and Burroughs hitched a ride back to Washington on an Air Force Jet Star that evening. Upon arriving in Washington, Stoughton went to his lab and had 8" x 10" prints made of all the swearing-in negatives, none of them showing any blood stains on Mrs. Kennedy's clothing. According to Stoughton, O'Donnell was being very protective of Mrs. Kennedy, and even though her stained clothes and stockings were very evident at the landing of Air Force One back at Andrews Air Force Base around 6:05 p.m., he did not want the swearing-in pictures to show such a scene, and had been reading into what the pictures showed without seeing the pictures themselves.[55]

Faith Stoughton, the mother of Cecil's three children, worked at the Pentagon, and when the first bulletin of the Dallas shooting was heard on Friday afternoon, Mrs. Stoughton was very upset and concerned, for she had envisioned her husband on the back step of the car, where he on numerous occasions had found a perch on such motorcades. She feared he might have been shot himself. Such speculation was not helped when a spurious report circulated for a time that an agent had also been shot at the scene. Faith breathed easier once her husband had spoken to her and was back in Washington.

The photographer was not ready to go home, however, and following his visit to the lab he went to the White House. He was there to record the body being escorted back into the Executive Mansion in the early morning of November 23. The next few days blur in Stoughton's memory. "I was going all day Friday, Friday night, and shooting pictures at 4 o'clock in the morning. I went back home, changed clothes, and went back to the White House for the visits of all the dignitaries to Johnson and all his meetings. Then the lying in state in the East Room and the Capitol and the funeral. And when we got to St. Matthew's on Monday, I was up on the steps as they were carrying the casket,

The casket entering St. Matthew's

and I could reach out and touch the flag, and I just collapsed at that point. But I carried on, went to the cemetery and shot everything there that I could. But I must have been going just on nerves."[56]

Following that long weekend Stoughton had expected to be interviewed by investigators concerning the assassination, but was not contacted. Concerning himself and other press photographers, he commented, "They think of us being there, and yet we're not there."

Stoughton remained on as White House photographer and felt his relationship with President Johnson was quite good. As he recalls concerning Johnson, "He liked pictures and I had something he wanted — a camera." In half-jest Stoughton remembers that he and the White House physician were the two most popular people with Johnson, and that his access to the President was much less restricted than under Kennedy. Remaining at the White House past the 1964 election and into the summer of 1965,

Stoughton requested permission to go to England for the dedication of a Kennedy monument at Runnymede. He explained that it would mean very much for him to be there.[57] A week following his return Stoughton abruptly received orders transferring him out of the White House. He worked out of a Pentagon office until his retirement from his Army career in April 1967, to become chief photographer for the National Park Service, retiring from his long government service in April 1973.

Biographer William Manchester interviewed Stoughton and scores of others for his 1967 book *Death of a President* ; and while Stoughton feels that most of Manchester's facts were correct, he does believe that Manchester embellished the conflicting mood and confrontational air aboard Air Force One during the time of the swearing-in ceremony. Manchester noted in his book and in subsequent interviews that most every Kennedy aide had insultingly circumvented the oath-taking. In February 1967 the *Boston Globe* published one of Stoughton's pictures depicting Kenny O'Donnell next to Mrs. Kennedy together with a story refuting the charge. A follow-up story about Stoughton and including reproductions of 19 of his pictures was published by *TIME* magazine two weeks later.[58]

Stoughton was on occasion approached by other assassination researchers, including David S. Lifton, who published a book, *Best Evidence*, in 1980 in which he claimed a possible casket switch and alteration of evidence on the President's body. Lifton used six of Stoughton's pictures and spoke to the photographer. Stoughton later succinctly commented on his opinion of Lifton's theory by saying, "You can rule him out." Though Stoughton admits to having read extensively about the assassination, he does not have any strong feelings about a conspiracy, save to say that it is hard to believe that one man could have done it; and that if there were a conspiracy, he hopes somebody got burned on it. None of the theories he has read, however, seems to have any great merit.[59]

Some twenty-odd years after the events of November 1963, a tanned and relaxed Cecil and Faith Stoughton live in retirement near Cocoa Beach, Florida. In 1973 he, along with Ted Clifton and *TIME* reporter Hugh Sidey co-authored a book of photographs and reminiscences titled *The Memories: JFK, 1961-1963*. Stoughton's dedication reflects the feelings he had for his unique job. "The 1,065 days of the presidency of John F. Kennedy were my golden days, filled with the special joy of living and working with young and vital people who had found a cause beyond themselves. Those days were not without personal sacrifices, prolonged periods of absence from my family were necessary. My wife Faith and children Bill, Jamie, and Sharon carried on cheerfully and gracefully, even though they could not share in my special experience. . . ."[60]

Concerning his anonymous contribution in recording presidential history on film, Stoughton, who has been described by friends as good natured, self-effacing, and loyal, comments simply, "The President knew I took them. I know I took them and my wife knows I took them. I guess that's enough credit."[61]

# CHAPTER NOTES

1.    Cecil Stoughton, *The Memories: JFK, 1961-1963*, p. 199.
2.    Letter, Stoughton to Trask, 5/6/1985.
3.    *Memories*, op. cit., p. 199; Telephone interview of Stoughton, 7/10/1985.
4.    Stoughton interview on ABC's *Good Morning America*, 11/22/1983.
5.    Telephone interview of Stoughton, 7/10/1985.
6.    *Memories*, op. cit., p. 137.
7.    Ibid.; Telephone interview of Thomas M. Atkins, 3/19/1986.
8.    Telephone interview, 7/10/1985.
9.    *Memories*, op. cit., p. 153.
10.   Telephone interview, 7/10/1985.
11.   Ibid.
12.   Ibid.
13.   Ibid.; *Memories*, op. cit., p. 153-155.
14.   Telephone interview, 7/10/1985; Letter, Stoughton to Trask, 5/6/1985.
15.   Telephone interview, 7/10/1985.
16.   Ibid.
17.   Letter, Allan B. Goodrich to Trask, 4/15/1985.
18.   Ibid.
19.   Telephone interview, 7/10/1985.
20.   Ibid.
21.   *Good Morning America*, op. cit.
22.   *Report of the House Select Committee on Assassinations*, p. 35-36.
23.   William Manchester, *Death of a President*, p. 62-63.
24.   Stoughton White House photo sequence, 525, #4-20; 524, #4-20.
25.   Stoughton White House photo sequence, C420, #36-38, 33; *Year: Encyclopedia News Annual*, 1963, p. [9].
26.   Stoughton White House photo sequence, C420, #31, 34, 32, 46, 45, 48, 47.
27.   Ibid., C420, #49, 50.
28.   Telephone interview, 7/10/1985.
29.   Ibid.; *Good Morning America*, op. cit.
30.   Stoughton White House photo sequence, C420, #51, 15, 16, 13-14.
31.   Ibid., C420, #19, 20, 17. This negative filmstrip was marked with a red serial number: 8 06018.
32.   Ibid., C420, #18, 23, 24; Telephone interview, 7/10/1985.
33.   Letter, Stoughton to Trask, 5/6/1985.
34.   Stoughton White House photo sequence, C420, #21.
35.   Telephone interview, 7/10/1985.
36.   Letter, Stoughton to Trask, 5/6/1985.
37.   Stoughton White House photo sequence, C420, #22.
38.   Letter, Stoughton to Trask, 5/6/1985; Telephone interview, 7/10/1985.
39.   Telephone interview, 7/10/1985.
40.   Telephone interview, 7/10/1985; Stoughton Parkland-AF1 photo sequence #2-5.
41.   Manchester, op. cit., p. 215.
42.   Telephone interview, 7/10/1985.
43.   Memorandum, To chief: U. S. Secret Service, From: ASAIC Thomas L. Johns, 11/29/1963, p. 2-3.
44.   Manchester, op. cit., p. 239.
45.   Stoughton Parkland-AF1 photo sequence, #6-16.
46.   John B. Mayo, *Bulletin From Dallas*, p. 118.

47.    Charles Roberts, *The Truth About the Assassination*, p. 113; Interview of Stoughton, 4/23/1986.

48.    Merriman Smith, *The Murder of the Young President*, p. [5]; Rufus W. Youngblood, *Twenty Years With the Secret Service*, p. 130.

49.    Manchester, op. cit., p. 322.

50.    Stoughton Tri-X film aboard AF1, photo sequence #0-5.

51.    Telephone interview, 7/10/1985; Interview, 4/23/1986; Stoughton 120 film aboard AF1, photo sequence #2 & 3.

52.    Stoughton Tri-X film, op. cit., photo sequence #6-9 and 120 film, photo sequence #4-7.

53.    Telephone interview, 7/10/1985.

54.    *The Clarion-Ledger* [Jackson, Mississippi], Nov. 23, 1963, p. 1.; *There Was a President*, p. 31. Also sent out was a copy of Stoughton's Tri-X #10 print which showed the President and Mrs. Johnson speaking to Mrs. Kennedy shortly after the oath. In the AP wirephoto caption it mentions, "Picture was made by Capt. Cecil Stoughton, official White House photographer, who was the lone cameraman allowed at the scene." (*Fort Worth Star-Telegram*, 11/23/1963, p.1).

55.    Telephone interview, 7/10/1985.

56.    Ibid.

57.    Ibid.; *TIME*, Feb. 24, 1967, p. 19.

58.    *New York Times*, Feb. 10, 1967, p. 15; *TIME*, Feb. 24, 1967, p. 20-21.

59.    Telephone interview, 7/10/1985.

60.    *Memories*, op. cit., dedication.

61.    Interview, 4/23/1986.

The President's last speech, Friday morning, November 22, 1963

# PART TWO

# THE AMATEURS

Like hundreds of others in Dallas, John Shroeder brought his camera to record the event. A navy man stationed in Dallas, Shroeder took several 35mm slides as the motorcade traveled down Main Street just a few blocks from Dealey Plaza.

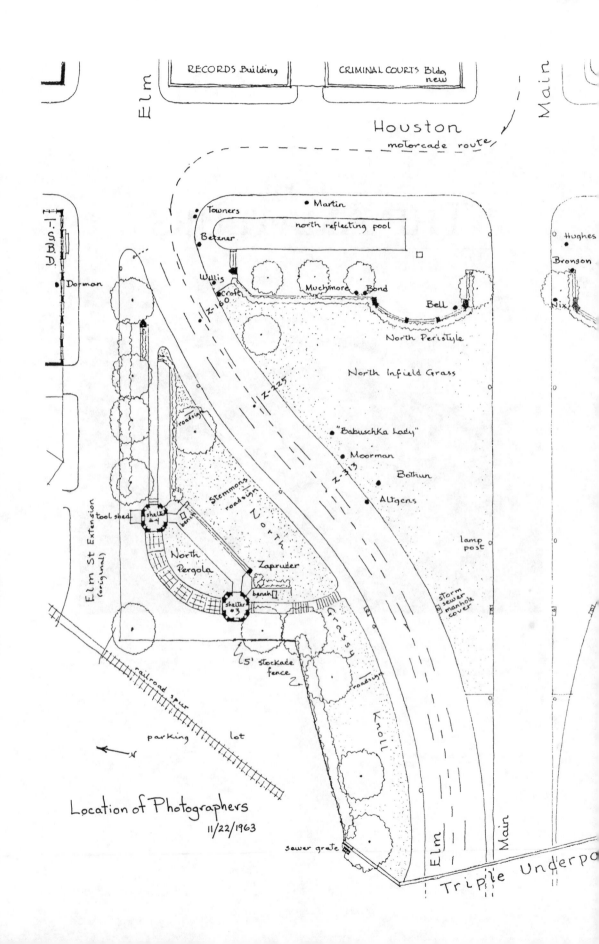

Location of Photographers
11/22/1963

## CHAPTER 2

# The Z Film

Question:    What average man who was neither a villain nor a hero, and who never personally met President Kennedy, has his name forever linked with the story of John F. Kennedy, and is even the subject of a question in the popular 1980s board game "Trivial Pursuit" relating to the death of the 45th President of the United States?

Answer:    Abraham Zapruder.

Question:    What is Zapruder's notoriety?

Answer:    He took a 26-second amateur movie film which recorded the shooting and death of President Kennedy, and which film is debatably the most famous motion picture sequence ever shot in history as well as the most examined piece of film ever developed.

~

Abraham Zapruder was born in Czarist Russia at the time of the Russo-Japanese War to Israel and Anna (Sauette) Zapruder on May 15, 1905, some dozen years prior to the Bolshevik Revolution. Of Jewish ancestry, Zapruder emigrated to the United States in 1920, obtaining a job in a New York dress manufactory. Moving to Dallas, Texas, in 1941, Zapruder became an employee at Nardis, a local clothing manufacturer. He and his wife Lillian found Texas to their liking and there raised two children, Henry and Myrna.

An affable, hard-working and shrewd businessman, Zapruder in 1949 went into business for himself creating "Jennifer Juniors, Inc., of Dallas," which manufactured and marketed a line of women's and young ladies' clothing. By 1963 the company occupied the fourth and fifth floor of the brick Dal-Tex Building, located at 501 Elm Street on the northeast corner of Elm and Houston Streets. This building was at the periphery of the downtown Dallas business district, and across Houston Street from the Texas School Book Depository Building. A freemason and a member of Temple Emanu-El Congregation, Zapruder, who still retained the accent of his heritage, lived on Marquette Street in the upscale University Park area of greater Dallas.[1]

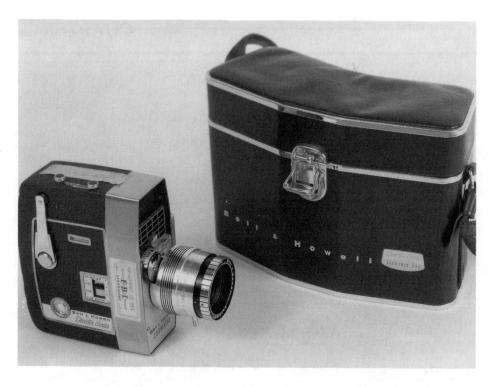

Zapruder's Bell & Howell camera and carrying case

Called "Mr. Z" by many of his employees, Zapruder, a cherubic, balding, bespectacled man in his late 50s whose features somewhat resembled book publisher and TV personality Bennett Cerf, was a strong believer in family values.  He kept pictures of his grandchildren in his office and delighted in their occasional visit to their grandfather's business.  In order to chronicle his family's growth, about a year earlier Zapruder had purchased from Peacock Jewelry Company on Elm Street, a top-of-the-line 8mm movie camera.  The Model 414 PD Bell & Howell Zoomatic Director Series Camera retailed for slightly more than $200, a set-up which included a Varamat 9 to 27mm F1.8 lens and a leather carrying case.  The camera's serial number was AS13486 and featured a built-in electric eye, a springwind indicator, and adjustable shutter speeds for animation (single-frame), run (16 frames per second), and slow motion (48 frames per second) filming.  The December 1963 *Consumer Reports* buying guide rated this model the best of the four zoom lens cameras tested.  It noted the camera's optical performance at the normal and wide-angle mode as "very good" and at telephoto as "excellent."  Its convenience, versatility, and speed consistency were also rated "excellent," while its useful running time for a fully wound camera was approximately 73 seconds, far better than any other zoom lens or turret model tested.  The camera was spool-loaded, necessitating the use of a double 8mm roll film which after the first 25 feet was exposed required the camera to be opened and the roll reversed.  In late November 1963 Zapruder's camera was loaded with Kodachrome II Safety Film and he had exposed the first 25 feet with scenes of family activity including sequences of a grandson digging beside a tree in a backyard patio.[2]

Zapruder's business receptionist, Marilyn Sitzman, would later recall that her boss was a tremendous fan of President Kennedy's. "He talked about him all the time, admired his politics. There just wasn't too much about him that he didn't think was just great." It became common knowledge in the Dal-Tex Building that on Friday, November 22, President Kennedy would be visiting Dallas. A lunchtime motorcade would take the presidential party right by the building on their way to a luncheon speech at the Dallas Trade Mart. Zapruder initially talked about bringing his movie camera to work on Friday to film the event. November 22 dawned overcast, however, and Zapruder left the camera at home, arriving at his fourth story office at around 8 a.m. As the morning wore on, the overcast lifted to a sparkling Texas autumn day and Zapruder's secretary, Lillian Rogers, asked him why he had not brought his camera. Offering that he probably wouldn't even get a chance to see the President, Zapruder was urged by Rogers to go home and get his camera as a President of the United States didn't ride by the office every day. Relenting to his secretary's good-natured badgering, by about 11:30 Zapruder had made the 14-mile round trip to his home and back. Zapruder first thought to film from his office window, but as the view was rather restricted, he decided to go down to Elm Street for a better view.[3]

Lunch break for the working women at Jennifer's was only 30 minutes long and many remained in the building deciding to glimpse the motorcade from the windows. Receptionist Sitzman opted to go down the short distance on Elm Street to the small but pleasant grass and concrete north side of Dealey Plaza where she sometimes ate her lunch. In her immediate area on the grassy slope and the adjoining sidewalk of Elm Street other individuals, many from nearby offices, were also marking time for the arrival of the presidential motorcade. Wearing his ever-present dark fedora and bow tie, Zapruder had also walked from his building to the north side of Elm Street seeking a good place to take his movies. He had turned his spool of film over to the unexposed second side and he positioned himself at first on the three narrow concrete steps leading to the north pergola area. Wanting to check if the camera and spring wind were operating correctly, Zapruder, noticing Sitzman, points his camera at her as she stands by a bench in front of the northerly concrete shelter. He squeezes off a few seconds' worth of film. Seated on the bench in this area were Charles and Beatrice Hester, the husband in a suit and tie and the wife wearing sunglasses. Sitzman, wearing a light colored dress and dark kerchief, turns to face towards Zapruder, waves with her right hand, and then turns away.[4]

Now nearing 12:25 p.m., Zapruder decided this location was not stable enough a perch for him. He noticed a rectangular concrete block some 4 feet high at the west end of the pergola steps. The top of the block was about 2½ feet wide by 4½ feet deep. This location would elevate him even higher than the surrounding knoll and give him a good sweeping view of Elm Street. Elsewhere in the Plaza amateur movie makers F. M. Bell and Charles Bronson earlier found similar flat elevated concrete pedestals where they too had seen the photographic advantage of an elevated position. Zapruder's concrete "crow's nest" was located some 185 feet from the southwest corner of the Texas School Book Depository Building and at its closest point, approximately 65 feet from the center of Elm Street. If he panned smoothly, Zapruder could take one continuous shot of the President's car from its first view at camera left as it turned from Houston Street on to Elm. By panning to the right he could follow the vehicle all the way to the extreme right as it approached a three- tunneled underpass. Only for a short time would a street sign adjacent to Elm Street partially impede Zapruder's view. After somewhat clumsily groping up onto the four-foot pedestal, Zapruder asked Sitzman to join him. As she later recalled, " . . . he wanted me to stand behind him so in case he got dizzy, I could hold onto him. So, I got up behind him and we saw the motorcade turn the corner at Main onto Houston." His camera fully wound and his lens set to maximum telephoto, Zapruder fingered the shutter control, ready to press it to its normal "run" mode for making regular speed home movies.[5]

DEALEY PLAZA – DALLAS, TEXAS

(1) Texas School Book Depository; (2) Dal-Tex Building; (3) Dallas County Records Building; (4) Dallas County Criminal Courts Building; (5) Old Court House; (6) Neeley Bryan House; (7) Dallas County Government Center (Under Construction); (8) United States Post Office Building; (9) Pergolas; (10) Peristyles and Reflecting Pools; (11) Railroad Overpass (Triple Underpass)

The first scene of the motorcade that Zapruder recorded on his film is a slightly over 7-second, 132-frame sequence of three lead Dallas Police Department motorcycles which were traveling one-half block ahead of the motorcade lead car. Unaware of the motorcade's makeup, Zapruder begins filming these cycles as the one on the west side of Houston Street is already into a sharp left turn onto Elm. Motorcycle Sergeant Starvis Ellis executes his left turn and proceeds down the sloping Elm Street, looking down at the controls on his Harley-Davidson dashboard. The other two cyclists are seen to begin a later and much wider left arc. As the middle cyclist makes his turn first he glances left, then into the turn looks right, and when finally on Elm Street, looks again to his left. Zapruder, whose camera panning is erratic, first moves the camera to the right, then to the left, then the right and again the left, trying to decide what to film. The cyclist on the Book Depository side of the street makes such a wide arc that Zapruder loses him in the shot and instead concentrates on Sgt. Ellis at camera right. Then he pans to officer W. G. Lumpkin, the middle cyclist. Zapruder abruptly stops his camera when Lumpkin is some 60 to 70 feet down Elm Street, Zapruder realizing this is not the sequence he is looking to shoot. Waiting just a few seconds, he picks up filming again when the now obvious sleek blue presidential convertible with its flags flapping in the wind is in a position on Elm Street just behind Zapruder's last frame location of the cycle cop.

Interviewed in 1966, Sitzman recalls of this scene, " . . . and we watched them as they came down Houston; and just as the motorcycles that were leading the parade came — started — came around the corner and started down the hill, he started taking pictures then . . . . There was nothing unusual until the first sound which I thought was a firecracker, mainly because of the reaction of President Kennedy. He put his hands up as to guard his face and leaned towards to the left, and the motorcade, you know, proceeded down the hill. And the next thing that I remembered correct — clearly, was the shot that hit him directly in front of us . . . . and we could see his brains come out, you know, his head opening; it must have been a terrible shot because it exploded his head more or less."[6]

In testimony before the Warren Commission, which was created by President Johnson following the assassination to determine the facts of the assassination, Zapruder, in July 1964, described for Commission Counsel Wesley J. Liebeler what he recalled witnessing. " . . . I heard the first shot and I saw the President lean over and grab himself like this (holding his left chest area) . . . . for a moment I thought it was, you know, like you say, 'Oh, he got me,' when you hear a shot. You've heard these expressions. And then I saw — I don't believe the President is going to make jokes like this, but before I had a chance to organize my mind, I heard a second shot and then I saw his head open up and the blood and everything came out and I started — I can hardly talk about it." Recalling the horror of the scene he had filmed, Zapruder began to cry. Following a brief pause so that he could compose himself, the businessman continued his recollection, " . . . Then I started yelling, 'They killed him, they killed him,' and I just felt that somebody had ganged up on him and I was still shooting the pictures until he got under the underpass — I don't even know how I did it."[7]

To call Zapruder's film "remarkable" is an exaggerated under-statement. It is, due to the subject matter and clear angle of view, undoubtedly one of the most important movie films ever made. To those who view it, it is a slice of gruesome reality, though a reality only experienced through the sense of sight, which sense is further restricted by a narrow angle of view and within the technological shortcomings of the 8mm film size. This amateur home movie, almost not made in the first place, would soon become one of the most well known artifacts of the twentieth century. As assassination researcher Josiah Thompson would later write, Zapruder " . . . had unwittingly become a prime source of history, and it would be largely through his camera that the world would come to know about this assassination in all its horror." Describing the film as containing ". . . the nearest thing to 'absolute truth' about the sequence of events in Dealey Plaza," Thompson wrote how it was not only of immense use to the Warren Commission, but has forever become the major piece of evidence utilized by innumerable independent researchers and critics.[8]

Yet inherent with the very existence of this film is the very important *caveat* that even though we see what the camera recorded, understanding what we see can be open to much subjective interpretation. Though this strip of film showed us in excruciating detail the fact that a President died, it also opened up to immense speculation the interpretation of the exact means of his death. Had the Zapruder film never been taken, or been lost to us, much of the later debate over the actual sequence of shots, the timing of the shots, and the victims' reactions to the shots would not have taken place. It is a dichotomy that much of these later controversies surrounding the facts of the assassination found birth in this the very piece of evidence that brought us the most truthful, visual record of the assassination itself. We all became spectators who could ponder various points of view of what the reality of the preserved images actually meant. As a result of this film's existence, a sub-culture of assassination investigators has delved into science and pseudo-science studying physics, ballistics, medicine, pathology, human reaction to stimuli, and photo interpretation — all to find the truth of the reality.

Without Zapruder we might have had simpler, though not necessarily any truer, answers than we now have; but perhaps answers that would have simplified the process and given our national psyche less trauma in the intervening years. But Zapruder we had, and his 26 seconds of film, though unavailable to the public for years, could not be suppressed in its original form forever, nor ignored by those who needed to know the truth or at least part of the truth of what and how the event occurred.

The complete Elm Street motorcade film sequence runs about 26½ seconds. The 486 frames, all later subsequently assigned individual numbers for investigative reference, had been exposed through Zapruder's telephoto camera lens at 18⅓ frames per second. The first 132 frames were of the motorcycle lead escort. When Zapruder started his camera again for an approximately 19-second uninterrupted run, his first frame showed the 4-ton presidential Lincoln already on Elm Street, having completed its Houston Street turn.

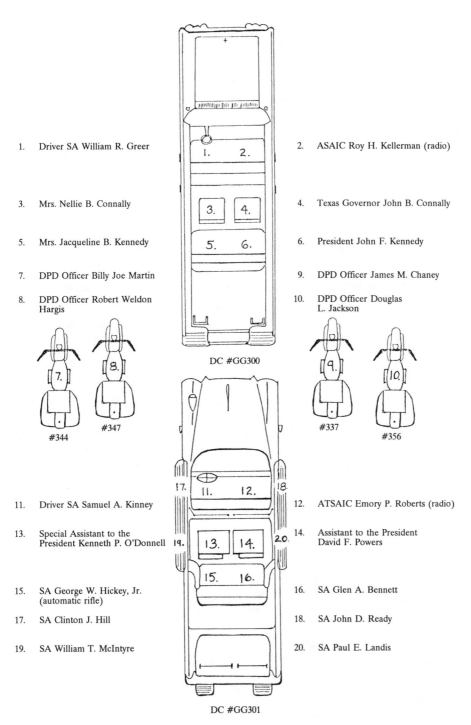

1. Driver SA William R. Greer
2. ASAIC Roy H. Kellerman (radio)
3. Mrs. Nellie B. Connally
4. Texas Governor John B. Connally
5. Mrs. Jacqueline B. Kennedy
6. President John F. Kennedy
7. DPD Officer Billy Joe Martin
9. DPD Officer James M. Chaney
8. DPD Officer Robert Weldon Hargis
10. DPD Officer Douglas L. Jackson

DC #GG300

#344 #347 #337 #356

11. Driver SA Samuel A. Kinney
12. ATSAIC Emory P. Roberts (radio)
13. Special Assistant to the President Kenneth P. O'Donnell
14. Assistant to the President David F. Powers
15. SA George W. Hickey, Jr. (automatic rifle)
16. SA Glen A. Bennett
17. SA Clinton J. Hill
18. SA John D. Ready
19. SA William T. McIntyre
20. SA Paul E. Landis

DC #GG301

Occupants of the presidential Lincoln, Secret Service follow-up car,
and presidential motorcycle escort in Dallas

President Kennedy is seated in the six-passenger limousine's back seat, right passenger side, which faces Zapruder's position. Early frames clearly show the President in the process of brushing his hair from his forehead with his right hand, which movement quickly turns into a waving motion towards the spectators at his right. The back sides of a line of spectators, mostly women, are seen in the frame's foreground standing on the north side of Elm Street, some of the ladies obviously applauding. Upon the southwest corner of Elm and Houston Streets many more spectators are now present than only seconds ago when Zapruder was filming the motorcycles, as many of these people had scurried just ahead of the Lincoln for a prolonged viewing possibility. Up near the corner a young man named Hugh Betzner, with camera in hand, is seen in light colored clothes preparing to make a picture of the vehicle. In the street Phil Willis, who has accompanied his family to see the President, at about Zapruder frame 139-142 (frames referred to hereafter in the text as Z139-Z142), takes a blurred picture of the occupants of the car as they pass parallel to him. He and his wife then step out of the street and back onto the sidewalk to avoid the motorcycle escorts. As the car proceeds very slowly, still recovering from the sharp left turn, Mrs. Kennedy, seated to the President's left in the back seat, looks towards her left. Texas Governor John B. Connally, seated in front of the President in a limousine jump seat and facing to his right, brushes back his wind- tousled hair, and at about Z142 is now looking slightly towards his left. On the south sidewalk just southwest of Willis is spectator Robert Croft, also with a camera and who takes a clear picture of the six occupants of the car at about Z161. President Kennedy is facing straight ahead and the back of his suit coat is visibly bunched up towards his neck, partially because of a back brace, which he usually wears for support due to his chronic back problem. His right arm is resting on the car's side body, also causing part of his suit coat's bunching. Between Z162 and 167, the Governor suddenly jerks his head to the right. The President continues to wave, though he has been moving right of center to about 45 degrees. Governor Connally now appears to move his body right following his head movement, possibly attempting to look at the President.

Zapruder movie frame Z183

Willis has begun to put his camera to his face again, and makes another color slide at about Z202. Beginning at about Z189, the President's hand acts in a manner inconsistent with his previous waving motion. Willis's 10-year-old daughter, Rosemary, in a red dress and white hooded jacket, had been running down Elm Street, and at about Z190, she suddenly stops and looks towards the direction of her parents and the Texas School Book Depository Building in the background. In an interview years later, Miss Willis recalled running to keep up with the President's car. She heard three shots which sounded as if they came from across the street, and from the direction of the Book Depository. Concerning why she stopped running at about Z190 she stated, "I stopped when I heard the shot." Appearing frozen in motion, the President at Z195 jerks his head suddenly to the left and looks towards his wife who is now also looking in his direction. At Z200 the Governor is lost to Zapruder's view by a street sign between Zapruder and the vehicle. The President disappears behind the sign at Z210.

At Z206 the tip of a dark umbrella is first seen in the Zapruder film frame adjacent to the right end of the sign. It is revolving slightly clockwise and moving up and then down until lost at the left of the camera frame at Z238. As the Lincoln convertible emerges on the right from behind the sign again into Zapruder's camera view, the presidential flag on the front driver side of the hood is flapping majestically in the wind, while the United States flag seems caught up on its staff. The governor is first fully visible at Z222 and in subsequent frames his body appears stiff and he has what seems to be a distressed look on his face. His body moves closer towards the car frame, his head facing right and his right shoulder turning left and downward. At Z226 his right hand, which is holding a Stetson hat, suddenly shows itself to the camera, and during the next two frames, his head turns forward. The hand and hat then rise to Connally's chin level, and in a fragment of a second between Z229 and Z230, he flips the hat over.

Full-frame 8mm image of Z228

Meanwhile as the car emerges from behind the sign, a spectator in the foreground and to the right of the man holding the umbrella has his right hand raised in a wave. In the frame's background on the opposite side of Elm Street and in a position where the President's car has passed their front viewing area, two black men are seen, one in a hat and the other wearing a work apron. They applaud as the vice-presidential portion of the motorcade comes into their view.

A cropped view of Frame Z225 as the President emerges from behind a road sign

The President emerges at Z225 from behind the sign in obvious distress as seen by the unusual movements of his arms. His right waving arm, with its hand and elbow on the same horizontal plane, moves unnaturally upward, the hand in front of his lower face. His left arm reacts just a bit slower, mimicking the movement of the right arm, though just below the other. Both arms pause in front of the President's nose-mouth area. The elbows rise above the level of the hands in an awkward position as if a marionette's hands and elbows were being manipulated upwards. Mrs. Kennedy has been turning and looking in the direction of the right towards her husband and at Z236 she begins to raise her right hand from her lap. Connally too has been turning right from Z231, and at Z237 and Z238 his cheeks suddenly puff and his right shoulder drops radically. His face likewise shows severe stimulus and his mouth is seen to be open during several subsequent frames. Mrs. Nellie Connally, in the left jump seat in front of Mrs. Kennedy on the driver's side of the car, also is turning right towards her husband, though her body is partially blocked from Zapruder's view by Assistant Special Agent-in-Charge Roy Kellerman in the front passenger seat, who is also looking towards the right.

As Mrs. Kennedy brings her right hand up towards the President, she noticeably glances at Connally, perhaps in reaction to his radical movement or his uttering of words. Mrs. Kennedy's right hand grasps her husband's left arm above the elbow as she looks again towards him. Then with her left hand she reaches under and clasps Kennedy's forearm. As she again looks towards Connally, who is writhing in obvious pain in the jump seat to her front right, the First Lady's torso moves towards the President. Her husband is turning slightly to the left, her motion seeming to be forcing his stiffened body down and slightly towards her side. Both his arms are being brought downward more horizontally, though they are still splayed in front of him. Her movement, if one can interpret such fragmental moments of time, is as if she were bringing him into her protection. Yet her attention is attracted to something very strange, which she is compelled to watch, which is happening in the jump seats in front of her.

The car was now traveling approximately 11 miles per hour and moving towards and almost parallel to Zapruder's camera position. Though very short in real time, as one views this sequence of Mrs. Kennedy solicitously holding the President's arm prior to the bullet impacting the President in the head, it also has a quality of appearing to happen in slow motion as the main point of interest seems unchanged. After viewing the sequence numerous times, one still can't help wishing that the car will swerve out of harm's way or that an agent will boldly offer protection. Instead, the President continues his unnatural, exposed position, head slightly down, hand still raised, his shock of puffy hair in place, save for the front locks wisping slightly in the breeze. It reminds one of a helpless and wounded animal.

Frame Z258

Mrs. Connally would later recall of the President following the first perceived shot, "I turned over my right shoulder and looked back, and saw the President as he had both hands at his neck . . . . He made no utterance, no cry. I saw no blood, no anything. It was just sort of nothing, the expression on his face, and he just sort of slumped down." Mrs. Kennedy seems transfixed for several moments at the writhing motion of the governor. In later testimony he recalled saying after he was shot, "Oh, no, no, no," and, "My God, they are going to kill us all." Mrs. Kennedy would relate about this scene, "But then suddenly Governor Connally was yelling, 'Oh, no, no, no.' I was looking this way, to the left [sic], and heard these terrible noises. And my husband never made any sound. So I turned to the right, and all I remember is seeing my husband, he had this sort of quizzical look on his face and his hand was up . . . ."

As the car virtually coasted down the Elm Street incline, Zapruder's panning to the right was catching much of the activity in and around the car. Assistant Special Agent-in-Charge Roy Kellerman, a 48- year-old, 23-year veteran Secret Service agent, began turning left to look into the back seat area. The car passes a street light pole in the foreground and Kellerman turns his whole body so that his back is against the door frame as he peers at the governor. Connally has his mouth open and is visibly still holding his Stetson in his right hand with a wrist now pierced and fractured by a bullet. A bullet had traversed Connally's chest coming out under his right nipple and creating a comminuted fracture of the fifth rib, laceration of the middle lobe, and hematoma of the lower lobe of the right lung. The bullet had then gone through the top of his wrist, shattering his radius and finally entered the top of his left thigh. Connally appears to have turned to face the south side of Elm Street and his head is facing the back of the car.

Mrs. Connally, looking to her right rear at Kennedy, now turns left and seems to meet Kellerman's gaze. Driver William Robert Greer, a Secret Service agent since

1945 and 54 years of age, also looks back to his right at Connally. The camera pans the north side of Elm Street while following the car, and blurry images of an unidentified woman in a scarf taking movies, and Charles Brehm and his young son pass by, followed by a view of Jean Hill and her friend Mary Moorman, who is aiming a Polaroid camera for a picture. Connally faces again back to the side, his wife looks towards him, and the two agents turn back towards the front. Kellerman recalls that as he again faced front he said to Greer, "Let's get out of here; we are hit." Grabbing his mike, he radios to the lead car some five car lengths ahead, "Lawson, this is Kellerman, we are hit; get us to the hospital immediately." Kellerman later recalled that he believes the head shot to the President occurred while in the process of broadcasting to agent Lawson. When later questioned by the Warren Commission as to his actions during these, the most critical few seconds of his professional life, Kellerman stated that he had done as he should have done. He appraised the situation and acted upon getting the car to medical assistance. "Did you consider presenting a further shield for the President at that time?" he was asked. "No, sir," he answered. He then stated powerfully, though self -servingly, "If I thought in my own mind that I was needed back there, there wouldn't have been an obstacle strong enough to hold me."

It is perhaps unfair to judge too harshly or from detached hindsight the actions of the agents in the vehicle, mindful of the quickness of the actual events of the shooting. Yet it still strikes one hard that these agents traveling in the car, sworn to protect their cargo and assumed always to be at the ready and possessing more keen skills and reaction time than the general public, appear in these sad Zapruder frames to be mere spectators to the events within the car itself. The vehicle does not jump into getaway speed or begin avoidance zig-zags during these very critical seconds. It is not until after the impact of the third shot, when all occupants felt, heard, and saw the results of a bullet hitting its mark, that the car quickly accelerated. Incredibly, Greer, following his initial turnaround and look into the back seat, and after Kellerman tells him to get out of there, again glances back into the rear of the car and is looking in that direction when the actual head shot occurs. Reflexes of these senior and older agents were not keen.

Of the fifteen Secret Service agents assigned to the first four vehicles in the Dallas motorcade, only Clint Hill, Lem Johns, and Rufus Youngblood made any movement to physically get to and protect their man. Youngblood, in the Vice-President's car, two cars behind the President's, on the first sounds, vaulted over his front seat position to put his body over Vice-President Johnson's. And while conditions in the President's vehicle, with a metal standing bar between the front and back seats and the Connallys physically separating Kellerman from Kennedy, would be more difficult a barrier for Kellerman to navigate, his just sitting there not knowing from where the shots were coming or how many were being fired, seems the depth of protective unprofessionalism.

Just as the camera pans past spectators Moorman and Hill in the background of the frame standing on the south Elm Street curb, Mrs. Kennedy takes her attention away from the moaning governor. She leans her head and body down and puts her face close to the President's. Run in real time, the shot that hits the President in the head occurs quickly, yet leaves a shocking, indelible impression on all who have witnessed it on film. Groups which see this clip usually audibly groan at the sight of seeing a man killed before of them. Twenty years after witnessing the assassination from the same location as Zapruder, receptionist Sitzman recalled that seeing the events on Zapruder's projector that next morning caused her to comment that, "The film was more gruesome than in real life." Reality gives you so much extra stimuli with which to react — sounds, smells, shifting points of reference. Watching a film, on the other hand, in which the point of reference is very centered and your attention is directed towards it tends to give one a super-real concentration.

Just prior to the moment of impact, the President's hands have drifted slightly lower towards his chin level and his elbows have also sagged appreciably. Just prior to impact Governor Connally, with his head tossing and his mouth fully opened, is facing towards the President. Mrs. Connally is looking in the direction of her husband. At impact they both instinctively turn away towards the front of the car. All four front occupants hunker down from the effects of the concussion and flying debris. Mrs. Connally testified about its effect, "The third shot that I heard I felt, it felt like spent buckshot falling all over us. . . .I could see that it was the matter, brain tissue, or whatever, just human matter, all over the car and both of us."

Within the next few frames the governor collapses to his left, and Mrs. Connally falls to the right covering him with her bouquet of yellow roses seemingly pushed over both their bodies in a futile gesture of protection. The First Lady of Texas seeing her husband still moving, though sure he is near death, keeps assuring him, "Don't worry. Be quiet. You are going to be all right."

Spectators in Zapruder's camera view also are seen reacting to the hit. A girl running towards the car from the grass infield stops in her tracks upon seeing the shot hit, while amateur photographer Richard Bothun and Associated Press photographer Jim Altgens hold their cameras, too shocked at the sight to take a picture. "When JFK's head exploded, sending substance in my direction, I virtually became paralyzed," confessed Altgens. And to the left of these cameramen, the falling body of Malcolm Summers hits the ground as he realized these are gunshots.

Z313 is the frame which shows the result of the bullet's impact upon the President. Zapruder would always remember that, "That was the horrible one." Mrs. Kennedy's head and the front face of President Kennedy are virtually hidden in a hazy orange-red ring of vaporized brain matter. Two distinguishable bursts containing bone

Frame Z313 at the moment of the impact of a bullet to the President's head

and matter shoot up and forward in the frame. As the film continues, the President's arm flops up from the impact, and then quickly falls lifelessly to his side, while his body travels slightly forward and then lurches powerfully backward and to the left. Several non-blurred frames show a seemingly inhuman form where once there was a face. Bright highlights show to the right of the ear and globs of matter seem to fall out in a clump. The back of the skull shows unnaturally disheveled hair.

The horror which Mrs. Kennedy witnessed would turn a heart of stone. One moment she is very close and looking into her husband's face, when in a fraction of a second she witnesses the disintegration of part of his skull and feels the concussion and scattering of fragments. It is hard to tell initially what she does with her hands. She instinctively backs off from the impact, but quickly appears to grab at his lower head and neck with her right hand. As he slumps further left towards her, the shock on her face and her open mouth are excruciatingly visible. Mrs. Kennedy later recalled of this, "And just as I turned and looked at him, I could see a piece of his skull and I remember it was flesh colored. I remember thinking he just looked as if he had a slight headache. And I just remember seeing that. No blood or anything. And then he sort of . . . put his hand to his forehead and fell in my lap. And then I just remember falling on him and saying . . . 'Oh, my God, they have shot my husband.' And 'I love you, Jack.' I remember I was shouting." From his stupor John Connally remembers hearing the First Lady's voice shouting, "They have killed my husband. I have got his brains on my hand."

Mrs. Kennedy was now in shock, a shock which would charitably in the future never allow her to remember much of the next few minutes. As her husband lay motionless with a gaping and glistening void in his right head exposed to Zapruder's camera, Mrs. Kennedy begins to rise in her seat, her white-gloved left hand pushing down on the President's head as she looks and leans towards the vehicle's trunk. In publicly deleted testimony before the Warren Commission, Mrs. Kennedy remembered as she traveled to the hospital, " . . . you know, you were trying to hold his hair on, and his skull on." It would appear from her actions of looking and then crawling on her hands onto the trunk of the moving vehicle, as well as the specific placement of her hands, that she was attempting to retrieve something on the trunk.

Clint Hill, the Secret Service agent specifically assigned to Mrs. Kennedy, ran from the front left running board of the Secret Service follow-up car after hearing a noise and seeing the President apparently hit the first time. Reaching the car just following the head shot, Hill was attempting to get a foothold on the back left step of the now accelerating Lincoln. Of Mrs. Kennedy's actions he would com-

Frame Z333 as Mrs. Kennedy begins to rise in her seat and Agent Clint Hill is seen at extreme left rushing to get aboard the vehicle

ment to the Warren Commission, "Mrs. Kennedy jumped up from the seat and was, it appeared to be, reaching for something coming off the right rear bumper of the car, the right rear tail, when she noticed that I was trying to climb on the car. She turned towards me and I grabbed her and put her back in the back seat."

Minutes later at Parkland Hospital anesthesiologist, Dr. M. T. Jenkins, would be handed something by what he best described as a "shell-shocked" Mrs. Kennedy. "I noticed that her hands were cupped in front of her, as if she were cradling something. As she passed by, she nudged me with an elbow and handed me what she had been nursing in her hands - a large chunk of her husband's brain tissues."

In an emotion-filled interview twelve years after the assassination, former agent Clint Hill, barely holding back tears and finding it hard to talk, told interviewer Mike Wallace that the reason Mrs. Kennedy went on the trunk of the vehicle was that, "She was simply trying to reach the head, part of the head. That's the only thing." Feeling that it was his personal fault that the President was not protected, Hill had this sad exchange with Wallace:

Hill:    If he [Hill] had reached about 5/10 of a second faster, maybe a second faster, I wouldn't be here today.

Wallace: You mean you would have gotten there and you would have taken the shot?

Hill:      The third shot.  Yes, sir.

Wallace:  And that would have been all right with you?

Hill:      That would have been fine with me.

Hill:      . . . If I had reacted just a little bit quicker, and I could have, I guess, and I'll live with that to my grave.


Hill was obviously very pained by his furtive actions and though one could explain that the fault was not his, and that he alone among the President's detail of body guards had physically acted, and perhaps had saved Mrs. Kennedy from falling from the accelerating vehicle into the path of the follow-up car, he contended that was not the point.  He had failed, no matter his intentions.

SA Clinton J. Hill being presented "The Exceptional Service Award" by C. Douglas Dillon

On December 3, 1963, at a ceremony at the Treasury Department with Hill's family and Mrs. Jacqueline Kennedy present, Agent Hill was given the Exceptional Service Award by Treasury Secretary Dillon.  The citation read in part:  " . . . for exceptional bravery in his efforts to protect the President and First Lady of the United States at the time of President John F. Kennedy's assassination . . . .  Agent Hill immediately ran from his vehicle while the bullets were still being fired, climbed on the rear of the President's rapidly moving limousine, and shielded the President and Mrs. Kennedy with his own body.  His extraordinary courage and heroic effort in the face of maximum danger reflect great credit on the United States of America, which can produce such men."  The award was deserved and one of the few incidents of the assassination of which the Service could be justifiably proud.  Yet Hill's self-blaming failure would sadly and irrationally remain with this very professional government agent for years to come.

Though Mrs. Kennedy never actually had her legs or knees fully out of the back seat, the scene of her groping onto the trunk, which began at Z345, was contrary to the elegant manner and poise to which Americans had grown fond.  Many who saw the pictures were very much affected by the pathetic scene.

Zapruder continued to pan right incredibly continuing to film while at the same time screaming, "They killed him, they killed him!"  The car was now speeding up and traveling away from Zapruder's location.  Other spectators on the opposite side of the street from the camera are merely tall blurs as Zapruder's cries unsteady any possibility of his smooth panning of the camera.  Hill is seen reaching the car at Z359, gaining a foothold in Z367, and then pushing with his right hand at Mrs. Kennedy who moves back into her seat. Branches and foliage begin to block Zapruder's view as he continues to pan at his extreme right until there is nothing else of the car to film as it disappears into the underpass. The 486-frame sequence has been exposed, and Zapruder would shoot no more of the now disintegrating motorcade as it confusingly passes below him. Twenty-three seconds of filming, and not incidentally, an era of American History had just ended.[9]

Zapruder now took his camera from his eye, and all but ignoring Sitzman, climbed down from the four-foot abutment and momentarily walked into the adjacent concrete pergola shelter. A photo made by AP's Jim Altgens shows Zapruder and Sitzman just getting off the abutment, while another picture taken moments later from a car in the motorcade by *LIFE* photographer Art Rickerby shows Zapruder in his easy-to-spot hat and bow tie within the shelter, which is also a temporary haven for Mr. and Mrs. Hester.

Zapruder and Sitzman have just gotten down from the pedestal, while the Hesters (at right) still sit on the ground

Charles Hester, later deposed at the sheriff's office that the shots, " . . .sounded like they came immediately behind us and over our heads. I immediately turned and looked at the Texas School Book Depository Building and did not see anyone. The shots sounded like the [sic] definitely came from in or around the building." During the shots Hester had grabbed and dragged his wife up next to the concrete embankment steps, threw her down and got on the ground with her.[10]

When interviewed by researcher Josiah Thompson two years after the shooting, Sitzman recalled a minor incident at the knoll area. Not mentioned by other witnesses in their accounts, her remarks have never been considered by serious critics in their scenarios of possible assassins lurking in the knoll area. A young black couple between 18 and 21 years of age had been sitting on a bench west of Sitzman near the knoll steps, and between the concrete retaining wall and the wood stockade fence. The bench, which is not visible from photos taken around the Elm Street area that day, faced toward the street and was similar to the one on which the Hesters had earlier been seated. The black couple were eating their lunch from small paper sacks and were drinking Cokes. Sitzman noticed them when she had first climbed on Zapruder's four- foot perch. "The main reason I remember 'em is after the last shot I recall hearing and the car went under the triple underpass, there, I heard a crush of glass and I looked over there and the kids had thrown down their Coke bottles, just threw them down, and just started running towards the back . . ." Thompson asked the secretary if she had turned in the direction of the stockade fence following the head shot, as Zapruder at the trailer of his film photographed the general area of the fence. Sitzman replied that he might have heard the crash of the bottles as it, "was much louder than the shots were." Her recollection was that she did not jump from the sound of the bullets and that concerning the loudness of the shots, "One would be startled by what one saw there rather than necessarily by what one heard." Her comments would add a different and perhaps unconsidered option to what other external stimuli might be relevant to a later developed "camera jiggle theory."

The existence of a bench at this location has generally not been acknowledged. No such object is visible in any assassination related photographs nor does it appear on any later plats made of the area. This author did, however, find verification. While looking through the photographic materials relating to the November 22 weekend coverage preserved at the *Dallas Morning News*, a black-and-white, 8" x 10" glossy print identified as being taken by Johnny Flynn was discovered. The photo shows two plainclothes men, one with a stenographer's note pad in hand, leaning over and examining a paper lunch bag and a wrapper marked "Tom Thumb 8 Buns 25 cents." The lunch leavings are resting on an old-looking metal frame slat bench positioned perpendicular to the concrete wall and next to the walkway leading to the stairs at the knoll. In the background is the pedestal where Zapruder was located, and further back still the Dal-Tex Building can be seen. Several police officers, a police cruiser and fire truck are visible on Houston Street at Elm. Though not specifically identified as such, this could well be the lunch left by the black couple observed by Sitzman. It is also of note that in a photo taken shortly after the assassination by Jim Towner, a glass pop bottle can be discerned on top of the end of the retaining wall, where the wall makes a right angle turn towards the knoll steps. Indeed, in her Warren Commission testimony, Mrs. Barbara Rowland, wife of Arnold, mentions that while she was in this area following the shooting, ". . . the policeman inspected a coke drink bottle that was there. . . ."[11]

If Sitzman had to make a guess from which direction the shots came, she would have guessed to her left. The two shots she recalls hearing sounded like firecrackers and, "I'm sure if the second shot [head shot] would have come from a different place, and the supposed theory is they would have been much closer to me and on the right side — I would have heard the sounding of the gun much closer and I probably had a ringing in my ear because the fence was quite close to where we were standing, very close."

The young black couple has not been identified. It is around this site where many later Warren Commission critics would assert that assassins had fired at the President. Unless the pair were assassins themselves, unlikely due to their seated position, lunches, and exposure, they would have been right on top of an assassin firing from either the concrete wall or at the adjacent stockade fence. Though a case cannot be made for what they saw, it would seem unlikely an assassin would set up his potential shot with witnesses so close. The pop bottles which Sitzman describes as "Cokes" and which, upon breaking, caused such a loud crash, might have added to the sound confusion of the area. The quick movement of the couple out of the area following the shots, and their possible shadowy features showing in related grassy knoll photos and films

Men examine a paper bag and food wrappers found the afternoon of November
22 on the bench adjacent to the north pergola walkway.  Marilyn Sitzman had
earlier noticed a young black couple having lunch here just prior to the shooting.

might lead some to find this movement sinister.  It could, however, be a simple  case of
reading too much into what could be a simple explanation.  The spilled liquid contents
might also be the result of what several later witnesses recalled seeing.  Some people
rushing to the area believed they saw spilled blood, but on reflection described it as a

In this poor quality frame, possibly from a clip by Mal Couch, a portion of the bench is seen at left. A pool of dark liquid is on the edge of the concrete walk.

spilled red drink or a melted slush concoction. This is the area in which this pool of liquid was noticed.

Getting down off the abutment, Sitzman could not locate Zapruder. She ran down the knoll and spoke with some men who had rushed to the scene. She assumed them to be Secret Service or CIA agents. When asked what had happened, she told them, "They killed him." Walking back up the hill, Sitzman then spoke with a man who she said identified himself as "FBI" and then she tarried for a bit in the concrete shelter before returning to her office. Deputy Sheriff John (Bill) Wiseman stated in his departmental report that when he had reached the knoll shortly after the shooting a man lying on the grass told him that the shots came from the Texas School Book Depository Building. He also talked with Sitzman who volunteered that her boss had taken movies of the shooting and that she then pointed out that the shots came from the direction of this same building.[12]

Zapruder had quickly started walking to his office, yelling as he made his way back, "They killed him, they killed him, they killed him!" He " . . . finally got to my office and my secretary — I told her to call the police or the Secret Service — I don't know what she was doing, and that's about all. I was very much upset. Naturally, I couldn't imagine such a thing being done. I just went to my desk and stopped there until the police came . . . ." Zapruder knew he had filmed something extraordinary. The camera was locked in a small office safe. Others in the company had also witnessed part of the events. Mrs. Margaret Burney, head of the shipping department, had been on Elm Street, heard two shots, and saw the car speed off. There had been pandemonium. "Everybody realized that the shots were coming from up high. People were running around cars and jumping over things. As soon as we were inside the building before any reports on the condition of the President, Mr. Zapruder had already told us, 'The President of the U.S. is dead.'" The news of the possibility of the existence of a film of the shooting began circulating. Early that afternoon Forrest Sorrels, Agent-in-Charge of the Dallas Secret Service field office, was informed by *Dallas Morning News* reporter Harry McCormack of Zapruder's film's existence. The two went to Zapruder's office. Sorrels spoke with the clothing manufacturer, asking if it would be possible to get a copy of the film. Apparently some media representatives were already there also. Sorrels described Zapruder as "real shook up. He said that he didn't know how in the world he had taken these pictures, and that he was down there and was taking the thing there, and he says, 'My God, I saw the whole thing. I saw the man's brains come out of his head.'" Even in the midst of the shock of events, however, Zapruder realized his film could be valuable. McCormack offered $1,000 for the film and others there were also interested. Sorrels later reported to Washington, "Mr. Zapruder agreed to furnish me with a copy of this film with the understanding that it was strictly for official use of the Secret Service, and that it would not be shown or given to any newspapers or magazines, as he expected to sell the film for as high a price as he could get for it."[13]

McCormack suggested his paper might be able to develop the film, and the three men and a Zapruder associate went the few blocks to the News building. There were no movie developing facilities there, so they walked over to the television section of the paper — WFAA — to see if the TV people could handle it. WFAA did develop black-and-white 16mm film for their news department, but were not set up for color or 8mm processing. They thus lost out on one of the most spectacular spot news scoops in history. At just around 2:00 p.m., Zapruder agreed to be interviewed live on WFAA by program director Jay Watson. Watson, who after having witnessed the motorcade and having heard the shots himself, had rushed back to the studio to break in with live coverage beginning at 12:45 p.m. The brief, somewhat disjointed interview with Zapruder, during part of which time Watson was obviously not paying attention as he listened into a telephone receiver, is nonetheless remarkable and the earliest interview of Zapruder.

> Watson: A gentleman just walked into our studio that I am meeting for the first time as well as you to the WFAA studio in Dallas, Texas. May I have your name, please, sir?
>
> Zapruder: My name is Abraham Zapruder.
>
> Watson: Zapruder?
>
> Zapruder: Zapruder, yes sir.
>
> Watson: Zapruder! And would you tell us your story, please sir?
>
> Zapruder: As I got out about a half-hour earlier to get a good spot to shoot some pictures. And I finally spotted one of these concrete blocks near the park, near the underpass. And I got on top there, there was another girl from my office, she was behind me. And I was [filming?] as the President was coming down from Houston Street making his turn, it was about a half-way down there, I heard a shot, and he slumped to the side like this. Then I heard another shot or two, I couldn't say whether it was one or two, and I saw his head practically open up, all blood and everything and I kept on shooting. That's about all. I'm too sick.

Watson:    I think that pretty well expresses the entire feelings of the whole world.  You have the film in your camera, we'll . . .

Zapruder:  Yes, I brought it to the studio.

Watson:    We'll try to get that processed and have it as soon as possible.

Watson then receives more information and shows a photo of the Texas School Book Depository attempting to locate on camera for the views the window from which it was believed the shots originated.

Watson:    . . . There is the picture of the window where the gun was allegedly fired from that killed President Kennedy.

Zapruder:  I must have been in the line of fire.

Watson:    Excuse me, go ahead sir.

Zapruder:  That must have been the line of fire.  Looking at that picture and where I was.  I was right on that concrete block up there.  As I explained before. [garbled]  It sounded like, when you make a joke, you hear a shot and somebody grabs their stomach.[14]

Hearing that the shots emanated from the Texas School Book Depository seemed to confuse Zapruder.  In his subsequent Warren Commission testimony he appeared unsure of how to answer as to the direction of the shots. He recalled police running behind him. "I guess they thought it came from right behind me."  When asked if he had an impression as to the direction of the shots, he commented, "No, I also thought it came from back of me . . . . Actually — I couldn't say what I thought at the moment, where they came from  . . . . — I assumed that they came from there because as the police started running back of me it looked like it came from the back of me." He also attempted to explain that as he saw the President hit on the right side of the head which faced him, that the shots had come from behind this location. It is unclear if Zapruder was reacting to what he perceived the police to be doing, or if the early identification of the Texas School Book Depository, contrary to his beliefs, clouded what he actually perceived as to the location of the shots. In the end, during his testimony taken months after the events, Zapruder opted out of trying to resolve for himself or for what he saw was what the "official line" was. Instead, he stated, "I have no way of determining what direction the bullet was going . . . . There is too much reverberation. There was an echo which gave me a sound all over."[15]

It was still not known at WFAA if Zapruder's undeveloped film would show anything, let alone the horror of the fatal shot about which Zapruder was so obviously upset. Personnel at the TV studio called ahead to Eastman Kodak Company about the need for processing, and Kodak agreed to process the film right away. A police cruiser took the men to the processing plant on Manor Way, and while there Sorrels met Phil Willis who had brought in his slide roll for development. Willis agreed to allow the Secret Service access to his transparencies. During the film's processing Sorrels was called away to police headquarters as a suspect named Lee Oswald had been picked up. Sorrels told Zapruder that he had to leave, but that he would contact him later about the film. Both Sorrels and Willis recount that Zapruder's film was processed at Kodak, though in an early December FBI report by Agent Robert M. Barrett, he quotes Zapruder as telling him the that film was processed by the Jamieson Film Company on Bryan Street. It should be noted there were other errors in this FBI report, including the size of the original film and the number of frames exposed per second by the camera. It is unclear if the mistakes were Zapruder's or the agent's in recording the conversation. It is also possible that both places were used, Kodak for the actual processing of the film, and Jamieson, with their optical printer, for making "timed" copies of the developed original. Later when some of these inaccuracies were reported by critics, Zapruder claimed he had never been interviewed about this, and the FBI produced this "interview." Zapruder noted, however, this was simply a conversation with the agent and not understood by him to be a formal interview. To further muddy the facts about the processing of the film, CBS Correspondent Dan Rather states in his book, *The Camera Never Blinks*, " . . . We helped arrange for Eastman Kodak to process the film. This job had to be done with the best equipment. It had to be done fast. And it had to be kept confidential." Since CBS's affiliate was KRLD, it would seem unlikely Rather had confused this with Zapruder and Sorrels' initial visit to WFAA. In the CBS program *Four Days in November* broadcast on November 17, 1988, during the 25th anniversary of the assassination, Rather stated concerning the Zapruder film, "CBS had the film briefly at the time, but for legal reasons, we could not broadcast it." According to assassination researcher and newspaper publisher Penn Jones, Rather saw the film when the FBI [more probably the Secret Service] brought it to CBS affiliate KRLD to use its facilities to look at the film during the November 22 weekend. Rather " . . . badly wanted to broadcast it . . . but CBS demurred." The Secret Service had previously utilized KRLD resources and its reporters Jim Underwood and Wes Wise in examining film taken of an assault on Ambassador Adlai Stevenson at a UN Day observance back in October 1963. No other information has been found relating to CBS or Rather's role in the development of Zapruder's original film.[16]

Zapruder had his original film developed together with an additional three first generation copies made of it. While at the processing lab he obtained assurances from the technicians that no additional copies had been bootlegged. Phil Willis in his later recollections notes that the film was previewed at the lab right after it was developed. Some time later that day Sorrels went back to Zapruder's office and received two of the three first generation copies of the film, again assuring Zapruder that they would be for official use only.

An official announcement of the death of President Kennedy had been made at 1:30 p.m. Central Standard Time. Events in the murder case were transpiring so rapidly that it was not always evident which pieces of evidence were going to be important. The various investigative units did not always follow through with potential evidence as well as they could have. Indeed, one FBI internal memo dated November 23 made note that Agent-in-Charge J. Gordon Shanklin of the FBI's Dallas field office: "Stated he did not believe that the film would be of any evidentiary value; however, he first had to take a look at the film to determine this factor." Talk about coming to a conclusion before the facts — and how wrong the agent was about the significance of this film! In this same memo it was assumed that the FBI had possession of the original Zapruder film and Cartha D. DeLoach, the FBI's Assistant Director in charge of the Criminal Records Division instructed that " . . . this matter would have to be treated strictly as evidence and later on a determination would be made as to whether the film would be given back to Zapruder or not." It was wishful thinking on the Bureau's part that they had snagged and wrapped up this original film as evidence, for by the time this memo was written Zapruder had sold the original film to a private party for big bucks. In the end the FBI would have to settle for a second generation copy of this most important piece of evidence. Whether or not the government could have actually seized the original film as a piece of critical evidence in a major criminal investigation was never followed through, perhaps as a result of the killing of the only suspect, Oswald, on Sunday, or perhaps due to the field agent not knowing the importance of an original versus a multi- generation copy of a film.[17]

Through Agent Sorrels' efforts, by the evening of November 22 the Secret Service now had two first-generation copies of Zapruder's film. At 9:55 p.m. Agent Max D. Phillips hastily hand-lettered a brief memo to Secret Service Chief James Rowley enclosing one of the two copies of the film to Washington. Phillips noted, "According to Mr. Zapruder, the position of the assassin was behind Mr. Zapruder." A quick, simple sketch of Elm and Houston Streets, the underpass, and Zapruder's camera position was also sent along.  Late that night or early Saturday morning the Secret Service, through Inspector Thomas Kelly, loaned the Dallas FBI the second first-generation copy of the film.  Unable to have copies made locally, some time after 5 p.m. on Saturday, Shanklin in Dallas was instructed by Washington to send the film immediately to FBI headquarters on a commercial flight.  That same night Shanklin forwarded the film requesting that the FBI lab make three copies — one for Washington and two for the Dallas FBI office. On November 26 the first generation copy was returned to the Dallas Secret Service, and on December 3 one second-generation copy was sent back to the Dallas FBI office informing them that, "It is felt one copy should be sufficient," and that "You are cautioned that the film is for official use only."  Although a *LIFE* magazine representative later stated that on Saturday, November 23, he had obtained both Zapruder's original and first- generation copy, he only bought print rights to the film and it is likely that Zapruder retained one copy, especially in light of the fact that Zapruder later testified that Sorrels came to his office quite a few times to show the film to different people. From Saturday afternoon, November 23, until about November 26, Sorrels did not have a copy of the film, the two having been sent to Washington, and he most likely needed to view Zapruder's copy.  It also seems probable that others, including CBS's Dan Rather saw the film in Zapruder's office on November 25 as the reporter broadcast a description of its contents that day as if he had just viewed it that same morning.[18]

The story of the actual sale of the original Zapruder film and rights is ambiguous in some details, in that for quite some time Zapruder purposely did not want to divulge the particulars.  There are also conflicts and contradictions in the comparison of parts of the story as told by *LIFE*'s Richard Stolley and CBS's Dan Rather, both of whom have written about aspects of the events leading to the deal.  Writing from a personal narrative perspective which does not take into consideration other players or events which might explain some of the ambiguities, Rather's account seems to be a result of telescoping events together and either having a poor recollection of specifics, or in the case of the description in his book, *The Camera Never Blinks*, relying too much on a co-author's narration.  In any event the following account tries to sift through the material to percolate the most factual account possible.

The Pacific Coast regional editor for *LIFE* magazine was Richard B. Stolley, whose bureau was located in Los Angeles, California.  An energetic, resourceful, Illinois native in his mid-30s, Stolley had been a rising star at the magazine during his 10-year tenure.  He had gained experience reporting on a plethora of subjects, including the race issue and the space program.  Shortly after 10:30 a.m. (Pacific Time) on November 22, the AP ticker in the *LIFE* Bureau sent out the first bulletin concerning the Dallas shooting.  Thomas "Tommy" Thompson, an intense, fast-track staff reporter quickly read and yelled out the news to Stolley.  As Los Angeles was the closest full-fledged *LIFE* bureau to Dallas, the pair wanted to get to the scene of this breaking news event fast. A quick call to New York confirmed they should go, and within an hour the two men, along with staff photographers Allan Grant and Don Cravens, were on their way.  Four hours later they and a large assortment of other California-based journalists landed at Dallas's Love Field. As *LIFE* earned its reputation as America's most popular weekly magazine by its unexcelled photographic coverage and straightforward writing, the L.A. staff members knew they would have to go the extra mile to ferret out angles others might miss. They always had to be on the lookout for those exclusives which *LIFE* prided itself in being able to attract. The magazine possessed a magical name draw and deep pockets. Tommy Thompson, through ingenuity and fantastic luck, managed to locate and exclusively interview Lee Oswald's mother and wife, keeping them hidden from the competition, and briefly from the authorities. *LIFE* was good at its job and knew it. Yet sometimes in the pursuit of a story the staff could border on interfering with the official process. Its staff sometimes treated everybody, including the government, as the dread competition, and the game was to try to outflank the competition. The fact is that *LIFE* was often perceived as, to beg a pun, "bigger than life." In both Thompson's temporary and exclusive capturing of the Oswald family and Stolley's eventual snagging of the original Zapruder film, we see the idea at work that the story is indeed the one-dimensional goal of these journalists. And if the authorities let this happen, or were not quick enough themselves to catch the prey, then tough for them. America should be able to read about and see the important events of the week and expected to do it through the pages of *LIFE* magazine. It was journalism at its best — or rather at its most successful. A rakish and talented man, Thompson, after *LIFE*'s 1972 demise, would go on to be a highly successful novelist and screenwriter, producing the best-selling novel *Blood and Money* and just prior to his untimely death, authoring the somewhat autobiographical volume *Celebrity*.[19]

Upon arriving in Dallas Stolley made for the Adolphus Hotel, Dallas's *grande dame* hotel located in the downtown business district, only blocks from City Hall and the scene of the assassination. As they often did when a major story broke at a location far from one of their bureaus, *LIFE* set up an interim bureau at a local site. Wire service teletypes could be set up, as well as office facilities for the staff. Stolley began making calls to local sources. Patsy Swank, a stringer correspondent who locally looked out for the magazine's interests and provided information and copy as needed, called Stolley with a tip. She had been on the lookout for information and film sources and had learned through a local Dallas police reporter that an amateur photographer whose name began with a "Z" had purportedly taken movies of the shooting. This might be just the kind of visual material *LIFE* would need for its story. *LIFE* staff photographer Art Rickerby, though in the motorcade, had been in a car too far back to record any pictures of the shooting scene itself, and *LIFE* often depended upon finding and then purchasing amateur spot news photos to round out a story. A short time later Swank called again with the information that the man was named "Zapruder" and he was a dress manufacturer. Reporter Harry McCormack, who had initially put the Secret Service in contact with Zapruder, had also alerted TIME-LIFE correspondent and friend, Holland McCombs about Zapruder, asking if *LIFE* would be interested. McCombs assured his friend that they would very much be interested, and the Dallas reporter eventually received a finder's fee of $1500 from the magazine.[20]

Picking up the local phone book, Stolley easily found Zapruder's residential address and phone number, and called him.  No answer.  During the next few hours at regular intervals Stolley persistently re-called the number, also calling *LIFE*'s director of photography, Richard Pollard, speaking to him about the possibility of this film being useful to *LIFE* and asking advice about the potential buying procedure.

After leaving his office, Zapruder had spent some quiet reflection time driving nowhere in particular around Dallas.  He was still in shock over the scene he had witnessed and was now the unwitting owner of a film which was both gruesome and yet apparently much desired by the press.  He arrived home late in the evening and some time around 11:00 received a call from the Adolphus Hotel.  Stolley explained who he was, that he represented *LIFE* and might be interested in Zapruder's film.  Zapruder was exhausted, his mind cluttered by the day's events.  He told Stolley that he was the first press representative to call him, confirmed he had the film, and that it did in fact show the shooting.  Stolley, not wanting to lose his apparent exclusive, and knowing that if he had found Zapruder others would be on his trail as well, asked the businessman if he could come out to the house and view it and talk.  Zapruder demurred, but Stolley detected even within Zapruder's obviously distraught feelings, a business sense of seeing what Stolley might have to offer.  Zapruder told Stolley to meet him tomorrow at his office at 9 a.m.

Fearing a media frenzy once Zapruder was discovered by his brother press, Stolley arrived at Jennifer's an hour earlier than requested.  He found himself with a small group of men who turned out, to his relief, to be Secret Service Agents and not journalists.  Zapruder, who had brought a projector into work, obligingly and almost apologetically projected the section of his 8mm film which graphically recorded the death of the President.  Recalls Stolley, "There was no sound, of course, except this rickety old projector grinding away. There was this tension because you don't know what he's got, but you know something awful is about to happen — and suddenly there is that head shot."  There was a real tension and sadness in the room as Secret Service agents watched in silence the horrific death of the President, the man who both they and their Service were established to protect from such an act.  As his eyes were transfixed by the images flashing on the screen before him, Stolley marveled, "It was the single most dramatic thing I've ever seen in my career as a journalist."[21]

Zapruder continued to replay the film.  Interest in it and its shocking scenes did not wane and more details revealed themselves in those repetitions.  Unfortunately for Stolley, as Zapruder replayed the film, some of the media Stolley hoped would not show up began arriving.  The press information network had been at work.  Representatives from AP, UPI and several magazines and other outlets arrived and also viewed the macabre motorcade.  When the show was finally over, Zapruder looked very ill at ease at both what he had shown and the number of people now interested.  Taking the initiative, Stolley asked to speak with Zapruder first and in private, since he had made the initial contact the night before. Though clamoring that he should not make up his mind before talking with the others there, the rest of the press had to cool their heels as Zapruder hurried Stolley into his cluttered inner office. Secretary Lillian Rogers was there and Stolley, using all the charm and good grace that he could muster, tried to ease the tension of the moment. He struck up a conversation with Rogers and learned that she too was an Illinois native with a home town near Stolley's. Rogers' demeanor had a calming effect on her boss and soon Zapruder was more comfortable talking about the matter at hand. "It was an unpleasant experience for Mr. Zapruder. This was a very sharp businessman, and I'm sure if we had been talking about sewing machine needles or fabric or something like that, he would have had my scalp. It was a very kind of elaborate conversation which sometimes avoided the sort of direct sense of we're bargaining over the film of a murder."[22]

The calm, reasonable talk in the inner office was offset at times by the near hysterical pitch exuding outside as the other gathered press stewed in the fear that *LIFE* with its prestige and pocketbook would leave them out in the cold on this opportunity.

In a 1973 article appearing in *Esquire* magazine, Stolley recaptured the events of one of the journalistic coups of the century:

> [Zapruder] was emphatic on two points: he wished he had not taken the film but now realized it could contribute to his family's financial security, and he was determined that it not fall into the hands of shoddy exploiters. Time and again he described what he feared most — the film's being shown in sleazy Times Square movie houses, while men hawked it on the sidewalk — and the revulsion on his face was genuine.
>
> For my part, I had to find out right away whether Zapruder understood the value of his seven seconds of film. I made a little speech about our being anxious to give the picture respectable display, just as he was, and nonchalantly added that we might go as high as $15,000. Abe Zapruder smiled. He understood.
>
> The negotiations between us were most cordial. I would mention a figure, saying I didn't think we could go higher. Zapruder would demur, and I would go higher. The wire-service representatives outside telephoned to ask fearfully why we were taking so long, the secretary brought in the business card of yet another bidder, this one from *The Saturday Evening Post*, and once when I told Zapruder I had to call my New York office for instructions he courteously left the room.
>
> In the end, *LIFE*'s reputation and our assurances that we would not sensationalize the pictures won Zapruder over before he had even talked to any of the other journalists, which of course had been my hope. At his desk, I typed out a crude contract which we both sol-

emnly signed. It called for payment of $50,000 for print rights only, an amount I'm sure he could have gotten, and possible more, from one of those anxious men outside. I picked up the original of the film and the one remaining copy and sneaked out a back door of the building. I wanted to be elsewhere when Zapruder faced my distraught rivals.[23]

Stolley, however, had only obtained the print rights to the film, and the potentially very valuable motion picture rights which *LIFE* magazine itself could not use, and which Zapruder feared could be used in a distasteful manner, were still Zapruder's for the selling. The original film was sent to *LIFE*'s Chicago plant, where it would be worked on for the now to be completely re-worked November 29 issue. Stolley states that the other Zapruder copy was sent to New York, meaning that Zapruder was left without possession of his film. As postulated earlier, Zapruder most probably did retain a copy, and in Chicago a dupe was made of the original and sent on to New York, along with duplicates of other photographic material initially being sent directly to Chicago.

According to later reports, *LIFE* publisher C.D. Jackson, upon seeing the film projected, was shocked and repulsed at the possibility of its morbid and graphically bloody scenes being shown to the public. For this reason, as well as to keep it from his competitors and to control all rights to this historic film, Jackson proposed TIME, Inc. purchase all rights. Those instructions were forwarded to Stolley by the end of the weekend.

In Dallas on Saturday, however, it soon became known that *LIFE* had purchased only the print rights, and the interest was still very hot to acquire motion picture and telecast rights. The *New York Times* on Sunday, underneath a photo distributed by UPI showing the Moorman Polaroid picture of the instant of the assassination, included a Richard J. H. Johnston by-lined article about TIME- LIFE's purchase from Zapruder. Though Zapruder declined to discuss the matter, the article quoted a secretary as saying that the Secret Service had permitted him to keep or sell the film. A TIME-LIFE New York editorial representative was quoted to say that the pictures would be published in black and white in their next issue which would appear on the streets Tuesday. They had been told the film " . . . depicted the impact of the bullets that struck Mr. Kennedy." Though neither Zapruder nor *LIFE* would comment about the deal struck, AP acknowledged that they had been in on the bidding, and that the winning figure was "well over $25,000 and close to $40,000."[24]

Zapruder was being hounded by the press about making a deal for his film rights. By the end of the weekend Zapruder's lawyer, Sam Passman, was now helping to handle the matter. CBS television's New Orleans Bureau Chief Dan Rather had been sent to Texas to help with the network coverage of the President's visit, and was near the scene at the time of the shooting. In his 1977 book, *The Camera Never Blinks,* Rather writes of his experiences with the Zapruder affair. His telling, however, seems to convolute some of the occurrences and he speaks of seeing and describing the film on television on Saturday when evidence points to its having occurred on Monday. In any

Dan Rather reporting from
Dallas on November 22

event, Rather, representing CBS, had been instructed to preview the film and bring it back to the station if he could. Rather recounts going to the lawyer's office and hearing the ground rules of viewing the film one time only, without benefit of taking notes and then giving a bid. "The first thing I am going to do," thought Rather, "is to look at the film, then knock the hinges off the door getting back to the station and describe what I had just seen. Then, and only then, would we get into the bidding."

Quickly leaving after the screening, Rather told the lawyer he would have to consult New York about the offer. He thought he had received a promise that the lawyer would withhold a decision until he could return. How many times Rather described the viewing of the Zapruder film is unclear. The earliest broadcast, however, appears to be one in which Rather speaks over CBS radio with Hughes Rudd and Richard C. Hotelett. In the Rudd reference of the Texas Attorney General's announcement and his later mention of "especially today" it seems to bear out a Monday, November 25 radiocast rather than a Saturday, November 23, date.

Hughes:    Dick, ah, Dan Rather just came into the studio, ah Dan we've just been discussing this statement just made by Texas Attorney General Waggoner Carr about a full and complete investigation that is going to be carried out and so on . . . what do you have that's new, anything?

Dan:    Well I'm not sure that this is the proper context in which to put it . . . but as you may know Hughes I, I . . . have just returned from seeing a . . . a movie . . . which clearly shows in some great detail the exact moments preceding, the exact moments of, the President's assassination which clears up some of the points that had been rather vague up until this time. Now may not be the time or the place to discuss that, perhaps Dick uh . . .

Dick:    No I think it is . . . uh, Dan . . . I think it fits right into the context of what we've been saying.

Dan:    Well let me tell you then, give you a word picture of the motion picture that we have just seen. The President's automobile which was proceeded by only one other car containing Secret Service Agents . . . the President's open black Lincoln automobile . . . made a turn, a left turn off of Houston Street in Dallas onto Elm Street, this was right on the fringe area of the downtown area. This left turn was made right below the window from which the shot was fired . . . as the car made the turn completed the turn went below the window from which this shot was fired . . . went on past the building keep in mind the window was on the sixth floor . . . it got about 35 yards from the base of the building that is if you had dropped a plumb line from the window to the sidewalk to the President's car was around 35 yards from that spot . . . President Kennedy had just put his right hand up to the side of his right eye, it appeared that he was perhaps brushing back his hair or rubbing his eyebrow. Mrs. Kennedy was not looking in his direction. In front of them in the jump seat of the Lincoln . . . were Governor and Mrs. Connally. The Governor as was the President was on the side of the car of the building in which the assassin was located. Mrs. Kennedy and Mrs. Connally were on the opposite side, two Secret Service men on the front seat. At almost the instant the President put his hand up to his eyebrow . . . on the right side of his face, with Mrs. Kennedy looking away . . . the President lurched forward just a bit, uh, it was obvious he had been hit in the movie but you had to be looking very closely in order to see it. Mrs. Kennedy did not appear to be aware that he was hit but Governor Connally in the seat just in front of the President . . . seemly heard the shot . . . or sensed that something was wrong . . . Governor Connally whose coat button was open turned in such a way to extend his right hand out towards the President and the Governor seemed to have a look on his face that might say, "What is it? What happened?" and as he turned he exposed his entire shirt front and chest because his coat was unbuttoned . . . at that moment a shot very clearly hit the part of the Governor. He was wounded once with a chest shot, this we now know . . . uh the Governor fell back in his seat . . . Mrs. Connally immediately fell over the Governor, uh, I say fell, she threw herself over the Governor . . . and at that instant the second shot the third shot total but the second shot hit President Kennedy and there was no doubt there, his head . . . went forward with considerable violence . . . Mrs. Kennedy stood up immediately her mouth wide open . . . the President slumped over against Mrs. Kennedy almost toppling her over as she was standing . . . Mrs. Kennedy then threw herself out of the back seat of the car onto the trunk of the car almost on all fours stretched out over the trunk of the car . . . there was a Secret Service man standing on the back bumper . . . it would appear that Mrs. Kennedy was either trying to get herself out of what she knew instinctively was danger or perhaps was trying to grab the Secret Service man and pull him into the back seat of the car for help at any rate Mrs. Kennedy was prone, uh face down on the back of the car on the trunk . . . the Secret Service man leaned over put his hands on her shoulders and shoved her back into the car she seemed to be in danger of perhaps rolling or falling off the back. A Secret Service man in the front seat of the car uh was already on the telephone perhaps he had been on the phone all along it was not clear and the car sped away.

Dick:      The car never stopped did it?

Dan:       The car never stopped, it never paused.

Hughes:    How long did all this take, Dan? In a matter of seconds?

Dan:       Well, the complete scene that I just described to you covers exactly 20 seconds that is from the time the car made the turn until the car disappeared onto an underpass.

Dick:      Is it clear, is it that the President was hit twice?

Dan:       It was very clear that the President was hit twice. He was hit, Governor Connally was hit and the Gov . . . uh the President was hit again.

Hughes:    How long a time did the actual three shots take from the first shot until the final shot, Dan?

Dan:       Not more than five seconds and I . . . am inclined to think slightly less than that perhaps.

Hughes:    There [sic] must have been very grim pictures to watch, especially today.

Dick:      What was the source of these pictures, Dan?

Dan:       An amateur photographer, had an 8 millimeter color uh camera he had positioned himself up off the side walk on an old street lamp base, he was above the heads of the crowd and was facing the automobile.

Dick: Of course he was focused on the automobile so there's no indication of where the shots came from.

Dan: No, he was focused on the automobile with his back or side to the window from which the shots came. Only the automobile was shown in the film.[25]

Later on the CBS Evening News Rather, with a lead in from Walter Cronkite, reported his observations over television:

Cronkite: Correspondent Dan Rather was permitted today to see some films of the actual assassination and here is his report from Dallas.

Rather: The films we saw were taken by an amateur photographer, who had a particularly good vantage point, just past the building from which the fatal shot was fired. The films show President Kennedy's open, black limousine, making a left turn, off Houston Street on to Elm Street on the fringe of downtown Dallas, a left turn made just below, the window in which the assassin was waiting. About 35 yards past the very base of the building, just below the window, President Kennedy could be seen to, to put his right hand, up to the side of his head to, either brush back his hair or cover up his eyebrow. President Kennedy was sitting on the same side of the car, as the building from which the shot came. Mrs. Kennedy was by his side. In the jump seat in front of him, Mrs. Connally, and Governor Connally, Governor Connally on the same side of the car as the president. And in the front seat, two Secret Service men. Just as the president put that right hand up to the side of his head, he, you could see him, lurch forward. The first shot had hit him. Mrs. Kennedy was looking in another direction, apparently didn't see, or sense that first shot, or didn't hear it. But Governor Connally, in the seat in front, appeared to have heard it, or at least sensed that something was wrong. The Governor's coat was open. He, he reached back in this fashion, back as if to, to offer aid or ask the president something. At that moment, a shot clearly hit the governor, in the front, and he fell back in his seat. Mrs. Connally immediately threw herself over him in a protective position. In the next instant, with this time Mrs. Kennedy apparently looking on, a second shot, the third total shot, hit the president's head. He, his head can be seen to move violently forward. And, Mrs. Kennedy stood up immediately, the president leaned over her way. It appeared that he might have brushed her legs. Mrs. Kennedy then, literally went on the top of the trunk, of the

Lincoln car, p-put practically her whole body on the trunk. It, it appeared she might have been on all fours, there, reaching out for the Secret Service man, the lone Secret Service man who was riding on the bumper of the car, the back bumper on Mrs. Kennedy's side. Uh, the Secret Service man leaned forward and put his hands on Mrs. Kennedy's shoulder to, push her back into the car. She was in some danger, it appeared of, rolling off or falling off. And when we described this before, there was some question about what we meant by Mrs. Kennedy being on the trunk of the car. Only she knows, but it appeared that she was trying desperately to, to get the Secret Service man's attention or perhaps to, help pull him into the car. The car never stopped, it never paused. In the front seat, a Secret Service man was, was on the telephone. The car picked up speed, and disappeared beneath an underpass. This is Dan Rather in Dallas.

Cronkite: The White House tonight announced a full investigation into the assassination of President Kennedy under orders from President Johnson. All Federal agencies have been advised to cooperate with the FBI.[26]

His on-air description of the Zapruder film would dog Rather later in his upward-moving career. If he had in fact only seen the film once, much of the description is quite detailed considering the shortness of the clip and the number of events occurring in the car among its occupants. In his book Rather bemoans his editing his comments about Mrs. Kennedy's movement out into the trunk as her possibly attempting to flee. He had done the tape that way once when he was urged in preparation for a second "take" to do himself a favor and leave out the part about her trying to flee. A compromise between the earlier radio and the later TV telecast indicates part of such a personal editing on Rather's part, an editing which Rather says he later regretted having done. The real controversy over Rather's description, however, was in his mentioning that upon receiving the final shot, President Kennedy's head moved violently forward. Rather wrote of his description, " . . . I did it as well and as honestly as I could under the conditions," but he did blow a piece of the description. To the eye, the head moved decisively and forcefully backward. His misstatement would follow him when later researchers found this backward movement to be consistent with what they thought to be a front, and not a back, gunshot entry. Many accused Rather of deliberate subterfuge on the American public who would not be given a chance to see the film and its backward head-snap, due to *LIFE*'s withholding of the broadcasting rights. Some thought Dan was thus part of the "cover-up."[27]

The rising CBS star correspondent was clearly not, however, tied into a nefarious plot to hide the truth from the American people. So intent on getting a major scoop, he even at one point entertained the notion simply to grab the film, show it on the CBS television station, and then let them sue him. Returning to the lawyer's office with authorization for an initial bid of $10,000 for the rights of a one-time showing on the air, Rather was shocked to find that Stolley had purchased all the rights. Calling into question the ethics of their selling prior to entertaining the CBS bid, Rather had no luck, as Zapruder ignored the raised voice and the heavy clopping of the correspondents' feet. Knowing what competition he faced, it seems a real mistake on Rather's part to have left Zapruder to the press wolves in order to describe what he should have first tried to secure. Certainly the real thing would have been far better than merely a flawed description of it. Supposedly CBS later offered *LIFE* $100,000 for a one-time showing of the film, but their request was rebuffed![28]

Stolley had called Zapruder that Monday morning indicating *LIFE*'s interest in bargaining for the entire rights package. Apparently Zapruder was more interested in making a deal with him than beginning the uncomfortable selling process with other strangers. The bargaining in the lawyer's office with the three men present was cordial, formal, and lasted almost four hours with Stolley beginning at $25,000 and working his way up. He knew exactly up to how much he was authorized to spend, and several times excused himself supposedly to check with New York about a new offer needed. These were done to add to the suspense and hopefully tilt the process a little towards his favor, much like a car salesman checking on a price offer with his boss.

The final agreement was typed out on three pages as a confirmation agreement addressed to *LIFE* publisher C. D. Jackson. The agreement called for Zapruder to sell the original and all three first-generation copies of the film together with all Zapruder's rights, title, and interest, "whether domestic, foreign, newsreel, television, motion picture, or otherwise" of the film. For this Zapruder, "or my heirs" as was written in and initialed by both parties, would be paid $150,000 with one installment of $25,000 being paid immediately, $25,000 being paid on January 3, 1964, and four other $25,000 installments being paid on subsequent January 3rds, up to 1968. Zapruder would also receive half of all gross receipts from all sources after *LIFE* had received back $150,000 worth of sold rights according to an included schedule. TIME, Inc., reserved for itself unlimited free use of the material in its own behalf. The agreement was to last as long as the copyrights secured the film rights, and that if these rights were sold or transferred, it would be done so subject to this agreement with Zapruder. TIME, Inc., also agreed to " . . . present said film to the public in a manner consonant with good taste and dignity," and in what seemed like a possible contradiction, "and agrees to exercise its best business judgment in the presentation, sale, leasing, licensing, and retail of said film consonant with your business custom and practice for the production of gross receipts therefrom." The letter of agreement was signed by Zapruder and accepted and agreed to for TIME, Inc., by Stolley's signature.[29]

Zapruder now found himself and his family financially secure as the result of an investment of less than $3 for a roll of film and his having taken the trouble to film a procession. He alone, among all of the scores of photographers of the motorcade, would unwittingly find financial stability in the death of the President. A few of the other camera-carrying spectators would also make money, but the most successful of these others would bring in only 1/30th the amount of the Zapruder windfall. All due to chance, location, and good reflexes, this very ordinary man had made such an extraordinary movie, one that he wished he had not taken, one that would hound him with bad memories and nightmares, and would make his name, if at all remembered, forever linked with the murder of JFK. Yet others close by the scene of the assassination would also have bad memories and nightmares, but it was Zapruder who now had $150,000. Yet even this large sum could have probably been improved upon by a more forceful man willing to engage in more distasteful tactics. For Zapruder it was both a no-win and a no-lose situation. And he was fully aware of that fact. Being Jewish and living in one of the geographical strongholds of right-wing activities, Zapruder was keenly aware of potential accusations of his profiteering from the assassination — or worse. Zapruder and the government would receive hate mail, the more paranoid of which would accuse "the Jew Abe" and international Jewry in general as being part of the plot. At least one man who contacted the FBI would accuse Zapruder himself of firing the fatal shot from his camera![30]

It wasn't just the nuts who would talk, however, for no matter who had done the filming and selling of the film, the fact of the sale and the amount gleaned from it would be criticized by many. To counter some of this, Zapruder asked that the amount not be revealed, and for years the actual amount was not known and was consistently under-estimated. Stolley recalls that attorney Passman suggested a grand gesture that was both sensitive and self-serving. In light of the delicate situation and the possible intensity of anti-Jewish sentiment, why didn't Zapruder donate the first installment of $25,000 to the fund for slain police officer J. D. Tippit, to benefit Tippit's widow and family? Tippit had been gunned down allegedly by Lee Oswald in a separate incident following the Kennedy shooting. Zapruder thought it a grand idea. An additional $25,000 was due on the agreement in less than 40 days.[31]

The donation was made public on November 27, and all the news outlets throughout the country publicized the generosity. Associated Press reported, "The man who received $25,000 for his color movie films of President John F. Kennedy's assassination gave the entire sum today to the family of Patrolman J. D. Tippit, slain by the man accused as the assassin of the President." Zapruder was quoted as saying, "I had intended for these films to be home movies for the future enjoyment of my family and friends. Now, from the revenue that has been offered for such a significant film, I wish to contribute to the well-being and future of the family that lost a very brave and gallant husband and father."[32]

Zapruder's actions were applauded throughout the country and the publicity it generated helped to increase further donations to the Tippit family. Though careful not to lie, Zapruder encouraged the interpretation that the entire sum had been generously donated. When in July 1964 Zapruder was being questioned by Warren Commission Assistant Counsel Wesley Liebeler as to how much he was paid for the film, one can almost feel his anxiety as he states, "Well, I just wonder whether I should answer it or not, because it involves a lot of things, and it's not one price — it's a question of how they are going to use it . . . so I will say I really don't know how to answer that." Liebeler replies he won't urge Zapruder to answer, he is only asking as " . . . the Commission feels it would be helpful." Zapruder then says, "I received $25,000, as you know, and I have given that to the Firemen's and Policemen's Benevolence with a suggestion for Mrs. Tippit." When then asked if he gave the whole $25,000, Zapruder replies, "Yes. This was all over the world. I got letters from all over the world . . . I am surprised — that you didn't know it — I don't like to talk about it too much." Indeed he didn't, either out of modesty or the desire for financial privacy.[33]

Zapruder would live until 1970 when at age 66 on August 30 of that year he died of carcinoma of the stomach at Dallas's Presbyterian Hospital. He was buried at Temple Emanu-El Cemetery on September 1. He had often told many of how he suffered nightmares, the whole grisly shooting events so often coming to him in his dreams. He never wanted a copy of his film and even found it emotionally difficult to pick up a motion picture camera. He agreed with the Warren Commission's findings, and it continued to amaze him that people didn't believe that a lone nut could do such a thing. He privately believed, however, that Oswald's main target was not President Kennedy, but rather Governor John Connally.[34]

*LIFE* Magazine's Volume 55, No. 22, issue of November 29, 1963, had been closed for publication on Wednesday, November 20. The action color cover featured Naval Academy All-American star quarterback Roger Staubach. Besides an article about Staubach, the issue featured a light photo essay on the current state of young American debutantes written by Brenda Frazier, a former *LIFE* cover girl whose own debutante experience had been the subject of a story 25 years earlier. Many of the ads for the issue were suggesting fine gifts for Christmas, including Webster's 7th New Collegiate Dictionary spotlighted in red on an otherwise black-and-white full page ad. Elsewhere Black and Decker suggested a number of power tool gift ideas at $19.88 each for your "No. 1 Man." A 6-page color art spread of painted self-portraits featured in a new book ($12.95) by Manuel Gasser, was spotlighted, along with part two of Theodore H. White's article concerning the Negro's increasing militancy highlighted on the cover with a question, "Negro Demands: Are They Realistic?" Color was a marketable quality, as both the new Polaroid colorpack camera giving a color print in only 50 seconds, and the RCA Victor's color Beauchamp all-wood French Provincial television console at $599.95 vied for the American consumer's dollar. An article on rare philately included on one page a color replica in actual and enlarged size of an 1851 2¢ Kingdom of Hawaii stamp. The reader would learn that this was the costliest publicly sold single stamp in history. "This pound-for-pound is the most valuable substance on earth," selling for $41,000 last May and weighing in at 1/2000 ounce and costing $1,995,833,395.61 per pound. Within a few days *LIFE* would be in the same league of acquiring one of the most valuable substances pound-for-pound in history. If someone cared to make the useless comparison by weight, the 478 frames of the Zapruder film would be worth over $7,200,000 per pound, not an inconsequential amount.[35]

By noon on Friday, November 22, this November 29 issue was in its printing run of over 7 million copies on huge presses in Philadelphia, Los Angeles, and Chicago. Thousands of bundles of completed copies were already being shipped to distribution centers. Then the news came of the assassination of the President. Only faltering shortly due to shock, the *LIFE* editorial team soon went to work. In New York, Managing Editor George P. Hunt made the decision to stop the presses. Assistant Publisher James R. Shepley had already taken it upon himself to begin notifying the plants to curtail printing. Within a few hours the senior editorial staff had decided to rip apart the original November 29 issue and, in the best tradition of the magazine, to hustle to bring out a credible report of what had occurred and was happening, all with timely narration and pictures. Editor-in-Chief of the TIME-LIFE empire, Henry R. Luce, was taken aback at the estimated near-million dollar cost for changing the magazine at this late date, but would later admit it was the best million he ever spent.

As Chicago's R. R. Donnelley printing plant was the location for creating the magazine's printing plates as well as the magazine's major print plant, Hunt sent a small group of New York-based editors there, for the most efficient front-line editing of format changes. All in the *LIFE* family pitched in, including numerous writers and photographers who searched for the right material that could be included in the new edition. Pictures and text that would somehow capture and interpret the events were sought after to give the *LIFE* readership that wider view than the mere scatter-gun approach of most newspaper reporting. Intimate pictures by Kennedy photographer Mark Shaw, a poignant essay by Teddy White, editor's notes, and an editorial, as well as a section about the new President, were put together. Numerous photographs including a last-minute insert photo by *Dallas Morning News* photographer Jack Beers showing the shooting of Oswald by Jack Ruby, and free-lance work by Dallas photographer Jim Murray and on-scene in Dallas *LIFE* staff photographer Art Rickerby, all went into making this a remarkable and memorable issue. All told, by late Sunday the revised copy included 37 pages of text and photos relating to the news since Friday. The new cover featured a color photograph by Yousuf Karash of a pensive President Kennedy, and included the hallmark white-lettered *LIFE* logo, usually on a red background, instead superimposed on top of a black background as a symbolic tribute to the slain President.[36]

Yet to most of the estimated 50,000,000 readers of *LIFE*, the items which stood out most in this remarkable issue were the article about Oswald and his background by Tommy Thompson, and the frames of the Zapruder death movie. As soon as Roy

Rowan, one of *LIFE*'s assistant managing editors who had led the edit team to Chicago, received the original Zapruder film late Saturday he went over the film, utilizing a movieola projector. Like all of the assassination coverage, save for one photo by Art Rickerby of President and Mrs. Kennedy at Love Field which was reproduced in color, there was not enough time to plate for any additional color pictures. The stills made from the Zapruder movie occupied page 24 through 27 of the issue and included twenty-eight 4¼" x 3", two 5¼" x 8", and one 10¼" x 13½" frames. The first double page had a heading proclaiming, "SPLIT-SECOND SEQUENCE AS THE BULLET STRUCK" and described the " . . . remarkable and exclusive series of pictures . . . ." The frame showing the President shot in the head (Z313) was not included. The second double page included sample frames from the sequence of Mrs. Kennedy's desperate crawl onto the car's trunk under the headline caption, "JACKIE CRAWLED FOR HELP." The issue was ready for subscriber mail distribution beginning Monday and hit many news-stands by Tuesday, November 26. Normally selling for 25¢ at newsstands, the demand was so great for the issue that in some locations copies were scalped for exorbitant prices. Few who saw this issue can forget lingering over these shocking frames, trying to understand what happened and pondering why. On November 30, under a "Courtesy *LIFE* magazine, Copyright 1963, TIME, Inc." sub-caption, six of the frames taken from the *LIFE* article were released for use "to the American press because of their historical importance."[37]

Demand for the November 29 and the next week's issue, which covered the Washington funeral, was the greatest in the magazine's history. The two issues were updated and combined, minus the advertisements, to produce an 84-page memorial edition. The 50¢ special issue had an initial run of 1.5 million copies and hit the news-stands in early December. In this issue the multi-image black-and-white pictures of the Zapruder film were replaced by nine large and vivid color frames on four pages, including at least five previously unused frames. According to the text narration and captions, the first bullet struck the President just as he passed behind the road sign and lodged in his body. The second shot struck the Governor and the third shot was fired about two seconds later and struck the President in the right rear of his head. The interpretation of the film had begun. There was some controversy among the editorial staff as to whether or not to include the graphic, yet important, head shot at Z313. After consider-able discussion, with some quite vehement over the question of good taste versus the right to know; in this edition good taste won out. Later, however, in the October 2, 1964, *LIFE* cover story reporting the conclusions of the Warren Commission, *LIFE* would publish in color and for the first time (in some editions), this disturbing frame. Other runs of the same issue substituted a later frame for this head shot, possibly as a result of the continuing internal controversy over appropriateness.

With the exception of the use of the frames by the government in its official investigation, the Zapruder movie stills were seldom available for public inspection. Besides using selected frames in its November 29, 1963, and October 2, 1964, as well as in the memorial edition, *LIFE* made occasional publication use of film frames, including the cover and seven pages devoted to the displaying of key frames in its November 25, 1966, issue. In this issue *LIFE* had asked Governor Connally to examine the film strip to determine at what point he was wounded. With a cover title, "DID OSWALD ACT ALONE? A MATTER OF REASONABLE DOUBT," the magazine, in what was the beginning of its own investigation into the assassination, stated at the end of its article in large black letters, "CONCLUSION: THE CASE SHOULD BE REOPENED." *LIFE*'s own investigation, however, was short-lived, and within a year would essentially evaporate. Always protecting its rights and investment, *LIFE* would never sell broadcast rights to the film, and seldom granted printing rights. Yet according to inside sources, in the 12 years of its ownership of the film, the corporation recovered over $100,000 in syndication fees from its original investment. Still, TIME-LIFE's dogged refusal to allow this key historical record and evidence of the assassination to be viewed by the public in any form save by what *LIFE* believed to be its own best interest, was the cause for many legitimate observers to condemn their cocky, intransigent attitude. This possessive and secretive attitude would help foster the belief among many observers that *LIFE*, aware of it or not, was significantly responsible for preventing serious non-governmental investigators from learning the entire truth about the assassination.[38]

From the moment of purchase, *LIFE* had attempted to keep complete control of the Zapruder film. The agreement with Zapruder specified that the three original copies were *LIFE*'s, and that following the use of the two handed over to the Secret Service by Zapruder, they should be given to *LIFE*. On January 7, 1964, *LIFE*'s Washington Bureau Chief wrote to Chief Jim Rowley of the United States Secret Service stating that *LIFE* had several copies of the film made up for government use. "I do want to stress that the film is the property of TIME, Inc." " . . . We of course expect the film to be returned to us whenever you agency has finished with them." Following a brief investigation of the circumstances under which the service obtained the film, Rowley wrote back at the end of January. The Chief stressed that *LIFE* should be assured that the film would not be shown to anyone unless for official purposes. The film however was acquired prior to Zapruder's selling of the original film, and Rowley had no knowledge of *LIFE*'S later arrangement with Mr. Zapruder. Calling *LIFE*'s bluff, Rowley then stated concerning the two first-generation films in their position, " . . . We consider it part of the official Secret Service file of the investigation of the assassination of President Kennedy." *LIFE* would not get these two copies back."[39]

*LIFE*'s possessiveness of the Zapruder film, however, did not necessarily assure the careful handling of this historically and analytically valuable record. During the tenure of the Warren Commission *LIFE* had volunteered to make available enlarged print copies of individual frames from the original film. The Commission staff requested copies of frames 171 to 334, and when the 26-volume Warren Commission *Hearings* was published in 1964, volume 18 of the set included these frames published in black-and-white format. Researchers soon noticed that frames 208, 209, 210, and 211 were missing from the series and a very obvious splice ran through frames 207 and 212. Speculation circulated that frames were deleted possibly because they showed something the

Commission did not want to be noticed. The frames depicted the President's vehicle at the critical time it was being blocked by the Stemmons Freeway sign.

In early 1967 the mystery was solved when *LIFE* announced that these four frames on the original film had been accidentally destroyed, while two other adjacent frames had also been damaged by *LIFE* photo lab technicians. It was not specified when the accident occurred or what type of an accident it was. If the film had broken, the individual frames could still have been retained. If a frame burnout had occurred, the incident might have destroyed at least one frame, and a not-thought-out splice repair might have been made affecting several others. The information on these frames had survived, however, in the form of the three first-generation copies, two of which the government possessed. The reason why the frames missing from the original were not published in volume 18 was that these stills had been made from the original film. Former Commission staff counsel Wesley J. Liebeler noted the lack of care in the layout of these items of evidence in the published *Hearings* volumes explaining that, "making up the volumes was viewed as a housekeeping function." In order to blunt criticism and controversy over the loss of these frames, *LIFE* released copies of these frames for general use and distribution. Unfortunately, the sloppiness of the technicians was not relegated to this one area of the film. Frames Z155 and Z156 are also missing and at Z157 there is another splice in the original film. As this portion of the film was not reproduced by the Warren Commission, its destruction received no public attention and *LIFE* has never given a public accounting of this further loss of part of the original film. Though accidents can happen during the most careful of procedures, the entire saga of corporate ownership of this piece of history, whose significance transcends most other evidence in the case, makes one feel uneasy that in such an important matter private ownership was allowed to stand above the concerns of the public's right to know. In a real sense public history was abused, hoarded, and became the object of profiteering, in the name of the sanctity of private corporate ownership.[40]

Dan Rather mentions that although the film was not allowed for viewing by the general public or other use by the media, that its control within the *LIFE* corporate community was lax. Executives could order up prints for viewing in their offices. Rather believes that during many of these informal orders bootleg copies would also be produced. Although sensitive to some people's contention that the film should not, out of decency, be shown during the period just following the assassination, Rather contends as do others, that much of the later built-up cynicism of the case, " . . . could have been eliminated, I always felt, if the public had been allowed to see the film soon after John Kennedy's death and in a clearer context."[41]

If the Zapruder film had significance as an historical artifact as well as investigative value, what of the camera that had created the film? According to Zapruder, in early December he had loaned the camera to the Secret Service as they wanted to do some checking of it. By that time the FBI had realized that a key fact in understanding the time frame of the filmed assassination events was a firm knowledge of the actual speed of the camera itself. On December 4 a local agent obtained the camera from

Zapruder and sent it to the FBI Washington laboratory. Zapruder requested that it be sent back to him when the test was completed, as he was going to give it to the Bell & Howell Company.[42]

Following a series of filmed clock tests utilizing the camera, the FBI lab on December 20 reported that " . . . It has been determined that this camera when operated at normal 'run' speed operates at 18⅓ frames per second." At the end of January 1964 however, the FBI was requested by Commission staff to determine the variation in the speed between the spring drive when fully wound and when run down. Checking the film speed at ten-second intervals, it was determined by the lab that for the first 10 seconds the average speed was 18.0 to 18.1 frames per second. Gradually increasing for the next 20 seconds from 18.3 to 18.5 frames per second, and decreasing to 18.1 frames per second for 10 seconds, the final 20 seconds was clocked at an average run of 17.6 to 17.9 frames per second. It was noted that as the Zapruder assassination film was exposed within the first half of the camera run, that the last 20 seconds were discounted, and that the inclusive figures still indicated the previous average rate of 18.3 frames per second.[43]

Bell & Howell's interest in the camera had begun with a query from their Illinois headquarters. They requested from the Dallas district manager to find out if Mr. Zapruder had in fact been using a Bell & Howell camera to record these historic scenes. If so, might he be interested to exchange it for a newer model, the original being an appropriate addition to the company's collection of historical products kept at their Lincolnwood, Illinois, archives. Cal Blaisdell contacted Zapruder who agreed to make the exchange of cameras. Following the return of the camera to Zapruder by the FBI, Blaisdell personally picked it up and sent it to Illinois. It was placed on display in the secure archives area, which was under the supervision of the patent department of the photo products group of Bell & Howell. Besides receiving a new model Director Series 8mm motion picture camera, Zapruder apparently also obtained through Bell & Howell a sound projector which was given to a local golden age group. Concerning this donation the Dallas businessman later commented to Warren Commission Counsel Liebeler, "I don't want anything for myself," continuing the false impression that he got nothing tangible from the result of his filming the assassination.[44]

The government was not quite through with its interest in the camera, however. On November 29, President Lyndon B. Johnson issued an executive order creating a special commission to investigate the assassination of President Kennedy. It was the Commission's task to evaluate all facts surrounding the shooting, as well as the subsequent murder of the accused assassin, Lee H. Oswald. The creation of this commission also successfully stopped in their tracks various other parallel governmental investigations. U. S. Supreme Court Chief Justice Earl Warren was named chairman and six other prominent present or past government officials were also appointed. These influential, respected, and very busy men, all with very little criminal investigation experience, would in general terms oversee the work of the so-called "Warren Commission" and put their stamp of approval on the resulting report to the President.

Meeting for the first time on December 5, the Commission agreed to ask former U. S. Solicitor General J. Lee Rankin to be chief counsel, who was sworn in at their December 16 meeting. Soon fourteen assistant counsels with much legal and investigative background were chosen by Rankin, assisted by a further support staff supplied generally from within other federal agencies. The senior counsels were prominent working lawyers who, on the whole, devoted much less than full time to the Commission. It fell to the young, bright, energetic junior counsels to perform the bulk of the work.

The Commission began its work severely limited as the result of two inherent weaknesses. First was the time constraint. The political and societal pressure necessitated that the report be completed as quickly as possible to allay public fears and rumors. Though not stated but acutely obvious was the need to complete the work in a safe time frame prior to the 1964 election season. Originally intending to have a completed report by June 30, the Commission would not deliver the final report until September 24, 1964. The second weakness of the investigation was that given the time and staff restrictions, the Commission could not, of its own power, conduct a truly independent investigation. They were forced to rely upon the services and manpower of the FBI and the Secret Service as its chief investigative wing. These two agencies, as well as others utilized from within the federal government, had their own points of view and areas of potential embarrassment. They would desire to protect themselves and handle potential controversy in the least hurtful manner. Yet given these two major flaws, the Commission staff worked diligently, dividing themselves to examine specific areas within the investigation. On December 9 the FBI provided the Commission with a four-volume summarization of its investigation, followed later by a fifth supplemental report volume. After receiving these volumes which included the FBI's conclusions, the Commission staff requested access to all supporting investigation materials created, and continued to call upon the agency for further investigations and follow-ups which the staff felt useful or necessary. These requests were generally met, though not always with enthusiasm, speed, or quite the precision or depth of investigation which the staff had desired. Raw data virtually hemorrhaged into the Commission, yet the sorting and appraisal of this information was a herculean task often ignored due to time constraints. Additionally the Commission and/or its staff took the testimony of some 552 witnesses. These "hearings" included many, but not necessarily all of the most important witnesses. Some of those deposed seemed of marginal significance. Edward Jay Epstein, in his 1966 book *Inquest* which researched the Commission and its procedures, noted that much of the Commission's work dealt with dispelling dangerous rumors. In the Commission's investigation, " . . . While known facts were substantiated, unknown facts were left unknown."[45] Later critics would contend that the hearings ignored witnesses who would not contribute to the fast-emerging government line of how the assassination occurred. According to these critics many of the staff would only question witnesses along narrow investigative lines, manipulating and cutting off testimony they did not want to hear. It was even later contended that in some cases testimony as published had been altered or deleted.

Up through December it was the general belief that President Kennedy had been shot first, followed by a second shot hitting Governor Connally, and then the third bullet striking the President in the head. Though this is the position touted in various FBI internal reports, their summary report released to the Commission would only state, "Two bullets struck President Kennedy, and one wounded Governor Connally." The Commission staff, however, sought more precision and detail as to the pattern of hits and their time frame. They felt that a close, precise examination of the Zapruder film would do just that. Indeed, Counsel Liebeler would months later volunteer to Zapruder, " . . . Your film has been one of the most helpful things to the work of the Commission that we could possibly have had . . . ." Yet upon early examination of the film it only seemed to muddy the neat ordering of the assassination, and might even indicate the presence of a second gun.[46]

Beginning on January 27 examination of the film commenced. FBI staff, including 14-year veteran Agent Lyndal Shaneyfelt, a document examiner and photographic expert assigned to the FBI laboratory, provided input, and a second generation copy of the film for examination. During the seven days in which the film was reviewed, Commission representatives were always present as were Secret Service agents. On April 14 the President's autopsy doctors and other government wound and ballistics medical staff were also called in. During the final April 21st work day with the film, Parkland Hospital doctors present on November 22, as well as other medical specialists and Governor and Mrs. Connally, were also given the opportunity to assist in the film interpretation.[47]

It was during the January 28 examination that Shaneyfelt told Commission staff counsels Joseph Ball and David Belin that a clearer print of the film could give more precise information about the data they were endeavoring to obtain. It was suggested to contact *LIFE* about the availability of the original film. It seems strange that one of the two Secret Service first generation films was never requested by the Commission staff or FBI, nor offered by the Secret Service for use in this official and joint examination process. By the February 25 joint meeting, Assistant Chief of *LIFE*'s photographic lab, Herbert Orth, personally brought the original film to the meeting and projected it several times for study, though never stopping it to look at individual frames, fearing possible burn damage. Orth did volunteer to make individual 35mm transparencies from the original, and during the two April meetings these slides were used in conjunction with the study. *LIFE* produced three sets of 159 slides, one each for the FBI, Secret Service, and Commission. The slides included Zapruder frames 171 through 334, which were thought to be the most pertinent in the film sequence.[48]

Those seven sessions during which the Zapruder film was analyzed were generally day-long examinations. The copy film would be projected at regular, slow-motion, and stop-frame. Those present attempted to discover in the reaction of the car's occupants or that of the spectators, the sequence of events and bullet strikes. The slides gave much more detail and were far clearer than the second generation film. The film by itself could not easily reveal when the shots struck a target, save for the head shot at

Z313. Nor by the use of the frames of the film itself could one obtain accurate information relative to the car's speed, the distance the car had traveled at particular points, or the exact timing of the shots. With these questions in mind, and given other less dramatic, though still revealing movies taken by other amateurs available to the Commission, the staff asked the FBI experts if these answers could be determined. As early as after the second joint meeting, Shaneyfelt indicated that with further testing and a survey made of the actual Dallas assassination site, much of this data could be discovered. A recommendation dated January 28 was so made, and on the ensuing typed FBI memorandum, a begrudging authorization was OK'd by FBI Director Hoover[49]

The film analysis was coming up with some complex problems. The FBI had established that Oswald's Mannlicher-Carcano rifle could not be fired twice in less than 2.3 seconds. With the film speed determined at 18.3 frames per second, that meant that at least 42 frames had to go through the camera before a single shooter could get off two shots. Preliminarily it was felt that as the President emerged from behind the road sign at Z225, he was obviously hit. It also appeared that this was the latest moment he could have been hit, and that he may have been hit as he first became obscured by the sign at Z208 or earlier, as at Z199 there appears some jerkiness in his movement. At Z204 through Z206 the examiners observed Kennedy's right elbow raised to an unnaturally high point. Several scenarios were talked out, including Connally hit through the chest by the first bullet which struck Kennedy and then hit secondly in the wrist by an additional shot. None of the explanations seemed to fit properly. The time between when President Kennedy was first possibly hit to the last possible frame prior to Connally's obvious reaction to being shot was less than the 2.3 seconds that Oswald needed to make two separate shots. Initially David Belin, a junior counsel experienced as a criminal trial lawyer and assigned to the investigation area identifying the assassin, was inclined to believe that the Zapruder information was proving that the same rifle could not have fired all shots, and thus there was a conspiracy.[50]

Arlen Specter, a lawyer and former assistant D.A. from Philadelphia, was a junior counsel assigned with Senior Counsel Francis Adams to study the basic facts of the assassination. Early on Specter found himself alone in this immense task as Adams played an insignificant role in the Commission's work. Acutely aware of the time problem as exhibited in the Zapruder film, Specter by early March was attempting to find a different solution that would still fit with the film evidence. Wrestling with collateral problems relating to President Kennedy's less-than-adequate autopsy, and the discovery of a near-pristine bullet on a stretcher at Parkland Hospital, Specter hypothesized that Kennedy and Connally had been hit by the same bullet.

Autopsy doctor James J. Humes in testimony on March 16, 1964, answered a Specter question with, " . . . I see that Gov. Connally is sitting directly in front of the late President, and suggest the possibility that this missile, having traversed the low neck of the late President, in fact traversed the chest of Gov. Connally." The doctor would not, however, agree that Connally's wrist wound could have been caused by the near-pristine bullet Specter postulated had gone through both men. Likewise Connally in his testimony to the Commission was adamant that he was struck by a second bullet, and not the one which first hit Kennedy. Upon viewing the Zapruder film, Connally stated his belief that he had been first hit at about Z231 to Z234. Connally's two doctors also gave separate opinions that he had been shot at about Z234 to Z236 and Z235 to Z237 respectively.[51]

Specter's evolving hypothesis nonetheless appeared worthy of pursuing, and though the evidence for it would later be described by co-Counsel Belin as "overwhelming," and Counsel Norman Redlich would call the theory the Commission's single most important contribution to the investigation, it still faced some major obstacles. For a time it was not clear if the first bullet that struck the President in the back had in fact exited his body. The FBI report spoke of the autopsy doctors not finding an exit point and that the bullet track stopped not far inside the entry point. This controversy, though messy, was cleared up to most everyone's satisfaction when the President's tracheotomy was described as having been made on top of an already presenting wound, and following the testimony of the Parkland and autopsy doctors as well as some physical evidence present on the President's shirt and tie itself. The question of the discovery of the so-called pristine bullet on a stretcher was not as easy. The discoverer of the bullet contended that it was from Kennedy's stretcher. Specter's hypothesis needed it (if found in its original location without having been moved or touched by others) to be found on Connally's stretcher, having fallen out of his last wound, the one in his thigh. Specter, and finally the Commission itself, chose to believe the stretcher had been Connally's, stating that the location of the President's stretcher was reconstructed to known locations precluding its being where the bullet was found.[52]

Commission Exhibit #399. Found on a stretcher at Parkland Hospital, this 6.5mm Western Cartridge Co. bullet was manufactured for the Mannlicher-Carcano rifle. As found it was slightly flattened and somewhat bent. Part of its soft lead inner core was squeezed out of the inside of the rear end of the jacket. Commission counsel Specter postulated it had traversed both President Kennedy and Governor Connally.

Could this only slightly misshapen, elongated and extruded bullet, which was traced to having been fired from the Oswald rifle, in fact have caused the wounds through Kennedy's back and throat, Connally's chest (breaking a rib), Connally's wrist (shattering it as it passed), and finally lodging in his thigh? It seemed hard to believe, and ballistic tests were requested to be made in late April to test the penetrating power of bullets through two objects. The tests and the premise that they were meant to study were flawed, however. Bullets were only shot through one object at a time. Figures on the loss of bullet velocity while passing through gelatine blocks and also through an anesthetized goat torso were calculated, but the calculations relied upon imprecise extrapolations. The bullet shot through a cadaver's wrist was significantly deformed and caused much greater damage to the experimental wrist than was the case with Connally's. The ballistics experts could not and would not specifically say that given their research that the single bullet hypothesis was in fact accurate. Though goaded into answering hypothetical questions put to them by Specter to help support his theory, the experts at best were non-committal as to whether their requested experiments could give validity to the hypothesis. Dr. Light, the Chief of Wounds Assessment Branch at Edgewood Arsenal, when pressed for his opinion of whether one bullet could have traversed both the President and the Governor, creating all the wounds and if this explanation was the most likely possibility, stated: "I think that is probably the most likely, but I base that not entirely on the anatomical findings, but as much on the circumstances." The other circumstances mentioned were the relative positions in the automobile of the two men, and that the bullet was found on the Governor's stretcher. Though not considered a problem to Specter, it might have appeared to these ballistics and medical experts that the experiments performed only addressed certain segments and unlinked portions of the question. In any event, a valid replication of such a series of wounds, where so many of the variables were unclear, was not attempted.[53]

A physical reconstruction of the assassination scene had been contemplated since late February. Utilizing the Zapruder film as well as two other films made of portions of the assassination filmed by Orville Nix and Marie Muchmore, it was hoped to test the single bullet theory. Other bits of information relative to car speed, angle, and distance to the target, etc., could also be gained. The reconstruction would include film and still pictures being made from these three camera positions as well as from the so-called assassin's window. In order to find the exact locations and to replicate the scene as best as possible, the amateur film makers' cameras would be of use. In early May Zapruder was contacted by the Dallas FBI requesting to borrow his camera again. Zapruder informed them that the camera had been given to Bell & Howell. After contacting Bell & Howell in Illinois, on May 12 the company volunteered to loan it to the FBI for their further use in the investigation.

The assassination reen-actment took place on Sunday, May 24, 1964. Various FBI agents took part, including Shaneyfelt, who directed much of the activity. Also present were Secret Service representatives and Commission staff, including Rankin,

FBI Agent Frazier at the sixth floor corner window with a
camera mounted to the rifle scope replicating the assassin's view

Redlich and Specter. FBI firearms expert Robert A. Frazier was positioned at the sixth
floor window of the Texas School Book Depository with the assassination rifle and scope-
set on a tripod to approximate the firing position. A camera was mounted to it providing a scope view. Utilizing the Zapruder frames for positioning, a stand-in Secret Service
vehicle and agents portraying Kennedy and Connally with marks on their coats representing bullet holes, were positioned at various pinpointed locations along the street.
Pictures were taken and measurements, including the distances and angles to the window,
were made. Both color and black-and-white still pictures as well as black-and-white and
color movie film were taken of these fixed points from the four locations. Several 11-
mile-per-hour run-throughs with the car were also made, being recorded on Zapruder's
and the other two witnesses' cameras. Later that afternoon further studies were made
in a nearby garage determining the angle a bullet might have traversed through both
bodies.[54]

The reenactment was very useful to Specter and, as far as he was concerned, supported his single-bullet theory. From the reenactment it seemed apparent that from the sixth floor corner window, an assassin had a clear view of the President's car as it rode down Houston Street towards the window and for the first 100 feet as it turned and proceeded down Elm Street. At about Z166 the President's position became obscured by the foliage of a large Live Oak tree. Visible again beginning at Z186 for an instant,

Commission Counsel Arlen Specter examines the angle at which the single bullet might have traversed through Kennedy and Connally

the stand-in President's head was quickly obscured by the foliage until Z210. Believing the foliage to have remained fairly constant since November 22, and that the assassin would not have fired through the obscuring tree foliage, the report would eventually state that it was probable that the President was not hit prior to Z210 because of this obstruction. The report would also conclude that Kennedy was probably hit by Z225 at an angle to the window of 20°11′ and at a distance of 191 feet. Utilizing much data from the reenactment, the final report would also state about this first shot, "The bullet that hit President Kennedy in the back and exited through his throat most likely could not have missed both the automobile and its occupants . . . . The relative positions of President Kennedy and Governor Connally at the time that the President was struck in the neck confirm that the same bullet probably passed through both men." According to Special Agent Frazier, both Kennedy and Connally were correctly aligned for a through and through shot between Z207 and Z225, assuming that the bullet had not veered in its course after hitting Kennedy. At some instant between Z235 and Z240 Connally turned out of a position to be able to receive his wounds from the gun at the sixth-floor corner position of the Book Depository. The Commission's final report carefully chose the most positive quotations from the various government gun, ballistic, and wounds experts' testimonies, at times quoting phrases of answers out of context. But the report did not emphatically state that the single bullet shot through both bodies had occurred beyond a doubt. It concluded about the reenactment, "The alignment of the points of entry was only indicative and not conclusive that one bullet hit both men. The exact positions of the men could not be recreated; thus, the angle could only be approximated."[55]

The report assumed that the earliest point at which the President could have been shot was at Z207, while Z313 was the last clearly discernable shot. Since it also believed three shots were fired, given the Zapruder film speed, this necessitated the shots

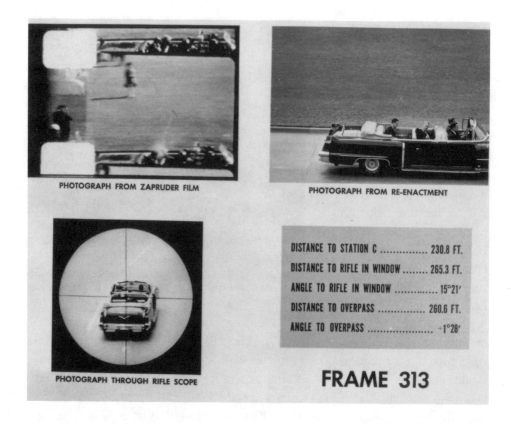

PHOTOGRAPH FROM ZAPRUDER FILM

PHOTOGRAPH FROM RE-ENACTMENT

PHOTOGRAPH THROUGH RIFLE SCOPE

| | |
|---|---|
| DISTANCE TO STATION C | 230.8 FT. |
| DISTANCE TO RIFLE IN WINDOW | 265.3 FT. |
| ANGLE TO RIFLE IN WINDOW | 15°21' |
| DISTANCE TO OVERPASS | 260.6 FT. |
| ANGLE TO OVERPASS | +1°28' |

**FRAME 313**

A portion of Commission Exhibit #902 depicting Zapruder frame 313 together with reenactment photographs and statistics.

to have been fired within 103 frames or 5.6 seconds. Much controversy would arise over Oswald's ability to get off three shots within that time span. The report also stated that it was inconclusive as to which of the three shots missed its target, though if it were the first or last one fired, it would have given more time for the shots to have been made. In the end Specter's single bullet theory was not adopted as conclusive. There were just too many problems with it, including Connally's apparent too-slow reaction to being hit, his and his doctor's testimonies, and the less-than-concrete findings of the expert witnesses. The Commission members themselves were pretty much split down the middle concerning accepting the assumption, and the final report relied upon compromise wording to allow room for both camps.

The report submitted to the President on September 24, 1964, stated in its conclusions concerning this area of the investigation:

Although it is not necessary to any essential findings of the Commission to determine just which shot hit Governor Connally, there is very persuasive evidence from the experts to indicate that the same bullet which pierced the President's throat also caused Governor Connally's wounds. However, Governor Connally's testimony and certain other factors have given rise to some difference of opinion as to this probability, but there is no question in the mind of any member of the Commission that all the shots which caused the President's and Governor Connally's wounds were fired from the sixth floor window of the Texas School Book Depository.[56]

Only a few of the Commission members themselves saw a projected first-generation copy of the film, and fewer still saw anything of the original. The Commission staff and FBI seemed complacent enough with the use of the less detailed copy film and the transparencies provided by *LIFE*. According to attorney and vehement Warren Commission critic Mark Lane, Rankin when later asked why the Commission had not subpoenaed the *LIFE* film is said to have given an answer that it was "private property" which he undoubtedly knew was one reason why the Commission had subpoena power. In 1975 some partial records were shaken loose during a Congressional investigation into intelligence agencies. These scraps of information from CIA files, which files were practically sacrosanct during the Warren Commission investigation, related to a Secret Service request of the CIA's laboratory at the National Photographic Interpretation Center to analyze the Zapruder film. It should be remembered that one first-generation copy of the Zapruder film had been retained by the Secret Service in Washington. Though the released documents are inconclusive as to when this examination took place other than in "late 1963," internal evidence does point out to its being performed after November 29 and probably before mid-December. Secret Service agents were apparently present during the analysis and took the film back when it was completed. At the time of the analysis, the frames per second speed of Zapruder's camera was unknown with figures for 16 and 18 frames per second used. Charts were drawn up outlining possible scenarios for the time frame of three shots being fired, including one utilizing *LIFE* magazine's published description. Several writer-critics have viewed this glimpse into the CIA's involvement with the Zapruder film as highly suspicious, at least one presenting the fantastic idea that the agency had the original film the night of the assassination. The researcher believes the CIA developed and tampered with the film as part of a plot, and then sent it back to Dallas. The available records, unfortunately, give us scant information as to what in fact the CIA or NPIC did with the analyzing of the film.[57]

The Zapruder film had given the Warren Commission investigators a large amount of data with which to study and manipulate. Yet so far as the Commission was concerned, this data, though able to tell much about the circumstances surrounding the assassination event, did not necessarily reveal substantially more about the sequence and timing of the shots themselves than would have been the case without the possession of the film.

The FBI returned the Zapruder camera to Bell & Howell on June 23, 1964, whereupon it was again put into the company's locked archives room. By late 1966 the company, for reasons unclear other than a statement of its being appropriate for the camera to be with other assassination materials housed in the National Archives, offered the original Zapruder camera as a gift to the United States. Former government investigator and Warren Commission critic Harold Weisberg contends that his public ridicule of non-essential items like Marina Oswald's nail file being housed in the National Archives collection, while the important Zapruder camera was not, spurred the company into making the gift. Before the transfer of the camera was made, Bell & Howell did its own engineering test on the speed of the film. This test was apparently spurred on by the comments of Weisberg that the film had actually been shot at 24 frames per second, thus invalidating the Commission calculations using 18.3 frames per second. According to a statement released by Bell & Howell President Peter G. Peterson, "Our results would appear to corroborate the FBI testimony before the Warren Commission that the average speed at which film passed through the camera was at 18.3 frames per second. In fact, our tests showed the camera speed should be within less than .1 of a frame per second from the figure reported by the FBI." The camera, along with its leather carrying case was turned over to federal authorities on December 7, 1966. It is now stored with other assassination exhibits within the National Archives.[58]

Volume 18 of the Warren Commission *Hearings* containing frames from the Zapruder film.

For months, except through the pages of *LIFE* magazine, the general public did not see any of the stills from the Zapruder film. With the publication of the Warren Commission *Report* in September 1964 and of the testimony and exhibits volumes by the Government Printing Office in November, a new source was available for looking at the frames. For $80 the 26 volumes of testimony and exhibits could be purchased, volume 18 of the series reproducing black-and-white copies of those frames provided from the transparencies given the Commission by *LIFE*. Thereupon began the initial public examinations of this film. Though the quality of the black-and-white reproductions was not excellent, more than one researcher quickly made crude filmstrips of the printed portion of the film utilizing motion picture cameras which had the capacity for single-frame exposures. In 1965 David Lifton, among others, noticed the transposition of frames Z314 and Z315 of the film in volume 18. This was taken up to be an attempt on the part of someone involved with the Commission to make the President's head appear to move forward rather than backward, being more consistent with the perceived movement of an object struck by a bullet from the rear. Using a woman's name and address, Lifton wrote Agent Shaneyfelt at the FBI about this discrepancy and received a response from none other than J. Edgar Hoover on December 14, 1965. Over Hoover's signature the letter responded, "You are correct in the observation that the frames labeled 314 and 315 of Commission Exhibit 885 are transposed in volume 18, as noted in your letter. This is a printing error and does not exist in the actual Commission Exhibit." It seemed too much of a coincidence to a growing group of suspicious critics that this would be the only so-called "printing error" made, and made to such a critical portion of the film exhibit. The difference in juxtaposition of frame 314 from 315, however, is not that revealing to the casual observer, and if anything, gives the impression of a quicker head back-snap. The manner in which the prints were published does in fact show a portion of the previous frame just above the frame being exhibited, with frame 314 mislabeled "315" showing in the very obvious head shot frame 313 above it. If deception were the true reason for the mistake, the portion of the previous frame should have also been deleted from the series. There is one other mistake which crept into the published record which no one seemed to pick up. Frame Z284 is actually a repetition of the one marked Z283. Part of the actual, and deleted, frame Z284 can be seen in the upper section of the picture depicting frame Z285.[59]

Though perhaps an unconvincing explanation to some, (this juxtaposition always seems to be brought up in critical literature on the subject), it was in all probability just sloppiness on the part of the editorial layout staff. It was apparent, however, even to the most casual and non-assassination buff, that while the exhibit volumes looked impressive in their depth and breadth of evidence produced, much of it was not very important, and some was downright unimportant. Missing was much of the photographic record of the assassination. Photographs and films of the assassination, much of which the public had seen in the media, were usually nowhere represented in these volumes. With the exception of a reprinting of a dozen pictures made by witness Phil Willis, which had not received wide distribution, and the inclusion of several cropped versions of other published photos, this seemingly inclusive set of records and exhibits relating to the death of the President had very little in the way of the best primary source material relating to the event — the photographic record. Even this author, as a 16-year-old, noticed the apparent lack of interest on the part of the government in gathering these photographic materials.

With the publication of the government's findings, a surge of published criticism, comments, apologies, and new theories was created in its wake. Several of these publications included more than just a cursory mention of the Zapruder film. The first writer to devote significant research space to the Zapruder film was a tenacious former U.S. Senate committee staff member who served as an analyst in the office of Strategic Services during World War II. A resident of western Maryland, Harold Weisberg has been described by friend and critic alike with such descriptive terms as "feisty, irascible, analytical, and curmudgeonly." He possessed a dogged determination to find and get at the raw data of the Kennedy investigation. In February of 1965 Weisberg completed a manuscript entitled, *Whitewash — the Report on the Warren Commission*. Though offering the text to over 100 book and media outlets, he was unable to find a publisher. Weisberg believed his strong accusatory text was politically too hot for publishers to touch.

It was indeed accusatory, and this and his other subsequent books would include premises that accused assassin Lee Oswald shot no one, that there was a major assassination conspiracy, the Warren Commission was a "palpably inadequate and entirely unsatisfactory official investigation," and that the FBI and other agencies carried out a systematic "whitewash." Finding no other outlet, Weisberg, in the best American tradition of letting one's opinions be expressed, engaged in self-publication. His typescript reproduced book, put out without the acknowledged benefit of a critical and professional editorial staff, and without the neatness of fine typeset and justified margins, did indeed find an interested audience. This and his subsequent volumes, several later published by the Dell Paperback Book Companies, enjoyed an eventual wide readership. Weisberg's research methods and his successful accumulation of documents became well known. Through persistence and later utilization of the Freedom of Information Act and court cases, much originally unavailable or suppressed primary source materials relating to the case was obtained through his efforts.[60]

A large 22,500 run of *Whitewash*, published with an April 1966 preface, was quickly followed by *Whitewash II*, published in December 1966. *Photographic Whitewash* followed in May 1967. Weisberg was a prolific writer, though much of his previous research and writing would be repeated in succeeding efforts. He tended to be caught up in minutia and details in which he would find conspiracy trails in the paperwork errors and omissions of the Warren Commission and the FBI. Highly accusatory in tone, much of Weisberg's criticism was leveled at the poor manner in which the FBI and the Warren Commission staff utilized photographic evidence. "Pictures don't lie — unless they are made to." *Whitewash* introduced and *Whitewash II* devoted expanded chapters to the treatment of the photographic works of Abraham Zapruder, Phil Willis, and Jim Altgens. A chief target for Weisberg was the Commission's junior counsels, particularly Wesley J. Liebeler, who had interviewed these photographic witnesses. According to Weisberg, Liebeler had carefully and deliberately manipulated the witnesses to extract only what he desired from them. In minute detail Weisberg took his readers through verbatim transcripts pointing out each lawyer's trick. In Commission documents he noted hidden meanings of inter-departmental messages. The author's writing is often folksy and humorous. Liebeler's style is described as " . . . running his witnesses through like autos off an assembly line and undoubtedly establishing a new speed record. . . ."[61]

Specter's single-bullet theory and its method of reasoning was violently attacked as a concocted charade, and the Dallas FBI-arranged reenactment was a deliberate hoax. The Zapruder camera had actually been running at 24 frames per second, as Zapruder had so stated to the FBI, and the FBI's 18.3 frames per second figure was used to allow a greater time span in the studied film for getting off the necessary three shots. Quoting Agent Barrett's interview with Zapruder in December 1963 when Barrett misunderstood or Zapruder apparently misspoke to say his camera "was set to take normal speed movies or 24 frames per second," Weisberg, ignored much other contrary evidence. He wrote, "This can mean only that the FBI and the lawyers on the Commission staff knowingly Weisberg couldn't concede that misinformation, mistakes, or just plain sloppiness of

,detail are as valid a reason for many of these discrepancies as is an immensely orchestrated conspiracy. When Zapruder was asked about this 24 frames per second quote by a *New York Times* reporter following up the Weisberg point, he stated he didn't believe he had ever been interviewed by the FBI, that the camera was set at 18 frames per second, and he didn't recall ever saying 24 frames per second. Zapruder, bothered by the question, then contacted the FBI about these discrepancies. The agency, ever covering their tail, explained to Zapruder that his conversation with Agent Barrett, even though not formally taken, was considered as an interview. The Bureau further said that the quoted 24 frames per second was, in fact, Zapruder's words. Zapruder, in a telephone conversation with Agent Robert Gemberling, the result of which was also typed up and filed, told the agent, " . . . that he did not recall exactly at what speed his camera was set and that this sentence had been taken by Harold Weisberg out of context in that Zapruder meant by these words that he did not know at what speed the camera was set, but that it was set at either normal speed, which would be 16 frames per second, or 24 frames per second." The slow-motion speed of the camera, which besides the single frame option was the only other settings on the camera, was 48 frames per second.[62]

It was believed by Weisberg that the FBI faked, destroyed, or ignored evidence. In his *Photographic Whitewash — Suppressed Kennedy Pictures*, Weisberg contended that, "At no point did the Commission make an analysis of what the Zapruder film shows. Instead, it used this film to argue that it was possible for a single bullet to have inflicted all non-fatal injuries on both the President and the Governor. The Commission knew this was impossible, for it had other and entirely unassailable evidence of it. . . . The FBI and Commission staff staged a fraudulent 'reconstruction' of the assassination in which they bastardized the Zapruder film . . . ." According to Weisberg the truth of the Commission's use of the photographs was that "None of the Commission's photographic evidence of the assassination is untainted. None of it was introduced into evidence properly. None of it was interpreted properly. None of it was used properly. None of it was complete in itself. Not a single motion picture, not the still pictures of a single photographer, was not 'edited' or 'cut.' And most of the pictures essential to any study of the assassination were rejected out of hand by the government . . . ."[63]

Weisberg was correct about the lack of care and regard that most of the photographic documentation received from the various lawyers in the investigation. Weisberg was of great assistance to others who wanted to pursue further the full story by accumulating, sharing, and forcing from the government much material that had previously been kept within. Along with 137 pages of text, *Photographic Whitewash* produced over 150 pages of facsimiles of Commission documents, many previously unaccessible. His shrill and convoluted attacks on technicalities, irrelevancies, and sloppiness in administrative housekeeping diminished to an extent the writer's credibility and impact, and caused many readers to find these and his other books interesting but not totally convincing. Yet he did focus attention upon the visual record, including the Zapruder film, which others in turn would take up in their own research attempting to get closer to what they believed to be part of the truth in this complicated subject.

By the mid 1960s, the Zapruder film in the only format available, a limited and static frame-by-frame reproduction, was being pored over by scores of citizens who wanted to discover the mystery behind the assassination. In late November of 1966, University of California physicist Luis Alvarez became intrigued with the challenge of applying scientific analysis to the Zapruder film when during lunch he heard graduate students arguing about the Warren Commission's findings. Alvarez was a Nobel Prize recipient who had also assisted in the development of the atomic bomb. As he was interested in both photography and shock wave studies, he decided to blend his interests into a look at the assassination photographs. After several days of examining the Zapruder color frames as published in *LIFE* magazine, as well as the frames available in the *Hearings* volume, Alvarez, armed with draftsmen's calipers and a sharp inquisitive mind, discovered what he believed to be internal clues about the shots fired. As the shock waves of the three shots reached Zapruder's position, Alvarez believed the cameraman had flinched. The jogging of his camera caused certain film frames to have streaks appear on the vehicles in the motorcade, which Zapruder was following in a right-panning movement. This shock reaction momentarily stopped the panning movement, resulting in a blur of the vehicles, but not of the stationary objects in the foreground or background. Alvarez plotted the horizontal spread of the streak highlights on each of the 165 frames and found three streaking peaks. This led him to believe that the three shots were fired around frame Z180, Z220, and Z313. The two later coincided with the Commission's findings, though the earlier possible shot point had not been noted by the Commission. Interestingly this Z180 point conformed with the point where for a brief instant a clear view was afforded to someone from the Texas School Book Depository's sixth floor corner window, through the obscuring branches of a tree below. If this were the first and probably missed shot, it would also give greater time (seven seconds) to be able to fire three shots rather than the 5.6 seconds (beginning at Z220) concluded by the Commission. Noting the controversy over the Zapruder camera film speed then in circulation, Alvarez made an additional observation. A man is clapping his hands in frames Z278 through Z296. Calculating his claps per second with various speeds for the camera's operating at 18.3, 27 and 36.6 frames per second, being 50% and 100% faster speeds, Alvarez pointed out the man's claps per second would be 4, 6, and 8. It was virtually impossible to clap at the two higher rates. The physicist concluded that the 18.3 frames-per-second figure, found to be the case by the FBI, was in fact a reasonable speed.[64]

Acquainted with CBS President Frank Stanton, Alvarez contacted him about his theory to see if the network would be interested in attempting to test his conclusions. CBS was working on a program dealing with the Warren Commission, and Stanton jumped for this fresh approach. Photoanalyst experts from Egerton, Germeshausen, and Grier, Inc., corroborated Alvarez's findings and found no evidence of additional shots. At the conclusion of the Commission investigation, the FBI copy of the Zapruder film and the set of slides had been deposited at the National Archives. Within certain restrictions they were available for on-site inspection. Alvarez, CBS, and E. G. & G.

representatives studied these materials there and found them consistent with Alvarez's earlier observations. Empirical tests utilizing subjects filming with cameras identical to Zapruder's during which a rifle was being fired at a position and distance relative to Zapruder's and the assassin's, replicated the involuntary movement and produced streaks on the test film resembling Zapruder's.[65]

CBS aired its news documentary, *The Warren Report*, in successive one-hour programs over four nights beginning on June 25, 1967. Though critical of certain aspects of the investigation, the report was basically in support of the principal Commission findings. Walter Cronkite narrated, "Our analysis of the Zapruder film suggests strongly that the first shot was fired at frame 186." Cronkite, contrary to Alvarez's "clap theory" said that, " . . . The Zapruder camera was quite possibly running slower than the Commission thought." The basis for this belief, which findings would have given the assassin more time in which to shoot, was CBS's examination of five cameras similar to Zapruder's, and clocking their run time. This test proved nothing about the actual Zapruder camera and its illogicality was later brought out by author Josiah Thompson in his book. In the television special report Cronkite summed up CBS's findings with the question and answer, "Did Lee Harvey Oswald shoot President Kennedy? CBS News concludes that he did." As for the Zapruder film and its lack of access, the CBS anchorman intoned: "There is one further piece of evidence which we feel must now be made available to the entire public — Abraham Zapruder's film of the actual assassination. The original is now the private property of *LIFE* magazine. A *LIFE* executive refused CBS news permission to show you that film at any price, on the grounds that it is an invaluable asset to TIME, Inc., *LIFE*'s decision means you cannot see the Zapruder film in its proper form, as a motion picture film. We believe that the Zapruder film is an invaluable asset, not of TIME Inc., but of the people of the United States."[66]

Perhaps one of the most influential and respected of the critical writings that came out of the post-Warren Commission flurry of books on the assassination was that written by Assistant Professor of Philosophy at Haverford College, Josiah Thompson. *Six Seconds in Dallas, a Micro-study of the Kennedy Assassination*, was published in late 1967 by Bernard Geis & Associates. An attractively laid out volume containing numerous photographs and an extensive and useful appendix, this book stayed clear of both shrill attacks or embarrassing apologies of the Warren Commission. It attempted to scrupulously examine and synthesize new and old evidence into a fresh look at the events in Dallas. In September 1966 Thompson had approached Geis Associates with a preliminary draft of his book which desired to examine the photographic record as it was "the only inviolable form of evidence." The approach much impressed the publisher and caused him to back this book project. In November 1966, *LIFE* magazine had editorially gone on record urging a re-examination of the assassination. Following an arranged joint meeting between the book and the magazine people, Thompson became a special consultant to *LIFE* assisting both their work and his own. The *LIFE* association, which lasted until February 1967, when *LIFE* cooled to the investigation, was immensely important for Thompson's work, as it afforded him access to the *LIFE* network of resources in Dallas, New York, and Washington. Most importantly it gave him free access to *LIFE*'s first-generation copy of the Zapruder film and their large format transparencies of individual frames. During Thompson's first screening opportunity of this first-generation copy, he quickly realized that this film was "infinitely brighter and clearer" than the National Archives copy. For the next several months in between trips to Dallas to speak with witnesses, Thompson spent literally hundreds of hours examining the Zapruder film and frames.[67]

Using the eye and ear witness testimony in relation to the photographic documentation available, Thompson evolved a scenario which amalgamated the hard facts with educated speculation. He chastised the Commission for its hasty evaluation of the photographic evidence. He attempted to use the photographs and films in his own study with care and by performing some scientific methodology upon them. Thompson concluded that in six seconds of shooting, each of the four shots fired had hit a body. The shooting had been made from three separate locations. With the Zapruder film as his basis of the scenario, Thompson concluded that the first shot was made at Z210-Z224, hitting and lodging in President Kennedy's back. The second shot, fired some ½ to 1½ seconds later, and some time prior to Z238, hit Connally causing all his wounds. From microscopic examination of the Zapruder frames, Thompson discerned the effect of the bullet upon Connally's body at Z238 by his cheeks puffing, locks of his hair being disarranged, and his right shoulder collapsing. He did not treat how the piercing bullet travelled through Connally's right chest, right wrist and left thigh, when Connally's hand during that time frame seems clearly out of line. This shot, according to Thompson, was most likely fired from an upper story of the Criminal Courts Building or another building on Houston Street.[68]

The interpretation of the fatal head shot to the President had become controversial almost from the initial release of the *Warren Commission Report*. Although the Commission had not seemed to take note of the movement of the head, researchers had. Philadelphia Attorney Vincent Salandria had described in an article the backward and left motion of the head upon impact, while Raymond Marcus and Harold Weisberg noticed the seeming double movement of the head beginning at Z312. Commission staff counselor Liebeler in 1967 confirmed, "It's only since the critics have raised this point that anybody has ever looked at it closely."[69]

In excruciating detail Thompson examined and, by means of plots and charts, detailed the movement and acceleration of the President's head during several seconds before and after the bullet struck. His conclusion was that a shot fired from the Texas School Book Depository Building had struck the President at Z312. Mirroring Isaac Newton's second law of motion, Thompson described that as the head was hit by the projectile, it was given a motion that had the same direction as the missile, and in Z313 and Z314 the head moved forward. At that instant a second projectile struck the right temple area of the President's head, fired from a position behind a stockade fence up on the knoll area on the north side of Elm Street. This almost simultaneous shot resulted, in just 1/18th of a second, in the double transfer of motion as the President's head reacted to this strike by rapidly being forced backward and to the left. Thompson laid out other supporting information by some eye and ear witnesses which also pointed to a shooter on the grassy knoll to the front right of the car.[70]

By the fall of 1967 the book was ready for publication, and Thompson requested of *LIFE* reproduction rights for a group of individual Zapruder frames which would graphically assist in explaining Thompson's chronology of the events. *LIFE* refused. Even when Geis finally offered to turn over all profits to *LIFE* in exchange for the right to use these frames in the text, *LIFE* still refused to make them available. Realizing the central need for pictorially representing what Thompson described, the publisher was forced to take a different, though not as satisfactory tack. Forty-nine charcoal replications of the critical frames were rendered as accurately as possible by an artist. To the public this would possibly pass for exposition of Thompson's theory, but to *LIFE* this end run was gross infringement upon their private property copyright.

The book was printed in late November with an initial run of 50,000 copies and excerpted in a cover story in *The Saturday Evening Post*. *LIFE* quickly filed suit against Geis Associates, Thompson, and the book distributor, citing copyright infringement and seeking to halt the sale and distribution of the book and to recover damages. *LIFE* claimed that Thompson, at the instigation of Geis, had "stolen surreptitiously" the material. Geis retorted, "Our sole motive in publishing this book was to correct a gross error in American history," and that in order to prove this, pictures from the Zapruder film were necessary even if only through the use of facsimile drawings. Publisher Geis allowed that he was willing to take this Federal Court suit through the process to the Supreme Court if necessary, further contending that at times the public interest supersedes the rights of private property. Such publicity only aided in interesting others in this volume and it took 10 months before the court finding was made.[71]

On September 24, 1968, Federal Judge Inzer Wyatt issued an opinion favorable to Geis that the *LIFE* copyright had not been violated. The opinion found, "There is a public interest in having the fullest information available on the murder of President Kennedy. Thompson did serious work on the subject and has a theory entitled to public consideration. The book is not bought because it contains the Zapruder pictures; the book is bought because of the theory of Thompson and its explanation supported by Zapruder pictures." The judge also found that the use of the pictures did not injure *LIFE* since the book and magazine were not in competition, and that the Zapruder frames' use in the book would, if anything, enhance the value of the copyright film.[72]

The Thompson book, which would eventually also be distributed in paperback form, was one of the first "theory books" that, through wide distribution and with an interesting graphic text and thoughtful reasoning, piqued the attention of many Americans who had up to then been turned off or ambivalent to the general tone of earlier critics. It also made many consider the intransigence of TIME, Inc.'s policy towards the film. Was the evidence of assassination conspiracy so visible in the film itself? Why, beyond greed, did *LIFE* not want the film shown? As Bernard Geis, in an unusual four-page introductory "Note From The Publisher" pointed out, "Surely, it is now time for

*LIFE* to release this unique body of evidence into the custody of its proper owners, the American people. The people must have all the evidence and all the facts . . . ."[73]

A significant number of citizens would not see the film as a result of *LIFE*'s deciding to concede to this public pressure, but rather as an indirect result of a messy and controversial investigation revolving around New Orleans District Attorney Jim Garrison. Garrison and his investigators turned up what they thought to be substantive evidence that New Orleans, a residence of Lee Oswald at critical times prior to the assassination, had been the scene of assassination plottings involving Oswald and two local men. Garrison's probe came to light in February 1967 and resulted in a blitz of media coverage and over-exposure. The D.A. made a case against prominent local businessman Clay L. Shaw and, following an arrest and indictment on the charge of conspiracy to kill the President, Shaw eventually went to trial. Part of the prosecution's game plan was to discredit the Warren Commission findings and explore the likelihood of a conspiracy in the actual assassination, and then to prove that Shaw was a part of that conspiracy.

In early February 1969 the D.A. subpoenaed the Zapruder film from TIME, Inc., which reluctantly released a copy of the film to New Orleans. At the Shaw trial in his opening statement before the court Garrison drove home the point of his belief in the importance of the film. "This film, which has not been shown to the public, will clearly show you the effect of the shots striking the President.  . . . you will be able to see him fall backwards as the fatal shot strikes him from the front — not the back but the front . . . ." Various Dallas witnesses to the shooting were also subpoenaed, including Abraham Zapruder, who appeared as a prosecution witness on February 13, 1969, and retold his story of the shooting. The film was then shown, though the first run-through was made without the jury present, in order for Zapruder to identify if it was, in fact, the same as his original. James Kirkwood, a writer who covered the trial and was partisan to Shaw, wrote a brilliantly narrated book on his observations and experiences. He described the reaction in court to this first projection of the film.

> . . . there was an insistent, almost panicky eagerness not to miss the first public showing of this widely heralded but little-seen film. . . . Many crowded to the side [of the courtroom] spilling over into the aisle and crouching down or kneeling, some on all fours, in their attempts to peer around and up at the white surface . . . . An intake of breath was heard in the courtroom, then a loud communal gasp when the President is hit a second time and his body jolts as the right side of his head literally explodes, sending a crimson halo of blood and matter spraying up into the air above him. Now short words and phrases filled the court: 'Oh, God !' 'Jesus!' 'Ahhh!'   . . . The first showing was bloodcurdling; one could barely take it in.[74]

The film was shown five times that Thursday, Kirkwood repulsed at both the obscenity of what horror the film depicted, and by the " . . . hungry look of salivating eagerness . . . ." with which many spectators viewed it. By the end of the prosecution's case, and over the insistent objections of the defense team, the film had been allowed to run ten times, once in frame-by-frame stop action.

The film display and the assassination testimony bolstered much opinion about the presence of a conspiracy, though the weak and flawed case against Shaw as a co-conspirator failed to win his conviction and resulted in a negative reaction by many as to the motives and the methods of the Warren Commission critics as a whole. While the Zapruder film was in Garrison's possession, many copies were covertly made. Garrison, sure positive of an assassination conspiracy, later admitted, "I persuaded Mark Lane to have 100 copies of the Zapruder film printed and distributed to colleges and universities all over the country and world."[75]

Soon bootleg copies were popping up around the country, obtained through an underground network of critics and amateur researchers. In November 1969 the editor of the liberal *Texas Observer* told his readers, "Whatever you believe, you owe it to your country to see the Zapruder film. If you do see it, you won't believe the Warren Report." He offered to make copies available to his readers at cost. The bootleg films, many as much as ninth or tenth generation copies, were soon being brought to college and other interested special audiences by self-styled experts. In the Boston area, beginning in 1973, a small group of politically active young men came together in a loosely knit group eventually known as the Assassination Information Bureau. Forming into lecture teams, the dedicated and proselytizing group of Kennedy assassination buffs would, over the next three years, spread their gospel of conspiracy and government coverup in a presentation entitled, "Who Killed JFK?" to about 600 audiences in over 45 states. The lecture featured "a provocative verbal and visual presentation, including the entire Zapruder film . . . ."[76]

The meeting's climax was always a showing of the Zapruder film and included the coaching by the speaker to watch for the obvious front shot to the head. The sickening sight of Z313 would occur and always take first-time viewers by shocked surprise, as audible moans from the audience would fill the auditorium. Audiences would be both shocked and titillated by the fact that they were seeing something most Americans hadn't seen. Following a long question and answer period, many would sign up for further information or sign petitions to reopen the investigation. They would leave feeling that the cost for admission or the passing of the donation bucket was indeed worth the chance to see this suppressed evidence. For $30 one could purchase from the A.I.B., a copy of the Zapruder film and a selection of slides. Concerning this package, the group's literature pointed out, "The visual material still remains the most effective way of informing persons of the inadequacy of the lone assassin theory. Hopefully such a package can be used as a tool for education and organization." Assassination writer and newspaper publisher Penn Jones even had available for $90 a sound version in which the viewer could witness a dual coverup. The suppressed film featured a married voice-over of Dan Rather explaining on TV what he recalled the film to show, including his comments that the head traveled forward as one saw it violently pitch backwards.[77]

Ten years had passed since the assassination. The public's general 1963 complacency with believing in the government had been shaken to its very foundations by other events. The terrible hemorrhage year 1968, with its assassinations, city unrest and riots, was fresh in the nation's collective memory. Vietnam, the race issue, Watergate, and trust in government were hotly debated topics. A good portion of Americans, fired by the critical literature, believed that their former President had been killed by a conspiracy, followed by a cover-up which many forces were still perpetrating.

Between 1969 and 1975 those relatively few people who had an opportunity to see the Zapruder film saw only a poor, multi-generation copy. In 1975 the public would have its first chance to see the film in all its chilling detail. Robert J. Groden, a young optics technician working for a New Jersey photo lab had come upon a copy of the Zapruder film. Though Groden was uncommunicative about the circumstances of his obtaining the film, several sources state Groden acquired it in 1968 when *LIFE* had sent the original out to the New Jersey lab for copying and copy slides. Groden says his copy was made directly off the original, and though he contends he did nothing wrong obtaining an unauthorized copy of this copyrighted film, he is careful not to mention who, if anybody, assisted him. Groden recalls, "When I saw it I was too afraid to do anything with it. I threw it in a bank vault." Over the next 10 years, he not only began studying it, but also enhanced it by reframing the individual frames utilizing fixed points, and thereby creating a new copy which removed much of the inherent shakiness of the original. This "rotoscoping" technique applied to a close-to-first-generation copy of the film greatly added to the clarity of the film, portions of which Groden also enlarged for even closer observation purposes. The Groden copy was indeed better than the primary copy from which the Commission staff and FBI had made their studies and observations.[78]

Becoming highly disturbed at what he believed the film to reveal, including a double shot to the President's head with one of these shots seeming by observation to have come from the front side, Groden began making contact with critics. He allowed some of them to view and study his work. Finally in 1975 the optics technician was convinced to show his enhancement of the film as part of a major 3-day conference on the Politics of Conspiracy, sponsored by the Assassination Information Bureau and held at Boston University. On January 31, 1975, Groden showed and discussed his work to a packed house. The conference received much publicity, including national coverage, and his film was quickly recognized as extremely important to the cause. Black comedian and gadfly activist Dick Gregory met with Groden and convinced him that he had to do more with it than just show it to a few people. It must be made public. Soon Groden, Gregory, and Ralph Schoenmann, were traveling around the country with the film, charging all sorts of conspiracy connections to the assassination, including CIA involvement. Groden had quickly emerged from obscurity to become a major player in the critics' circle. His ease at speaking, his often flip remarks and cockiness, yet sincerity of beliefs, made him an important spokesman.[79]

An April article in *Rolling Stone* titled "A New Look at the Zapruder Film," and Groden's publicly showing the film for its first time-ever broadcast on television on NBC's *Good Night America* hosted by Geraldo Rivera on March 6, 1975, brought a flurry of bookings and interest. It also caused pressure to be exerted by citizens upon their congressmen to open up a new investigation. A constituent letter to Congressman Robert Leggette of California in response to the TV airing is typical. The correspondent wrote his congressman, "John F. Kennedy was not murdered by Lee Harvey Oswald. Anybody who has seen the Zapruder film taken in Dallas that day can easily see that the shots were fired from the front, not the behind . . . . I am *convinced* that a massive conspiracy murdered JFK and in the process, a revolution took place right under our noses of which we were totally ignorant. Please do what you can to re-open the investigation of his death."[80]

In early February Groden had appeared before the Rockefeller Commission, screening his print of the Zapruder film. The President's Commission on CIA Activity Within the United States had been formed by President Gerald Ford to look into possible abuse and gross improprieties by the government intelligence community. As information had surfaced about possible CIA connections with Oswald and the Kennedy assassination, this avenue of the investigation was pursued by the Commission. Former Warren Commission Counsel and staunch supporter of the report's findings, David W. Belin, was appointed Executive Director of the Commission. To many observers this seemed a cynical and manipulative appointment to a supposed independent panel. Realizing the conflict in regard to the Kennedy assassination aspect of the investigation, Belin removed himself from direct responsibility, turning that part of the work over to Senior Counsel Robert B. Olsen. At the Groden screening, however, Belin was present. He described Groden's visit in his book *Final Disclosure*, calling the use made of the Zapruder film by critics as "the vehicle used to gain publicity by assassination sensationalists . . . ." According to Belin, Groden's copy of the film, " . . . was not nearly as clear a copy of the original Zapruder film as was available to the Warren Commission in the initial stage of its investigation. (Ultimately the Warren Commission obtained the original print.)" Groden pointed out the head of a man along with a possible gun visible behind some foliage at Z413 and Z458-478. Belin recalled, "as the film was running several times, Grodin's [sic] comments became more and more ludicrous. Grodin [sic] would yell out, 'There's the rifle,' or 'There's the gunman,' yet no rifle or gunman could be seen. It was as if Grodin [sic] were seeing a Rorschach ink blot in interpreting what he saw." Groden on the other hand remembers the meeting in a slightly different context. In his 1976 paperback book, *JFK: The Case for Conspiracy* co-authored with writer F. Peter Model, Belin is described as entering the room, looking bored, and undoubtedly expecting to view a poor quality version of the Zapruder film typical of those bootlegged copies in circulation since 1967. The Groden second-generation copy was bright and clear, and that upon seeing it, Belin bolted upright at what he saw. At the time when the head shot was projected and the President's head snapped to the rear, according to Groden, Belin jumped up and motioning to the projected image, shouted out, "Neuro-spasm, neuro-spasm!" Two totally different interpretations of events as seen by men with opposing viewpoints.[81]

Congress slowly had come to realize the dramatic mood swing of the public, as now not only did a great many believe that the Warren Commission was not correct, but now they demanded action from Congress. Virginia Congressman Thomas N. Downing and the other members of the Old Dominion State's congressional delegation were convinced to see the Zapruder film. On April 15, 1975, they met Groden and viewed the movie. Recalled Downing, "It convinced me that there was more than one assassin." Two days later a House Resolution was offered by Representative Downing, and after a year of stalls and false starts, in September 1976, House Resolution 1540, co-sponsored by Representative Downing, called for the creation of a Select Committee of the House to reopen the investigation of the assassination of President Kennedy. To many of the critics who had been working so diligently all these years, their efforts had come to a climax, partially through the efforts of Groden, who had enhanced and then had the opportunity to display this visually powerful "best evidence" of the assassination. Groden's work and success was grudgingly congratulated by many of the critic community, whose field work had matched or surpassed Groden's, but which had not the flash of his enhanced film.[82]

Groden would serve as a consultant to the House Select Committee on Assassinations and the photographic panel, advising it on issues raised by the photographic evidence. He gave testimony at the Committee hearing on September 6, 1978. In his introduction of Groden before the Committee, Chief Counsel G. Robert Blakey said of Groden that the " . . . results of his studies played no small part in convincing many members of Congress that the Kennedy case should be reopened." In his testimony Groden articulated the important photographic issues raised by the critics, and presented his film to the Committee and the national PBS television audience, who watched the proceedings. Though Groden was never considered an insider or had as full an access to the staff research and findings due to his being so extreme and oblique in many of his assassination beliefs, he was given the right to comment in the published Committee appendices upon a number of points where he disagreed with the photo panel. Though he changed his beliefs in some areas of the case with the introduction of new evidence, Groden's thoughts relative to much of the case had remained constant. He chose not to publicly air his more sensational opinions during his testimony. He was of the opinion that six wounding shots were fired in Dealey Plaza from at least four separate locations. On a 1979 radio talk show, he gave his views of accused assassin Lee Harvey Oswald by commenting, "I want to find the truth no matter where it falls. And as yet I have not seen one piece of evidence in 16 years to show that Oswald was even remotely involved in the murder except as a patsy." Claiming he was fired from a 14-year job in a photo lab due to his association with the assassination investigation, Groden also believed he had been blackballed from the industry. He maintained that his phone was tapped for at least three or four years, and his mail at times has been gone through. The autopsy photographs of President Kennedy, which were studied by the House Select Committee on Assassinations and found to be authentic, Groden believes to have been faked to suppress evidence about the President's wounds. So too, Groden is of the opinion that Lee Harvey Oswald's back yard photos showing him holding the Mannlicher-Carcano rifle are also fake.[83]

*High Treason. The Assassination of President John F. Kennedy: What Really Happened?*, written by Groden and co-author Harrison Edward Livingstone, was published in 1989. The book is a somewhat disappointing conglomeration of facts, allegations, and some new as well as some old and invalid information. Without a unified writing style, the book seems to have been put together using scissors and a glue pot. Included are numerous photographs including some distasteful autopsy views of the slain President. Much of the work simply states facts and opinions as truth without weighing their evidentiary value. Later released in popular paperback format, the book was an intellectual disappointment.[84]

Spectacular interest had been generated by Groden and others with the first televised and succeeding public showings of the Zapruder film beginning in early 1975. The always controversial film's virtual suppression by *LIFE* had consistently been criticized by interested investigators and the media. Now as a result of the resurgence of interest which had been somewhat dormant after the Garrison fiasco, TIME, Inc. felt the heat of controversy as never before. Groden and the other assassination buffs repeatedly pointed to the President's so-called head snap towards the rear of the car as obvious to all who could see as proof positive of conspiracy. As David Belin observed, TIME now wanted to get rid of this "hot potato." Some within the organization desired to donate it to the National Archives, though the final solution taken by the publishing empire was to turn it back to the Zapruder family.[85]

TIME had made initial contact with the National Archives and Records Service as early as June 1974 concerning a possible transfer of the Zapruder film, and in February 1975 Paul Welch of TIME had had a conversation with the audio-visual archives director about donating the film and transferring its rights to the archives or some other institution. Due to legal obligations stemming from the original agreement with Zapruder in 1963, TIME found that it was unable to donate the film and all its rights. Abraham Zapruder had died in 1970, and it was his two children, Myrna Hauser of Dallas and Attorney Henry Zapruder, along with the father's wife Lillian who became the recipients of the original film and its May 15, 1967, registered copyright. The assignment of copyright took place on April 9, 1975, upon payment to TIME, Inc. of $1, followed on April 11 by the three Zapruder family members assigning the copyright to a created partnership for this purpose known as LMH Company. Later, upon the request of the family, the National Archives gave courtesy storage of the film though with no public access to it.[86]

The same day that TIME transferred the copyright to the family by deed of gift, it donated the one of three original first generation copies of the film, together with a second generation copy and a set of transparencies made from the film to the National Archives. The deed read that, "Each of the above items are to be retained in perpetuity for the benefit, enlightenment, and scholarship of the people of the United States." The material was restricted in use, however, by making it available for viewing only to individuals on the premises. The gifts were accessioned into the motion picture collection of the National Archives, the first generation copy noted at that time by an archivist to be of poor quality.[87]

Thus the Archives now had at least one copy of the film, most probably the FBI second-generation print, originally from the Warren Commission files, which had been available at the Archives from the time of the transfer of the Commission's records. It also had, as of 1975, one first and one second generation copy together with the original, which was now stored at the Archives, but not available. Just what became of the two first generation Secret Service copies is not known, though it is known that an additional copy of the Zapruder film came to the Archives with the files of the House Select Committee on Assassinations.

Although news accounts reported that the LMH Company would make the film available to students and researchers, a hefty fee would be required for any publication or telecast use. CBS became the first media outlet to take advantage of the new ownership of the Zapruder film. The network purchased rights for its use from the family for a projected fall *CBS Reports Inquiry* titled *The American Assassins*.

In the summer of 1975 the network approached Itek, a Massachusetts-based photo optics company. They requested Itek to study the Zapruder and other assassination related films utilizing new and sophisticated image analysis techniques to try and answer some of the vexing questions raised by the community of assassination critics. Questions which a new examination of the Zapruder film might aid in answering included when the first shot was fired, when Governor Connally was hit, if both Kennedy and Connally could have been hit by the same bullet, information concerning the dramatic head shot at Z313, as well as several ancillary questions consistently raised by critics. CBS had acquired not only the telecast rights to the film, but also the use of the original film in the scientific query by Itek. This would be the first ever actual physical examination of the original film of anything other than cursory viewing.[88]

Over the next several months some dozen technical specialists at Itek examined the film in various high-quality black-and-white, false-color, and color print frames as well as with motion picture copies. Different methods of image analysis were applied to looking into the various questions. Among techniques used were: (1) stereophotogrammetry, being the analysis of stereo pairs of frames for depth profiles of the President's limousine and occupants; (2) precision photographic processing; (3) spectral enhancement and coherent spatial filtering, which allowed for special prints which gave more detail in critical, though inclusive areas including the enhancement of edges of objects; (4) mensuration, being precision measurements made directly from the film itself; (5) digital plotting of this measured data for overlay plotting of frames to assess motion; and (6) the more subjective and totally human photo interpretation, being the visual observations of frames and sequences performed by five trained analysts. They sought overall impressions and qualifications of what the film actually showed.[89]

Given the filming rate of 18.3 frames per second, each frame was taken at .0546 seconds, with an exposure time of .025 seconds per frame. The camera lens set at full zoom had an effective focal length of 27mm or .089 feet. The quality and clarity of individual frames was influenced by the changing scale of the filmed limousine and occupants as it traveled down Elm Street, Zapruder's panning ability as he followed the car, and most critically, the mechanical procedure of the film itself traveling through the camera. In a 4 or 5 frame cycle, a pattern was found of a good frame preceded and followed by several less sharp frames. The use of the original film and Itek's creation of precision copies of it, in the report's words, " . . . resulted in dramatic increases in information derived from these films."[90]

Itek's 94-page report with appendices was titled, *John Kennedy Assassination Film Analysis*. The following is a synopsis of the major findings using or relating to the Zapruder film made by Itek. The following information is verbatim from the report, but the sequence is changed to reflect to the chronology of the event.

There is no indication from the Zapruder film that the President was struck by a bullet before he was blocked from Zapruder's view by the Stemmons Freeway Sign. He is clearly reacting to a wound by frame 225 which probably occurred between frames 212-223 while he was behind the sign.

One noticeable fluctuation was found on both sets of plots for the car and JFK. It was centered at about frame 190 and lasted for about 4-5 frames or about ¼ second.

The positions of President Kennedy and Governor Connally in the car at about 1 and ¾ seconds before (i.e., frame 186 vicinity) President Kennedy was struck by a bullet (i.e., frame 218 vicinity), and the locations of their wounds are consistent with the hypothesis that both were struck by a single bullet traveling on a trajectory from the sixth floor corner window of the Texas School Book Depository.

Governor Connally exhibits a rapid change in appearance and position which begins at about frame 225 and is most obviously characterized by a sudden vertical movement of his arm and a flip of his hat held in his right hand, which flip is most discernable from frames 228-230.

Governor Connally's hand movement lags President Kennedy's by about 2 frames or about 1/9 of a second.

. . . the explosion from the bullet impact [on the President's head at frame 313] radiates matter in all directions. However, the major, or large particles which are actually measurable on the film, and have contiguous boundaries which hold together during flight, all radiate in a forward direction.

Figure 3.3.16

PRESIDENT KENNEDY FRAME 313
SHOWING EJECTED PARTICLES

Frame 313 shows what appear to be two major trajectories radiating upward and forward from the President's head. Study of frame 314 revealed two other trajectories which radiate forward and downward, into the car.

This spray of fine matter dissipates fairly rapidly but traces of it can be observed hanging in the air as late as frame 316.

The particles traveling upward and forward are traveling very rapidly at velocities on the order of 80 mph.

It is believed that those particles are 2 or 3 fragments of bone.

At 312-313 [the President's] head goes forward approximately 2.3 inches, his shoulder about 1.1 inches.

Immediately prior to the impact at frames 312-313 [the President] was moving very slightly in a forward direction.

Prior to impact at frame 312 [Mrs. Kennedy] moved in toward the President and was in contact with him with both hands as she attempted to assist him. At impact she felt the force of his body being driven forward, and she was hit by the exploding matter from the wound. The ensuing action on her part was purely instinctive to duck down and shove backward in one continuous motion. Her motion appeared somewhat periodic as her arm extended and she performed a

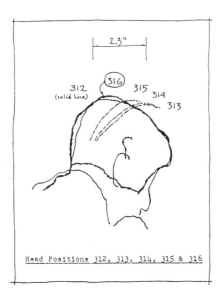

Head Positions 312, 313, 314, 315 & 316

push and shove-off type of motion. She alternates between pushing backward and then having the force of the collision push her forward.

Mrs. Kennedy moves forward in amount similar to JFK at 312-313.

Mrs. Kennedy then reverses her direction and moves rearward with greater magnitude at 313-314 than does JFK.

JFK's shoulder and elbow lag the backward movement of his head. The shoulder reverses in a smooth turn at frame 315-316, followed by the elbow at 316-317.

JFK continues backward in a relatively uniform manner, while Mrs. Kennedy undergoes another motion reversal, and greater accelerations than he and then continues to push away from him.

His backward motion after 313, as characterized by the momentum changes he undergoes and the impulses of the force(s) is significantly different than the forward motion. Mrs. Kennedy's motion after 312-313 indicate she caused her own movements and strongly influenced or caused JFK's backward motions.

This cause-effect hypothesis is subject to interpretation and must remain heuristic in nature since we cannot prove it beyond all doubt. However, we are certain that she does exhibit one reversal of her elbow and two of her shoulder in this very brief interval after 313, and that he is subject to a significantly different impulsive force after 313 than before.

> . . . [The President's] backward motion is clearly in progress by frame 315 and is virtually completed by 321.

> There is an object present in a few frames [around 414] which looks like the head of a man in the bush in about the right center of the frame.

> It is our belief that the object is a head probably that of one of the bystanders seen in the Nix film standing on the steps.[91]

The CBS News special, *The American Assassins* aired its first one-hour segment on November 25, 1975, with Dan Rather as its host. Extensive use of both the Itek study and the Zapruder film clip and stills from it were made during the program. Rather introduced this piece of evidence by stating, "What we have here now that we did not have in 1967 [during the first CBS program dealing with the assassination] include the original film Abraham Zapruder made of the murder . . . . It is not pleasant viewing for you or your family. We have attempted to keep on-the-air use of it to a minimum. But many conspiracy theories are based on this film, so we believe it must be shown, sometimes at slow speed, in order that you may follow our examination of it."[92]

Through attempted replications of the firing of three shots in 5.6 seconds, interviews with David Belin, ballistics and medical people relating what the recovered bullets and the autopsy revealed, and a review of the autopsy photographs by an expert, CBS made a case that although we still don't know all the answers, the basic facts relating to the assassination confirm the Warren Report findings.

As to evidence which revolved around the Zapruder film, Rather commented concerning the point at which Governor Connally was struck by a bullet, "Unlike Professor [Josiah] Thompson, Itek scientists don't claim to know the precise moment Connally was hit. Even with microscopes, computers, and the original film, they say the instant simply can't be pinpointed. They did find unusual reactions in Connally including facial expressions and movement of the hand and hat, which raises serious doubts he was wounded as late as Thompson claims. The Itek findings indicate Connally may already have been reacting to a bullet strike only ⅓ second or less after the President. If this is true, it increases the possibility that the same bullet hit both men." As to the single bullet theory, Rather declared, "We think the available evidence shows the single bullet theory is at least possible — that's the most that can be said."[93]

Earlier Rather had introduced the controversy over what many critics believed the Zapruder film to show as a double bullet shot, or at least one bullet hitting the President in the head at Z313, fired from the front. Rather introduced and explained this portion of the Itek report:

> The Zapruder film does indeed show the President lurching backwards, after moving forward. This is what the unaided eye sees.

CBS News asked Itek Corporation, world-renowned for film analysis to study the film scientifically using the best modern techniques and equipment. It is important to remember that Itek, for this first-time-ever study, had not copies of the Zapruder film, but the original. According to John Wolf, president of Itek's optical systems division, this is what they found. When the fatal bullet struck, the President's head went forward with extreme speed, almost twice as rapidly as it subsequently traveled backwards. [Wolf] "So in the three frames following 313 he reversed his direction and came back where he was before — it took him three frames to do it, so he's moving considerably slower moving back than he moved forward." [Rather to Wolf] "No matter how many times you look at it, that's not the impression one gets just sitting in a room and looking at the film. The very clear impression is that his head tilts backward faster than it went forward." [Wolf] "That of course is the whole point of doing this kind of — applying this kind of technique. It's to get away from the subjective impressions that are developed by looking at a blurred motion picture. My answer to your implied question is I don't know what I see, I know what I measure."

What Itek measured in head movements is an important indication that the fatal shot struck President Kennedy from behind. That's point 1 — Now point 2. Computer analysis shows that all major particles from the President's head traveled away from him — forward. Another strong indication that the fatal shot came from the back. [Rather] "Any doubt that the particles are moving forward?" [Wolf] "No doubt." What about Mrs. Kennedy? what if anything do her movements indicate? Additional computer analysis of the film measuring motions, direction and the velocity suggest the following: She may have pushed her husband backward while pushing herself forward away from him as a reflex reaction to the fatal shot hit. If true, that could help account for some of the backward movement of his head and body [discussion of another film taken by Robert Hughes].

But the key conclusion of this complicated computerized study of the films analysis of the President's head movement and the direction of the particles blown from his head both indicate that the bullets that hit him came from behind. That is one of the most important results of the new CBS investigation.[94]

Many critics were not surprised at CBS's conclusions as regards the interpretation of the Zapruder film. As far as they were concerned, this broadcasting company was known to be at the beck and call of CIA and governmental interests. Most chose not to believe Dan Rather's comment that as a news reporter nothing would have assisted his career or influence more than cracking the Kennedy assassination case and proving that a conspiracy did in fact exist. Rather and the CBS powers-that-be were, if not directly, then indirectly in the pocket of those who desired to perpetuate the coverup. Itek could not do an unprejudiced study and chose to ignore facts that would have proven conspiracy. In the words of one critic Itek "still faces the problem of being permanently tied to the CIA, the Pentagon, and the rest of the Invisible Government through a variety of important contracts." The CBS explanation of the backward head movement as having been caused chiefly by Mrs. Kennedy's actions was not given much credence by most critics.[95]

Luis Alvarez had been unimpressed with the manner in which the original 1967 CBS investigation had simplified and not been very convincing in interpreting his streak findings. He now used the vehicle of an article in the *American Journal of Physics* to expand upon his original findings. His original observations that Zapruder's neuromuscular system was set into a temporary spasm by the sound of the rifle which resulted in the blurs observed on the frames, was honed into specific findings. The streaks in the film proved the precise timing of a first and missed shot which was fired at Z177 and a wounding shot at Z215.5. He noted but chose to ignore, "two small accelerations between frame 245 and 280," judging that the smears were possibly caused by the imperfections of the half-tone process replicating the film frames. He believed the smear exhibited at Z290 was caused by Zapruder reacting to the sound of the follow-up car's driver setting off the vehicle's siren, which was reported to have started just prior to the fatal head shot striking. Alvarez also noted, utilizing observational techniques never picked up upon by the Warren Commission photo analysts, that just about this time [Z290] the Zapruder film showed that the President's car suddenly decelerated for about ½ second from 12 to 8 miles per hour as Chauffeur Agent Bill Greer, probably in reaction to the siren noise, lifted his foot from the accelerator pedal. If the siren sound became apparent to Zapruder at Z285, Alvarez would expect him to react at Z290.[96]

The most important observation made by Alvarez was in relation to the President's head movement. For years critics had been vociferously arguing that the laws of physics required that the observable backward direction which the President's head and body took following the shot resulted from a shooter positioned to Kennedy's front, and not his back. A body would fall away from and not toward the direction of the shot. Alvarez strongly stated that this "both theoretically and experimentally is simply incorrect." Through calculations Alvarez concluded, " . . . that the retrograde motion of the President's head . . . is consistent with the Law of Conservation of Momentum if one pays attention to the Law of Conservation of Energy as well, and includes the momentum of all the material in the problem. . . . My analysis involves three interacting masses, the bullet, the jet of brain matter observable in frame 313, and the remaining part of the head. It will turn out that the jet can carry forward more momentum than was brought in by the bullet, and the head recoils backward, as a rocket recoils when its jet fuel is ejected."[97]

To prove his theoretical calculations, at the urging and with the assistance of graduate student and assassination buff Paul Hoch, Alvarez requested professional associate and gun enthusiast Sharon Buckingham to fire a rifle into melons reinforced with filament tape. After initial positive results, the experiment was filmed with, to the surprise of various observers, six out of seven melons recoiling in a motion towards the gun when it was struck by a bullet. Though some questioned the procedures and setup used, to Alvarez the point was that there was a documented counter-example that qualitatively showed that the head could indeed jerk backwards. Though the results of the experiment seemed to run counter to logic, Alvarez had shown that the Zapruder film's evidence could have an alternative explanation from what people would assume should be the case.[98]

In September 1976 the House Select Committee on Assassinations was finally authorized by a vote of the U.S. House of Representatives, acquiescing to the pulse of the public. The resurgence of interest in the Kennedy case was assisted by numerous public showings of the Zapruder film. A Gallup Poll taken at the time indicated that over 80% of the American people believed that a conspiracy was responsible for the deaths of President Kennedy and the Rev. Martin Luther King, Jr. A Select Committee of 12 was chosen with Rep. Tom Downing appointed as its chairman in October. Downing, however, had decided not to seek reelection to the House and would retire at the end of the 94th Congress on January 3, 1977. This Committee was controversial from the outset, and for months was plagued with an uncertainty of leadership and funding difficulties. Texas Representative Henry Gonzalez became the new chairman, but fell into contentiousness and conflict with the Committee's outspoken Chief Counsel Richard Sprague of Pennsylvania. A nasty and sophomoric power struggle ensued, resulting in the resignation of Gonzalez, followed by that of Sprague. Finally on March 8, Rep. Louis Stokes of Ohio was named chairman, while Rep. Richardson Preyer of North Carolina headed the task force looking into the Kennedy case. Funding was a constant stumbling block, and what had been looked to as a fresh chance for an impartial, meticulous and truth-seeking congressional investigation, had been ground into a political quagmire fraught with inbred weaknesses. By June 1977, the Committee had overcome most of its organizational difficulties with Professor Robert Blakey of Cornell University, who possessed extensive experience in the Justice Department, chosen as the new Chief Counsel. Blakey began to give the Committee direction. There was neither time nor money for what many critics hoped would be an intensive independent reinvestigation of all facts and leads in the cases, a style favored by Sprague, but not the style temperament of Blakey.[99]

The Committee believed the most reliable means of investigation was the reliance upon scientific study of the evidence in hand. By setting up special panels of leading independent experts, questions were posed and answers sought. These experts in the fields of photography, acoustics, ballistics, forensic pathology, and other disciplines meticulously pored over the physical and other evidence. The Committee and staff also attempted to address the major points of criticism and confusion as postulated by a number of people from the critic community. In order to prevent speculation and premature judgments, for months the Committee worked without press releases or allowing the public to know of its progress.[100]

According to House Resolution 433, adopted in March 1977, the Select Committee would end January 3, 1979, at the conclusion of the 95th Congress. To be addressed were the questions of who the assassins of President Kennedy and of Rev. King were, did the assassins have any aid or assistance in the crimes, and did the United States government adequately perform its duties before the assassinations in protecting Kennedy and King and in conducting the investigations into their deaths. Also to be considered was if any new legislation was necessary as a result of the Congressional investigation. The questions addressed were significant and complicated. Under the restraints of the congressional committee system, the Committee in and of itself could not decide upon legal matters of guilt or innocence, nor apply legal sanctions. Such an activity is a judicial function. Responding to the public concern and allegations of conspiracy in the assassinations as well as possible governmental coverups in their aftermath, the Committee believed that in its pursuit of the truth, its procedures could be as elastic as necessary to find answers, and that " . . . its informing and legislative function required an independent determination and public disclosure of the facts." Through later open hearings and the publication of a report, "The Committee had the responsibility to state who it believed participated in each assassination, and what the factual basis was for that conclusion." They could also make recommendations to the Department of Justice to pursue prosecutions or follow-up leads.[101]

Given all of the internal and external restraints thrust upon the Committee, it made significant headway in clearing up old problems, expunging to its own satisfaction much mis- and dis-information, and clarifying, through scientific study, much of what the evidence could reveal. Yet it was constantly under the constraints of working within a finite time frame and limited resources. Although technically functioning over a 30-month span, the initial 6 months were eaten up by false starts and political in-fighting. March to December 1977 was utilized as an exploratory phase of the investigation, as staff became familiar with the subject and sought the comments of the critical community. Roughly from January to July 1978 the staff and consultants concentrated on the fact-finding phase, and from August to December it held some 36 public hearings. During this last phase the Committee and staff questioned key witnesses and the public saw the new information and tentative conclusions being drawn out. Unfortunately, newer and possibly more useful information continued to be uncovered down to the last moments of the Committee's existence, but neither time nor money for the examination of this new evidence, such as disclosure of new assassination films, was available to judge the significance of the new evidence. Congress was eager to put a conclusion to this ever-controversial committee.[102]

Just weeks before its demise, and after reaching draft conclusions that Lee Harvey Oswald was the assassin of President Kennedy and that there was insufficient evidence to find that there was a conspiracy to assassinate the President, the Committee was given new and startling information. Some time earlier critic Gary Mack, among others, had drawn the attention of Committee staff to the possibility that the noise of gunfire might have been inadvertently recorded on Dallas Police Department dispatch transmissions made on November 22, 1963. The original recordings of these transmissions, made over two separate police radio networks, were located in the possession of a Dallas official. Police transmissions had been recorded on Department Channel 1 by means of a Dictaphone belt recorder and the day of the assassination this channel was used primarily for normal police activities. Channel 2 was used that same day as a communications link for the presidential motorcade. It was voice-activated and recorded on a Gray Audiograph Disk at headquarters. Though Channel 2 was apparently not in use during the period when the actual assassination occurred, by a fluke of a microphone transmitter on a motorcycle or other vehicle being stuck on the "On" position, approximately 5.5 minutes of the noises in and around the vehicle were recorded by the Dictaphone belt, including around the time of the shooting.[103]

Though unclear to the unaided ear what among the various noises recorded on the Dictabelt meant, several critics postulated that among the clatter were a number of possible gunshots. The Committee decided to give this problem over to acoustics experts. These respected acoustics scientists would analyze the nature and origin of the suspect sound impulses on Channel 1 to determine if sounds of shots had been recorded; and if so, how many, the time interval, and point of origin. In May 1978 the Committee contracted with Bolt, Beranek and Newman, Inc., to attempt the analysis. By means of sophisticated and, to the layman, complicated scientific analysis of the recordings, chief scientist Dr. James Barger located 6 impulse sequences which could have been caused by a loud noise such as a gunshot. The Committee was urged to conduct an acoustical reconstruction of the assassination at the Dallas site. Realizing that Barger's initial findings, if true, pointed to a probable assassination conspiracy, the Committee sought an independent review of his analysis by Queen's College, New York, professor Mark Weiss and his research associate, Ernest Ashkenasy. Barger's analysis and methodology for the reconstruction were concurred by the two others, and on August 20, 1978, an elaborate test in Dealey Plaza was conducted. Microphones were strategically located at 36 separate positions to record test shots fired from the sixth floor southeast corner of the Texas School Book Depository Building window and from the area behind the stockade fence on the grassy knoll from where various witnesses believed shots to have been fired. A total of 432 shot impulse sequences were recorded. These "acoustical fingerprints" were then laboriously compared with the six impulses noted on the original recording for a total of 2592 comparisons. This analysis was not completed until days before Barger's public hearing on September 11. Though cautioning that the match he had found did not prove conclusively that the impulses on the 1963 recordings represented gunfire, Barger testified that his studies showed that the 1963 recording contained four sounds attributed to probable gunshots. Three of the impulses matched an origin point at the Texas School Book Depository sixth floor, and one impulse, the third in the sequence, matched an origination point on the grassy knoll. He further conditioned his findings of the grassy knoll sound to a probability of 50 percent.[104]

Asked by the Commission to further study Barger's work to obtain more certain results of his possible grassy knoll shot, Weiss and Ashkenasy put together an analytical extension to refine the estimate. They studied Dealey Plaza determining which structures were likely to have caused echoes received by the microphones. By identifying these echo-generating sources around the vicinity of the knoll, they were able to predict what "sound fingerprints" would have been created by a shot from the grassy knoll location when picked up by an open microphone. Each location of a microphone relative to a shooter's location would, by echoes generated off constant structures, produce a unique sound travel pattern which they referred to as a "sound fingerprint." The experts were confident that their precise calculations, taking numerous variables including air temperature in 1963 and buildings constructed after 1963 into consideration, gave them a certainty factor of 95% or better, that impulse #3, previously identified by Barger, was in fact a shot fired from the grassy knoll.[105]

There were some problems to this seemingly neat and highly dramatic acoustic study. Whose motorcycle from within the motorcade had been the one whose microphone had recorded the shots? The Committee concluded that it was probably that of

McLain at police headquarters on Friday evening

Officer H. B. McLain. But McLain did not agree, nor did a number of other researchers who examined the photographic evidence. So too, the recorded noise on the stuck microphone included siren noise increasing and then diminishing, the lack of crowd noise, and what sounded like a carillon bell, all of which didn't seem to fit with the actions and sounds expected to be picked up by a motorcycle officer riding within the motorcade itself. Later there would be several reports and published stories that the stuck mike was actually on a cycle further along the motorcade route or out by the Dallas Trade Mart, over a mile from Dealey Plaza. Anticipating such possible questions, the Committee report commented, "It is extremely unlikely that the echo patterns on the [1963] tape, if received from elsewhere, would so closely parallel the echo patterns characteristic of Dealey Plaza." It had further been determined by the acoustic experts that the grassy knoll impulse was marked by an N-wave, an impulse characteristic of a supersonic bullet.[106]

As the Zapruder film had been taken in real time during the assassination, a corroboration of the acoustical findings might be possible matching the information obtained from this film. Prior to the development of the acoustics evidence, the Committee had done a major re-examination of the Zapruder film. It attempted to answer those same questions previously addressed by the Warren Commission, the critics, and the Itek study — When did the President and Connally first show a reaction to severe external stimulus, and was the relative alignment of Kennedy and Connally in the vehicle consistent with the single-bullet theory?

The photographic evidence panel, including outside contractors (a total number of some 20 individuals), studied various forms of the Zapruder film, including the original film, a first-generation Secret Service copy which included those frames missing from the imperfect *LIFE* original print, the Groden enhanced version of the film, as well as enhancements of individual frames. The new enhancement work was conducted by the Los Alamos Scientific Laboratory of the University of California, under the direction of D. H. Janney. The object of this study was a " . . . computerized clarification of obscure details on selected films so that a visual analysis would be more satisfactory in assessing the positions of persons in the presidential limousine, facial expressions, and the details of motion." After studying the individual frames for blur consistency, a total of 16 key frames were processed for de-blurring in a three-step process of digitization of the frames into numerical data, computation to clarify the image, and reconstruction and reproduction of the adjusted digitization. The frames studied included those around potentially key points of the film where questions had arisen.[107]

The panel, meeting both collectively and in smaller units, reviewed the Zapruder film and the frame evidence on some 100 different occasions culminating in a final conference in July 1978. Analysis of the film evidence indicated that the initial reaction by occupants of the vehicle to "severe external stimulus" began to occur around frames Z162-Z167. Connally looking to his left, turns his head 60 degrees to his right in 1/9th of a second followed by a further movement of his head turning to his rear, followed by a shift of his upper torso in the same direction. In Z168-Z170 he appears to be looking upward. Though other occupants do not seem to react like Connally, except Mrs. Kennedy who does begin a right-hand turn at this point, the panel noted that at about this time a young girl [Rosemary Willis] running along the grass, " . . . suddenly began to stop and turn sharply to her right, looking up the street in a direction behind the limousine." Willis later told researchers she had stopped running in reaction to having heard a gunshot. Though there was no evidence that a bullet had impacted people in the limousine at this time, the panel believed Connally's reaction to be significant as it conformed to his original Warren Commission testimony that he had turned in response to having heard the first shot and was struck soon thereafter.[108]

The first suspicious movement seen in the President's reaction is at approximately Z200, when Kennedy's movements suddenly freeze and his right hand abruptly stops in the middle of a waving motion. His head also rapidly moves from the right toward his wife on his left. By the time Kennedy disappears behind the sign at Z207, the panel found, " . . . he is evidencing some kind of reaction to a severe external stimulus," and emerges from behind the sign at Z225 clearly having been shot. So too, Connally's movements as he emerges from behind the sign at Z222-Z224 indicates he is also reacting to severe external stimulus. He is frowning and his shoulders and upper trunk are rigid. A rapid change in his facial expression and his head movement follow. The panel noted that both men show simultaneous reaction-type movements, Connally lagging some

.16 seconds behind Kennedy in these movements. Further visual analysis assisted by computer-enhanced frames Z187 and Z193, which were stereoscopically examined, showed Kennedy's and Connally's position within the limousine to be aligned and consistent with the single-bullet theory. This evidence was further supported by independent scientific study performed by the trajectory and ballistics experts. The trajectory analysis based on studying Z190 indicated that the trajectory of two shots intercepted the plane of the southeast corner of the Texas School Book Depository around or near the sixth floor.[109]

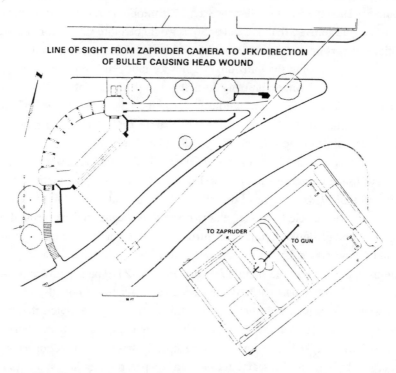

Approximately six seconds after emerging from behind the road sign, the President is struck in the head at Z312. By that time Kennedy was about 70 feet from Zapruder's position, the camera 13 feet higher than the President's head and Kennedy was turned about 25 degrees past the 90 degree profile direction from Zapruder. His head was tilting away from Zapruder by about 15 degrees and nodding forward by about 11 degrees. Extrapolating backward, considering the 265 feet to the building and the speed of Zapruder's camera, the shot was fired at approximately Z310, hit at Z312 and its explosive results shown at Z313. Members of the photographic panel voted on their conclusions based on examination and studies of the Zapruder film as follows: (1) by 12 to 5 they concluded Kennedy first showed reaction of severe external stimulus at Z207 as he was being obscured by a road sign; (2) by 11 to 3 that Connally showed reaction by Z224 virtually immediately after emerging from behind the sign; (3) by 15 to 1 that the relative alignment in the vehicle was consistent with both having been hit by a single bullet; (4) at least two shots spaced approximately six seconds apart were fired at the presidential Lincoln, but that there was insufficient evidence based on the reactions of persons as seen in the Zapruder film to reach conclusions about other shots.[110]

An analysis was also made of the so-called "jiggles" present in the Zapruder film to see if these could be interpreted as the cameraman's reflex reaction to the noise of gunshots. These studies, measuring the pan errors made by Zapruder while filming, were undertaken independently by two panel members, William Hartman and Frank Scott. Hartman measured the elongation of small highlight images present on the limousine in each film frame in which small, round shapes were evident when there was no panning error, but becoming elongated and blurred when there was an error. Plotting these points on a chart, and ruling out less significant errors as normal panning errors inherent with a cameraman hand-holding a camera while attempting to follow a moving vehicle, Hartman drew a threshold line above which were the greatest or most unusual errors. Scott, in his report, alluded to the danger of attributing film jiggles to specific events, as this can be speculative and subjected to prejudicial interpretation. He illustrated the point by commenting that if the event was not of an assassination, some of the jiggling could have been explained as Zapruder's attempting to initially locate the President in his viewfinder and as his frustration in filming and tracking the car as it went behind and re-emerged in front of the road sign. Yet Scott concluded it reasonable to believe that the larger jiggles could probably be ascribed to involuntary physical actions by Zapruder in response to the sound of gunshots. He was fairly confident to conclude that the jiggles occurring immediately after Z313 were involuntary reactions to hearing the fatal head shot, and that the jiggles beginning at Z331 may be attributed to Zapruder's reaction to actually seeing the results of the hit. The three long-term jiggles between Z335 and Z370 were most probably the result of Zapruder's yelling as he continued to film. Scott admitted that correlating jiggles with events prior to Z310 were much more speculative. He provided the Committee with a frame-by-frame plotting of background points on the film, correlating them with his measurements of the jiggles recorded on the film. These errors in the smooth tracking of the President's limousine were then reconstituted by Hartman from his connected, erratic, forward-moving line into numerical measurements represented on a chart which drew a horizontal line between minor smooth panning errors and the more unusual errors.[111]

These two differing approaches by Hartman and Scott towards the jiggle analysis were then matched to the earlier work of Luis Alvarez, who in his published study had measured the difference in blur between frames and had calculated the rate of change in these blurs. The two parallel sets of conclusions and the Alvarez study were then charted on one single graph which noted a time line calculated at zero for the head shot at Z312-Z313 with – and + seconds marked for before and after, and the Zapruder frame numbers also indicated. The magnitude of the panning errors or blurs were tracked for all three studies. These showed up as larger vertical peaks along the horizontal time line.

A number of jiggle errors were noted in the studies, the greatest of which occurs between Z312 and Z334. The next greatest magnitude of error occurs between Z189 and

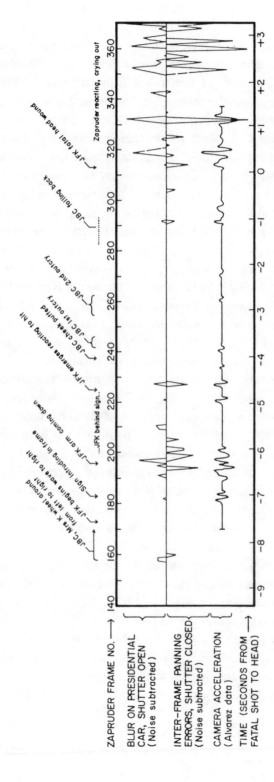

FIGURE II-5.—A comparison of the three independent records of largest blurs or tracking errors, in the Zapruder film, as derived by W. K. Hartmann (top, above line), Frank Scott (top, below line), and L. Alvarez (bottom). Magnitude of blur or panning error is indicated by length of curve upward or downward along direction of vertical axis. Frame numbers and times in seconds are given at top and bottom along horizontal axis.

Z197. In closely examining the peaks of these errors, the photographic panel concluded, " . . . that the shot may have been fired between frame 181 and 192 and impacted the limousine between frames 182 and 193." As for whether or not the other blur episodes represented additional shots being fired, the panel found that difficult to determine. They did point out three other episodes as noteworthy. One episode occurs at Z220-Z228 just prior to Connally's cheeks puffing out. It follows two apparent outcries in which the governor appears to be shouting. Another blur is evident at Z158-160 on the two Committee studies (Alvarez not having been able to study this earlier section of the film). This point conformed to the panel's notation of a visual reaction on the part of Connally quickly turning his head. The final major blur occurs at Z290-293, represented as fairly small by Hartman and Scott, though quite substantial by Alvarez. No visual indications on the film were noted to coincide with this error event. In its report, the panel concluded that there were two pronounced series of blurs found on the film. The one at Z189-Z197, coupled with the panel's visual observations, suggested this as being the time when the President was first shot, while the blur series at Z312-334 could be reasonably attributed as Zapruder's startled reaction to the sound and observation of the head shot. Time between these two possible shots was approximately 6 to 7 seconds.[112]

As Scott had commented in his report, subjective prejudice could ascribe too much emphasis on the single stimulus of shots being fired and Zapruder reacting to these to the exclusion of other reasons why jiggles could be found on the film. The razzle-dazzle of scientific studies with impressive looking charts and graphs could be over-emphasized. Not taken into consideration in any of the studies was Zapruder's secretary's (Mary Sitzman's), recollection about the crashing bottles close to the right of her and Zapruder's position. She had described these as being louder than the gunshots themselves. This event, taking place some time after Z313, was perhaps the cause of some major panning error seen after Z313. The panning error analysis was interesting, but only an indicator of panning errors, and not conclusive evidence of shots being fired.

One other task relating to the Zapruder film which the photography panel addressed was the question of the head of a man associated with a distinct linear feature which some believe to be a gun. This image showed up in the latter frames around Z413, though partially obscured by bushes. Many critics saw this as a possible assassin captured on film by Zapruder, the location of which was hidden behind a concrete retaining wall. Alvarez, in his independent study, had dismissed the controversy by showing that the man was actually one of those men standing on the very visible steps leading from Elm Street up to the knoll area. The panel concurred after studying the issue in depth. Through computer enhancement of Z413, it was found that the head shape was in fact real, though the pulled-down brim of a hat which some frames appear to show was only "a coincidental juxtaposition of leaves near the head." The frames also were examined photogrammetrically in order to find how far distant the head was in relationship to Zapruder's position. By this means it was determined that the closest possible point of the figure to Zapruder was in the middle of the stairs, and the farthest point some 10 to 15 feet beyond the sidewalk. The linear feature seen by some in this frame was similar in direction to other features noted in the frame, and from computer enhancement imagery it was seen that a narrow part of it passed in front of leaves in the bush. It was in fact only one of a number of twigs of the bush and located close to Zapruder and many feet in front of the head position.[113]

The photographic evidence panel and its hired contractors had done much to further quantify the information from within the Zapruder film. These findings were coupled with other panels' work to help determine just what happened during those 20 odd seconds in Dealey Plaza. Trajectory analysis had found that the position of Kennedy and Connally were consistent with the possibility of the single-bullet theory, and that the track of the separate back and head wounds had its place of origin within the bounds of the sixth floor corner area of the Texas School Book Depository. The forensic pathology panel, having certified the authenticity of and examined the autopsy photographs and x-rays of President Kennedy, determined that the President was struck by two and only two bullets, each of which entered from the rear, with one causing the head trauma. Nerve damage from the bullet penetrating the President's skull, " . . . could have caused the back muscles to tighten which, in turn, could have caused his head to move toward the rear." The nature of the back wounds of Kennedy and Connally and Connally's wrist and thigh wounds were consistent with the possibility that one bullet could have done all that damage. The so-called pristine bullet could have, according to a wound ballistics expert, caused all the wounds to Kennedy and Connally without becoming any more deformed than it was. Though there continued to be differing recollections of eye and ear witnesses as to the location or locations of shots fired, with the above data and other pieces of information relating to Oswald and his gun, the Committee was pretty much prepared to report to the American people that the President had been struck by two bullets that were fired from above and behind, and that, " . . . the available scientific evidence is insufficient to find that there was a conspiracy to assassinate President Kennedy."[114] All this changed, however, at the closing phase of the Committee's existence when the acoustics evidence was presented on December 29 indicating a 95% possibility of a single shot having been fired from the grassy knoll area. With little time remaining to further examine this and the other evidence, the Commission staff scurried to integrate these new conclusions into the other body of evidence.

Except for the grassy knoll shot pattern discovered by the acoustics analysis, the conspiracy theory was not solidly corroborated. A possible factor in corroboration of the acoustics evidence would be to see if it would fit into the pattern of shots and possible events discovered by the photographic panel's visual examination and jiggle studies of the Zapruder film. The attempt was made to fit the observed reactions of President Kennedy and Governor Connally in the film to the four gunshot impulses found on the recording. After considering various event scenarios, the Committee found a comfortable correlation between the Zapruder film and the acoustics pattern. The first impulse would have occurred at Z157-161 from the area of the School Book Depository followed 1.66 seconds later, at Z188-191, by a second impulse at the same general source location. At Z295-296 there was an impulse originating from the grassy knoll area followed within a split second at Z312 by a fourth impulse from the School Book Depository. "When the tape and film are so synchronized, the sequence on the film corroborated or substantiated the timing of the shots indicated on the 1963 tape." As to the sticky question of two shots being fired from the area of the School Book Depository within 1.66 seconds, when the minimum time required to shoot two shots had been established by the Warren Commission at 2.3 seconds, the Committee came up with a new answer. A ballistics expert testified that the Mannlicher-Carcano rifle being used with the open sights on the rifle itself, rather than the inaccurate scope mounted to the rifle, could be fired with two shots being gotten off in 1.66 seconds. There were many ear and eye witnesses to the shooting. A portion of these witnesses had described the shots as being fired from the knoll area. The Committee tended to give least weight to this type of evidence, however, due to the passage of time since the event, the intervening publicity, and the acknowledged poor accuracy of much of this type of evidence, especially given the physical nature of the Plaza area and the surprise of the incident itself. Unlike the School Book Depository shooting location, there was no physical evidence on the knoll, and no forensic evidence to identify this location as a source of a shot. The Committee concluded concerning the importance of the acoustics evidence: "In summary, the various scientific projects indicated that there was a high probability that two gunmen were firing at the President. Scientifically, the existence of the second gunman was established only by the acoustical study, but its basic validity was corroborated or independently substantiated by the various other scientific projects."[115]

This meshing of the untimely, and to some not fully developed, acoustics analysis evidence with the previous evidence of two shots at Z190 and Z312, did not negate the body of the medical, ballistics, photographic, and neutron-activated analyses of bullet fragments previously developed. If the acoustics evidence had not fit so well into the visual and jiggle analysis of the Zapruder film, one would not have had to embrace it. But as it seemed to fit so well, an extra assassin had been discovered! This new evidence forced the Committee to change its first draft report finding of December 13, that insufficient evidence of a conspiracy existed. The December 29 finding now indicated that the acoustical evidence established a "high probability" that two gunmen, including Oswald in the Texas School Book Depository, fired at President Kennedy.

The final printed presentation of the House Select Committee on Assassinations *Report* filed with the clerk of the House of Representatives on March 29, 1979, included much new and revealing information about the Kennedy assassination. It had cleared up to most reasonable persons' satisfaction numerous questions posed by critics over many years. The Warren Commission supporters still had a guilty Lee Harvey Oswald, and an intact and scientifically supported single-bullet theory, while the President's head snap had been relegated to a minor controversy within the bulk of the other evidence. So too, the critics had the conspiracy they always believed there was, though except for an inaudible impulse found through scientific wizardry, nothing else was known about the assassin and his activity. And his bullet had not hit any limousine occupant. Yet no one was satisfied. The Committee had self-destructed at a point where its efforts should have been redoubled, and a solution to the murder was as far away now, and wrapped in other ambiguities, so as to frustrate any observer in the seemingly never ending quagmire of the case. There were dissenters from within the Committee with regards to the entire acoustics evidence. Congressman Christopher J. Dodd could not agree with the finding that Oswald fired the first and second shots within 1.66 seconds, stating either the acoustics study was flawed in all or in part, someone else fired one of those first two shots, or Oswald was able to fire faster and more accurately than anyone else who had attempted it for the Committee. Stating for the record that following careful study and probing questions, his skepticism of the acoustics evidence persuaded him of its validity, he acknowledged that it would remain the subject of debate for years to come. Dodd strongly recommended that a general review of this evidence be conducted by the National Science Foundation or similar body, a recommendation echoed by the full Committee itself in their recommendations.[116]

Members Samuel L. Devine and Robert W. Edgar disagreed with the acoustics evidence stating, "This is a conclusion that must be rejected. Unless supported by other evidence, it is not sufficient to establish conclusively there was indeed another shot, another shooter, or a conspiracy." Edgar, in a separate dissenting view, went on to emphatically state that he believed the Committee rushed into its conspiratorial conclusion and did not have sufficient time or expertise to ask the tough questions. "We did a great job up to the last moment, when in our focus on the acoustics, we failed to give proper weight to the other findings of the investigation." Representative Harold S. Sawyer, in a lengthy dissent also strongly disagreed with the acoustics findings, concluding his statement by commenting, "I do not accept the acoustical testimony and the conclusions flowing from it." The remaining seven members concurred with the report's final conclusions that in fact there was a high probability that two gunmen fired on President Kennedy.[117]

True to Congressman Dodd's prediction, the acoustic evidence has remained the subject of debate since first brought forth. In the fall of 1980, the National Research Council (NRC), in a response to a Justice Department request, established a Committee on Ballistic Acoustics to review the work of Barger and Weiss, examining the methodology and recommending other possible tests to better refine the process. Chaired by Norman F. Ramsey, the Higgins Professor of Physics at Harvard University, the panel consisted of 11 other national experts, including Luis Alvarez, whom many critics described as a prejudiced anti-conspiracy spokesman. The chief challenge to the acoustics evidence was not initiated by the eminent scientists, however, but arose from an unlikely source. Young Ohio assassination researcher Stephan N. Barber was attempting, like so many of his critic friends, to find the truth behind the events. He had obtained an excerpt of the tape from the July 1979 issue of *Gallery Magazine*, a slick "girlie" magazine which had included an exclusive tear-out 5½" diameter 33⅓ rpm disk with the recorded "gunshot evidence that destroyed the lone assassin theory!" Narrated by critic Gary Mack, the inexpensive record included approximately 3 minutes of narration and police dispatched sounds as recorded from the stuck microphone. Listening to the recording time after time, trying to figure out which of the motorcycles had had the stuck mike and attempting to hear the gunshot impulses, Barber in September 1980 heard what no one else, experts or sleuths, had detected.

At the time of the recorded shooting sequence, between the second and third shot, Barber picked up the faint but audible voice of what turned out to be Sheriff Bill Decker. In the motorcade's lead car Decker instructed his men to "hold everything secure. . . ." Decker was using Channel 2 though his voice was being picked up on the stuck-open Channel 1 microphone in a phenomenon referred to as "cross talk." Some-one monitoring Channel 2 was close enough to a Channel 1 mike so that the Channel 2 transmission was picked up and recorded on the Channel 1 recording at headquarters. Barber later found several other examples of cross talk on the Channel 1 recording. The problem was that Decker had not given this order until over a minute after the shooting had taken place. So the gun shots could not have occurred in the midst of Decker's instruction following the shooting. The acoustics evidence was invalid. Barber wrote to the Committee about his findings, and they realized its importance relative to the accuracy of the acoustics study. Though the phrase fragment found on Channel 1 at the time of the assassination sounded like the transmission sent out after the assassination on Channel 2, that was not sufficient proof. The Committee made arrangements to obtain sound spectrograms or voiceprints of the two segments. Analysis of these voiceprints conclusively showed them to be identical. The Committee unanimously agreed that the original two acoustic studies performed for the Select Committee were flawed in matters of inclusion and exclusion, that the Barger analysis had completely missed the identification impulse that Weiss considered to be the primary one, and that factors within the recorded sounds greatly suggested that the open microphone was not even located in Dealey Plaza. In conclusion the Committee unanimously found, " . . . that the acoustic impulses attributed to gunshots were recorded about one minute after the President had been shot and the motorcade had been instructed to go to the hospital, and that reliable acoustic data did not support a conclusion that there was a second gunman."[118]

The NRC report was a heavy blow to critics, many of whom reacted strongly with the old, convenient "cover-up" accusations. Barber and his supporters were looked upon as dupes at best, traitors to the cause of truth at worst. Gary Mack, the man who had brought the potential importance of this tape before the House Select Committee, consistently stood up in support of the original acoustics analysis, and continued to find areas of research and possibilities of NRC undeveloped reasoning on which to hang his beliefs. He wrote Barber concerning the NRC report prior to its release. "This report will be believed, especially if it says the acoustics is wrong. And the media will say, 'Let's not hear any more conspiracy talk.' There was a conspiracy — you know it and I know it. But the public doesn't know it. And if this dies, they'll never listen to JFK research-ers again. I hope you can live with that. Your theory may be right, but if it isn't, some-one is using it to conceal what really happened to President Kennedy. Think about what you've done." Others, however, weren't so accusatory towards Barber's efforts, and admired the fact that a critic was more interested in the pursuit of truth than in simply supporting an interesting, though flawed theory.  And he may not have always been completely comfortable with those from whom he received accolades.  Former Warren Commission Counsel and ever consistent and fervently devoted apologist David Belin wrote Barber thanking him very much, " . . . for your important contribution to the work on the Committee.  It is a wonderful example of citizen participation in government."[119]

Though government agencies had had enough of the Kennedy case, interest in it by critics and the public alike, did not wane following the House Select Committee on Assassination issuing their report.  One of the most interesting volumes to appear in the post-HSCA era was a large format, highly illustrated book titled, *Kennedy and Lincoln, Medical and Ballistic Comparisons of their Assassination*.  An attractively laid out, though curious and somewhat morbid book, its combination of research into these two most famous presidential assassinations was a novel approach.  The book suffered from the so-called fascinating but overworked noting of similarities between the two assassinated Presidents, their families and murderers, and this "strange fact" syndrome tended to divert from the basic premise of the Kennedy half of the book.  Yet much of its content and use of empirical experimentation on questions relating to bullet wounds and medical evidence was quite remarkable.  The book's strong anti-conspiracy reasoning was sure, however, to give it little attention or interest from among the critical community, who disregarded it with enthusiasm.

Authored by Dr. John K. Lattimer, chairman of the Urology Department of the College of Physicians and Surgeons at Columbia University, his title and area of specialty caused many critics to find him unimpressive as a medical expert.  His solid background included being a former military combat surgeon and a firing range officer.  His knowledge and interest in ballistics and autopsy work, his access to a fine laboratory complex, and his strong determination to find answers to the often posed questions of the Kennedy case, led this President Lincoln buff to be the first non-government sponsored medical man to be allowed to examine the original Kennedy autopsy and x-ray evidence at the National Archives.

During a 17-year span Lattimer gathered information including interviewing the doctors associated with the Kennedy assassination.  He and his sons became frequent users of the Mannlicher-Carcano rifle in numerous experiments, including firing 700 rounds of the same lot of ammunition used in the assassination. Although the doctor does make occasional mistakes in specific facts relating to the assassination story, his work in describing the President's and Governor's wounds are precise.  His work in field experimentation attempting to understand and replicate those wounds and the conditions which created them, caused Lattimer to utilize mock-ups and test-firings into similar materials.  The tests were remarkably revealing.  In many cases he was able to contrive his experimentation so that it more represented the reality of the  assassination conditions, than any previous private, critic, or governmental testing.[120]

Like all researchers, Lattimer made extensive use of the Zapruder film. He also obtained the rights from the family-controlled LMH company for reproduction of many of the frames of the film within his book. Lattimer reasoned that Oswald took deliberate intervals of approximately five seconds to fire his three shots. The first shot was made by him from the sixth floor corner window through a partial obscuring of tree branches. The assassin in his anxiety had yielded to the temptation to fire, seeing his target so close. He fired and missed, Governor Connally reacting to the shot by quickly turning his head to the right rear. From the reaction of President Kennedy in Z225, it being the first frame showing the President visible after emerging from behind the road sign, Lattimer estimates he was struck in the back at about Z220. His reasoning for this is the sudden upward jerk of Kennedy's elbows. Lattimer concluded from examining the President's x-rays that there was compelling evidence that the President's spinal cord had been struck, grazed, or brushed by the assassin's bullet as it traversed through the lower neck area, causing a traumatic lesion. The result of this strike could be graphically seen in the Zapruder film as Kennedy's elbows flew up in a reflex motion to the bullet tipping his spine. Within half of a second of the hit, the strange position of his arms and elbows presented a position which had in the 19th century been described and illustrated by Dr. William Thorburn, a reflex known as the "Thorburn position." As Kennedy's right elbow was slightly higher than the left, it indicated to Lattimer that the President had been struck on the right side of his spine. As the reflex is so quick, and the President did not exhibit signs of it when first obscured by the sign, yet showed the reflex action beginning by Z225,

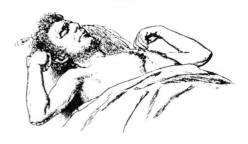

CASES OF INJURY TO THE CERVICAL REGION OF THE SPINAL CORD.

BY WILLIAM THORBURN, M.D., B.S. (LOND.), F.R.C.S.
1889

"The Thorburn Position"

Lattimer thus drew the conclusion that Kennedy had been hit while behind the sign at about Z220. This spasmodic contraction lasts some 90 frames, though the elbows begin to downturn. It is interrupted and terminated when the President was struck in the head. Unfortunately, due to his bad back, the President was wearing a wide corset back brace with metal stays laced tightly to his body by a broad elastic body wrapping bandage. This apparatus tended to keep him propped up after the initial shot.[121]

Lattimer went into much forensic, ballistic, and experimental detail to show that this first bullet traversed Kennedy, then went on to cause all of Connally's wounds. As relates to the Zapruder film, Lattimer noted that by Z230 Connally's right hand is recorded to have risen high enough so as to be out of the path of his being wounded there in conjunction with his other wounds. In intricate detail Lattimer describes Connally's wounds and what Zapruder records of his reaction to them. "After about one and a half seconds, in frame 236, Governor Connally's mouth can be seen to open wide, probably as he recovers from being stunned by the chest wound and attempts to take a breath. This attempt generated severe pain in the cut rib and nerve endings of his chest and the sickening feeling of not being able to draw enough air into his lungs because of his torn-open pleural cavity." Connally's reflex reaction to the shots had been to press his right elbow  against his gaping, painful wound.[122]

Lattimer had been very interested in the work done by Dr. Alvarez in explaining the backward movement of the President's head following the third shot. Alvarez had used a high muzzle velocity, 3,000 feet per second, rifle with soft-nose exploding ammunition in his experiments firing into melons wrapped in heavy tape. He had found a very severe backward movement to the melons being shot. For his experiments, Lattimer used the Oswald-type rifle firing 6.5 full-metal jacketed projectiles at 2,200 feet per second. His targets were human skulls packed with solid melon and white paint and then taped and sewn tightly together. He hit them in the same location as the Kennedy wound. Of the 12 experiments made and filmed, each skull fell towards the shooter's direction in a jet-recoil effect and with large skull fragments flying upwards and forward. The backward motion was not as severe as was the case with Alvarez's higher velocity and soft-nose bullets, but he found that the skull wounds so produced were strikingly similar to what happened to the President. Lattimer's explanation of the effect was that, "More of the heavy wet brain substance flies out through the large wound of exit on the front right of the head, causing a jet-engine effect in helping to drive the head backward in a jet-recoil effect. This backward motion was due in even greater part to the neuro-muscular reflex that stiffened Kennedy's back and neck muscles and arched his back in a final spasm caused by the bullet in the brain."[123]

In November 1988 the award-winning PBS science series *Nova* broadcast a one-hour inquiry titled, *Who Shot President Kennedy?*, utilizing what they described as "previously unavailable technology," to look into the 1963 assassination. As part of the program an extremely clear copy of the Zapruder film was used on several occasions, including a dramatic and sickening close-up and enhanced sequence of the fatal shot.[124]

Robert Groden in his 1989 co-authored book *High Treason* included an extreme color blow-up of Z335, showing the President's head moments following the fatal shot. Groden described the picture as showing the effect of a front shot blowing out a portion of the back of the skull, a fact which he contended was subsequently covered up by someone faking the autopsy photos.[125]

At a November 1991 3-day conference in Dallas attended by several hundred assassination researchers, a new wrinkle developed in the study of the Zapruder and other related photographs. During an evening presentation Tom Wilson, a 30-year veteran engineer for U. S. Steel who currently performs private consultations, addressed the gathering about his personal findings developed since 1988. Claiming to have perfected an industrial image processing and computer analysis system similar in methodology to how industry examines the interior of metal ingots to test for flaws, Wilson spoke of his process which could be used on photographic images. Explaining that while humans can discern only 30 shades of gray, industrial technology has improved the human detection so that 256 shades can be observed. Wilson's seemingly unbelievable premise was that utilizing this technology he had developed a system whereby he could examine any image for material detection and identification (metal, glass, ice cream, pizza) and strip away layers of the gray images to reveal underlying information.

In a convoluted presentation, Wilson then proceeded to solve most of the questions relating to the assassination by using the Zapruder and Orville Nix films and the Polaroid photograph taken by Mary Moorman with his system. Commenting, "Either I'm a fake or I'm for real," Wilson explained a scenario of two grassy knoll shots made by an assassin, the first shooting a through-and-through bullet piercing the front of Kennedy's neck, followed by the shot to his head entering at the right front and exiting at the top right side. Another shot was fired at the head from the School Book Depository, though not from the sixth-floor southeast corner window. With many in the audience incredulous concerning the data, Wilson also described how he can reveal whether any photograph has been retouched. He also stated that through his process he can look past the surface wounds of President Kennedy into the wounds themselves. He further concluded that if he had the original Moorman photo, through his process of looking at the brown iris of the knoll assassin, " . . . I think I could look in and see what he's seeing."[126]

To most familiar with the imprecise findings of much of the best of science when put to use in examining the assassination, Wilson's claims seemed absolutely incredible and too good to be true. Yet many did not want to slough off what might be a revolutionary new technique. Though assassination critics are ever skeptical of the government, many have a hearty optimism when it comes to flashy new potential research technology. Wilson sounded and looked credible and he promised to lay his technology before impartial scientists and keep the process public with nothing done "behind closed doors."

For the next two years information relating to Wilson and his technology was scant. In November 1993 Wilson again appeared at an assassination conference in Dallas to answer some of his critics and to indicate that potential articles about him and his work had been at first suggested and then rejected by *Newsweek*. He had then submitted an article to the "My Turn" section of the magazine, outlining his conclusions but not their proofs. In it he requested to present his findings to the Kennedy family and would then provide a complete description of his image processing hardware, software, and protocol to several credible institutions. At this Dallas conference, Wilson time and again asked for a public forum to explain and prove his technology, but when urged to do so there by several in an audience composed of many sympathetic listeners, he begged off, causing a number of listeners to vocalize their skepticism. Wilson continued to display his beliefs and conclusions, but while giving lip service to wanting to make public his methodology, he continued not to do so.[127]

In the early 1990s the Zapruder film was yet again examined utilizing state-of-the-art computer-enhancement technology developed and presented by Failure Analysis

Associates, Inc., of California. Their findings were presented at the 1992 annual meeting of the American Bar Association. Notable among the conclusions was the discovery of Governor Connally's right front suit lapel bulging forward from his chest at Z224, the probable result of the tumbling bullet and tissue particles exiting his chest.[128]

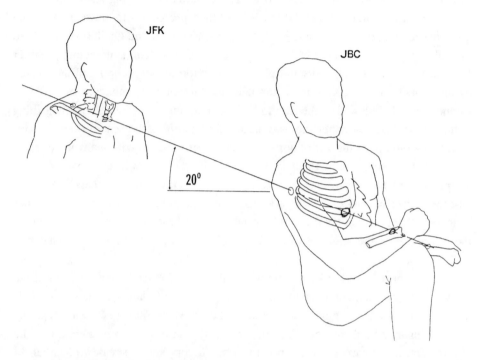

Schematic drawing by Todd Wayne Vaughan and James Michael Vaughan, Jr., showing the projected path of bullet CE399 traversing both President Kennedy and Governor Connally according to photographic and medical findings.

These new findings were synthesized by Dr. John K. Lattimer with his previously held observations of the Zapruder film and experiments into a succinct 1993 article in *The Journal of the American Medical Association*. The first shot had been fired at about Z160 and had missed. Approximately 3½ seconds later the second shot was fired. This shot wounded both Kennedy and Connally, striking them at about Z223-224. Both begin to react to the shot at Z225 as their right arms begin an upward jerk. Almost 5 seconds later the third shot is fired and strikes President Kennedy in the head at Z313. This timing scenario allowed 3 shots and 2 bolt-action sequences to be performed in over 8 seconds, enough time for an assassin to have fired such a rifle.[129]

A brief review of the major studies of the rifle firing sequence and its impact upon the President's vehicle shows the progression of theorizing based primarily upon observations of the Zapruder film. The Warren Commission found the President's position as seen from the Book Depository was obscured by tree branches from Z166-210, though momentarily clear at Z186. The alignment of Kennedy and Connally was consistent with a double hit by a single bullet from Z207-225. Kennedy was hit by the time his form emerged from behind a sign at Z225 and might have been hit at Z208 or earlier. At Z199 there was a jerkiness to his movement. Connally believed himself to have been hit at Z231-234 and two of his doctors believed him to have been hit at Z234-236 and Z235-237 respectively. In 1966 Dr. Alvarez noted his belief that shots were fired at Z180, Z220 and Z313. Josiah Thompson postulated in 1967 that Kennedy was first hit at Z210-224 and Connally was hit secondly and independently prior to Z238; and that two shots by separate assassins hit the President in the head between Z312 and 314. Itek's 1975 study saw a noticeable fluctuation at Z190 and that Kennedy was reacting to his first wounding at Z225, which probably occurred between Z212-223. Between Z186 and 218 the positions of Kennedy and Connally in the car were consistent with a through-and-through shot, and Connally exhibited a change of appearance and position at Z225. By 1975 Dr. Alvarez had refined his earlier data to postulate a missile shot at Z177 and a first wounding at Z215.5. The House Select Committee's intensive study saw a first reaction to severe stimuli exhibited by people at Z162-167, Kennedy's movement froze at Z200 and when he disappeared from camera sight behind the sign at Z207, he was reacting to severe stimulus. Connally was reacting to stimulus as he emerged from behind the sign at Z222-224. The jiggle theory was interpreted to see a shot fired at Z181-192, and another significant blur at Z158-160. Dr. Lattimer in his 1980 book noted the assassin fired roughly at 5-second intervals; the first shot being a miss due to firing into the tree, the second shot hitting Kennedy and Connally at about Z220 and the third shot striking President Kennedy at Z313. Finally in the 1992 study, it was believed the first shot was a miss at Z160, the second shot hit both men at Z223-224, and the final hit was at Z313.

The Zapruder film remains one of the key pieces of historic evidence in the assassination of the President. Its reality has been seen by millions and studied by hundreds of people over the years. Abraham Zapruder was trapped in the dichotomy of having hated to have filmed it, yet having taken advantage of its monumental monetary value. Various government agencies, major corporations, and institutions of higher learning have been caught up in the interpretation of this film's meaning, while scores of objective and subjective amateur sleuths have attempted to exact from it elusive truths. It is perhaps the best evidence of what happened to this President, but even as the best evidence, it falls far short of our learning or being able to comprehend exactly what happened and who did it. As Richard Stolley, that shrewd journalist who captured the movie sequence for *LIFE* magazine once commented about this film clip, "Depending on your point of view, it proves almost anything you want it to prove."[130] The film, though compelling and undoubtedly bound to be studied and interpreted for years to come, is truly obscene. Like Abraham Zapruder, many who see it have trouble getting the vision of horror out of their mind or dreams, for it truly exhibits one of our worst national nightmares.

## CHAPTER NOTES

Attempting to obtain good quality reproductions of a sampling of Zapruder frames, this author contacted the attorney representing the current owners of the film requesting to purchase one-time photo rights. The author provided all information requested. Assurances of following up the request on the part of the attorney did not take place after various letters and phone calls over a number of months. Though the Zapruder film is available for visual inspection within various television programs and books, the author believed it important to include representative frames to accompany this chapter. The result is that the text is forced to rely upon inferior quality reproductions printed in the Warren Commission exhibits available through the National Archives. Having been informed that if permission for reprinting these materials from the 1964 government publication were necessary, the author was told he would be so contacted. No such notice was forthcoming. Several Zapruder frames are thus provided as a minimal visual help in illustrating the text.

1.  "A. Zapruder Dies," *Dallas Morning News*, 8/31/1970; Bureau of Vital Statistics, Abraham Zapruder Certificate of Death, file #6013, 9/1/1970.
2.  *Consumer Reports*, 12/1963, p. 312-313; Harold Weisberg, *Photographic Whitewash*, p. 148-150; FBI Airtel, To: Director, FBI, From: SAC, Dallas, file #62-109060-3184, 5/25/1964, obtained by Trask through FOIA request #277,782, 11/1986; FBI interview of Zapruder by Robert M. Barrett, 12/4/1964, through FOIA,Ibid.; Photograph of the Zapruder Bell & Howell camera obtained through the National Archives.
3.  *Hearings Before the President's Commission on the Assassination of President Kennedy*, v. 7, p. 570; Richard B. Stolley, "What Happened Next," *Esquire*, 11/1973, p. 134-135; *The Story Behind the Story*, television broadcast; Josiah Thompson, *Six Seconds in Dallas*, p. [3]-4.
4.  Transcript of Josiah Thompson audiotape interview with Marilyn Sitzman, 11/29/1966, p. [9]; *Hearings*, op. cit., v. 7, p. 570-571.
5.  Transcript of Sitzman, op. cit., p. 1; FBI interview of Zapruder, 12/4/1964, op. cit.; Photo of camera, op. cit.
6.  Transcript of Sitzman, op. cit., p. 1-2.
7.  *Hearings*, op. cit., v. 7, p. 571.
8.  Thompson, op. cit., p. 6-7.
9.  The foregoing description is taken chiefly from numerous painstaking observations of the Zapruder film seen in real time, slow motion and stop action. They are described as objectively as possible, only commenting on what the frames seem to show clearly, and utilizing only the frames themselves as a reference. Subjectivity probably does enter into some of the description, though opinions of what outside, non-visible influences had on the scene are avoided as much as possible. One problem with amateur and even professional photo interpretation is the making of too many assumptions of what is occurring when individual frames are magnified beyond clear recognition.

Also hopefully avoided was the pitfall of ascribing emotions, reactions and feelings to an image of a human made during only a fraction of a second. Too often some writers dwell over what one isolated frame reveals, not remembering that real-time reactions and stimuli aren't divided into separate, independent and minute stories of events, but is a flowing and evolving process. If this author has erred, it is probably in being too conditional in the phrasing. Yet it is better in this realm of photo interpretation to be too cautious rather than too subjective. In one professional study of the film conducted by Itek, it was noted that of the best and sharpest frames present in this film strip, one can minimally distinguish objects or details of a size from between .70" and 4", depending upon the quality of the particular 8mm frame. The

Zapruder camera seemed to go in a cycle whereby a clear frame was proceeded and followed by less sharp frames in a 4 or 5 frame cycle.

When believed relevant, the author has included references to what various of the car occupants later recalled about the event. Among references used for this were: *Hearings*, v. 2, p. 74, 104, 138; v. 4, p. 133-134, 147; v. 5, p. 180; v. 7, p. 575; Robert Groden and Harrison Livingstone, *High Treason*, p. 16; David Lui, "Boy's Quest for Clues to the JFK Killing," *Los Angeles Times*, 6/5/1979; *LIFE*, 11/1983, p. 52; Dennis L. Breo, "JFK's Death, Part II," *The Journal of the American Medical Association*, 5/27/1992, p. 2806; Interview of Clinton J. Hill by Mike Wallace on the television broadcast *60 Minutes*, 1975; Original copy of award announcement sent to Trask by Clinton J. Hill, 1964.

10.  *Hearings*, op. cit., v. 19, p. 478; James Altgens and Arthur Rickerby photographs, 11/22/1963.

11.  Transcripts of Sitzman, op. cit., p. 2-10; *Dallas Morning News* photo library, 8x10 print by Johnny Flynn; Jim Towner photo #3, 11/22/1963; *Hearings*, op. cit., v. 6, p. 184. Part of the bench can be seen in several photos made that afternoon by Jim Murray.

12.  Transcripts of Sitzman, op. cit., p. 3; *Hearings*, op. cit., v. 19, p. 535.

13.  *The Story Behind the Story*, op. cit.; Peggy Burney, "I Saw Him Die," *Dallas Times Herald*, 11/23/1963; U.S. Secret Service, "Zapruder film, . . . Attention Inspector Kelley, [From:] SAIC Sorrels, #CO-2-33-030, 1/22/1964, as provided by Paul Hoch from documents found by Philip H. Melanson at the National Archives in 1982; *Hearings*, op. cit., v. 7, p. 352, 571. In transcribed but unattributed notes within the records of the *Dallas Times Herald*, one reporter obviously spoke to Zapruder prior to the announcement of the death of the President. These notes record in part: "Abraham Zapruder . . . heard 3 shots /// after first one Pres slumped over grabed stomac . . . hit in stomac . . . two more shots /// looked like head opened up and everything came out . . . blood splattered everywhere . . . side of his face . . . looked like blobs out of his temple . . . forehead . . . . Jackie first reached over to the Pres. and after second shot . . . she crawled over to back of car . . . after that she was lying. . . . looked like she was trying to crawl; of car. . . out of rear. . . cars moving so fast, he didn't see how it happened . . . Mr. Zabrudd taking film with 8mm camera. . . he has whole works on film . . . swants to give to police . . . (he is at Jennifer Junior Company . . . . RI8-6071)."

14.  WFAA-TV videotape of interview of Abraham Zapruder, 11/22/1963.

15.  *Hearings*, op. cit., v. 7, p. 572.

16.  Ibid., v. 7, p. 352; Dan Rather, *The Camera Never Blinks*, p. 124; Mitch Tuchman, "Kennedy Death Films," *Take One*, 5/1978, p. 21; CBS television broadcast *Four Days In November*, 11/17/1988.

17.  U.S. Secret Service, "Zapruder film, . . ." op. cit.; FBI Memorandum, To: Mr. Mohr, From: C. D. DeLoach, file #62-109060-453, 11/23/1963, through FOIA, op. cit.

18.  Ibid.; *Hearings*, op. cit., v. 7, p. 575; Thompson, op. cit., p. 311-312; FBI Memorandum, To: Mr. Mohr, From: C. D. DeLoach, file #62-109060-68, 11/23/1963; FBI Memorandum, To: Director, From: SAC, Dallas, file #62-109060-1094, 11/23/1963; [To:] SAC, Dallas [From:] Director, file #62-109060-1094, 12/31/1963, through FOIA, op. cit.

19.  Loudon Wainwright, *The Great Magazine*, p. 318-320, 323-328; *Life In Camelot*, p. 13-14; Curtis Prendergast, *The World of Time Inc.*, p. 122-124.

20.  Ibid.

21.  *The Story Behind the Story*, op. cit.

22.  Ibid.

23.  Stolley, op. cit., p. 135. Dave Taylor, who represented Associated Press that morning, recalls he was only authorized to offer $1,500 for photo rights. He soon realized he was helplessly outdone by what he knew was *LIFE*'s ability to pay. Later Zapruder asked him just how much AP would have spent for it. He gave the satisfying answer, "Mr. Zapruder, you'll never know." (Dave Taylor account to the "Reporters Remember" Conference in Dallas, 11/20/1993).

24.  *New York Times*, 11/24/1963, p. 7.

25.     "CBS radio description of Zapruder film by Dan Rather," from a transcript from the Richard Sprague Papers, Special Collections Division, Georgetown University Library, Washington, D.C., p. [1-3].

26.     Gary Mack, "The $8,000,000 Man," *Continuing Enquiry*, 8/22/1980, p. 3-4.

27.     Rather, op. cit., p. 124-128.

28.     Ibid., p. 125-127; Robert Slater, *This Is CBS*, p. 221. As noted earlier in the text, Rather's description of the events surrounding his seeking the Zapruder film is fraught with impreci- sions, and as his book is the only description extant concerning his role, it is presented ac- knowledging those imprecisions. Attempts at requesting clarifications from him were unsuccess- ful.

29.     Letter of agreement addressed to C. D. Jackson, Publisher, *LIFE* Magazine, c/o TIME, Inc., 11/25/1963.

30.     Miscellaneous letters received and reports filed by the FBI relating to Abraham Zapruder, through FOIA, op. cit.

31.     Stolley, op. cit., p. 135, 262.

32.     *New York Times*, 11/28/1963, p. 23.

33.     *Hearings*, op. cit., v. 7, p. 575-576.

34.     *Dallas Morning News*, 8/31/1970, op. cit., p. 3; Zapruder Certificate of Death, op. cit.; Stolley, op. cit., p. 262-263.

35.     *LIFE*, original issue, 11/29/1963.

36.     *LIFE*, second issue, 11/29/1963; Wainwright, op. cit., p. 311-318.

37.     *LIFE*, second issue, op. cit.; Wide World and UPI photos on microfilm, roll #10 & 15, John F. Kennedy Library, Audio-Visual Department. The 11/29/1963 release of these photos stipulated the copyright holder, " . . . restricts use of these photos to newspapers only in U.S.A and Canada. They may *not* be used on television nor magazines. They may not be retouched or altered in any way. Mandatory credit . . . ."

38.     *LIFE*, 11/25/1966, p. 40-48, 53; Wainwright, op. cit., p. 323.

39.     Letter, Bureau Chief Henry Suydam, to James Rowley, 1/7/1964; Letter, Rowley to Suydam, 1/27/1964, both as provided by Paul Hoch, op. cit. As a curious aside, in December 1964 Director Hoover wrote Warren Commission Chief Counsel Rankin with a request made by the CIA that the FBI copy of the film be loaned to them, " . . . solely for training purposes." Rankin apparently spoke with TIME, Inc. representatives and informed the FBI that they would get in touch to "make their own arrangements." Harold Weisberg, *Photographic Whitewash*, p. 143.

40.     *Newsweek*, 2/6/1967, p. 17; *New York Times*, 1/30/1967, p. 22; Thompson, op. cit., p. [216]-218.

41.     Rather, op. cit., p. 127-128.

42.     Memorandum, To: A. H. Belmont, From: I. W. Conrad, file #62-109060-1132, 12/4/1963; Memorandum, To: Director, From: SAC, Dallas, file #62-109060-2111, 12/5/1963, through FOIA, op. cit.

43.     FBI laboratory, To: FBI, Dallas, 12/20/1963; Memorandum, To: Mr. Conrad, From: W. D. Griffith, file #62-109060-2360, 1/31/1964, through FOIA, op. cit.; Weisberg, op. cit., p. 140.

44.     Ibid., p. 148-150; *Hearings*, op. cit., v. 7, p. 576.

45.     Edward Jay Epstein, *Inquest*, p. 42, 83.

46.     Ibid., p. 113; *Hearings*, op. cit., v. 7, p. 576.

47.     Memorandum, To: Mr. Conrad, From: W. D. Griffith, file #62-109060-3282, through FOIA, op. cit.; *Hearings*, v. 5, p. 141-142.

48.     Ibid., v. 5, p. 138-139; Weisberg, op. cit., p. 142, 144. In the published *Hearings* Shaneyfelt is quoted as saying the frames chosen went up to Z434. This is an obvious misprint as the published frames went up to Z334. This would include 163 frames which, if excluding the four which *LIFE*'s original film did not now include, would represent 159 frames. This is the number

this author used as valid, rather than the 169 frames quoted in Hoover's letter as the number provided to the investigation by *LIFE*.

49.    Memorandum, To: Mr. Conrad, From: W. D. Griffith, file #62-109060-2405, 1/28/1964, through FOIA, op. cit.

50.    Epstein, op. cit., p. 13, 17, 43-45, 113-114; Thompson, op. cit., p. [305]; David W. Belin, *Final Disclosure*, p. 51-53.

51.    *Hearings*, op. cit., v. 2, p. 375; v. 5, p. 157; v. 4, p. 114, 128.

52.    Epstein, op. cit., p. 112; Belin, op. cit., p. 52; *Report of the President's Commission on the Assassination of President John F. Kennedy*, p. 79, 81, 87-92.

53.    Epstein, op. cit., p. 119-122; *Hearings*, op. cit. v. 5, p. 77-87, 92-97.

54.    Ibid., v. 5, p. 143-148.

55.    Ibid., v. 5, p. 148-155, 167-169; *Report*, op. cit., p. 97-107.

56.    Ibid., p. 19.

57.    Copies of National Photographic Interpretation Center documents provided by Paul Hoch, #177; Mark Lane, *Rush to Judgment*, p. 66; *Hearings*, op. cit., v. 5, p. 176.

58.    Weisberg, op. cit., p. 25-26, 146-151; Peter Kihss, "Critic of Warren Commission Disputes Film Timing," *New York Times*, 12/8/1966.

59.    Weisberg, op. cit., p. 145; *Hearings*, op. cit., v. 18, p. 55-56, 70-71.

60.    Harold Weisberg, *Whitewash*; Harold Weisberg, *Whitewash II; The FBI-Secret Service Cover Up*; Weisberg, op. cit.

61.    *Whitewash*, op. cit.; *Whitewash II*, op. cit., p. 207, chapter 11-13, 17.

62.    Airtel, To: Director, FBI, From: SAC, Dallas, file #62-109060-4376, 1/6/1977, through FOIA, op. cit.; *Whitewash II*, op. cit., p. 294-295; Kihss, op. cit.

63.    Weisberg, op. cit., p.14-18.

64.    "New Clues in JFK Assassination Photos," *The Magnet*, 7/1967, p. 1, 6-7.

65.    Ibid., p. 6.

66.    Thompson, op. cit. p. [292]-294; Florence Graves, "The Mysterious Kennedy Out-Takes," *WJR [Washington Journalistic Review]*, 9-10/1978, p. 25.

67.    Thompson, op. cit., p. xii, xv-xvii, 6-9, 14.

68.    Ibid., p. 30, 50, 53-56, 69-79, 179-195.

69.    Ibid., p. 86-87.

70.    Ibid., p. 86-98.

71.    "*LIFE* Sues to Halt Book on Kennedy," *New York Times*, 12/9/1967, p. 61.

72.    "Time Inc. Looses Suit on 'Dallas' Photos," *New York Times*, 10/1/1968, p. 22; "JFK Assassination Films: Court Rules 'Fair Use,'" *Publishers Weekly*, 10/14/1968, p. 39.

73.    Thompson, op. cit., p. xviii.

74.    "Garrison Subpoenas Film of Kennedy Assassination," *New York Times*, 2/5/1969, p. 20; "Zapruder Film of Kennedy Shown at Shaw Trial," *New York Times*, 2/14/1969, p. 20; Teletype, To: Director, From: New Orleans, file #62-109060-6751, 2/14/1969, p. 1-6, through FOIA, op. cit., James Kirkwood, *American Grotesque*, p. 207, 315-316, 319.

75.    Jim Garrison, *On the Trail of the Assassins*, p. 239.

76.    [Washington] *Evening Star*, 11/26/1969, p. A-8; David Williams and Harvey Z. Yazijian, "The Grassy Knoll Papers," *Boston Magazine*, 3/1979, p. 83, 121; "Who Killed JFK?" [flyer] May 29 [1975].

77.    "From Penn Jones" [flyer, 1978]; "Dear Friend" [Assassination Information Bureau form letter, 1975].

78.    Robert B. Cutler, *Seventy-Six Seconds in Dealey Plaza*, p. 2, 42; Gary Shaw, *Cover-Up*, p. 33; Talk given by David Lifton at the Assassination Symposium on Kennedy at Dallas, Texas, 10/23/1992; Audio tape of Robert Groden interview on WPIX, New York, 11/5/1979; Letter, Richard E. Sprague to R. B. Cutler, 1975.

79.    Ibid.; Williams, op. cit., p. 124.

80.   *Rolling Stone*, 4/24/1975; Letter to Hon. Robert L. Leggett, file #62-109060-7172, 3/1975, through FOIA, op. cit.

81.   F. Peter Model and Robert J. Groden, *JFK: The Case For Conspiracy*, p. 281-287; Belin, op. cit., p. 178-179.

82.   WPIX, op. cit.; Model, op. cit., p. [1]; Robert J. Groden and Harrison Edward Livingstone, *High Treason*, p. 294.

83.   WPIX, op. cit., Cutler, op. cit., p. 2-3; Model, op. cit., p. [2-3]; Groden and Livingstone, op. cit., p. 47-48, 88-89, 148-149, 322-323; *Appendix to Hearings Before the Select Committee on Assassinations*, v. 6, p. 294-318.

84.   Critic Paul Hoch presented a balanced overview of the volume's strengths and weaknesses in his newsletter *Echoes of Conspiracy*, 11/24/1989, p. 3-11.

85.   Belin, op. cit., p. 181-182.

86.   Memorandum by Meyer H. Fishbein regarding Kennedy film, 10/15/1974; Memorandum from Director of Audiovisual Archives James W. Moore, to Archivist of the United States, 4/6/1975; Assignment of copyright from TIME, Inc., to Zapruder, 4/9/1975; Assignment of copyright from Zapruder to LMH Company, 4/11/1975, all from material provided Trask by National Archives, 3/4/1985; "Time Yielding Custody of Kennedy-Death Film," *New York Times*, 4/10/ 1975.

87.   Deed of gift, TIME, Inc., to National Archives and Records Service, 4/9/1975; James W. Moore, Final report on transfer, 4/29/1975, all from material provided Trask by National Archives, 3/4/1985.

88.   Itek, *John F. Kennedy Assassination Film Analysis*, p. 1; CBS television broadcast, *The American Assassins, Part I*, 11/25/1975.

89.   Francis Corbett, "John F. Kennedy Assassination Film Analysis," p. [1-3]

90.   Itek, op. cit., p. 5, 27-28.

91.   Ibid., [in order of items quoted] p. 50, 35, 3, 50, 3, 56, 52, 62-63, 78, 64, 81, 84-85, 66, 90-91.

92.   CBS broadcast, *The American Assassins*, op. cit.

93.   Ibid.

94.   Ibid.

95.   Rather, op. cit., p. 128; Christopher B. Sharrett, "Review of Itek John F. Kennedy Assassination Film Analysis," p. 1.

96.   Luis W. Alvarez, "A Physicist Examines the Kennedy Assassination Film," *American Journal of Physics*, 9/1976, p. 815-819, 823-826.

97.   Ibid., p. 813, 819.

98.   Ibid., p. 820-822.

99.   *Report of the Select Committee on Assassinations*, p. 9-10, 494-495, 534-561.

100.  Ibid., p. 18-19, 42.

101.  Ibid., p. 10-11, 15-16, 556-557.

102.  Ibid., p. 18-19.

103.  Ibid., p. 66-67; *Science*, 10/8/1982, p. 127.

104.  *Report*, op. cit., p. 68-72; *Science*, op. cit., p. 127.

105.  *Report*, op. cit., p. 72-75.

106.  Ibid., p. 74-79; *Dallas Morning News*, 4/14/1982, p. 1A, 9A.

107.  *Appendix*, op. cit., v. 6, p. 15-16; D. H. Janney [Report] 6/27/1978, p. [1-8]

108.  *Appendix*, op. cit., v. 6, p. 17; Letter, Frank Smith to Jane Downey, 8/15/1978, p. 6.

109.  *Appendix*, op. cit., v. 6, p. 17-18, 32-42.

110.  Ibid., v. 6., p. 16-17, 38.

111.  Letter, Smith to Downey, op. cit.; *Appendix*, op. cit., v. 6, p. 20-22.

112.  Ibid., v. 6, p. 26-30.

113.  Ibid., v. 6, p. 131-133.

114.  Ibid., v. 6, p. 32-45; *Report*, op. cit., p. 43-45, 495.

115.  Ibid., p. 79-84.

116.   Ibid., p. 483-487.

117.   Ibid., p. 491-508.

118.   *Science*, op. cit., p. 127-133; Letter, Steve Barber to R. B. Cutler, 12/22/1981; Audio disk recording insert in *Gallery*, 7/1979.

119.   Letter, Gary Mack to Steve Barber, 3/4/1982; Letter, David Belin to Steve Barber, 9/17/1982. The controversy continued, as evidenced in the 1989 Groden co-authored book *High Treason*, in which he contended that the shots are authentic and the cross-talk superimposed. A privately published rebuttal by Steve Barber titled *Double Decker* was published in the summer of 1989.

120.   John K. Lattimer, *Kennedy and Lincoln, Medical and Ballistic Comparisons of Their Assassinations.*

121.   Ibid., p. 146, 167-171, 244-245.

122.   Ibid., p. 168-169.

123.   Ibid., p. 174, 248-259.

124.   PBS television broadcast, *Nova*, "Who Shot President Kennedy?" 11/15/1988.

125.   Groden and Livingstone, op. cit., p. 88-89, opp. p. 387.

126.   Presentation by Tom Wilson at the ASK Conference in Dallas, 11/15/1991.

127.   Presentation by Tom Wilson at the ASK Conference in Dallas, 11/20/1993.

128.   John K. Lattimer, "Additional Data on the Shooting of President Kennedy," *The Journal of the American Medical Association*, 3/24-31/1993, p. 1544-1545.

129.   Ibid., p. 1544-1547.

130.   Audio tape of WJR radio interview of Richard Stolley, 11/22/1983.

## CHAPTER 3

# Images in Black and White

Many of the spectators who were in and around Dealey Plaza on November 22 to view the presidential motorcade worked at nearby businesses. As the Plaza was located adjacent to the railroad yards and the Union Railway Terminal, a number of the spectators were railroad employees. One such person who, unlike his co-workers, brought a camera to record the event was Richard Bothun.

Richard Oscar Bothun was born on May 31, 1921, in Albert Lea, Minnesota, the son of Bennie A. and Beatrice (Swenson) Bothun. Following service in World War II in the Navy-Marine Air Corps, Bothun moved to Texas in about 1949 and took up a position with the Fort Worth & Denver Railroad.[1]

In 1963 Bothun was living in Dallas with his wife, the former Janet Smeby, and their son and daughter. An amateur photographer who enjoyed developing and printing his own pictures, Bothun owned a camera which his wife recalled to be a Nikon or Pentax.[2] Although not politically active, Bothun did want to take some photos of the President Kennedy visit to Dallas. In the late morning of November 22, he located himself south of the center line on Main Street just east of where Main and Houston intersect. His location was virtually the same as that taken up by Associated Press cameraman James W. Altgens. From comparison of subsequent photographs taken by both, it would appear that Bothun may have mirrored Altgens's later movement to a position on Elm Street in order to take additional pictures.[3]

Apparently using a 50mm lens and his camera loaded with black-and-white film, Bothun took two photos of the motorcade from the same Houston Street position. With the granite County Criminal Courts Building facade showing at left and a corner of the old Dallas County Courts Building at the right, Bothun captured in his first picture the three lead Dallas police motorcycles of the motorcade driven by Officer J. B. Garrick, Sergeant S. G. Bellah, and Officer G. C. McBride. Numerous spectators on both sides of the street are leaning forward to see the President's vehicle which is some two blocks further up Main Street.[4]

Moments later the presidential Lincoln was in view, and Bothun took another photo showing the vehicle heading in his direction. The car is in shadow so that the occupants cannot be made out, except for one of Mrs. Kennedy's white-gloved hands. In the Secret Service follow-up car Agent Clinton J. Hill, on the driver's side front

running board, is looking forward. Agent John D. Ready, on the front passenger side running board, is looking up towards the tall buildings on his right, where over a dozen people can be seen watching the procession pass below. Indeed, numerous windows are open in various surrounding buildings.[5] The Secret Service agents carried only handguns, with the exception of Agent George Hickey, Jr., in the back seat of the follow-up car, who also had custody of an AR-15.223 automatic rifle. The agents were required to train only with small arms and were not familiar with the sounds of high powered rifles. They could do precious little in the event of shots being fired from above, except to try and run to the President's vehicle and physically act as a shield upon the person they were sworn to protect.

Bothun's third photo was clicked as the presidential vehicle made the swing from Main to Houston Street. Taken a split second after professional photographer Jim Altgens's third photo, the Bothun picture is somewhat blurred, possibly due to too slow a shutter speed, while he swung the camera left. The picture does, however, show a broader view than the Altgens photo, a result of Bothun's wider lens. Two women spectators can be seen on the other side of the car, one in the process of taking a photograph, while the other appears just to have taken a photo and is lowering her camera.[6]

After making this picture Bothun sprinted westerly across the infield grass of Dealey Plaza, some 220 feet. In about half a minute he took up a position on the east side of Elm Street about ten feet from the curb in time for another view of the President's vehicle.[7] After making a sharp left-hand turn onto Elm Street and past the Texas School Book Depository Building, the President's car proceeded at about 11 miles per hour toward Bothun's position. At a point of only a few feet to the right of Bothun, the fatal bullet hit the President in the head, and its horror stunned the spectators, who until that moment did not know an assassination attempt was in progress. Beginning at frame Z330 of the Abraham Zapruder film sequence, Bothun, in a tie and dark jacket, can be observed for a few frames, holding his camera frozen at his chest level, while the presidential vehicle passes and Mrs. Kennedy gets out of her seat and onto the trunk of the car.[8] Years later, Mrs. Bothun recalled that her husband was very shocked at the sight of the President being hit in the head and that he had been close enough to hear Mrs. Kennedy "holler."[9]

Many seconds passed before Bothun came out of his momentary shock and reacted again with his camera. Seeing a family lying on the grass across the street from him, he raised his camera and took a picture of the scene.[10] This final photograph that Bothun took and the only one he shot at the assassination scene, shows the grassy knoll area and the Pergola about half a minute after the last bullet struck the President.

A full view of Officer Bobby W. Hargis and his Harley-Davidson motorcycle is seen at left. Hargis had been traveling on the driver side of the President's vehicle, the closest cycle to the President when the head shot occurred. Just after the shot, Hargis dismounted from his cycle, and ran to the north side of Elm Street, quickly looking for evidence of a culprit. In the photo he has just gotten back on the cycle and will proceed to the underpass, still looking for sinister activity. He soon thereafter would travel back to the Book Depository area.[11] Hargis was the only one of the four cycle cops traveling near the presidential Lincoln who wore dark glasses and gloves that day. To the right of the picture and just coming into view is another cycle, this one most likely ridden by Officer Clyde A. Haygood.

Bothun's photograph #4 taken of the assassination aftermath on Elm Street

Sixteen people can be seen on the north side of Elm Street, including a later self-identified Louie Witt and an unknown black eyewitness, both sitting on the curb.

Bill Newman and his wife are prone on the ground, protecting their children. The Newmans' protective gesture became a focal point in just about all witnesses' memories, and the drama of the scene focused people's attention to that spot. Jim Altgens is at the left of the Newmans proceeding towards the sidewalk, while White House movie cameraman Tom Atkins is focusing his camera on the Newmans. CBS cameraman Tom Craven is also moving onto the scene with camera being raised, while Dave Wiegman of NBC is moving onto the sidewalk, having already taken a few feet of film of the Newmans and is now focusing in on the motorcycle coming his way. On the grass further to the right, UPI photographer Frank Cancellare, partially obscured by the highway sign, is also making his way to the action to record it with his still camera. With the exception of Altgens, the four visible cameramen had been passengers in Camera Cars within the motorcade. When the cars slowed down near the corner of Elm and Houston, they jumped out and ran in the direction of where they perceived the action to be. Two teenagers near the pergola shelter are also visible, having run to that position from the curb after the shots were fired. Also on the grass area just above the Stemmons road sign are Mr. and Mrs. John Arthur Chism, Mrs. Chism with her three-year-old son in her arms. Mr. Chism would later recall, "As the motorcade passed directly in front of us, the President was standing and waving to the crowd. As he made an apparent gesture to sit down, the final shot was fired but was mistaken by us as a backfire or a firework display. We saw Mrs. Kennedy jump up, pull the President down into her lap and cover him." Behind the waist-high wall located east of the shelter one shadow figure, apparently walking away from the area, is seen in the Bothun photo .[12]

Like millions of other Americans that day, Bothun used the telephone to let a loved one know about the tragedy; but unlike the rest, Bothun told his wife the terrible news from first-hand experience.[13]

Shortly after the shooting Mr. Bothun apparently went back to work. He seems not to have been stopped or questioned as a witness at the scene, and apparently did not volunteer information to any official.

On November 23, a cropped version of Bothun's fourth photo appeared in the *Dallas Morning News*, his wife believing that he might have brought the picture to the newspaper. The caption under it read, "Suspense at scene of assassination. A mother and father shield their small children from bullets on Elm approaching the triple underpass Friday moments after President Kennedy and Governor John Connally were felled by rifle slugs near the Texas School Book Depository Building. Startled photographers race to the scene, as this photo by Richard O. Bothun vividly demonstrates, not knowing the President was fatally wounded."[14]

Eventually the full uncropped version of this photograph surfaced. Years later newscaster Wes Wise of TV station KRLD made an on-the-air appeal for new photographic evidence, looking for evidence to support an assassination conspiracy. Bothun gave Wise a copy of his photo. Wise, an anti-establishment candidate, was later elected Mayor of Dallas in 1971.[15] Bothun was also helpful to other researchers, making prints from his negatives, and even allowing a negative to be borrowed by Massachusetts researcher R. B. Cutler.[16]

Remaining with the railroad into the 1980s, Mr. Bothun held the position of Director for Freight Claims and Prevention and had his office at 701 Commerce Street. On January 5, 1981, Mr. Bothun died at St. Joseph's Hospital in Fort Worth of a heart attack.[17] Unfortunately Bothun, a very close witness to the events of the assassination, was never sought after or deposed by police or other officials as to his eyewitness account.[18]

## CHAPTER NOTES

1. Telephone interview of Mrs. Jan Bothun, 11/26/1984.
2. Ibid.
3. Comparison of Altgens photographs, roll #1, #2-4, with Bothun photographs #1-3, and the position of Altgens and Bothun as seen in Abraham Zapruder film, frame Z344.
4. Richard O. Bothun photograph #1, 11/22/1963.
5. Ibid., #2.
6. Ibid., #3.
7. Diagram of Dealey Plaza, Bothun to R. B. Cutler, 7/1976.
8. Abraham Zapruder film, 11/22/1963.
9. Interview of Mrs. Bothun, op. cit.
10. R. B. Cutler, *Seventy-Six Seconds in Dealey Plaza*, p. 68.
11. *Hearings Before the President's Commission on the Assassination of President Kennedy*, v. 6, p. 294-295.
12. Bothun photograph, #4; Letter, John A. Chism to Trask, 1/29/1965.
13. Interview of Mrs. Bothun, op. cit.
14. Ibid.; *Dallas Morning News*, 11/23/1963, section 4.
15. Richard E. Sprague, *The Taking of America, 1-2-3*, p. 90-91.
16. Letter, Richard O. Bothun to R. B. Cutler, 1/4/1977 & 1/14/1977.
17. Fort Worth Bureau of Vital Statistics — Certificate of Death for R. O. Bothun.
18. Interview of Mrs. Bothun, op. cit.

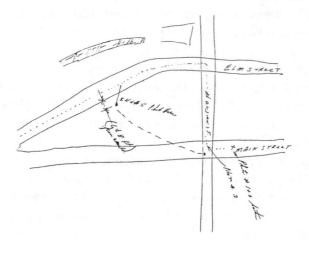

A diagram by R. O. Bothun of Dealey Plaza showing his camera positions

## CHAPTER 4

# "A Firecracker Going Off"

Twenty-two-year-old Hugh William Betzner, Jr., resided at 5922 Velasco Street about 4½ miles northeast of Dealey Plaza and near the Lakewood Country Club in Dallas. The young man worked afternoons at Railway Express Agency, Inc., at 515 South Houston Street, and on the morning of November 22, had decided to go downtown early to view the visit of President and Mrs. Kennedy to Dallas.[1]

Betzner took up a position at the Dealey Plaza area on the curb of the west side of Houston Street near the north reflecting pool and some 70 feet to the south of Elm Street. He had brought with him what he later described as "an old Kodak camera" and which an FBI report later identified as "a small Kodak 120 camera."[2] This box camera contained a roll of 120 black-and-white film and required one to turn the film advance knob carefully watching the film window for the next exposure number to be centered. Betzner had previously taken pictures on this roll and having three exposures left, he wanted to capture a view or two of the presidential motorcade. This was the first time he would be seeing a President of the United States.[3]

After standing on Houston Street for quite some time, Betzner could finally tell by the ripple of noise and applause from the crowd further down Houston Street that the motorcade was approaching. He could see first the motorcycles and then the pilot car make their turns from Main to Houston Street. Betzner waited until the sleek and gleaming presidential Lincoln was almost in front of his position before he took his first picture. The entire vehicle fills the negative frame with President and Mrs. Kennedy, while not looking his way, clearly visible. In the background of the photograph a few spectators are seen standing in front of the double entrance to the garage between the Dallas County Records Building and the Courts Building.[4]

After taking this picture, Betzner recounts, "I looked down real quick and rolled the film to take the next picture. I then ran down to the corner of Elm and Houston Streets, this being the southwest corner. I took another picture just as President Kennedy's car rounded the corner. I was standing back from the corner and had to take the pictures through some of the crowd."[5]

This second picture shows the presidential vehicle partially obscured by three members of the Towner family who are standing between Betzner's position and the car. Jim Towner is at the left, having just taken a picture of his own of the car

The President's car turning onto Elm Street
in front of the Book Depository Building

during its turn. Daughter Tina is in the process of filming the car with her father's movie camera, pivoting towards the left as the car passes her position. Mrs. Towner stands to their right. Mrs. Kennedy is visible, virtually obscuring the President next to her. On the opposite side of the street from Betzner some 20 people can be seen. Behind them the west side of the Dal-Tex Building and the southeast corner of the Texas School Book Depository Building is evident. Such is the pity that Betzner had not shifted his camera to reveal the upper stories of the School Book Depository, for such a picture might have obviated many of the controversies which arose following the assassination. But since the action was in the street, only the easternmost first three stories are visible in Betzner's negative.[6]

Betzner then moved to his left, trying to keep the President in view while winding his camera and making his way through a cluster of spectators. Taking a position near the curb and sandwiched between others also jockeying for a view, Betzner took his third picture and then, ". . . started to wind my film again, and I heard a loud noise. I thought that this noise was either a firecracker or a car had backfired."[7]

This last photo Betzner took would have been considered a throw-away shot under normal circumstances. It was taken at a time when the event was now passing him by. But the excitement of the moment dictated trying to take that one extra photo. About one-third of the photograph is taken up by another spectator obscuring part of the camera's view on the left. Only the almost unidentifiable rear of President Kennedy's head is visible in the Lincoln, with the Cadillac follow-up car and its covey of Secret Service agents and presidential friend Dave Powers visible. Special Agent George Hickey, Jr., in the rear driver's side, who had custody of the Colt AR 15.223 automatic rifle is looking to his left. On Elm Street, opposite Betzner's position, an excited undulation of hand-waving is seen within the crowd as the President passes.[8]

Fifteen feet west of Betzner's position, amateur photographer Phil Willis has his 35mm camera to his eye. As the motorcade proceeds between 13½ and 15½ feet further down Elm Street, Willis (a little less than a second after Betzner) presses his shutter and records in color a scene nearly identical to Betzner's.[9] Both men also captured on their respective photographs, Abraham Zapruder on an abutment near the north Pergola, filming his own home movies of the motorcade. Part of Zapruder's film shows Betzner aiming his camera. It was later established that Betzner's photograph #3 was taken at the time Zapruder frame #Z186 was exposed.[10]

Betzner's photo #3 taken just a moment before a bullet strikes the President in the back

After taking his last photo and hearing a noise, Betzner "looked up and it seemed like there was another loud noise in the matter of a few seconds. I looked down the street and I could see the President's car and another one, and they looked like the cars were stopped." Though Betzner's memory of what happened in the ensuing seconds was vivid, he was unclear as to its sequence. "I heard at least two shots fired and I saw what looked like a firecracker going off in the President's car. My assumption of this was because I saw fragments going up in the air." This statement, made later that same Friday afternoon, is descriptive of his seeing something that he just could not clearly discern from his perspective — it was the result of the bullet striking the President's head. Betzner also observed, "a flash of pink like someone standing up. . . ," and a man in either the President's car or another car pulling out what looked like a rifle. He also observed what appeared to be a nickel revolver in someone's hand somewhere in the President's car or around it.[11] The flash of pink was undoubtedly Mrs. Kennedy's dress as the term is used similarly by other witnesses. The rifle Betzner observed was brandished by Special Agent Hickey in the follow-up car. Assassination researcher Richard E. Sprague wrote Betzner in November 1967 inquiring about the pistol Betzner mentioned. Betzner wrote back, "It was in the car just behind Kennedy's, and it was not fired."[12] It should also be noted that both the Mal Couch film and a Jim Towner photograph show a police officer near the Betzner position kneeling while pointing a revolver towards the street shortly after the presidential vehicle had left the scene.[13]

After the car carrying the mortally wounded President had sped through the underpass, Betzner watched police and spectators run up the grassy knoll area to a wooden stockade fence. He then walked to the area where the President's car seemed to stop, and observed plainclothed and uniformed officers "digging around in the dirt as if they were looking for a bullet."[14] Free-lance photographer Jim Murray also observed plainclothes Deputy E. R. (Buddy) Walthers and Patrolman J. W. Foster doing this probing. He recorded their activity in a number of black-and-white photos including several frames with Betzner in them.[15]

Betzner crossed Elm Street and went up the knoll embankment to the stockade fence, and there he heard the rumor that this was the area from which the shots had been fired. He thought that the fence might be visible in the third picture he had taken. Seeing some men he thought were officers, Betzner approached them about his photos. Deputy Sheriff Eugene Boone had run to this area after hearing three shots from his location in front of the Sheriff's office at 505 Main Street. After contacting superiors, Boone escorted Betzner to the Sheriff's office in order for him to make a statement. After asking Betzner to wait for someone who could take his statement, Boone took the Kodak camera to the ID Bureau and asked that the film be developed.[16] Betzner's camera was returned to him and he was told that as soon as they were done with the film, they would return it to him also. Later Betzner was given the developed negatives, although the police did not give him prints of his pictures. They indicated that they were interested in a couple of the pictures.[17]

Apparently, by the time the film was developed, the police emphasis on the case had shifted from the grassy knoll area to the Texas School Book Depository. As Boone later testified before the Warren Commission, "Later on we were able to ascertain that the shots had come from the building from that southeast corner over there. And he [Betzner] had some photographs, but they didn't extend past the second floor on the building."[18] Boone himself, after leaving Betzner at the Sheriff's office, went over to the Texas School Book Depository to help search the building, and on the sixth floor, it was he who found a rifle hidden among book cartons.

According to Boone, Dallas Police Officer Homer Reynolds obtained a statement from Betzner and a two-page voluntary statement notarized by Aleen Davis on a Sheriff's Department form was taken. Betzner's statement is longer than most others taken that afternoon, and though obviously not in polished form, it, when compared to others taken that day, is very detailed as to what Betzner saw and perceived to be happening.[19]

Betzner (center, holding jacket) is interviewed at the Sheriff's Department.
To the right of Betzner are Larry Florer and the three members of the Chism family.

Chief Deputy Sheriff Allan Sweatt was given the Betzner photographic prints, which he included in the files on the case. Sweatt also made available to the Dallas Police Department a complete set of all statements taken that day.[20] Before the end of the day, Betzner was interviewed by FBI Agent James W. Anderton about what the photos showed. Betzner agreed to lend the negatives to the FBI and the next morning brought them to the Dallas FBI office and turned them over to Agent Anderton. Betzner's negatives were returned to him prior to the next Wednesday, and Anderton apparently contacted Betzner once more before December 20, in order to obtain a statement from him that he had never known either Lee Harvey Oswald or Jack Leon Ruby.[21]

Betzner was not again contacted by investigative agencies. He was not called by the Warren Commission, and his photographs were neither published nor found among the Commission files, although a facsimile of his statement to the Sheriff's Department was reproduced twice within the *Hearings* set.[22]  To many persons who trudged through the 26-volume set of *Hearings* when they were published in 1964, references to the Betzner photographs sounded intriguing, and many questioned why the photographs themselves had not been published.   Several researchers and Commission critics who saw at least sloppy evidence-gathering and sharing procedures and even possible governmental cover-ups of evidence, postulated that the Betzner photographs were "suppressed" as what they did show might be contrary to the government's conclusions.

Harold Weisberg, of Frederick, Maryland, a relentless critic of the Warren Commission, wrote among other self-published volumes a 1967 book titled, *Photographic Whitewash: Suppressed Kennedy Assassination Pictures.*  Although Weisberg makes a number of valid arguments about the unprofessional manner in which the case's photographic documentation was managed, he also fell into the trap of postulating what various referred-to, but unseen photographs might reveal.  Such a descriptive device is of questionable validity.  It broaches upon the sensational, and usually reads, through postulating description, to be of more significance than the actual photograph exhibits when finally seen.

In writing of Betzner's unseen "Photograph #1," Weisberg states, "What this picture, therefore, should show and show clearly and from just across the street is those people in the doorway [Texas School Book Depository Building] and around it.  This means it could show where the various employees and others called as witnesses were standing and it could show clearly those who should have been called and were not.  This picture should show the doorway from the southeast in a very desirable angle just opposite to that of the picture taken by AP Photographer James W. Altgens."[23]  The photograph in question, actually the second of the sequence and not the first, could indeed have shown the views that Weisberg postulated — had the camera been pointed otherwise — but it was not, and all of Weisberg's "could's" and "should's" and "show clearly's" just did not pan out upon examination of a print of the Betzner photograph.

Weisberg was informed in 1966 by letter from the Archivist of the United States that the Betzner photographs were not among the records of the Warren Commission, and he concluded in his published section on the Betzner photographs that, "There is no reason consistent with a thorough job for the Government not to have kept the Betzner pictures. Only a contrary motive is reason for not doing so."[24]

Responding in 1965 to a query to Betzner by this author (then a teenager) Betzner indicated, "I still have the photographs," and in early 1967 Betzner's father wrote that "Bill has been approached many times for copies of his pictures with negative results. . . ."[25]  In the meantime, Hugh, Jr., had joined the Navy, being stationed for a time on the U.S.S. *Richmond K. Turner*, serving as a lieutenant junior grade. Contacted in February 1967 he was, ". . . not sure exactly where they [pictures] are located. Probably in some book or something at my parents' home."[26]

Staff at *LIFE* Magazine were at this time trying to locate unpublished assassination photographs, and according to Managing Editor George P. Hunt, a reporter was able to see the Betzner pictures in Kansas at the home of Betzner's parents, but *LIFE* could not publish them without the son's approval. This approval was obtained when Gayle Rosenberg of the Los Angeles Bureau located Betzner's ship and made arrangements with him for that purpose.[27]

Independent assassination photographic researcher Richard E. Sprague was told in a 1967 letter from the senior Betzner that, "*LIFE* has purchased the negative and rights for the third photo and has option until November 30, 1967, for the purchase of the other two."[28] Indeed the public had its first opportunity to view the third Betzner photo when it was published in *LIFE* on November 24, 1967, also including a photo of Betzner and a short description of how a photo-optical electronics firm, Itek, had used various techniques to glean further information about the Betzner and similar Willis photographs.[29]

In 1976 the House Select Committee on Assassinations examined a first-generation print of Betzner #3, and published an uncropped print in volume 6 of their appendix. It was also noted that "no enhancement processing was performed as the original negative was never located."[30]

It is unclear if *LIFE* magazine had this negative at the time, or whether the House Committee staff contacted Mr. Betzner. In recent years, H. W. Betzner, Jr., is polite but does not want to be bothered by outside inquiries concerning the assassination. He only remembers his camera as being "an old Kodak," does not remember the kind of film that was in it, does not now own the camera, nor knows where it is. He has a set of negatives, but does not know if they are the originals. It is hoped that the original negatives may eventually be archivally preserved for their historical documentation.[31]

## CHAPTER NOTES

1. Letter, Betzner to Trask, 7/21/1986.
2. *Hearings Before the President's Commission on the Assassination of President Kennedy,* v. 19, p. 467; FBI report by James W. Anderton concerning Betzner, file #Dallas 89-43, 11/23/1963.
3. FBI, op. cit.
4. Betzner photograph #1, 11/22/1963.
5. *Hearings,* op. cit., v. 19, p. 467.
6. Betzner photograph #2, 11/22/1963.
7. *Hearings,* op. cit., v. 19, p. 467.
8. Betzner photograph # 3, 11/22/1963.

9.    *LIFE,* 11/24/1967, p. [93]; *LIFE - Itek Kennedy Assassination Film Analysis,* 11/20/1967, p.6. An error in Itek's original measured distance was corrected in the Christopher Scally manuscript, "So Near . . . And Yet So Far," (p. 51 and 96), as per an Itek vice-president's letter of 1969.

10.   *Appendix to Hearings Before the Select Committee on Assassinations,* v. 6, p. 50.

11.   *Hearings,* op. cit., v. 19, p. 467.

12.   Letter, Richard E. Sprague to Hugh Betzner, Sr., 11/14/1967; Letter, Hugh Betzner, Jr., to Richard E. Sprague, 11/28/67 from the Richard E. Sprague Papers, Special Collections Division, Georgetown University Library, Washington, D.C.

13.   James Towner 35mm photographic transparency #2, 11/22/1963.

14.   *Hearings,* op. cit., v. 19, p. 467.

15.   Jim Murray photographs, roll 1, #13-19, 11/22/1963.

16.   *Hearings,* op. cit., v. 3, p. 292; v. 19, p. 508.

17.   Ibid., v. 19, p. 468.

18.   Ibid., v. 3, p. 292.

19.   Ibid., v. 19, p. 467-468.

20.   Ibid., v. 19, p. 532-533.

21.   FBI document, "Individuals known to have taken photographs, . . ." 12/19/1963, p. 1; FBI report by James W. Anderton Concerning Betzner, file #Dallas 89-43, 11/23/1963; file #DL 89-43, 11/23/1963; file #DL 44-1639, 12/20/1963, obtained by Trask through FOIA request #263,248, 6/11/1985.

22.   Letter, Betzner to Trask, 8/27/1985; *Hearings,* op. cit., v. 19, p. 467-468, v. 24, p. 200.

23.   Harold Weisberg, *Photographic Whitewash,* p. 44.

24.   Ibid., p. 45.

25.   Letter, Betzner to Trask, 1/2/1965; Letter, Hugh Betzner, Sr., to Trask, 1/7/1967.

26.   Letter, Betzner to Trask, 2/14/1967.

27.   *LIFE,* op. cit., p. 3.

28.   Letter, Hugh Betzner, Sr., to Sprague, 10/30/1967.

29.   *LIFE,* op. cit., [p. 93].

30.   Appendix, op. cit., v. 6, p. 508.

31.   Letter, Betzner to Trask, 8/27/1985, 7/21/1986. In Deputy Sheriff Boone's November 22, 1963, report, he describes the film as "35mm film" while all FBI records indicate it is 120 film. The Itek analysis of assassination-related films done for LIFE magazine, dated November 20, 1967, describes the Betzner negative they did studies on as an "original size 127 black-and-white negative."

## CHAPTER 5

# The Major

Like millions of Americans, Phillip L. Willis was a self-styled amateur photographer who enjoyed taking pictures of trips, family activities, and special occasions. Thus, when he learned that President John F. Kennedy would be visiting Dallas, Willis wanted to make sure to see this man whom he so admired, and take some pictures of the President's visit to the city.[1]

Willis was forty-five years old, having been born on August 2, 1918, in Kaufman County, Texas, some fifty miles from Dallas. Prior to America's entry into World War II, Willis had joined the Army Air Corps and in August 1941 was commissioned a second lieutenant. Willis was stationed at Bellows Field, Oahu, Hawaii, on December 7, 1941, when the Japanese attacked Pearl Harbor. Assigned to the 86th Observation Squadron, he managed to get his plane airborne during the first attack. His plane was destroyed on the ground by hostile fire during the second attack, and on December 8, Willis was assigned to beach patrol, being ranking officer in charge of the unit.[2]

Besides launching an air attack, the Japanese had sent to the area a special attack unit consisting of five midget submarines. These two-man subs did no damage, save to themselves, and one of them, piloted by Ensign Kazuo Sakamaki, ran onto a reef off Bellows Field. After attempting to scuttle the vessel, at 6:40 on the morning of December 8, Sakamaki and his companion tried to swim for shore some 200 yards away. Only Sakamaki survived the raging surf; and upon regaining consciousness from the watery battering, he found himself a prisoner of Willis's beach patrol, becoming the first enemy prisoner-of-war captured by the United States.[3]

Through 1943 Willis saw action in the Pacific Theater as a B-17 bomber pilot, including serving at the Battle of Midway and the Guadalcanal Campaign. He flew 52 combat missions, was credited with sinking four ships, including a large Japanese troop transport, and walked away with no crew loss from two downed bombers. Among his numerous decorations is the Silver Star for gallantry in action. Marrying his "sweetheart" Marilyn in 1943, Willis retired as a major as the result of war combat disabilities in 1946. He soon ran for and was elected to the Texas State House of Representatives. He served two terms representing Kaufman County until 1950, and during that time became acquainted with rising national figures Lyndon Johnson and Sam Rayburn.[4]

In April of 1960 Willis moved to Dallas, and in September of that year he and his wife Marilyn had a chance to meet presidential candidate John F. Kennedy at a political luncheon.  By November 1963, Willis, his wife, and two daughters, Rosemary (age 10) and Linda Kay (age 14) were residing at Ava Lane, some 6½ miles east of Dealey Plaza.

The morning of the 22nd of November, the Willises had seen the news reports of the visit of President and Mrs. Kennedy to Fort Worth; and they were aware of the general route of the presidential motorcade through Dallas.  As this was a special occasion, and since Mrs. Willis's parents, Mr. and Mrs. William H. Stubblefield, were visiting from San Antonio, it was decided that they would all go and see the motorcade, including the two children, who were kept out of school for the event, since Willis "wanted my children to see the President."[5]

Mr. Willis in 1984 holding his original
Argus 35mm camera

Willis left the house that morning, taking with him his Argus 35mm Autronic I, Model 35156-M camera with an F 2.8 Cintar lens.  Purchased in June of 1962 at a post exchange in San Antonio, the camera had three settings — "flash," "scene" (for still photos), and "action" (for moving shots).  It was loaded with Kodachrome slide film with an ASA rating of 25.  The first three frames of this roll were taken prior to the motorcade and included shots of Mrs. Willis's mother and dad.[6]  As it looked like the day might remain overcast due to persistent rain showers, Willis did not bring the camera's sun filter with him.[7]

Employed as an executive salesman for Downtown Lincoln-Mercury and Ford Motor Company, Willis drove to the business showroom located at 118 Commerce Street. He spent the morning at work and planned to meet his family so that they could all go and see the presidential procession. At about noon the family met Willis at the business.  Willis later remembered, "We left my Lincoln at the dealership and let a serviceman drive us over and take the car back." They were dropped off near the corner of Main and Houston Streets, "so we would have a good place about at the end of the parade route, where we would have a chance to see him without being in a jammed-up crowd.  I figured that would be the ideal spot.  I wanted them to see him and get some pictures.  I had no idea what I was getting into."[8] Willis could see that if he stationed himself on the northwest corner of the cross street, he would have a good position for taking pictures as the motorcade slowed to make its right-hand turn onto Houston Street.  With a bit of luck, Willis could then quickly travel up Houston and perhaps get another few slides of the procession on Elm Street.  The children would remain with their father, while Mrs. Willis and her parents opted to move down to the colonnade area on the south side of Elm Street.

Mrs. Willis recalls that they waited in the area some 30 minutes before the parade passed.  "Curious things happened, though.  There was an old loan truck called 'Honest Joe.'  He was a pawn shop operator and his old black car was painted with all kinds of signs on it and it had a great big gun mounted on the top of that car. And he drove up Houston towards the Depository and pulled in behind somewhere back there and turned around and came back." She also recalls seeing a man having an epileptic seizure and a woman dipping her handkerchief in the water of the reflecting pool and wiping his face with it. She believes that "he got up and walked away before the ambulance got there. I thought it was very strange."[9]

At about 12:25 p.m. the sounds of the approaching motorcade were apparent. As it came closer toward the junction of Houston Street, a careful observer could see the many cars and three busses strung out almost a half a mile up the slope of Main Street. The three press convertibles, as well as several other vehicles were provided through Earl Hayes Chevrolet, while seven other cars in the party, including the Vice-President's steel gray 1964 Lincoln convertible, were made available through Dick Fisher of Downtown Lincoln-Mercury, where Willis worked.[10] Few people, however, directed their attention to these many cars, with their subordinate passengers, for the main attraction was the luxurious presidential Lincoln and it was to this object that Willis, after taking two quick pictures of the three lead motorcycles and Chief Jesse Curry's lead car, aimed his camera.

The limousine traveled up adjacent to the stately 1893 Victorian Romanesque Dallas County Courts Building, with its jutting towers supporting conical roofs. Under the building's semi-circular entrance arches and on the balcony above, as well as from numerous windows set into the walls, various secretaries, court officials, and others viewed the motor-

The limousine on Main Street

cade making its way past them. The wind fluttered the Lone Star flag, set prominently in front of the building, and as the limousine neared its right hand turn, Willis could see the President's large crop of hair blowing in the wind.[11] He snapped his picture, and immediately moved onto the Houston Street sidewalk, scurrying some 60 feet north and almost next to John Martin, Jr., who was recording the same scene with an amateur movie camera.

In his fourth slide, Willis captured the limousine as it is finishing its turn onto Houston Street. Governor and Mrs. Connally are looking toward the Willis position, while Mrs. Kennedy is holding down her hair and hat from the wind, thus obscuring her face from the photograph. The President's hair is still in motion as he looks in his wife's direction. The bright noon sun is fully in evidence, some of its glare reflecting off the

While the President's car turns onto Houston Street, the Vice-President (arrow) is seen in the background on Main Street.

polished chrome and metal of the Lincoln, while blurred images of the side motorcycles, spectators, and white pedestrian lines, are reflected off the car body. Being a friend of Lyndon Johnson, Willis was anxious to get a picture of him in the motorcade. Whether by chance or by design this picture includes on the extreme left side, the Johnsons' convertible, with Lyndon in the back seat, passenger side, the last identifiable photograph showing the 35th President and his Vice-President in the same picture.[12]

Moving about 40 feet further up Houston Street, Willis took a fifth picture, now showing the limousine from the rear as it passed between the Dallas County Criminal Courts and County Records Building. Motorcycle officer Bobby W. Hargis is seen on the left of the picture riding cycle #347, while the presidential follow-up Cadillac, code named "Halfback," is visible with its agents on the running boards, looking to their sides. Special Agent Glen A. Bennett, sitting in the rear right side of the vehicle is looking up to his right at the Criminal Courts Building. No one, at least in this fraction of a second, is looking up front toward the Texas School Book Depository Building, some 200 feet ahead.[13]

Traveling along Houston Street

Remembers Willis, "Then, I immediately ran across the Plaza, raced over to Elm Street and stationed myself on the curb in front of the Texas School Book Depository."[14]

On Elm Street

With his children following behind, Willis had traveled the 120 feet in time to snap a blurry photo of the passengers in the limousine, only some 15 feet from his position. Both Mrs. Connally and Mrs. Kennedy are looking to Willis's side of the street while the governor and the President are patting their wind-disheveled hair back into place. In the background can be seen the white concrete pylon that delineates the east end of the north pergola wall system, and to the right and rear of that, one can see the white cutout block design of the first floor west front of the Book Depository. Reflecting on that picture 23 years later, Willis commented,

"Had I only enough sense to look up, but that's hindsight. I would have been famous if I had raised my camera up at that time."[15]

Standing on top of a concrete abutment some 180 feet to the northwest, Dallas businessman Abraham Zapruder was now filming the presidential convertible turning on to Elm Street. Concerned only with filming the President and First Lady, Zapruder nonetheless also recorded Willis in the process of taking his sixth slide. Willis is seen standing in the street as the first Zapruder frame showing the presidential limousine is exposed. After taking his picture, Willis stepped back onto the sidewalk to avoid the approaching motorcycles, all the while following the President's vehicle with his eyes, and again putting his camera viewfinder to his face. Willis's daughter Rosemary is also observed, wearing a red skirt and a white pull-over top. She was attempting to keep up with the car as it traveled down Elm Street when, as seen in the Zapruder film at about Z197, she abruptly stops. Many years later Rosemary would tell a researcher that she had stopped "when I heard the shot."[16]

The Willis slide taken moments before the President is hit

The most important of the series of Willis slides was his seventh in the sequence. Later government research placed this photograph as being taken at about the same time as Zapruder frame #Z202.[17] Less than three seconds after his sixth picture, Willis had moved slightly down Elm towards the departing presidential vehicle. He raised his camera to his eye, and remembers, "As I was about to squeeze my shutter, that is when the first shot rang out and my reflex just took that picture at that moment. I might have waited another full second . . . but being with my war nerves anyway — when that shot rang out, I just flinched and got it." From his military and hunting experience, he knew the sound was that of a high-powered rifle, and that the bullet had hit.[18]

This photograph of the Willis series would have been a very disappointing slide under normal circumstances. The President's car is not the prominent feature, and only the backs of the heads of the Kennedys and the Connallys can be glimpsed. Instead, the bulky Secret Service follow-up car and two motorcycles on the left are the prominent feature of this somewhat blurred picture. The action on the street has obviously passed Willis by.[19] This photo most likely should have been the last of Willis's sequence showing the President's motorcade in Dallas, and not the best of his views of the subject. Instead, due to what happened just as this picture was taken, it has been studied by numerous researchers, both governmental and private. Some critics have discovered in it what they believe to be the dastardly "hit team" who orchestrated the President's assassination. An examination of the photograph does reveal the controversial "Grassy Knoll" area at the time when the assassination begins. It is taken some six seconds before the President's fatal head wound occurs. At this point no one in the photograph appears to be reacting to any unusual stimulus. The six visible Secret Service agents in the follow-up car are looking in various directions, but appear stationary. Also in the car is Kenny O'Donnell, the President's trusted advisor. He is looking straight ahead, seemingly perched on the end of his seat and with his hands on the car rest to his front. The balding head of presidential assistant Dave Powers can be glimpsed to O'Donnell's right. The backs of motorcycle officers B. J. Martin on cycle #344 at the right and Bobby W. Hargis on cycle #347 to his side are clearly visible. The number of spectators is thinning out the further left one looks. A cluster of women office workers, some applauding and waving, are visible at the right along with a construction worker in a silver hard hat.[20]

Near the Stemmons Freeway sign are the Chism family and a man in a dark suit holding over his head a black umbrella. Later picked out by many observers, this man was the only one in the area using an umbrella on a now sunny 68-degree-Fahrenheit day. Following the assassination, his identity remained unknown.[21] It was an unusual stance to say the least, and many saw in his open umbrella a possibly sinister motive. The Zapruder film sequence in which a portion of the umbrella is visible, seems to show the umbrella being moved in an up-and-down and twirling motion. Since this man's position was close to the spot where the assassination action began, some later observers saw in his umbrella and movements a possible signal to other plotters to begin the assassination. In 1976, Massachusetts architect and researcher Robert B. Cutler postulated that the umbrella was a portable, miniature rocket launcher equipped with a self-propelled flechette that was fired and caused the President's throat wound.[22] To even the most staunch non-believer in conspiracy theories, this man and his umbrella were an enigma. Why the umbrella? Did he have a skin condition aggravated by the sun? Why did he not step forward to squelch the speculations about his activities?

Fifteen years after the assassination, the House of Representatives Select Committee on Assassinations circulated to the news media a blow-up of a portion of a photograph taken by *LIFE* cameraman Arthur Rickerby from his position in the motorcade. The picture showed a more clear view of the "umbrella man" sitting on the curb just after the assassination. The Committee requested information about the man's identity. Through a friend, the identity of Louie Steven Witt was made known to the local Dallas press, and Witt was requested to give testimony at the House Select Committee hearings in September of 1978.

A blow-up of the "umbrella man"

Witt, an insurance salesman, told the Committee that he was, indeed, the "umbrella man," and had opened the umbrella during the Kennedy motorcade in order to heckle the President. He had been told that the open umbrella "was sort of a sore spot with the Kennedys," since it symbolized Prime Minister Neville Chamberlain's and United States Ambassador to Great Britain Joseph P. Kennedy's apparent appeasement of the Nazis prior to World War II. Witt was surprised no one had questioned him right after the shooting. He did not step forward partly because of his embarrassment at the protest he had made at the time of the shooting, and because of the climate in Dallas following the assassination. Until he had read the account in the newspaper and had seen his picture, he did not realize the interest in the umbrella; but even then, he did not come forward of his own accord, and was discovered through the talking of a friend. As Witt said in his closing statement before the Committee, ". . . I think if the *Guinness Book of World Records* had a category for people who were at the wrong place at the wrong time, doing the wrong thing, I would be No. 1 in that position without even a close runner-up."[23] The same could have been said about the President, but Witt's uneasiness in his embarrassing situation was very evident.

To the left of Witt in the Willis photograph can also be seen a black man in a white shirt and dark cap, who following the assassination sat down close to Witt and kept repeating something like, "They done shot them folks." This man was never identified by government agencies. Further down the street can also be seen a cluster of six other people near the curb including the four members of the Newman family. Also captured on film just to the right of the Stemmons Freeway sign are Abraham Zapruder and Marilyn Sitzman, who are standing on a concrete pedestal in the process of filming the scene. Two men, including Plaza grounds keeper Emmett Hudson, are likewise seen standing on the walkway halfway up from the street.[24]

Also evident in this Willis photograph is a dark human-like shape seemingly just inside the retaining wall at the top of the steps. Many researchers noted this shape, which was also recorded in a photo by Hugh Betzner. It became known as the "Black Dog Man," due to its superficial shape reminding some of a dog sitting on its haunches. This mysterious image does not show up in the next Willis slide. A 1967 study initiated by *LIFE* magazine concluded, through the utilization of other photographic evidence, that this person, ". . . joined two other persons on the steps by the time the car was at point 313," which was at the time of the head shot. In 1978 the House Select Committee on Assassinations, following up questions concerning possible assassins in the area around the Grassy Knoll, had this shape investigated. The University of Southern California and the Aerospace Corporation performed a number of state-of-the-art photographic tests on this shape. The photographic panel concluded, ". . . that the object was most probably an adult person standing behind the wall." A distinct straight line feature near the region of the hands and extending from lower right to upper left could not be identified due to the blurring extending in the same direction as the feature.[25] The identification of this person, like so many others in the Plaza that day, is unknown. Might it have been one of the two unidentified blacks whom Marilyn Sitzman saw eating their lunch in this general area? Could the straight object have been a pop bottle? Photos taken only several minutes later, particularly one made by Jim Towner, seem to show a glass bottle at this position on the wall.

The "Black Dog Man" (upper left) as seen in the Betzner photo

After taking this picture, events moved quickly, and Willis remembers exclaiming about the President, "Someone is shooting at him!" He remembers hearing two additional shots being fired at about two second intervals, though he could not see the President during this time. Willis later stated, "They did not ring out long like a bullet shot that is fired into mid-air in a distance. I knew it hit something, and it couldn't have been a firecracker or anything like that. . . ."[26] Willis's two daughters had been running alongside the presidential limousine and, fearing for their safety, their father hollered for them to come back. The girls had stopped in their tracks during the shots and headed back to their mother, who was some forty feet away, inside the open block concrete wall which was part of the north peristyle area.[27]

Marilyn Willis had watched the motorcade pass her position on Elm Street. Looking out of an opening in the peristyle at the receding presidential vehicle, she heard a noise that sounded to her like a backfire or a firecracker. She remembers that enough time elapsed between the two first shots to be able to remark, "Was that firecrackers?" A few seconds later she heard another report and saw the top of President Kennedy's head "blow off and ringed by a red halo." She turned to her companions and said, "My God, they've shot him." Hearing what she believes were three shots in all, Mrs. Willis then glanced at her watch, which indicated 12:35.[28]

Following the shots, Phil Willis remembers screaming to "ring the building," meaning the Texas School Book Depository, as he was sure that that was from where the shots had come. As confused pandemonium broke out at the scene, Willis observed people and police on the triple underpass as well as people falling on the ground and police officers racing up the Grassy Knoll.

Willis shoots the scene as the motorcade begins to break up.

Approximately half a minute after the President had received his fatal head wound, Willis now took an eighth photograph from a position approximately 10 to 15 feet further down Elm Street. This photograph exhibits over half a dozen men on the south side of Elm Street running in the direction of the triple underpass. The VIP vehicles have already sped off en route to Parkland Hospital, and motorcycle policeman Clyde A. Haygood has parked his cycle by the north curb of Elm Street and is seen near the Fort Worth sign running up the incline towards the overpass. A portion of the motorcade, including from left to right, dignitary cars 2 and 3 (convertibles), dignitary car 4 (a sedan), a wood trim Mercury station wagon, and the first press bus seem to have stalled in the road with a passenger on the driver's side of the station wagon opening the door and getting out. Willis believes this to be Governor John Connally's press aide, Bill Stinson, getting out to see what was happening. An older black man in light clothes and a workman's apron is walking up Elm close by the Continental Trailways bus. He can be observed earlier in the Zapruder film on the south side of Elm Street applauding as the President's car had driven by. The Willises recall this "old newsman" strolling up the street, "oblivious to everything. Just no interest at all." All the observable witnesses on the north side of Elm Street are on the ground, still in shock over to the horrifying events. Associated Press photographer Jim Altgens, who has been quickly deserted by members of the motorcade press who had moments earlier jumped from their vehicles to photograph the cowering witnesses, can be seen on the north Elm Street sidewalk, looking towards the street.[29]

The first press bus leaves as AP photographer
Jim Altgens crosses Elm Street

Seconds later, and still further down the street, Willis took a ninth photograph, this one revealing many of the backs of the men he captured in his previous photo. Also evident are some 20 additional people looking towards and beginning to cross the street. The so-called "Babushka Lady," an unidentified woman in an over-coat and a scarf who had apparently been taking film of the shooting scene, is evident in this photograph. Motorcycle officer Haygood has now almost reached the wall above the knoll, while Altgens, with camera in his right hand, is crossing Elm Street, content that the action is over in that area.[30]

At about this point Willis rejoined his family, his daughter Rosemary telling him, "Oh, Daddy, they have shot our President!"[31]

Years later, Willis described the scene following the shooting: "After the gunfire, we could not believe what we had seen! Someone had a small battery-powered radio and people crowded around to listen. The broadcasters did not know any more than we did at that time. It was a very emotional scene — weeping and praying — people running everywhere, and Dealey Plaza swamped by people rushing to the scene." Mrs. Willis added to her husband's recollection, "It's a terrible feeling to see it and then it all goes away, and then you're just left not knowing. Then the people began to just pour in. Actually I don't suppose there were over 100 people at the most. It just seemed like forever before the police and firemen really got there." Mrs. Willis also recalled seeing a little boy out in the grass between Elm and Main Street who was crying and saying to no one in particular, "I just saw a man pick up part of his skull down in the grass."[32]

As Willis had believed that the gunfire originated from the Book Depository Building, he went up to that area and began taking pictures of police activities near the front of the building. The family remained in this vicinity for the next hour, Willis taking some 15 additional photographs.[33] His thirteenth photo and the first taken around the Depository area is very blurry, and while showing uniformed policemen and others, the heads are cut off from view.

Slide 14 shows a crowd of citizens and police outside the Depository's main entrance. Noticed by Willis at a later date, as well as by various critics of the government probe, was a balding man in dark glasses. He is located at the far right of the 35mm transparency. In November 1964, Willis was interviewed by a member of the Citizens' Committee of Inquiry, a group critical of the government's handling of the investigation. According to critic Mark Lane in his book *Rush to Judgment*, Willis showed the man the slide and commented that it appeared to be Jack Ruby, Oswald's killer. Willis remarked that the figure looked so much like Ruby that it was "pitiful," and that when Willis had seen Ruby later in court, he believed the picture looked just like Ruby. Willis also reported that FBI agents who had questioned him, had mentioned the man's presence in the photo before Willis did, and that they thought it was Ruby.[34]

Scene at the Depository front entrance before the civilians were pushed back from the area.

Many who saw this picture thought the man in dark glasses at the extreme right was Jack Ruby.

A photo taken by Jim Murray around the same time as the Willis slide #14 reveals the man in dark glasses not to be Jack Ruby.

The man with the receding hairline in the Willis photo does indeed look like Ruby. Another photograph, a black-and-white print taken by Jim Murray at about 12:50 of the same Book Depository doorway shows a police cruiser in the foreground with this man on the other side. This Murray photo positively shows that the man, when seen from a different angle, is not Ruby. Photographic evidence can at times be as misleading as it is informative.[35]

Willis photo 15 was taken to the right of the entrance at the corner of Elm and Houston, looking down Houston with the Dal-Tex Building in the background. Parked motorcycles, spectators and a cameraman carrying a 16mm movie camera are visible. The sixteenth photo is taken of the upper three floors of the Book Depository Building, including one open window, but not including the side window where the assassin's perch was supposedly found. Photos 17 through 21 were taken at the same general spot on the south corner of Houston and Elm, after Willis and the other civilians had been pushed back away from the building by the police. These five photos show the Depository entrance and the Houston Street area between the Depository and Dal-Tex with numerous police and their vehicles as well as a fire truck at the scene.

Photo 22 is a blurry close-up, probably of Larry Florer, an apparently intoxicated man who was acting suspiciously at the scene and was escorted to the Sheriff's office. Photo 23 is taken further south in the middle of Houston Street, looking to-wards the Depository and the crowd that has gathered behind roped crowd lines in front of the reflecting pool. Photos 24 and 25 are taken on Main Street looking over the infield grass to the Depository with Elm and Elm Street Extension visible includ-ing parked cars and police officers. The 26th photo shows the full Depository Building taken from the north peristyle, while the 27th photo is taken from Com-merce Street, near the entrance of the triple underpass, looking back at the entire Depository and the Dal-Tex buildings.

A previously unpublished Willis slide showing activity around the northeast corner
of Elm and Houston, including a TV cameraman (possibly Sanderson) at extreme right

Remaining around the area for about an hour after witnessing the shooting, none of the family was questioned by law enforcement personnel, nor volunteered information. The girls were very much upset and at one point Willis ended up "laying down on the ground and vomiting due to my old war ulcers." Some of the others went and got the car and came back after Mr. Willis. They then drove to the Kodak processing laboratory at 3131 Manor Way, arriving about 2:45 in time to see Air Force One, with the slain President's body aboard, taking off from nearby Love Field. Shortly after Willis arrived at the photo lab, Abraham Zapruder also came in with his film as did Forrest D. Sorrels, Chief of the Secret Service Bureau in Dallas.

Within half an hour, the film was developed. According to Willis, "We viewed them for the first time and went home after dark — very sick. However, on the way home, we stopped at the *Dallas Morning News* and the photo department showed our slides for the second time."[36]

The rest of the weekend was spent in the Willis home with them keenly viewing the television coverage around the clock, following the events as they unfolded. The following Monday Willis loaned his slides to Sorrels. They were returned to him in January of 1964.[37]

Finding that few pictures of the assassination scene were available, Willis decided to market 12 of his best slides, feeling "compelled to make them available to the public." Incorporating under the name Phil Willis Enterprises, Willis had 1,000 sets of these 12 slides made and packaged them in cellophane under the title, "Assassination in Dallas — November 22, 1963. The Last 25 Seconds of Happiness in the Life of President Kennedy — and the Tragedy." A two-page description of the slides was included with the package.[38]

As with the case of several other photographers, government investigators had not interviewed Willis or shown much interest in his photographs, until it was evident that publicity concerning his photographs was being generated. In June 1964, seven months after the assassination, Willis and his wife were interviewed by FBI Agent A. Raymond Switzer. On July 22, 1964, Willis and his daughter Linda Kay gave testimony in Dallas to the Warren Commission, represented by staff attorney Wesley J. Liebeler, whose area of responsibility centered around Lee Harvey Oswald's background. Concerning his interview with Liebeler, Willis states, "He just asked what he wanted to know and that's all. He told me not to elaborate, he didn't want too much information, just what he asked me. And you know me, I'm liable to start rattling."[39]

The six pages of testimony revolved chiefly around Willis's photo of the President's limousine at about the time of the first shot, and the number and direction of the shots. There is no evidence that Liebeler was aware of the full series of the Willis photographs, nor knew or cared about his film type and equipment. It is unclear if the full frames of the slides were examined by investigators to see all photographic evidence. Only the 12 commercially available slides were depicted in volume 21 of the Commission *Hearings*. These photographs were printed in cropped format, including obliterating from the then controversial slide the area showing what many critics believed to be Jack Ruby.[40] The treatment of Willis's slides as evidence, and the lack of interest in him or his family as close eye-witnesses to the assassination, is quite evident in hindsight, with no government agency apparently following up on such potentially important material.

Willis's reaction to the Warren Commission is, "I was never, neither was any other photographer in Dallas, subpoenaed before the Warren Commission. They subpoenaed people who were two blocks away that didn't know a damn thing about it, but not one single photographer, not one. . . . We know there was a lot of cover-up to get over with in a hurry."[41]

Willis never sold his slides to a news agency and copyrighted the 12 he marketed. Somewhat evasive as to just how many slides he took that day, this for years encouraged speculation about what these unseen slides might reveal, adding fuel to critics' speculation. In 1967 *LIFE* magazine published three of his slides from the original set of 12 transparencies in an article about the amateur photographers in Dealey Plaza. Cropped versions of several of his commercial photographs have subsequently been printed in various publications.

Both Mr. and Mrs. Willis were subpoenaed and gave testimony during the Clay Shaw trial in New Orleans, and they were interviewed in Washington, D.C., by a staff member of the House Select Committee on Assassinations. Mr. Willis brought his original transparencies with him, but did not allow them to get out of his custody.[42] The original slides are kept in a bank lock box in Dallas, and Mr. Willis still retains his original Argus camera with its carrying case.[43]

Daughter Rosemary, 16 years after the event, confirmed that she had heard three shots during the assassination which came from the direction of the Book Depository Building. She added, however, that it was her opinion that Oswald was at the window on purpose, so people would believe he was the assassin. She believed that other shots, particularly the one that hit the President in the head, were fired from elsewhere, possibly from a silencer.[44]

Willis is "truly surprised" about the continued interest in the President Kennedy assassination, and personally agrees with the assassination explanation put forth by Josiah Thompson in his book *Six Seconds in Dallas*. After having viewed the Zapruder film numerous times and reflecting on the events 18 years later, when this author visited the Willises in their Dallas home in 1985, Phil Willis states, "I don't care what any experts say. They're full of baloney. I've shot too many deer. I've hit a deer in the head and his horns fly 20 feet with the direction of the bullet. No one will ever convince us that the last shot did not come from the right front, from the knoll area."[45]

## CHAPTER NOTES

1.  *Hearings Before the President's Commission on the Assassination of President Kennedy*, v. 7, p. 492.
2.  Letter, Willis to Trask, 6/29/1984; Willis interview, 11/22/1985; Biographical sheet entitled "Phillip L. Willis, Major, USAF, Retired."
3.  Walter Lord, *Day of Infamy*, p. 210-214.
4.  Letter, Willis to Trask, 6/29/1984; Willis interview, 11/22/1985.
5.  *Hearings*, op. cit., v.7, p. 492; Federal Bureau of Investigation interview of Mrs. Phillip L. Willis, by A. Raymond Switzer, 6/19/1964, p. 1; Willis interview, 11/22/1985.
6.  Letter, Willis to Trask, 6/29/1984; Letter, Dave Hawkins to Trask, 8/28/1984.
7.  Harold Weisberg, *Photographic Whitewash*, p. 178.
8.  Letter, Willis to Trask, 6/29/1984, p. 1; FBI interview of Phillip L. Willis, by A. Raymond Switzer, 6/22/1964, p. 1; Willis interview, 11/22/1985.

9.    FBI interview of Mrs. Willis, op. cit., p. 1; FBI interview of Willis, op. cit., p. 1; Mrs. Willis interview , 11/22/1985.

10.    *Hearings*, op. cit., v. 17, p. 608.

11.    Willis, 35mm photographic transparencies, #4-6, 11/22/1963.

12.    Ibid., #7.

13.    Ibid., #8.

14.    *Hearings*, op. cit., v. 7, p. 493.

15.    Willis photographic transparency, #9; Willis interview, 11/22/1985.

16.    Abraham Zapruder, movie, frames, #Z135-ca. Z212; David Lui, *Los Angeles Times*, "Boy's Quest for Clues to JFK Killing," 6/5/1979.

17.    *Hearings*, op. cit., v. 15, p. 695-697; *Appendix to Hearings Before the Select Committee on Assassinations*, v.6, p. 44.

18.    FBI interview of Willis, op. cit., p. 1; Willis interview, 11/22/1985.

19.    *Appendix*, op. cit., v. 6, p. 121.

20.    Willis photographic transparency, #10.

21.    Josiah Thompson, *Six Seconds in Dallas*, p. 227-228.

22.    R. B. Cutler, *Seventy-Six Seconds in Dealey Plaza*, p. 58-105.

23.    *Appendix*, op, cit., v. 4, p. 428-453.

24.    Willis photographic transparency, #10.

25.    *Life-Itek Kennedy Assassination Film Analysis*, p. 9; *Appendix*, op. cit., v. 6, p. 121-125; David Garber, Image Processing Institute, "The Black Dog Debate," p. [13-14].  Christopher Scally in his manuscript, "So Near . . . And Yet So Far," (p. 51-52), has contended that by a careful examination of this Willis slide, that three men were already on the stairs, and that the Itek explanation of this figure behind the wall was not valid.  A close examination of a second-generation Willis transparency, however, seems to show two, not three, men on the stairs.

26.    *Hearings*, op. cit., v. 7. p. 495.

27.    Ibid., v. 7, p. 493-497; FBI interview of Willis, op. cit., p. 1-2.

28.    FBI interview of Mrs. Willis, op. cit., p. 1-2; Mrs. Willis interview, 11/22/1985.

29.    Willis photographic transparency, #11; Willis interview, 11/22/1985.

30.    Ibid., #12.

31.    *Hearings*, op. cit., v. 7, p. 496.

32.    Letter, Willis to Trask, 6/29/1984; Mrs. Willis interview, 11/22/1985.

33.    Letter, Dave Hawkins to Trask, 6/27/1984.

34.    Mark Lane, *Rush to Judgment*, p. 348-349.

35.    Jim Murray photograph, roll 1, #27, 11/22/1963.

36.    Willis interview, 11/26/1985; Letter, Willis to Trask, 6/29/1984.

37.    Ibid.

38.    *Hearings*, op. cit., v. 7, p. 493; Phil Willis Enterprises [slide set] 1964.

39.    Willis interview, 11/22/1985.

40.    *Hearings*, op cit., v. 21, p. 765-776.

41.    Willis interview, 11/22/1985.

42.    Letter, David Hawkins to Trask, 7/27/1984; Willis interview, 11/22/1985.

43.    Weisberg, op. cit., p. 178; Letter, Willis to Trask, 6/27/1984.

44.    *San Francisco Examiner*, "Girl Tells Mystery Figures Near JFK Assassination," 6/5/1979, p. 8.

45.    Willis interview, 11/22/1985.

CHAPTER 6

# A Gunman in the Shadows?

The black spool of unprocessed movie film was indistinguishable from the dozens of others sent to a local photo lab for processing. Like thousands of others before and after this particular roll, the 25-foot long double-width film would be developed, split, and spliced to produce a 50-foot roll of 8mm amateur format film. Wound onto a 3-inch diameter plastic reel, the film would be ready for packaging and sending back to its owner. If a photo lab technician had bothered to carefully inspect the images on this film during processing, he would have seen much of its approximately four minutes worth of film to be the typical subject matter for home movies. The latter half of the reel was taken up with a high school football half-time program in which cute uniformed majorettes were the camera's subject. The middle sequence of the movie included hopelessly dark scenes, as if taken at dusk, of a park-like area with white concrete structures and tall buildings close by. Atop one building was a prominently displayed electric time and temperature sign alternately reading "7:28" and "36°." The briefest segment on the film was near its beginning. And it was this section which made this amateur film so exceptionally different from the other scores of films processed at the lab in late November 1963. The 380-odd frames included in one brief snippet, scenes of the death of President John F. Kennedy.[1]

It is unclear if any film processing technician noted the brief, dramatic event recorded on this particular movie, and then made the authorities aware of its content. It is known, however, that the various film processors in the Dallas area had, shortly after the weekend of November 24, been requested to insert printed notices into all their completed orders asking that if people had taken pictures of the assassination to please contact the local FBI office. The owner of this film which indeed included scenes of the assassination was Orville O. Nix, who also was friends with Forrest V. Sorrells, Special Agent-In-Charge of the Dallas District Office of the Secret Service.[2]

Realizing the potential importance of this film, on December 1 Mr. Nix voluntarily turned it over to FBI Agent Joe B. Abernathy. Nix also gave the special agent information as to its content and the type of camera he had used. Although desiring to be of assistance to the investigation, Nix emphasized that he wanted the film to be returned to him immediately. The Dallas FBI office thereupon had a copy of the Nix film made through the Jamieson Film Company at their production studio in Dallas. The original was quickly returned to Nix on December 4.[3]

The copy of the Nix film was forwarded to the FBI laboratory in Washington, where an additional copy of it was made and retained in the Administrative Division, the first copy being sent back to the Dallas office.[4]

Orville Orheal Nix, Sr., was a 6'6" native Texan, having been born in April 1911 to James Allan and Myrtle (Mabra) Nix. An air-conditioning engineer for the United States General Services Administration (GSA), which had its offices at 1114 Commerce Street in the Santa Fe Building, some seven blocks east of Dealey Plaza, Nix was married to Ella and had a grown son named Orville, Jr.  Mr. & Mrs. Nix resided in 1963 on Denley Drive, a residential neighborhood to the south of downtown Dallas in close proximity to the Cedarcrest Country Club.[5]

The camera Nix had used on November 22 was a Keystone Auto-Zoom Model K-810 8mm camera.  Manufactured by the Keystone Camera Company of Boston, Nix's model had a suggested retail price of just under $200.  In the decade of the 1960s these built-in electric eye cameras were fast becoming the most popular amateur movie cameras, allowing for self-adjustment to light sensitivity.  The zoom or "infinity-variable-focal-length lens" was quickly replacing the older 3-lens turret camera, though the complicated optics involved in a zoom lens made this type of camera much more expensive.  Zoom lenses on the less expensive side often produced poorer quality pictures. The well respected purchasing guide *Consumer Bulletin* rated this Keystone Auto-Zoom K-10 series as an "intermediate" between their recommended and non-recommended listings.  The zoom lens had a 9mm to 27mm focal length and the quality of the lens was rated as "fair" at normal and wide angle settings, but "poor" when used on the telephoto setting.[6]

The film used by Nix on November 22 was not a good choice.  Though the camera was loaded with Eastman Kodak's Kodachrome II, a brand rated substantially better than other 8mm films, Nix was using Type A Tungsten film.  This film was designed for indoor use with photo-flood light.  If used for daylight application, the lens should be equipped with a compensating Type A filter.  Nix did not do this, and the ASA film speed rating for exposure control was 40 rather than 25.  These factors resulted in film that would be darker and grainier than if the correct outdoor film or correcting filters were used.[7]

Sometime around noon on November 22, 1963, Nix had walked down to Dealey Plaza and had positioned himself near the curb of the southwest corner of Main and Houston Streets. As the presidential motorcade traveled down Main Street and turned right onto Houston, Nix began filming.  His initial sequence of approximately 115 frames, or a little over 6 seconds, recorded the President's limousine proceeding north on Houston Street away from Nix's position.  His camera view is partially obscured several times by the shoulders and bodies of other nearby spectators.  As the motorcade moves along Houston Street towards the Dallas Records Building, Nix loses view of the President and shoots the President's Secret Service follow-up car, one of the motorcycle escorts, and the Vice-President's convertible with Senator Yarborough and Vice-President Johnson fleetingly visible.  The lens becomes more and more obscured by spectators' bodies at camera left.

Figuring he might get a chance for another view across the grass infield towards Elm Street, onto which the motorcade is turning, Nix, according to an FBI report, ". . . proceeded to a point about 20 feet west of Houston Street on the south side of Main Street and made the latter series across an open area which was in view of his position, using the zoom lens completely open." A later study would determine Nix to be at the south curb of Main Street approximately 200 feet from the center line of Elm Street at the point where President Kennedy was shot in the head. His zoom lens allowed an angular coverage of 11°, which covered approximately 75 feet of the grassed knoll area to the north of Elm Street.[8]

Frame #24 at the time the President was hit in the head. The image behind the knoll wall at the spot above the flapping flag on the presidential limousine would later be the subject of much speculation and controversy.

The approximately 122 frames in this second film sequence lasted only slightly more than 6½ seconds. An examination of the frames reveals that the camera is tilted to the right of the horizon, making it appear as if the President's car is traveling upwards, rather than down the Elm Street road grade. The presidential Lincoln enters the scene at camera right. The camera pans left, following the full length of the President's car as well as the following police cycles and the front portion of the follow-up car. At camera right a girl wearing a long coat is observed running from the infield grass towards the car. At about frame #29 the girl stops dead in her tracks and thereafter leans hard back towards her right in a graphic recoil motion. The cause of her reaction is a shot hitting the President's head, which impacts around frame #24-27.

Frame #66 showing SA Hill attempting to stay with and climb aboard the now accelerating vehicle

At about Frame #37 Agent Clint Hill is seen at camera right running towards the President's vehicle. The outboard motorcycle closest to the camera overtakes the second cycle, which has abruptly stopped. At Frame #50 Mrs. Kennedy is rising from her seat, beginning to stretch out with her hand towards the trunk area, as if to grab something. On Nix's side of Elm Street AP photographer Jim Altgens is noted at Frame #73 in a picture-taking stance. At Frame #61 a man in a red shirt standing on the steps of the north side of Elm Street is noted running up the steps, while on the opposite side of the street Malcolm Summers, who fell to the ground upon hearing the shot, is visible in that position beginning at Frame #65. Agent Hill manages to begin to climb aboard the President's vehicle at Frame #88. The car picks up speed and races toward the triple underpass beginning its unscheduled rush to the hospital.[9]

Seconds pass. Nix scurries 35 feet west on Main Street, now moving some eight feet into the street itself. He presses the camera shutter and blurry frames of the street's pavement quickly are replaced by a view of Elm Street and the stairs leading up to the concrete pergola area.  People are rushing across Main Street and the area is being literally inundated by a mob of humanity coming from camera right towards Elm Street.  UPI photographer Frank Cancellare is spotted taking a picture of a family of four who are prostrate on the ground.  Summers slowly rises from the ground.  Part of the motorcade is still on the street.  A blue Chevrolet convertible with cameramen aboard travels down Elm, followed by the third camera car convertible.  This final of the filmed assassination scene sequences lasts some eight seconds.[10]

In late 1966 Nix would tell in a short filmed interview of hearing three shots during the assassination.  It was his belief at the time of the shooting that all three shots came from the fence area on top of the knoll.[11]  It is noted that in both Nix's film and in examination of his filming locations, that the Book Depository Building was obscured to him, blotted out by the cement column of the north peristyle to the northeast.  The entire focus of Nix's camera was on the Elm Street and knoll area of it, and the place to which all early activity within his point of reference radiated.

Nix told the 1966 interviewer, known to him as Robert Blake, but in reality attorney and vehement Warren Commission critic Mark Lane, that though at the time he believed the shots to have come from the fence, he now in 1966 believed the Warren Commission.  The interview became a part of a 1967 film.  Directed by radical documentary film maker Emile D. de Antonio, the film was meant to complement Mark Lane's book *Rush to Judgment*.  It was produced by both Lane and de Antonio, who eventually had a severe falling out.  Responding to Lane's low-key incredulity, part of the exchange between Lane and Nix went like this:

> Lane:   Did you think at that time that the shots came from Book Depository Building?

> Nix:    No, I thought it came from a fence, uh, between the Book Depository and the railroad track.

> Lane:   Did anyone else whom you know or have spoken with also believe that the shots came from there?

> Nix:    Most everyone thought it came from the fence behind the Book Depository.  Between the Book Depository and the railroad track.

> Lane:   At the present time where do you think the shots came from?

> Nix:    It came from the Book Depository because there's proof it did come from there. . . .

> Lane:   And what is the basis of your belief?

Nix:     Several witnesses that said Oswald was in there, the Warren Report
         and the police and so forth proved he was there, so— [12]

Except for an interview with CBS, the out-takes of which have never been
released, this is the only known time that Nix's direct recollections and opinions were
recorded.  Save for two FBI reports which only recorded his film information, and
despite his willingness to testify as a witness, Nix was never called nor deposed by the
Warren Commission or its staff.  Critics of the Warren Commission contend that Nix's
1963 beliefs in the location of the shooter made him an unwelcome witness, whom they
chose to ignore.

Either during the evening of November 22, 1963, or during the following day,
Nix returned to Dealey Plaza to film views of the area, including shots similar to what
he took at the time of the assassination, "to see what it would show."  The film shows the
Hertz sign atop the Texas School Book Depository with a temperature indication of 39°
and a time of 7:28.  Later Nix's son, Orville, Jr., borrowed the camera to take pictures
of his daughter performing as a majorette at a football game.[13]  The Dealey Plaza
sequence is dark.  Though it cannot be discovered from the film what day it was taken,
it was probably taken in the evening of the 22nd, as the sunrise on November 23 was at
approximately 7:00 a.m., with sunset at about 5:30 p.m.  The recorded low temperature
in Dallas on November 22/23 was 36°.[14]

Following the assassination, the news media scrambled for any possible visuals
of the shooting scene itself.  *LIFE* magazine was able to snatch rights to the film taken
by Abraham Zapruder, and it soon became known that they had paid a hefty price for
photo rights.  Burt Reinhardt, General Manager of United Press International's Newsfilm Division, flew to Dallas to attempt to acquire other possible film of the assassination.  Reinhardt connected with Nix in early December, while the Nix film was on loan
to the FBI.  He indicated an interest by UPI Newsfilm in it, and Nix realized his film
might be of some monetary value.  Nix also contacted *LIFE* about his film.[15]

Once the film was back in Nix's possession from its loan to the FBI, he called
Reinhardt, who had returned to New York.  Inquiring if UPI was still interested, Nix
related that *LIFE* also was, and he was flying to New York to discuss a deal.  Reinhardt
convinced Nix to agree to see him before consummating any sale, and upon Nix's
meeting with him, UPI Newsfilm was able to acquire the original film for $5,000 (the
same amount Time Inc. offered) with a good dinner and a new hat thrown in to sweeten
the deal.  On December 7, UPI sent out to subscribers a sampling of frames from the
Nix film with a text indicating, "This photo sequence which has just become available was
taken as the late President Kennedy was assassinated. . . . This black-and-white sequence
is taken from 8mm color film."[16]

The original film was not of the highest quality.  It suffered some significant
scratches and due to it being tungsten film stock, the colors were dark, the grain structure heavy, and the picture itself not very sharp.  By the time UPI Newsfilm acquired the
strip of film, the assassination story itself was somewhat old news and as a film format,

it was sparingly used. Fox-Movietone did include the Nix assassination sequence in both full-frame and close-up format in a wrap-up newsreel about the weekend events, and two frames were reproduced in color in the UPI-American Heritage souvenir hardcover book *Four Days*, published and widely distributed in early 1964.[17]

UPI Newsfilm also obtained a fee for the use of this Nix film in a documentary produced and directed by Mel Stuart for Wolper Productions and released in October 1964 by United Artists. Titled *Four Days in November*, the 122-minute, black-and-white film included Nix's two film sequences taken on Elm Street. Later still in the 1973 conjectural conspiracy film *Executive Action*, produced by Edward Lewis and starring Burt Lancaster and Robert Ryan, a color version of Nix was used as the movie's only authentic assassination scene sandwiched between theatrical re-enactment scenes.[18]

In Washington during the early weeks of 1964, the newly established Warren Commission staff was putting together its method of operations for investigating the case. The FBI was to act as its chief investigative source and any requests for assistance from the FBI technical and lab support staff had to be approved through the Bureau's chain of command.

Special Agent Lyndal L. Shaneyfelt, a photographic expert in the Document Section of the FBI laboratory, met with Commission staff to go over their requests regarding the known assassination films. The Commission asked that a study be made to establish the speed of the President's car, the distance traveled during the assassination, and the location of Nix and Zapruder during that time. Shaneyfelt stated this could be accomplished by examining the films and cameras involved, ". . . accompanied by a survey of the actual site in Dallas." An FBI memorandum was generated with a recom-

mendation to request to obtain Nix's camera for lab examination followed by a study in Dallas of the site. Approval was given at the bottom of the typed memorandum in the form of a scrawled handwritten statement reading, "Okay, it sounds like a lot of poppycock to me. H." Director J. Edgar Hoover had indicated his less than enthusiastic approval of the study. He undoubtedly believed the Commission

Hoover's less-than-enthusiastic approval
of the FBI assassination scene study

should simply take as gospel the investigative conclusions which the FBI had arrived at in their early December 1963 supplementary report on the case, rather than going through an expensive and work-intensive study, wasting his resources.[19]

Contacted on January 29, Nix made his camera available. "Mr. Nix advised the FBI was welcome to use the camera for experimental purposes and that he would be available as a witness if needed."[20]  In early February the FBI laboratory reported that the average film speed of the Nix camera was 18.5 frames per second, which information was forwarded to the Warren Commission.[21]

Beginning on January 29 and on at least three other days during as many months, Shaneyfelt and other FBI representatives met with staff of the Commission and agents from the Secret Service.  On these occasions they specifically examined the Nix film in concert with motion picture films taken by Zapruder and Marie Muchmore. Following these meetings, on May 23 and 24, the FBI took primary responsibility in the survey re-enactment of the assassination at Dealey Plaza.  The location of Nix at the time of his filming was ascertained and throughout several run-throughs all three amateur movie cameras were used to film the staged re-enactment from their November 22 positions.[22]

PHOTOGRAPH FROM NIX FILM                    PHOTOGRAPH FROM RE-ENACTMENT

It was established at the re-enactment that of the 122 frames of the assassination sequence as filmed by Nix, frame #24 coincided with Zapruder frame #313, being the moment when the shot impact to the President's head became visible.  Seven of Nix's frames were reproduced in the published Warren Commission *Hearings*.  Except for these inferior quality reproductions, two FBI reports and several minor references to this and the other films being displayed to members of the Commission, there was no further mention of Nix and no testimony recorded concerning him.[23]

For his part, Mr. Nix contacted the FBI Dallas office in mid-March, requesting the possibility of acquiring a print of his movie from the Bureau.  In the subsequent report relating to Nix's request, "He stated that the copy of the film which was returned to him by the Bureau does not appear as clear as his usual pictures and that it may be partially due to the fact that in viewing his present copy he has frequently stopped the film in the projector."[24]

In internal communications during this time and later still in 1966, the Bureau always maintained that "Mr. Nix's original film was returned to him on 12/4/63." Save for the few days it took to copy the original, the FBI never took permanent possession of the original film. That original film was purchased by UPI Newsfilm in December, and Nix might have obtained his copy from them or made one for himself prior to their purchasing it. In any event, Nix was not happy with his copy and requested another, which the FBI provided, ". . . since his own copy has deteriorated."[25]

Though Mr. Nix had provided his camera to the FBI in early February, he had apparently assumed they would not need it very long. Beginning in early March 1964 Nix made inquiries to the Dallas FBI office about when he could expect it back, as vacation time was approaching. He told the agent with whom he spoke that in the event the camera was still needed, ". . . he could get along without it and wanted to cooperate in every way possible." Mrs. Muchmore, who had also loaned her camera to the FBI, was also getting itchy about its being returned to her, not able to understand why it was needed so long. Thus began a period of several months during which much paperwork was generated internally by the FBI, which was chagrined by the Commission's not following through by authorizing the cameras' return. The Bureau also did not like being the middleman in this go-around, and the tone of memos indicates their wanting to pass the situation directly on to the Commission rather than their being the brunt of increasing displeasure on the part of the two citizens. The language of the memos and letters generated are also somewhat self-serving on the part of the FBI, and include an undercurrent tone of annoyance with the Commission. Finally the Commission informed the FBI that the cameras were needed for the field work at Dallas in late May. Nix was told that if his camera was not available by the time he needed it beginning in early June, he could rent one, charging it to the Commission.[26]

By far the largest amount of paperwork generated concerning Nix had nothing to do with his witnessing the assassination, but with regard to his borrowed camera. Finally on June 2 the Nix camera was personally delivered to him by Special Agent Gemberling. That evening Nix called Gemberling at home complaining about the condition of the camera, including a missing take-up spool, loosened screws, and an inoperable footage indicator. Within a day Nix was instructed to bring the camera to a local shop to put it "in first-rate working condition." The repair bill of $4.50 was paid by the local FBI office.[27]

Over a year passed with little further interest generated from the Nix film until a researcher hit upon something. Jones Harris was a comfortably well-off New Yorker who had become interested in the assassination events. His research led him to conclude that the government had participated in a cover-up conspiracy, and that Oswald was probably innocent. His interest included the photographic evidence, and in 1965 Harris came upon frames of the Nix film. The frames seemed to show that at the time of the assassination a figure of what appeared to be a man was positioned to camera left of the pergola atop the grassy knoll. The figure seemed to be in a classic shooting

A conjectural drawing of what some saw as a gunman firing from behind the grassy knoll

position, standing behind what looked to be a station wagon, leaning on it, and taking aim with a rifle. His head, shoulders, and arms were all visible. An associate of Harris's, photographer Bernie Hoffman, wanted to assist in further verifying this serious and possibly key observation. Harris approached UPI Newsfilm Managing Editor Maurice W. Schonfeld and General Manager Burt Reinhardt, who had originally acquired the film from Nix. Realizing the importance of this potential find and the fact that if it were borne out, then the film's market value would be tremendous, the men cooperated. The film was made available for individual frame reproduction and enlargements. Into 1966 the men pursued the matter attempting to verify the existence of a gunman on the knoll. The image seemed real enough to Schonfeld for him to be caught up in the exhilaration, yet worried that maybe they were really onto something much bigger than a typical news story. He wondered if this information made them vulnerable to unknown forces.[28]

Hoffman's photo work was impressive, but not conclusive, as he was not able to do anything else with the material more sophisticated than darkroom work. UPI sent staff correspondent Jack V. Fox to Dallas to follow up. His resulting article was sent out via the UPI network in June 1967. The article stated that the image in question did appear to be a rifleman with sunglasses leaning on the roof of a station wagon, yet also cautioned that from examining the image, ". . . one can also imagine a white-faced steer staring down."[29]

Thereafter followed a period of unstructured meandering and an uncertainty of how or where to proceed. Though Harris wanted the quest for authentication to continue, he was reluctant to do so personally. UPI did not want to front the expense of having this relatively unknown film studied with the possible result of a non-story, and was at the same time reluctant to give up its possible exclusivity to other media. UPI, however, was a news service, and not in the position of being able to develop such a potential story as well a magazine could. Schonfeld, though not wanting to lose control of this story, still wanted to see it pursued, rather than its possibly withering from non-activity. He approached several national magazines, but with little success. The story, however, was finding its way into the information loop of the assassination buffs, while an undercurrent of interest was emerging from within the media.[30]

In November 1966 *Esquire* magazine published in its December dated issue, an article by Edward Jay Epstein, outlining numerous of the assassination theories being proposed as indicators of a conspiracy. The three UPI men were named as proponents of the "over-the-fence theory." A Nix frame and blow-up of the area of the "rifleman" was included together with text briefly outlining the story of its discovery, and the fact that witnesses Lee Bowers, Jr., and S. M. Holland seemed to confirm the possible presence of a shooter at that location.[31]

Though Jones Harris had given the information to Epstein, he did not want to be identified by name, and had suggested the UPI men be listed as proponents of the theory. *Esquire's* P.R. people, building on what they presumed to be a high point of the article, overstated the case by releasing a statement that the picture, "appears to confirm the existence of an assassin now at large." *Esquire's* Associate Editor John Berendt, when confronted by other members of the press concerning this statement, back-pedaled indicating the release was "perhaps a bit too positive." The initial press release and subsequent availability of the December issue caught much media and public attention.[32]

Though displeased to be listed as proponents of the theory, Schonfeld was nonetheless eager to follow it to a conclusion. He was contacted by an RCA executive who suggested that an examination of frames utilizing recent innovations in photo analysis could be quite helpful. RCA, it turned out, was not interested, given the controversial nature of such a project. Schonfeld was discouraged by the continuing lack of progress. About this time he saw the newly released commercial movie *Blow-Up*. Directed by Michelangelo Antonioni, the film concerned a photographer, played by David Hemmings who, while photographing at a park incidentally caught on film what might have been a murder. Studying his film, frame by frame, Hemmings' character became obsessed with blowing up the fuzzy negatives in an attempt to find the reality of the event. In what must be a classic case of an art form imitating life, which is then in turn used as a catalyst for real-life activity, Schonfeld, ". . . made up my mind to give the Nix film one last try."[33]

A further search for companies that might be able to examine the frames finally landed on the Massachusetts firm Itek. After a meeting with company officers, Itek agreed to do the study free as a "public service." Such a study would demonstrate the sophisticated techniques Itek had developed for classified governmental work. It would hopefully bring prestige and other possible business applications to this lesser known company which performed advanced photographic image enhancement work. The Itek people did not slough off the image as easily refutable, and all involved appeared serious to see just what the image was.

Shonfeld personally carried the original film from its vault location in New York's Chase Manhattan Bank to Lexington, Massachusetts, for laboratory use and various methods of copying. He also made available UPI's facilities to produce reference photos and measurements of pertinent Dealey Plaza features.

The Itek study was conducted between January and May of 1967. The resulting 55-page analysis was released on May 18, much of it explaining the investigative procedures, methodology, computations and including charts and illustrations reflecting this process. Primary objectives of the study included identifying the shape of the "gunman" and "vehicle" and its line of sight to the area on Elm Street where President Kennedy received the fatal head wound. The Itek technicians found that the Nix film was not optimally produced. Whereas, ". . . low contrast resolution levels close to 100 lines per millimeter can be obtained on Kodachrome II film," the optics of the camera itself were not impressive, and the film was of an indoor artificial light class, used without a filter. The resulting resolution levels were at about 25 lines per millimeter.[34]

Image improvement was thus the first task pursued. Procedures included contrast-controlled reproduction methods utilizing special high-definition film and processing, and special printing and enlarging techniques. These techniques were used to create black-and-white prints which better brought out image detail in the shadow areas of the frames. Included in this task method was color separation. In this technique a separate filtration is made of each of the three color layers of Kodachrome film, producing three independent black-and-white pictures. Each new picture registers distinct information without interference from the other two layers. Another technique used for image improvement was the creating of four-image integration prints. Information from four separate Nix frames (color or black-and-white) are combined into a single frame, minimizing grain characteristics and random features of individual frames, while accentuating edge characteristics to improve imagery.[35]

With these more accurate images in hand, and utilizing ancillary information from study photos of the knoll and Plaza, measurements assisting the study could be made of significant features and distances. Analysis of the images could now be made through visual photo interpretation of each Nix frame. Besides analysis of individual frames using enlargements and optical magnification, stereoscopic analysis was also performed.

Nix had filmed the primary scene from a distance of some 300 feet. Between his two film sequences — at the time of the assassination and at a time moments later when the President's limousine had departed — Nix had moved about 18 feet to the left of his original position. This distance allowed the Itek researchers a sufficient minimum separation in the two viewing vantage points to allow a stereoscopic analysis, much the same as photo interpreters use when examining stereo pairs of aerial photos.[36]

The study came up with interesting, though not startling, conclusions. The "assassin with a rifle" shape to the right of the concrete pergola ". . . was found to be shadow and highlight details created by the sun casting shadows of tree branches on the wall of shelter 3." Stereoscopic study revealed the shape did not possess a three-dimensional form, while improved imagery buttressed the conclusion that they were patterns of shadows and highlights. Furthermore, important components of the shape disappeared and appeared faster than is humanly possible. The "vehicle-like" object was about five feet high, and was located some 20 feet behind these shadows in the parking lot behind the knoll. It possessed the appearance and size of a vehicle, but no person could be associated on or near it. If a shooter had been at this position, he would have to be nine feet above the ground to get an unobstructed view of Elm Street, and his line of sight view of the President would have been limited to less than 1/30 of a second before the fatal shot was fired, due to vertical obstructions to his left. No person was found in the Nix film frames in the area of the stockade fence, concrete wall, or shelter #3. The average speed the President's car traveled as viewed by the Nix film at the 20-feet-close-to-the-head-shot frame was 8.7 miles per hour.[37]

The "assassin with a rifle" feature was evident in the Nix assassination sequence during the first 77 of the 122 frames, the camera panning out of its field of view after frame #77. However, when Nix began to film after the President's vehicle had left, and during a time when scores of people were streaming into the area, the same "assassin" image was still present. This fact was yet another proof that the human form was an illusion and not a reality.[38]

Schonfeld and Jack Fox put together a copyrighted feature story for UPI regarding the Itek findings. Though turning out to be the non-story Schonfeld had earlier postulated as a possible result, the report's opening paragraph gave it a broader interpretation. "An analysis by one of the nation's top photographic laboratories has demolished a widely circulated theory that a second gunman was involved in the assassination of President Kennedy."[39] Itek and UPI had interpreted the entire grassy knoll area which many had claimed to be the location from where shots were fired, as exclusively limited to the area Nix had filmed the "assassin with a rifle" shape. Contrary to their sweeping conclusion that no rifleman was present on the knoll, the study only seriously examined this area close to the mystery image. Many legitimate assassination researchers had previously discounted the "assassin with a rifle" shape. They felt that all the earlier hoopla generated about it was disinformation. Mark Lane was quoted by UPI to say, "I don't think the study proves anything." Researcher Harold Weisberg noted that these conclusions written up in the article about this proving there was no second gun was a ". . . disgracefully slanted and entirely inaccurate story."[40] The print press reporting of the Itek analysis generated sweeping headline conclusions in many newspapers including: "A Second-Assassin Theory Fades on Film," "Film Tests Explode Myth, No 2d Gunman in JFK Plot," and "Idea Spiked on Kennedy 2nd Gunman."[41]

After this flurry of newspaper stories on May 19, except for a brief article in *Time* magazine on May 26, the story quickly died. Shonfeld in writing of his odyssey with the film in the *Columbia Journalism Review*, tells of his later discovery that not only was Howard Sprague, Schonfeld's contact man with Itek who was assistant to the corporation's president, a former CIA employee (as he had told Schonfeld early on), but so was Itek president Franklin T. Lindsay a former CIA agent. Many assassination researchers knew of the deep connections between Itek and the government, which gave the firm 60% of its business through the analysis of aerial photos for intelligence purposes. Did this mean the analysis was tainted? Schonfeld, more out of credulity than a firm belief in conspiracy wrote, "I gave up. Enough was enough. But I love to tell the story on myself, and maybe on all of us, of how, in the end, the only people I could get to investigate a picture that might (by a stretch of conspiratorial imagination) involve the

CIA were people who worked for the CIA."[42]

By 1973 Schonfeld had one more run-in with image enhancement of the Nix film. Electronic analysis had advanced since 1967, and at California Institute of Technology at Pasadena a computer image processing was done on 35mm color transparencies made from the film. The results were then analyzed by Dr. Kenneth Castleman and Alan Gillespie of the Cal Tech's Jet Propulsion Laboratory. In early 1975 a report was drawn up stating that there were no errors found within the original Itek report and that the conclusions reached in the 1967 report were most likely correct. It did caution, however, that due to the poor image quality of the film, and given the availability of other hiding places in and around the grassy knoll, especially in deep shadows behind the stockade fence, that such a possibility of an assassin being there and not seen in the Nix film could not be ruled out. The film analysis did not strongly support such a possibility, however.[43]

In late 1971 Mr. Nix had suffered a heart attack, and on January 17, 1972, succumbed to a fatal attack. He was 60 years old and was buried at Edgewood Cemetery in Lancaster, Texas.[44]

Areas studied by the HSCA included the "gunman" image above the concrete wall
and movement within the dark shadows above the wall at its culmination on the left.

During the House Select Committee on Assassinations investigation in 1978 the Committee's photographic panel and their contractors, including Los Alamos Scientific Laboratory and Aerospace Corporation, examined the questions previously raised concerning the Nix film. In regard to the image "interpreted to be a rifleman in the classic military posture for firing a rifle," magnification of this area proved to be indistinct and blurry even after computer enhancement. "Frame-averaging" techniques were utilized whereby frames are registered on computer tape, added together to reduce the noise [blur or artifacts not part of the scene itself] and then enhanced into a final product. There were no human flesh tones associated with the "gunman" object, unlike others present in the film, and the feature was almost uniformly white and identical in appearance to the other white tones of the concrete wall. It was also observed in one of the frames examined that the "right arm" of the object disappears, reappearing in the next frame, a characteristic virtually impossible for a human, though, "conceivable for tree branches casting a shadow pattern on a wall." Also reviewing the previous Itek study as to its methodology and conclusions that the "gunman" was a pattern of light and shadows on the concrete shelter, the House Select Committee panel, ". . . agrees with those conclusions."[45]

The panel also took a look at a feature which appears to show movement in the dark shadow near the end of the retaining wall where the steps lead to the Elm Street sidewalk below, which is camera left of the "rifleman" image. Some type of perceived quick motion appears to take place there during the Nix film sequence. Several of these frames were scanned and input into a computer for enhancement of the edges and sharpening of details. The resulting report stated, "The enhanced Nix film shows an object that can be construed as having a shape similar to that of a person. It is also possible to interpret this object as being of the same general shape as the person identified at the wall in the Willis #5 photograph. Nevertheless, the person in the Willis photograph displayed distinct flesh tones in the computer display of the image. No such pattern of flesh tones is visible in the enhanced (or original) Nix frames." The panel's conclusion was that they could not verify that the image was the same as seen seconds earlier in the Willis slide, that it was not identified as a human being, and was more likely the result of light and shadows.[46]

At the tail end of 1991 there was a renewed flurry of popular interest in the assassination story predicated on the release of the Oliver Stone movie *JFK*. Mr. Nix's granddaughter, Gayle Nix Jackson, appeared on several television programs at the time, telling of her grandfather's experience. In conjunction with the much-believed popular theory that a shooter had fired from the top of the knoll area, the granddaughter reiterated that the Nix film is the only film which exhibited the entire grassy knoll area. Emphasizing that if there is something in this film that reveals a second gunman, she told one interviewer, "Let's find the truth and let it be known and let our lives go on." Claiming that the government kept the original film and still refuses to make it available to her, Mrs. Jackson also said that her grandfather believed that the government altered the footage and the copy returned to him, though she simply doesn't know the truth.[47]

On a late November 1991 edition of the *Geraldo* TV talk show, Mrs. Jackson told the host that it was her personal opinion that the original film showed something that the government didn't want people to see. Also on the guest panel was Robert Groden, photographic researcher who had advised the House Select Committee photo panel and frequent lecturer who holds strong beliefs of an assassination conspiracy. Displaying a good quality Nix film sequence with extreme blow-ups, freeze-frames and repetitive loop action, Groden told of his discovery 12 years earlier of the movement behind the concrete retaining wall next to the steps. He stated that he informed the Select Committee about this figure one can see in motion behind the wall. Mrs. Jackson, obviously impressed and commenting that today is the first time she had seen this feature, interrupts to say that she doesn't know if it is some guy throwing hot dogs, but it is definitely something. The multi-repeated loop of the blow-up does show two to three light areas in motion, one light area descending rapidly during part of the sequence, and all obviously not merely photographic artifact.[48] The implication given to those seeing this film so displayed is that this is movement — the movement must be a human — and the human movement must be that of an assassin. The logicality of such reasoning, though attractive, is unfounded. If it is in fact human movement why could it not be more logically another of the numerous spectators at the scene? Must every unknown shape or movement be construed as that of an assassin? If a mundane explanation is a plausible explanation, is it not intellectually more justified to seek out those explanations before jumping to the conclusion of more bogeymen being present?

The little known comment of Marilyn Sitzman, the woman who stood on the pedestal a short distance to camera right of this site with Abraham Zapruder while he filmed the assassination, is important here. Sitzman recalled distinctly that a young black couple between 18 and 21 years of age were sitting on a bench only several feet behind this concrete wall in question. She remembered that right after the last shot, ". . . the kids had thrown down their Coke bottles, just thrown them down, and just started running towards the back. . . ."[49] Though not as satisfying or as sensational an explanation for this possible event, this explanation does jibe with actual observed actions of the people at the scene.

## CHAPTER NOTES

1.      Maurice W. Schonfeld, "The Shadow of a Gunman," *Columbia Journalism Review*, p. 46; National Archives copy of the Orville O. Nix film, 11/22/1963. Researcher Harold Weisberg first obtained permission in 1966 from UPI to examine the copy of this film deposited at the Archives. Subsequent to this, and contrary to the wishes of UPI, the Archives interpreted this initial use as justifying other on-site examinations of the film by researchers.

2.      Interview of Nix by Mark Lane from the film *Rush to Judgment*, produced by Emile de Antonio and Mark Lane, Impact Films, 1967.

3.      *Hearings Before the President's Commission on the Assassination of President Kennedy*, v. 24, p. 539, exhibit #2109; FBI Memorandum, To: Director, From: SAC, Dallas, Attention FBI Laboratory, #62-109060-2063, 12/5/1963, obtained by Trask through FOIA request #266,203, 1/1986.

4.      Ibid.; SAC, Dallas [from] Director, 12/19/1963, through FOIA request, op.cit. Although the paper trail indicates that a copy of a copy was retained in Washington, it would seem appropriate that when this film was needed for examination, that the best copy available would have been used.

5.      *Dallas Morning News*, 1/18/1972, p. 4 D; *Dallas Times Herald*, "Assassination Films Maker Succumbs," 1/19/1972, p. A 25; Orville O. Nix Certificate of Death, file #704, recorded 1/24/1972.

6.      *Consumer Bulletin Annual, 1962-63*, p. 53-54; *Hearings*, op. cit., v. 24, p. 539, exhibit 2110.

7.      *Consumer Reports*, v. 28, no. 12, 12/1963, p. 307-308; Itek Corporation, *Nix Film Analysis*, p. 2.

8.      Ibid., p. 2, 5-11; *Hearings*, op. cit.

9.      Nix Film, 11/22/1963.

10.     Ibid.

11.  *Rush to Judgment*, op. cit.

12.  Ibid.; Mark Lane, *A Citizen's Dissent* (Fawcett Crest p.b.), p. 64-65.

13.  Schonfeld, op. cit., p. 48-49; Notes by Richard Sprague of phone interview with Mrs. Orville Nix, Jr., from Sprague Papers, Special Collections Division, Georgetown University Library, ca. 1968.

14.  *Dallas Times Herald*, "World Wide Weather," p. 10 A, 11/23/1963.

15.  Schonfeld, op. cit., p. 46-47.

16.  Ibid., p. 47; UPI photos on microfilm, micro-copy NK-46, roll 15, UPI NXP 1404 338 at Kennedy Library.

17.  United Press International and American Heritage Magazine, *Four Days, The Historical Record of the Death of President Kennedy*, p. [21].

18.  Wolper Productions, released by United Artists, *Four Days In November*, 1964; National General Pictures, *Executive Action*, 1973.

19.  Memorandum, To: Mr. Conrad, From: W.D. Griffith, Request by Investigating Commission, #62-109060-2405, 1/28/1964, through FOIA, op.cit.

20.  *Hearings*, op. cit., v. 24, p. 539, exhibit #2110.

21.  Memorandum, To: Mr. Conrad, From: W.D. Griffith, #62-109060-2383 & 2397, 2/3 & 2/5/1964; Memorandum, To: Mr. Belmont, From: A. Rosen, #62-109060-2465, 2/20/1964, through FOIA, op. cit.

22.  Memorandum, To: Mr. Conrad, From: W.D. Griffith, #62-10960-3282, 6/10/1964, through FOIA, op. cit.

23.  *Hearings*, v. 5, p. 137, 139-141, 159-160, 162, 177; v. 17, p. 901; v. 18, p. 81-83, 95; v. 24, p. 539.

24.  Airtel, To: Director, From: SAC, Dallas, Attn: FBI Laboratory, 3/17/1964, through FOIA, op. cit.

25.  Airtel, To: SAC, Dallas, From: Director, #105-82565-2722, 3/24/1964; Memorandum, To: Mr. DeLoach, From: A. Rosen, #62-109060-4275, 11/18/1966, through FOIA, op. cit. This memo was generated to refute the contention of Mark Lane which was made on a 11/12/1966 television program that Nix had told him the FBI damaged his film and camera. The memo reviewed the history of both items concluding: "Mr. Lane's comment is not accurate."

26.  13 Airtels, memos, and letters regarding the camera; all dating between 4/7/1964 and 6/2/1964, through FOIA, op. cit.

27.  Airtel, To: Director, From: SAC, Dallas, #62-109060-4265, 11/18/1966, through FOIA, op. cit. The last known communication between Nix and the FBI was in the summer of 1967 when he requested the Bureau to provide him with some documentation indicating the serial number of the camera at the time he provided it to them in early 1964. It appeared that Nix wanted proof that his present camera was one and the same, as he was approached by someone who wanted to buy the original assassination camera. An FBI report noted, "No purpose will be served by assisting Nix in any such negotiations." (Memorandum, To: Mr. Wick, From: M. A. Jones, 7/24/1967). A record of the serial number of the Nix film is not included in the released Nix FOIA files.

28.  Schonfeld, op. cit., p. 47-48.

29.  *New York Times*, 11/15/1966, p. 35.

30.  Schonfeld, op. cit., p. 48.

31.  *Esquire*, 12/1966, p. 206.

32.  *New York Times*, op. cit.; Schonfeld, op. cit., p. 49. In a January 1967 issue of the *Saturday Evening Post* a large color blow-up of one of the Nix assassination frames was included with a caption which read, "Some witnesses insist they heard firing from the grassy knoll. In the upper left of this picture others see a man aiming a rifle from a car roof just as the shots hit." (*Saturday Evening Post*, 1/14/1967, p. 22-[23]).

33.  Schonfeld, op. cit., p. 49.

34.  Itek, op. cit., p. 17, 24.

35.  Ibid., p. 16-19.

36.     Ibid., p. 19-21.
37.     Ibid., p. iii-iv, 42-46.
38.     Nix film, 11/22/1963.
39.     UPI Teletype "225A Assassination 5/18 NX," 5/18/1967.
40.     [Boston] *Record American*, 5/19/1967, p. 19; Harold Weisberg, *Photographic Whitewash*, p. 124.
41.     *Boston Globe*, 5/19/1967, p. 2; *Dallas Morning News*, 5/19/1967; *The* [Washington] *Evening Star*, 5/19/1967, p. A 3.
42.     Schonfeld, op. cit., p. 50.
43.     Ibid.; Robert Sam Anson, *They've Killed the President!*, p. 147-148.
44.     Nix Death Certificate, op. cit.; *Dallas Times Herald*, 1/19/1972, p. A 25.
45.     *Appendix to Hearings Before the Select Committee on Assassinations*, v. 6, p. 128-131; *Report of the Select Committee on Assassinations*, p. 86.
46.     *Appendix*, op. cit., v. 6, p. 126-128.
47.     *Inside Edition*, [Television Program] 12/27/1991.
48.     *Geraldo*, [Television Program] 11/19/1991.
49.     Transcript of Josiah Thompson taped interview of Marilyn Sitzman, 11/29/1966, p. [9].

## CHAPTER 7

# The Justin McCarty Women

Among a number of the female employees of the Justin McCarty Manufacturing Company, the impending presidential visit through Dallas on Friday was a subject of some excitement. Located just four blocks south of Houston and Main Streets, upon which the presidential motorcade would pass, Justin McCarty was one of several local ladies' dress wholesale manufacturers. Besides the excitement of possibly seeing the young, handsome President, many employees looked forward to catching a glimpse of Jacqueline Kennedy, whose clothing taste and flair was the talk among those interested in fashion and design.

At about 11:30 a.m. on November 22 a group of six Justin McCarty employees together walked the few blocks to Dealey Plaza to take in the excitement of the motorcade. Two of this group of co-workers brought personal cameras with them to record the event. Mrs. Marie Muchmore was a native of Oklahoma who lived on Randy Lane in Farmers Branch, a part of metropolitan Dallas, located about 10 miles northwest of her place of employment. She brought from home that day a Keystone K-7 zoom lens 8mm movie camera. The camera was about a year old, originally costing some $150, and it used roll-type movie film. Its serial number was 20648.[1]

Miss Wilma Irene Bond was a 42-year-old native of Indiana who worked as a bookkeeper at Justin McCarty. She lived north of downtown Dallas on East Lovers Lane and had brought with her on that Friday a 35mm camera loaded with a 36-exposure roll of color transparency film.[2]

At about 11:45 the women arrived at Dealey Plaza and positioned themselves about 30 feet north of the northwest corner of the Main and Houston Streets intersection at a location where the parade would make a right turn from Main onto Houston Street. Though there was red, white, and blue bunting attached to street lights, including on the pole just on the opposite side of Houston from their position, and though there were a few people gathered around the corner, there was not much else in evidence that the President would soon be passing by. Muchmore put her camera up to her eye and shot three brief scenes, totaling only about eight seconds, of activity at this cross-street. Several cars are stopped at a red light on Main Street, while a station wagon travels north on Houston through the intersection. There are some people on the sidewalk waiting for the procession and Muchmore, in her last pre-motorcade sequence, shoots toward the old redstone Dallas Court House as a black man crosses the intersection.[3]

By about 12:30 a respectable size crowd had now gathered around the intersection. The court house sidewalk was lined with people. Others stood on the building's entrance steps while a group of court employees also had a view from a second-floor balcony and from adjoining windows. Looking up Main Street one could see a large mass of people paralleling the street. Though Bond and Muchmore did not have a specific view up Main, they could see in the movement of people opposite them that something was approaching. Soon they heard the roar of motorcycles and readied their cameras.

Cyclists turn the corner from Main to Houston Street

The lead motorcycles were five in number, traveling just ahead of the white lead car driven by Dallas Police Chief Jesse Curry. The cycles had remained in a single rank as they had cruised down most of Main Street, though as they now approached Houston, three formed a wedge shape as they neared the corner. Muchmore, thinking that this approaching activity was possibly the President's vehicle, began to film as the three cycles turned right, followed close behind by two others coming up to make their turn. After less than five seconds, Muchmore realized this group did not include the President, and she stopped her camera. Bond, to Muchmore's immediate left, took her first slide as the two cyclists approached her position. Across Houston Street, while several spectators are looking towards the cyclists, most are craning their heads to their left in anticipation of the President. A man in a suit holds a camera near his chest.[4]

As the President's Lincoln came into view on Main, making its turn onto Houston Street, Muchmore began what would be her longest film clip. The ten seconds of film follows the vehicle's turn and pans left as it comes parallel with her position. Several times spectators momentarily block part of Muchmore's camera view, including one man with a camera who may be Phil Willis. The President's Secret Service follow-up car is seen and Muchmore's camera, trying to keep up with the action, shifts left. A momentary pause in filming occurs, followed by a little over five more seconds of film taken of the Vice-President's convertible and its occupants, a quick view left of the President's car with the Dallas Records and the Dal-Tex Buildings in the background. Jostled by the shifting crowd, Muchmore finishes the sequence with frames of the Vice-President's follow-up car. Its rear driver's side car door is seen slightly ajar. The camera is now tilting to the right about 30°, at which point Muchmore stops filming.

Meanwhile Bond has taken two more still photos, one as the President's vehicle is almost parallel to her position. This photo is flawed, however, as the back of Muchmore's head obscures the President and First Lady, though the Connallys can be observed looking to Bond's side of the street. As the car passes her position, Bond does get off a photo showing most of the President's car with both him and his wife in view, the President smiling and looking in the direction of Mrs. Kennedy. Parts of all four cyclists traveling behind the convertible are in the frame, as are various people in first story windows of the County Criminal Courts Building in the background, one man gesturing with a friendly wave. One of the people in the windows of this building is free-

The President's car on Houston Street

lance photographer Jim Murray. Ten spectators are widely scattered on the eastern sidewalk below the windows of the Courts Building, seemingly passive in their actions while observing the President, save for one man in a suit and hat, who applauds as the car travels past him.[5]

Once the President was effectively out of sight, a number of people around the intersection moved quickly to locate another possible view as the Kennedy vehicle turned a sharp left and began traveling down Elm Street. Bond and Muchmore turned around and rushed to the low concrete wall facing onto Elm Street. At a location where the waist-high wall intersects the tall, elliptical shaped north Peristyle, the two women found a good viewing position. While the women were proceeding the 80 feet northwest to this location, the President's Lincoln convertible had turned the sharp corner onto the Elm Street straightaway and shots had rung out.

In the only known report of Bond's activities, recorded in the third person by two FBI agents almost three months after the assassination, it was reported, "She stated that due to the excitement she did not obtain any photographs at the time of the shooting. She also advised to the best of her knowledge, she heard at least three shots fired at the time of the incident, but that due to the excitement, she does not recall the exact number."[6]

In a statement taken by the FBI of Mrs. Muchmore, the same day as they interviewed Miss Bond, "Mrs. Muchmore stated that after the car turned on Elm Street from Houston Street, she heard a loud noise which at first she thought was a firecracker, but then with the crowd of people running in all directions and hearing the two further noises sounding like gunfire, she advised that she began to run to find a place to hide.

She related that she panicked and does not recall the setting on the camera or what she did after learning that the noise was gunshots."[7]

Muchmore had in fact filmed a little more than three seconds of the assassination scene on Elm Street, including the moment of the fatal head shot to President Kennedy. This brief but important sequence appears to have been made with the camera on its telephoto setting. It is quite erratic, with a number of individual frames extremely blurry. The first frame is virtually unidentifiable, while the second reveals the limousine visible in the frame as far as its rear wheel, Mrs. Kennedy seen on the extreme right. An unidentified woman filming close to Elm Street, generally referred to as the "Babushka Lady" for the scarf that she was wearing on her head, is at camera left. By frame #12 the full vehicle is visible and as Muchmore pans left, the backs of spectators Charles Brehm and his son, the "Babushka Lady," Jean Hill in a red coat (frame #18) and Mary Moorman (frame #26) taking a Polaroid photograph herself, are observed on the near side of the road. On the opposite side of the street and facing Muchmore are the four members of the Bill Newman family (frame #23 being the last showing them). On the northern knoll stairs three men are observed beginning at frame #22, with the man in the reddish shirt reacting in panic to the shooting at frame #49. At frame #24 a motorcycle cop is in view at right, while Secret Service Agent Clint Hill is also observed beginning at frame #41 and seen running from the follow-up car at frame #45, reaching the President's car at frame #56.[8]

A frame from the Muchmore film showing the assassination scene on Elm Street

According to her later interview by the FBI, Muchmore, ". . . said she panicked after this shot and ran back to the office, later becoming deathly sick over the incident when learning of the President's death."[9] "She related that the incident upset her so much that she had to take sick leave for the next four days."[10]

In a 1975 article concerning United Press International's dealings with the Orville Nix film, author Maurice Schonfeld wrote that Mrs. Muchmore visited the Dallas UPI office on November 25 with her roll of film as yet undeveloped. Burt Reinhardt, the UPI News Film general manager, was in Dallas from New York for the purpose of obtaining possible films for UPI. When told by an employee that a woman was in the building professing to have movies of Dealey Plaza at the time of the assassination, Reinhardt, probably only half kidding, told the desk man, "Lock the door."[11]

Enthusiastically welcoming Mrs. Muchmore, the UPI executive indicated an interest in the film and offered to develop it and see its content and then to make an offer to purchase it. Or, if Mrs. Muchmore preferred, he would make a $1,000 offer to purchase it sight unseen. As Mrs. Muchmore still appeared not sure of just what she had filmed, or if it were exposed properly and in focus, she agreed to the $1,000 offer.[12]

Following its development at the Eastman Kodak lab in Dallas, the film was sent to New York City. Those who examined it found the film to have some fair pre-assassination scenes of the motorcade, and a short, jerky snippet of the assassination. This portion of the film transpired so quickly as to be difficult to follow or to comprehend. The most highly visible use to which this film was made by UPI was in the early 1964 souvenir book *Four Days*, co-produced by UPI and *American Heritage*. Unattributed as to the creator, the text described, "These startling pictures, taken from an 8mm color film, show the brief terrible moments that shook the world." Three pages were devoted to a single frame each from the Muchmore film. Bordered in black and reproduced in color in the predominantly black-and-white photo picture book, these large scale frames were dramatic in both layout and content. The only credit source mentioned concerning these was that they were from UPI news film.[13]

Thousands of readers saw these pictures in this book for the first time. It was evident that the position of the cameraman was across the street from the position of Abraham Zapruder, whose film *LIFE* magazine had acquired and utilized. One group of people who took a keen interest in these newly printed color pictures was the FBI. On February 10, 1964, the Bureau contacted UPI about the pictures and were informed that they were taken by Marie Muchmore, and that the stills used in the book were the result of a ". . .special finished film product . . . far more revealing than is the original film." UPI's Reinhardt offered to make copies available to the Bureau.[14]

Muchmore had actually been interviewed by the FBI previously. The week following the assassination was Thanksgiving Day, and Mrs. Muchmore had visited her family in Oklahoma. While there she told them of her experiences and through a family member the FBI was notified. In early December 1963, an agent spoke with Mrs. Muchmore and issued a brief two-paragraph report. Whether Muchmore was playing coy or her story was misunderstood, the report, while mentioning she had a movie camera with her at the time, indicated she herself, "did not get any pictures of the assassination." It seems that the interviewer, Special Agent Robert Basham, did not follow up on the film's content. A December 19 FBI listing of photos and films of the assassination only describes hers as "moving pictures; original in her possession."[15]

Here it was that the supposedly premier investigative agency in the country had blown such potentially important visual evidence, only to stumble upon it in a souvenir publication put out by a major news gathering source. The facts of the foul-up must have reverberated through several layers of FBI bureaucracy. Internal FBI paperwork is devoid of any embarrassing mention that Muchmore had been contacted earlier. The Dallas office was instructed to, "immediately interview Marie Muchmore and obtain her camera for examination by the laboratory."[16]

In mid-February activity was quickly re-generated on the Muchmore matter. Mrs. Muchmore was interviewed. The resulting report added only slight information to her December description, including that she took approximately four or five feet of film as the motorcade passed her, and that she only heard three shots, though she knew not from what direction. Nothing was mentioned concerning her three seconds worth of assassination film or her description of it. The camera she used was voluntarily given over to the FBI for their examination, though she specifically requested its return after completion of the examination.[17]

Meanwhile the Bureau was pursuing a copy of the film itself. In a memorandum on February 18, W.D. Griffith mentions that the existence of the film previous to seeing frames from it in the souvenir booklet had not been ". . . brought to our attention." There had obviously been a snafu and lack of communication and follow-up on the part of the field agents. UPI sent a 16mm copy of the film to the Bureau, but declined to make available the original. Following other contacts, the FBI accepted for their investigation, ". . . an exact copy of the original 8mm film in lieu of the original." While making the film available for viewing to the Warren Commission, it was the FBI's opinion that, ". . . aside from assisting in pinpointing the third shot, the film is of little additional value."[18]

Upon examination of Muchmore's Keystone camera, it was determined by the FBI laboratory that when fully wound, the camera would expose some 35 seconds of film at an average speed of 18.5 frames per second.[19] The examination of the UPI copies of the film found 66 frames had been made at the time of the assassination with an elapsed time of approximately 3 seconds. "The third shot is recorded in the forty-second frame of this sequence."[20]

By early March Mrs. Muchmore was becoming concerned over the return of her camera, as she had promised it to her brother for his use on a trip to Europe in mid-April. A month later, following several contacts to the FBI, Mrs. Muchmore was obviously put out by the camera's not being returned. An FBI report concerning the matter stated, ". . . that she could not understand why the President's Commission needed her camera for the period of time they have had same. . . ." She also mentioned that she might ask Texas Congressman Bruce Alger, a close personal friend, to check into the matter. With vacation time fast approaching, on April 7 Mrs. Muchmore called the FBI to say that a similar camera had been rented from W. H. Parr at Glendale Camera Shop for a period of seven weeks. The Warren Commission would cover the rental fee, Mrs. Muchmore was told.[21]

Muchmore's camera, along with those of Orville Nix and Abraham Zapruder, were used by the Commission during a May re-enactment at Dealey Plaza conducted chiefly by the FBI. The cameras were positioned in their November 22 locations and film was exposed through them of at least one of the ride-through re-enactments. On June 2 Special Agent Ivan Lee personally returned Muchmore's camera to her.[22]

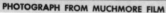

PHOTOGRAPH FROM MUCHMORE FILM

PHOTOGRAPH FROM RE-ENACTMENT

Muchmore frame #42 which coincides with Zapruder frame #Z313 at the time President Kennedy was hit in the head. At right a photo made during the May 1964 reenactment replicating Muchmore's location and frame #42.

The original film was retained by UPI, never having been examined by the FBI or Warren Commission. Muchmore was not a witness before the Warren Commission, nor were any of her statements as recorded by the FBI included within the 26 volumes of hearings. The only material relating to her is in testimony by FBI photo expert Lyndal L. Shaneyfelt when he exhibited the three amateur assassination films for the Commission. A map indicating Muchmore's location during the filming of the assassination scene was included in one of the *Hearing*'s volumes, as were a sampling of three of her movie frames — #19, #42, and #55.[23]

While most researchers would concede that Muchmore's experiences and recall of the assassination events, as gathered by the government, were pitifully sparse; the record of Wilma Bond's recollections, as gathered by the government, are virtually non-existent. Except for her FBI interview taken on February 14, 1964, after her existence was apparently made known to the FBI by Marie Muchmore, no other record of her has been found to exist in the Warren Commission papers or FBI files of 1963 or 1964. She is not mentioned anywhere within the *Warren Commission Report* or the 26 volumes of hearings. Though agents looked over her slides made on November 22, no copies were apparently requested, as the agents were only interested if pictures included the Texas School Book Depository.

It would be the media and assassination buffs who would eventually take an interest to locate Bond and more critically examine her slides. When non-published Commission documents were subsequently released to public access, the Bond interview of February 1974 was located by several researchers. *LIFE* magazine, in a November

1967 issue featuring amateur photos made by nine by-standers, published near full-frame color views of three of the Bond post-assassination photos. Almost concurrently, the *Saturday Evening Post* excerpted portions of Josiah Thompson's new book *Six Seconds in Dallas*, and included two of the color pictures reproduced in *LIFE*, though cropped at the sides.[24]

At the time of the shooting, Miss Bond had moved over to the concrete wall facing the grass infield and overlooking Elm Street at the same position as Mrs. Muchmore. Though Muchmore did take a sequence of the President's car on Elm Street at the time of the assassination, and did not remember doing so, Bond said that due to the excitement, she made no photos of the shooting or of the presidential vehicle. Within 20 seconds of the last shot, however, she began to take a sequence of six photos at intervals of approximately 5 to 10 seconds each. She later wrote a researcher, ". . . When I once started snapping, I was consisted [sic, consistent] to the end of the parade." Bond later discovered that though she had stopped taking pictures when the camera meter read 20 exposures, she had previously loaded her camera with a 36-exposure roll, and not a 20-frame roll.[25]

Bond's first post-assassination photo

Bond's first transparency in the sequence of post-assassination pictures shows Elm Street with the grassy knoll, the stockade fence, the west concrete shelter and a section of the arching pergola. No automobiles are visible in the street, though two 2-wheeled motorcycles are in frame left. At extreme left, Hollis B. McLain, who rode in the motorcade on the left side near the press cars, had, upon hearing shots, revved up his engine. He attempted to catch up to the fast-departing vehicles at the head of the column, now speeding their way on to Parkland Hospital. Also astride his Harley-Davidson cycle was Officer J. W. Courson originally located at the left side near the first motorcade bus. Catching up to McLain, Courson followed the presidential party to the hospital.

In the middle of the street, Robert Weldon "Bobby" Hargis is seen just returning to his parked cycle. One of four of the police cycle escorts just behind and astride the presidential Lincoln, Hargis was riding on the left inside position. He later gave an account of his actions at the time that the President was shot in the head.

> . . . I felt blood hit me in the face, and the presidential car stopped immediately after that and stayed stopped about half a second, then took off at a high rate of speed. I racked my cycle and jumped off. I ran to the north side of Elm Street looking to see if I could find where the bullets came from. I don't think the President got hit with the first shot, but that I don't know for sure. When I heard the first shot, it looked like he bent over. I feel that the Governor was shot first. I could be wrong. Right after the first shot, I was trying to look and see if the President got shot. When I saw the look on Connally's face, I knew somebody was shooting at the car. . . . The fatal bullet struck the President in the right side of the head. I noticed the people in the Texas School Book Depository were looking up to see the top. I didn't know if the President stopped under the triple underpass or not. I didn't know for sure if the shots had come from the Book Depository. I thought they might have come from the trestle. I couldn't locate anyone who looked suspicious, so I waited a few seconds then ran back to my motorcycle and went to the triple underpass to see if I could see anyone, but I didn't observe anything.[26]

Among those seen in the background of this Bond slide and located on the north side of Elm Street are the Newman family lying on the ground and being filmed by NBC-TV cameraman Dave Wiegman and White House cameraman Tom Atkins. Associated Press's Jim Altgens, behind the Newmans, is walking up the knoll incline. On the steps at camera left are plaza groundskeeper Emmett Hudson and another man in a red shirt, both sitting on the steps. On the sidewalk curb at camera right a man in a cap, light shirt and dark pants also sits. On the near side of the street Charles Brehm and his son, and Jean Hill and Mary Moorman sit in shock, while the "Babushka Lady" in a long, light-colored coat and head scarf stands with camera poised near her chest and stares at the activity before her field of vision. In the immediate foreground a uniformed cop runs towards the street, while a black man in suit coat and hat wanders into the scene.[27]

In the second photo of this Bond Elm Street sequence, all taken at the same locale with minor shifts in pointing of the camera, the first of the three motorcade busses is in full view.  Carrying press representatives and marked with a large placard on its side reading "White House Press," the Continental Trailways bus includes as a passenger Fort Worth *Star Telegram* photographer Harry Cabluck.  Cabluck took three pictures at about this same time from the right side of the bus which, as in the Bond slide, showed several kids running down the incline from the pergola area.  At the upper left of the Bond slide, cycle officer Clyde A. Haygood is seen running up the knoll incline towards the north corner of the overpass.

The first press bus coasts down Elm Street

Haygood, an eight year veteran of the Dallas Police Department, was a solo motorcycle officer in the presidential escort riding near the first motorcade bus.  On Main Street, just approaching Houston, when he heard the first of three shots, "I made the shift down to lower gear and went on to the scene of the shooting. . . .  When I first got to the location there I was still on Houston Street, and in the process of making a left turn onto Elm Street I could see all these people laying on the ground there on Elm. Some of them were pointing back up to the railroad yard, and a couple of people were headed back up that way, and I immediately tried to jump the north curb there in the 400 block which was too high for me to get over. . . .  And I left my motor on the street and ran to the railroad yard."[28]

On Elm Street in front of the bus is a wood panel 1964 Mercury Colony Park station wagon.  In it were traveling presidential military aides, Army Major General Chester V. Clifton and Air Force Major General Godfrey McHugh.  On the south side of Elm Street, facing towards the bus, which is just passing his position, cameraman Jimmy Darnell of WBAP-TV, who had jumped out of Camera Car 3 just following the shooting, takes movie film of the scene.  To Darnell's left in a long dark coat and white pants, Mary Moorman, now back on her feet, is looking westerly down Elm Street, her Polaroid camera seemingly visible in her left hand.  From the right, the beginning of an influx of spectators pours into the area.[29]

Seconds later Bond clicks off another shot as the first bus approaches the underpass.  A sedan carrying *Morning News* reporters, which had unofficially managed to squeeze into the motorcade between two busses, is in the camera's view.  The Newman family at frame right, has gotten up from the ground.  The major movement

Bond photo #6

Bond photo #7

in this slide, however, is the rush of many spectators across Elm Street and up the knoll following Haygood, who is climbing upon the underpass abutment in the background. Some ten men are running up the hill, while others still are in the street or on the south side, heading in that direction. UPI photographer Frank Cancellare is on the south side sidewalk just west of the Fort Worth road sign.[30]

In the next Bond photo people are still seen running towards the police officer. In the street the second press bus has reached this position with a motorcycle officer, most likely Sergeant R. Smart, alongside the bus as it proceeds towards the underpass.

Bond photo #8

Within about six seconds Bond takes her eighth photo. Some people are now running in the direction of the steps leading up to the pergola. Bill Newman has his arm wrapped around the shoulder of his wife Gail; the so-called "umbrella man" is seen on the right of the frame with his umbrella closed, he looking to the east. On the Bond side of the street, Jean Hill, Mary Moorman, and the "Babushka Lady" stand, seeming to be looking across the street. A Chevy hardtop is at frame left, followed by a black 1957 Ford hardtop Western Union car. This car has distinct tail fins and a light colored sign attached to the driver's door. It is obviously moving due to its blurry shape in relation to other fixed objects. Within several seconds of this, Bond takes her ninth photo, which shows the third bus carrying the official party of White House, vice-presidential, and governor's staff members, appearing from the right. The "umbrella man," clasping the folded umbrella staff in his hand, now has turned and is looking to the west. Spectators continue to wander the area. Believing her roll of film to be used up, Bond takes no more photos.[31]

Bond photo #9

With the exception of the single February 18, 1964, FBI interview, Bond was not contacted by anyone else in authority. Though shy herself of publicity, Bond allowed her slides to be seen and published. In 1969, during the Clay Shaw trial in New Orleans, District Attorney Jim Garrison's prosecution team called her as a witness, thereby putting two of her pictures into the trial record along with the implication that the federal government had attempted to suppress them. In her testimony Bond recalled hearing three shots which sounded like firecrackers. She also recalled seeing people, "running toward the grassy knoll." On cross-examination she stated that the sounds she heard came from her right, which she acknowledged was the same general area as the Texas School Book Depository.[32]

In 1975 and 1976 architect and assassination researcher Robert B. Cutler contacted Bond regarding his research on the "umbrella man," who he contended was, "along with a dark complected man standing next to him, a participant in the assassination conspiracy." Bond made available to Cutler first-generation copies of her slides, which Cutler used in his book *Seventy-Six Seconds in Dealey Plaza*, along with accurate and attractive plans showing the camera's line of sight, to further outline and develop his theory. Bond wrote to Cutler that about a year earlier the advance mechanism on her 35mm camera had broken, and the repair was too expensive for her to make. Her original slides were kept in a downtown Dallas bank vault.[33]

Miss Bond died at the age of 58 on January 8, 1980, at Baylor Hospital in Dallas. She was buried in her home state at the Garland Brook Cemetery in Columbus, Indiana. In the Dallas area she was survived by a sister and several nieces.[34]

## CHAPTER NOTES

1.     Report by SA Robert E. Basham, 12/4/1963; Report by SAs Robert M. Barrett & Ivan D. Lee of Mrs. Marie Muchmore, 2/18/1964, CD 735, p. 8; Airtel, To: Director, From: SAC, Dallas, #105-8255-3184, 4/7/1964, p. 1; For: Mr. Conrad, From: W.D. Griffith, Reenactment of film, 6/10/1964, all obtained by Trask through FOIA request #266,202, 1/1986.

2.     Report by Barrett & Lee, of Miss Wilma Bond, 2/18/1964, CD 735, p. 7, obtained by Trask through FOIA request #266,201, 1/1986; Dallas Health Department Certificate of Death,

Wilma I. Bond, File #238, Recorded 1/9/1980; Letter, Wilma Bond to Robert B. Cutler, 7/6/1976.

3.    National Archives copy of the Marie Muchmore film, 11/22/1963.

4.    First generation copy of Wilma Bond transparency #1, 11/22/1963; Muchmore film, op. cit.

5.    Bond transparency #2 & 3, op. cit.

6.    Report by Barrett & Lee of Bond, op. cit.

7.    Report by Barrett & Lee of Muchmore, op. cit.

8.    Muchmore film, op. cit. The specific number of frames taken by Muchmore in the sequence is a matter of contention. Several sources and an examination of other copies of the film count 59 and 61 frames respectively, with several splices evident. One report by the FBI Laboratory indicates the sequence to consist of 66 frames, though it agrees with other sources that the result of the head shot is recorded at frame #42.

9.    Report by Basham, op. cit.

10.    Report by Barrett & Lee of Muchmore, op. cit.

11.    Maurice W. Schonfeld, "The Shadow of a Gunman," *Columbia Journalism Review*, p.46.

12.    Ibid.

13.    United Press International and American Heritage, *Four Days, The Historical Record of the Death of President Kennedy*, p. [16-17] 20 [144].

14.    Memorandum, To: Mr. Mohr, From: C. D. DeLoach, #62-109060-2472, 2/11/1964, through FOIA request #266,202, op. cit.

15.    Report by Basham, op. cit.

16.    Teletype, To: SAC, Dallas, From: Director, FBI, #62-109060-2436, 2/13/1964, through FOIA request #266,202, op. cit.

17.    Report by Barrett & Lee of Muchmore, op. cit.; Memorandum, To: Director, FBI, From: SAC, Dallas, #105-8255-2153, 2/14/1964; Teletype, To: Director, From: Dallas, #62-109060-2461, 2/14/1964, through FOIA request #266,202, op. cit.

18.    Memorandum, To: Mr. Conrad, From: W.D.Griffith, #62-109060-2468, through FOIA request, Ibid.

19.    To: FBI, Dallas, [From:] FBI Laboratory, Washington, 2/26/1964, through FOIA request, Ibid.

20.    Report by SA Robert P. Gemberling #[?]-2579, 3/10/1964, through FOIA request, Ibid.

21.    Airtel, To: Director, FBI, From: SAC, Dallas, #105-82555-3184, 4/7/1964, through FOIA request, Ibid.

22.    Airtel, To: Director, FBI, From: SAC, Dallas, #62-109060-3201, 6/3/1964, through FOIA request, Ibid.

23.    *Hearings Before the President's Commission on the Assassination of President Kennedy*, v. 5, p. 137, 140-141, 159-160, 177; v. 17, p. 901; v. 18, p. 84-85, 95.

24.    *LIFE*, 11/24/1967, p. 3, 94-95; *Saturday Evening Post*, 12/2/1967, p. 28-29.

25.    Letter, Bond to Cutler, op. cit.

26.    From undated typescript copy of interview with B.W. Hargis within photograph collection of the *Dallas Times Herald*, Belo Corp.

27.    Bond transparency #4, op. cit.

28.    *Hearings*, v. 6, p. 297-298.

29.    Bond transparency #5, op. cit.

30.    Bond transparency #6, Ibid.

31.    Bond transparency #7-9, Ibid.

32.    Teletype, To: Director, From: New Orleans, #62-109060-6746, 2/15/1969, through FOIA request #266, 201, op. cit.

33.    R. B. Cutler, *Seventy-Six Seconds in Dealey Plaza*, p.69, 79, 87, 89, 93, 95, 97; Letter, Bond to Cutler, op. cit.; Letter, Cutler to Bond, 8/10/1975; Note, Bond to Cutler [7/1976].

34.    Death certificate, op. cit.; *Dallas Morning News*, 1/8/1980, p. 5D.

## CHAPTER 8

# The Bobby Soxer and Her Dad

Tina Towner was a typical young teenager who enjoyed the company of school girlfriends, was becoming interested in boys and not at all thrilled with junior high school. Like tens of thousands before and after her, this thirteen-year-old would occasionally feel ill enough at school to request to go home. In later years Tina would concede that these bouts with sickness during school hours were mostly psychosomatic and tending to occur when a test or other adolescent pressures made absence more attractive than being around an unpleasant situation.

Tina lived with her parents in the Oak Cliff area of Dallas just northeast of Red Bird Airport. Her dad, James M. Towner, was a civil engineer. When Mr. Towner learned of the impending visit and motorcade of President Kennedy to Dallas, he asked his wife and daughter if they would like to go into town to see the excitement, as such a rare event was one not to be missed. Tina had little interest in politics, though when she learned that her father would allow her to miss school for the motorcade, as Tina would later recall, "Those were the magic words."

On November 22 Tina wore a light colored blouse, dark skirt, and her ever present white bobby socks to school, also carrying a light blue sweater as a guard against the fall chill. She also had with her a note from her mother requesting that she be excused from school at ten o'clock. Though excited to be missing much of the school day, Tina was nervous about being questioned over the appropriateness of such an excuse. She soon learned, however, that many other kids were getting out of school for the same purpose, and that the school considered this event worthy of an excused absence. It was then she realized that the President's visit was a really big deal, and she became caught up in the excitement felt by her parents and other adults.[1]

Jim was enthused about seeing the President and brought two cameras to record the event. He would use his own 35mm camera to take slides of the motorcade. As Tina had some experience using the family's 8mm movie camera, her father let her handle taking the movies, getting her into the flow of the event by assigning her some responsibility. Unfortunately the meter which indicated the number of unexposed feet left in the movie camera was broken. Not knowing how much remaining film was left on the spool, Mr. Towner cautioned his daughter not to waste film before the President's arrival.

Jim decided the best place to get a good view of the motorcade would likely be near its end, and after picking his daughter up at school, the family of three drove down by the Union Railway Terminal. After parking the car, the Towners walked through the busy terminal, the bustle of which Tina always enjoyed. They walked the four blocks north to the southwest corner of Elm and Houston Streets, directly across from the Texas School Book Depository, arriving there around eleven o'clock.

Now all they could do was wait, and to a young, squirmy teenager with nothing do to, waiting was interminable. Every few minutes Tina would ask the time and quiz her father about when the President was going to arrive. Temporarily escaping his questioning daughter, Jim walked down Elm Street searching out any better viewing sites. Feeling a little sickly, Tina rested a while on a folding stool her father had brought along, and sat in the shade of a tree in the area by the north reflecting pool. Jim returned to tell the women that he had found a better viewing location closer to the triple underpass. But the two women wouldn't budge from their corner position, and Jim, seeing he was hopelessly outnumbered, settled in to wait with them.[2]

Several times Jim directed his family's attention to all the people looking out of the windows of the buildings around them including several in the Book Depository Building, commenting how these spectators had a real bird's eye view. To break the monotony Tina on several occasions walked across Elm Street to the front of the Book Depository Building. All three noticed the commotion on the east corner of Houston and Elm Streets when someone in the crowd collapsed from what they guessed to be a seizure or fainting spell. Shortly an ambulance with sirens wailing arrived and then quickly departed with the stricken spectator.[3]

Finally, real excitement! Tina and her parents heard the spectator commotion building to their right and rear as the police escort cars and motorcycles turned into Houston from Main Street. Jim repeated advice he had given many times before to his daughter on how to hold the camera while filming. Within moments the family's boredom dissipated in the excitement of seeing the President and First Lady. The Towners were now standing in the street. They were several feet from the corner's long bending curb which ran from Houston into Elm Street. Jim had seen that this position would give them a longer view than simply a position on a straightaway. Raising camera to eye, Jim made a color transparency as the long, sleek presidential Lincoln began its wide arc turn. Following the movement of the car with his camera, Towner captured all six occupants in fairly good focus. The three men on the passenger side of the car are looking towards their right with President Kennedy's full profile in view. Driver Greer, Mrs. Connally and Mrs. Kennedy look to their left. Mrs. Kennedy is smiling and glancing straight at the Towners, whose distorted shapes can be just recognized in the shining reflection of the car's highly polished side body. In the background looms the Dal-Tex Building and at street level there are over two dozen spectators whose forms are horizontally misshapen due to Jim's panning his camera along with the movement of the car. At the east corner of Elm Street a trailer truck and a van can be seen over the heads of the spectators, stopped at the intersection while the motorcade passes.[4]

To her father's right and a half-step in front, Tina has the movie camera to her eye. "As soon as the front of the limousine came into view from behind the crowd, I began shooting the film. . . . What I remember most was Jackie Kennedy's beautiful, beaming face. She was so gorgeous with the brightest, happiest look in her eyes. . . . Her hair was blowing in the wind and the whole feeling she conveyed was framed by her pink suit ensemble. What's more, she was looking at me — no one else, just me."[5]

Tina had begun filming when the car was just beginning its turn, and in her earliest frames the Dallas County Records Building is in the background. She continued to pan left as the car traveled around the corner. Her film includes the front entrance of the building across the street with a sign over the entrance reading, "Texas School Book Depository," and as the car travels away from her down Elm Street first cycle officer Martin and then cycle officer Hargis momentarily break the view of the limousine. Her film sequence lasts approximately 11¼ seconds and includes some 200 8mm frames.[6]

Mrs. Kennedy in front of the
School Book Depository entrance

While Tina continued to film, Jim began quickly walking down Elm Street to try to get another picture. Just after she stopped filming, Tina would later relate, "Now I was beginning to leave when I heard the sky fall in — the loudest crack of a rifle I had ever heard! At that time I had the least notion that it was a gun. The truth of the matter was that I thought it was a fire cracker." She commented to no one in particular, "Some dummy is lighting fireworks!" Hearing another boom she, ". . . looked around to see where they were coming from. Finally, the third and last boom and, with that one, I turned to look at the School Book Depository Building to see who was throwing fireworks out the window. I didn't see anything, though I was fairly sure that was where they were coming from. As I looked up, some man with his wife and children grabbed my arm and pulled me down beside a small wall."[7]

Jim Towner had rushed a number of yards further down Elm Street. Somewhere along the way he became aware that the noise was caused by a high-powered rifle. As the presidential, vice-presidential, and follow-up vehicles had quickly departed, he now took a picture of the activity further down Elm Street. Several occupants of the convertible Camera Car 1 had bolted out of the car and ran down to the opposite side of the street. Towner's photograph shows the back of three men in the foreground gazing down the street, while further down Towner's side of the road a uniformed police officer is kneeling with his service revolver drawn. Closer to the underpass police officer

Clyde Haygood is turning his cycle into the north curb of Elm Street, while closer to Towner's position Camera Cars 1 and 2 are in view. In the second camera car White House Photographer Cecil Stoughton is seated partially on top of the back door and seat of the convertible. On the north side of the street a cluster of cameramen are encircling the Newman family who are lying prone on the ground. UPI's Frank Cancellare is observed running down the slope toward them. A couple, Mr. and Mrs. Hester, are in the north pergola area and what may be Abraham Zapruder's shape can be discerned inside the concrete shelter.[8]

Jim Towner's view on Elm Street showing Camera Cars 1 and 2

Several minutes later Towner walked further down Elm Street and took his third photo of the day. Officer Haygood's cycle is now parked at the curb as he, with civilians trailing behind, ran to the north abutment wall of the triple underpass. The Newman family, partly obscured by a light pole, are now standing up. Meanwhile a darkly complected man wearing a cap and a light-colored jacket who following the shots had sat next to a man who carried an umbrella, appears to be walking slowly down the street. He has his hands in his back pockets. A bus, the second of the motorcade, has just entered the underpass and someone near the concrete shelter looks to be gazing over the fence in the direction of the parking lot. Seconds later spectator Wilma Bond took the ninth slide in her series, which allows us to establish the time sequence for the Towner pictures.

Returning to his family, Towner told them that someone must have tried to shoot the President. Crowds were now gathering in clusters and numerous police vehicles were arriving at the intersection of Elm and Houston Streets. Jim walked down to the opposite side of Elm Street where one large cluster of people were gathered near the steps leading to the knoll area and the north pergola. In the midst of this group a trembling Charles F. Brehm stood relating to no one in particular and almost incoherently what he had moments earlier seen from his vantage point on the infield grass area. He was telling those around him that the President definitely had been hit by a bullet. Towner took his last photo in the day's sequence of Brehm and the numerous other people around him. The photo is blurred and in the background is the triple underpass and part of a cement truck traveling down Elm. Traffic was incredibly re-opened shortly after the shooting. Towner then walked north to the parking area where rumors had it that that was the direction in which the assassin had run. Finding nothing but a lot of directionless people milling around, Towner returned to his wife and daughter.[10]

Tina took one additional film sequence some ten minutes after the shooting, panning right from the knoll area to the Texas School Book Depository. Unfortunately, upon later developing, it was found that her earlier film, as well as this sequence, was somewhat over-exposed, being darker than normal.[11] Tina, having experienced far more excitement and shock than she had bargained for, was beginning to feel nervous and shaky, and the three soon left the chaos behind. When they arrived at their car they turned the radio on for news. It was not until they arrived home and as Mrs. Towner was making sandwiches for a now late lunch, that the official news came over the home radio that the President had been shot and was now officially declared dead.

Towner later contacted *LIFE* magazine stringer Patsy Swank about his and his daughter's pictures, but they were not used until in 1967, when in *LIFE*'s issue containing an article on amateur photographers of the assassination, Jim's first and second photos were used as well as three frames of Tina's movie.[12]

Massachusetts architect and self-styled "assassinologist" Robert B. Cutler espoused a theory that one of the several assassins at Dealey Plaza on November 22 was the umbrella carrier who was positioned on the north side of Elm Street near the Stemmons road sign. According to Cutler's theory, this man had shot a self-propelled flechette from the open umbrella. Cutler's self-published volume, *The Umbrella Man*, was printed in 1975 and included highly detailed and accurate plats of the Dealey Plaza area, which he had researched and drawn up. Cutler attempted to find any and all photographic information that would show this man as well as another man who stood next to him. The second man, swarthy of complexion and wearing a cap, was believed by Cutler to be a possible accomplice. In 1976 Cutler made contact with a now married Tina Barnes and was able to acquire use of her father's photo #2, which showed both of these men sitting on the curb right after the shots. By the time Cutler published his 1978

TA

Blow-up and overlay sketch of a man in Jim Towner's third photo

book, *Seventy-six Seconds in Dealey Plaza*, he had also obtained the Towner photo #3. This was the first publication of the photo. The "umbrella man" is just visible walking down the street towards the underpass, while "the accomplice" is seen on the north sidewalk, closer up to the photographer's position. This man, sporting a cap and wearing a light-colored jacket, has his hands at his back pockets, and seems to be slowly walking down the street away from Towner. At Cutler's request, Boston photographer George M. Cushing and fellow assassination researcher and photo technician Jack White made extreme blow-ups of these two men from the Towner and other amateur photos, including Wilma Bond's series and a photo taken by Richard Bothun. In both a Bond slide and the Towner photo Cutler believed he could see a piece of equipment visible in "the accomplice's" back side. According to Cutler, "Jack White's blow-up of TA [the accomplice] clearly shows the working part of the light-colored w-t [walkie-talkie] equipment protruding and being steadied in his pants rear pocket, as the accomplice hurries off down Elm towards the safety of oblivion." An overlay sketch of the blow-up outlining the equipment was also provided by Jack White and printed in Cutler's book so that those who had difficulty seeing or imagining this equipment would be given assistance.[13]

Cutler's theory is one of the more imaginative of those of the critics, and prior to the probable identification of the umbrella man in 1978, it gave a possible explanation to the enigma of an open umbrella during the sunny presidential motorcade. Though some believed Cutler's Flechette explanation too "James Bond-ish," Cutler found evidence of similar devices which were later admitted to by the CIA. Cutler's theory, particularly after the hearings of the House Select Committee on Assassinations found little universal appeal by other assassination researchers, however.

Neither the Towner family, nor their pictures, were examined during the Warren Commission investigation, and the films were not considered to have been taken late enough to be of assistance in the House Select Committee on Assassinations investigation. In the 1970s, Tina Towner became Mrs. James R. Barnes and her family remains in possession of both the transparencies and the movie.

## CHAPTER NOTES

1.  Tina Towner, "View From the Corner," *Teen*, 6/1968, p. 46-47; "Last Seconds of the Motorcade," *LIFE*, 11/24/1967, p. 3.

2.  *Teen*, op. cit., p. 48.

3.  Ibid.; *LIFE*, op. cit., p. 90.

4.  James M. Towner photograph #1, 11/22/1963.

5.  *Teen*, op. cit., p.49.

6.  Tina Towner 8mm film, 11/22/1963. In Hugh Betzner's second black & white photo made of the President's vehicle, it includes in the foreground the backsides of all three Towners as they look towards the President. Tina is obviously in the process of filming the scene in front of her. From a fourth floor window of the Texas School Book Depository Building Elsie Dorman, filming with her husband's camera, also records the Towners in the street below, Tina with camera pointed and shooting.

7.  *Teen*, op. cit., p. 49; *LIFE*, op. cit., p. 91.

8.  James M. Towner photograph #2, 11/22/1963.

9.  Ibid., photograph #3.

10. Ibid., photograph #4; Letter, Mrs. James R. Barnes [Tina Towner] to R. B. Cutler, 6/14/1976; *Teen*, op. cit., p. 90.

11. Letter, Tina Barnes to R. B. Cutler, 8/26/1976; Letter, Ken _____ to R. B. Cutler, 9/13/1976.

12. *LIFE*, op. cit., p. 3, 90, 91, 94.

13. Correspondence file of R. B. Cutler relating to Tina Barnes, 1976; R. B. Cutler, *Seventy-Six Seconds in Dealey Plaza*, p. 62-63, 80-81, 90-91, 100-101. Further information on the identification and actions of the "Umbrella Man" may be found in Chapter 5.

## CHAPTER 9

# The Missionary

While most of the amateur photographers who took up positions in Dealey Plaza wanting to snap pictures of President and Mrs. Kennedy lived in the greater Dallas area, one of the photographers was there purely by traveler's happenstance. Robert Earl Croft was a twenty-year-old missionary for the Salt Lake City, Utah, based Church of Jesus Christ of Latter Day Saints. He was traveling alone on his way to Denver, Colorado, following a missionary assignment in Little Rock, Arkansas. Croft was in Dallas awaiting an early afternoon train connection leaving from the Union Railway Terminal located off Houston Street only a few blocks away from Dealey Plaza. He had never before been in Dallas, didn't know a soul in the city, and was only waiting for his train connection.

Almost twenty-five years after that Friday in November of 1963, Croft recalled that upon arrival at the station, "I didn't have any idea that anything was even going on. I just happened to walk down to the Plaza because I heard some of the people in the train station talk about the presidential motorcade. And I went down there and watched it and then hustled back to get on the train."[1] Croft had decided that he might have just enough time to snag a view of a President of the United States, and get back to the station to make his connection. He secured his belongings in a storage check at the station except for his camera which he took with him. Croft had with him an Argus C3 35-mm camera loaded with a roll of 36 exposure Kodachrome-X daylight color slide film, of which 16 exposures had already been taken.[2] Croft recalls that, "I never had a camera in my life until I bought this camera at a second-hand store just before I went out into the mission field. It was the old original Argus C3." The camera did not have a built-in light meter, and Croft would "just eyeball it" when taking pictures.[3]

At around 12 noon the young missionary made his way northerly up Houston Street from the Union Railway Terminal to the major intersection of Houston and Main Street. The west side of the intersection of Main Street had been closed off to traffic, and a fast-growing crowd of spectators was strung across the street, peering up toward the eastern direction of Main Street, looking for signs of the procession. Croft found a spot in the street near the northwest curb corner of Main Street. Near his location, other amateur photographers who had also seen the viewing advantage of this spot, had also gathered, including Dallasites Phil Willis, Richard O. Bothun, and Wilma Bond.

Also very close to Croft's position was Dallas Associated Press photographer Jim Altgens, who had come here to get a shot of the motorcade for possible use by AP.[4]

Shortly after 12:20 Croft and the others around him could see the motorcade in the far distance preceded by a phalanx of five motorcycles. They could also hear the outbreak of applause and cheers descending slowly down the street at a pace with the vehicles. Not knowing the order of the motorcade, Croft took his first slide view of the activity as a couple of the lead cycles were approaching his position at Main Street. Near the corner of Main Street, the five lead cycles had broken up with three remaining with the motorcade while two rode off to get ahead and cover the Stemmons Freeway traffic lanes. The first Croft photo shows one of the lead cycles beginning a right turn onto Houston Street followed by a second cycle somewhat obscured by the deep shadows of the old County Courts Building at the left. As spectators lean out onto the street to see the approaching motorcade, the white lead Ford sedan, driven by Police Chief Jesse Curry, is discernible with its two red lights on the front grill brightly shining. Behind the Ford one can just make out some other features of the motorcade, including Secret Service agents standing on the running board of the presidential follow-up car located behind the President's vehicle.[5]

Lead cycles approaching Houston Street

Seeing that there were still a few moments before the President would arrive at Croft's corner, he wound his camera, and waited for a clear view. The sleek Lincoln Continental approached the corner and took a sweeping right turn, revealing the occupants to Croft and his camera. At just about the same instant both Croft and AP's Jim Altgens took a photograph of the vehicle. Altgens, located some few feet to the right of Croft, was using a 105-mm lens to capture the occupants of the car while Croft, using a 50-mm lens, took in more of the scene. A comparison of the two photos shows the spectators located on the other side of the car at almost the exact instant of time. In Altgens's view, however, a woman appears to be snapping a photograph while in Croft's she has lowered her camera from her face. The slight difference in the angle between the two photos also reveals a man who in the Croft shot is also taking a picture, while in Altgens's this man is partially hidden by the car visor. Smiling broadly, the President is looking in Croft's direction, as is Mrs. Connally, while the Governor is waving his left hand. Mrs. Kennedy is trying to steady her pink pillbox hat against the effects of a cross street breeze.[6]

Croft takes his second photo as the limousine turns from Main to Houston Street

As the President's vehicle passes Croft's position, Croft "just kind of followed the car along, as I remember, on the left hand side of the car." He quickly walks to the north along the Plaza's north reflecting pool and takes up a position near the south curb of Elm Street about 190 feet from his original location. Dressed in a dark suit and hat, Croft is just some six feet to the left of picture taker Phil Willis, who also scrambled to this position from the corner of Houston and Main Street. From across the street, Dallas businessman Abraham Zapruder is filming the motorcade with his 8-mm camera, and from an examination of his film sequence, Croft can be seen aiming his camera to take a picture as the President's vehicle again passes him.

Whereas in his previous photo, the First Lady's face was obscured by her hand and arm, in this third Croft photograph taken only about 15 feet from the car, Mrs. Kennedy appears to be looking right at Croft. The President is looking straight ahead, and Mrs. Connally's bouquet of yellow roses can be seen in the photo, Croft being slightly elevated over his subjects. The picture includes three glare spots where the bright noon sunshine reflects off the car's chrome. Across Elm Street a group of over a dozen spectators line the curb smiling and applauding, while in the background adjacent to the walkway which leads to the concrete shelter and pergola, four others sit on the wall and wave. In the far background a truck and several cars are parked along the dirt Elm Street Extension, located adjacent to the Texas School Book Depository Building, while even further back are railroad passenger cars parked on a spur-track.[7]

Croft's third picture, taken from the south curb of Elm Street

Quickly winding his camera, Croft takes another picture of the vehicle as it passes by his position. As he makes this fourth photo, he hears a shot, and believes that this picture was "taken simultaneously with the shot which killed the President."[8]

Following the shots, pandemonium broke out all around the Plaza. People ran from place to place with little sense of direction, as the remainder of the motorcade continued down Elm Street. Speaking of the events a quarter of a century later Croft explains, "I can't tell you at this point anything about the shots, numbers, or where they were. I was on my way back, as I remember, before the car ever got — it was kind of going down a hill and under a railroad track. And I noticed what time it was and took off, because I was going to be late for the train. I kind of jogged back to the station and got my baggage out of check and took off."[9] Croft then boarded his train and, leaving Dallas behind, was on his way back to Denver.

The morning of Saturday, November 23, found Croft at the Western States Mission Home on Clarkston Street in Denver when at 10 a.m. the mission president told him that two FBI agents were downstairs and that Croft needed to go talk with them. Croft recalls: "Concerning the weekend events I have almost no recollection of the details. That's why I say I really don't know how they came up with what they did so fast. They put things together awful quick. We went through this interrogation back and forth for I don't know how long. I got tired of it I know." Croft is now unsure of how the FBI knew about what he had witnessed at Dallas since he did not contact the agency, and does not recall speaking with anyone at Dealey Plaza following the shooting.

Perhaps someone in Denver or on the train made the contact. An unsigned typed note on an FBI report dated at Denver on December 3 states that Croft ". . . voluntarily appeared at our Denver office on 11/23/63, and was interviewed and furnished undeveloped 35 mm film which he had taken on 11/22/63."[10]

The FBI contact report itself of the November 23 interview relates that Croft brought with him the undeveloped film from his camera and explained to the agent-in-charge that he had taken four pictures of the presidential motorcade in Dallas. The report further states that Croft said he believed his last picture was taken simultaneously with the shot that killed the President. Mr. Croft allowed the FBI to borrow and develop the film. In keeping with his wishes, it was reported to the FBI in Washington that: ". . . all photos except those which may have evidentiary value are to be returned to Denver so that they may be returned to Croft. Photos of possible evidentiary value may be retained until completion of prosecution at which time they must be returned to Croft without any duplicates or copies having been made."[11] That same day the Denver office sent the undeveloped roll of film via registered air mail to the FBI lab in Washington.

The roll of Kodachrome-X transparency film received in Washington was apparently not able to be developed at the FBI lab. It was sent to be processed at a local commercial Kodak laboratory. In the FBI's December 3 report an explanation was given of how the processed slides came back. "Twenty-two frames were developed and only three frames, number 16, 17, and 18, may have some future pertinence to this case. Frame number 4 was apparently skipped in numbering by the Kodak laboratory. While there are only 22 frames, the slide numbers go to number 23. This would account for the skipped number. However, this early sequence no doubt relates to personal shots taken by Mr. Croft at an earlier time, and he should be in a position to verify the sequence when the film is returned to Denver. Frame number 18 is completely blank and might possibly have been occasioned by a malfunction of Croft's camera or some other error on the part of the photographer."[12]

If Croft had believed that his film would receive extra special handling through the auspices of the FBI, he was sadly mistaken. He undoubtedly could have had as good service for this special set of slides if he had taken them to the local drug store to be developed. Just what the problem was with the blank slide, which Croft believed he had taken at the time of the shooting, is unclear. The FBI report did not indicate whether it was a black over-exposure or a washed-out under-exposure or anything. The intimation is that it held no image on it at all. Not now recalling the details of the photographic slides, Croft remembers that not having a light meter in setting the aperture on the camera, "I just guessed on that camera all the time. . . . I wouldn't think I'd be changing the f-stop on it much [while taking pictures] between the corner and down on the side. I don't know why it was blank."[13] Realizing by December 3 when the memo was sent to Denver that prosecution of Oswald was now a moot point, as Oswald had been killed on November 24, the author of the memo did point out that: ". . . while there is no foreseeable need for the above-specified frames, it is possible that subsequent developments in this highly involved case might require review or presentation of these photographs before a congressional committee or presidential commission; therefore, you are requested to contact Croft and endeavor to obtain his permission for the Bureau to make appropriate copies of the above three frames for our use to cover the eventualities mentioned above."[14]

On December 4 Croft traveled to the Denver FBI office at the request of Agent John Broughton. Croft recalls, ". . . they had made some big prints of the slides and wanted me to look at them to see if I could tell them anything. That's the only time I was down their place." During this visit Croft signed a document allowing the Bureau to make and retain copies of the slides for potential future investigative use. Once in January and again in February 1964, the package of Croft's 22 slides were borrowed for brief periods of time. On both occasions Croft was given a dated and signed Secret Service "Receipt for Contraband."[15]

The FBI presently has on file prints of the three Croft slides in slightly cropped black-and-white format. Neither Croft's name nor his pictures appeared within the 26-volume Warren Commission *Hearings*, and a request and search of his name failed to turn up anything in the records of the Commission papers now on deposit at the National Archives.[16] It was not until the House Select Committee on Assassinations was underway in 1978 that any of the Croft pictures were looked upon by official investigators as having any relevance to the case. The Committee staff apparently discovered his presence and photographs after looking through old FBI files. An outside contact report dated September 11, 1978, is reported to have been made with Croft. Mr. Croft states, however, that "I know I wasn't contacted [by the HSCA]. I moved up here about that time and I never had any contact. I'm positive that there was no contact made then because that hasn't been that long ago."[17] The original slides were not utilized by the photographic evidence panel of the House Select Committee. His recollections seem accurate, as the panel report indicated, after explaining their policy of "working with transparency images as much as possible as distinct from prints that are on an opaque base," that copy prints were used of the Robert Croft color photographs.[18]

The third Croft photograph of the Kennedy motorcade sequence became an important piece of evidence used by the photographic panel and by the House Select Committee on Assassinations during the 1978 hearings. A careful study of this picture was made to determine much about the physical placement of the President and Governor Connally within the presidential limousine. Used in conjunction with other photographic evidence, this photo was able to help in the reconstruction of the possibilities of directional shooting paths of bullets into the vehicle.

During public hearings before the Committee, C. S. McCamy of the photo analysis and enhancement panel, in explaining studies made in attempting to reconstruct the bullet trajectories testified that, "The positions of the people in the motorcade were determined by study of a large number of photographs. Incidentally, some of these photographs have just come to be known, so there is some new evidence. At least one recent photograph is a very clear photograph of the side of the limousine, taken by a man standing right on the curb. . . . This is the Croft photo."[19]

During the panel's investigation it was determined that at about the time of the first bullet hitting the President, "the best record of Kennedy's posture, torso inclination and shoulder 'hunching' is a photograph taken by Robert Croft at about the time of the Zapruder frame 161. . . . In Croft's picture, Kennedy and other persons in the limousine are seen from a perspective that permits a reasonable determination of their posture and orientation." The President ". . . was hunched forward somewhere between 11 and 18 degrees forward of the vertical in the upper torso, and his shoulders were either facing straight ahead in the car or were turned slightly to the right of straight ahead." The distance between the President's neck and governor's back was determined to be about 60 cm, and the height difference between the two was 8 cm, Kennedy sitting higher. It was also noted that even though the panel believed that the first bullet to strike the President occurred at about the time of Zapruder frame 190 (Z190), the position of Kennedy in the Croft photograph had not changed significantly to alter the data, and that results of trajectory studies would not be altered significantly if the shot had even possibly occurred some frames later.[20]

In further studies during the early 1990s it was postulated by Dr. Lattimer and others that the first shot, which was a miss, had been fired at approximately Zapruder frame Z160, just about the instant that this third Croft photo had been taken. It was believed by Lattimer that the second shot struck both Kennedy and Connally at about Zapruder frames Z223-224.[21]

By utilizing the Kennedy autopsy photographs and x-rays in conjunction with the Zapruder film and slides taken by Phil Willis and Croft on Elm Street, the panel concluded that the alignment of Kennedy and Connally in the limousine during this period was consistent enough to account for both being wounded by the same bullet. The panel further concluded that the backward tracing of the path of the bullet trajectory from the President's neck entry wound would intercept the Texas School Book Depository at an area corresponding partially within the sixth floor window area. Thus one of the Croft pictures, ignored for almost 15 years, was able to eventually aid in the inquiry of what transpired at Dealey Plaza, and to assist in strengthening the evidence of the single bullet theory.

By the late 1980s Mr. Croft was living in the western United States. Somewhat reluctant to speak of the events in Dallas, Croft states, "I haven't talked about or reviewed any of it for over twenty years, and have made no attempt to maintain any of the details. I haven't even told [my wife] about it other than mentioning the generalities of it. It's not one of those things that I had any reason to remember." He still has his original slides, but until requested to locate them by this author in conjunction with this study, hadn't seen them for a long time. He hasn't given the various assassination conspiracy theories much thought. "It's not been something I've discussed with my wife or my kids or anybody. I doubt there are few people that you can find that even knew I was even around there. Other than my immediate family that knew I was there, I've never discussed it with anybody." Croft concedes that the event of the assassination did have an impact on him. "I think it wasn't until a long time after, that it really soaked in as to what it was. It was the kind of thing you might read about but never visualize yourself standing on the sidewalk witnessing something like that."[22]

## CHAPTER NOTES

1. Telephone interview of Robert E. Croft, 4/20/1988.
2. Airtel To: Director, FBI, from SAC, Denver, file #62-109060-1388, 11/23/1963, through FOIA request #263,250, 6/1985.
3. Croft telephone interview, 4/20/1988.
4. Croft slide transparencies #16 & 17, 11/22/1963.
5. Croft slide transparency #16.
6. Croft slide transparency #17; James Altgens photo #4, 11/22/1963.
7. Croft slide transparency # 18.
8. Airtel, 11/23/1963, op. cit.
9. Croft telephone interview, 4/20/1988.
10. Letter, Croft to Trask, 12/2/1988; Croft telephone interview, 4/20/1988; Airtel, To: SAC, Denver, From: Director, FBI, Re. Other evidence, file #62-109060-1388, 12/3/1963, through FOIA, op. cit.; Note, Croft to Trask on rough draft, 4/1/1988.
11. Airtel, 11/23/1963, op. cit.
12. Airtel, 12/3/1963, op. cit.
13. Croft telephone interview, 4/20/1988.
14. Airtel, 12/3/1963, op. cit.
15. Croft telephone interview, 4/20/1988; Letter, Croft to Trask, 12/2/1988; "Receipt for contraband," 1/15/1964, 2/4/1964.
16. Letter, Trask to Marion Johnson, National Archives, 12/11/1984; Letter, Johnson to Trask, 12/27/1984.
17. Croft telephone interview, 4/20/1988.
18. *Appendix to Hearings Before the Select Committee on Assassinations*, v.6, p. 12,312.
19. *Hearings*, v.2, p. 150-151.
20. Ibid., v.2, p. 175-176, 184-185, 195-196; v.6, p. 45, 54.
21. John K. Lattimer, "Additional Data on the Shooting of President Kennedy," *The Journal of the American Medical Association*, 3/24-31/1993, p. 1544-1545.
22. Croft telephone interview, 4/20/1988.

## CHAPTER 10

# The Polaroid Pictures

One of the most familiar of the assassination photographs made at Dealey Plaza was taken with a Polaroid camera by a Dallas housewife. Of immense spot news importance, the photo was quickly copied and then distributed by Associated Press and United Press International on November 23, yet subsequently all but ignored by the Warren Commission investigation.

Mary Ann Moorman was a 31-year-old Dallas native married to a local plumber, and a close friend to Jean Lollis Hill. Hill was a 32-year-old native of Ferguson, Oklahoma. Following her marriage to serviceman Bill Hill and the births of a son and daughter, Hill earned a B.A. degree from Oklahoma Baptist University in 1955. Teaching seven years in the Oklahoma City school system, in August 1962, Jean Hill moved with her family to Dallas, her husband obtaining a new position with Science Research Associates. Mrs. Hill occasionally substitute taught in the Dallas school system. Her marriage was faltering, and the couple was in the process of getting a divorce, which would be finalized in August 1964. For several weeks Hill had been regularly seeing a married Dallas Police Department motorcycle officer, Billy Joe Martin. Martin was one of the cycle officers who had been assigned escort duty in President Kennedy's motorcade on November 22. Mary Ann Moorman also knew several of the officers taking part in the motorcade, as they had attended high school with her. The women decided it would be fun to see the President and their officer friends, and maybe get a picture of them in the procession. Hill also wanted to be sure Martin saw her, so she wore her full-length red coat for the occasion. The two women parked Mary's two-door 1961 Thunderbird on Houston Street near the "Old Red" sandstone court house around 11:00 a.m. and bought a package of film for Mary's Polaroid camera at a nearby store. Mary had impressed on Jean that they had to beat any potential traffic jam out of the area, as Mary disliked driving in heavy traffic.[1]

The Polaroid camera Mary had with her on November 22 was the result of the brilliant inventiveness of Dr. Edwin H. Land. Land had created a company which, utilizing scientific technology, was in the forefront of polarized light usage and high-quality photographic work. He had helped the Eisenhower administration in the secret development of the camera and film system which was effectively used for the photographic reconnaissance work of the U-2 spy plane. Numerous spy flights were made over the Soviet Union until the Francis Gary Powers shoot-down in May 1960. Even after that incident the plane and camera equipment continued to see good use, including critical reconnaissance flights over Cuba during the missile crisis of 1962.

Within the area of popular photography, Land's idea of a self-contained camera and print developer for near instant photography was first marketed in 1948. At the Jordan Marsh department store in Boston the Polaroid Land Camera Model 95 was demonstrated and sold to a quickly enthralled crowd. The camera's inner workings resembled nothing like that of the traditional camera. Company literature proudly described the resulting process. "Within one minute after taking a picture with a Polaroid Land camera, it will deliver to you a dry, finished, excellent print of your subject. No other camera can do this." Two connected film rolls were composed of a strip of a negative on one roll and a strip of a positive sheet on another, and included eight pods of a viscous development reagent. Once the exposure had been made, the end of the film roll was pulled, at which time rollers pierced the foil envelope of the first chemical development pod. The film sheet was drawn between the chemicals. Cooked in the development solution for 60 seconds, the photograph was then removed from a rear film door. The print was peeled away from its frame, thereby stopping further development. There were initial problems with the print's sepia tone and the image's extended life. Land had to improve upon the product in newer camera models in order to hold and expand his market. The improvements, though attaining more stability of the print, were a step back, however, from the one-step process, as it required the introduction of a film coater. The packaged Polaroid film now included in each box a glass vial containing a 3-inch applicator with a sponge surface which had to be carefully and completely run across the just-developed picture. The applied coating of a polymer and acidic solution prevented further development and provided the image with a durable surface. If the procedure was not performed, the picture was liable to darken and fingerprints could mar the picture's surface.[2] Many a coating too quickly applied to the print would result in translucent over-exposure which would quickly take on a brownish tint. Yet for all its extra fuss, the more than double cost of the Polaroid versus traditional black-and-white prints, and the generally poorer quality of snapshots produced, the camera and the system was nonetheless an immense success. Quickness of results was a trait twentieth century Americans appreciated.

By the fall of 1963 50-second color Polaroid film was in limited production, and the Cambridge-based Polaroid Company was a major player in the camera industry. Black-and-white prints had for a number of years been available at a company specified developing time of 10 seconds, reduced from the original 60 seconds. The process of coating the print and correct drying for best results of the finish was still in the range of from two to five minutes. All black-and-white models took eight exposures to a roll. Models available in 1963 included the Pathfinder Model 110B at $172, the popular Model 150 at $113, the simpler J66 taking Type 47 film and costing $93, and the least expensive J33 using Type 37 film and priced at $75.[3]

Mary Moorman's Polaroid was known as the "Highlander," a Model 80 series folding camera, first put into production in 1954 as a smaller, lighter, and cheaper version of the Model 95.  Using series 30 film, this camera produced eight of the smaller 2¾" x 3½" prints which retailed for $1.19 per roll.  Continuing in production until 1957, the camera had a 100mm focal lens, and shutter speeds of 1/25 to 1/100 second.  One consumer publication described the lens's quality as "mediocre," and that "the pictures obtained with this camera were about of the quality one would expect to obtain by use of an inexpensive box camera in the $6 to $15 price range."[4]

Display at JFK Assassination Information Center featuring a Polaroid camera
similar to Moorman's, a copy of her Photo #5 and two prints of
the women at the car parked on Houston Street

In 1988 Jean Hill located two long-forgotten Polaroid prints made back on November 22, 1963, prior to the motorcade.  One photo shows Hill poised on the seat by the Thunderbird's open passenger door; the other pictures show Mary Ann Moorman, wearing a pair of sunglasses and long coat, standing by the same open car door.  The car is parked on the east side of Houston Street.  In the background across the street the Plaza's obelisk can be seen in front of the north peristyle, while a portion of the Texas School Book Depository is visible at far right.  Hill recalls that Moorman gave her these Polaroids that day, that they were the last exposures on a roll already in the camera, and that they were left in the car when the women went to see the motorcade.  A fresh roll of film was purchased at a nearby store.[5]

Walking to the corner of Elm and Houston Streets near the front entrance of the Texas School Book Depository Building, the women struck up a conversation with

Patrolman W. E. Barnett, the officer assigned to work traffic and crowd control at that corner in anticipation of the presidential motorcade. Barnett fixed Hill's cigarette lighter, which was malfunctioning. Recollecting to writer Jim Marrs many years later, Hill remembered getting into a, "cops and robbers frame of mind," and when she saw an odd vehicle with the sign "Uncle Joe's Pawn Shop" being allowed to cruise within the motorcade area, she kiddingly remarked to Moorman, "Do you suppose there are murderers in that van?"[6]

Nearing the scheduled time for the motorcade, the two women decided to take up a position on the south side of Elm Street near the street's curb and some 200 feet away from the southwest corner of the School Book Depository. Hill, wearing her red raincoat, was at Moorman's right side. She was ready to take any exposures made by Moorman, coat them and put them into her pocket for safe keeping. Moorman was wearing a blue coat.

The presidential vehicle was preceded in the motorcade by a number of other vehicles. Informally, Perdue Lawrence, captain of the police traffic division, traveled some half-mile ahead of the motorcade, alerting the traffic officers of the imminent arrival of the caravan. The first official part of the motorcade was a pilot car driven by Deputy Chief George Lumpkin, containing two detectives, an advance man, and an army lieutenant colonel. The three-man advance motorcycle unit followed, traveling three to

four blocks ahead of the presidential party and headed by Sergeant S. G. Bellah in the middle, flanked by J. B. Garrick on his right and G. C. McBride on his left. Officer Glen McBride was a good friend of Moorman's from her high school days and it is of him astride his Harley-Davidson two-wheel response cycle #340 that she took her

Moorman's Polaroid photo of Cycle Officer Glen McBride

first Polaroid photo of the motorcade. McBride was looking straight in her direction. Across the street numerous spectators are seen, including two young men in jackets on the left side of the print who, following the shooting, would first run up the knoll to the east concrete shelter and then run westerly in the direction of the underpass. Appearing in the right background of the picture is the front of the Book Depository Building with portions of the first five floors visible, excluding the last set of windows on the east side of the building. On the fifth floor, the lower sashes of four windows can be seen to be open, one slightly and three almost fully, including the second to last window, where Depository employee James Jarman, Jr., was watching the motorcade. At the extreme left of the photo one can make out the rear wheel, antenna, and tail section of another cycle, most probably Bellah's. This Polaroid exposure marked #3 on its reverse, was quickly peeled out of the camera, wiped and put into Hill's pocket.[7]

Following the advance unit, the lead motorcycles of the escort began to come into view. Originally five in number, these cycles were under the command of Sergeant Starvis Ellis, and traveled some one-half block in front of the lead car. These cycles were used primarily for crowd control, opening up any street area filled in by exuberant crowds. All down Main Street the advance unit rolled in single rank with occasional sweeping gestures being made by cycle officers, indicating to those ahead to clear out road space. By pre-arrangement, near the end of Main Street when the motorcade turned right onto Houston Street, two of the escort cycles broke away, to travel down ahead and onto Stemmons Freeway in order to stop traffic. They were then to fall in at the rear of the motorcade preventing any vehicles from passing the presidential party. The remaining three cycles continued the route of the motorcade, and included W. George Lumpkin, another Moorman school friend. A 33-year-old motorcycle officer who had joined the force in 1953, Lumpkin always used Cycle #343, a 1962 Harley-Davidson. He was assigned police radio call #152.

In an interview with Lumpkin many years after 1963, the officer recalled that he was in the middle of Elm Street with Sgt. Ellis on his left and L. E. Gray on the opposite side. Lumpkin told how the cycle engines were getting quite hot due to traveling so slowly, and that it was hard to steer them when they were going that speed. Backfires were also more frequent when the motor overheated, and there were quite a few that day. Lumpkin had known Mary Moorman for many years, and knew she took a picture of him. He thinks he stopped on Elm Street and briefly spoke with Moorman and Hill. Moorman believes she took this frame #4 picture about two minutes before the assassination. She indicated to a researcher that this photo did, upon later examination, show the "assassin's window" in the Depository (east end, sixth floor) as in this photo Lumpkin was closer to the Elm and Houston Street corner than McBride's location in the earlier photo. Following the assassination, Moorman recalled that on more than one occasion she counted floors and windows, and neither she nor others in her presence ever found anyone discernable in any of the windows. As there were at about that same time others in open windows of the Depository, the absence in the photos of any identifiable persons in the windows was more likely due to the small scale of the features and the simplistic optics of the camera, rather than no one being there. Proceeding on, Lumpkin, prior to entering the triple underpass, heard three noises which he took to be engine backfires to his rear. Then, upon hearing Chief Curry on the police radio and realizing an incident had occurred, Lumpkin motored to Parkland Hospital, the prearranged location in the event of a problem. He rode ahead of the cars and stopped at the emergency entrance to prevent unauthorized vehicles from entering.[8]

In 1964 Moorman gave Lumpkin the picture she had taken of him the day of the assassination. Lumpkin eventually mislaid the photograph. In 1978 he was contacted about this picture, and though he looked for it, he could not find it. In one query he mentioned that at the time his kids were living with him, and they might have lost it, but that he has a lot of photographs around. Concerning the assassination, Lumpkin who was the last of the 1963 cyclemen to see active police duty, retiring in 1981, believes that Oswald did the shooting from the Texas School Book Depository. He knew that some of his fellow officers disagreed with him about this.[9]

Zapruder frame Z303 showing Moorman poised to take a picture. Hill is at left.

The two young women were now caught up in the excitement as Chief Curry's lead car passed, and was followed soon behind by the noise, blinking lights and sight of the President and First Lady traveling down Elm Street towards them. Perhaps waiting too soon between taking the last photograph and this next one, or simply caught up in the excitement of the moment, Moorman didn't snap her exposure #5 of the roll until after the President passed in front of her position. The vehicle was only some 20 feet to her left front when Moorman made her picture. At about that instant the two women heard obtrusive noises and saw the violent reaction of the President and Mrs. Kennedy to the assassination. As the car quickly sped off, Moorman and Hill, like most of the spectators around them, instinctively fell to the ground to get out of harm's way. After several long moments, and as the tail end of the motorcade passed in front of them and scores of spectators streamed into the area, many crossing to the north side of Elm and up the embankment, Hill followed suit, trying to locate someone she had seen who seemed suspicious.[10]

Moorman's Photo #5

At one point Hill saw what she thought to be blood near the knoll's concrete path, and she thought someone had wounded a culprit. The dark puddle turned out to be some type of liquid like soda pop, Kool-Aid or a melted slush cone. After a short, fruitless look-about in the area of the railroad tracks where many other spectators were also now milling around, Hill, realized "I didn't want to be in on anything," and returned to Elm Street. Mary Ann was standing at her original position, but now joined by a man. The man, *Dallas Times Herald* court reporter James Featherston, had seen Moorman with her camera and realized she was not only a witness, but might have pictures. Moorman was crying and Featherston had hold of her arm and possession of her camera, urging her to go with him. Hill rushed over, highly agitated, trying to shake his hand loose and grab the camera, saying they had to leave.

In later re-writes for possible inclusion within the November 22 late editions of the *Dallas Times Herald* Featherston described the encounter: "A *Times Herald* reporter was at the intersection of Houston and Main. 'I heard what seemed to be a series of firecrackers go off. Everyone seemed stunned and a great mass of people ran over toward the scene. I ran over and caught these two girls and somebody told me they thought these women had seen it and I got them to talk to me.'" In a separate re-write it states, "Minutes later Mrs. Moorman developed her picture and delivered it and her story to a *Dallas Times Herald* reporter."[11]

Featherston, realizing he had an important part of a breaking story, insisted they go with him. Hill recalls he practically ran them up to the corner of Main and Houston Streets. Featherston brought the women to the press room in the Dallas County Criminal Courts Building, which also housed the Sheriff's Department. This building became the focal point that afternoon for taking witnesses' statements, and for press and various officials to visit in an attempt to find out what was happening. The atmosphere in much of the building took on an excited and confused air as scores of people filled the press room trying to get a hold on the story. Assassination witness Charles Brehm recalls seeing two women together there, one wearing a highly visible red coat. To Hill the difference between the press asking her to tell her story and her trying to be cooper- ative with the authorities blurred in her mind. She later testified, ". . . We didn't know that we were in a press room. We just knew we were in a court house and with police. I mean, this was to us a police station." And it appears Featherston and other press had no intention of explaining the situation clearly to Hill. Hill described Featherston's actions: "He kept standing in front of the door and he would let a camera in or some- one to interview us and they were shooting things in our faces, and he wouldn't let us out." The two women remained at the Court Building until some time after 6:00. Moorman, a Dallas native who knew some of the people with whom she came into contact that afternoon, recalls their stay as not quite as unnerving and confused as Hill. Years later it would be pointed out in a biography about Hill that Moorman's memories of that period immediately after the assassination, ". . . do not necessarily coincide" with Hill's. Both had the chance to use the telephone, and they were not physically prevented from leaving. Both briefly stepped outside, but were firmly requested by sheriff's deputies to return for questioning. Though the women generally knew the difference between press interviews and investigators' questions, they apparently felt compelled or pressured to be as cooperative with both.  And they tired of answering the same questions over and over again.[12]

Thirty years after the event Jim Featherston commented at a reporters' gathering concerning his locating Mary Ann Moorman. "I wanted that picture, period.  At the time I thought that was the only picture [of the assassination] in existence.  Mary Moorman agreed to give me the film.  I asked both of them to come back to the press room with me — which they did.  I interviewed them, called the rewrite desk.  In their own words they said what they had seen.  Later Jean Hill told the Warren Commission I was down there and I grabbed her; Mary Moorman, she was crying and I wouldn't let her go, and I took them to a strange room.  Of course that was the Press Room — it *was* a pretty strange room at that time.  She also told them they couldn't leave — that's all nonsense."[13]

Initially, it appears that the two witnesses were the figurative captives of the press, though by some point in the afternoon the Sheriff's Department took brief statements and examined Moorman's pictures.  It is from the initial press interviews that one can hear the most complete eyewitness impressions of the two women.  Their accounts were on occasion colored by misperceptions, though this frequently occurs with fallible eyewitness memory of stressful events.

One of the first broadcast interviews of an assassination witness was one WBAP television newsman Jimmy Darnell arranged with Hill.  Darnell had been in the motorcade, and following the shooting had remained at the scene.  Darnell came upon Hill in the press room.  At 1:21 p.m. CST, WBAP's Tom Whalen played over the NBC network an interview arranged through Darnell, which he had just audio-taped a few minutes earlier.

Whalen :     Did you see the shooting?

Hill:     Yes, sir. . . . They were driving along and we were the only people in this area on our side, and the shots came directly across the street from us, and just as the President's car became directly even with us, we took one look at him and he was — he and Jackie were looking at a dog that was in the middle of the seat, and about that time two shots rang out just as he looked up — just as the President looked up and these three shots rang out and he grabbed his chest, looked like he was in pain and fell over in his seat.  And Jackie fell over on him and said, "My God, he's been shot!"  After that more shots rang out and the car sped away. . . .

Whalen:     Where did the shots come from?

| | |
|---|---|
| Hill: | The shots came from the hill — it was just east of the underpass. We were on the south side. |
| Whalen: | Did you look up there where the shots came from? |
| Hill: | Yes, sir. |
| Whalen: | Could you see anyone? |
| Hill: | I thought I saw this man running, but I looked at the President and you know for a while and I looked up there and I thought I saw a man running and so right after that I guess I didn't have any better sense — I started running there too.[14] |

Darnell was later joined at the Court Building by NBC cameraman Henry Kokajan, who had brought with him WBAP's only sound camera which had originally been set up at the Trade Mart. By about 3:16 CST, NBC was again reporting through its WBAP affiliate on witnesses to the shooting, and Moorman's photo of the President was shown on camera followed by a filmed interview of the two women.

| | |
|---|---|
| Hill: | Just as Mary started to take the picture and the President came right even with us, two shot — we looked at him and he was looking at a dog in the middle of the seat — two shots rang out and he grabbed his chest and a look of pain on his face and fell across towards Jackie and she, uh, fell over on him and said, "My God, he's shot!" And there was an interval and then three or four more shots rang out. By that time the motorcade sped away. |
| Interviewer: | What prompted you to take the picture at that particular instant, Ma'am? |
| Moorman: | Well, that's the only chance I had. Mine is a Polaroid and I can only take one every ten seconds, and that was at that time when I took it. |
| Interviewer: | Did you know he was shot? |
| Moorman: | No, I didn't. I must have snapped it immediately when he slumped, 'cause in the picture that's the way she's there and he's slumped over. |

Interviewer:     Did you see the person who fired the — ?

Hill:            No, I didn't see any person fire the weapon, I only heard it. I looked up and saw a man running up the hill. No, I had no idea, nothing to go by, I mean I don't think it dawned on me for an instant that the President had been shot. I mean, I knew and yet it just didn't register.

Interviewer:     Did you get a look at the suspect, the assassin?

Moorman:         No, I had taken a picture and then the shots and I decided it was time to fall on the ground.[15]

Hill (left) and Moorman at the Courts Building

ABC's Bill Lord interviewed the two women for later broadcast on WFAA. Moorman related, "My picture when I took it was at the same instant that the President was hit, and that does show in my picture . . . it shows the President he, uh, slumped. Jackie Kennedy was leaning towards him to see I guess. It all happened so suddenly, I don't think anyone realized, you know, what had happened." Asked about the shots, Moorman then stated, "There was three or four real close together, and it must have been the first one that shot him, 'cause that was the time I took the picture, and it was during that time after I took the picture, and the shots were still being fired, I decided I better get on the ground. . . . I was no more than fifteen foot from the car and in line of fire evidently."[16]

Lord's interview of Hill took place later in the afternoon just prior to her speaking with FBI agents. Hill again mentioned the fact of a dog in the car between the President and the First Lady, which she later learned was not there. She explained it subsequently to a Warren Commission staff attorney saying she had just barely glanced and noticed something white and fuzzy in the seat between them, and assumed it was a small dog.  After the shooting and while on her way to the Courts Building, Hill remarked to Moorman that she could understand Liz Taylor or the Gabors traveling with dogs, but not the Kennedys.  She later reconstructed in her mind that what she had seen the President and Mrs. Kennedy looking at were the roses in the seat.  Her mixup concerning the dog remained quite embarrassing to her and was made even more painful by her husband making fun of it saying, "Of all people in the United States, you would have to see a dog."  She was also embarrassed by her Oklahoma twang, and referring to Mrs. Kennedy as "Jackie."  Though Hill continued to mention the dog in interviews on November 22, she began leaving out the part of her story about following after a man who was running, because reporter Featherston told her she was wrong about that, and not to say that anymore on the air.[17]

Lord's interview of Hill was broadcast as follows:

Lord:   This is Mrs. Jean Hill of Dallas.  Could you tell us what you saw?

Hill:   Yes, Mary and I had come downtown to see the President this morning, and we tried to get a place where we could be away from everyone and we, I guess, succeeded.  As the car came down the hill towards us he was on our side of the street, and the President and Mrs. Kennedy were in the back seat, had a little dog between them looking at it, and just as the car came right in line with us, the President looked up and just as he looked up two shots rang out and he grabbed his chest and this real odd look came over his face and he pitched forward onto her lap.  And she jumped up over him at that, and screamed, "My God, he's been shot!" and there was just an instantaneous sort of an instant pause and the motorcade momentarily halted and three or four more shots rang out and they sped away real quickly and by that time I became aware of Mary tugging on my foot saying, "Get down, they're shooting," and it hadn't registered, I had been so busy looking at the President.

Lord:   You were at a very advantageous spot to see the President?

Hill:   To see the President, but also to get shot.

Lord:   How do you feel now, it's been several hours later, you've talked to the police, given your story several times.  Do you still believe that something like this really did happen to you?

Hill:     I don't think I could have believed it unless I had actually seen it, and when I saw the look come across his face I knew that he'd been hit. But I don't think I could have believed it if I hadn't been right there and seen it.

Lord:     Well, you are going to have to talk to the FBI now and I understand you have some home chores as well?

Hill:     Breakfast dishes and everything.

Lord:     I think there are an awful lot of homes here in Dallas that have breakfast dishes to be done today.

Hill:     Well, that's right but uh I made a call to my friend in Oklahoma and he told our governor of Oklahoma right away. Guess that's the first thing I wanted to do was get those people in Oklahoma told about it.

Lord:     Thank you very much.[18]

Hill later in her testimony to Warren Commission staff lawyer Arlen Specter recalled that late in the afternoon she was located by a Secret Service agent who had specifically been looking for two women who had been wearing a red and a blue raincoat and were close to the scene of the assassination. Hill told the agent that she had heard from four to six shots. According to Hill he responded, "'Mrs. Hill, we were standing at the window and we heard more shots also, but we have three wounds and we have three bullets. Three shots is all that we are willing to say right now' . . . then, he asked me — I was asked did I know that a bullet struck at my feet? And I said, 'No, I didn't,' and he said, 'What do you think that dust was?' and I said, 'I didn't see any dust.'" Hill most likely mixed up part of her recollections, as the mention of a Secret Service agent standing at the window at the time of the shooting seems to be more logically the statement of a deputy positioned in one of the county buildings, as no Secret Service agents were in buildings in Dealey Plaza.

Hill probably did speak with a Secret Service agent late that Friday afternoon. Moorman "advised," in the words of an FBI report made out by Agents Perryman and Gemberling that day, that she had given a photo she had taken of the police motorcycle showing the Texas School Book Depository to Secret Service Agents John Joe Howlett and Bill Patterson shortly before 4:00. In the same report Moorman is paraphrased to indicate how she had made the photo of the motorcycle escort, as well as the one of the President at which time she heard what sounded like a firecracker. The report states, "She knows that she heard two shots and possibly a third shot." This second-hand statement is at variation to what Moorman is recorded to have told news media, and her remarks that she heard three or four shots in all as recorded in her Sheriff's Department statement. The statement Hill gave to FBI Agent Robert Wish was typed up into two short paragraphs, briefly mentioning, "Jean Hill advised she heard something like a rifle shot, and observed President Kennedy crumple in his seat in the automobile." This scanty report reflected little of what Hill had told national television. Hill also made a voluntary statement to the Sheriff's Department. The Sheriff's Department statement was very close to that given the TV reporters, including a mention of wanting to take a picture, the dog in the car, the President grabbing his chest, the two separate groupings of shots, and her running across the street. The only item not mentioned in the film interviews was that she said, "I thought I saw some men in plain clothes shooting back, but everything was such a blur. . . ."[19]

As reporter Featherston had been the one who discovered these two ladies who turned out to be talkative news sources, he initially questioned them for his own reporting purposes and looked over their pictures. The women later recalled that at the press room they allowed the pictures to be examined, and they were out of Moorman's physical custody on several occasions. According to researcher Gary Mack, who spoke extensively with Moorman some 20 years after the events, the assassination photo was quickly taken to the *Dallas Times Herald* offices, which shared a photo lab with UPI. The photo was copied there and returned to Moorman at the Sheriff's Office. Moorman's Polaroids had all come out light and the copy pictures were darkened to bring out better the President's and the car's features.[20]

The evening extra edition of the *Times Herald* included an article entitled, "Candid Snapshot: Picture of Death" featuring Featherston's early interview of the two women, including a statement that, "They glanced up to see a man run up the hill across the street from them and another (near the motorcade) pepper bullets at the running figure."[21]

The specific custody and location that afternoon of Moorman's Polaroid pictures is now impossible to reconstitute. From a Sheriff's Department investigative report by Deputy Sheriff John (Billy) Wiseman, we learn that he asked Moorman to see all of her pictures, specifically mentioning having seen the photo taken at the time the President was shot. He also saw the picture taken of the lead motorcycle officer. ". . . In the background of this picture was a picture of the Sexton Building [Texas School Book Depository] and the window where the gunman sat when doing the shooting." This latter picture was turned over to Chief Criminal Deputy Sheriff Sweatt, who in turn gave it to Secret Service Agent Patterson. Patterson thereupon gave Moorman his card, saying he would return the picture to her. The FBI took temporary custody of the shooting picture.[22]

Copies of Moorman's assassination photo had been made by the press, possibly without Moorman's permission. Hill remembers the scene as very highly charged with her and her friend gradually realizing that the prints had monetary value, and their not knowing where the original was for large blocks of time. According to Hill, Moorman, ". . . sold the rights, the publishing rights of it, not the original picture, but they had already — AP and UPI had already picked it up because Featherston stole it."[23]

Moorman, it turned out, had not been the only person using a Polaroid in the Dealey Plaza area. One other "instant picture" photographer was Jack A. Weaver, who worked at the Fidelity Union Life Building and had traveled to the southeast corner of Main and Houston Streets at lunch time that Friday in order to see the procession. As the President's convertible was making its right turn onto Hous-ton, Weaver, when the two escort motorcycle cops in his viewing foreground passed his position, pushed the release button and made an exposure. The photo showed the back sides of the car's passengers, including the President patting down his hair from the sudden effects of a cross-street wind. His

The Depository Building looms in the background as the President's vehicle turns onto Houston Street

hand was reaching to that portion of his head which in only a matter of seconds would be punctured and fractured by a high velocity bullet. Covering the upper third of the Polaroid print's background is the prominent Texas School Book Depository Building. All floors are seen from the first floor front entrance steps up to the bottom half of the massive Hertz sign atop the structure. Included are all of the first six double sets of windows on each floor beginning at the east side. On Houston Street one can see Chief Curry's lead car, while at least one of the lead cyclists is seen swinging left onto Elm. In the crowd of spectators opposite Weaver, at least one person and possibly two others appear to be taking pictures. None of these possible photographs have come to light.[24]

Weaver appears to have volunteered this picture to the Dallas FBI office on December 3, and the Dallas office sent it to the FBI Washington Laboratory for examination. A brief "result of examination of the Polaroid, labeled "Q220," was typed up on December 6, stating that it ". . . does not contain sufficient detail in the area of the corner sixth floor window of the Texas School Book Depository to determine if an individual was within the view of the camera at the time this picture was made. The form recorded by the photograph in this window does not conform to the form of people which are visible in other windows recorded by this photograph. This form is the samegeneral shape of boxes later located in the window in question." Josiah Thompson included the photo in his book *Six Seconds in Dallas* in both the text and in the back dust jacket, it having been discovered among FBI records by researchers just prior to the book's publication.[25]

FBI laboratory enlargement of the Depository Building from the Weaver Polaroid

At least one other Polaroid camera was used that day to record part of the drama of the assassination events. James Troy Hankins was an employee at the production department of Sound & Music on Cole Street in Dallas, just west of Stemmons Freeway. With a Polaroid camera in hand, Hankins decided to view the motorcade and he walked over to the expressway and took up a position on the median strip facing northeast and just opposite a sign advertising Pearl Beer. Observing a car he believed to be the President's approaching his position at a speed of 60 to 70 miles per hour, Hankins took a picture of the car. Shortly thereafter, Hankins learned from someone with a portable radio that the President had been shot. The Hankins photograph shows a slightly blurry view of the entire presidential Lincoln traveling down the freeway. Agent Clint Hill is partially in the back seat, his hands spread eagle over the back seat. All the back seat occupants are a jumble of undiscernible bodies low in the car. In the front seat Agents Greer and Kellerman are facing forward. Above the street is a frame with two freeway signs positioned in the direction of oncoming traffic, while across the street from Hankins' position are several clusters of spectators.[26]

The presidential convertible on Stemmons Freeway rushing to Parkland Hospital

Hankins' name seems apparently to have come to the attention of the FBI, not through his picture, but through a report filed with the Miami FBI office. On December 3 one Thadeus Zielonko reported to the FBI that in mid-April 1962, while employed as an electrician's technician for Arma Corporation, he had worked on a project at Dyess Air Force Base at Abilene, Texas. Zielonko became acquainted with another Arma employee working there named Hank Hankins, a native Texan. In a conversation one day Hankins reportedly remarked to Zielonko that "There is a plan in Dallas to get rid of Kennedy." When asked what kind of a plan, Hankins went on to comment that there was at least one official in on it, and that Dallas was involved because, "That's where they make things happen." Though Zielonko gave the opinion that possibly Hankins was at the time attempting to impress Zielonko and others, he decided it proper now to report the incident. On March 4, 1964, Hankins was interviewed in Dallas by Agent Alfred D. Neeley. In the brief report filed that same day, Hankins confirmed he had been working at Dyess for about two weeks in 1962, but that he very definitely never made any such statements, and that he was not the type of person who discussed politics. He had no recollection of having a discussion with anyone there about President

Kennedy. Whether or not this interview was the spark which drew Hankins to inform the FBI of his photo, or if he did it independently on March 10, is not clear. Except for internal papers logging in the photo and indicating the making of a copy negative and prints of it, publicly accessible information concerning its further use or significance is lacking. A follow-up report was made concerning Hankins shortly after March 30, in which the FBI had checked into Hankins' former employment history. He was born in 1923 at Grandview, Texas, was part Indian, and married with three children. His military records indicated he served in the Air Force until 1946 as a radio operator mechanic. A credit bureau report of 1962 reflected favorably on him and commented that he had a reputation as a talker and could hold the floor in a group. No arrest record on him was found. It was apparently decided that there was no further necessity to investigate Hankins. No further records about him were found in a Freedom of Information Act request made by this author in 1985 and no records were reported as withheld at that time. Though never published, the FBI retained the copy negative made from the Hankins photograph.[27]

No press knew about Weaver or his Polaroid that day, but numerous information-hungry journalists knew of Moorman and her small 2¾" x 3¼" underexposed Polaroid print. Her picture was the first assassination print to be developed and was usable only seconds after the last shot had been fired. And for all its technical shortcomings, this Polaroid has turned out among the millions of Polaroid prints to see the light of self-development, to be the most famous and still one of the most controversial Polaroid pictures ever taken. Though the picture itself lacks all that a well composed photograph should have, and the point of its interest is nebulous, once the viewer understands the time frame in which it was taken, its significance is revealed. Like the Weaver photo, none of the occupants' faces are in view. In the back seat Mrs. Kennedy is leaning to her right toward the President, who is obviously tipping unnaturally to his left. Only his full bushy hair and right shoulder are discernable. According to later studies, Moorman made this picture at about 1/5 of a second after the fatal head wound had occurred. At the right of the picture cycle Officer Bobby Hargis (foreground) and probably Officer James Chaney (extreme right) are evident, as is the windshield and a hand of Officer B. J. Martin (Hill's friend) whose body is just outside the exposure zone. Spectator Bill Newman is just visible behind Chaney on the sidewalk opposite Moorman's position. Park employee Emmett Hudson (second from left) and two unidentified men also stand on the steps. Abraham Zapruder and Mary Sitzman are on top of a pedestal at the upper right corner of the print, while the five-foot-high grassy knoll stockade fence and a concrete retaining wall are in view across the street from Moorman's position.[28]

Displayed on NBC-TV about 3:15 CST that Friday afternoon, by Saturday Moorman's photo was being carried by scores of newspapers around the country through the UPI and AP wirephoto networks. One curious use of the photo is found in the Saturday issue of the *Boston Traveler*, which though credited to UPI wire photo, is printed backwards and heavily touched up so that the cycle cop in the foreground is

A slightly cropped version of Moorman Photo #5

metamorphosed into what looks like a nurse with a white cap and cape walking down the street.     Only the President (arrow pointing to him) is visible in the car. The caption reads, "TERRIBLE INSTANT — This picture made with a Polaroid camera and taken from newsreel film belonging to WBAP-TV Dallas, shows President Kennedy at the very instant he was shot. Traveler artist touched up photo to reduce haziness, but detail is accurate in every way. Woman on foot is not identified."[29]

A curious version of the Moorman photograph

By the time Mary Ann Moorman left the Sheriff's Department in the early evening of November 22, the FBI had, with her permission, kept her picture of the President in the car.  According to Secret Service Agent Patterson, she surrendered to him for use in the investigation, ". . . a Polaroid picture of the Texas School Book Depository," presumably the photo showing cycle Officer McBride.  In his report Patterson later stated that as it was not known to him at the time exactly from where in the building the shots had come, he could not tell if the picture was of value or not.  "The next day I learned which window the shots had been fired from and after checking the picture, determined that the photograph did not show this window at all.  In fact, the picture was of such poor quality that no detail of the building, windows or surrounding areas, was distinguishable."  At the request of the local FBI office, within a day or two, the picture was turned over to them, and subsequently given back to Mrs. Moorman.[30]

Given the confused state within the Criminal Courts Building that Friday, it seems strange, though possibly understandable, that each federal investigative agency would take custody of one photograph.  Stranger still is the fact that the third photo, that of Officer Lumpkin (marked Photo #4 in the roll sequence) which Moorman would later state did show the Texas School Book Depository Building, including the so-called sniper's window, was not mentioned in any report nor offered to any agency.  Although oblique references are later made in official records as to the possible existence of more than two Moorman photos, a fact first brought to light in the research community by Harold Weisberg, all FBI and Secret Service reports refer only to the two (#3 and #5 in the roll sequence) photos.[31]

In early December the Dallas FBI was shown the two Moorman photos (at least one a copy and not the original) by the local Secret Service, and on March 18, 1964, Warren Commission General Counsel J. Lee Rankin requested of FBI Director Hoover a copy of the motorcycle photo for examination by the Commission.  He requested that if the FBI did not have a copy, they should obtain the photo from Mrs. Moorman.  Thereupon follows a paper trail of five additional directives and reports from Hoover et. al. concerning obtaining the two Moorman photos previously examined by the agency.  This heightened interest was developed mainly in response to the testimony of an attorney, Mark Lane, who managed to embroil himself in the growing controversy over the assassination facts.  Moorman later indicated to one researcher that she had been asked in early 1964 to appear for a Warren Commission interview, but that having recently injured her foot, she asked for a few days' delay, which was granted.  She never heard from the Commission again.  Once published and released, neither the Warren Commission's *Report* nor the 26 volumes of hearings and evidence, included any of Moorman's pictures in any form.[32]

Though Moorman did not get the opportunity to have her testimony taken, Jean Hill did, though as much interest was generated over what she had said to New York lawyer and self-styled attorney representing the interests of Lee Oswald, Mark Lane, as for what she had witnessed during the assassination.  Lane had spoken with Hill by telephone on February 18, 1964.  In testimony before the Warren Commission itself in

Washington on March 4, Lane told Chief Justice Earl Warren, Senator John Sherman Cooper, and Representative Gerald R. Ford that Hill had heard some four to six shots fired from the grassy knoll area and not from the Texas School Book Depository. He further stated that she had seen a man run from behind the general area of the concrete facade on that grassy knoll, and that Hill said a picture taken by her friend Moorman might, ". . . include the entire Book Depository Building, taken just precisely a second or less before the shots were fired." Finally Lane, in speaking about Hill, mentioned that in her questioning by Secret Service agents, ". . . they indicated to her what her testimony should be, and that she only heard three shots."[33]

Powerful stuff for Lane's advocacy, but only hearsay testimony. The photo in question was sought and examined by Commission staff and Hill, whose only official FBI interview had been recorded within two short paragraphs must now be re-interviewed by the government. On March 13 she was interviewed by Dallas FBI agents. Hill now told the FBI what she had repeated so frequently to the press on November 22. ". . . When the car occupied by President Kennedy was passing Mrs. Hill, she recalls shouting, 'Hey!' She stated that President Kennedy was looking down when she shouted, and when he turned to look at her a shot rang out and he slumped towards Mrs. Kennedy. Mrs. Hill heard more shots ring out and saw the hair on the back of President Kennedy's head fly up. She stated she thought Mrs. Kennedy cried out, 'Oh, my God, he's been shot!' . . . Mrs. Hill stated she heard from four to six shots in all and believes they came from a spot just west of the Texas School Book Depository Building. She thought there was a slight time interval between the first three shots and the remaining shots." Though Hill was sticking to her original impressions of the number of shots fired, she did not seem pleased in her statement to the FBI with how Lane amplified her remarks about what happened at the Sheriff's Office. "Mrs. Hill stated that from reading some of Lane's statements regarding this conversation she determined that Lane had taken some of her remarks out of context, thus changing the meaning of her replies. He had not used her full answers to some of the questions, and had misquoted her in this conversation."[34]

Following her FBI contact statement, on March 24, 1964, Hill testified before assistant counsel to the Commission and future United States Senator Arlen Specter at the U.S. Attorney's office in the Post Office Building in Dallas. In the 18 pages of recorded testimony, Hill reads to be very ill at ease, defensive, and unclear about many facts. Specter appears patronizing at times and presses her hard on certain subjects, especially trying to get specifics from her when she only has vague impressions. At times she seems easily led, and she speaks of being influenced by what others have said. She is consistent in believing she heard four to six shots, the first three seemed to be paced long enough for one person to have done the firing, and she recalls that it was on the third shot that the President's hair rippled. The second sequence of shots was different from the first. She described it as "quicker — more automatic." She speaks of jumping to the edge of the street to see the President, and following the shots, "just stood there and gawked around." Following the shots she saw a man across the street running from the direction of the School Book Depository towards the railroad tracks. ". . . He was the only thing moving up there." And she initially chased after him. "I never saw a weapon during the whole time, in anyone's hand," but, ". . . his moving made me start after him." She tells Specter, "I frankly thought they [the shots] were coming from the knoll." Specter at one point asks and answers, "Did you think perhaps they [the shots] came from the knoll exclusively because you saw the man run away, and you said you thought that might be the case?" To that Hill responds, "Could be." Hill admits that a television interview "left me very doubtful and confused," yet Specter's questions could have had the same result. At one point Specter goes off the record when Hill obviously needs a moment or two to compose herself and relax. She admits she thought the man she saw running looked like Jack Ruby, (who on Sunday, November 24, shot Oswald) and that she was mistaken about the dog in the car with the Kennedys. Concerning the Lane interview, Hill tries to explain that the conversation on November 22 at the Courts Building was with some of the press, and that although some of the things were emphatically said by persons she presumed to be Secret Service agents, they never said she had to say them — she was not coerced by the Secret Service! Specter continues to question her on this point until he receives the statement he wants. It seems plain that Mrs. Hill was not overjoyed by the testimonial wringer she was forced to endure.[35]

Hill spoke with Attorney Lane once more when in March 1966 Lane visited Dallas. In his work *Rush to Judgment* Lane wrote that Jean Hill said that after she had talked with him in February 1964 that FBI agents were there for days. She had told the truth for two years, but they didn't like what she said. She could not believe the *Warren Report* and knew it all to be lies, because she witnessed the event. Yet being a school teacher and with two children to care for, she couldn't talk about it anymore.[36]

Undoubtedly Jean Hill always believed she did tell the truth as she saw and remembered it. Yet two eyewitnesses to the same event often see and perceive what occurred quite differently. Besides the obvious mentioning of seeing a dog in the President's car and seeing the President shot in the chest, the still and film sequences of other photographers show Hill's reactions as somewhat different, at least in real time, than Hill recalls. Shortly after the actual shooting, when some of the President's escort cycles were still in the immediate area, both Moorman and Hill are on the ground. Hill does not rush across Elm Street looking to find a suspicious man for quite some time following the shooting, and then not until just about everyone in the area is back on their feet and numerous other spectators have arrived and crossed Elm Street and are streaming up the grassy knoll towards the railroad yard.[37]

Many of Mrs. Hill's recollections of the events have undergone embellishments and changes over the years. In 1965 Mrs. Hill wrote this author, "I had jumped into the street and yelled, 'Mr. President, we want to take your picture!' He raised his head and turned it in our direction. Just as the beginning of a smile creased his face, the first shot rang out and he slumped forward into Mrs. Kennedy's lap." Possibly a recollection thought to be true, but contrary to what the film shows. Over time Hill's account of the events began to take on new and more dramatic form.[38]

Portion of a Bond post-assassination photo
with both Moorman and Hill sitting
on the grass in the center foreground

By the mid-1980s as interest in the Kennedy case was picking up with the approach of the 25th anniversary, Jean Hill emerged from a self-imposed exile of discussing the assassination. She was sought out by several researchers and the media. Hill's new version of the events could have been colored by her knowledge of what new researchers and theories were claiming. She admits to having been so influenced in her testimony back in 1964. Free-lance writer and noted Kennedy researcher Jim Marrs had assisted Hill to come out of her shell. There were many people who believed and admired her. In Marrs's 1989 book *Crossfire*, he quotes Hill as telling him that she saw a man fire a gun from behind the wooden fence on the opposite side of the street. She also now claimed to have seen a puff of smoke and movement on the grassy knoll where the man was located.[39]

On November 22, 1988, the 25th anniversary of the shooting, Hill appeared on both the *Oprah Winfrey Show* and *Geraldo*, two network television talk show programs. On *Oprah Winfrey* Hill displayed her fear as well as her resentment towards the official investigation. She now contended that right after the shooting one and then two Secret Service agents confronted her, one asking her to go with him, while putting a very painful hold on her neck. To Geraldo she added that she tried to jerk away several times, but the other agent put the same hold on her other shoulder and said, "You will walk with me," and to "smile." In an office within 15 minutes after the shooting, Hill was told by two other men when she said to them that she had heard four to six shots that, "No, you really didn't see that, and you really didn't hear but three shots." Detained until 9:00 or 10:00 that evening, Hill recalled that in the months that followed her phone was tapped, her mail tampered with, and she was followed everywhere. She also told the audience that she was not interviewed by Specter where the official testimony says, but rather as a means of intimidation at Parkland Hospital. In subsequent writings, she elaborated on this to state that Specter treated her terribly. While "off the record," he claimed to know all about her and her shabby extra-marital affair and accused her of being a totally unreliable witness. According to Hill, much of her testimony as recorded in the Warren Commission *Hearings*, was fabricated, distorted, and heavily edited.[40]

Back in 1967 and 1968, Hill was fearful enough of outside influences not to cooperate in the Jim Garrison investigation, but after 25 years she believed that time enough had passed. Yet she felt some of those old fears creeping in. To Oprah she confessed that she began to have those feelings of uneasiness when recently talking with some high school students. There was a man in the crowd who made her very uncomfortable. Suddenly she began to experience those feelings like she had after 1963 when various odd things happened to her.

In the *Geraldo* interview she recalled that as the series of shots had rung out during the assassination, she thought she saw someone firing from behind the fence on the grassy knoll. Questioned by Rivera if she thought she saw someone shooting from that direction, Hill became even more emphatic. "Yes, sir. He did. I know he did." A moment later she exclaimed, "And there was a rifle blast from behind the fence on the grassy knoll." Rivera asked, "Just behind? Do you feel you saw that?" And Hill replied, "Yes, I know I did."[41]

In a 1992 book authored by Bill Sloan, "with Jean Hill," Mrs. Hill's life and experiences are narrated. Her account of the shooting is now fully developed to conform to the most recent theories, as well as fitting very nicely with the scenario film director Oliver Stone portrays in his rich movie spectacle *JFK*. Jean sees "A muzzle flash, a puff of smoke, and the shadowy figure of a man holding a rifle, barely visible above the wooden fence at the top of the knoll still in the very act of murdering the President of the United States."[42]

Witnessing the shocking death of your President right before your eyes would unnerve anyone, and both Hill and Moorman were, within minutes, thrust into an unfamiliar and intense atmosphere of being inundated with news media, all wanting a piece of them for their story. The environment was chaotic, and both women were under some amount of pressure over a number of hours, attempting to be helpful to people whom they assumed to be investigators, as well as media types hanging on their every word. Because of some of her comments to the press that day, Hill was teased by her husband and felt foolish about certain things she had said. She selectively ceased to repeat items from earlier interviews at the urging of others, though she consistently stood by her recollections of hearing four to six gunshots. She appeared to get confused and later irritated by the interest generated by her observations. She was also pressured by the contrary positions espoused by some government critics and government investigators, people who, in her eyes, continued to hound her.

To an outside observer it seems that Hill's initial taped interviews are the best record of what she saw at about 12:30 on November 22, before others influenced her to change, or before she repeated the story enough to fix the telling of it in her own mind. From these, her initial impressions, it would appear that her powers of observation under stress were not keen, and that her recollection 30 years after the events of observing someone actually firing from the grassy knoll is not substantiated by any of her statements made on the day of the event and thus without foundation.

Many others besides Hill, however, had noticed movements on the knoll at the time of the assassination. The Moorman picture, which included this area in the background, quickly became the subject for many researchers' magnifying glasses and conspiratorial theories. Given the Polaroid print's small size and its physical condition upon development, as well as the simple optics of the camera's lens, this was not an ideal photograph. Couple those factors with the small area on the print taken up by the fence and tree line, together with the confusing texture of the tree line itself, investigation of this area by a photo interpreter would be quite difficult. When researchers look at this area, their observance can be as fanciful a search as a person making out animal forms in clouds. In point of fact, even if there were assassins lurking in this area, the problems with this particular Polaroid print would make identifying them quite difficult.

Researcher Raymond Marcus was one of the first to publicize the potential importance of this photo's angle of view, and he believed that human forms could be made out in its confusing black-and-white-and-gray background. In May 1965 David Lifton, a graduate engineering student at UCLA, brought a copy of this picture published in a souvenir photo history of the assassination to Marcus's attention. Lifton believed he could make out at least one hitherto unknown person within the scene. After obtaining a negative of the picture from the publisher, an additional person was located in the print by Lifton. Among his observations was a belief that one of the plantings on the grassy knoll was artificial and used to hide snipers. The exercise of identifying figures, however, can be compared with the experiences of Percival Lowell. A noted 19th century astronomer, Percival Lowell made direct observation of the planet Mars through a large telescope and drew sketches of his observations. Lowell perceived canals or channels on the Martian surface and recorded them in numerous sketches. A man of integrity who believed that a former civilization might have at one time inhabited the red planet, his mind let him see through unclear viewing what he desired to see, even though his grand, long canals were not really there. David Lifton soon became a dedicated seeker of the truth behind the assassination. In a book touting his assassination theories published in 1980, Lifton after describing his discovery of figures in the background of the Moorman photo was bold to concede, "It became evident that those who were already in disagreement with the Warren Commission conclusions found it far easier to 'see' people on the knoll than those who believed in the Report. I could even apply this reasoning to my own observations; How certain could I be that my basic processes of perception were not hopelessly biased as a result of my believing in, say, the head-snap evidence? I really did not believe that was the case, but I couldn't prove it was not, either. Eventually, I concluded that photographic enlargements had very limited use as evidence."[43]

College professor and well respected assassination researcher Josiah Thompson in his 1967 book *Six Seconds in Dallas*, systematically examined much of the photographic evidence, including the Moorman photograph. Emmett Hudson, one of the three men who had been standing on the knoll steps, had told the FBI that the shots sounded as if they had been fired to his left, behind and above him, which Thompson saw to be the corner of the stockade fence. Thompson found in the area just above the stockade fence, as seen in the Moorman photo, two anomalous shapes to the west of the corner. One turned out to be a top portion of the railroad signal tower, located some distance to the rear, while the other one did not seem present in a nearly duplicate photograph made for this comparison at a later date. Signal supervisor S. M. Holland had been viewing the procession from the railroad overpass, and during the shooting he had noted what he referred to as a "puff of smoke" in front of the stockade area. He had heard four shots, the third and fourth fired so close together as if they were a double shot. Feeling that a shot had originated near the corner of the fence, he and two companions ran over to this area. "I was looking for empty shells or some indication that there was a rifleman or someone over there." When Thompson, later doing field research, took Holland to the area of the assassination, and requested that he stand in the position where he had described what he had seen, Holland's head appeared in the exact position where the second anomaly was located in the Moorman photo. Holland had earlier been shown a copy of the Moorman photo and had declared, "Well, do you know, I think you are looking right down at the barrel of that gun right now!" Interestingly, in the photo reproduced in the Thompson book portraying Holland at the fence position and seemingly replicating the view of the Moorman photo, the signal tower is not in evidence.[44]

In late November 1967 under the headline, "Blow-up!! November 22, 1963," the *Los Angeles Free Press*, an alternative tabloid newspaper, published an article by Raymond Marcus including illustrations of five ever-increasing enlargements of the area where Lifton and Marcus had found a man behind the concrete wall near the Zapruder position. After chastising the Warren Commission for not publishing the Moorman photo, Marcus then described the finding of the figure. From the sketches the figure appeared to be a youngish balding man of medium build and with his right elbow elevated and extended to his right with a straight object apparently held in his hands. One can seem to make out the figure in the photo used by Marcus, though other prints of the Moorman film examined by the author do not seem to show the figure at all. Inherent in photo examination are possible outside factors — be it photographic artifact, the use of multi-generation copies, or darkening of the print — all possibly affecting the observation. As part of his article Marcus asked 12 persons holding professional photography positions to comment on what, if anything, they did see when presented with this portion of the photograph. Marcus reported that ten recognized the image of a man, two could not detect a discernable shape, and four of the men were willing to furnish a statement as well as a sketch of what they saw, the sketches reproduced in the article all showing similar characteristics.[45]

In a subsequent *Free Press* issue Josiah Thompson wrote to refute Marcus's alternate "assassin" sighting saying, among other things, that in the original print the image is invisible. Marcus's response was to attack Thompson's sighting, stating of the Thompson figure, "This spot is TOTALLY indistinguishable as a human figure, or any other definable object. Because this spot does not appear in a test photo taken in Dealey Plaza three years after the assassination, Thompson believes it represents a man. It is, of course, possible that his guess is correct; but surprisingly, he chooses not to apply this same reasoning to the far more compelling Number 5 man — who, similarly is not present in test photos taken last year."[46]

More and more figures were seemingly being found by various researchers examining the same photo. In 1976 authors F. Peter Model and Robert J. Groden in their book *JFK: The Case for Conspiracy* included three pictures made at the time of the assassination with blow-ups and sketches showing possible assassins firing rifles at the President's car.   One of the three was the Moorman picture in which this time the assassin's position is at the end of the concrete wall which, ". . . shows the indistinct face of the man seen in Z[apruder frame]-413." The word "smoke" and an arrow point to the area in the sketch made from the photo blow-up, so no one will be confused as to where the figure is located.[47]

Unlike the Warren Commission inquiry of 1964, the 1978 House Select Committee on Assassinations investigation included research into and the gathering of photographic materials relating to the assassination.   The two Polaroids still in the possession of Mary Ann Moorman, who by then was remarried, were loaned to the Committee's Photographic Panel for examination. The panel report noted that the photo showing President Kennedy ". . . had suffered from handling during the intervening years," and that "a number of large and small defects were visible on the photograph when the panel examined it." Due to the nature of the photo image and the absence of an original negative, image scanning of transparencies could not be used.   The panel decided that there was little merit in using computer processing on it, instead asking Rochester Institute of Technology to make a high quality copy negative.   Enlargement prints with varying contrast and brightness were then made, but failed to produce significant increases in detail.   No evidence was found of a person at the position at the concrete wall as had been indicated in the Willis #5 transparency, and due to the poor quality of detail near the stockade, the panel did no work on that area.   Robert Groden, the assassination critic as well as consultant to the Photographic Panel, criticized the panel for relying on the faded original print rather than the higher quality negative that was taken of the Polaroid and used back in 1963 by AP and UPI.[48]

In the Committee's final report, which included a finding that, based on acoustical research done by two separate experts, a shot most probably originated from the fence area, the report again reiterated the lack of tests and results from the Moorman photograph. Then stating that the significance of the picture might be largely negative, the report went on to comment that if figures were not found behind the fence, it would be, ". . . a troubling lack of corroboration for the acoustical analysis." Finally, covering all bases without needing to bother with the Committee's own lack of follow-through, the report concluded, "At the same time, the Committee noted, the Department of Justice might consider further enhancement, if it is deemed to be feasible," to which most critics would surely respond, "Sure they will!"[49]

Yet while the second official government inquiry still could not find anyone among the foliage on the grassy knoll, critics had no problem continuing to populate the Polaroid with potential assassins.

In 1982 while examining a transparency made of a good quality print of the Moorman photograph, Texas researcher Gary Mack almost immediately noted a figure standing behind the knoll's stockade fence, which at that point looked to be a part of the concrete wall.  Asking for the assistance of co-researcher and photo technician Jack

White, the two found in the White-enhanced pictures what appeared to be the forehead, eyes, nose, and upper body of a man. Partly obscuring his face was what might be taken to be a muzzle flash and smoke from a rifle. The man also seemed to be wearing on his left chest and arm a badge and insignia similar to those worn by Dallas police officers. Later still the two researchers identified what they interpreted as a man wearing a hard hat standing to the left of the first man, glancing towards the direction of the Book Depository as well as a man to their right, possibly in a military soft hat and taking pictures with some sort of camera.[50]

Attempting to interest a major photo lab in pursuing the study of this photo, Mack relates that in late 1983 Massachusetts Institute of Technology agreed to work on the question with computer enhancement technology. According to Jim Marrs in *Crossfire*, they were told that the picture did reveal a man firing a gun, but a day later without explanation the chairman of the department gave the materials back and said that the school would no longer participate in the study.[51] Undaunted, the two enlisted the aid of the Jet Propulsion Laboratory [JPL] under the auspices of former House Select Committee on Assassinations photo panelist Robert Selzer. According to Selzer, Mack made his request through the JPL public information office, which allowed Selzer to examine the material without charging a fee. Selzer remembered receiving, "a whole series of copies of prints." The photo images were extremely grainy, and noisy, and Selzer ". . . tried various types of linear computer filters to try and suppress the noise to some extent without wiping out everything that's in the image. You sort of have to find a balance. It's difficult because you're not quite sure what you are looking for. We've run through a whole gamut of methods on some of the earlier pictures that he sent, and we felt the noise was too high to do anything with — to do anything useful."[52]

An intriguing sidebar to this tale is the story told by one Gordon L. Arnold some years after the assassination. In 1978 Arnold was interviewed by *Dallas Morning News* reporter Earl Golz, who had written many stories relating to the assassination. Arnold claimed that back in 1963 as a 23-year-old soldier on brief leave prior to shipping out three days later for a post in Alaska, and dressed in uniform, he had brought his mother's camera to Dealey Plaza to take movies of the President's motorcade. Chased out of a position high on the knoll near the triple underpass by a man who showed him Secret Service credentials, and who told him he could not stay up there, Arnold went to a tree on the road-side of the fence, high on the grassy slope and to the west of the colonnade. As the motorcade rolled by and he was taking his movie, a shot whizzed past his left ear from behind. Knowing someone was firing live ammunition, Arnold hit the ground. Following a second report, ". . . While I was laying on the ground, it seemed like the gentleman came . . . and I thought it was a police officer because he had a uniform of a police officer, but he didn't wear a hat . . ." The officer demanded to know if he was taking photos. A second officer who was shaking and crying also appeared and was waving a long gun. Arnold, seeing the weapon in the officer's hand, immediately gave him the exposed film and quickly left.[53]

*Populating the Moorman Polaroid with Potential Assassins*

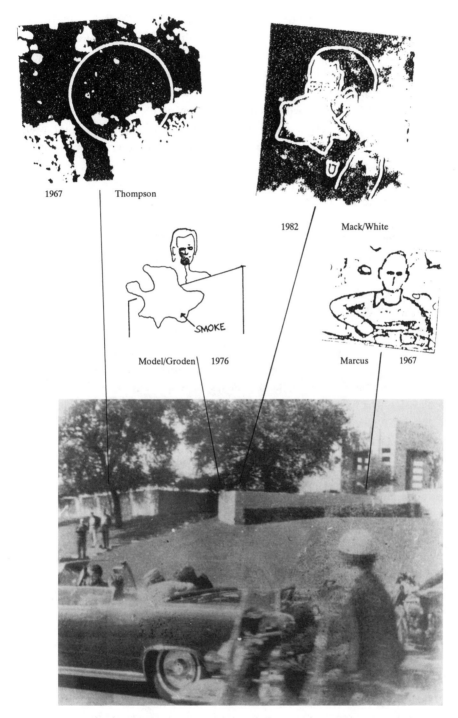

Various researchers have found figures within this Moorman photograph,
which they have interpreted as possible assassins.

Intriguing as the story is, especially when coupled to the figures Mack and White believed they had identified, Arnold's story, to a healthy skeptic, is soft on proof. Although it is true that some of the people visible on the knoll area that day are still not publicly identified, their being at the scene is readily visible in various photographs and films. Neither the distinctive dress of Arnold's, nor his purported location, nor that of the police officer who rousted him is recorded in any existing photograph, and no one else recounts seeing such an event transpire during the moments after the shooting. Getting off the ground, speaking with a cop, and removing his film from the camera would have taken some seconds at a time when other people streamed into the area. Why didn't Arnold report the firing of the weapon to his rear, or the actions of the weird cop? Alaska is a faraway place, but not the end of civilization, and he was around for several days after the event. Didn't he tell any family or friends about his experience who could corroborate his story? Supporters claim the fact that Senator Ralph Yarborough commented about seeing someone drop to the ground following the shooting and thinking, "There's a combat veteran who knows how to act when weapons start firing," refers to Arnold. Yet it could refer to several men who dropped to the ground at the sound of shots, including the highly visible Bill Newman.

In a 1988 British TV program looking into the assassination, the producers extensively reviewed the "badge man" evidence developed by Mack and White. Arnold is interviewed, and when shown the fuzzy blow-ups of the ¼-inch square area where the images of these three men are purportedly located within the Polaroid, hesitatingly and then emotionally Arnold takes us slowly, point-by-point, through the realization of his presence at the shooting scene, being the one closest to an assassin. Then, in a dramatic piece of television, the former soldier faultily declares that if he had known about this evidence, he probably would not have agreed to do this interview. It's a chilling scene, but whether it is Arnold's true reaction or just plain acting leaves one unsure. As with so much involving the case, Arnold's story makes a cautious person not want to give the benefit of a doubt without other more substantive facts than one man's 15-year-late confession and a noisy, multi-generation, poor quality Polaroid print showing cloud figure assassins.[54]

In November 1988 PBS's award-winning series *Nova* took on the Kennedy assassination. A copy negative made from a print of the Moorman photo was examined by Polaroid and MIT technicians, especially relating to the area where the "badge man" was described. In this brief segment of the program their verdict was that the figure of the "badge man" could be a man, but the gun flash within the image was more likely the effect of sunlight filtering through the trees. One technician somewhat frivolously commented that he thought seeing the figure required a little bit of imagination, but that he believed you could see that there was something there about the right size. In describing this segment Mack contends about the *Nova* test that they used a crummy print and poked fun at what should be a serious question.[55]

Mack, who has spent some 11 years attempting to resolve the truth about the possible figures with the Moorman picture, has written that the odyssey with his observations has gone from "simple and startling" to "complex and frustrating." Though some may not agree with his visual interpretation, his efforts to request and obtain serious scientific study for this picture have been well documented. He genuinely wants to resolve the issue and has met various personal and technological roadblocks. Due to the fixative coating having been applied improperly or much too late back in November 1963, the Polaroid's fine detail has substantially faded and will continue to fade until the image is invisible. By late 1993 Mack was debating whether or not to recommend a radiation-enhanced procedure available in Japan which might create an identical image with detail to match the original print, but at the cost of radioactivity contaminating the original Polaroid.[56]

The Moorman picture, like so much else with the case, does not appear to give us simple, definitive answers. While we wonder as Mary Moorman did many years later, if hidden away in her 24¢ print, ". . . Something could have been there all this time and no one cared to do anything about it,"[57] we still are left with a less than ideal piece of evidence.

## CHAPTER NOTES

1.	Gary Mack, ed., *Coverups!*, 11/1984, p. 2; *Hearings Before the President's Commission on the Assassination of President Kennedy*, v. 6, p. 215, 222-223; Bill Sloan with Jean Hill, *JFK, The Last Dissenting Witness*, p. 19-20, 35, 48, 74, 143; Conversation with Jean Hill in Dallas, 11/15/1991.
2.	Peter C. Wensberg, *Land's Polaroid*, p. 98-99, 132-133, John Wolbarst, *Pictures in a Minute*, p. 4-5, 130-133.
3.	*Consumer Reports*, 12/1963, p. 309, 322; *Consumer Bulletin Annual 1961-62*, v. 36, p. 87.
4.	Ibid., Information provided by Ronna Berezin, Polaroid Corporate Archives, 10/25/1990, 10/31/1990; a view of the Moorman camera is seen in the 1988 BBC-TV production, *The Men Who Killed Kennedy*.
5.	Conversation with Jean Hill in Dallas, 10/22/1992. The frame number on the reverse of the first Polaroid print which Mary Moorman made of the motorcade is #3. Moorman now has no recollection of the content of the apparent first two frames on the fresh roll, believing they didn't turn out and were probably thrown away. It seemed probable from the discovery of the two Houston Street portraits, that they might be the missing frames. Yet Hill distinctly recalls them being remnants from another earlier roll. Another factor which seems to confirm Hill's recollection that these two were from an earlier roll is that according to the camera's instruction manual, the numbers of frames run from 2 to 9 rather than 1 to 8, as in previous cameras, and thus on a new roll the first frame would be #2.
6.	FBI report by E. J. Robertson and Thomas Trettis, Jr., on Jean Hill, 3/13/1964; *Coverups!*, op. cit. p. 2; Jim Marrs, *Crossfire*, p. 37-38; Harold Weisberg, *Photographic Whitewash*, p. 164-168.
7.	Mary Ann Moorman Photo #3, 11/22/1963, obtained from FOIA request 10/1985 and 1/1986; *Coverups!*, p. 2; *Hearings*, op. cit., v. 20, p. 489.
8.	W. George Lumpkin telephone interview with Trask, 2/26/1987; *Hearings*, op. cit., v. 20, p. 489, v. 6, p. 303; and v. 7, p. 579-580, 582; *Coverups!*, op. cit., p. 2-3.
9.	Lumpkin interview, op. cit.

10.  Wilma Bond transparencies #4-8, 11/22/1963; and F.M. Bell film sequence 11/22/1963.
11.  *Hearings*, op. cit., v.6, p. 212, 214-216; Typescript copy of rewrites within the collection of the *Dallas Times Herald*, [JFK] file #8, Belo Corp., 11/22/1963.
12.  *Hearings*, op. cit., v.6, p. 213-216; *Coverups!*, op. cit., p. 2; conversation with Charles Brehm in Dallas, 10/22/1992; Sloan, op. cit., p. 30.
13.  Remarks by James Featherston at Reporters Remember Conference, Dallas, 11/20/1993.
14.  NBC telecast, 11/22/1963, from videotape at The Kennedy Library, TNN255-R1; *There Was a President*, p. 5.
15.  NBC, ibid., TNN-222; 5; *There was a President*, p. 25.
16.  WFAA telecast, 11/22/1963, from the telecast *The Kennedy Tapes*, broadcast 11/1983.
17.  *Hearings*, op. cit., v. 6, p. 214, 221-222. It is noted that in recent reviews of film coverage made at Love Field, Mrs. Kennedy was apparently presented with a small stuffed animal and also with a portrait. Though she may have kept the stuffed toy among the roses with which she was also presented, it cannot be specifically seen in overhead views made of the back seat of the Lincoln.
18.  WFAA, op. cit.
19.  FBI report of S.A. Robert C. Lish, 11/22/1963; *Hearings*, op. cit., v.6, p. 220-221; v. 22, p. 838-839; v. 9, p. 479; v. 19, p. 487.
20.  Lecture of Gary Mack at the Pittsburgh, PA, conference, 11/19/1988; *Hearings*, op. cit., v. 19, p. 487.
21.  *Dallas Times Herald*, 11/22/1963, p. A-17.
22.  *Hearings*, op.cit., v. 19, p. 533, 535-536; v. 22, p. 839.
23.  Ibid., v. 6, p. 219-220.
24.  Jack A. Weaver Polaroid photograph, 11/22/1963, obtained through Trask FOIA request #254,888 and #254,889, 11/30/1984.
25.  Ibid., FBI report, file #DL100-10461, 12/3/1964.
26.  James T. Hankins Polaroid photograph, 11/22/1963, and file obtained through Trask FOIA request #208,085, 4/17/1985; Commission Document 397, p. 37.
27.  Ibid.
28.  Moorman photo #5, 11/22/1963, from various sources.
29.  *Boston Traveler*, 11/23/1963, p. 3.
30.  Weisberg, op. cit., p. 163.
31.  Ibid., p. 30-39.
32.  Trask FOIA request #263,249 for Mary Moorman papers, 10/29/1985; *Coverups!*, op. cit., p. 2.
33.  *Hearings*, op. cit., v. 2, p. 42-43.
34.  Weisberg, op. cit., p. 164-166.
35.  *Hearings*, op. cit., v. 6, p. 205-223.
36.  Mark Lane, *Rush to Judgment*, p. 285.
37.  Bond transparencies and Bell film, op. cit.
38.  Letter, Jean Hill to Richard Trask, 1965. Mrs. Hill also indicated on a simple diagram of Dealey Plaza provided to her that at the Texas School Book Depository "shots from here" and including an "X" at that location.
39.  Marrs, op. cit., p. 38; Sloan, op. cit., p. 207-214.
40.  Journal Graphics, *The Oprah Winfrey Show: Remembering President John F. Kennedy*, transcript #572, 11/22/1988, p. 4-5; Journal Graphics, *Geraldo: The Killing of JFK*, transcript #309, 11/22/1988, p. 2-4; Sloan, op. cit., p. 100-102.
41.  *The Oprah Winfrey Show*, op. cit., p. 5; *Geraldo*, op. cit., p. 3.
42.  Sloan, op. cit., p. 23. A very interesting paper titled "Eyewitness Testimony, Memory and Assassination Research," was published by Dennis Ford and Mark S. Zaid in 1993. Explaining proven experimental data gathered through numerous psychological studies, the paper demonstrates the caution that must be used with eyewitness testimony and suggests that researchers must be more analytical in their evaluation of witnesses' statements. Discussing long and short

term memory, the process of information retrieval and forgetting, as well as the role of interference and the presentation of new information to witnesses, the authors through independently examining Mrs. Hill's statements over the years, state that she has developed into a most unreliable witness to the assassination. Her memories, possibly through the influence of the critic community, have become unreal or scattered throughout by false memories. (Paper presented at the Second Research Conference of "The Third Decade", June 18-20, 1993.)

43.    Richard Warren Lewis, *The Scavengers and Critics of the Warren Report*, p. 172; David Lifton, *Best Evidence*, p. 11.

44.    Josiah Thompson, *Six Seconds in Dallas*, p. 120-123, 126-129.

45.    *Los Angeles Free Press*, "Blow-up!! November 22, 1963," 11/24-12/1, 1967, p. 1-2, 31.

46.    Ibid., 1/19/1968.

47.    F. Peter Model & Robert J. Groden, *JFK: The Case for Conspiracy*, p. [186].

48.    *Appendix to Hearings Before the Select Committee on Assassinations*, v. 6, p. 125-126, 296.

49.    *Report of the Select Committee on Assassinations*, p. 84-85.

50.    *Coverups!*, op. cit., 10/1982, p. 1-2; Marrs, op. cit., p.79-80; British Central Television telecast, *The Men Who Killed Kennedy*, 10/1988.

51.    Marrs, op. cit., p. 80; Mack lecture, op. cit.

52.    Robert H. Selzer telephone interview with Trask, 7/1987.

53.    British Central Television telecast, op. cit.; Anthony Summers, *Conspiracy*, p. 58-59; Henry Hurt, *Reasonable Doubt*, p. 111-113.

54.    British Central Television, op. cit.

55.    WGBH Transcripts, *Nova: Who Shot President Kennedy?*, transcript #1518, 11/15/1988, p. 12-13; Mack lecture, op. cit.

56.    Gary Mack, "Eyes Closed: The Case Against Gerald Posner," *The Fourth Decade*, 11/1993, p. 17-18.

57.    British Central Television, op. cit.

Polaroid's Model 80 "Highlander"

## CHAPTER 11

# The Terminal Annex Men

Among the amateur movie makers who were present in Dealey Plaza at the time of the assassination were two employees of the federal government, Bob Hughes and Mark Bell, who though they did not know each other, worked out of the same building. From their separate locations and angles of view, neither man captured on film the actual shooting itself, though both had been filming up to only moments before the shots echoed in the Plaza. Likewise they both resumed filming the now wild scene in front of them within seconds after the last shot had been fired.

Robert Joseph Elmore Hughes was born on April 15, 1938, in Mt. Pleasant, Iowa. Married in 1959 and moving to Dallas, Hughes and his wife Maureen were living in an apartment on Hursey Street in the University Park section of Dallas in 1963. Maureen was a schoolteacher in Richardson, a northern suburb of Dallas, while Robert was a customs examiner for the United States Treasury Department, employed at the Terminal Annex Post Office, located at the corner of Commerce and Houston Streets on the southern boundary of Dealey Plaza.[1]

Also working out of the Terminal Annex was F. M. "Mark" Bell. A native of Limestone County, Texas, Bell had been born on March 6, 1918, and had seen combat in the 1st Marine Division during the Second World War. By 1963 the 45-year-old Bell lived with his family some five miles southwest of downtown Dallas on South Oak Cliff Boulevard. A letter carrier for the United States Postal Department, Bell prepared his daily deliveries at the Terminal Annex and then delivered them on a walking route taking him into the nearby downtown commercial area.[2]

Maureen Hughes recalls that her husband, who passed away in the fall of 1985, owned a Bell & Howell 8mm movie camera in 1963. He loved taking home movies and would usually have the rolls developed at a local Sears Roebuck store. In late November 1963 Hughes had a partially exposed roll of Kodachrome color film in his camera, including scenes of working on a family car, shots taken from the observation deck of a tall building, and of family members going to church. The last sequence taken prior to Hughes using the roll to film the President's visit is a prankish shot of a woman hiding behind a photograph of another woman.

Mrs. Hughes knew her husband planned to go out at lunchtime to take movies of the presidential motorcade. He was an avid amateur photographer, and couldn't pass up such a momentous event occurring just a stone's throw from his office. Mr. Bell's reason for filming the parade had a very different slant.

Bell owned a simple one-lens 8mm Kodak movie camera, not so much for himself, but for the family. He virtually cants a litany of reasons why he took family movies explaining — "I'm not interested in pictures, because I can see the actual thing, and I don't dwell on pictures. My wife does, but I don't. When we are on vacation, I only take pictures for her. I don't for myself. My wife insists on taking pictures, but I don't take pictures for myself. I don't like taking pictures."

A reluctant photographer at best, Bell, like many other amateurs, was at times caught in the typical, but unenviable position of seeing special events through the often minuscule and obscure camera viewfinder. He would not have been the first family photographer who would rather enjoy the reality of the event rather than have to try to record it on film for the family.

On November 22, Bell's 16-year-old daughter wanted to be excused from school so she could see the downtown presidential motorcade. In an obvious personal dichotomy, Bell didn't want his daughter to miss school, so he agreed to take a movie of the parade so she could see it later. "My daughter wanted to go, and I refused to let her get out of school and I took the pictures just because of that. She wanted to attend the parade and I wouldn't let her."[3] And thus an historic piece of film was created by a reluctant photographer who was also a strict, but sympathetic father.

At around noontime, Bob Hughes walked northerly up Houston Street and picked a spot on the southwesterly curb at Main and Houston Streets to await the procession. Pointing his camera at the red sandstone upper floors of the old Dallas County Court House, he squeezed off about three seconds' worth of film, then pointed his camera up Main Street in the direction of an under-construction steel skeleton skyscraper in the distance. Then for some six seconds of film he first tilts down to the street and then pans left bringing into view the gathering spectators on the Houston and Main Street corner diagonal to his position. Two other short takes are made. There is a

Pre-motorcade scenes
by Hughes

quick view of Main Street followed by pictures of a young man and a woman in the group of spectators to Hughes's immediate right.[4]

Bell has in the meantime also broken for lunch, and alone he walks up from the Annex Building to the north cement peristyle, one of the decorative features delineating were people around taking pictures. I was standing up on a pillar that was made for aesthetic purposes, I suppose, and I was standing on top of that. It was about four feet tall."[5] These concrete peristyle endposts afforded an elevated position above the crowd, and though unnoticed by Bell, on the southern peristyle endpost and parallel to his position, another amateur photographer, Charles Bronson, had also discovered this good viewing location. Some 240 feet northwest of Bell, yet another amateur movie maker, businessman Abraham Zapruder, was atop a similar concrete post in the north pergola area. All three perches would offer a dramatic view of the ensuing events.

Like Hughes, Bell took a few seconds to record the view up Main Street towards the direction of the anticipated procession. At about 12:30 the blinking red lights of the motorcycles and the presidential caravan were in camera range. Bell and Hughes and the numerous other still and movie camera amateurs began to click and purr their cameras away as the President's sleek Lincoln convertible ran the gauntlet of excited waving and clapping hands.

As the car turns right at Houston, Bell records some 15½ seconds of the scene, picking up the view again as the car swings left around to Elm Street and passes the front door of the Texas School Book Depository Building. About 62 frames are made of this Elm Street sequence, until Bell's view is obscured by his panning left into the trees parallel to the street. "Between me and the President's car there was a tree. I

Bell records the limousine in front of the Depository

jumped down from the thing that I was on and ran around to the end of it so that I could get a better picture. That's when the shots were fired, while I was down. Probably not more than 5 to 10 seconds."[6]

Hughes has meanwhile been filming about 16 seconds of the President's car coming up to and turning right onto Houston Street. As he pans his camera to the left following the now receding Lincoln convertible and the police motorcycle escort, the spectators on Houston Street and on the lower floors of the County Court, County Records, and Dal-Tex Buildings on the east side of Houston Street are in the camera view. Also turning onto Houston Street and into Hughes's camera view are the Secret Service follow-up car and Vice-President's blue convertible. Releasing the shutter button momentarily, Hughes, seeing the President's car beginning to turn onto Elm Street, resumes filming. This time his camera is aimed slightly more to the left, revealing both sides of Houston Street and much of the facade of the Texas School Book Depository

Building. This approximately 5-second, 88-frame sequence displays on the left side of the frames a view of the east side of the Depository Building up to the sixth floor. Hughes stops filming just as the President's car is beginning to travel in front of the Depository Building itself. He redirects his camera towards the right and films the middle section of the motorcade, including the camera cars and a motorcycle turning onto Houston Street. After 72 frames of this activity are exposed to his camera, Hughes stops filming since the major part of the motorcade has now passed him by.[7]

In a letter to his parents written that Friday evening, just hours after the assassination, Hughes tells them of his recollections and reaction to what occurred next:

"Just a minute before the shooting everybody was clapping and cheering Mr. Kennedy as he passed. . . . About five seconds after I quit taking pictures we heard the shots. . . . Some of the people dropped to the ground at the first shot, but most of us just stood where we were. Nobody knew for sure who had been hit. My first reaction was that somebody was shooting firecrackers. Then the lady standing next to me said, 'They're shooting at him.'

"The car had just turned the corner to go under the triple underpass beneath the railroad tracks. I saw Mrs. Kennedy then. She seemed to be in about a half-standing position with her arm behind her on the back of the car. I couldn't see the president. After a minute's hesitation, the car roared off through the underpass, and the crowd began to run towards the scene.

"About half-way through all that, I realized what had happened and began taking pictures again. I may have some movies of the car leaving the scene, but there was so much confusion that I don't really remember.

From a position at Main Street,
Hughes films activity on Elm.

"However, I know that I have shots of the crowd as the first reaction set in. The people ran towards where the shooting took place, and also towards where the shots seemed to come from."[8]

Upon hearing the shots, Hughes had rushed down some 80 feet westerly on the south sidewalk of Main Street to better watch the commotion on Elm Street, and from this location he began filming. Looking between and beyond the backs of three men in the camera's foreground, the lens discerns a rush of people traveling towards Elm Street. Two convertible camera cars are very slowly traveling towards the underpass. Panning left and then right, the camera picks up motorcycle officer Clyde A. Haygood, just getting off his cycle, setting it down and running up the embankment toward the railroad overpass. Navy cameraman Tom Atkins is made out running back towards his car, Camera Car 1 having stopped and the second car overtaking it on the left and then passing it. The first camera car then starts off, followed by the third camera car. In Hughes's next sequence taken at the same spot several seconds later, one and then another three-wheeled motorcycle is seen speeding westerly down Main Street, one of the cycle officers being D. V. Harkness who, following the shots, cycled down Main Street to obtain a view between the railroad tracks and Industrial Boulevard.[9] In the background, the infield area between Elm and Main Streets is filling up with people as the first of the motorcade busses is seen traveling down Elm. Hughes then shifts his attention back to the corner of Main and Houston Streets, where people are walking and running westerly towards the action. Several minutes pass as Hughes travels to the area behind the grassy knoll fence. Many spectators had gravitated to this location following the shooting, believing the shots originated here. Then a panoramic sequence is made by Hughes of the buildings surrounding Dealey Plaza including the southwest corner of the Texas School Book Depository Building. The final of the ten sequences Hughes made following the shooting is of the front

Hughes films the parking lot and Depository.

entrance of the School Book Depository with a milling crowd around it, including construction worker Howard Brennan. Brennan told the authorities he had seen a rifle being fired from the sixth story corner window of the building, and Hughes's film captures Brennan on the steps of the building.[10]

Mark Bell had just gotten off of his camera perch and was moving to the end of the north peristyle to resume filming when he heard shots. In 1967 researcher Josiah Thompson asked Bell about the number of shots Bell had heard. Bell recalled hearing three shots, two of which were bunched, but he could not tell which ones. He explained to Thompson that anyone there could have been mistaken as to the bunching of the sounds as it had all happened within several seconds and that emotion, fear and excitement were involved in the mix. When asked about the number of shots many years later, Bell who was quite familiar with the Plaza area, having worked from there so many years, volunteered, "I will tell you the same thing I told Josiah Thompson, that is a natural bowl, and there are echoes in it, and I don't believe that any individual person can exactly tell how many shots were fired, because of the echoes. I'm not an authority, but considering the amount of shots I've heard during the war, I don't believe anyone could recognize the difference between the number of shots, and the number of echoes."[11]

Just after the shots had been fired and upon reaching the end of the peristyle, Bell immediately began filming. "In the process of moving you lose some of your senses. You know something had happened because the President's car took off like a bat out of Hades, and I got a shot of it going under the underpass — so you know something had happened. A motorcycle was lying down where a cop was behind it trying to see what was going on.

Vehicles rush through the underpass.

People were running in all directions. You knew something was happening, but had no way of knowing what. I just kept shooting pictures."[12]

Bell's film captured the action in three erratic but dramatic film sequences. The first sequence opens with his camera blurrily swinging to pick up the scene, including fast pans to the left with the motorcade lead car being overtaken at the underpass by the President's car. The follow-up car, Vice-President's convertible, and sedan escort are following behind. At this moment Bell apparently had to rewind his camera spring. When he again begins filming, he captures the activity around the grassy knoll with spectators including the Newman family, Jean Hill, Mary Moorman, Charles Brehm, and Marilyn

Bell directs his camera to activity on the knoll area.

Sitzman identifiable, while motorcycle cop Bobby Hargis, off his cycle, is running back to it as another escort cycle rushes past. Other later sequences are made from this same camera location. The camera cars travel down Elm Street, while more and more spectators arrive in the area, cross the street, and run up the knoll to the area around, adjacent to, and behind a stockade fence. After recording a few more seconds of film, Bell, knowing his lunch hour is now about over, walks back to the Post Office Annex Building. Bell did not speak with any police authorities and remained at his building until the end of his shift. Before he resumed work, however, from an overlooking upper story window of the Annex he took some film of the School Book Depository and Plaza area with its flurry of post-assassination activity.[13]

Returning home that evening Bell recalls being "extremely affected" by what he had seen, and he and his family watched much television that weekend. Other things were also pressing on his mind as his son-in-law was in the hospital following an emergency appendectomy. Bell recalls that everything got quite confusing. "There was a lot of personal things going on at the time, and that was more important to me than anything else."

Bell's last personal link with the assassination story took place early Sunday afternoon when he witnessed the live on-air shooting of Oswald by night club owner Jack Ruby. "I saw it on television as it happened. I was acquainted with Jack Ruby, and not surprised at anything that happened. He was on my mail route, and I just was acquainted with him delivering mail to him at his business. I don't doubt it [the shooting] was a spur-of-the-moment thing. He was that type of a person."[14]

The next week Bell brought his film down to a camera store on Main Street to have it developed. Although he is presently unsure of just how or when *LIFE* magazine first found out about his film, a 1967 *LIFE* article indicated Bell brought his film to Dallas correspondent Patsy Swank. This occurred probably in early 1967. It seems clear that Bell never let it be known to authorities that he was a witness or had film, and it wasn't until 1967 that his film received any public notice. Josiah Thompson, on a research and writing assignment of his own, as well as assisting an assassination investigation conducted by *LIFE* magazine, made contact with Bell. The resulting effort included *LIFE* publishing a story titled, "Last Seconds of the Motorcade" and including a picture of Bell and one frame his movie. Thompson's book *Six Seconds in Dallas* came out that same fall concurrent with an article about it in *The Saturday Evening Post*, which included one color frame from the Bell film. Thompson's publication used some five frames from the Bell movie footnoted to indicate that the film had never been looked at by authorities, and that several frames were published in his book for the first time ever.[15]

Whereas Bell's film and content was unknown for quite some time, the Hughes film took a different course. Maureen Hughes describes her husband as "a very conscientious person who would always do the right thing." She believes that following the assassination he heard on television that those who had taken film were urged to let the authorities know. In point of fact, on Saturday afternoon, November 23, Captain Glen King of the Dallas Police Department, being interviewed on live television in a corridor at the police station made a plea. "The Federal Department of Justice has asked us, and we join in with them in requesting that any person who was in the vicinity of the assassination yesterday who was taking pictures, bring these pictures to the police department here. . . . It's logical, I think, that since the President's motorcade was going through, someone in that area might have had cameras and might have been taking pictures. We don't know of anyone, but if there are such persons, we certainly would urge that they bring their film to the police department." Later still that afternoon Police Chief Jesse Curry in a similar television interview made the same request.[16]

By Monday Hughes had his film developed. Although Oswald was now dead, and the police department's role had diminished, Hughes voluntarily and personally delivered his roll of Kodachrome film to the Dallas FBI office. He also gave the agents a description of from where he had taken it. In one of two reports filed by the local FBI to headquarters in Washington, it was pointed out that the film included frames of the front of the Texas School Book Depository and that, "from the photographs there appears to be a person in the sixth floor window. . ." The second report stated, "On the sixth floor of the room where the rifle and cartridge cases were located one figure can be seen in the window."[17]

Sent on to the FBI laboratory in Washington, the film was copied and examined. Still prints were made of the window in question in order to determine, ". . . as to whether any individuals could be observed in the window from which the murder shots were fired." On December 9 the FBI laboratory reported concerning that question — "There are no images in any of the exposures of Q104 [number assigned to the Hughes film specimen] which show the corner window of the sixth floor of the Texas School Book Depository Building from which the assassin's gun was fired that can be interpreted as the form of an individual. The forms recorded in this window can be interpreted as in the same general shapes as boxes, found at and just behind the window in question."[18]

By December 19 Hughes received back his original film, after which the government had no interest in it. Except for what seemed to be a somewhat cursory examination by the FBI, this perhaps very key piece of film was subsequently all but ignored by the investigation.

Maureen Hughes recalls that her husband would occasionally express the wish that he had been in Abraham Zapruder's shoes. He, by the chance of his location, had recorded such an historic piece of film for which he was able to acquire a great sum of money. She thinks *LIFE* magazine first located her husband in 1967 and, "Of all those who have contacted him about the film, Tink Thompson was my favorite. He came down and spent time with Bob. He was very thorough." The film, rediscovered by *LIFE* through released Warren Commission documentation, generated significant interest as it showed that critical window locale, taken only seconds before the first shot. Through various new examinations of the film by the media and others, both Hughes and his wife were interested to learn, "If somebody would show up in that window at the Book Depository."[19]

In November 1966, *LIFE* magazine published an article urging the reopening of the investigation into the assassination as part of its third anniversary issue coverage of the President's death. The magazine then committed itself to an investigation of its own. Upon hearing of the activities of Josiah Thompson, an assistant professor of philosophy at Haverford College, who had been doing some interesting and relevant research, *LIFE* invited Thompson to join with them, while at the same time pursuing his own research for a book on the subject. Then abruptly at the end of 1967 *LIFE* all but abandoned its previously committed intensive investigation. Its only major published investigative result was a November 24, 1967, issue which included an article by Governor John Connally and a photographic sampling of pictures taken by amateurs during the events of the assassination. The magazine had, during the ensuing year, gathered together a number of prints and films taken by amateur photographers, including Bell and Hughes. It had then requested Itek, a Massachusetts photographic interpretation firm which had previously done a study of the Orville Nix film for the United Press International, to conduct a study of some of the gathered photographic materials. The objectives of the study were defined by *LIFE*. By means of time-lapse viewing of the Hughes sixth floor window sequence under high magnification, Itek concluded that "A rectangular shape with the long dimension vertical can be seen slightly to the right of center in the half open, right hand window of the Texas School Book Depository Building. In the Hughes sequence, the shape appears to change in size as the car approaches the corner of Houston and Elm Streets. It seems to decrease in size from left to right and from top to bottom." Stereo viewing of these same images indicated to Itek that, "The rectangular shape is definitely recessed from the window and would appear to be a stack of boxes." Other varied observational methods performed by Itek, while not bringing out any further new information, seemed to support the first two observations. There appeared to be movement in the critical window. Just what that movement meant, however, [were the boxes themselves moving?] was not definitely stated. While *LIFE* printed an extreme blow-up of the last of Hughes's frames showing the sixth floor corner window with the motorcade below, its couched caption ignored Itek's confusing findings, yet at the same time reaffirmed Oswald's apparent guilt. The caption read, "The window where it was established that Lee Harvey Oswald waited is at the far right on the top floor. Boxes behind which he presumably was hiding are visible."[20]

While *LIFE*'s interest in the assassination was waning, and its 1966 investigative interest had resulted in this non-controversial 1967 picture essay, Thompson's major project was in the production phase at Bernard Geis Associates. Thompson's view of the significance of the Hughes film was far different from that of *LIFE*. In his book Thompson critiqued:

> . . . The FBI apparently studied one frame from the film and decided it could not make out the shape in the corner window. There is no record that anybody on the Commission itself ever looked at it, that anybody ever compared this frame and the later frames to see if the shape moved, or that much attention was paid to a rather curious configuration in the window next to the one at the corner.[21]

Thompson castigated the FBI for not comparing the 88 frames made showing the Texas School Book Depository window against each other. "Had they performed this elementary comparison, they would have recognized that the box-like shape in the window changed in width — getting narrower as time went on. Although the form cannot be distinguished

One of 88 frames Hughes made showing the Depository's southeast facade

as a human figure, it must be animated since it changes in time. It is almost certainly the gunman Brennan saw, slowly turning to his right (thus presenting a profile to Bob Hughes's camera) as he moves into firing position."[22]

Thompson also observed something which Itek had not been asked to look into, an observation which, if correct, completely changed the complexion of the government's lone assassin theory. "There is also photographic evidence supporting the contention that there were two people on the sixth floor rather than one. . . . The other figure appears 10 or 12 feet to the left in the second pair of windows from the corner. The outline of what seems to be a head appears above the first lintel in the window frame. In some of the eighty-eight (88) frames that picture the Depository, this figure appears clearly. In others its outlines blur, and it becomes scarcely visible. This change may be a natural function of the camera — some frames clear and others fuzzy — or it may be due to the figures moving toward and then away from the window." Thompson displayed three of the Hughes full-frames, and three blow-up frames showing the Depository and the window area. He wrote that these three representative frames covered four seconds, the last being when Hughes stopped his camera at approximately seven seconds before the shots.[23]

An extreme close-up view of the two pairs of windows on both the fifth and sixth floors of the southeast corner of the Depository Building

Thompson's conclusions of what the Depository windows revealed were apparently the result of his and others' direct view and interpretation of the film itself and of blow-ups of the frames. The window feature on the actual 8mm film is smaller than the head of a common pin. With the decrease in sharpness for every incremental enlargement or additional generation copy of the film's frame, as well as the possible variations inherent in the film or camera at the time of the filming, visual observations of such minute features are helpful, though fraught with possible misinterpretations. Thompson's book, while controversial with its theorizing of more than three shots and more than one shooter, was looked upon by a significant number of thoughtful people as opening up new areas of evidence. His book found a national audience which was beginning seriously to question what were perceived as major flaws in the government's 1964 investigation.

It wasn't for quite some time, however, that interest was refocused on possible revelations of the Hughes film. When that interest was renewed, Itek was again chosen as the examiner, a fact which did not square well with ever-suspicious assassination researchers. Itek Corporation did much of its specialized photo interpretation work as contractors for the federal government, and it was widely held that much of its sensitive work included that performed on CIA-related projects. Such a close relationship between the company and "The Company" led many to believe that any conclusions by Itek involving such a sensitive topic as the assassination would be extremely suspect.

Columbia Broadcasting System was preparing for a special television re-examination of the Kennedy assassination, and as Itek was well known for its previous work with assassination-related films, the TV producers approached Itek in the summer of

1975. A new film study was deemed appropriate since the relatively new and sophisticated image analysis techniques, such as digital image processing, were now available and might reveal new information concerning the Hughes and Zapruder assassination films. The objectives addressed in the proposed Hughes analysis were whether any objects could be detected or recognized in the sixth floor corner or other windows of the Texas School Book Depository, and could what was happening there be seen.

Utilizing both optical and digital analysis on the original 8mm and newly made fine quality copies of the Hughes film, over a dozen technical specialists performed a number of procedures. One technique utilized a digital processing method of sharpening and then integrating 22 frames of the film sequence into 1 frame, followed by an additional overlapping integration of 22 more frames, until 7 integrated images were produced. These 7 frames were then duplicated 5 times each and projected in order to detect motion. A slightly different technique was then used whereby computer-processed images were first binarized and then printed. A movie was made of this result. Also by optical means a computer-generated superimposed outline was created of frames 13 and 84 of the window sequence to show similarities and differences between the first and last part of the film sequence. The result of these studies indicated to Itek that motion of an object or person was detected in the sixth floor corner window, though the specific identification of this object was not possible.

Itek reported the shape, "... goes from an appearance and position of lower and nearer the right side to one of narrower, taller, and at the center of the window." Three people were also detected in the corner pair of windows of the floor below. One person was leaning out from shadows and becoming more visible, while another was raising his right hand as if in a wave. No changes were

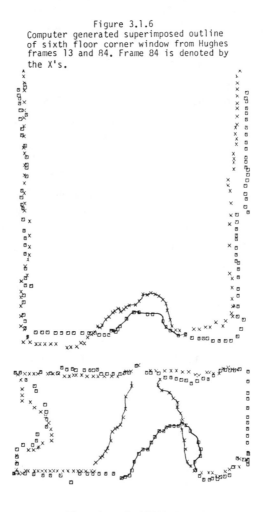

Figure 3.1.6
Computer generated superimposed outline of sixth floor corner window from Hughes frames 13 and 84. Frame 84 is denoted by the X's.

Figure from the 1976 Itek study

observed in the window adjacent to the sixth floor window where Josiah Thompson thought he had observed one or two men.[24]

With the exceptions of the corollary questions of the other windows, which had not been addressed in the earlier Itek report, and which seemed to refute Thompson's earlier analysis, this new Itek study contained basically the same information about the sixth floor corner window as before, except that a more sophisticated digital examination had been used.

In 1978 the House Select Committee on Assassinations, whose mission it was to re-examine both the Martin Luther King and President Kennedy assassinations, put together a photographic panel of experts whose object it was to look into the various problems and questions regarding photographic evidence. Among other areas, the panel looked afresh at the Hughes film of the Texas School Book Depository windows. Aerospace Corporation was hired as a contractor to the panel and it made a new study of the critical 88 Hughes frames. The frames were processed for computer enhancement and motion analysis. Following the scanning of the sixth floor corner windows, the images were viewed on a precision television soft-copy video-display computer system which could adjust contrast of the images displayed. The object in the window, observed by numerous people and by the Itek studies as having movement over the approximate 5-second filmed interval, was determined by Aerospace to be partially in the sun and partially in the shadows. As the individual images on the video-display were manipulated as to the amount of contrast, the perceived shape of the object also changed. The theory which grew out of this observation was that, ". . . the contrast of each frame of the unenhanced Hughes film was not constant in the region of the sixth floor window and that this was causing an apparent change of shape that appeared to be motion in the film sequence." Further study confirmed to the panel that the contrast of the window images was in fact changing from frame to frame. Adjusting by computer the photographic contrast as equally as possible for each individual frame, the technicians at Aerospace came up with a sequence in which much of the apparent motion which hadn't been identified in the Itek study, now disappeared.

The remainder of the perceived images on this film strip were then examined by a computer reading the coordinates of the center of the object in the window and then calculating the change in the position of the center of the object from frame to frame. Their conclusion of this aspect of the study was that the perceived motion was apparent rather than real. The motion pattern did not display a consistent direction, but seemed to be either random motions or purposeful motions of a very complex type. Considering the time intervals between the positions examined, the motions appeared to be very rapid to the tune of up to 18 inches per second. During three frame sequences, the object itself disappeared and reappeared, which is inconsistent with human motion and could be only explained as a photographic anomaly.

The House Select Committee on Assassinations report on the Hughes film concluded:

In summary, a pattern of changes in the object in the sixth floor window is visible in the computer processed images of the Hughes film. Nevertheless, the panel did not attribute this pattern of changes to the motion of any recognizable object such as a person. While the overall pattern is not necessarily inconsistent with human motion, the panel still concludes that the perceived motions are attributable to photographic artifact. The closed sixth floor windows adjacent to the sixth floor window were also examined. The same type of artifacts were present.[25]

A memo was printed within the Select House Committee on Assassinations *Hearings*, by film expert and assassination critic Robert J. Groden, who also served as a consultant to the photographic panel. The memo stated that an examination and optical enhancement of the then recently discovered Charles Bronson film showing the same sixth floor windows as in the Hughes film, but made a few minutes earlier, also revealed definite motion in at least two of the windows in question. "The two most obvious are the same two windows (Nos. 1 and 3) that show movement in the Robert Hughes film and at the beginning of the actual firing sequence. Also, the Hughes and Bronson films both show the man in window No. 1 to be wearing a bright reddish shirt (or so it appears) and the man in window No. 3 to be wearing a neutral colored shirt." Groden went on to criticize, "As you know, I was sorry to hear the wording of the representative of the photo panel who testified that the moving shapes in these windows could not be identified as human one way or another from the Hughes film. The fact that the shapes are indeed moving and stereo views show them to be well within the windows but not in as far as the boxes in the background, and that there is nothing else that these shapes could possibly be except human movement, should at least have prompted the wording to allow for a fairer comprehension on the part of another party concerned with the issue at a later date. . . ." Groden closed his memo, which was printed in the Committee *Hearings*, with a suggestion for yet another look at the Hughes film.[26]

Implied in Groden's criticism was the fact that the so-called photographic anomalies found in the Hughes film seemed to match what Groden himself observed in yet another film taken by a different person at a different position and at a slightly different time. Would these anomalies register the same on a totally different photographic setup? Groden was sure he could observe human activity behind the window. The Aerospace study indicated that you can't believe what you see, but only what you can measure; and that the scientific measurements seemed to preclude human activity. A new question was what would the Bronson film add to this dilemma. And thoughtful laymen who at first blush found fascinating the apparent wizardry of modern scientific technology, when confronted with various seemingly contradictory scientific findings, could only question just how exact current science can be.

At the time of the thirtieth anniversary of the assassination in 1993 yet a new study was performed on the Hughes film. The Public Broadcasting Service program

*Frontline* confronted the question of the life and guilt or innocence of Lee Harvey Oswald. One facet of the investigative special was a segment looking into the assassination itself. *Frontline*'s producers had the critical windows at the Book Depository as seen in the Hughes sequence just seconds prior to the assassination examined by current sophisticated image processing analysis. The examiners included Francis Corbett and Robert A. Gonsalves, both reputable analysts with past experience in examining assassination related materials. Corbett had participated in previous Itek studies.

After enhancing the window areas of the frames in question and playing the enhancement in motion, the technicians concluded that the human-like appearance in the window adjacent to the "sniper's nest" double windows was not present. The form of a figure (Harold Norman) was more clearly brought out in the window below the "sniper's window." Norman was in the process of waving at the President as the presidential convertible passed below. In the suspect sixth floor corner window itself, this study concluded that there is movement which indicates a person being present there just seconds before the shots commenced.[27]

The Hughes family remained in Dallas until 1968. Robert had allowed his original film to be examined by supposedly credible organizations, but became angry about how the film was carelessly handled by some, including some frames being cut out of the original. Mark Bell remained in Dallas, and recalls his film also being examined by many. "The U. S. House of Representatives had it for a while, *LIFE* magazine has had it a couple or three times. I've got a couple copies of them, but I don't know if one's original or if both are copies. I don't dwell on stuff like that, as it's not important to me anymore."[28]

Concerning his thoughts on the truth of what occurred in Dealey Plaza back in November 1963, Bell, in the late 1980s stated, "Most of the theories are people looking for publicity. I'm not in a position to say what happened. I know what happened, but the reasoning for it is political, and I don't have enough information to make a judgment on it, and would not. The situation being what it is and what I do know of people, I don't question it, because in the first place questioning it wouldn't do me any good, and in the second place if it's not going to do any good, then it's a waste of time!"[29]

## CHAPTER NOTES

1.    Telephone interview of Mrs. Maureen Hughes, 3/28/1989.
2.    Telephone interview of F.M. Bell, 3/13/1989.
3.    Ibid.
4.    Robert Hughes film, 11/22/1963. The films examined in this study were a third generation 8mm copy acquired from the FBI through a FOIA request, as well as a 16mm copy of the original loaned by Mrs. Hughes.
5.    Telephone interview of Bell, 3/13/1989.
6.    Ibid.; F.M. Bell film, 11/22/1963.
7.    Hughes film, op. cit.

8.  "Former Indianola Man Assassination Witness," *The Record Herald and Indianola Tribune*, 11/28/1963, p. 1; Josiah Thompson, *Six Seconds in Dallas*, p. 181, 195.

9.  *Hearings Before the President's Commission on the Assassination of President Kennedy*, v. 6, p. 309.

10. Hughes film, op. cit.

11. Thompson, op. cit., p. 26, 28, 269; Telephone interview of Bell, 3/13/1989.

12. Telephone interview of Bell, 3/13/1989.

13. Bell film, op. cit.; *Appendix to Hearings Before the Select Committee on Assassinations*, v. 1, p. 720.

14. Telephone interview of Bell, 3/13/1989.

15. *LIFE*, 11/24/1967, p. 3; *Saturday Evening Post*, 12/2/1967, p. 29; Thompson, op. cit., p. 28, 103, 119, 185, 189, 224.

16. Telephone interview of Mrs. Hughes, 3/28/1989; WFAA-T.V. videotape of interview of Captain Glen King and Chief Jesse Curry, 11/23/1963.

17. FBI memorandum, To: Mr. Belmont, From: A. Rosen, 11/28/1963; Report of Special Agent Robert M. Barrett, file #DL100-10461 (Commission exhibit 2591), 11/26/1963.

18. FBI memorandum re. lab report, 12/9/1963; File #62-109060-1899, 12/13/1963; Undated memorandum, file #DL100-10461 RPG:S1 quoting "Result of examination."

19. Telephone interview of Mrs. Hughes, 3/28/1989.

20. *LIFE*, op. cit., p. 89-90; *LIFE-Itek Kennedy Assassination Film Analysis*, 11/20/1967, p. 1, 10, 12.

21. Thompson, op. cit., p. 11, 13.

22. Ibid., p. 136-137.

23. Ibid., p. 245-246.

24. [CBS-Itek] John Kennedy Assassination Film Analysis, 5/2/1976, p. 1, 3, 5-7, 10, 23-26; Francis Corbett, "John Kennedy Assassination Film Analysis," *Optics in Law Enforcement*, 4/1977. The C.B.S. special *The American Assassins*, Part 1, was aired on November 25, 1975. Narrator Dan Rather said of the Itek study: "C.B.S. News also had the scientists examine a strip of 8mm film taken by Robert Hughes just as the motorcade turned onto Elm Street seconds before the assassination. This is the only known film in which one is able to view together the motorcade, the School Book Depository Building, and the sixth floor window. Through use of a computerized process called 'image integration' Itek experts first sharpened the visual context of the Hughes film. Then they studied the frames for movement. In one four second span they found what they called 'definite signs of movement in the window.'"

25. *Appendix to Hearings*, op. cit., v. 6, p. 115-120.

26. Ibid., p. 309.

27. The PBS-TV broadcast *Frontline*, 11/16/1993.

28. Telephone interview of Mrs. Hughes, 3/28/1989; Telephone interview of Bell, 3/13/1989.

29. Telephone interview of Bell, 3/13/1989.

## CHAPTER 12

# Enigma in the Window

It was four a.m. and Charles Bronson could not sleep. One of the loneliest hours of darkness, the sun would not begin to lighten the Texas skies for at least another hour. Sunrise was three hours into the future. Six miles away, Lee Harvey Oswald was securely locked in his fifth floor cell at Dallas City Jail, unaware he had only some nine more hours to live. Thirteen hundred miles and one time zone east, the body of President John Fitzgerald Kennedy lay in its coffin in the East Room of the White House in Washington, D.C. Within seven hours the coffin would be ceremoniously carried by caisson to the Capitol Building's rotunda where tens of thousands of citizens would begin to pay their last respects to their slain President. Less than 40 hours ago, Lee Oswald was an unknown, but free man, and John Kennedy was a breathing, vibrant Chief Executive. And Charles Bronson was going to fulfill a dream and get his first glimpse of a President of the United States.

Now Bronson, unable to sleep for the second night in a row, had decided to put down in a letter to his sisters what he had witnessed in Dallas on Friday, November 22, 1963.

Dear Sisters and Family,

Memory is a most blessed and wonderful thing, but when a world-shaking tragedy of such national and international significance and implications has been indelibly stamped within the recesses of the mind by seeing with the eyes that horrible event, then memory haunts you incessantly and robs you of restful sleep. Frances and I were eyewitnesses to that untimely and awful event from a distance of only 50 or 60 yards.[1]

Charles Leslie Bronson was chief engineer of Varel Manufacturing and he and his wife Frances lived at 3874 Dunhaven Street in Dallas. Born in Centralia, Illinois, on February 28, 1918, Bronson was the son of coal miner Albert Bronson and his wife Edith. Always interested in photography, Bronson as a youth often helped his mother, who worked in a photographic studio, and he recalls having printed and enlarged pictures by the hour.[2] Bronson attended Greenville College where he was yearbook photographer, and Bradley University in Peoria, Illinois. He graduated in 1946 with a double major in chemistry and mathematics. He had met his future wife in Centralia, Frances having been born in 1922 in a town some 9 miles south. Bronson worked in the Metallurgy Department of R. G. LeTourneau, Inc. in Peoria, Illinois, for six years and was transferred to the new plant in Longview, Texas, where he spent the next ten years as Chief Metallurgist. In 1956 he accepted a position and was later named vice-president of Research and Development with Varel Mfg. Co., a rock bit manufacturing firm in Dallas, Texas.[3]

Continuing his letter to his sisters, Bronson wrote:

> That morning [November 22] at breakfast I told [Frances] of my plans that would see the fulfillment of a dream harbored since boyhood — getting to see the President of the United States and his Lady waving and smiling. The newspapers on Thursday evening had given a detailed map of the parade route and the timing of events from the moment the President landed until he was to depart. . . . I asked her to meet me at the Union Station parking lot at about 12:10 p.m. I left work about 5 minutes before the noon hour, and in about 15 minutes I met Frances and we parked the cars and walked about 4 blocks to the little park area at the foot of Elm, Main and Commerce Streets.[4]

Bronson had chosen this location due to the adjacent parking area and knowing that the downtown area would be full of people and cars. This site turned out not to have too many people because, "It was more or less the end of the parade route."[5]

Concerning his choice of a vantage point to view the parade, Bronson noted in his letter to his sisters:

> On either side of Main Street in the park area are these stone abutments, the height of which is 4½ or 5 feet and about 2 feet x 5 feet in area on top.
> We chose the one on the left (as viewed from those in the parade) as it not only afforded us a view up Main Street, down which the parade was to come, but we could watch it make the right turn on Houston Street over to Elm and left on Elm Street down to the underpass. And for some reason there were less than a dozen people from the colonnade area on Elm Street down to the underpass, which really gave us an unobstructed view at that point.[6]

The couple climbed on top of the concrete abutment, Mrs. Bronson tearing one of her stockings as she got on top. They had a good sweeping view of the entire Plaza area.[7] The Bronsons had come well prepared to view and record the President's pass by.

Mrs. Bronson had brought with her a pair of 7 x 40 binoculars, while Mr. Bronson had both a still and a movie camera.

Bronson's Leica camera

Bronson's still camera was a classic of sorts, and probably the oldest one used in the Plaza that day. Purchased by mail order from Sears in May of 1938, the chrome trimmed, black-bodied 35mm Leica Model III-a, serial #259903, cost Bronson $169.95. The Leica camera was the first successfully marketed 35mm miniature camera manufactured, beginning in 1925 by Ernst Leitz Company at the optical works at Wetzlar, Germany. The III-a series was manufactured from 1935-1950. Bronson's camera possessed a 50mm f2.0 lens with serial #379429. He had loaded it with daylight Kodachrome A transparency film with an A.S.A. rating of 25, and had the shutter speed adjusted to 1/100 of a second.

His movie camera was a new acquisition, since he purchased it only a week or so earlier at a pawn shop on Elm Street in Dallas. The brown leatherette 8mm Keystone Olympic K-35 camera with serial #774192 was mounted with a 3-lens turret, including wide-angle and telephoto lenses. An f-stop guide was attached to one side of the camera, indicating to the film maker what stop was best for bright sun or snow, hazy sun, cloudy-bright, or open shade. Today, the f-stop was at f-8 for bright sun. On the opposite side of the body was the spring motor wind, a foot indicator, and a speed adjustment, allowing the cameraman to film

Bronson's movie camera photographed
on the abutment at Dealey Plaza

at 12, 16, 24, or 48 frames per second. Normal film speed for 8mm film was 16 frames per second, although today Bronson would set the speed at 12 frames per second because, as Bronson said, "I was kind of stingy with my film because I couldn't afford too many rolls."[8]

A developed roll of Kodachrome film produced, when projected, approximately 4 minutes of film. The roll of Kodachrome Type A film Bronson had with him on November 22 had already been half used and the spool already turned over. A proud grandfather, Bronson had taken some 21 separate exterior sequences of his first grand-daughter doing some newly learned out-of-doors walking. When the two minutes of the first side of the film was used up, Bronson had turned the film over and recorded about 22 seconds more of his granddaughter, this time with her happily scurrying around indoors. Thus, when he arrived at Dealey Plaza, Bronson had approximately 100 seconds of projected time left on his roll.

The first film sequence Bronson made of November 22 was not even mentioned in his letter to his sisters on November 24, nor did it seem important at the time. Bronson recalled some 22 years after the event about this first Dealey Plaza film sequence. "Approximately 6 minutes before President Kennedy arrived in the Dealey Plaza area there was a commotion diagonally across from the School Book Depository Building on Houston Street. An ambulance, with its lights flashing, arrived on the scene, and they evidently loaded someone in it that needed hospitalization. I thought I would capture that little bit of excitement as I aimed my movie camera, so I moved my movie camera in that direction and shot [92] frames as I recall. I thought I had my tele-photo lens in place, but instead I had my wide angle lens engaged. My experience at that time

Slide view taken by Bronson on November 23, 1963 with his Leica of his view from the day before

with photographic equipment told me that telephoto lenses were long and wide angle lenses were shorter. But as I found out later, just the reverse was true on my movie camera. And that is the reason those frames that I shot of that ambulance and the commotion also included part of the School Book Depository Building and also the window that Oswald is alleged to have fired the fatal shots from."[9] The potential signif-icance of the scene would not be brought to light, however, until 15 years after it was filmed.

About 10 or 15 minutes after the Bronsons had climbed onto the abutment, the motorcade could be seen traveling down Main Street towards their location. Bronson took a five second sequence with his movie camera which shows people pressing closer to the street while at least one motorcycle officer begins turning the corner from Main to Houston Street. Bronson then switched to his Leica and made two pictures of the Kennedy vehicle as it came to the corner of Main and Houston Streets. The first Leica transparency Bronson took from his perch reveals a cloudless blue sky below which hundreds of spectators are standing by the curb or in the street on Main Street and across Houston Street, looking towards the oncoming motorcade. Deep shadows from the old Dallas County Courts Building are cast on Main Street with shadows of the turrets pointedly reaching up to the second story of the Dallas County Criminal Courts Building. These shadows have obscured many of the details of the motorcade. The President's and Vice-President's cars and their follow-up vehicles are discernable, but individuals are hard to pick out. The red lights of three of the escort police cycles do, however, clearly stand out.

Bronson's second still photo taken of the motorcade

Pivoting slightly to his left, Bronson snapped another picture as the President's vehicle emerged from the building shadows, and was beginning its turn onto Houston Street. The American flag on the front of the President's Lincoln is clearly visible flapping in the breeze, and Mrs. Kennedy can be seen wearing a pink hat and with her white-gloved left hand raised to steady it from the wind-tunnel effect of the cross streets. At least one woman on the northeast corner of Houston and Main Streets can be seen with camera to her face. From Bronson's elevated position, he looks down upon a city bus stopped on Main Street west of Houston. To camera right one can count within his slide transparency the backs of some 50 spectators forming an arch in the street around the southwesterly Main and Houston intersection. In building windows diagonally across the street a number of spectators are also looking down upon the excitement below.[10]

Mrs. Bronson wanted her husband to take the binoculars so he could get a good view of Mrs. Kennedy, "In her bright pink suit highlighted by the brilliant Texas sun." Instead he told her to keep looking while he switched back to the Keystone movie camera, taking a 7½-second film sequence as the car moved along on Houston Street and stopping just before the Book Depository Building came into view.[11]

At the Texas School Book Depository and now out of Bronson's view, the presidential automobile made a sharp left turn onto Elm Street. Meanwhile Bronson, with his Leica in hand, got ready to make a picture of the vehicle as it emerged into view at his left. In his letter to his sisters 40 hours after the event, Bronson recalled he was taking a picture with his Leica:

> . . . As they were about halfway down to the underpass. And then it happened! My first impression was parade — celebration — fireworks when I heard the first two shots ring out in rapid succession and a slight pause before the third shot rang out. My next thought was that the crack Secret Service men had no doubt fired at someone who was about to cause real trouble. I remarked to Frances, "Is that fireworks or is someone shooting?"
>
> As I said [this] I was looking through the viewfinder all the time. The parade was en route, so I couldn't see any details. But right after my remark Frances said, "President Kennedy is bent over and Jackie has her arm around him and Governor Connally is lying down." Then I looked and saw a few people lay flat on the ground just as the presidential car stopped for a split second and then take off. I told Frances, "Let's get out of here before we get caught in crossfire!" And we did.[12]

Some 22 years later, in 1985, Bronson revisited Dealey Plaza with this author and vividly recalled the still picture he was about ready to take of the limousine on Elm Street. He realized that the pictures he had made of Main Street included crowds of people, and he wanted to get a full, unobstructed photo of the limousine as the car traveled down Elm Street.[13] "I was waiting till the limousine got into full view at about right angles [to my position], but the shot rang out just before. I wasn't quite ready, but I had my finger on, and I had enough pressure on it so when the shot rang out. . . I instinctively jumped and snapped it at the same time, and that's the reason you will notice that the picture is a little blurred up and down."[14]

Bronson's shutter was set to expose at 1/100 second, and the Leica was equipped with a focal-plain shutter that, when the trip button is depressed, the shutter would expose the film from left to right. Bronson's transparency shows blurring throughout, although noticeably more blurring takes place the further right one looks on the transparency.

Charles Bronson on November 23, 1985,
recreating with his camera his filming
location of 22 years earlier

This picture exhibits quite a bit of detail concerning the triangular infield area. To the foreground left may be seen branches of a tree on the south side of Main Street and to the left of Bronson's location. Across Main and Elm Street the white concrete pergola, including both end shelters, is clearly visible with the figures of Abraham Zapruder and Mary Sitzman standing on a pedestal at the left end. Also visible on the north side of Elm Street are Mr. & Mrs. Hester up by the right hand shelter. There are some 23 other people down by the curb, including Mr. & Mrs. Newman and their two children and Mr. & Mrs. Chism and their child. Louis Stephen Witt, the man later self-identified as the "Umbrella Man" can be seen standing at the rear of the sidewalk with his black umbrella held unfurled and high above his head. On the south curb of Elm Street from left to right may be observed Mary Ann Moorman with her hands raised towards her face preparing to take a Polaroid snapshot; her companion in a red coat, Jean Hill, Charles F. Brehm and his five year old son, Joe, and the unidentified woman, later referred to as the "Babushka Lady" in a brown coat, taking what appears to be movie film of the President's car coming towards her. Three women and four men are seen on the infield grass hurrying towards Elm Street to get a glimpse of the President, while another woman and man are on the gravel area by the southwest corner of the north peristyle, also quickly walking to catch a view. These nine people most probably viewed the President at the Houston and Main Street corner and opted for an additional chance to see the President's vehicle. At the extreme lower right of the transparency one can make out the shoulder of one of the other occupants of Bronson's perch, while a blurry glimpse of the roof coving of the School Book Depository is discernable at the upper right frame.[15]

Assassination on Elm Street

From examination of a plan of Dealey Plaza, this Bronson picture seems to correspond at about Zapruder frame Z220-Z225 at a time that the limousine was obscured from Zapruder's view by a sign. Measuring the distance between Bronson and the alleged assassin's window at the Texas School Book Depository for the distance of sound to travel, together with a .2 second reaction time, it would appear that the shot to which Bronson had reacted occurred approximately at Zapruder frame Z211. Philip Willis's reaction photograph (#5) was made at Zapruder frame Z202, or only 9 Zapruder frames, or .5 seconds earlier. None of the calculated figures used in this type of measurement can be precise, but they would seem to indicate that both Willis and Bronson reacted to the same noise.

About five seconds after taking the Leica picture, Bronson grabbed for his movie camera and began filming. The presidential limousine had now traveled about 70 feet and was in line between the Zapruder location and Bronson's camera. The follow-up car is also fully visible, while a man in the foreground can be seen crossing Main Street. Mrs. Kennedy is bending over the President when a bullet hits him in the head, and the First Lady begins to rise from her seat. Bronson's filmed action is becoming obscured by the tree branches to Bronson's left, but this is not the reason for his stopping the filming of this very brief two-second sequence. Bronson, while peering through the small camera viewfinder, could not accurately see the action, but his ears were telling him something was wrong. As he related much later, ". . . then when the second and third shot rang out, that's when I decided they were rifle shots; and of course by that time people started running down there, and I told my wife, 'Let's get down from here. Those are rifle shots,' and a little chubby girl in a pink dress, she was in the picture, and she came running across just before we got off of here and she said, 'Oh, my God, they shot the President!'"[16]

In 1978 Bronson recalled for researcher Dave Hawkins the sounds of these shots. "When the first shot rang out it sounded like somebody had thrown like a cherry bomb — it sounded like they tossed it out between the School Book Depository — out of one of the windows — and on the opposite side of Houston Street. It sounded like it went off between the buildings because there was an echo. . . .Then when the second and third shot went out, then it's when I realized that it wasn't any firecracker, it was rifle shots. . . ." Bronson also recalled that all the sounds were alike.[17]

In his letter to his sisters Bronson told of the aftermath of the shooting:

> As we hurried to the cars we tried to believe that if it really were gunshots that we heard, that no one in the presidential car was hit. We turned on our car radios as we headed for home and the plant, and it was just a matter of a few minutes that we learned that both the President and the Governor were shot. But somehow it was just too unreal to believe that such a thing could happen on such a beautiful day here in our own beloved city of Dallas.
>
> Shortly after I got back to work did we learn that President Kennedy was dead and the Governor was critically wounded. And what a terrible feeling came over me as I thought that just a few minutes ago I was getting to see the President of the United States and his First Lady smiling and waving to cheering Dallasites numbered in the thousands. And the three loud shots still echoing in my ears and, yes indeed, the parade was over.
>
> Whether we want to face facts or not, one era in our national history was ended with that first shot of deadly accuracy. Another day is dawning. Just what is in store we all wait in anticipation. . . .
>
> I know you are all praying that God in his infinite wisdom, mercy, and grace will see us through in these days of national and international tension. Lots of love, Charles.[18]

The Bronsons were "very shook up" over the events and could not sleep at all Friday night. On the afternoon of November 23, Mr. and Mrs. Bronson and their daughter Charlette drove back to Dealey Plaza and he finished up his roll of film taking for the last approximately 1½ minutes of film in his camera, "pictures of the places, buildings, people, and the many wreaths of flowers that different ones had brought there." He also took slides from the same vantage point as the day before.[19]  Around 4 a.m. on Sunday morning, November 24, Bronson drafted his letter to his sisters about what he had witnessed, and later that morning the family went to church as usual in Oak Cliff.

Later that Sunday Bronson began thinking that maybe he had some pictures that might be worthwhile, and which might even show the School Book Depository, as he could not remember between his two cameras and the speed of the events, just what he had taken.  He took two movie rolls and a roll of slides to the Eastman Kodak Processing Plant at 3131 Manor Way in Dallas on Sunday evening, and included with his undeveloped film a note indicating that he had been in the vicinity of the assassination and might have a picture that might be important.[20]

Walter Bent, sales service manager at the processing center, found Bronson's film and letter on Monday morning and telephoned the Dallas FBI. He related Bronson's note to Agent Milton A. Newsom and that in it Bronson indicated his willingness to cooperate with proper authorities.  Bent also relayed that the material "Should be processed and ready for viewing by 3 p.m."[21]  Bent then, at around 9 a.m., called Bronson and indicated that the film would be processed as quickly as possible and that the FBI would like to look at any pictures taken at that area, but that Bronson did not have to let anyone look at them if he chose not to.  Bronson said that they were welcome to look at them, and at around 3:00 in the afternoon Mr. and Mrs. Bronson and their daughter went down to the processing plant.  The women were asked to stay in the waiting room while Bronson, Bent, Agents Newsom and Emory E. Horton went into a room where a movie and slide projector had been set up.  The four looked at the movie at normal and slow speed, and Bronson was asked "a lot of questions."  The agents focused their interest on the assassination sequence, saying that they couldn't see that there was anything there that was important.[22]

In his internal departmental memorandum, Agent Newsom reported "These films failed to show the building from which the shots were fired.  Film did depict the President's car at the precise time the shots were fired; however, the pictures were not sufficiently clear for identification purposes."  He did note that in the transparency of the car on Elm Street it depicted, "A female wearing a brown coat taking pictures from an angle, which would have, undoubtedly included Texas School Book Depository in the background of her pictures.  Her pictures were taken just as the President was shot."  The agent also reported that each package of film received for processing by Eastman Kodak would be returned to the owner with a slip of paper requesting if any pictures included scenes of the President's assassination to notify the local FBI office.[23]

As for Bronson and his pictures, that was the last contact he had with any investigative official.  No agency contacted him again, no copies of his pictures were requested for study purposes, and the cursory examination of the film and slides by these two FBI agents satisfied any interest in the Bronson eyewitnesses or the film and pictures.  Although it cannot be doubted that at the time the FBI had more leads and investigations than it could handle, the report of the two agents who were neither photographic experts nor probably fully conversant with the details of the Dealey Plaza layout, apparently got lost in the mass of bureaucratic paperwork.  Such evidence should, of its very nature, have been examined again at a later date by investigators who had become more familiar with the case and possible leads.

In the very least the Bronson film complemented the Zapruder, Nix, and Muchmore films, while revealing a wider angle of view.  Most importantly, the agents had not noticed that in Bronson's first film sequence taken at the time the ambulance had arrived at Dealey Plaza to aid a seizure victim, the sixth floor corner window, the alleged assassin's perch, had also been filmed at a time less than six minutes prior to the assassination.  This fact would remain unknown for years to come.

Bronson expected that both he and his wife would be contacted by the Warren Commission investigators, but the only outsider to contact him was UPI, a representative of which called him to look at his film.  No offer was made by them, however, for use of his pictures.  The original assassination films were put in with the rest of Bronson's film and slides, and once in a while some friends and relatives saw them, but as Bronson recollects, "I got so many pictures that people got bored looking at all my pictures."[24]

~

During the next decade and a half, Bronson's career took him to Durant, Oklahoma; back to Longview, Texas; and in April 1977, to Ada, Oklahoma; were he became vice-president for Research and Development for the Gault Tool Company. Bronson read in the newspapers about the hearings being held in Washington by the House Select Committee on Assassinations, and he "Started to write them and tell them that I had some pictures I had taken at the time, and thought maybe they . . . might want to hear from me — my version, because my wife and I had a little better vantage point than a lot of people, because we had an unobstructed view at all times."  Upon reflection he then decided that if they wanted to get a hold of him, they could, and he dropped the proposed letter.[25]

In December 1977 and January 1978, 90,000 papers relating to the assassination of President Kennedy from within FBI files were declassified and made available. Although many of these were duplicates of papers already within the Warren Commission records located at the National Archives, a good number were of previously undisclosed material.  Researchers began poring over these papers for new leads.  It was as a result of this declassified material that Bob Ranftel, a researcher associated with the Washington-based Assassination Information Bureau, found a memo from the FBI's Dallas field office referring to a previously publicly unknown film.[26]  Earl Golz, a reporter for the *Dallas Morning News* with extensive writing background on the Kennedy case, was contacted to see if he could locate Bronson and his film.

It took Golz a few weeks to locate Bronson in Ada, Oklahoma, and on November 6, 1978, Bronson was contacted by Golz and local assassination researcher Gary Mack, who worked at radio station KFJZ in Fort Worth. They asked Bronson if they could come and speak to him about his film. Bronson invited them down and on November 9 they visited Bronson's home. From about 6:00 to 11:30 p.m. they examined Bronson's film and slides and showed Bronson a copy of the Zapruder film. The two visitors were very excited with Bronson's film, particularly the scene taken prior to the motorcade's arrival. As Bronson had mistaken his wide-angle lens for the telephoto lens, the film scene took in more area than would have been the case had he used even a normal lens. His film speed was set at 12 frames per second, due to his wanting to conserve film, so the projected action is slightly faster than normal. A total of 108 frames of this first sequence show Houston Street approximately six minutes before the assassination with a number of people on the northwest corner of Houston and Main Streets looking up Houston Street at activity near the corner of Elm. A white ambulance with red blinking dome light

Bronson's pre-assassination movie view of Houston Street
with the Depository Building's sixth floor at upper left

is in the street and movement can be discerned in that area. Meanwhile, five cars are observed traveling west down Elm Street past the Texas School Book Depository Building, the corner of which up to and including the sixth floor front corner windows can be observed in 92 frames.[27]

Golz and Mack were very excited with this part of the film, for it appeared to them that there was discernable movement within the sixth floor window. Golz asked Bronson if he could take the film for enhancement studies, with the *Dallas Morning News* paying for the study and having the right of first publication of the results. A letter of agreement was written out by Golz protecting Bronson's rights, and the reporter was given the film from which to make copies and an enhancement study. Subsequently attorney John L. Sigalos of the Dallas firm Sigalos and Levine, which specializes in patents and copyrights, was retained for Bronson in order to protect his interests. The

Bronson film and his third slide taken on November 22 were copyrighted and the originals later housed in a bank vault. Thereafter Mr. Sigalos represented Mr. Bronson's legal and commercial interests with regard to these "Kennedy assassination slides and film."[28]

The *Dallas Morning News* commissioned Robert J. Groden of Hope Lawn, New Jersey, to make an enhancement study of the Bronson photographic materials, agreeing not to retain any copies of the material following his contractual analysis. A film technician, Groden had done some extensive work on clarifying and stabilizing the Abraham Zapruder film, and his showing of the film and co-authoring a book, *J.F.K.: The Case for Conspiracy*, was instrumental in gaining public pressure which resulted in the House of Representatives Select Committee on Assassinations being formed. Groden had been hired as a staff consultant for the House Subcommittee on Photographic Evidence, though not selected to be on the panel itself. During three days of independent examination of the Bronson film, "Groden used a microscope arrangement to focus in and enlarge minute parts of the 8mm movie film and make slides of what he saw." He found that the film grain interfered with the image, as the size of the windows on the 8mm frame took up about as much space as half the size of a pinhead.[29]

The Sunday, November 26, 1978, edition of the *Dallas Morning News* broke its story about the Bronson film in several copyrighted articles by Earl Golz and Kent Biffle, and included reproductions of nine black-and-white highly enlarged copies of photographs taken of the windows. A headline declared, "J.F.K. Film May Reveal Two Gunmen." Groden was quoted, "There is no question that there is movement, and I am sure, given time and money, a computer could probably clarify the images a bit more." Groden reported that one of the persons in the window pair was wearing a magenta, or purplish-red, shirt and, "You can actually see one figure walking back and forth hurriedly. I think what was happening there is the sniper's nest was actually being completed just prior to the shots being fired."[30] Associated Press picked up the story, and that same day the *New York Times* included a seven paragraph story titled, "New Evidence Is Hinted In Assassination Film." Groden said in the story, "I can make out figures moving simultaneously in both sets of windows." He described the second person as wearing a brownish-tan or olive shirt.[31]

On that same Sunday afternoon in Washington the Assassination Information Bureau, an organization critical of the Warren Commission, and which also was recommending that the House Select Committee on Assassinations continue its inquiry past the December 31, 1978, deadline, held a press conference of its own. Director Carl Oglesby chided the government body for failing to have discovered this film when his own non-profit organization was able to do so. The film and slide enlargements were shown to the gathered press representatives, though no photographs of these were allowed to be taken. Bronson's attorney, John Sigalos, was present to represent Bronson's interests, and he stated that Mr. Bronson was not claiming that the film disclosed anything new or startling, but that he was simply cooperating with the newspaper and the A.I.B., "Because he has no reason not to."[32] Groden stated that, "It is beyond question there is more than one person up there," but Wendell Rawls, Jr., reported his skeptical observations in his *New York Times* article that, "If they disclose anything to the layman's eye, it is perhaps one figure in one window."[33]

On November 28 another news briefing, but this time including Charles Bronson and arranged by Sigalos and Levine, was held at the Republic National Bank in Dallas. Again, no photographs were allowed of the viewing of Bronson's film. Following the initial press disclosures, Bronson was deluged by the media, including the three television networks and phone calls from radio stations including as far away as Melbourne, Australia.[34] Several news agencies bid for use of the frames including UPI for $100, being their "Normal free-lance rate," and AP, through news photo editor David Taylor, bidding $1,000. The sensationalistic tabloid *National Enquirer* offered $2,500 for exclusive North American rights. Bronson referred most of these contacts to his lawyer, and these offers were not pursued.[35]

Following the exclusive *Dallas Morning News* stories on the Bronson film, by a prior signed legal agreement any and all photographic images of the film were to be destroyed or returned by the paper to Bronson. Unknown to the *News* or Sigalos, reporter Earl Golz had surreptitiously kept negatives of various of the frames. In early 1979 Golz sent these along to assassination photo researcher Richard Sprague to see what he could learn from examining them. Cautioning to "Keep their existence under wraps for now," Golz requested Sprague to let him know if he found anything, as it "Could be a good story."[36]

The first inkling the government might have had that the Bronson film could hold some possibly important information came from Golz himself. Originally in contact with the local Dallas FBI office in October 1978 when trying to locate Bronson, Golz spoke with an agent again on November 14 prior to the Bronson story being published. In a follow-up report dated November 27 an FBI agent wrote that according to Golz, " . . . at one point where Bronson had apparently moved the camera in a swinging motion, the Schoolbook Depository Building could be seen. He advised that by slowing the film the sixth floor window could be seen but the picture was very blurred. A figure could be seen in the window and an additional figure which might have been crates or boxes could also be seen."[37]

By November 27, 1978, staff of the House Select Committee were finally officially aware of the Bronson film. Committee Chief Counsel G. Robert Blakey, in a letter dated that day outlining the understanding reached for examination and analysis of the film, agreed and assured Lawyer Sigalos that there would be no unauthorized use or exhibition of the film by the House Committee.[38] Arrangements were made with the Committee staff to see the film, but House Committee Chairman Representative Louis Stokes indicated that the panel was out of time and money for a sophisticated computer analysis of it. It was commented by a photo panel committee member that an analysis by computer scanning process would take from four to six weeks to accomplish at a cost of from $60,000 to $90,000.[39]

On December 2 a meeting was held at the Aerospace Corporation's Digital Image Processing Laboratory in Los Angeles, California. Arranged by Jane Downey of the House Select Committee, present were three lawyers representing Bronson and ten photographic and digital image processing technical experts, five of whom were serving on the photographic evidence panel of the House Select Committee. The original 8mm Bronson movie, several 35mm enlargements, and a 16mm copy of the movie which had been processed by Groden were on hand. Several frames of the original film were viewed under microscope and one frame was scanned in color in a Photo Digitizing System's company microdensitometer.[40]

Among the conclusions outlined in a letter from Charles J. Leontis, Director of the Optical Systems Department, to Michael Goldsmith of the House Select Committee was that the experts, ". . . could not say conclusively whether or not the frame-to-frame changes in the sixth and fifth floor windows were due to real motion behind the windows." They disagreed unanimously with Groden's comment that, "You can actually see one figure walking back and forth hurriedly," and felt that ". . . the apparent motion in the windows seems to be random, and therefore it is not likely to be due to human motion behind the window." Finally, it was pointed out, "Computer analysis of the Bronson film similar to that applied to the Hughes film may clarify this issue, especially since the Bronson film is of superior quality to the Hughes film."[41]

A few days later Robert Selzer of the Jet Propulsion Laboratory, a Committee member who participated in this same meeting, also wrote a letter to Goldsmith. He indicated no disagreement with the first letter, but more strongly recommended computer processing of the film as it, ". . . is the only possible evidence of movement behind the two closed windows adjacent to the half-opened window." Such a study could clarify the situation. He also noted that new equipment and the good quality of the original Bronson film as compared to the poorer quality Hughes film and the Groden copy of the Bronson film would only better serve to aid in such a study.[42]

Time and money, however, had run out for the House Select Committee. The photographic panel, in its published report, while pointing out that the apparent motion was not likely to have been caused by humans, also stated that, "No firm conclusion could be reached without applying digital image processing. . . ." Robert Groden, in a dissenting view published in the same photographic evidence volume, reiterated his opinion of definite movement in at least two windows. He also wrote that he now believed that there is a third ". . . distinctly different person who is probably handing boxes to Man #1." He took issue with the photo panel's wording and stated that ". . . The shapes are indeed moving, and stereo views show them to be well within the windows, but not in as far as the boxes in the background, and that there is nothing else that these shapes could possibly be, except human movement. . . ."[43]

In its eventually published report issued in 1979, the House Select Committee on Assassinations, under its recommendation for further investigations, neatly "passed the buck," stating that "The Department of Justice should contract for the examination of a film taken by Charles L. Bronson to determine its significance, if any, to the assassination of President Kennedy."[44]

Writing to Attorney General Griffin B. Bell in early January 1979 specifically concerning the Bronson film, Chairman Stokes directly urged the Justice Department to perform the digital image processing work. He wrote that, "The Bronson film is potentially significant because it may show movement of more than one person in the vicinity of the sixth floor southeast corner window. . . ." The congressman also noted that Mr. Bronson, through his lawyer, was willing to cooperate fully if the study was pursued.[45]

By early May, however, Sigalos had heard nothing from the Justice Department. After attempting to contact the department several times, he wrote Bronson, "I, frankly, am very disturbed that they have not had the courtesy of a return call stating what their position is."[46]

Meanwhile, others were interested in what the film might reveal. In early 1979 Sigalos had been contacted by Fran Corbett of Itek Corporation and Dr. Robert A. Gonsalves of Boston's Northeastern University. They proposed a two-phase image processing study of the Bronson film to be ". . . done with the highest degree of professionalism." Though volunteering participant time, the projected computer time needed for the study would cost some $5,000, which it was hoped could be raised. Pending contact from the Justice Department, Sigalos did not follow up the proposal at that time.[47]

By 1980 Bronson's lawyer had become exasperated by the government's inaction. Conditioning his client's cooperation on the premise agreed to by the Select Committee that the film be protected from public domain use, Sigalos was met with bureaucratic stalling and inaction by the Justice Department. In late 1980, wanting to address the issue of possible movement in the Depository windows, Sigalos entered into an agreement with Gonsalves to perform a study, and the original film was made available to him. Explaining the situation to Bronson, Sigalos wrote, "We went forward on this only after reaching the conclusion that the Justice Department and FBI are really not serious in doing anything with your film. . . . All in all, I get the very strong feeling that the government is not interested in pursuing all the facts of the Kennedy assassination." Though the Gonsalves project initially sounded promising, it too appears to have fizzled.[48]

When this author began researching the photographic history of the assassination, the official follow-up to the recommendation of the House Select Committee as regards the Bronson film seemed an important aspect of the study to understand. Letters addressed to the Attorney General beginning in August 1986 asking of the results of the film's examination were finally given a written response in late December. Lawrence Lippe, chief of the Legal Advice section of the Justice Department, linked any potential significance of the film with the analysis of the acoustical evidence. During the Select Committee hearings an acoustical analysis of a recording purportedly made by the Dallas Police Department during the time of the assassination appeared to indicate a second shooter had fired a shot on the "grassy knoll" behind the picket fence in Dealey

Plaza. Though there could be a connection with a master conspiracy between someone behind the fence and others in the Texas School Book Depository, the significance of more than one person seen in the sixth floor southeast corner Depository window was not dependent upon the accuracy of the acoustical study. More than one person in the Depository window would be significant by itself and indicate a possible conspiracy. The letter from Washington further stated that the department did not obtain the film, ". .

due to our inability to reach an agreement with the film's owner regarding restrictions. . . ." Lippe assured the author that details of the department's efforts in this regard would be included in a report to Congress, "Likely to be completed in the near future."[49]

The tone of this letter seemed a put-off. Though Mr. Sigalos was scrupulously careful to protect the rights and potential profitability and exclusivity of Mr. Bronson's film, perhaps too legalese in his approach for some tastes, he and Mr. Bronson had always indicated a willingness to allow a thorough examination under mutually agreed-upon restrictions. It appeared that if the Justice Department could not do it their way, and indeed never seemed to indicate what constituted their way, this was a fortuitous excuse to ignore the film study and blame the other party.

This author did not know Mr. Sigalos, but had developed a friendly and mutually respectful relationship with Mr. Bronson, a gentleman in all regards. It seemed important to examine all evidence, if only to prove a negative. Mr. Bronson was approached concerning the Justice Department letter. By 1987 the film itself was not even necessary to examine, as the frames in question relating to the Depository windows had been digitized and stored on tape by Robert Selzer of the Jet Propulsion Lab, an original member of the House Select Committee's photo panel.

After contacting Mr. Selzer and Mr. Bronson, in August 1987 the author sent off another letter to the Attorney General with copies to the principals. The letter read in part:

> I have been researching the assassination for the past four years, not as one attempting to prove a pet theory, but as a study into photographic history and interpretation. I have no preconceived opinion of what the film shows, or does not show, but believe that such a potential piece of evidence should not be ignored.
>
> I have been in contact with Mr. Robert H. Selzer of the Jet Propulsion Lab who has informed me that digitized images of the original Bronson film frames in question were put on tape, and that "I am willing to do further work on the Bronson film — the problem is to obtain funds for one of our engineers to spend about a month to do the job properly." He also indicated that "If someone else wants a copy of the digitized images on tape, we'll be glad to provide them if Bronson or his attorney approve." Mr. Selzer was a member of the HSCA photographic panel.

I have also contacted Mr. Bronson who has stated to me, "I have never been contacted by the Justice Department or Mr. Sigalos over the use of the film. I certainly would have no objection to any qualified individuals studying the Selzer tape. I for one would like to know if anything would show that would shed light on the events of that fateful day. Feel free to do whatever is necessary to study the tape — as you certainly have my permission."

It has been over eight years since the Select Committee made its report and recommendation that the Justice Department have further research done on the Bronson film. It is amazing to me that the Justice Department has not been able to make arrangements to examine crucial frames of this film. Both Mr. Bronson and Mr. Selzer have indicated to me, a private citizen, a willingness to have the work done. I will be happy to provide their addresses to your department.

I sincerely believe that the Justice Department should rejuvenate its abortive study into the question of the Bronson film, as there seems to be no external obstacle blocking the study. This matter should be addressed, even after these many years, if for nothing more than to fulfill the Select Committee's recommendation, and for the historical record.[50]

Following 2½ months of no reply, the author again wrote the Attorney General with copies sent to several congressmen. Following an inquiry to the Justice Department by a Massachusetts member of congress, a second letter from Lawrence Lippe arrived in late February 1988. The letter reiterated the previous inability to reach an agreement over public access restrictions. Such reasoning now appeared to be a moot point. As a study by the National Academy of Sciences had resulted in the conclusion that the original acoustical study was flawed and inaccurate, this separate issue, through a perverse use of logic, was linked to the significance of the film. According to the Lippe letter Congressman Stokes, the Chairman of the House Select Committee was, ". . . promptly advised of the Department's decision to cease to further pursue the acquisition of the original film absent Congressional assistance in obtaining the film were some subsequent indication of its potential value to the investigation." Lippe indicated that Stokes had not objected to that position. [51]

A response from this author's congressman also arrived explaining, "According to Assistant Attorney General John Bolton, the Justice Department feels that the subsequent conclusions of the National Academy of Sciences, which disproved through scientific acoustical analysis the Select Committee's sole basis for its conspiracy theory, contributed to their current belief that expensive analysis of the 'Bronson film' would not be worthwhile."[52]   Again the illogical linking between the acoustics study and the possibility of more than one person in the assassin's window area of the Texas School Book Depository. The study would be too wasteful a use of taxpayers' money!

Though many Americans aware of the House Select Committee's recommendations concerning the Bronson film were awaiting the study results, it became clear to this author that years earlier the Justice Department had begged off on any such study. And no new avenues or opportunities would shake the department from its course of inactivity. Only "lip service" was now being given to the question.

Interestingly, shortly thereafter the long-promised Justice Department report, in the form of an undated letter addressed from Assistant Attorney General William F. Weld to Chairman Peter W. Rodino, Jr., of the House of Representatives Committee on the Judiciary finally was produced with a cover letter. The cover letter dated March 28, 1988, and written by Acting Assistant Attorney General Thomas M. Boyd stated, ". . . matters occasionally come bubbling to the surface from the depths of the bureaucracy. An example of this phenomenon is the enclosed report which relates back to the activities of the Select Committee on Assassinations. While this is long overdue, it may no longer be of interest, I am forwarding it to you for your information and appropriate disposition." Thus, through a flip cover letter, and an undated, long in coming report originally requested by a Select Committee of the United States to further investigate the murder of an American President, this response was disposed of in a short five page report some nine years after the initial request.[53]

It was not until September 1988 that the report itself was made known to the public through the efforts of a California ophthalmologist who shook it out of the bureaucracy following a Freedom Of Information Act request. In the report it was revealed the Justice Department had dropped any interest in the Bronson film by April 1981 due to their perceived problem with Lawyer Sigalos's privacy stipulation. Upon notice to Congressman Stokes of their intended inaction unless specifically requested by Congress to do differently, ". . . the Department has taken no further action in this regard." The Justice Department had made a half-hearted effort and then put the onus back upon Congress, through Representative Stokes, to request further action. No response by Stokes' office was taken as an excuse to simply drop the issue.[54]

Contacted by Associated Press in early September 1988 to comment upon the conclusions of the official probe, House Select Committee on Assassinations aide Kevin Walsh blasted the Justice Department's inaction. "All these years later we found out they've been doing nothing. Members themselves had faith that the Justice Department was going to pursue this, and now we see all these years later that their faith was misplaced." Walsh went on to criticize the handling of the Bronson film, calling this inaction the "most egregious sin." "If you have film footage that bears on a murder case, you subpoena it. They didn't even consider it."[55]

Though the Reagan Justice Department had no intention in discovering if the Bronson film revealed a potential murder conspiracy, others did. Lawyer Sigalos, though always keeping tight rein on his client's copyright protection and any unauthorized copying or displaying, attempted within those parameters to have the film available for serious study.

The month prior to the 20th anniversary of the assassination CBS news corre-spondent Terry T. Drinkwater had contacted Sigalos about a possible study and broad-cast story relating to the Bronson film. It was agreed that Itek Optical Systems in Massachusetts could perform a non-destructive examination of that portion of the film revealing the Depository windows. While all images generated in the study remained the property of Mr. Bronson, CBS would at its expense underwrite the cost of the study and would have an exclusive one-time televised showing of the resulting enhanced version.[56]

Delivering the original film to Itek on Friday, October 28, 1983, Sigalos received word on Monday of the preliminary findings that the film did not conclusively establish that there were two men at the assassin's window just minutes prior to the arrival of the motorcade. The technicians at Itek had made 32 Polaroid photomicrographs of selected frames of the film depicting enlarged images of the window area. Upon studying these black-and-white still images it was concluded that the perceived movement in the windows was due probably to the movement of the film in the gate of Bronson's camera as the movie strip was being recorded. Their recommendation to CBS was that no further study be done.[57]

It was agreed by CBS and Sigalos that Robert H. Selzer of the Jet Propulsion Laboratory should review the Itek enhancements and the original film to see if he would corroborate the Itek opinion. Before this could be done, however, Drinkwater and Sigalos had a serious difference of opinion over the stated agreement concerning the copying and telecasting use of the original Bronson film, resulting in the film and en-hancements being returned directly to Sigalos.

On the November 7, 1983, *CBS Evening News*, the first of a three-part segment on the assassination anniversary was aired. While showing researcher Gary Mack switching on a movie projector, and a reverse sequence of the Bronson film being projected on Mack's living room wall, Drinkwater narrated:

> Recently, conspiracy advocates have pinned their hopes on these blurry, never fully analyzed pictures from a home movie taken minutes before the shooting. Some thought they could detect move-ment of not one, but several people in the sixth floor windows of the Texas School Book Depository. But the Itek Corporation, photo enhancement experts, studied the film for CBS News and decided that whatever movement there is was caused by the jumping of the film in the camera, and not by shadowy figures behind the window panes.[58]

The quickly generated Itek study was the first serious attempt at a scientific examination of the film, though a number of knowledgeable researchers believed that Itek did not take the time or the thoroughness to make a valid study. The examination of only one-third of the frames in question, and these not consecutive, as well as the ignoring of the perceived colors of the objects in the windows, made researchers believe further testing was essential. At the time Selzer had not been given the opportunity to assess the Itek study or make his own observations. Sigalos subsequently gave Selzer the original film from which he digitized all the 92 frames and stored them on magnetic tape by September 1984. Working on the project only in spare time, which was not often, Selzer by 1987 had performed frame averaging and attempted some filtering. His progress to that point was not successful in finding anything new.[59]

A close-up view of the fifth and sixth floor corner windows. White blocks at right are part of the obelisk between Bronson's camera and the building.

It was in July 1987 that this author discussed with Selzer his work and opinion with regard to the Bronson film. As a member of the House Select Committee on Assassinations photo panel, Selzer recalled learning about the film at the tail end of the Committee's existence. As to Groden's contention that the film revealed movement in the window, Selzer commented, "At the time my feeling was that it was very ambiguous. The film is extremely noisy when you get it to that kind of enlargement. It seemed quite likely, or possible, that that could be just random fluctuations in film grain. . . . Since then we've worked on the film, but not extensively. We've made a couple of tries at it, and haven't really come up with anything that really contradicts that." Though he did not want to endorse the Itek study, Selzer conceded that at that point he did not have anything to contradict their conclusion.[60]

Selzer then went on to explain the best method for examining the film scientifically. After the frames have been digitized and stored on tape, one should not rely on examination of still frames or series of still frames, but rather should reproduce these in motion as a motion picture, by taking a computer frame and putting it on a video disk one frame at a time. By the lengthy process of putting one frame at a time into a loop mode, one should then be able to examine 50 or 100 frames. In order to cut down on the noise of each frame, a group of frames should be registered and then averaged.

Thus with 100 frames you average the first 5 frames together and then average frames 2 through 6, then frames 3 through 7, and so on to create a new movie which is a composite, this should help suppress the noise. If there were any movement present, it would be carried along in the frame averaging, so one could see it.[61]

And if this study were made of the frames in question, what would Selzer expect in the way of results? "From what I've seen of the film so far, my best guess is that you are going to end up the same place we are now after we process it. If you want to believe one side, you'll believe it, and if you don't, you won't. The results are not going to be definitive. Nobody's going to suddenly pop out. A human form is not going to suddenly appear. The more likely thing is you might be able to prove the negative, you might clearly establish that there is nobody there. But I don't think you would be able to prove the positive."[62]

A thoughtful person who appears careful to examine all sides of questions, Selzer admits to having joined the photographic panel of the House Select Committee not believing that Oswald had acted alone, and that with all the disturbing contradictions to the case, he still is inclined to that opinion. Interestingly, he is emphatic to point out that none of the so-called photographic proofs of a conspiracy, from the backyard photos of Oswald, to the assassination-related materials, were ever found by him to support a conspiracy or a cover-up.[63]

Though not planning to do any further independent enhancement of the Bronson film, Selzer was very cooperative in offering to make his digitized material available to any serious researcher, subject to Mr. Bronson's approval.[64]

In 1988 a further examination of the Bronson film was conducted. Nigel Turner of Central Independent Television in England was producing a large-scale multi-hour television documentary concerning the Kennedy assassination. In a legal agreement drawn up by John Sigalos, representing Charles Bronson, Turner agreed to a non-destructive technical analysis made of the window sequence with the non-exclusive right to use the material within his production.

Dr. Don Monroe of Imperial College in London performed the study. According to a one-page report, the film was first converted to a slow-motion high-quality video tape capable of playing back individual frames. Eighty-four of those successive frames which included the Book Depository windows in question were then digitized and software was adapted to align these frames to the same point within the display area. "To improve the signal to noise ratio, sequential frames were added in pairs, pairs of pairs, and so on to give a large number of composite results. Best results were obtained with about 16 frames combined." By combining frames, a reduction of interfering noise or "snow" was accomplished together with an extended range of contrast. Those resulting best frames were then magnified and had their contrast manipulated to display details within the windows.[65]

Dr. Monroe's conclusions were as follows:

The rightmost window frame [the so-called assassin's window] is partially opened throughout the 84 frames processed. I examined original frames and results and can detect no significant motion. (It would be possible to process the pictures to highlight motion.) In the rightmost window frame is a figure, brighter at the bottom, and lighter above where it is partially obscured by the open window frame. It is possible that the lower part of the figure is the shoulder of a person seen from the side close to the window in light clothing, with the head less distinctly visible above and partially covered by the window frame.

The next frame over, still in the right-hand window, is closed. Visible behind it is a shape which seems to have straight edges and does not appear to be a human form.

The left-hand window is partially obscured by leaves diring [sic] parts of the sequence and is recessed and in shadow. However, by stretching the contrast, a shadowy form appears in this window which is the size and shape of a human figure.

Further processing of this picture is possible. Within the available budget I could not attempt to compensate for the response of a camera lens and the characteristics of the enlargement process used by Mr. Percy. Doing this could sharpen the original frames, and make the alignments of the frames more accurate. Both these effects would give a less-blurred result, but with more noise. It is doubtful that features of the rightmost figures could be extracted. However, it is possible that both figures could be improved enough to be more certain of their human form.[66]

The results of the preliminary study, though not conclusive, were nonetheless interesting. Not interesting enough, however, to continue the expensive scientific analysis. Turner reluctantly canceled further study and the matter was not mentioned in the television documentary. Were these types of studies an exercise in examining a Rorschach-like digitized, highly contrasted dark and light picture? The three attached versions of the enhancement provided with Dr. Monroe's report looked very much to a layman like such a Rorschach test. Were the "two figures" noted by Dr. Monroe human forms? As with so much of the discovered evidence in the Kennedy case, few hard and fast conclusions could be drawn. As Selzer alluded to earlier in 1987, such a study as this left it possible for both sides to read what they wanted into the findings. Further tests might clarify the findings. If Monroe's observations and language were correct, however, it did indicate possibly two human forms in the two pairs of windows at the sixth floor southeast corner of the Book Depository were present only minutes before the motorcade arrived. The findings, couched in cautionary phrases, certainly did not locate the three men at work which Robert Groden had supposedly discovered in his earlier examination, yet enough was found to point out that such potential evidence as this film should have been more carefully considered by the Justice Department.

John Sigalos, though often looked upon as the heavy, the spoiler, the uncooperative one in the literature of the critics and within the records of the Justice Department, was always looking out for the protection of the rights of his client. Though a case could be made that he was too legalistic and unwavering in his various agreements made with those who desired to utilize or study the film, he was true to his profession and to his client. Failure of duty in the story of the Bronson film rests clearly upon the federal government which chose not to follow through on a potentially important piece of evidence. Mr. Bronson always was willing to cooperate. In 1963, right after the assassination the FBI agents who contacted Bronson failed to appraise the potential value of the film properly or even to acquire a copy of it for reference. Once it was rediscovered by a private citizen, the House Select Committee on Assassinations, with little time and money left, chose the simple path of passing the buck on to the Justice Department. Considering all the evidence to which this author has been privy, it seems clear that the Justice Department chose merely to give the request passive lip service before dropping any interest in pursuing it as was so emphatically requested by the House Select Committee and the photo panel. And when confronted with the possibility of doing a study in 1987, something they claimed was impossible to do earlier in the decade, the Justice Department simply obviated the issue and chose to repeat shallow excuses of the past.

Mr. Charles Bronson told this writer back in 1985, "My personal opinion from what I've seen is that you can't see anything. As far away as that was in the film and the motion you had at the time, I don't think there is any way in the world you could get a definition of what was up there."[67] In the final analysis he may be correct in his opinion.

The well known and often controversial PBS investigative series *Frontline* produced a three-hour study on Lee Harvey Oswald, which was broadcast in November 1993. Among the impressive background research done for the program was a scientific enhancement of that portion of the Bronson film showing the suspect windows. Image processing analysts Francis Corbett and Robert A. Gonsalves, who had previously in the late 1970s proposed a scientific study, conducted this new research on the film. It was noticed that in the window pair west of the sixth floor corner window, there appears to be a person standing there, and some have speculated that successive frames indicate someone walking back and forth. According to Gonsalves, however, when the color images were processed to reduce the grain noise, all these images throughout the various frames appeared approximately the same. Gonsalves concluded in simple language that no one is walking about behind that window, but rather ". . . that's grain noise walking about."[68]

This *Frontline* study might be the end of the controversy, but like so much else in the case, definitive answers have a way of becoming only more words with which to take sides. One of the most unsettling aspects of this Bronson film matter is the failure of the government to do what citizens have been forced to attempt themselves. To understand that with such a potentially important piece of evidence available, people within our government did not think it worth the effort or the expense to attempt by all legal means possible to examine that evidence, is abhorrent. The incident in November 1963 is not simply a matter of petty criminality, but the murder of our nation's chief executive. He and we deserve better and more responsible care, interest, and treatment on the part of our government.

## CHAPTER NOTES

1.     Charles L. Bronson draft letter, 11/24/1963.
2.     Letter, Bronson to Trask, 5/2/1985; Bronson interview with Trask, 11/23/1985; Kent Biffle, "Lens Error Caught Image," *Dallas Morning News*, 11/26/1978.
3.     Bronson interview, 11/23/1985; Biffle, op. cit., 11/26/1978.
4.     Bronson draft, 11/24/1963.
5.     Bronson interview, 11/23/1985.
6.     Bronson draft, 11/24/1963.
7.     Ibid.
8.     Letter, Bronson to Trask, 5/2/1985; Photographs of Bronson's cameras provided to Trask; Bronson interview, 11/23/1985.
9.     Letter, Bronson to Trask, 5/2/1985.
10.     Bronson 35mm transparency #1 & #2, 11/22/1963.
11.     Letter, Bronson to Trask, 5/2/1985, p. 2; Bronson draft, 11/24/1963.
12.     Ibid.
13.     Bronson interview with Dave Hawkins, tape #100, 12/1978.
14.     Bronson interview, 11/23/1985.
15.     Bronson 35mm transparency #3, 11/22/1963.
16.     Bronson interview, 11/23/1985.
17.     Bronson interview with Hawkins, 12/1978.
18.     Bronson draft, 11/24/1963.
19.     Letter, Bronson to Trask, 5/2/1985; Letter, Bronson to Trask, 9/11/1985.
20.     Bronson interview, 11/23/1985.
21.     FBI Memorandum, To: SAC, Dallas, From: S. A. Milton L. Newsom, file #89-43-518, 11/25/1963.
22.     Bronson interview with Hawkins, 12/1978; Bronson interview, 11/23/1985.
23.     FBI Memorandum, op. cit.; FBI Memorandum, To: SAC, Dallas, From: SA Milton L. Newsom, file #89-43-493.
24.     Bronson interview with Hawkins, 12/1978.
25.     Ibid.
26.     Wendell Rawls, Jr., "New Film Suggests an Oswald Cohort," *New York Times*, 11/27/1978; *Boston Magazine*, 3/1979, p. 127.
27.     Bronson film, 11/22/1963.
28.     Bronson interview, 11/23/1985; Handwritten agreement by Earl Golz, 11/9/1978; Agreement between Charles L. Bronson and A.H. Belo Corp., 11/15/1978; Letter of agreement between Charles L. Bronson and Sigalos & Levine, P.C., 11/17/1978.
29.     Agreement among Charles L. Bronson, A.H. Belo Corp. & Robert Groden, 11/14/1978; "Optical System Utilized Microscope," *Dallas Morning News*, 11/26/1978; Gary Mack, *Coverups!*, 11/1983, p. 2.
30.     Earl Golz, "JFK Film May Reveal Two Gunmen," *Dallas Morning News*, 11/26/1978.

31.  "New Evidence is Hinted in Assassination Film," *New York Times*, 11/26/1978, section 1.

32.  Wendell, op. cit.

33.  Wendell, Ibid.; George Lardner, Jr., "Film in JFK Assassination Reassessed," *Washington Post*, 11/27/1978.

34.  Sigalos & Levine, "News Briefing," 11/28/1978; Attendee's list, 11/28/1978; Bronson interview with Hawkins, 12/1978.

35.  Letter, Craig Mailloux to Charles L. Bronson, 11/30/1978; Letter, David Taylor to Sigalos & Levine, 12/1/1978; Mailgram, John L. Sigalos to Michael J. Hoy.

36.  Letter, Earl Golz to Richard Sprague, 2/28/1979, 4/18/1979, from Western New England College, Sprague Collection.

37.  FBI Memorandum regarding "Assassination of President John F. Kennedy," File #62-109060-7984, 11/27/1978, obtained by Trask through Freedom of Information Act request #288,783, 8/24/1987.  Typically names of informants are blacked out prior to FOIA releases.  This particular item did have a brown magic marker like black-out, though the underlying typescript could readily be read.

38.  *The Continuing Inquiry*, 3/22/1981, p. 3.

39.  "JFK Panel Moves to Analyze Film," *Dallas Morning News*, 12/1/1978; Earl Golz, "Time Running Out for Committee," *Dallas Morning News*, 12/18/1978, p. 4A.

40.  Letter, Charles J. Leontis to Michael Goldsmith, 12/11/1978.

41.  Ibid.

42.  Letter, Robert H. Selzer to Michael Goldsmith, 12/11/1978.

43.  *Appendix to Hearings Before the Select Committee on Assassinations*, v. 6., p. 120-121, 308-309.

44.  *Report of the Select Committee on Assassinations*, p. 7.

45.  Letter, Louis Stokes to Griffin B. Bell, 1/8/1979.

46.  Letter, Sigalos to Bronson, 5/7/1979.

47.  Letter, Sigalos to Bronson, 1/22/1979, 2/5/1979; Letter, Gonsalves to Sigalos, 2/5/1979.

48.  Letter, Special Council Robert L. Keuch to Sigalos, 4/23/1980; Letter, Sigalos to Bronson, 12/22/1980.  The only movement with regard to Bronson's photographic take involved his transparency view taken of the Elm Street area.  In the late summer of 1980 researcher David Lifton secured rights to reproduce this third Bronson slide for his new book, *Best Evidence, Disguise and Deception in the Assassination of John F. Kennedy*, this being the picture's first publication. (*Best Evidence*, photo 11; Letter, Lifton to Bronson, 12/14/1979; Letter, Sigalos to Lifton, 7/22/1980; Letter Lifton to Sigalos, 8/26/1980; Letter, Lifton to Bronson, 9/17/1980.)

49.  Letter, Trask to Edwin Meese III, 8/12/1986, 11/28/1986; Letter, Lawrence Lippe to Trask, 12/23/1986.

50.  Letter, Trask to Edwin Meese III, 8/26/1987.

51.  Letter, Lawrence Lippe to Trask, 2/26/1988.

52.  Letter, Congressman Nicholas Mavroules to Trask, 3/14/1988.

53.  Letter, Thomas M. Boyd to Congressman Peter W. Rodino, Jr., 3/28/1988, through Paul Hoch #1988.75.

54.  Letter, William F. Weld to Peter W. Rodino, Jr., n.d., through Paul Hoch #1988.74.

55.  *Washington Times*, 9/5/1988, p. A3; *Sacramento Bee*, 9/4/1988, p. A18.

56.  Receipt signed by Itek Vice-President Richard J. Wollensak, 10/28/1983; Handwritten agreement signed by Terry T. Drinkwater, 10/29/1983.

57.  Telex, Richard J. Wollensak to Sigalos, 11/1/1983; Letter, Sigalos to Bronson, 11/8/1983.

58.  *Coverups!*, op cit.

59.  Letter, Robert L. Selzer to Trask, 4/14/1987.

60.  Trask telephone interview with Selzer, 7/1987.

61.  Ibid.

62.  Ibid.

63.     Ibid.

64.     Letter, Selzer to Trask, 8/20/1987.

65.     Letter and attachment "Film sequence," Sue Winter to Sigalos, 11/29/1988.

66.     Ibid.

67.     Bronson interview, 11/23/1985.

68.     The PBS-TV broadcast *Frontline*, 11/16/1993.

# PART THREE

# THE PROFESSIONALS

*LIFE* photographer Art Rickerby (in light coat) and NBC cameraman Dave Wiegman (wearing hat) are among the professionals recording the Love Field reception.

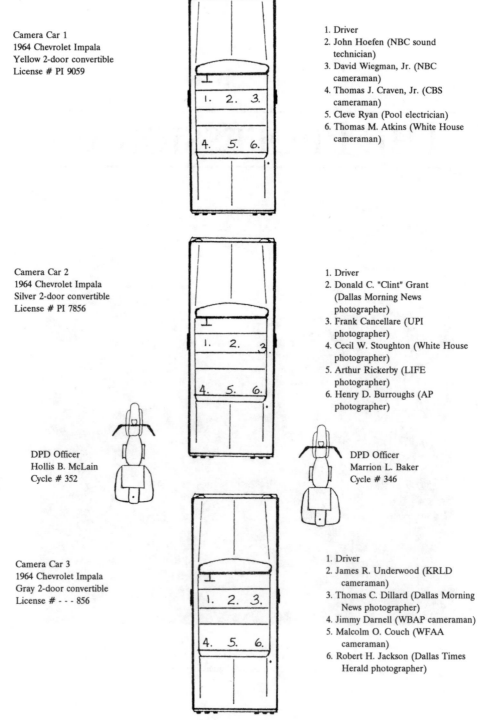

Camera Car 1
1964 Chevrolet Impala
Yellow 2-door convertible
License # PI 9059

1. Driver
2. John Hoefen (NBC sound technician)
3. David Wiegman, Jr. (NBC cameraman)
4. Thomas J. Craven, Jr. (CBS cameraman)
5. Cleve Ryan (Pool electrician)
6. Thomas M. Atkins (White House cameraman)

Camera Car 2
1964 Chevrolet Impala
Silver 2-door convertible
License # PI 7856

1. Driver
2. Donald C. "Clint" Grant (Dallas Morning News photographer)
3. Frank Cancellare (UPI photographer)
4. Cecil W. Stoughton (White House photographer)
5. Arthur Rickerby (LIFE photographer)
6. Henry D. Burroughs (AP photographer)

DPD Officer
Hollis B. McLain
Cycle # 352

DPD Officer
Marrion L. Baker
Cycle # 346

Camera Car 3
1964 Chevrolet Impala
Gray 2-door convertible
License # - - - 856

1. Driver
2. James R. Underwood (KRLD cameraman)
3. Thomas C. Dillard (Dallas Morning News photographer)
4. Jimmy Darnell (WBAP cameraman)
5. Malcolm O. Couch (WFAA cameraman)
6. Robert H. Jackson (Dallas Times Herald photographer)

Motorcade Camera Cars

These vehicles, provided by Earl Hayes Chevrolet, were
positioned 6th, 7th, and 8th respectively behind the presidential Lincoln.

## CHAPTER 13

# The AP Man

Numerous photographers were on hand to record the last moments in the life of the thirty-fifth President of the United States. Most of these picture-takers around Dealey Plaza were non-professionals who had simply wanted to capture on film a fleeting glimpse or two of the infrequent visit of an American President to their state and city. If the event had turned out to be just a typical motorcade, these amateur pictures would soon have been relegated to the near obscurity of the family photo album or stored in a slide box tucked away into a bureau drawer or on a bookshelf.

A number of White House, national, and local press photographers were traveling in the motorcade from Love Air Field to the Dallas Trade Mart in vehicles many car-lengths away from the presidential Lincoln. These professionals would occasionally take a few feet of movie film or a photo of the large downtown crowd with the VIP vehicles barely visible up ahead. Yet of the scores of people, both amateur and professional, who would take pictures of the events before, during, and after the few seconds of shots that would sidetrack the course of American history, no other photographer was at the scene with more premeditated camera planning than Jim Altgens, a man not originally even scheduled to be viewing the parade.

~

James William Altgens, known as "Ike" to his friends and co-workers, was, except for his service during World War II, a life-long resident of Dallas, having been born there on April 28, 1919. Orphaned as a child, Altgens was brought up by a widowed aunt. In 1938, at the age of 19, he began his long career with Associated Press. Initially working at odd jobs in the local bureau including keeping track of payments for "stringers," and doing occasional sports writing, by February 1940 Altgens began to work for the wirephoto department. In 1945, following his return to Dallas from Coast Guard service and his marriage to Clara B. Halliburton in July of 1944, Altgens began making photographs for the Associated Press News Bureau. A graduate from high school, Altgens, while working for AP, attended Southern Methodist University night school. He completed his academic work after six years and earned a Bachelor of Arts degree, majoring in speech with a journalism minor. During those early years Altgens was often sent out of town on assignments and would have to bring his books with him so he could study when he had a chance. "I just kept plugging, and got through it and got my degree."[1]

James W. Altgens

By the 1960s, Altgens, a genial Texan with large facial features, a low melodic voice, and a receding hairline with a rake of white hair on top, served the Dallas Bureau of the Associated Press as a wire photo operator, though often functioning as a photographer, and sometimes filling in as news photo editor. He also enjoyed occasional work acting in television commercials and doing modeling for magazine and newspaper advertisements. Residing with his wife Clara about two miles north of University Park, Altgens covered numerous local events, including sports photography of AFL and Bowl games. He had photographed John F. Kennedy once before. In November 1961 the new President, accompanied by former President Dwight D. Eisenhower, arrived at Perrin Air Force Base to attend the funeral of Speaker of the House of Representatives Sam Rayburn, in Bonham, Texas. Just prior to this assignment, Altgens had climbed to the twenty-ninth floor of the Dallas Mercantile Bank Building to take a picture of the rescue of a girl trapped in a burning elevator. The only photographer making the climb, Altgens phoned in the story to his bureau before beginning the exhaustive trek back to the ground floor.[2]

Some twenty-three years after the event Altgens recalled how he came to be at the scene of the President's assassination in 1963. "On November 21, 1963, my work assignment was in the office. While I was originally assigned to work as photo editor on November 22, I urged the assignment editor and bureau chief to let me go down to the triple underpass to make a scenic view of the presidential caravan with the Dallas skyline in the background."[3] This was an area where there was no scheduled photographic coverage. With some reluctance News Photo Editor Dave Taylor gave Altgens this requested assignment. Taylor reassigned the night photo editor to come in early and relieve Altgens. Late that Thursday afternoon Altgens went to the Bloom Advertising Agency, which was taking care of press credentials for the presidential visit. He picked up his press identification badge which was marked "No. 196" on the back. On Friday work began early, as at 4:45 a.m., Altgens was assigned as wirephoto operator shifting at 6:15 a.m. to news photo editor.[4]

Wanting to find and be in position in plenty of time for his making photos of the motorcade, at about 11:15 a.m. Altgens walked over to the triple underpass where Main, Elm, and Commerce Streets travel under the railroad tracks. Altgens brought with him his personal 35mm Nikkorex-F single lens reflex camera. He had purchased the camera mounted with a 50mm lens in January 1963 from Medo Photo Supply Corp. of New York, through the Associated Press. It cost $157 and was marked with serial

#371734. Today the camera body was mounted with a 105mm telephoto lens and loaded with Eastman Kodak Tri-X pan film. Altgens also carried a gadget bag with extra lenses and other camera paraphernalia. On major assignments photographers were usually given motor-driven cameras, but due to Altgens not having been originally assigned as a photographer, he took his own hand-cocked camera, which did not lend itself to speed shooting. As Altgens knew, "This meant that what I took I had to make sure it was good — I didn't have time for second chances."[5]

accepts interchangeable Nikkor lenses & Nikon F accessories

Two uniformed police officers assigned from the Traffic Division, J. W. Foster and J. C. White, were stationed on top of the underpass. Foster came over and challenged Altgens if he was a railroad employee. Altgens said "No," showed him his press tag, and explained that he had a Department of Public Safety ID Card, and was assigned by AP to take some photos of the motorcade. His 2¼" x 3½" white press card printed in black ink with the word "PRESS" printed below in blue ink was pinned to his left coat lapel. It did not help. The officer was adamant that this was private property, and no one but railroad personnel were permitted in the area. Noting that the area seemed pretty well protected with these two cops here, and another one on the Stemmons overpass, Altgens nonetheless decided not to press the issue, and moved on to find another photographic vantage point. The officer had not denied access to the area for security reasons, but with the fact that it was private property.[6]

PRESIDENT KENNEDY'S
VISIT TO DALLAS
NOVEMBER 22, 1963

PRESS

Altgens's Press Badge

Altgens walked the short distance across the overpass into the Texas School Book Depository Building's parking lot, over to Elm Street at Houston, crossing Elm and traveling south on Houston over to the corner of Houston and Main Street. To his seasoned photographer's eye, Altgens could see some potential photo opportunities as the motorcade would be traveling down the sloping grade from upper Main Street towards this point at Houston and Main. The immense "Texas Bank" roof sign was up the street on the right, and there were tall buildings on both sides of this heavily commercial district. This view might, if the building shadows did not over-contrast the light areas, make for a usable shot of the motorcade in the middle of a large Dallas crowd with the tall buildings giving a cavernous mood to the picture. After a few possible pictures here, Altgens saw that he could then run across Dealey Plaza and again catch the motorcade on Elm Street as it proceeded towards the triple underpass.[7]

It was now about 11:30 a.m., and as Altgens fiddled with the focus of his camera and marked time as he had done so many times before while on photographic assignment, waiting for the "photo opportunity" to arrive, the crowd began to build at this major cross-street area.  At about 12:15 Altgens and many others watched as a young white man fell into an apparent epileptic seizure on Houston Street, opposite the north reflecting pool.  Aided by uniformed police, the man was finally transported away in an ambulance, and as the ambulance traveled down Elm Street and under the triple underpass, Altgens noticed about a dozen people on top of the railroad bridge.  He thought to himself, "What the heck are all those people are doing up there," at the spot where he was not allowed to stay and take his pictures.  "And just as the ambulance was clearing the triple underpass, you could see the red lights as the motorcade cut onto Main Street."[8]  Rechecking his camera, Altgens could now hear the distant applause and cheers rippling closer towards him as he looked at the scene in his viewfinder.  Positioning his camera at the vertical plane which best showed the tall buildings towering over the motorcade, Altgens took his first shot of the procession as it traveled towards him.  He waited to make his exposure just at a point when the President's car hit a sunlit break between the building shadows.[9]

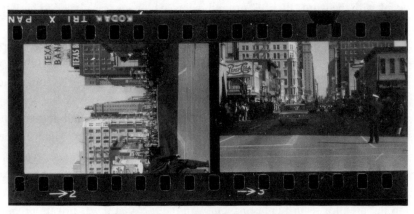

Contact prints of Altgens's first two photos

Quickly winding his camera, a few moments later he readied for another shot, this time with the camera at the horizontal. Waiting long enough for the lead motorcycle escort to pass his position, Altgens pushed the shutter button again, capturing the light-colored motorcade pilot car in the foreground being followed by the presidential limousine and trailed closely behind by the Secret Service follow-up car.[10]  Yet Altgens's instinct told him this wouldn't be the picture he wanted.  Readjusting his focus, he waited for a clear view of the presidential limousine.

All around Altgens at slightly different angles, amateurs, including Phil Willis, Wilma Bond, Marie Muchmore, Richard Bothun, and Orville Nix, were taking movies and still pictures of essentially the same views as the AP photographer.  Most of the amateur pictures, however, would be just slightly out of focus or were of too slow a shutter speed causing a slight blurring of features of the limousine and its occupants.

Waiting for the pilot car to turn onto Houston and out of the camera's view, yet not waiting too long so that the motorcycles might obscure details, Altgens looked for the right moment to click. As the massive, shining blue-black Lincoln swung the corner with Secret Service driver William Greer turning the wheel, both Governor and Mrs. Connally were looking towards Altgens's side of the street. He didn't even notice their glance, for the couple in the back seat were the celebrities, and the President was looking towards

Full frame of Altgens's third photo

the camera and raising his right forearm in a wave. "Jackie Kennedy was looking at me, but the wind had just gotten up catching the First Lady's hat." She instinctively reached to hold it with her white-gloved left hand, obscuring her face to Altgens's lens. Though

Cropped version of the third photograph as sent out by AP

Mrs. Kennedy's face was not in the picture Altgens took, the others were, as were the features of over 20 smiling spectators located across the street, on the northeast corner of Houston and Main, all captured on the film in a frozen moment of time and light. Among these spectators *Dallas Morning News* artist Merle Robertson wearing dark glasses and with a scarf around her head can be picked out. She had come on her lunch break to see the motorcade. Another newspaper employee can be seen to her right.

James Featherston, a reporter for the *Dallas Times Herald* was there on assignment. He was to pick up film thrown to him by Bob Jackson, a photographer in Camera Car 3 further on in the motorcade, so it could be rushed back to the paper for processing and possible use in the paper's late edition. One older woman can be seen waving with her right hand held high, while near her another woman is in the process of taking a picture of the famous American couple.[11] This Altgens photo would, in various cropped forms, be published in hundreds of newspapers across the country within the next six hours, with the caption to the photograph alluding to the last few moments of happiness before the horror.

Cocking his camera again, Altgens took one more photo of the President's car and the Secret Service follow-up vehicle as they moved away from him and were passing the Dallas County Criminal Courts Building.[12] Grabbing his gadget bag Altgens sprinted down the sloping grade in a northwesterly direction over the grassed infield area of the Plaza. He reached the curb of the south side of Elm Street, about 240 feet from the northerly corner of Elm and Houston Streets, where the motorcade was making a sharp left-hand turn. Still using his 105mm lens, since he had no time to get into his gadget bag and change lenses, Altgens had the cameras' aperture at F-11 with a shutter speed of 1/1000 of a second.[13]

Stepping off the curb into the street, Altgens looked into his viewfinder and, just a fraction ahead of his clicking the shutter, he heard a noise that sounded like a firecracker going off somewhere from behind the approaching car. The noise was extraneous to Altgens and held no significance to his task. He took no notice of how many noises occurred following this first one.[14] Later estimating he was about 30 feet from the car when he took his photo, a comparison of this picture with frames from the Zapruder film indicates that it was taken around Zapruder frame #255, which would actually make his location about 60 feet from the presidential limousine.

This photograph is, along with the Moorman Polaroid, perhaps the most well-known of any still photograph made at the assassination scene. Along with Altgens's next photograph, it would be published in papers the world over.

Spot photographers don't typically have the benefit of time to study their subject, as things happen so quickly around them. As Altgens would vividly describe to this author at this same site some 23 years later, "My first instinct was 'Well, they're shooting firecrackers up there,' or some kind of celebration on behalf of the President. And then I hear it again as the car comes on down. No one had the foggiest idea that something was taking place."[15]

His developed picture, however, showed in detail what eyes and mind could not so quickly comprehend. Because Altgens was using the 105mm telephoto lens, there is a foreshortening of features within the picture, so that people standing near the Elm and Houston Street intersection look almost the same size and distance away as people on the north side of Elm Street and the sidewalk some 120 or more feet away. In examining the photograph one can identity over 55 spectators watching the motorcade. All except two of these people and the shadows of a few more are on the north side of Elm Street. Many are still looking toward the President's car, which has by this moment passed their position, while other people have diverted their attention to the Vice-President's convertible.

Portions of the first two stories of the front northeastern side of the Texas School Book Depository are seen with at least four persons viewing the procession from the front entrance. So too, parts of three stories of the westerly Houston Street side of the Dal-Tex Building are in view with three spectators leaning out of a second story window, while another person can be seen apparently sitting on the second floor fire escape. This man, a Black by appearance, can also be seen in Altgens's fourth photo, sitting on the fire escape.[16] Two women are photographing the motorcade. One woman to the left of the lamppost on the left side of the picture is aiming towards the Vice-President's convertible, while another woman, perhaps using a movie camera, can be seen in the crowd between the Secret Service agents standing on the right side of the follow-up car running board, and the middle-pictured motorcycle policeman.

Many of those spectators at the Elm and Houston Street intersection have diverted their attention completely away from the front of the motorcade, while on the extreme right of the photo the hands of Charles Brehm, who is standing about 160 feet from Houston Street, are applauding the President's appearance. While the spectators seem oblivious to anything wrong, the occupants of the President's car have had their attention diverted from these friendly onlookers. In the front seat Secret Service Agent-in-Charge Roy Kellerman's face is virtually lost in the shadow, while driver Greer's is hidden by the flapping presidential flag. Mrs. Connally's face is also obscured, but the Governor has turned sharply to his right and seems to be wincing. The eyes and nose of President Kennedy are obscured by the limousine's rear-view mirror, but his lips appear pursed and he is cocked slightly to the left with his left arm horizontal to the plane of his mouth. His fingers are clenched. The white-gloved right hand of Mrs. Kennedy is cradling his arm. Motorcycle officer Chaney, on the left side of the picture, has turned his head sharp right, while the other two visible motorcycle men seem to be looking towards the limousine.

In the "Queen Mary," the Secret Service follow-up car, driver Kinney and Agent-in-Charge Roberts, both sporting dark glasses, seem to belooking towards the President,

A near-full-frame print of the fifth Altgens photo

while Agents Ready and Landis, on the passenger running board, are looking hard to their right, perhaps toward the sound of the report. So too, is Agent Hickey in the back seat. Agent Clint Hill, on the driver's forward running board position, and presidential assistant Dave Powers, his forehead obscured by the rear-view mirror, seem to be looking directly at the President. In the Vice-President's Lincoln convertible, only a glimpse of Lyndon Johnson's head can be observed, while Lady Bird's smiling face can be clearly discerned, as she sits between her husband and Senator Ralph Yarborough.

The Vice-President's follow-up Mercury sedan is directly behind. As he had done along much of the parade route, Agent Warren W. Taylor has kept his rear passenger side door ajar in case he has to exit quickly in order to protect the Vice-President.[17] The Altgens picture captures the scene just a few seconds into the assassination of the President, when save for the victims themselves, few have had time to react to the intrusive noise they had just heard.

Still in the midst of taking his pictures and oblivious to the danger around him, Altgens stepped back onto the curb. He quickly wound his film to the next frame, adjusted his focus to 15 feet, and raised the Nikkorex to eye level, wanting a good closeup of the President and Mrs. Kennedy. The limousine came towards him at about 12 mph, and as it passed just about 15 feet a little to the front of him, and as he was about ready to snap the picture, Altgens heard another report. A high-velocity bullet punctured the

Altgens, with his camera poised, witnesses the horror of the head shot. The man to his right, also with a camera, is Richard Bothun.

rear of the President's head. "Fragments of his head fell right at my feet. That was some heck of an explosion when it hit his head. His skull just disintegrated and bone and flesh flying. . . ." The horror was unexpected, Kennedy's head was covered with blood, and according to Altgens, "It stunned me so at what I saw, that I failed to do my duty and make the picture that I was trying to make." Mrs. Kennedy then grabbed the President and Altgens heard her cry, "Oh, no!" as his body slumped over into her lap. Altgens also heard on the radio from within the car, "we've been hit, get us to the nearest hospital," the words coming out as Altgens emphasized, "loud and clear."[18]

Speaking of the event over two decades later, Altgens's memory is still vivid of the horror of the moment and the later criticism by some. "The big showdown came at the time J.F.K. received the shot to the head. I had prefocused, had my hand on the trigger, but when J.F.K.'s head exploded, sending substance in my direction, I virtually became paralyzed. This was such a shock to me that I never did press the trigger on the camera. The sight was unbelievable, and I was surprised I recovered fast enough to make the picture of the Secret Service man aiding Mrs. Kennedy. This, to me, was an awesome experience. Yet, many news people say I should have taken the picture anyway, regardless of the circumstances. Perhaps they are right. Nevertheless, they must put themselves in the identical, same position before they criticize." When, on a day shy of the twenty-third anniversary of the assassination, Altgens revisited his original location at Dealey Plaza, he again tried to convey the horror and, at the same time, his frustration concerning this missed photo. "I really can't tell you in a way that anyone will truly understand. But to have a President shot to death right in front of you — and keep your cool, and do what you're supposed to do — I'm not real sure that the most seasoned photographers would be able to do it. . . . It's not that I'm looking for any excuse, it's just that there is no excuse for this. I should have made the picture I was set up to make. And I didn't do it."[19]

The photographer's shock and disbelief at such a ghastly sight was momentary, and the veteran's instinct took hold. Altgens stepped out to the curb, aimed his camera at the now quickly accelerating presidential vehicle. He shot a forlorn scene in which agent Clint Hill is on the limousine rear step. Mrs. Kennedy is moving back into the car. The white pilot car is a few lengths ahead, just starting into the shadow of the overpass on which some ten spectators can be seen peering down at the horror taking place below.[20]

With the presidential Lincoln disappearing into the underpass, Altgens made a picture of the activity across Elm Street showing amateur movie maker Abraham Zapruder and his secretary Mary Sitzman just after they had gotten down from the concrete wall from where he had filmed the assassination. In the middle of the frame are Mr. & Mrs. Charles Hester hunkered down in front of the colonnade area.[21] Altgens then quickly crossed the street. The area was in "utter confusion" as uniformed policemen went racing up the incline of the grassy knoll. Says Altgens about the scene, "Well, I thought they were onto something. I was satisfied that the shot came from the rear, but I didn't know where in the rear. So I figured they had spotted the guy somewhere and they had chased him up here, and I wanted to come over and get a picture of the guy — if they had such a person in custody. And I came over here and by the time I can get up to the hill, they're turned around and are coming back. And they hadn't found anything." He then took a "good look" around the area to see that no one else had been shot, and observed a family of four sprawled out on the ground, parents protectively covering their two children. Cameramen from the motorcade had in the meantime jumped out of their vehicles and were scurrying to this area, taking pictures as they approached. Altgens however took no more photos. After a few moments he crossed back Elm and retrieved his gadget bag. "My main concern from that point on was getting my stuff back to the office."[22]

Altgens takes a photo of the colonnade.

Realizing the extreme importance of what he had seen and the pictures that he made, Altgens sprinted back to the Dallas News Building. Part of the way he was in the company of WFAA-TV personality Jerry Haynes. Altgens caught the correct signal lights at each intersection and even an elevator waiting on the first floor. Arriving at the third floor AP wirephoto office, he picked up the interoffice phone which rang automatically in the news office. Dallas AP Bureau Chief Robert H. Johnson, Jr., came on the line to hear Altgens blurt out, "Bob, the President has been shot!"

"Ike, how do you know?" Johnson incredulously asked. "I saw it, there was blood on his head, Jackie jumped up and grabbed him and cried, 'Oh, no!' The motorcade raced onto the Freeway."

"Ike, you saw that?" cried Johnson.

And Altgens affirmed, "Yes, I was shooting pictures and then I saw it."

Johnson yelled, "Bulletin!" as he typed the most important lines of his career. Night editor Ron Thompson pulled the bulletin from the typewriter and quickly handed it to wire operator Julia Saunders. At 12:39 CST the bulletin was on the wire. "Dallas, Nov. 22 (AP) — President Kennedy was shot today just as his motorcade left downtown Dallas. Mrs. Kennedy jumped up and grabbed Mr. Kennedy. She cried 'Oh, No!' The motorcade sped on." The bulletin was received in newsrooms and government offices throughout the nation. Undoubtedly the first public media outlet to broadcast the AP report was Dallas TV station WFAA, which interrupted its regular programming to begin coverage at about 12:45. Program director Jay Watson read the shocking news from a quickly rushed-in bulletin — "An Associated Press photographer, James Altgens, reports he saw blood on the President's head. The AP man said he heard two shots, but thought someone was shooting fireworks, until he saw blood on the President. He also said he saw no one with a gun."[23]

Altgens remembers that while the bulletin was being readied, "Someone grabbed my camera, removed the film and took it in to process it, because they wanted me on the telephone reporting what I saw. We did an extraordinary good job, because within 20 minutes of the assassination we had a picture rolling on the wire — and that's good. All the wires were connected together, which means they got it in Africa and London, all over the world, at the same time that people got it in the U. S. of A. It was fantastic. I saw some of the cable photos that came back in that night, and one or more of the pictures I had taken were on page one of many of the world newspapers."[24]

The photo caption of the motorcade under fire, one of three Altgens photos sent out on the wirephoto network, read: "(DN2) DALLAS, TEX., NOV. 22 — KENNEDY SHOT IN DALLAS — President John F. Kennedy was shot today just as his motorcade left downtown Dallas. He was taken to Parkland Hospital. Secret Service men are looking from where the shots came from (AP Wirephoto) (cel61303 stf — jwa) 1963." The AP photo code at the sign-off indicated that Carl E. Linde (cel) was the caption writer, 6 indicated the day was Friday, 1303 that it was sent at 1:03 p.m., and the photo was taken by staff member James W. Altgens.[25]

Staying long enough to provide identification of what he had photographed, Altgens relates that "After my pictures cleared the wirephoto network, I was sent to Parkland Hospital to work with AP Washington photographer Henry Burroughs. We stayed until President Kennedy's body was removed from the hospital to Air Force One at Love Field. I then was sent back to the assassination site to make photos that could be diagrammed. I later was sent to City Hall to pick up photos made by photographer Ted Powers and bring the film back to our office to process. These were pictures made of Oswald in police custody, and this was the first and only time I saw Oswald." Altgens got a glimpse of the suspect as Oswald was being taken from the interrogation room at Police Headquarters to another room. To Altgens, the accused looked exhausted, "Like they had put him through the interrogation ringer."[26]

A little after 5:00 p.m. Altgens returned to Dealey Plaza and took a series of 21 photographs of the Book Depository, triple underpass, and pictures from the point where he had taken his first photo of the motorcade under fire. Altgens's original negatives of the motorcade were sent to Associated Press headquarters via an airline pilot on a commercial flight to New York, where a special messenger picked them up and delivered them to the AP office.[27] Altgens had been so busy, that he had not gotten prints of his photos and had to request copies from New York, but apparently he never acquired a whole set of his pictures.

In later years Altgens became unsure of the number of photographs he took that day of the assassination, and has been reluctant to acknowledge authorship of all seven since he is very adamant about not wanting to take credit for someone else's work. In discussions with him, it is evident that he is sure or reasonably sure that he took five of the photos, but admits to leaving things to AP's judgment. In testimony six months after the shooting, he did mention that he made one or two pictures of the caravan coming down Main Street, but with the length of intervening years and the fact that he possibly never saw in print form all his pictures before the negatives were sent to New York, this explains some of his caution about authorship of the photos.

An examination of the negative sequence, however, shows quite conclusively that these seven pictures are Altgens's, a fact first noticed by researcher Richard E. Sprague, who found the individually cut negatives at AP in New York. The film is of the same type (Tri-X), is numbered sequentially, is chronological, and taken from the same vantage points at which Altgens is known to have been located. Mr. Altgens's personal caution is refreshing, but in light of the evidence, not problematical to the evidence.

Although it was obvious from the published photographs circulated all over the nation and world that an AP photographer was present at the assassination, no government official contacted Altgens or the Dallas AP about the events that he had witnessed. Altgens tried to get his bureau chief to give him permission to notify the authorities to let them know he had been in the area, but his boss never got permission for him, and Altgens did not feel he had the authority to act on his own. Yet, although the official investigations resulting from the murder seemed uninterested in Altgens's account, others were very interested in one of his pictures.

A number of people spotted the uncanny resemblance of accused assassin Lee Harvey Oswald to one of the men standing in the doorway of the Book Depository Building, peering out at the motorcade in Altgens's photo #5. If this man were Oswald, how could he be accused of doing the shooting? Three days after the assassination, Mike Shapiro, manager of WFAA-TV in Dallas, brought this observation to the attention of the FBI, stating that, ". . . an individual in the Associated Press office at Pittsburgh, Pennsylvania, had noticed the similarities between the individual in the doorway and Lee Harvey Oswald."[28] Others also noticed. Mrs. Helen Shirah of Jacksonville, Florida, wrote in January 1964 to the Secret Service, pointing out the man "who bears a striking resemblance to Lee Harvey Oswald," from a photo in a magazine picture she had purchased. Stating that she was sure they were very thorough in their investigation, ". . . and had probably checked out all available pictures. . . ," she had no idea of how cavalier the investigation was with gathering photographic evidence.[29]

The FBI was, however, checking out this identity question. On November 25 agents had interviewed Roy S. Truly, Warehouse Manager of the Book Depository, who identified the person in the doorway as employee Billy Nolan Lovelady. They also spoke to Lovelady, who confirmed that the person in the picture was indeed him, admitting that there was a resemblance between Oswald and himself. Lovelady would later tell an interviewer that when the agents had shown him the Altgens picture, "Right away I pointed to me and they seemed relieved. One had a big smile on his face because it wasn't Oswald. They said they had a big discussion down at the FBI and one guy said it just had to be Oswald."[30] On January 30, 1964, Assistant Manager William H. Shelley was also interviewed. He stated that the person in the photo was indeed Lovelady, and that he, Shelley, had been standing next to Lovelady that day.[31]

Billy Lovelady, in circle, resembled Lee Oswald enough
to make this Altgens photo the subject of much speculation.

Although critics of the 1964 Warren Commission investigation continued for years to question the identity of the man at the Depository entrance, spurred on by a mixup of what shirt Lovelady was wearing that day, the evidence is quite overwhelming that it was in fact Lovelady. This conclusion was only strengthened as a result of the House Select Committee on Assassinations work in 1978.[32]

The question of the identity of the man in the Altgens photo aside, investigators had not apparently even attempted to find and interview Altgens, a witness to the assassination who might shed light upon other important matters. On May 11 and 14, 1964, Altgens received phone calls at his home from a Dom Bonafede, who was preparing a story on the controversial Altgens photograph.[33] This Bonafede article was published in the magazine section of the *New York Herald Tribune* on May 24, 1964, under the title "The Picture with a Life of Its Own," referring to the Oswald look-alike. Bonafede described the Altgens photo as "the Classic assassination photo," and noted that even though the photographer could recall the shooting in great detail, Altgens had never been questioned by the FBI. The following day a column by Maggie Daly, "Daly Diary," published in the *Chicago American* asked: "Isn't it odd that J. W. Altgens, a veteran Associated Press photographer in Dallas, who took a picture of the Kennedy Assassination — one of the witnesses close enough to see the President shot and able to describe second-by-second what happened — has been questioned neither by the FBI nor the Warren Commission?"[34] The Chicago FBI reported this column to Washington. Finally and undoubtedly as a result of critical comment by the press, on June 2, 1964, over six months after the assassination, Altgens was finally interviewed by an FBI agent, resulting in a five-page report.

On July 22, 1964, Wesley J. Liebeler, Assistant Counsel for the Warren Commission, took testimony from Altgens at the Dallas Post Office Building. According to the record, the testimony amounted to 9 pages, and took only some 15 minutes for the questioning. Liebeler centered his questioning around the circumstances of Altgens taking his photographs, his movement in the Plaza, the number, spacing, and direction of the shots, his distance from the limousine, and questions relating to Altgens's being able to identify anyone in his well known photograph #5. The testimony reads as non-confrontational and Altgens comes off as a cooperative witness feeling somewhat guilty of not stepping forward to make the authorities aware of his presence at the assassination and wishing that he had been able to give his testimony when it was fresh in his mind.[35] Until the news stories about their negligence surfaced, the investigative bodies made no effort to contact Altgens. Instead of actively seeking out this man who had obviously been an important witness to the killing, the government had to be prodded into action by newspaper questions.

There is no evidence to show that the original negatives or first generation full frame prints were requested or obtained by the FBI or Warren Commission, save for their use of cropped Associated Press wirephoto prints of his fifth photograph of the series. All this is consistent with the nonplus attitude on the part of the government towards potential photographic evidence during the entire 1963-1964 official investigation into the assassination.

At the time of the New Orleans trial of Clay Shaw on the charge of conspiracy in the death of President Kennedy, Altgens received a subpoena from District Attorney Jim Garrison's office to appear as a trial witness. Altgens, having read about the controversial investigation, was not eager to become involved. "I really didn't want to go, because Garrison's reputation had already been pretty well established, and most of the things that he was doing were self-aggrandizement." Altgens was concerned that given the reputation of the D.A.'s investigation, Altgens's testimony could be badly twisted. A subpoena from another state jurisdiction had to be examined by a Texas state court to judge if it should or should not be honored. Altgens appeared before Judge Holland's court with a copy of one of his photos, and an explanation that the picture and his testimony before the Warren Commission attorney was the sum and substance of his information. He voiced his reluctance to the judge about going to Louisiana, but the judge nonetheless told Altgens he thought he ought to go and urged the photographer to, "have a fun time in New Orleans."[36]

Several weeks later a check for $300 for plane fare to New Orleans arrived with a notice that he would be contacted about when to make the trip. "About a week or two later, when I was down in Houston, I happened to run into John Connally. I had known him from past times when I had to cover him in office, and also had been out at his ranch a time or two." Asking of Connally's health, the former governor responded that he was pretty well, although the wrist that had been shot through during the assassination still hurt him quite a bit. Altgens asked him if he too had received a subpoena from Garrison. The governor replied, "Oh Hell yes! But I'm not going." Connally decried Garrison and the standing of his case, remarking that he had cashed his travel expense check and spent it. He urged Altgens do the same, which advice was soon thereafter taken. Later it was reported by the press that Governor Connally and James Altgens of AP would not be called to testify in the Shaw trial, as they were hostile witnesses. Thus ended Altgens's connection with the Garrison case.[37]

Ike Altgens took early retirement from Associated Press in September of 1979 in lieu of a transfer, wanting to remain in his native Dallas. Working a number of years as a field representative of Ford Motor Company for their Display and Exhibit Department, Altgens has often been sought out by assassination buffs for his recollections. He freely concedes that, ". . . there will always be some controversy about details surrounding the site and shooting of the President," but wonders whether at this point in time it is possible to uncover something that investigators have overlooked. He says he has yet to see indisputable evidence to the contrary that Oswald did not kill the President.[38]

Ever a polite and affable gentleman possessing a sense of history and enjoying the sharing of stories of his varied and interesting career, Altgens is careful not to embellish his recollections. Emphasizing, "I don't have any authority to speak about something of which I don't know," Altgens does not suffer gladly the eyewitnesses to November 22, 1963, who have changed and embellished their stories over the years. He is bemused and perplexed with many of the conspiracy theorists who spend much of their time devising intricate scenarios, and who attempt to convince him with detailed diagrams and rambling letters that what he saw and experienced is incorrect, and what they have imagined is the truth. "Until those people come up with solid evidence to support their claims, I see no value in wasting my time with them." [39]

The original Altgens negatives which were created on November 22, 1963, are deposited with other negatives on the subject within the vast Wide World Photo operations in New York City. Some of the original seven negatives have had copy negatives in cropped format created, while others of this historically valuable set unfortunately appear to be misidentified, misplaced, or even missing.

## CHAPTER NOTES

1.      "Lone 'Pro' On Scene Where JFK Was Shot," *Editor and Publisher*, 12/7/1963, p. 11, 61; *Hearings Before the President's Commission on the Assassination of President Kennedy*, v. 7, p. 516; Altgens interview with Trask, 11/21/1985, 10/23/1992.

2.      "Lone," op. cit., p. 61.

3.      Letter, Altgens to Trask, 3/31/1984.

4.      Ibid.; Letter, Altgens to Trask, 6/21/1986; "Lone," op. cit., p. 11.

5.      Letter, Altgens to Trask, 6/23/1984; Letter, Altgens to Trask, 6/21/1986.

6.      *Hearings*, op. cit., v. 6, p. 249-50; v.7, p. 516.

7.      Ibid., v. 7, p. 516-517.

8.      Ibid., v. 7, p. 524; Altgens interview, 11/21/1985.

9.     Altgens photograph 11/22/1963, roll 1, #2 (first photograph in the series was frame #2).

10.    Ibid., roll 1, #3.

11.    Ibid., roll 1, #4; Altgens interview, 11/21/1985.

12.    Ibid., roll 1, #5. This photograph was the subject of speculation by some critics who believed it pictured among the spectators on Houston Street, Joseph A. Milteer, a right-wing organizer alleged to have been a possible conspirator. Consultants for the House Select Committee made a study of this photograph (*Appendix to Hearings Before the Select Committee*, v. 6, p. 242-257) which study supported the conclusion that the man was not Milteer.

13.    *Hearings*, op. cit., v. 22, p. 790; "Lone," op. cit., p. 11; Altgens interview, 11/21/1985.

14.    *Hearings*, op. cit., v. 7, p. 517-518.

15.    Altgens interview, 11/21/1985.

16.    Altgens photograph, op. cit., roll 1, #6. Several researchers noticed in this Altgens photograph a rifle-shaped object protruding out of the second floor of the Dal-Tex Building at the fire escape landing. Indeed, some claimed to see at this location a rifle with silencer together with a pillow propped on one of the metal fire escape steps. Robert J. Groden, a critic who served as a consultant to the HSCA photography panel, examined the original negative of this photograph and reported that "using my technique of vario-density cynexing, I was able to enhance the image in the window to the point of clarity where the figure in the window is now identifiable as a black man leaning on the window sill with both hands, and with no gun in view." (*HSCA* v.6, p. 307)

17.    *Hearings*, op. cit., v. 18, p. 777, 782. A number of researchers have noted the VP follow-up car's open door and have explained it as evidence of a quick response of the Vice-President's protectors, in contrast to the President's agents. Some others have seen in this super-fast reaction a sinister foreknowledge of the event. These explanations are examples of persons reading more into the reality of photographs than is necessarily there. Agent Taylor's report of his activities indicated, and photos taken earlier in the motorcade, including a picture by Cecil Stoughton in Camera Car 2 of the motorcade on Main Street, as well as a film sequence made by Marie Muchmore of the motorcade on Houston Street, revealed that this door was ajar during much, if not all, of the motorcade.

18.    Ibid., v. 7, p. 518; v. 22, p. 791; Altgens interview, 11/21/1985.

19.    Letter, Altgens to Trask, 6/23/1984; Altgens interview, 11/21/1985; Letter, Altgens to Trask, 6/21/1986. In a 1993 letter Altgens mentioned he recalled not seeing any blood on the right side or face of the President, ". . . But there was plenty of blood on the left side and rear of his head. I noticed this as he slowly fell down onto the seat next to Jackie Kennedy." (Letter, Altgens to Trask, 8/11/1993.)

20.    Altgens photograph, op. cit., roll 1, #7.

21.    Altgens, Ibid., roll 1, #8.

22.    Altgens interview, 11/21/1985.

23.    Bob Johnson, "Too Busy for Tears," *The AP World*, 8/1972, p. 18-19; *The Torch is Passed*, p. 14; Altgens interview, 11/21/1985; WFAA-TV coverage, 12:45-12:48 p.m. CST, 11/22/1963.

24.    Altgens interview, 11/21/1985.

25.    AP Wirephoto caption "cel61303stf-jwa," 11/22/1963; Letter, Altgens to Trask, 6/21/1986.

26.    Letter, Altgens to Trask, 3/31/1984; Letter, Altgens to Trask, 4/21/1984.

27.    Letter, Altgens to Trask, 3/31/1984.

28.    Harold Weisberg, *Photographic Whitewash*, p. 188. By December 2 Associated Press would, in fact, distribute an enlargement of this Altgens photo to its subscribers with a circle around the mystery man. Titled "Photo arouses new interest," the caption concluded with the fact: "Authorities said the man in the picture is not Oswald but another employee of the Depository." (*New York Herald Tribune Magazine*, 5/24/1964, p. 9)

29.    Ibid., p. 189-191.

30.    Ibid., p. 189, 191-192; *New York Herald Tribune Magazine*, 5/24/1964, p. 10.

31.     Weisberg, op. cit., p. 191. Altgens was later contacted by Lovelady, via telephone, who re-
        quested a copy of this famous photograph. Altgens was happy to comply, but could not secure
        from the elusive Lovelady an interview or photo session. He was told by Mrs. Lovelady, whom
        he met shortly afterwards, that Lovelady's elusiveness was due not so much to the assassination's
        events, as to threats on himself and his wife's children by a former husband, whom the family
        was attempting to avoid. By November 1971 *Dallas Times Herald* photographer Bob Jackson
        was able to have a photo session with Lovelady. Wearing the same shirt he'd had on the day
        of the assassination, Lovelady posed on the steps of the Book Depository Building for several
        copyrighted pictures. At a distance of eight years from the original event, it was still readily
        evident that Lovelady was one and the same in both the 1963 and 1971 photos. (*Dallas Times
        Herald* photograph files, JFK #9)

32.     *New York Times*, 5/24/1964, p. 7; *Appendix to Hearings Before the Select Committee on Assassi-
        nations*, v. 6, p. 286-293.

33.     *Hearings*, op. cit., v. 22, p. 791-792.

34.     *Chicago American*, 5/25/1964, p. 7.

35.     *Hearings*, op. cit., v. 7, p. 517-525.

36.     Altgens interview, 10/23/1992.

37.     Ibid.

38.     Letter, Altgens to Trask, 4/21/1984, 6/23/1984.

39.     Altgens interview, 11/16/1991; 10/23/1992; Letter, Altgens to Trask,12/19/1991.

An enlargement of Altgens's Houston Street photo, his fourth in the series

## CHAPTER 14

# The Star-Telegram

The hallmark of good newspaper reporting is that it be topical, timely, and accurate, whether it is the reporting in a large daily circulation metropolitan newspaper, or a story in a modest 1500 circulation rural weekly. And all newspapers, no matter what their size or prestige, are also judged and supported by their local readership on the quantity and quality of local events coverage.

In the early 1960s there were in the United States a significant number of newspapers with circulation figures and advertising revenues hefty enough to support large and effective editorial and reporting staffs. These papers not only covered local and regional events, but also, in addition to receiving wire services, were committed to independent reporting of national news and topics. Among those major American dailies which had an acknowledged reputation for their national coverage were the *New York Times*, *Los Angeles Times*, *St. Louis Post-Dispatch*, *Washington Post*, *Chicago Sun-Times*, *New York Herald-Tribune*, *Chicago Daily News*, *Wall Street Journal*, *New York Daily News*, *Baltimore Sun*, *Philadelphia Bulletin*, *Cleveland Plain Dealer*, *Kansas City Star*, *Chicago Tribune*, and *Detroit News*.

In the Lone Star State, the highest circulation newspapers included the *Houston Chronicle* and *Houston Post*, the *Dallas Morning News* and *Dallas Times Herald*, and the *Fort Worth Star-Telegram*. As important daily newspapers in the host state and host cities during President John Kennedy's three-day visit, these five papers would be covering what to most editors would be the closest thing to an ideal assignment — a local story of national interest. The excitement and importance of a presidential visit could not help but spark up the creative skills of many a local editor, reporter and photographer. All eyes would briefly be upon their city. Reporting on a rare presidential visit would be a short though exciting change from the perhaps interesting, though usually categorically repetitious local news events. As cub news photographer Jarrold Cabluck would later recall of his covering the visit, "To the national press it was just another subject to cover, but when I saw the President, it was a very big deal."[1]

No one could have foreseen that this essentially political visit would turn out to be the setting for the public murder of the Chief Executive of the nation. And when that murder occurred, the local press found themselves in the midst of the major story of their generation. The manner in which this turbulent story was covered exposed the local newspapers' best and most creative side. It also laid open any major flaws in its capability of fast news-gathering and in its ability to disseminate such breaking news to the public. One paper whose success in this coverage was due largely to an aggressive and cooperative staff, was the *Fort Worth Star-Telegram*.

As was typical of any number of major-city newspapers, the *Star-Telegram* of 1963 was the evolutionary result of mergers of earlier papers. The city's first paper, the *Fort Worth Telegram*, had its origin in 1880, when much of the western frontier was still unsettled and Fort Worth was barely a quarter of a century old. In 1906 promoter and salesman Amon Carter became the driving force for the establishment of a new Fort Worth newspaper called *The Star*. Boasting of "more local news than any other in the city," the *Star* had a rough time financially as head-to-head competition with the *Telegram* often made its existence tenuous at best. Always willing to take risks, Carter is purported to have said when told the *Star* was bankrupt, "If we're going broke, let's expand." With frontier brashness and entrepreneurial skills, Carter managed to borrow money, and with an offer of $100,000 purchased the rival *Telegram*. On January 1, 1909, the presses rolled with the first issue of the *Fort Worth Star-Telegram*.[2]

The newly combined *Star-Telegram* proclaimed on its masthead, "Fort Worth, Texas — Where the West Begins," and its emphasis for decades was as a newspaper which catered to the needs of the scattered towns and ranches of west Texas. By train, truck, and bus as many as 13 daily editions were sent out across 84 rural counties with a territory as large as New England. West Texas news was emphasized and the paper utilized a network of some 600 local correspondents. An attempt in the late 'teens by newspaper czar William Randolph Hearst to buy the successful paper away from its local owners failed, as did his trying to bankrupt it by purchasing and pouring money into the *Fort Worth Record* in an attempt to run the *Star-Telegram* out of town. Not catering to the local concerns of the strong west Texas readership, the *Record* failed in its squeeze play. In 1925 Hearst quit the fight and sold the *Record* to the *Star-Telegram*. Into the early 1950s the *Star-Telegram* was the largest newspaper in Texas.[3]

As the population and economic importance of Fort Worth increased, the *Star-Telegram* shifted its news coverage and circulation emphasis to that of the community and Tarrant County. During the 1920s the paper had expanded into the fast-growing radio industry, and in 1928, the *Star-Telegram*'s WBAP radio station affiliated with the National Broadcasting Company. Then in 1948 the newspaper acquired a license to run WBAP television, which also soon became an NBC affiliate. The newspaper remained closely linked to the city, always offering editorial and financial support to any project which appeared to be good for the progress and development of Fort Worth.[4]

By 1963 a leaner *Fort Worth Star-Telegram* than its 1950s version was published by Amon G. Carter, Jr., the son of the co-founder. It included a five-star morning and an evening edition. Costing 5 cents and including an average of some 26 to 36 pages, it also published a large, 20-cent Sunday edition. The paper was a member of Associated Press and proclaimed itself, ". . . an independent Democratic newspaper supporting what it believes to be right and opposing what it believes to be wrong, regardless of party politics; publishing the news fairly and impartially at all times."[5] The paper serviced the city and county westerly as far as 200 to 300 miles out, and had a steady circulation of around 20,000.

The photography department was located on the third floor of the *Star-Telegram* building on 7th Street. It shared the floor with the newsroom. An irregularly shaped area carved out of the center of the floor space included three fully supplied  dark rooms. Joe McAulay was the chief photographer and had a long association with the paper, having begun as a copy boy. He headed a young and enthusiastic staff of twelve. Though several staff concentrated on farm and ranch photography, and others had their own specialties, the news photo staff itself could be called upon to do any assignment needed.

Among the photo staff were Jackson, Mississippi, native George Edward Smith, a 35-year-old veteran aerial photographer who had served in the Army Air Corps in the South Pacific in World War II, and in 1956 had graduated from Texas Christian University. He had begun working part-time at the paper in 1953 and became full-time upon earning his degree. Norm Bradford came to work for the paper in 1959 following assignments with two other Texas papers and a brief stint as a wire service photographer with United Press. Al Panzera was originally from New York, and following a tour of duty in the Air Force, had joined the staff primarily as a sports photographer. Port Arthur, Texas, native Wilburn G. Davis was one of the older photographers at 51, while Fort Worth-born Jarrold Cabluck, known as Jerry, was the youngest at 21. Also on the staff was Jerry's 25-year-old brother Harry, also of Fort Worth. Tony Record started out as an office boy with the *Star-Telegram* during the late 1940s. Following college he returned to work at the paper and had been a photographer for four years prior to 1963. Rounding out the photographic staff was the newest staff photographer, Dale Blackwell, who performed much of the photo lab work, being the least senior member.[6]

Photo assignments were the life's blood of the department. Recalls Norm Bradford, "The City Desk would send back a photo assignment card, basically telling what they wanted covered. Joe McAulay would kind of say, 'You go here, you go there.' A guy would just grab the assignment he wanted, and away he would go. A lot of it was also determined by who was working the late shift, and who was in early. It was a really compatible group, though we had competition, and that probably also helped. A couple of us got into a run one time to see who would stay on the front page the longest without a break. Harry was working morning and I was working evening."[7]

With the scheduled arrival of President and Mrs. Kennedy at Fort Worth in the late evening of November 21, as part of his 3-day trip to Texas, the *Star-Telegram* became poised to cover this local and national event in depth. Reporter Robert Hilburn of the *Star-Telegram*'s Washington Bureau had accompanied the White House press to Texas, while Austin Bureau Chief Sam Kinch picked up the story by joining the entourage upon its arrival. Most of the reporting staff were given leads and story possibilities to pursue by their editors. As photographer George Smith relates of the President's visit, "We unloaded the whole department on the visit." Bradford remembers, "I went to Carswell Air Force Base to cover the arrival. The deal was I would shoot the arrival and run like heck for the paper and turn out photos to make the 11:35 edition. That was the cover photo for the next morning, Kennedy and Jackie waving from the steps of the airplane."[8]

The November 22 morning edition included the headline, "WELCOME, MR. PRESIDENT!" pasted in reverse white letters against a night photo of the Fort Worth skyline outlined in gleaming Christmas lights. Just below was a four-column photograph credited to Norman Bradford and captioned, "Hello Fort Worth." This was a telephoto shot of the President and Mrs. Kennedy emerging from the hatchway of Air Force One. The lead story by Ed Johnson was titled, "JFK Lands Amid Roar of Cheers," while Sam Kinch's front page article, "Democratic Party Split Increases," told of the continuing Senator Ralph Yarborough and Governor John Connally political rift. The editorial page featured a drawing by cartoonist Harold Maples's titled, "HOWDY!" and showing a head identified as Fort Worth, wearing a gigantic Texas ten gallon hat with a sign in its hatband declaring, "WELCOME MR. PRESIDENT." On the same page an editorial beamed, "Fort Worth is honored this morning to have as its guests the President of the United States, the Vice-President and their wives, all at the same time." No less than seven other articles, two AP photos, and a mood photo by Harry Cabluck of people awaiting the arrival of the President at Carswell, rounded out the coverage of the evening before.[9]

As the morning edition was being sold on the streets of Fort Worth, the soon to be well remembered events of November 22 were already underway downtown. They were being covered by a large contingent of the *Star-Telegram* staff. According to their assignment schedule, Smith and Bradford would cover an early morning rally at the parking lot opposite Hotel Texas with photo chief McAulay, while Panzera, the Cabluck brothers, Davis, and Record would shoot the ensuing Chamber of Commerce breakfast event and presidential speech. Davis would then take up a position to make a picture of the motorcade on its way back to Carswell Air Force Base, while Smith and McAulay would get to the tarmac at Carswell itself to record the President's departure. Meanwhile, the Cablucks would swiftly ride the thirty miles over to Dallas and photograph the President's official airport arrival at Love Field. Harry would ride in one of the press busses in the winding motorcade to the Dallas Trade Mart, the location of a major noonday speech, while Jerry would drive there by a direct route arriving prior to the motorcade. The others would remain back at Fort Worth processing the morning film take at the newspaper's photo lab, preparing for what should be a very full and well covered evening edition.[10]

The photo department by 1963 was generally using 35mm cameras rather than the larger format, bulky, and slower Speed-Graphic cameras. Some used Rolleiflex cameras, but the most typical cameras were generally of 35mm format with the department owning a number of Leica M2s. Jerry Cabluck recalls using a department-owned Bell & Howell Photon. This was a range-finder camera with a spring-driven motor drive which could shoot up to 11 frames with a wand. The youngest member of the department, Cabluck bemoans, "The only reason I got to use it was nobody else wanted it."[11] The preferred film to use was fast speed Tri-X, and although the photographers had available to them a number of company and personal lenses, including 50, 90, and 135mm, the preferred size for general newspaper use was the slightly wide-angle 35mm lens, which gave a view wider than the human eye, but with virtually no discernible distortion.

It had been raining during the early morning hours. Wilburn Davis, before he made his way into the Hotel Texas to take up a position for the scheduled 9 a.m. breakfast program, made a shot of a young girl sporting a wide smile and with an adult's light-colored overcoat partially resting over her head. This later-published photo would be captioned, "Raindrops which spattered spectators awaiting President Kennedy's appearance outside Hotel Texas didn't bother Carol Chappell, 11 . . . . She and others were rewarded by the President's appearance and the almost simultaneous cessation of the rain." A cute, human interest-type of photo, when it did appear in the *Star-Telegram*'s evening edition of November 22, its innocent cuteness would be juxtaposed with an extra's blaring headline reading, "KENNEDY SLAIN."[12] Once inside the ballroom, Davis found that "People in authority wouldn't let us move around, we just had to be in a certain place."

After briskly walking out the hotel entrance under a marquee proclaiming, "WELCOME MR. PRESIDENT" Kennedy, with entourage trailing behind, proceeded the short distance to the parking lot across the street. Smith recalls that the President, ". . . did the perimeter pretty well, shaking an awful lot of people's hands. It had sprinkled earlier in the morning, but when they came out there it had quit at that stage, so he was out there probably longer than they had intended."

Bradford had found a spectacular location for creating an overview photo. "I went to the top of the Hotel Texas and made a shot down on the parking lot across the street from the 14th floor of the Hotel. I'm still wondering why I wasn't shot off the side of the building at that time. When I got up there and was shooting down, I just happened to glance around, and all I could see on all of the roofs of the buildings around were yellow raincoats with people with high-powered rifles. There I was, standing on the 14th floor of the Hotel Texas, and not a soul, it was not protected, and it was not sealed off. I was very surprised. I just stepped out on the balcony and started shooting — no problem. I did, however, get off the balcony pretty quick." Using the photo technique known as "bracketing" to assure at least one frame with a perfect exposure, Bradford clicked off some six shots at varying f-stops. The dramatic picture displayed a cluster of thousands of heads within the parking lot. Surrounding the sea of humanity was a perimeter of parked cars, one section kept clear for the arriving dignitaries, and a triangle of open space set up as a security perimeter. The photographers and various security men are visible clustered around the speakers' platform, where Representative Jim Wright is introducing the dignitaries. Following these exposures, Bradford went into the hotel to cover the breakfast crowd. They were seated on both sides of narrow tables which filled up the cavernous ballroom.[13]

McAulay and Smith had taken various sequences of the President and his entourage making their way to the parking lot as well as the shots of the soggy though

Norm Bradford shoots the parking lot event from 14 stories up.

enthusiastic crowd. Following the brief fifteen-minute outside program, at about 9:05, the President entered the hotel's Grand Ballroom for the Chamber of Commerce breakfast. He was belatedly joined by Mrs. Kennedy. Davis, Record, Bradford, and Panzera recorded the breakfast event along with numerous other photographers, reporters, and live television broadcast cameramen.

The final public chance for Fort Worth to see the President was in a motorcade he took through the city on the way to the Carswell airfield. Davis, ". . . had gone out to White Settlement, that's a section of town that the President and his group passed through, and I photographed them when they were passing there. And then I came on back to the office to develop and print my pictures."[14]

Smith was at the air base itself and made pictures of the President and First Lady boarding the plane, Kennedy turning and waving at the top of the gangway. From there Smith also returned back to the office to process his photo assignment.

As the President was on his way to Carswell, Jerry Cabluck was motoring to Dallas to take up position at Love Field for Air Force One's arrival. Harry had missed his auto ride to Dallas and with the permission of Jenks Fauver, he was allowed to fly on the press plane to Dallas. Cabluck recalls that from "wheels up" to "wheels down" the flight lasted eight minutes.

With the President's arrival in Dallas both Cablucks worked the scene with their cameras. After several minutes of photo coverage Jerry noticed Governor Connally waiting in the President's limousine and walked over to him to say hello as he had known the Governor for years. Raising his camera, Cabluck made a vertical exposure of a smiling Governor who is standing in the car and looking straight at the lens. Thereupon follows an 11-frame sequence of the Kennedys approaching, entering and settling into the back seat. Connally gentlemanly doffed his hat upon their approach.[15]

Meanwhile brother Harry, along with *Star-Telegram* reporter Jim Vachule, boarded the first of two Continental Trailways busses, marked with a lettered sign on its side, "WHITE HOUSE PRESS." The 30-minute motorcade ride would snake down through the Dallas business district, and then on to the Dallas Trade Mart for the luncheon engagement. Harry's bus was separated by some twelve vehicles from the President's special Ford Lincoln, so that when the motorcade left Love Field at about 11:55 it was only on occasion that a few passengers in the front of the bus could even glimpse the sleek convertible far up ahead. Crowds in the business district were very large and enthusiastic. No one expected the deadly shooting incident which occurred nearing the end of the parade route. *Star-Telegram* writer Ed Johnson, also on one of the two press busses, reported

Governor Connally poses in the presidential limousine for Jerry Cabluck. Rep. Jack Brooks looks on at left.

his impressions of the scene at the place of the assassination in an article appearing in the second of four evening extras published by the *Star-Telegram* that day. "The sound of shots that struck President Kennedy and Governor John Connally in Dallas Friday was heard by members of the press accompanying the motorcade. I was in the press bus as it wound under the triple underpass where Main, Elm, and Commerce Streets converge, separated by six or seven [sic] cars from the open-air convertible in which the President was riding. We in the bus did not know immediately what had happened. We could see spectators lining the route fall to the ground as the shots rang out. A woman roughly knocked two children to the ground. A man, apparently her husband, lay beside them, pounding his fist into the earth. Reporters were hollering for the bus to stop. It kept going. . . . As it passed through the area from which the shots apparently came, we on the bus could see Dallas motorcycle officers jumping from their vehicles and running up the nearby hill."[16]

Harry Cabluck's first bus photo

Harry Cabluck was carrying a Leica M2 with Leicavit outfitted with a 35mm lens and loaded with a roll of 36 exposure 400 speed Tri-X film. It was a near-fresh roll with only a few exposures made, including one distant shot of the deplaning with Mrs. Kennedy being greeted by the official party. It was while the busses were turning onto Houston Street from Main Street that the President's vehicle, already having turned onto Elm Street, was fired upon. Seated on the right side of the bus, Cabluck saw the commotion to his right when the cumbersome vehicle finally turned the sharp left onto Elm Street. He clicked off three quick pictures through the bus window. In the first shot, two boys are seen running down the steps adjacent to a decorative 1930s concrete pergola towards the street and ahead of the bus. In the foreground two other boys are running forward past the bus, one on the sidewalk and the other on the grass, veering towards the incline. Five women spectators are standing, looking in the direction ahead of the bus. Moments later Cabluck made a second shot as the bus had proceeded a few dozen feet further along Elm Street towards the triple underpass. In this second photo, the four running boys are in view on the grass scurrying along at full speed. A woman, later self-identified as Cheryl McKinnon, is sitting on the grass with her hand to her face. Young Clayton and Billy Newman are partially hidden by their parents, Bill and Gayle, all four on the ground facing away from the street and towards the concrete pergola at the top of the knoll. Mrs. Newman is looking down the street while Mr. Newman is caught by the photographer's lens in a motion of pounding the ground with his fist. A man in a suit is rushing along the sidewalk past them, glancing in their direction as he passes. This

A second photo made an instant later

man is quite possibly *Dallas Morning News* reporter Kent Biffle, who was a passenger in a car between Cabluck's and the next bus. Biffle later recalled that after he jumped out of his car, "A rush of men and women swept by me. They were running away from the sounds of the shots. A few of us ran towards the shooting. People were crouched behind the concrete structures in the plaza on the grassy slope that drops down towards the underpass, several figures were flat on the ground. . . . Some teenagers followed. One of them darted ahead and hit the fence before I did. I remember thinking, 'This nutty kid is going to get his head blown off and he's not even getting paid for it.' Puffing, I followed him."[17]

On the left edge of the Cabluck photo, James W. Altgens, an AP photographer who moments earlier had taken a photo sequence of the shooting, is now at the curb with camera in hand watching for a break in the motorcade, so he can cross the street and get back to his bureau. Two figures, possibly including Abe Zapruder, are glimpsed in the concrete shelter while two other figures can be seen in shadow sitting on the steps leading from Elm Street to the pergola. Motorcycle police officer Clyde A. Haygood, his abandoned cycle back at the curb, is seen running in the background towards the overpass, looking for culprits. As the bus proceeds further down Elm Street, Cabluck

Cabluck's last photo made from the bus

shoots his third picture inadvertently also including some of the bus window frame. In this photo Haygood has climbed up the overpass concrete support wall and is looking left. Some six men are standing on the railroad bridge.

Cabluck would later recall of the scene, "The Dallas motorcycle policeman shown in the far background of one of the frames left his vehicle and ran up the hillside. He hurdled the concrete banister at the top of the hill. I have wondered if he saw anything. I did not see anything that might confirm or deny the findings of the Warren Commission. . . . The press bus was more than a hundred yards away from the assassination site when the shots were fired. The bus stopped for a few seconds — only a few of the press got off the bus, then we continued to the planned luncheon site at the Dallas Market Hall. Vachule and I then hitched a ride to Parkland Hospital." The next photos Harry would take on this roll would be of the empty Vice-President's car and other scenes at Parkland Hospital. The three photographs made by Cabluck from the bus window captured some of the confusion in a crucial area shortly after the shooting, and are also interesting in that they are the only photographs that have come to light made by anyone on the press busses. As Jerry would later say of his brother's quick reaction on the bus, "The 'local yokels' down here were interested in covering the story. The national people were riding a bus to another meeting. They weren't ready for anything."[18]

While Harry was on the bus which was now plodding its way to the scheduled speaking location, his brother Jerry was at the Trade Mart waiting to pick up the motorcade's arrival at the luncheon. "I parked my car across from the freeway and had to cross the freeway during traffic. And when I crossed it, I saw the motorcade come by. Parkland was probably half a mile away. And it was the only time I ever stopped a car and said, 'Follow that motorcade.' I gave them five dollars to do that. John Maziotta, chief photographer for the *Times Herald*, and I were in the car, and they took us to the emergency entrance. I ran in and all we heard was the President was hit with a beer can. At that point we didn't know anything. I ended up being in Trauma One for about 10 seconds. As a young kid mesmerized or petrified, I didn't do anything. I was in there very briefly and the Secret Service threw me out. Then the rest of the White House press was there. We shot people going in and out. I made shots of a policeman carrying plasma in there, and of Ralph Yarborough and other politicians and newsmen gathered around to get their comments. A lot of the general public was milling around."[19]

Back in Fort Worth those *Star-Telegram* photographers who had covered the morning activities had returned to the photo department. Though it was his day off, Blackwell had come in that morning to help process and print the early film from the breakfast event. Bradford relates, "At this point Blackwell, Davis and Joe went back into the darkroom and were turning film out as we sent it in. We had developed a courier service. Whoever was next to go in or had their shot and was going in with their film would pick up everyone else's film and go in. Smith, myself, and Record were all sitting on the counter in the darkroom. The phone rang and they said Kennedy had been shot.

Ed Johnson, a writer, was calling in. He had no details. At this point we just grabbed whatever film and cameras we could grab and jumped into two cars — Record's and Smith's cars — and headed for Dallas down the toll road as hard as we could drive. We went directly to Parkland. Made it in 20 minutes. I was in the car with Tony Record and he kind of threw the money at the toll keeper. I don't think he got below 55 miles per hour when we went through the toll gate. Harry was already there, and he was photographing Ralph Yarborough and some of the politicians standing around the outside door. I made a shot of one of the limousines with flowers down on the floor of the car and a hat on the dashboard with the emergency room in the background. At that point I saw the caravan with [now President] Johnson in it frantically driving up and down Harry Hines Boulevard. They go towards Love Field and turn around and go back towards downtown. Then they turn back around and go back towards Love Field. They

President Johnson, sitting in the back of Chief Curry's car, being whisked from Parkland Hospital back to Air Force One

did not know what to do." One *Star-Telegram* photo sequence shows Mrs. Johnson, Congressman Homer Thornberry and Secret Service Agent Rufus Youngblood at a car door, followed by several shots through the back window of President Johnson in the middle of the car's back seat.[20]

Dr. Kemp Clark had declared President Kennedy dead at 1:00 C.S.T., but White House Assistant Press Secretary Malcolm Kilduff was instructed for security reasons not to make an official announcement until after President Johnson had left the hospital. Smith had arrived at Parkland with several reporters, having made a stop for gas in Arlington, and when he arrived he ". . . went into the area they had set aside for the [press] conference. It wasn't until after we got there that they actually came in and had that brief release that the President had been declared dead."[21]

Covering the exciting, though closely choreographed visit of the President of the United States to Texas had suddenly been transformed into a tale of horror, sadness, shock, and confusion. Within seconds this story had evolved into the major event in most of these reporters' careers, though to most of them it was happening too quickly for them to fully grasp its scope. And the story with its many fragmented facets and locations had to be quickly evaluated and acted upon while still in the process of unraveling. Focusing on and covering a breaking story is what good newsmen are trained to do, and during those first hours of confusion, the scattered photographic and reporting staff of the *Star-Telegram* did their job well in a city that was not their normal beat.

Recounts Bradford:

> Everybody was really kind of operating on their own at that point. We were just working among ourselves. Since Harry had Parkland pretty well covered, George took off for downtown and went to the School Book Depository. Tony Record went to the Police Station. I hitched a ride out to the airport, but couldn't get through barricades. When I found out I wasn't going to do any good at Love Field, I went from there to where the banquet was going to be at the Trade Mart, and made an overall photo of the empty hall. From there to the Book Depository then to the Police Station. . . . We were just working out coverage as we went. Sam Kinch was our state reporter, and he was kind of giving indications of who should go where, what might be a good possibility. Everybody on the team had a good news sense. We had very good coverage, which about blew everybody else out of the tub. It was just good teamwork. There wasn't any one person trying to dominate the story. Everybody was just trying to work together. Jerry Cabluck, for example, had a horrible fear of heights. He said, 'OK, I'll get into a plane and shoot an aerial of Dealey Plaza' — which he did, and it was a good shot, but he was as sick as a dog and scared to death. Everybody pitched in. Nobody minded working the darkroom or anything else."

Tony Record had driven his 1950 Chevy, which had no radio, to Dallas. Initially he went to Love Field with reporter Jim Vachule, but arrived after Air Force One had departed. Traveling down town some time after 2:00, he met up with George Smith and later that afternoon went to the police station. Calling his paper, he was told to wait outside for the arrival of suspect Lee Oswald's mother. "My instinct got the best of me and I went up to the floor where Oswald was being booked in. They brought him out and it was the only time that day that I got pictures before the halls of the police station were crowded with reporters and cameramen."[22] By the end of the day the *Star-Telegram* had set up a reporting task force with an appointed straw boss working out of a downtown Dallas hotel.

Upon arriving in Dallas from Fort Worth, photographer Smith had parked his car on the street near the hospital, but due to the immense traffic jam, he decided to leave it there and hitch rides with others. He remembers it being, "wall-to-wall with cars," and during the next few hours in the back of his mind he worried that with the city's notorious towing reputation, his car might be hauled away. Taking several photos of the exterior of Parkland and of a portion of the press conference, Smith was using the same two cameras still loaded with film on which he had recorded the President's morning Fort Worth departure. Smith could see that the hospital scene was well covered by others. "We were back on the fringe of it, surveying the situation. That's when we decided to head downtown and we cut out before it was finished."[23]

Sometime before 2:00 Smith went down to the Sheriff's office on Houston Street and stopped in the press office there, "to see what the situation was at that time. That's when we decided the best thing to do was head on over to the School Book building located catty-corner across the way." At the Depository the crowd had been moved back.

Smith generally used 36-exposure rolls of Kodak Tri-X film. "This was back in the days when you shoot everything that moved. You took pictures first, and thought about them later. If you thought you were getting down to the end of the roll and had definite breathing time, you would go ahead and pull it out of there and put a fresh one in. So a lot of my rolls wouldn't have been full."[24]

Lieutenant Johnson holding
the recovered bag and bottle

Smith looked around for camera subjects. An early sequence made of the Depository Building shows the Hertz sign on the roof with the time display clearly reading "2:19." Seven frames were taken of uniformed officers W. E. Barnett and J. M. Smith at the Depository's front entrance, while two photos were taken of police Lieutenant Johnson standing in front of the building being questioned by a reporter. In one hand the lieutenant holds a stick on which an empty inverted Dr. Pepper bottle rests, while in the other hand he grasps what looks to be a used paper lunch bag. Both these items had been retrieved from the building as possible evidence. Two additional shots were taken of Lieutenant Montgomery holding a long and narrow paper bag, which authorities would later claim was the handmade bag used by Lee Oswald to secret his Mannlicher-Carcano into the building on the morning of the assassination.[25]

While outside on the sidewalk near the front of the Depository, and prior to his taking the photos of the police detectives with their gathered evidence, Smith made two pictures of three men being escorted by uniformed Dallas police officers. These photos were made after 2:19, though just how long after that time can not be discerned from Smith's photos themselves or by his recollection. Also recorded by *Dallas Times-Herald* photographer William Allen, and *Dallas Morning News* photographer Jack Beers, this event was largely forgotten by those in Dealey Plaza at the time due to other more pressing developments continuing to occur. It would only be much later following other subsequent events that the identities of these three men would undergo much speculation. Smith recalls, "Somewhere else along the road they came by with these tramps they had flushed out somewhere. Anybody that was where they shouldn't have been was getting hauled in. For all I know, some characters had given them some back-talk. The police weren't in any mood for any back-talk at that stage. There were a few I saw warned to get back and stay back. I just saw three guys in custody going along, and I took their picture."[26]

Following the assassination at 12:30, the School Book Depository and the area around it, particularly the parking lot and railroad yards to the west and northerly of the building, were the subject of large scale police activity and searching. At least an hour and a half after the shooting a freight train was leaving the rail yard and Lee Bowers, Jr., the railroad tower man for the Union Terminal Company stationed within the fourteen foot high switch tower, stopped the train to give the police a chance to search it. In a later interview with Warren Commission critic and attorney Mark Lane, Bowers stated, ". . . I pulled the train up immediately opposite the tower after alerting the police that I intended to do so, and I stopped the train and gave them a chance to examine it and to be sure that there was no one on it. As a matter of fact, there were three people on it who appeared to be winos, and perhaps were the most frightened winos I've ever seen in my life, since there were possibly 50 policemen with shotguns and Tommy guns and various weapons, shaking them out of these boxcars. . . ."[27]

Dallas police sergeant D. V. Harkness later testified before a staff member of the Warren Commission that he was told to search all freight cars that were leaving the yard, and that ". . . we pulled some people off of there and took them to the station."[28] Deputy Sheriff Harold E. Elkins, in a deposition filed on November 26, stated ". . . a City of Dallas policeman came to our office with three prisoners who[m] he had arrested on the railroad yards. I took these three to the city jail and turned them over to Captain Fritz."[29] From this point until the 1990s there was no known extant documentation as to the identities, or questioning of these men. And due to their photos not having been published, this incident was largely forgotten by the relatively few who had witnessed it at the time.

The two Smith photos of the "tramps" were the first in a series of seven known still shots made of their being escorted over to the Sheriff's office on Houston Street. His first photo was made looking northwesterly towards the sidewalk area just in front of the high chain-link gate driveway adjacent to the west side of the School Book Depository. The full bodies of two of the tramps are visible, while only the hat and feet of the third man is seen behind the second. Two uniformed police officers, one in front and one behind the men, carry pump shotguns, though not in a threatening manner. From an examination of all seven photographs, it would appear that three escort cops are identifiable in the series, although never more than two are seen in any one photograph. One researcher has identified one of these cops as Harkness, while another

Officer M. L. Wise leads the three tramps

researcher has indicated that the officers in the photos were Patrolmen Billy L. Bass and Marvin L. Wise, both of the Second Platoon's 8 a.m. to 4 p.m. shift. Smith pivoted his upper body to the right and positioned his camera on the vertical plane to make his second photo as the three men in custody walked by him on the sidewalk at the front southwest corner of the Book Depository Building.[30]

The man who first brought the "tramp" pictures to public attention was Richard E. Sprague. Sprague was a business computer expert who had become deeply immersed in the photographic documentation of the assassination. He believed that through the analysis of this photographic evidence, one might be able to find proof if a conspiracy did exist, as he believed that photographs, when properly interpreted, don't lie. During 1966 and 1967 Sprague ferreted out much photographic material relating to the assassination. He became the leading authority on the subject, compiling a list of all known media and amateur photographs and films, and obtaining copies of as much of this primary source material as possible. As a partner in charge of business systems for Touche, Ross, Bailey, and Smart of New York, Sprague combined numerous business trips around the country with an opportunity to research for photo sources and photographers.[31]

Sprague was able to discover and view the "tramp" photos in Dallas and Fort Worth and acquired copies of several, including the two Smith photos. From his personal research Sprague was a confirmed believer in an assassination conspiracy in which at least two, and probably three assassins had fired shots. He circulated these photos among Warren Commission bashers and to others within the circle of assassination research.

In February 1967 New Orleans District Attorney Jim Garrison exploded onto the national scene when the media broke the news that his office was investigating the Kennedy assassination in relation to a conspiracy involving persons within Garrison's geographical jurisdiction. Sprague contacted Garrison and sent him copies of some of the "tramp" photos. Garrison would in the late 1980s recall how the photos up until the late 1960s had never been published. It was Sprague's conviction (embraced by Garrison) that if the "tramps" or the officers were identified, it might unlock some of the assassination's mysteries.[32]

On January 31, 1968, Garrison was invited to a guest appearance on NBC's popular late night Johnny Carson *Tonight Show* to tell about his investigation. In a typical Garrison flourish, the D.A. exhibited one of the "tramp" photos towards the camera, a move not overly appreciated by the talk show host, who was obviously out of his subject element. Garrison then proclaimed in an accusatory and knowing voice that, "Those arrested men you just saw were never seen again. They all got away."[33]

The May 1970 issue of a Massachusetts-based computer periodical, *Computers and Automation*, carried a lengthy article by Richard Sprague concerning the assassination under the subtitle, "The Application of Computers to the Photographic Evidence." Only lightly touching the relevance of computers to the subject, it seemed a way of justifying editor Edmund Berkeley to publish what he conceived to be an important topic. Sprague was thus afforded a vehicle to publish a comprehensive list of photographers and photos of the assassination scene as well as a few of the photos he had collected. The subject of the "tramps" was spotlighted in a half-page of text along with full-page copies of the two Smith as well as two of the Allen photos. In his text Sprague pointed out the lack of any official information about these men. He also focused in on one of the police officers escorting the three, pointing to what he saw as inconsistencies in how the officer was dressed. Sprague also drew attention to what he believed was an earpiece or radio communication device in the cop's right ear as seen in the first Smith photo. Sprague's tramp segment closed with a plea: "If any reader of this article notices any person resembling any one of the 'tramps,' or the 'phony' policeman, it would be useful for him to send information to me."[34]

With this first availability of a list of assassination photographs, as well as the publication of some of the "tramp" pictures, speculation about these photographs abound.

The old tramp (with hat), "Frenchy," and the tall tramp (right)
Some later identified the tall tramp as Frank Sturgis.

Most of the research community of amateur sleuths saw much of significance in the content of these photos, coupled with the seemingly unbelievable lack of an arrest report, fingerprints, statements, or even names having been taken down of these mystery men. The more the photos were circulated and examined, showing a real-time event stopped and captured by the camera, the more incredulous many researchers became of the lack of any other information. Men obviously arrested are let go with no records being kept! It seemed a sinister act on the part of someone in authority. Incredibly, if not for these photos, nothing about the incident would have come to light. The physical characteristics of the "tramps" were closely scrutinized. As one researcher wrote, "They appear to have had recent barber shop haircuts, their clothing is not as worn as a tramp's would be, and the soles of their shoes are thick." The tramp with the upturned collar began to be referred to by researchers as "Frenchy" due to his perceived continental clothing style. Many researchers became convinced that he was in fact a member of the assassination team![35]

Then the Watergate scandal of the Nixon presidency occurred, and by the spring of 1974, a few people, notably Michael Canfield and Alan J. Weberman, saw striking similarities between two of the tramps and Watergate "plumbers" E. Howard Hunt and Frank Sturgis. Comedian and gadfly social activist Dick Gregory obtained copies of the photographs and received much media coverage over his charges of a CIA link with the assassination, all of which was superficially investigated by the Rockefeller CIA Domestic Activities Panel. In 1975 Canfield and Weberman published their conclusions of the identities of two of the "tramps" as being Hunt and Sturgis in their book *Coup D'Etat in America, the CIA and the Assassination of John F. Kennedy*, which was received with something less than enthusiasm, and in some cases by heavy criticism from the assassination research network.

By 1977 when the House Select Committee on Assassinations was established, one area of investigation pursued by a sub-committee was whether or not the "tramps" were any of those individuals identified by various researchers as ones who might have been involved in a plot. The Select Committee's study briefly made note of the separate FBI and CIA examination of some of the photos which had been compared with photos of Hunt and Sturgis to a negative conclusion. As the validity of these two earlier studies were suspect by some, the new committee explained that ". . . Warren Commission critics still view this issue as unresolved, and the identity of the three tramps is still regarded as an important part of the conspiracy theories. In addition to the Hunt and Sturgis connection, three other individuals, Thomas Vallee, Fred Lee Chrisman, and Daniel Carswell, who had been named as possible co-conspirators, have been suggested as likely tramp candidates."[36]

The entire thrust of the Select Committee in regard to the "tramp" issue focused on the comparison by forensic anthropologists of photographs of the tramps with photographs of the suspected individuals to see if any of these five individuals could "be positively identified or excluded as one of the three tramps." By means of examining photos of the identified men in question (most provided by assassination researchers) and utilizing no other materials, the report concluded, "Daniel Carswell, E. Howard Hunt, Frank Sturgis, and Thomas Vallee were not the tramp(s) with whom they were being compared. Fred Chrisman strongly resembles one of the tramps, but, without analysis of additional photographic materials, no positive identification can be made."[37]

The Committee's examination of the tramp photographs included a description of the trio as to approximate age, gait, and dress. While critics thought a couple of the tramps dressed too well, the Committee's analysis found, "All three men are shabbily dressed, befitting their status as vagrants," and that, "while such clothing might be a disguise, their footwear seems consistent in their classification as vagrants." The analysis even went to the point of whimsical exaggeration in describing the oldest tramp, exclaiming, ". . . from his battered fedora to his worn-out shoes, [he] has managed to achieve a sartorial effect similar to what one would expect had he been fired from a cannon through a Salvation Army thrift shop."[38]

Through comparisons of facial and other morphological features including nasal form, the forehead, ear and lobe length, hair, eyebrows, physique, mouth and chin, and by assigning point values from standardized indices, a resemblance value between tramp and comparison subjects could be discerned. The only person which the study could not rule out as a candidate among the three tramps was Fred Lee Chrisman. Chrisman was a right-wing activist who had been implicated during the fizzled Jim Garrison investigation. The analysis between him and the older hat-wearing tramp showed that "Chrisman resembles Tramp C rather strongly in both metric and morphological features. These similarities, derived from the analysis of a single undated photograph of Chrisman, are in no way sufficient to establish a positive identification. Nevertheless, they are strong enough to suggest that further analysis, based on more fully documented Chrisman photographs, should be considered, unless independent evidence excludes Chrisman's presence in Dallas on November 22, 1963."[39]

The Committee did not attempt to identify and get statements from the police officers visible in the photographs whom researcher Canfield had cursorily identified as officers Bass and Wise from a comparison with photos in a 1963 Dallas Police Department yearbook.

In 1991 in the process of writing a book about a notorious, unsolved Houston, Texas murder case, John R. Craig, a former legal investigator with ties to various local and federal enforcement agencies, came across what he believed to be important information. Charles Frederick Rogers, a mystery man with possible connections to the CIA and possessing a checkered personal life, was the suspect in the 1965 killing and cutting up for disposal of his elderly parents. Through circumstantial evidence and a possible link with Charles V. Harrelson, a convicted assassin of a Federal Judge, the two were identified by a 70-year-old career criminal named Chauncey Marvin Holt as the 1963 Dealey Plaza "tramps." Holt in 1991 came forward with a confession that he was the older of the tramps, even though he was only 42 in 1963. Harrelson, a Texas hit man, had previously been identified by certain researchers as one of the three tramps. In 1980 while high on cocaine, and during a six hour stand-off with police, he had admitted to killing Judge John Wood and also to participating in the Kennedy assassination.

Holt claimed that in 1963 he was under orders from the CIA to deliver fake IDs and hand guns at Dealey Plaza on November 22 for what he believed to be some sort of staged incident. At the scene Harrelson introduced himself to Holt, who knew him by reputation. Holt also knew Rogers, another participant, to be a contract CIA agent and known to Holt as "Montoya." Following the shooting the three ran to a train boxcar and hid there till discovered by police. Showing fake ATF IDs, the three were escorted out to check on their identity papers. They were supposedly later released on the OK of Dallas FBI agent-in-charge Shanklin.

To test the identification of these three with the "tramp" photos, author Craig elicited the assistance of Houston Police Department forensic artist Lois Gibson. She utilized only visual, facial structure features including bone and muscle shape, ear wrinkle, and hair patterns in her study. Gibson, who had attracted much popular media attention for her previous work and her cases involving skull reconstruction, positively identified all three men from several earlier photos supplied to her. Photos of Rogers were only available of him as a teenager, yet Gibson stated her belief that both he and the other two named men were in fact the 1963 "tramps."[40]

Just who these three 1963 men actually were, where they were situated, and what they might have seen at the time of the assassination, were intriguing, unanswered questions. It appears that these men were not picked up as early after the shooting as researchers have assumed, and thus, were not flushed out shortly after the event. Rather, they were detained sometime after 2:19 and closer to 2:30. The questions of whether or not they were typical 1963 tramps, the significance of the thickness of their shoe leather or trimness of their hair, or the quality of their clothing, are all subjective value judgments, since there exists no dress code for tramps, if in fact that is what they were. The only solid evidence we have are the photographs of an incident, which coupled with the lack of documentation or even reasons for the lack of documentation allows a questioning mind to be even more suspicious. Photo interpretation can indeed be useful, but it is often more an art than a science. Sherlock Holmes could have solved the meaning of the incident, if it indeed had significant meaning, merely by his powers of deductive reasoning, having gleaned all of the information the photos could reveal. Reality, however, is both more complicated and more trivial than a fiction writer's pen, and very much, or perhaps very little, can be seen when one examines a finite slice of time from a cameraman's lens with its limited angle of view. Like so many other loose ends in the events of November 22, 1963, this incident could have very real significance, or could simply be an exercise in paranoia.

Then in early 1992 a major break in the story occurred. On the media hyped heels of the release of the Oliver Stone movie *JFK* in which the "tramps" are portrayed as having a sinister role in the assassination, the Dallas City Council opened the formerly restricted police files dealing with the Kennedy case. Within the Dallas City Archives police arrest reports from November 22, 1963, had sat unexamined for decades. No one had thought to check these records, or through lackadaisical bureaucracy, researchers had been told that no such arrest records existed. As is often the case with governmental records, those having custody over them don't necessarily know what they have and are not inclined to do search tasks unless pointedly instructed to do so. All the wasted effort and money on the part of Federal government committees could have been saved if someone had taken the time to gain access and physically look through the police paper work. It had been taken as gospel that no such arrest records were extant, all adding to the mystique of the "tramp" incident.

Upon examining these newly released files it was discovered that on November 22 three railroad yard arrests near Elm and Houston Streets had been duly recorded at 4:00 P.M. on official arrest forms. John Forrester Gedney, age 38, with no home address given; Gus W. Abrams, age 53, with no home address given; and Harold Doyle, age 32, of Red Jacket, West Virginia, had all three been arrested together. According to the details of arrest on two of the forms, "These men were taken off a box car in the railroad yards right after Pres. Kennedy was shot. They are passing through town. They have no means of support." The arresting officer of record was W.E. Chambers and according to the record, they were released on Tuesday morning, November 26.[41]

In exceptional investigative work Ray and Mary LaFontaine

Arrest report on Howard Doyle discovered by researchers in 1992

traced the one man who had given an address of West Virginia, first to that state and then to Amarillo, Texas where at least one neighbor recalled his telling of his arrest in Dallas in 1963. Doyle, a now balding, pudgy, affable character with a "man of the road" manner of expressing himself, was finally located in Klamath Falls, Oregon where he had a small apartment and worked part time in a local pool hall. He told his story to the LaFontaines who sold this exclusive to the sensationalistic television program, *A Current Affair*. The taped piece ran on February 25, 1992, with a follow-up segment in early March. In a seeming first, a tabloid-like, often exploitative genre TV program was laying to rest, rather than promoting or instigating, a long held possible conspiracy theory. It was fascinating television, and as soon as the now 61-year-old Doyle appeared in view, his face was recognizable to many who had seen the "tramp" photos during years of research. His story was not sensational, but rang of truth.

Beginning the day at a homeless shelter in the vicinity of Dealey Plaza, Doyle and his two companions had decided to hitch a train ride to Fort Worth. ". . . before we went to the railroad yard, sirens and everything was going on and all, and we asked somebody what happened and they said the President been shot. Then all at once someone said, 'Don't make a move.' We looked up the end we were sitting in and the far end down the side we were surrounded by policemen with guns drawn and they said, 'Don't make a move.'" The three were pulled out of the box car. Doyle remembers that the police, ". . . took us through the park. All the people was going on and the sirens was going and people was taking pictures of us coming over this a way. Hell there was all photographers, people hollering, 'Are they the one that done it? Are they the one that done it?'" At the police station Doyle was at one point across a desk from the recently arrested Lee Oswald, and someone said to the vagrants, "You boys are sure lucky. You see the guy that killed the President in person."[42]

Doyle had known about the "tramp" controversy for some time, having kept a copy of at least one article including a photo published about the mystery. Not the type to come forward to authorities about his role on November 22, he has feigned notoriety stating, "I'm a plain guy, a simple country boy, and that's the way I want to stay. I wouldn't be a celebrity for 10 million damn dollars." Believing the controversy over the photos of the tramps might imply his having taken part in a conspiracy, Doyle emphasized, "But like I said, I had nothing to do with it. Don't bother me whether they believe me or not. If they want to think I did it, its up to the individual. . . . But like I said, the "tramps" had nothing to do with it."[43]

Subsequent inquiries by the government as well as by researchers located John F. Gedney in Melbourne, Florida. A respected 67-year-old municipal officer, Gedney had not been driven to speak to outsiders about this earlier, harder, vagabond time of his life. At that time in 1963 he was making his way towards Alaska where there seemed more work opportunities. He is not now enthusiastic about all of the new notoriety and crazy speculation. Of the incident in Dallas he told one reporter, "We were taken away, put in jail for three or four days and found not guilty of anything except vagrancy." Gus Abrams was 76 when he died in Ohio in August 1987. Contacted by a researcher, Abrams' sister, with whom he had lived for the last 15 years, knew nothing of his being in Dallas the day of the assassination. She recalled that back in those days, "he was always on the go hopping trains and drinking wine." She speculated he didn't even know who the President was. When presented with a picture of the November 22 "tramps" she confirmed to the researcher, "Yep that's my Bill!"[44]

Still some diehard critics, notably Michael Canfield and Alan Weberman whose reissued volume *Coup D'Etat* was expanded in 1992 to include more recent information, don't accept the Doyle revelations. In the new edition of their book they contend that while Doyle and the other two were arrested that day, though earlier than the second group of three "tramps," they are not the "tramps" in the famous pictures. According to the authors, Doyle ". . . does not look like the tramp by any stretch of the imagination," and his story is not consistent with the known facts. The writers, with years invested in a conspiratorial theory, suspect intricate disinformation on the part of the FBI.[45]

To the author, however, the painstaking discovery of Mr. Doyle, his and the other two mens' stories, and the evidence of Doyle's own face all come together into a more than credible explanation. It's an explanation which counters what active imaginations, coupled with the Dallas police department's previous disinterest in sharing information with the public or the government, created as a breeding ground for fantastic, though seemingly possible speculation.

On November 22, 1963, Fort Worth photographer George Smith recalls gaining entry to the Texas School Book Depository Building sometime between 3:00 and 4:00 along with members of the Dallas press.

> We didn't have a bit of trouble getting on up to the building and then right on in. There were Dallas reporters and police, and we just tagged right along with them. Everywhere they went, we went. Nobody seemed to object or anything. We went inside to the sixth floor, took pictures and no one tried to stop us. Probably thought we were with the police. [I took] all sorts of pictures of where the boxes were stacked, sandwich wrapper leavings — just everything. Even took some pictures out the window towards the motorcade route. . . . I took pictures probably of the ceiling, just burn up the film and then examine it later and see what you actually have. I knew where the little stack of boxes was, and the window was open. You knew you needed to get a picture of that, too. There were a dozen people up there at that time. With the building secure, they were looking for anything that might be there just like at a normal shooting, when they come back and start going over everything with a fine-toothed comb. It looked like they were checking everything around the place. I believe the weapon had been found earlier. I think they finally found out we weren't supposed to be up there, and invited us back out.

Smith's interior shots included one overall view of the sixth floor corner window with its wall of cardboard boxes, and three frames looking out the supposed assassin's window towards Elm Street below. He also took exposures of some of the text books lying on top of open boxes with the titles *History of a Free People*, *Of More Days and Deeds*, *The New Basic Reader*, and *Think and Do Book* clearly readable. Four frames also captured a police officer on the sixth floor near the stairway, followed by two other photos by Smith of Lt. J.C. Day pointing at the location of where the rifle had been found among boxes near the stairway. Six other bracketed pictures were taken looking out of a rear window at the train yard below and including a cop talking to a civilian dressed man. Smith finished up his interior photo series with two shots of building superintendant Roy Truly being interviewed on the first floor.[46]

Smith had by now accumulated quite a bit of exposed film, and knowing that it might quickly lose its newsworthiness with the fast pace flow of events, he wanted to swiftly ship it back to Fort Worth. "One of the TV people was coming back to town and I gave him my film." His various rolls, primarily of the plaza area, and including the "tramp" photos as well as his sequence taken of inside the Depository Building, made it back to the station in Fort Worth, but as Smith bemoans, "The idiots on the desk were too busy to send somebody after it, and didn't have sense enough to have a cab bring it in. I had to retrieve it the next day when I finally got back to Fort Worth." This slip-up

Lieutenant Day points out the
hiding spot of the rifle to the press

resulted in none of Smith's good, live coverage photos, including the view of the assassination scene from the Depository window, making it into the Friday or Saturday editions, although one or two shots were used later in a wrap-up story.[47]

When finished in the Dealey Plaza area, Smith went downtown to police headquarters and took several photos of Oswald being escorted through the jam-packed corridors of the homicide department. Tony Record had been at police headquarters early enough to capture a number of frames of a grim photo opportunity when the Italian 6.5mm rifle was carried through the corridor and held overhead by crime lab Lieutenant John C. Day.

Smith and Record remained at the station until late that night, when at the urging of the press, Oswald was brought out to be seen and photographed. Record recalls an interesting footnote to the event: "When I went into the room designated, people were already standing on top of desks. I was stuck between two rows, and asked the man in back of me if I could get up there in his place. He was holding a reporter's pad like most of the reporters and I said that he did not need to see Oswald, but I did. He emphatically denied my request and a TV cameraman for Channel 11, Dutch Morrison, told me to get next to him. I thought nothing of this until the Warren Commission Report came out and I discovered a picture of the man that I had been talking to. It was Jack Ruby."[48]

Around 3:00 Bradford had ". . . heard from the City Desk that reporter Bob Schieffer had picked up old lady Oswald and was bringing her over to the jail. I met them at the curb of the city hall." When he learned where Oswald had a rented room, which was out near where Bradford had grown up, "I got in the car with Jimmy Jones and went out to the house on Beckley and photographed and interviewed the eight or so people who lived there." By about 8:00 that evening Bradford returned to Fort Worth with a batch of film taken by him and his colleagues.[49]

Some time in mid-afternoon on that Friday, Jerry Cabluck was sent out to Bell Helicopter located half-way between Dallas and Fort Worth with the assignment to take aerial photos of the scenes of the shooting in Dallas. Bell pilot Clem Bailey flew Cabluck to Dealey Plaza. Recalls Cabluck, "I left Parkland with all of the film for my paper and met somebody half-way and dropped the film off at Bell Helicopter. They furnished us a helicopter and I did aerials. I didn't even know where the killing happened, so I photographed Stemmons Freeway and a whole lot more because I didn't really know where it was. Then the helicopter took me to downtown Fort Worth and dropped me off. Since everybody else was out, it was up to me after I got back from the flight to develop all the film. I remember sitting there for 2 or 3 hours just turning out film. The librarian, Dorothy Hooper, came in to help, as did others too."[50]

Dealey Plaza the afternoon of November 22, 1963

Harry Cabluck had left Parkland Hospital soon after the death announcement and went to Dealey Plaza to spot for his brother's aerial photos. While in the Plaza area, Cabluck took several photos of police officer James W. Foster who was near a manhole cover, by the infield curb of the south side of Elm Street in an area believed to be where a bullet had struck and ricocheted out. Foster later testified that the projectile, ". . . caught the manhole cover right at the corner . . . where it penetrated the turf." Cabluck was later quoted as saying concerning the scene, ". . . There was more than one piece of turf knocked up. But that was the biggest piece turned up, like someone shoved a screwdriver in and peeled it back a little bit." He also indicated that a second gorge looked the same, "but not as big." Cabluck now took several frames of the area near the corner of the concrete rectangle, using a pencil to point to the upturned turf. The resulting photos were imprecise in detail, though one was included in the Saturday evening edition of the paper. A photo editor included a fanciful description: "One of the rifle bullets fired by the murderer of President Kennedy lies in the grass across Elm Street from the building in which the killer was hiding and from where he launched his assault." Though including a circle to indicate the bullet within the photo frame, no such object can be specifically seen.[51]

The fact of the shooting in Dallas had been flashed by UPI and AP teletype within minutes of the attack. Network television coverage quickly picked up the story and soon preempted all its regularly scheduled programming for continuous real-time broadcast. The event would become a milestone in media coverage. And with this blanket coverage, television, for one of the first times in its history, would edge out the traditional press as the primary news vehicle for the public. Yet much of this coverage was relegated to marking time with repetitious stories, forced studio chatter, and the rescreening of film clips between news developments. Americans still looked to traditional newspapers for expand information and to put events into a retainable and seemingly reliable and factual format. The *Star-Telegram* had the set-up, know-how, and staff to gather and disseminate this information. Being a morning and evening paper, its facilities were geared to run 24 hours, and thus could cover a day-long news story with more immediacy than a one-edition daily.

When news of the shooting reached the City Desk in early afternoon, much of the evening edition had been "put to bed." Quickly, 2½" letters were typeset for a startling headline — "KENNEDY SHOT," while 1½" letters on the second line declared, "CONNALLY WOUNDED." A short six paragraphs, taken primarily from the initial AP wire story was inserted over the by-line, "Bullet Strikes President's Head," and positioned to the right of a full-face photo of Mrs. Kennedy taken by Tony Record during the morning breakfast. This extra edition indicated that the President was still alive, but in critical condition. Shortly after beginning the run of this first extra, an updated second extra edition ran with a new headline declaring, "KENNEDY DEAD; CONNALLY ALSO HIT." By the time this second extra edition was set staff writer Ed Johnson's recollection of the shooting scene from his vantage point aboard the press bus was also inserted, while Thayer Waldo and Jerry Flemmons both contributed short news updates. A stock official photo of the President was the only photograph included on this second extra edition's front page. Yet an additional extra was sent out when more visuals were available. In this third extra the headline read, "KENNEDY SLAIN." All old news of the pre-assassination event were now removed from the front page, replaced by a portion of a Dallas street map indicating with an arrow the approximate location of the incident, together with an AP photo made by Jim Altgens of the President's Lincoln moving out after the shots were fired. The final *Star-Telegram* EXTRA published for distribution that Friday included a front-page story by Thayer Waldo identifying Lee H. Oswald as a suspect in the murder of a Dallas police officer and possibly also in the Kennedy shooting.  Included was a photo of Mrs. Marguerite Oswald, mother of the suspect.

The rifle at police headquarters

The Saturday morning edition included among its heavy photographic and news coverage of the events, a McAulay photo of President Kennedy at the Friday morning outdoor reception at Hotel Texas, a Panzera shot of President and Mrs. Kennedy at the Chamber of Commerce breakfast, a Record photo of Lieutenant Day displaying the assassin's rifle, and one of Jerry Cabluck's aerial photos captioned, "Ambush Angle," with a circle around the sixth-floor corner of the School Book Depository with a line running from it to a circled X on Elm Street below.  Also published was an uncredited photo by Harry Cabluck of Patrolman Foster, captioned, "Witness to Tragedy — Dallas Policeman J. W. Foster, eyes closed, kneels near spot where Kennedy was shot.  'I heard 'em both (Mrs. Kennedy and Mrs. Connally) scream,' he recalled, his voice trembling."[52]

Most of the photo staff had been working since early Friday morning, and with the tragic events occurring that afternoon, all the staff continued to work on the story both on scene in Dallas and with photo developing and editing work back in Fort Worth. In Fort Worth Joe McAulay also had photographically covered the local arrest of a man suspected of possible involvement in the assassination, a report of which had briefly been given in the paper's third Friday extra.  Those cameramen in Dallas stayed with the events at the police station into the night and early morning hours, and continued to follow leads and assignments into Saturday. George Smith later recalled that he had reported to the paper 6:30 Friday morning and did not return home until 8:00 p.m. Saturday night.  After driving back from Dallas on Saturday night he recollects being dog-tired when he arrived back at the photo department with his most recent batch of exposed rolls.  "I just printed the stuff, took it out, dumped it on the desk and said, 'I'm going home,' and just kept going."[53]  By evening deadline on Saturday the staff had put in many hard hours, and as Jerry Cabluck puts it, "The paper at that time was just mortified with overtime."

The photo coverage in Dallas on Sunday morning by the *Star-Telegram* for the transfer of Oswald was non-existent. Smith remembers, "We didn't have a photographer over there. I was sitting at home watching the transfer on TV, bemoaning the fact we didn't have photographers over there, and the doggone shot went off.  As soon as I saw the shot, it made me a little sicker — the authorities had goofed again.  And it couldn't have been a minute later when my phone rang, and it was the office telling me to get on down to the office."[54]

Tony Record also witnessed the shooting on his home TV. Calling the paper, he was told to get to Parkland. Upon arriving there after Oswald was pronounced dead, Record took shots of the commotion. "Oswald's family arrived after I got there and I remember his mother opening the door and attempting to hand the baby to a police officer. He refused to take the child and I thought at this time this poor kid is going to have a tough time in life."[55]

Professionally some of the photographers must have been disappointed at missing the opportunity to photograph such an historic scene, especially as both the Dallas newspapers had photographers there, one of whom, Bob Jackson, subsequently won a Pulitzer for his photo of Jack Ruby shooting Oswald. Yet even though the event was broadcast live on at least one television network, getting the story out in newsprint was the name of the game for all newspaper men, and the *Star-Telegram* staff outdid themselves in that regard.

Bradford explains that following the shooting, ". . . everybody just kind of heard it and showed up, and we're all looking around and realize, 'Hey, we've got enough people here to put out an edition.' The pressmen came in, the typesetters came in. They made enough papers to make a truckload, threw it on a truck, took it to Dallas and started selling it off the truck on the downtown streets." Proud of his newspaper's ingenuity, Bradford also recalls that the *Star-Telegram* had the AP wirephoto taken from *Dallas Morning News* photographer Bob Jackson's picture printed in the Fort Worth paper and for sale in Dallas prior to its being used by the Dallas paper itself. This newspaper scoop also apparently resulted in the Dallas City Council shortly thereafter passing a resolution that the Fort Worth paper could not have news racks in Dallas.[56] As a result of their weekend effort, the *Star-Telegram*, along with the *Houston Chronicle*, won the 1963 Texas Associated Press first place award for its in-depth coverage of the assassination.

As with many major local stories, only a few of the numerous photographs taken while covering the story ended up being published in the *Star-Telegram*. Due to the large number of exposures made, and the hurried manner in which they were often run back to the paper, many of the exposures were unidentified as to who made them. Also, with the rush in photo editing to use the most newsworthy shot, some of the negative strips were misfiled in the process.

Following the issuance of the Warren Commission *Report*, various researchers and critics attempted to dig deeper into the facts of the event, believing the government's version was fatally flawed. Researcher Richard Sprague visited, was given some access, and had a number of prints made from the files of the *Star-Telegram*, among them the eventually famous "tramp" photos by George Smith. Interest grew in what sinister or perhaps key facts photographs might reveal, and various serious as well as sensation-seeking individuals clamored for any new information they might be able to discover.

Concerning the status of the Texas visit and assassination-related photographs within the *Star-Telegram* files, George Smith explains, "It was a fairly open newspaper in those days. They would make contact prints on just about everything. A lot of that photographic stuff disappeared out of our files. I understand that a lot of the contact prints disappeared, and some negatives have been clipped out and the sequence broken. No idea by who or when or exactly what. It could even have been done at night, as it was an unprotected area. Nowadays you can't hardly get into the building. I do understand most of the negatives are still around, however. As far as I know, all my negatives are still filed, but I never have checked nor printed them since." According to the paper's photo sales department, since about 1976 the pictures concerning the Kennedy assassination have been closed to the public, and some of the paper's original negatives from that series are in fact missing. Today the paper's reference library contains the photo negatives, prints and contact sheets of the coverage of Kennedy's visit to Fort Worth and Dallas. The contact sheets alone of just the Fort Worth and Dallas coverage up to the early evening of November 22 number over 30.[57]

George Smith left the photo department in 1968 for an 11-year stint, first as assistant city editor, then as editor of the morning paper. By the mid-1980s he was still very active at the paper, writing for the "action line" as well as their military and retirement columns. Concerning his feelings about the assassination conspiracy theories, Smith says, "I have stuck to the official line all these years. I think Oswald probably did it all by his lonesome. Conspiracy theories never washed with me. You get that many people involved in something, it usually gets fouled up." Having examined and viewed out of the corner window where the shots are believed to have been fired less than two hours after the incident itself, Smith comments, "I'm no great shakes with a rifle. I'm not that bad either. I still think it could be done." His most vivid memories of that weekend 1963? "I remember more than anything that wave by President Kennedy from the top of the stairway at Carswell, and that smirk on Oswald's face when they were bringing him around the hall in the police station. I don't think I'll forget either image."[58]

Harry Cabluck, who in the 1980s worked with Associated Press in Dallas as photo editor, shares Smith's belief that Oswald did the shooting, and recalling the traumatic events, states, "I think we lost one of the top eight presidents this country has had. I felt great sympathy for the Kennedy family. I think the event drew the country together in a spirit of togetherness not seen since World War II."[59]

Brother Jerry, eventually became owner of his own photographic studio. He sees the question of conspiracy slightly differently. "My opinion is it was just too incredible. It was wonderfully done if a plot, and if it was just a lone assassin, he was really lucky." Concerning the continual interest, theories, and counter-theories of the assassination, he comments, "It's the best murder mystery you will ever read. If anybody says this is exactly what happened, it will be disputed."[60]

The *Star-Telegram* photo staff had done an outstanding job of covering a terrible and highly newsworthy event. Few had or would in the future cover such an impacting story. Yet being a young staff, their work was done not in a vacuum, and the true importance of what they witnessed, though perhaps not fully understood in the hours of their coverage, would soon become apparent to them. As Jerry Cabluck would put it some twenty years later, "I was just a kid who saw history happen in front of me."[61]

A wave good-bye at Carswell taken by George Smith

## CHAPTER NOTES

1.   Telephone interview of Jarrold Cabluck, 11/4/1985.
2.   Phillip J. Meek, *Fort Worth Star-Telegram*, p. 9-12.
3.   Ibid., p. 14-15.
4.   Ibid., p. 16, 18, 21.
5.   *Fort Worth Star-Telegram*, 11/22/1963 (Morning edition), p. 6.
6.   Telephone interview of Norm Bradford, 6/12/1989; Telephone interview of George Smith, 4/30/1987; Telephone interview of Jarrold Cabluck, 11/4/1985; Telephone interview of Wilburn Davis, 3/30/1987; Questionnaire filled out by Harry Cabluck, 11/14/1985.
7.   Telephone interview of Bradford, 6/12/1989.
8.   Ibid; Letter, Tony Record to Trask, 11/9/1993.
9.   *Fort Worth Star-Telegram*, 11/22/1963 (Morning edition), p. 1, 6, 9.
10.  Telephone interviews of Davis, 3/30/1987; Smith, 4/30/1987; Bradford, 6/12/1989; and J. Cabluck, 11/4/1985.
11.  Telephone interview of J. Cabluck, 11/4/1985.
12.  *Fort Worth Star-Telegram*, 11/22/1963 (Evening edition, third extra), section 2, p.2.
13.  Telephone interview of Bradford, 6/12/1989; *Fort Worth Star-Telegram* contact sheet "51" of photographs taken by Norm Bradford, 11/22/1963.

14.    Telephone interview of Davis, 3/30/1987.

15.    Note from Harry Cabluck, 3/9/1990; Telephone interview of J. Cabluck, 11/4/1985; *Fort Worth Star-Telegram* contact sheet "A", "D", & "45" of photographs taken by the Cablucks, 11/22/1963.

16.    *Fort Worth Star-Telegram*, 11/22/1963 (Evening edition, second extra), p.1.

17.    *Dallas Morning News*, 11/4/1981, p.1AA; *Fort Worth Star-Telegram* contact sheet "CA72826" of photographs taken by H. Cabluck, 11/22/1963.

18.    Ibid.; Questionnaire filled out by H. Cabluck, 11/14/1985; Letter, H. Cabluck, 3/15/1990; Telephone interview of J. Cabluck, 11/4/1985. Two of these Cabluck photos were reproduced, but without a credit line, in J. Gary Shaw's book *Cover-Up* while a print of the third shot is included in the exhibit at "The Sixth Floor" in the former School Book Depository Building in Dallas.

19.    Telephone interview of J. Cabluck, 11/4/1985.

20.    Telephone interview of Bradford, 6/12/1989. The author was given access in 1991 to view the *Fort Worth Star-Telegram* contact sheets of the coverage of Kennedy's Texas trip, and examined them for several hours to better understand the photographers' shooting sequences. Though many could be identified to specific authors, the proof sheets often have more than one photographer represented on a sheet, and unfortunately frame numbers were not replicated. Among the various sheets which contained Parkland Hospital sequences were sheets marked "CA72826", "4," "11," "16," "40," "22," and "32."

21.    Telephone interview of Smith, 4/30/1987; *Fort Worth Star-Telegram* contact sheet "11" of photographs taken by George Smith, 11/22/1963.

22.    Telephone interview of Bradford, 6/12/1989; Letter, Record to Trask, op. cit.

23.    Telephone interview of Smith, 4/30/1987; *Fort Worth Star-Telegram* contact sheet "11" & "40."

24.    Telephone interview with Smith, op. cit..

25.    Ibid.; Richard E. Sprague, "The Assassination of President John F. Kennedy," *Computers and Automation*, 5/1970, p. 53; *Fort Worth Star-Telegram* contact sheet "11." *Dallas Morning News* photographer Jack Beers was with Smith both inside and outside the building, he taking similar views. One of the Beers photos was later published in a UPI souvenir volume titled *Four Days* in which the caption read, "The sniper had dined on fried chicken and pop while waiting patiently to shoot the President." The evidence, held by a detective outside on the sidewalk, actually belonged to another worker. Both Beers and Smith made photos of this incident.

26.    Telephone interview of Smith, 4/30/1987.

27.    Michael Canfield, *Coup D'etat in America*, p. 60. According to an official transcript made of police radio channel #1, just before 2:00 p.m. the dispatcher was contacted by caller 61 identified as patrolmen G. W. Temple and R. E. Vaughn. They reported that they had information that the train which had been stopped by a train agent on the overpass had a man hiding in the ninth boxcar from the engine, "hunkered down inside." (*Hearings*, v.23, p. 878.)

28.    *Hearings Before the President's Commission on the Assassination of President Kennedy*, v.6, p. 312.

29.    Canfield, op. cit., p. 279.

30.    Sprague, *Computers*, op. cit., p. 38-39; *Hearings*, op. cit. v.19, p. 124; *Fort Worth Star-Telegram* contact sheet "11."

31.    Biography of Richard E. Sprague issued in conjunction with an article from *Gallery Magazine*; Letter, Sprague to Trask, 4/10/1984; Unpublished typescript by Richard E. Sprague, "The Kennedy Assassination," 5/1/1967; Telephone interview of Richard E. Sprague, 12/1987.

32.    Jim Garrison, *On the Trail of the Assassins*, p. 208.

33.    Ibid., p. 213; *New York Times*, "Garrison declares Ruby was sighted near assassination," 2/1/1968, p. 75.

34.    Sprague, *Computers*, op. cit., p. 36-41.

35.    J. Gary Shaw, *Cover-up*, p. 82-84.

36.    *Appendix to Hearings Before the Select Committee on Assassinations*, v. 6, p. 257-258.

37.    Ibid., p. 259.

38.    Ibid.

39.    Ibid., p. 265.

40.    Tape recording of a presentation before "The Assassination Symposium on John F. Kennedy" by John R. Craig, Phillip A. Rogers & Lois Gibson at Dallas, 11/16/1991. See also Jim Marrs, *Crossfire*, p. 333-336 concerning the Harrelson question.

41.    Dallas Municipal Archives and Records Center, "Arrest Report on Investigative Prisoners," 11/22/1963.

42.    *A Current Affair,* 2/25/1992.

43.    *A Current Affair,* 2/25/1992, 3/3/1992.

44.    Billy Cox, "John Gedney: JFK Player Gets Bitten Publicity," Kenneth W. Formet, "Gus Abrams: 'Yep, That's Bill!,'" *Dateline: Dallas*, Winter, 1993, p. 24-25.

45.    *Coup D'Etat in America*, (revised edition © 1992), p. 351-353.

46.    Telephone interview of Smith, 4/30/1987; *Fort Worth Star-Telegram* contact sheet "11" & "40."

47.    Telephone interview of Smith, 4/30/1987.

48.    Letter, Record to Trask, op. cit.

49.    Telephone interview of Bradford, 6/12/1989.

50.    Telephone interview of J. Cabluck, 11/4/1985.

51.    *Hearings*, op. cit., v.6, p. 252; Gary Mack, ed., *Coverups!*, 2/1983, no.7, p.5; *Fort Worth Star-Telegram* 11/23/1963; *Fort Worth Star-Telegram* contact sheet "15" of photographs taken by H. Cabluck, 11/22/1963.

52.    *Fort Worth Star-Telegram*, 11/22/1963 (all editions); 11/23/1963 (Morning edition).

53.    Telephone interview of Smith, 4/30/1987.

54.    Ibid.

55.    Letter, Record to Trask, op. cit.

56.    Telephone interview of Bradford, 6/12/1989.

57.    Telephone interview of Smith, 4/30/1987; Letter, Dorothy Hooper to Trask, 5/30/1986; Letter, Kristin Sandefur to Trask, 3/24/1989; *Fort Worth Star-Telegram* contact sheets, 11/22/1963.

58.    Telephone interview of Smith, 4/30/1987.

59.    Questionnaire filled out by H. Cabluck, 11/14/1985.

60.    Telephone interview of J. Cabluck, 11/4/1985.

61.    Ibid.

## CHAPTER 15

# Camera Car 1

For better or worse, today's American society depends heavily on television for its knowledge of national and world news. During the last few decades, the packaging and presenting of news has been a dominant fiefdom of the television industry. Steady technological advances in the industry, including the development of faster, more sensitive photographic films, universal color broadcasting, the introduction of videotape and mini-cameras, and the capability of satellite feeds from almost anywhere in the world for nearly instantaneous viewing, have all contributed to make this an immediate, flashy, and when used well, insightful medium. Television, however, is often attracted to those news events which best lend themselves to visual images; and if television doesn't cover a news story, for a large percentage of the population, the event might as well not have occurred. Likewise, many non-events or relatively obscure stories are covered by television due to the potential of good visuals, and marginally significant events run the risk of being perceived by the television viewers as more important than they are simply because of the presence of the TV camera. The assassination of President John Kennedy in the fall of 1963 is acknowledged by students of the mass media as a watershed event in the history of news reporting in America. Prior to that traumatic episode, the reporting of world and national news was the primary function of traditional print journalism. As one media observer commented concerning the assassination coverage, ". . . TV journalism came into its full maturity" as a result of the event. Television broadcasting picked up and reported the shooting within minutes of the incident, and during the next 72 hours it attempted to cover in a heretofore unprecedented completeness, the events as they unfolded in real time. From that time on, television would emerge as the major source by which a large segment of the population would obtain their news information.[1]

A White House and two TV network cameramen were on assignment in the motorcade on November 22, 1963, at the time of the shooting, and we shall look at the events of the assassination as witnessed and recorded by these three film makers.

~

By 1963 motion picture film had been on the world scene for some 70 years. The inventive genius of Thomas Alva Edison is credited with developing in the late 1880s the first practical motion picture camera.

With the growing acceptance and popularity of motion picture film following its introduction to paying audiences in the United States in 1896, various film producers such as Edison and Biograph attempted to record newsworthy or interesting events. At times they even reverted to faked reenactments when the technology or distances involved did not allow for on-location filming. Probably the earliest film sequence showing a United States President is a March 1897 Edison movie of an inaugural parade at which outgoing President Grover Cleveland is filmed. This was allowed by the scene of the oath of office being given to President-elect William McKinley.[2]

McKinley proved to be the third United States President killed by an assassin's bullet. In 1901, during his second term, McKinley visited the Pan American Exposition at Buffalo, New York. At a reception in the Palace of Music on September 6, McKinley was mortally wounded at point-blank range by anarchist Leon Czolgosz, who crudely concealed his gun in a cloth-covered hand at a time when the President was standing, shaking hands with the public. Vitagraph cameraman Albert Smith later claimed that he was present and filming during the assassination, but neither surviving frames nor other reports confirm his comments. It would be another 62 years before such a traumatic presidential event would be recorded on film. Though not present at the shooting scene, the various film companies did recorded other aspects of the story including the arrival of Vice-President Roosevelt at Buffalo and the funeral and burial of McKinley. French film maker Georges Melies exhibited a realistic reenactment of the assassination on film, though not apparently trying to fool his audience into thinking that it was a film of the actual event.[3]

During the next half century the American public's desire for motion picture news of important and spectacular world events was satisfied by the product of numerous newsreel companies including Pathe, Vitagraph, Hearst, Fox, Paramount, and Universal. Ten-minute news packages were gathered as often as twice weekly for distribution to thousands of motion picture theaters around the nation.

Two of the most sensational events ever captured on newsreel film occurred during the 1930s. In October, 1934, King Alexander I of Yugoslavia was visiting Marseilles, France, when during a motorcade he and the French Prime Minister were shot and mortally wounded by an assassin who had jumped on their car's running board. Present at the event was a Fox Movietone camera crew. The audio and visual circumstances of the incident, including the cutting down of the assassin by a sword-wielding mounted French officer, and closeups of the vehicle after the attack, were all dramatically captured on film and had a great impact on moviegoers.[4]

Perhaps the most famous newsreel story of all time was filmed on May 6, 1937, when four newsreel crews were present and filming at the grand but seemingly uneventful docking of the German dirigible *Hindenburg* at Lakehurst, New Jersey. At 7:20 p.m., after a lengthy delay and during intermittent showers, the hydrogen-filled giant balloon was just touching the mooring mast. Most of the newsreel men had just begun cranking their cameras when an horrific ball of fire consumed the *Hindenburg*'s skin and steel hulk. This unexpected disaster features possibly the most spectacular film sequence ever made which Paramount editor Max Klein later described as ". . . an unmatched example of newsreel spot coverage."[5] Even today these dramatic film sequences are shocking and memorable, even to people who know the facts of the events.

Any professional cameraman, though not wishing a disaster to occur, still hoped that if a spectacular event did take place, he would be there with his camera containing a full spool of film, a fully wound spring, and enough available light. For a number of decades newsreels continued to be the only outlet for recording and distributing action and movement in the news, and the best cameramen had to possess both the eyes of a photojournalist and the flair of a film storyteller.

In May of 1939, for the first time ever, newsreel and television cameras recorded side-by-side during the opening ceremonies of the New York World's Fair. Although at the time television was regarded as a curiosity and did not seem to be a serious competitor of the newsreel film, within a decade the advancement of television would be a major factor in the demise of the newsreel film business.[6]

In the spring of 1948 the National Broadcasting Corporation network introduced the "Camel News Caravan," television's first popular news program. Shown five nights a week between 7:30 and 7:45 p.m., the program consisted primarily of an announcer reading news copy, interspersed with the broadcast of silent newsreel provided by Fox Movietone. The American Broadcasting Company and the Columbia Broadcasting System followed with their own versions of 15-minute news programs, ABC into the 1960s continuing to rely on outside sources for news film work.[7]

By September 1963 the waning of the newsreel format became quite evident with Fox Movietone News relinquishing its regular movie theater newsreel service. On Labor Day 1963 the CBS network expanded its nightly news format from 15 to 30 minutes including newscaster Walter Cronkite conducting a special interview with President Kennedy.[8] Many newsreel-trained cameramen were fast slipping over to the television medium.

The popularity of television had mushroomed during the late 1940s and early 1950s with new stations and markets opening in major cities throughout the nation. The Dallas-Fort Worth area of Texas was looked upon in the television industry as a single market area, Dallas ranking 21st and Fort Worth 42nd nationwide in city population. Each of the three major local television stations, all begun during 1948 and 1949, had national affiliations. WBAP-TV, headquartered in Forth Worth, was an affiliate of NBC, KRLD-TV in Dallas was the local CBS affiliate, and WFAA-TV in Dallas, the affiliate for ABC. Each of these local stations was owned by an area newspaper. Also present in the market area, which ranked 14th in the United States, were independent commercial stations KTVT-TV in Forth Worth and Dallas Educational Station KERA-TV.[9]

All three of the major Dallas area TV stations had good-sized news staffs, facilities for videotape recording, in-house 16mm movie film processing labs, and remote truck units with cameras able to broadcast from outside the studio.[10]

The announcement of President Kennedy's three-day trip to Texas for November 1963 would be extensively covered by Texas television. In the Dallas-Fort Worth area plans were made by the major stations to have full coverage of the Fort Worth events, the arrival at Love Airfield in Dallas, and the noontime speech delivered by the President at the Dallas Trade Mart. The Texas trip was looked upon as not simply a local event, as the visit was one of the first taken by President Kennedy in the upcoming presidential election season. His message and popularity could be viewed and measured, and the strong political side of the events could not be ignored. Therefore, besides the expanded local Texas TV coverage, the major networks would need to cover the trip, and made arrangements for support among their area affiliates.

CBS sent five network production crews to Texas with chief southern correspondent Dan Rather and Nelson Benton sent over from New Orleans to assist. Traveling with the President in the White House press corps was veteran CBS correspondent Robert Pierpoint and cameraman Tom Craven, Jr. NBC often relied upon WBAP for program feeds, and they also had available an assigned southwest area cameraman, Moe Levy, who worked out of Dallas. Acting NBC White House correspondent Robert MacNeil and Washington cameraman David Wiegman, Jr. were covering the story for the network, augmented by four reporter-photographers at WBAP, Levy, and an additional free-lance cameraman, Henry Kokajan. ABC had the weakest network film coverage for the trip, as it did not have a strong reservoir of cameramen. It often relied on outside contracts for such work together with assistance from its affiliates. Thus ABC White House Correspondent Bob Clark had no film crew along with him, and the needed film coverage would be provided by WFAA-TV.[11]

Thursday, November 21, was the first day of the tightly scheduled Texas visit, and at 11:00 a.m. Eastern Time, the gleaming white-with-blue trimmed Boeing 707 jet referred to as "Air Force One" departed Andrews Air Force Base outside of Washington, D.C. It carried the President and his official party towards its first stop in San Antonio, Texas. Taking off minutes after Air Force One was a back-up twin jet to the President's #26000 Air Force craft which carried additional members of the large presidential party. An additional plane, a chartered jetliner with

A capricious shot taken aboard the press plane on the short trip to Dallas

about forty of the White House press corps, as well as photographers, technicians, and some additional White House and government employees, followed closely behind the first two. The three jets arrived at San Antonio at 2:30 p.m. Centra Standard Time. Following a full schedule of public events at various locations, the official party arrived at Hotel Texas in Fort Worth near midnight.

Friday, November 22, dawned drizzly. Prior to the Dallas visit, the President's itinerary included an outside public address in a parking lot adjacent to the Hotel Texas, followed by a breakfast address in the hotel, sponsored by the local Chamber of

Commerce. A short motorcade through Fort Worth to Carswell Air Force Base preceded a 13-minute flight to Dallas at 11:20. Air Force One took off, followed by the press plane and the back-up plane, now officially referred to as "Air Force Two," due to Vice-President Johnson's being aboard. In mid-air these two trailing jets were allowed to overtake Air Force One and arrive at Love Field in Dallas, with the press plane landing first, and then the Vice-President's jet. This leap-frogging was done to assure an orchestrated ceremonial presidential arrival which would be recorded by the traveling as well as the local press. Arriving aboard with the press plane were three cameramen who had been chronicling the Texas trip on motion picture film since leaving Washington the previous day. Two of the film makers, CBS's Tom Craven and NBC's Dave Wiegman, were television's version of the old newsreel cameramen. These two cameramen were part of their respective network news crew who, along with the correspondents and technicians, traveled with the President to obtain the rough footage and comments that would be packaged for television viewing by millions of Americans. These crews worked hard and fast and needed the support of local television affiliates to get their reports out while the events were still newsworthy. The third cameraman aboard the plane was Tom Atkins, who worked not for the media, but the White House, and whose position was quite new to presidential history. His work was primarily for internal White House consumption as well as for the historical record, and it generally would not be seen by the public.

Craven filming in the Oval Office in October 1963

Thomas Joseph Craven, Jr., was born in Queens, New York, in August, 1930, the son of a former newsreel cameraman. In February, 1955 he obtained a job with CBS, and was eventually assigned to the Washington area as a cameraman. In 1963 he lived with his wife Jane and four children in Falls Church, Virginia, a short commute to Washington. Recalling his early 1960s film assignment areas, Craven relates, "In those days I think there were four cameramen, and we rotated one month on and three months off at the White House. We also covered general assignments — hurricanes, rioting, the marches around Washington, civil rights demonstrations — general news assignments and sports." On many occasions Craven had covered John Kennedy from the days the President had been a Massachusetts senator.[12]

The camera Craven brought with him on the Texas trip was a 16mm FILMO Bell & Howell 70 DL. The three-turret lens system was mounted with 10-, 25-, and

50mm lenses. A manually cranked spring-wind kept the film looping by the shutter mechanism at a steady 24 frames per second. Although television was beginning to broadcast some programming in color, news was not in that category, and cameramen invariably used black-and-white film. Craven's film was Dupont 936 negative film with an ASA of 250 used with ND filters.[13]

The other network cameraman traveling with the presidential party was Dave Wiegman, Jr., of NBC. Wiegman was born in 1926 in Baltimore. Always possessing an interest in photography, Wiegman in his early 20s did free-lance photography as well as work as a watch repairman. His father-in-law was a professional photographer and Wiegman worked as an assistant to him as well as getting involved in both still and occasional movie work on a free-lance basis in the Baltimore area. Starting a family, Wiegman desired a steady union job with good pay. He recalls of that period, "I told my wife if I didn't get a good job at what I want to do in a year, I'd go to work in a shipyard where I could get seniority. I was going to switch completely." His first "break" came when as a result of an automobile accident, Tom Craven, who was working on a story for CBS, was hospitalized for a few weeks, and a Washington cameraman was needed. As Wiegman lived only 50 miles from the Capital, and was willing to commute for a few weeks, the network asked him to fill in rather than have to pay hotel bills for someone from New York. Remembers Wiegman, "So they called me up and I got two weeks' work in Washington. That was the beginning." By January, 1956, the Wiegmans had moved to the Washington area and he was hired by Julian Goodman, then Bureau Manager for NBC and later President of RCA. Wiegman always remembered Goodman's instructions about how to cover a story. "If I send you to do a hurricane and you get there and the hurricane's over, I want you to bring me back a picture of the puddles of water." The point carried home, and Wiegman would remember the advice that no matter what kind of event you're covering, you've always got to turn in some kind of footage. In Dallas this ingrained training would come in handy.[14]

In Washington Wiegman was one of two cameramen, the other being Brad Cress, Wiegman's senior, who taught him much, but did not enjoy the White House coverage. Wiegman explains concerning this news beat, "Strange philosophy about the White House. It's entirely different coverage. A lot of men choose to do it because it's actually spot news all the time. You don't build a feature story or have time to use cinema ability. You just have to shoot the story. And it's really news. I've always said — it's press photography — 90% press and 10% photography. And press becomes shove many times. It's a very physical job at the White House." NBC did not have a rotation system, and Wiegman covered the White House every day for about eight years. His coverage included President Eisenhower and part of the campaign of Vice-President Nixon until the November 1960 election, when thereafter Wiegman was sent to cover the new President-elect at Palm Beach, Florida, shortly after the election.[15]

Wiegman's camera was a FILMO, almost identical to Craven's, except that Wiegman did not use a handle. Speaking of shooting techniques, Wiegman explains, "You shoot with the left eye. The finder's on the left side of the camera, naturally, and you shoot with the left eye, and that puts your nose and your forehead right against the back of the FILMO. The amateur picks up a FILMO and would put his right eye at the viewfinder and then the whole thing's wobbling out there, and you're off center. We filmed so your elbows are right against your ribs, equidistant. The camera's straight in front of you and you're resting it on your head. You're cushioned with your arms and head, that's the technique." The wide angle lens he used varied from a 9mm, 10mm, or 13mm though on the Texas trip Wiegman thinks he used a 10mm. He also carried with him a box to hold the camera and up to six rolls of film. The box also served as a 10-inch platform to extend Wiegman's 5'8½" height in a crowded situation. The typical 936 negative film used in failing light could be pushed from 250 to 400 or even 800 ASA back at the lab if Wiegman so requested. Wiegman wore an ever-present dark Fedora hat as his hair was thinning, and "When I got into a convertible in motorcades, this fine hair would blow every way and I'd look like a wild man." Though a dress code is nonexistent in today's media coverage of the White House, back in the early 1960s most cameramen went in pin-striped suits, and although hats were not *de rigueur* in the Kennedy White House, the Fedora was one of the few acceptable types of headgear available when decked out in a suit.[16]

When working a major story, a cameraman would never leave the action to get his film processed. Instead at key events or at sites along a motorcade route, pick-up couriers would be stationed ready to whisk away the exposed film to a local television affiliate where it could be processed and edited for possible network feed. As these pick-up "stringers" were not always known to the cameramen and could easily be lost in a crowd, they carried mesh bags similar to those in which onions are packaged, and made of distinctive, eye-catching colors. CBS always used yellow bags, while NBC used red and white mesh bags with "NBC" printed on the side.[17]

Whereas the network cameramen were always aware of drop points and news deadlines, the third motion picture cameraman on the trip from Washington was filming with a far different set of needs in mind. Tom Atkins was a Navy officer on assignment to the White House. Born on March 24, 1934, in Mannington, West Virginia, Thomas Maurer Atkins graduated with a B.F.A. from Ohio University in 1956. Upon joining the Navy and completing boot camp, Atkins was stationed at the Naval Photographic Center in Washington. After attending Officer Candidate School at Newport, Rhode Island, Atkins, now an ensign, returned to the photographic center. Atkins comments, "I always wanted to work in still photography because that's what my degree was in, but the Navy put me in motion picture work."[18] As a film production supervisor, Atkins worked around the country on Navy training films with small film producers, followed up in 1960 by a two-year tour of duty in Hollywood, California, at the Navy Motion Picture Office.

In January, 1963, Atkins was able to transfer to a potentially very interesting assignment. He was scheduled to replace a Navy chief who did still photography work out of White House Navy Aide, Captain Tazewell Shepard's office. Recalls Atkins, "The chief didn't leave, and I thought, 'I'm going to be on a ship or something if I don't make a job for myself,' so I started shooting movies because nobody on the White House staff had shot movies before." Somewhat modestly, Atkins comments about his then new job, "I did not study to be a motion picture cameraman, and I just sort of picked it up. I was probably the only person who had on-the-job training at White House expense." With Captain Shepard's approval Atkins began filming events fairly regularly after March, 1963. "Up through Dallas, I was just getting established, taking a few films of heads of state visits and that sort of thing. We would make a 10-minute film with sound and music of the arrival of the dignitary at the White House including the speeches. And then, 24 hours later, when the President had his office meeting with the head-of-state, we would show the film. Then he would give the film to the dignitary as a gift. And occasionally, he would give the projector also, and I would have to go out and buy a new one. If it was a country where they did not have that sort of thing, he'd give them the whole kit and kaboodle."[19]

Captain Shepard also had Robert Knudsen on his staff, who worked primarily with a still camera. Earlier, White House Military Aide General Chester V. Clifton had engaged Captain Cecil Stoughton as White House photographer, and Stoughton also occasionally worked in motion as well as still photography. Atkins recalls concerning inter-service rivalry at the White House, "I think that rivalry was more between the military aides — Clifton and Shepard. I think what Clifton put in there, Shepard was going to put in, and I think that's probably why I got there." Atkins's typical workday could be from 9 a.m. to 5 p.m. or 5 a.m. depending on what was happening with the President. On most weekends Atkins followed the President to Newport, Hyannis, or Camp David. Atkins accompanied the presidential party on a poverty tour through the Appalachian area, and on another trip through the West to the Pacific coast, making films of the tour.

The camera most frequently used by Atkins was a German-made 16mm Ariflex-S movie camera which held a 100-foot load of film and had a 3-lens turret with 10mm, 25mm, and 50mm mounted lenses. He preferred the turret system to the zoom lenses as, "I could spin the turret, cut out camera stops and not have all the zooming in and out." An often-used piece of equipment for this rather bulky camera was a metal tubular support; a shoulder pod. This frame could be used from off the shoulders to get smoother and more steady shots. Though it looked bulky, Atkins remembers that, "It weighed just nothing." Unlike the television cameramen who worked almost exclusively in black-and-white for broadcasting reasons, Atkins usually shot in color, and his was often the only 16mm color professional film taken at many presidential events. On the road Atkins would usually carry about 10 rolls of daylight film along with 2 or 3 tungsten rolls, most stored in a gadget bag which could be slung over the shoulder.[20]

Recalling his activity covering events outside of the White House, Atkins recounts, "It was very hectic coverage. I was surprised at some of the stuff I would get under fluorescent lights. I would just shoot, and we would [later] color-correct it as best we could. I wasn't trying to do a Hollywood production. You didn't have a sound man, you didn't have lights. So other than a light meter, a camera and film, that's all I carried. You would get into situations with crushing crowds where you would practically lose the gadget bag or the camera. It could be an unbelievable situation. You always had to watch yourself so that you didn't get cut off by the crowd. The party would leave, and you would be stuck out in the sticks, thumbing your way home."[21]

While broadcast cameramen took film to record breaking news, centering on the subject of the moment, the White House photographers usually had more flexibility and freedom of expression in what they could shoot. Local press and television cameramen invariably focused their attention on the President. Atkins's perspective was slightly different. "My philosophy was to try to be the President's and First Lady's eyes. When they are in a public situation like that, you can be very tensed up, you see faces and shake thousands of hands. I don't think they really saw anything, so I tried to be their eyes. I would show them at an event, but I would also show faces of people they shook hands with, places they went, so that they could look back later on and be reminded of where they had been." Even then, it took some getting used to for the new White House movie man not to be impressed with the access his new job gave him to the President and his family. "They were quite a magnet. It was hard to take the camera away from them to get those extra shots, but I knew I had to have them."[22]

According to Atkins, the President loved film. "All I had to do was let Mrs. Lincoln or Marvin Watson know I had a film ready, and the first time the President had a chance, I'd take the projector in. I had a little rear-screen projector, and would put it on the coffee table [in the Oval Office] between the couches, and set it up and play it right there in the office."[23]

Concerning his presence during the President's trip to Texas, Atkins relates that, "Generally we wouldn't get involved movie-wise with trips that were 100% political, but that trip was a quasi-political foray, I guess, and I went." Knowing the itinerary for the trip and the various presidential stops, Atkins roughed out in his mind an outline of the type of establishing shots he would need to put a short film together, so when later editing it he could have a coherent sequence. Like Cecil Stoughton, who would also be on the Texas trip, Atkins generally traveled as part of the press package, following along with the working press on their plane and in cars assigned to them in the motorcade. At events, however, the White House photographers generally had much better access and movability. Atkins took a good number of Ektachrome color rolls of the Texas events of November 21, including at their arrival, late night scenes in Fort Worth of tall buildings decked out with Christmas lights arranged in geometric patterns, gleaming brightly against the black backdrop of night.[24]

A mounted Ranger outside Hotel Texas

Utilizing the remainder of the roll of film begun the previous night, Atkins picked up his coverage of Friday morning, November 22, with a view of Texas Rangers on horseback in front of Hotel Texas, waiting in anticipation of the President to walk out of the hotel to address a gathering crowd. A shot looking over the horse and rider towards the hotel entrance exposing a sign, "Welcome to Fort Worth, Where the West Begins," was next followed with a closeup of the eye and side view of the horse's head, and then a local color closeup of a ranger sporting a pencil moustache and topped with a ten-gallon hat.

By means of wide, medium, and telephoto shots, and the panning and tilting of the camera, spotlighting scenes around the main event, Atkins was utilizing his knowledge of film making. He was gathering together clips possibly to be used during editing to create a simple, yet colorful and visually interesting story of where the President was, what was happening around him, and what he was doing. This and a second full roll was exposed of the outdoor activities, while an additional two rolls were taken of the reception and presidential speech in the hotel at the Forth Worth Chamber of Commerce breakfast, followed by clips made of the motorcade to Carswell Air Force Base.

Aboard the airborne press plane Atkins made shots from his window of clouds with the flat Texas landscape below, together with a sequence of the landing at Love Field. These could possibly be used later in editing to give the impression of the view from Air Force One coming into Dallas. Once on the ground and prior to Air Force One's landing, Atkins took some general shots of spectators. Some can be seen holding Texas and Confederate flags and hand-made signs, waiting in

Landing at Love Field

anticipation for the Kennedys. Atkins's fifth roll of the day records the President's plane landing, taxiing, and the President and Mrs. Kennedy stepping down the gangway and being greeted by the official party. The Kennedys unexpectedly veered towards where the public were sequestered behind a chain-link fence. This photo opportunity was not wasted on the scrambling photographers, who jockeyed for good camera positions. All the while the public showed their exuberance and Secret Service agents, conspicuous by their less animated presence, watched over this swarm of activity.[25]

In unstructured, unscheduled events like this, the press had much closer access to the President than at formal events. Cameraman Craven recalled about his relations with the Secret Service prior to the assassination, "I've traveled with those guys for a good many years, and you get to know them pretty close. They know every one of us. Every one of us has a White House pass, we've had background checks, and we're not out to kill the President, we're out to make him look good. Today they keep you as far away as possible. To the Secret Service years ago, the first line of defense was to keep the photographers up front." Only partially in jest, Craven mentions, "For a good many years, Chiefs of the Secret Service used to say, 'Get the photographers up close, if anybody's going to take a shot at the President, they'll have to hit one of them first.'

And it's the truth — get those idiots in there, and we're another line of security." Craven, like many of his colleagues had much respect for the presidential Secret Service detail, believing them under-appreciated and underpaid for the job they performed.[26]

Craven (standing, left) and Wiegman (wearing hat) filming the Love Field arrival

Atkins' impressions of the airport reception are that, "Everyone was in good spirits, the weather was nice, lots of smiles!" CBS's Craven remembers, "It just so happened this day that the President walked the fence and shook hands with a lot of people, which is not highly unusual, but it just seemed unusual for that trip. It was just an everyday, run-of-the-mill arrival. The only thing that I recall is that I shot two rolls of film that day. It seemed we had an awful long time at the airport. We were just killing time."

Concerning the President's walking towards the fence and the crowd of spectators, Wiegman explains, "We semi-anticipated shots like that. You didn't get yourself on the other side of the President, you got towards where he may tend to go. We walked backwards for a way." None of the three cameramen remembers undue tension or anticipation of a bad incident, although at least one member of the print press believed the President was spending the extra time and exposure at the airport to show his unconcern for the reputation of Dallas as unwelcoming of Kennedy. If there was any trepidation on the part of the President or his advisors towards Dallas, the warm airport reception must have relieved it. Contrary to some later reports, there is little evidence from the photographs and film clips made at the airport that the reception was anything less than cordial and enthusiastic.[27]

While the President was still shaking hands, Atkins turned his camera for a moment towards the "Queen Mary," the large Cadillac Secret Service convertible which follows directly behind the President's Lincoln in motorcades. These two gleaming-clean White House vehicles had earlier been flown to Love Field for use in the Dallas procession. Aboard the specially outfitted buff interior of the follow-up car, presidential aides Kenny O'Donnell and Dave Powers are at their jumpseats, happily observing and undoubtedly politically assessing the reception scene. Atkins captured Powers taking home movies of the event, holding a black-bodied 8mm camera in his hands. Noted political reporter and presidential observer Hugh Sidey would later recount of Powers at the Hotel Texas earlier that day, "Somebody kidded about his avid pursuit of home movies. Just the day before a professional photographer complained that Dave got in his way. He laughed, but pointed out what an expert photographer he was becoming. The President recently had gone to the White House projection booth for a movie, and Dave had slipped in his home-made movies of the trip to Ireland. The surprised President had watched, then said to Dave, 'These are terrific.'"[28]

Presidential Aide Dave Powers
shooting home movies at the airport

There is much evidence that Powers continued to take movie film from his unique vantage point directly behind the President's vehicle during the Dallas motorcade. Secret Service Agent Paul E. Landis, Jr., who was seated just behind Powers in the follow-up car, noted in a statement made November 30, 1963, that "At various places along the route I remember Mr. Dave Powers standing up and taking movies of the President's car and crowd," while some photographs taken of the motorcade by spectators show Powers standing with the camera to his eye.[29] Photographic evidence indicates that Powers was not filming by the time the motorcade reached the end of Main Street, nor during the assassination itself, and he probably did not film anything after the shooting, nor on the trip to the hospital. Powers's early motorcade film would be, however, by itself, historically important, due to the event and time it was being filmed. It might also help answer the question posed by some researchers as to if the dent in the presidential Lincoln's chrome windshield trim was present prior to or as a result of the assassination. Powers, an affable and loyal staff member and friend to President Kennedy later became museum curator at the John F. Kennedy Library in Boston. The audio-visual library does not have this film, and when contacted about the type of film and camera he used, and the scenes he took that day, Powers would only comment, ". . . I do not discuss the assassination or contribute in any way to articles and books on the assassination. As the Secret Service agents knew, I often did take pictures during my many trips with President Kennedy. I consider these to be my own personal property and would not allow them to be used by anyone else. However, I was not standing up taking pictures at the time of the actual shooting and if I had been these too would be for my use only."[30] It is hoped that his home movies of the Texas trip will eventually be preserved for the public record in an institution such as the Kennedy Library, where many less historically privileged individuals have donated private materials for preservation and public access.

By now the President and his wife had broken off from the crowd at the fence and walked the short distance to their waiting limousine. All three film makers triggered a few feet showing the Kennedys and  Connallys settling into the back of the Lincoln convertible, and then quickly made for their own assigned positions in the motorcade. A yellow 1964 Chevrolet Impala convertible (license plate P1 9059) had been reserved for the "reel car" which was positioned just behind the Bell Telephone press pool car. The reel car, often referred to as "Camera Car 1," was the sixth vehicle behind the President, and the closest of any vehicles with photographers aboard. Convertibles were always the car of preference for photographers, as the camera people could stand up and shoot crowds and the motorcade over the windshield, and make a quick exit if an unscheduled stop proved photogenic. Craven recalls of parade spectators, "You look and see people oddly dressed or holding any signs. A lot of people try to run alongside and the police or Secret Service agents would jump off the follow-up car and stop them."[31]

Aboard the "reel car" Atkins got into the rear passenger side and Craven took the rear driver's side. In between them sat Wiegman's sound man, John Hoefen. At the Dallas stop the NBC sound cameras had not been scheduled to be taken off the plane, as the Trade Mart speech was to be handled by a separate NBC team. Explains Wiegman, "That was called 'hopscotching,' and we did that a lot. We might make a three-stop trip and we would cover that one which logistically we could get the sound equipment knocked down and back to the plane before 'The Man' left. And we'd do one of them maybe, and they would supplement with another crew in the area and hopscotch them. Our gear would be knocked down by the sound man and any help we could get. I would go in the motorcade and when I pulled up at the ensuing stop, the tripod would be right there and all I'd have to do is put the camera on the tripod, thread it up, and I'm ready to shoot. In Dallas Johnny didn't have an assignment, but he went along in the motorcade — fortunately."[32]

In the front seat the driver was a hatted Texas Ranger while Wiegman positioned himself in the passenger seat, at times sitting on the door frame itself for a better filming position. Craven recalls the sixth occupant of the car was White House electrical technician Cleve Ryan. "There was just room in the car. Usually Cleve went ahead on the baggage truck with the White House transportation people and helped unload our gear. But there was room in the car and he rode with us. He was well known to everyone. I think Cleve was in the front seat." Ryan was a pool electrician who worked for and received a check from all the networks, as well as from other news agencies which chipped in when they used his services. Ryan had been called over to the F.D.R. White House during the earlier newsreel days when the need for a union electrician was realized. Originally from a stage production background, the genial Irishman who arrived at the White House sporting a derby hat and spats, had soon made his presence invaluable to the press, doing courier jobs and the like. As Wiegman points out, "Cleve knew where he was needed and made sure he was there."[33]

With the motorcade off, all three movie makers scanned the crowds looking to take a few representative feet of activity. Still in the outskirts of downtown Dallas, Atkins shot a view of the motorcade vehicles in front of him, and clips of the crowd to his right, including someone with a homemade sign reading, "Howdy." Just after a brief glimpse of people in windows of buildings along the parade route, Atkins recognizes his film was about depleted and wasted the last few feet of film. Now inserting his sixth reel of the day, Atkins squeezes off a few feet of waste film to check the camera mechanics and get into virgin film. The motorcade is now in the business district. At a right turn ahead, Atkins's lens just manages to catch Kennedy and his wife six cars ahead. Scenes of the downtown area with spectacular crowds and red, white, and blue bunting over the street make for some good shots. A telephoto shot of the motorcade going down a seeming cavern of lights and shadows created by the tall building, is followed by a

Atkins turns around and films Camera Car 2. Art Rickerby is in a light coat and Cecil Stoughton (at right) is raising his camera.

backward shot of Camera Car 2, in which White House cameraman Cecil Stoughton can be picked out aiming his camera for a shot of the scene in front of him. Further down Main Street Atkins takes his last shot of the motorcade sequence showing kids waving, and he pans back towards them.[34]   Both Craven and Wiegman had taken similar sequences of the large and energetic downtown crowd.

Atkins describes what next transpired. "We came to the end of [Main Street] and made that right-hand turn, and were going directly at the [Texas School Book] Depository. Just as we turned, I remember looking at my watch, and it was 12:30, and just as I looked at my watch I heard an explosion. The thought that ran through my mind, 'Oh, brother — somebody lit a cherry bomb. I bet the Secret Service are jumping out of their britches.' And then immediately following there were two more quick explosions, and my stomach just went into a knot. The explosions were very loud, like they were right in front of me."

Craven was also sitting in the back seat. "It was just as we were making the turn. We thought it was a motorcycle backfiring. There were motorcycles abreast of cars, riding in the motorcade. It was stop and go, and those things backfire quite frequently. Somebody, I think, casually said, 'Jeez — that sounds like shooting or shots,' — and none of us really knew." Events transpired quickly. Atkins says concerning the three shots he remembers hearing, "You know when kids play cowboys and Indians and they go Bam — Bam Bam! The last two [shots] clustered together." Craven believes he heard three shots, but adds, "To tell the truth, I wouldn't be really positive. I could have sworn they were backfires."[35]

Seated in the front right side of the car, NBC Cameraman Wiegman's instincts were finely tuned that day. His recollections of his activities were spoken about 25 years later.

We were in that straight-a-way heading down to what I now know as the Book Depository, and I heard the first report and I thought like everybody that it was a good size fire cracker — a cherry bomb. Then when I heard the second one, the adrenaline really started pumping because there was a reaction in the motorcade. I was sitting on the edge of the [car door] frame, which I sometimes did. I keenly remember right after the incident that my feet were on the ground during one of the reports. I don't think I was fast enough to react to the second, but I think on the third one I was running. The car had slowed down enough for me to jump out. I swung my leg over and jumped while the car was still moving, but it was very slow. I jumped and I remember running and I remember the third shot. When I got out I knew I better get around the corner. The car was stopping. I'd better run around there and see what was happening. I knew the reaction was to run forward. I'd done this before in other motorcades because a lot of times the President will stop and do something. He might just shake a hand. He might look at a sign. So you're doing no good sitting in your car, and you can always retrieve your car as it goes by. . . . It was a technique I've used and I've gotten some good pictures that way. That may have been built in to get out and run and get up there to see what the heck's happening. The motorcade has stopped, plus you heard a report. I don't think I thought on the first or second [shot], but when the third one went off, I really thought I felt the compression on my face — I really thought I felt it. Then I thought "Somebody is shooting."

The idea of turning on the camera, I don't know where that came from. I've turned in some real sloppy work over the years that went into editing because I believed that sometimes you're not photographing what's happening as much as a moment. It's a slice of time. And something told me, "hey look , what have I got to lose. I've got a full spring and just turn it on." I can't stop and plant my feet, so I put it against my chest because you can't run with a Filmo up to your eyes. So I just slid it down under my chin and looked forward and ran as fast as I could and took in everything I could."[36]

Of Wiegman's quick action, Assistant Press Secretary Malcolm Kilduff, seated in the press pool car in front of Wiegman's later commented, "I remember seeing one cameraman off to the right running up the grassy slope to get some pictures of this couple huddled together at the top of the hill." When Wiegman ran around the corner he did not recall seeing the President at all, and his attention was drawn to a police officer getting off his motorcycle and running up the incline up ahead on the right. "I figured he knows something's up there, so I ran up there. I found myself there with Lem [Johns, a Secret Service agent originally in the Vice-President's follow-up car who had jumped out of the vehicle at the sound of the shots] close by, a few feet away. Then I saw the people lying on the side, and I saw nothing up there [on the slope]. Lem was sort of looking around. Couldn't see anything. I knew now I'd better get something — I've got to get some footage. I saw these people lying on the ground, and I took them. I saw a lady being pulled down to the ground. . . . You could sense she just wanted to get away from there, and somebody pulled her down."[37]

The Wiegman film sequence of the activity around the shooting scene lasts approximately 36½ seconds. It is filmed in real time without any breaks in the sequence. Though jumpy and blurry as a result of the cameraman's running while the camera was rolling, it is nonetheless a remarkable clip of film in the best tradition of newsreel cameramen. Wiegman's reaction to the stimulus of the unknown noise, and assessing and taking action, even without benefit of knowing or being able to see the President or his vehicle, is quicker than most anyone else in the entire motorcade. It would appear through careful analysis of this film, and aided by research done by Richard Sprague and Gary Mack on the timing of the sequence, that Wiegman began filming a little over three seconds prior to the President being hit in the head.[38]

Wiegman probably first pressed his camera trigger just after the second shot. The action captured on this remarkable film clip begins as Wiegman's car is approaching the Texas School Book Depository, while the telephone car in front begins making the left turn. The camera swings to the left, then to the right. An examination of these individual frames show various spectators on the steps of the Book Depository Building as well as others on the sidewalk. Many are looking forward towards the presidential vehicle while some are gazing back at the vehicles coming in their direction. The frames blur and tilt as

Wiegman begins filming as the crowd in front of the Book Depository reacts to noise

Wiegman jumps out of his car, a portion of its metal body appearing in a few frames. He begins traveling a few steps down the street, then veers off towards the knoll to his right. Though not evident in watching the sequence in real time, close scrutiny of some less blurred individual frames show that the camera briefly panned Elm Street. In the street is motorcycle officer Hargis, one of the four cycle escorts who were located adjacent to the back of the President's vehicle in the motorcade. At the time of the shot which struck the President in the head, Hargis stopped his cycle, got off and ran across the street to his right. To Hargis's right cycle officer Martin, approximately 20 feet ahead, was following the presidential car. The telephone car takes up much of this Wiegman frame, though to its front left may be seen the Vice-President's follow-up car, while two white "blips" on the roof of the telephone car are quite possibly glimpses of the helmets worn by motorcycle escort officers Jackson and Chaney ahead of and mostly obscured by the pool car.

Two separate frames taken close together afford a panoramic view of the scene.

The President's vehicle can just be made out traveling towards the triple under-pass, while near the sidewalk at the right of the frame some spectators are crouched on the ground. As Wiegman races towards the concrete pergola above the grass plot to the right of the street, his camera jiggles left to right to left to right. Spectator Mrs. Charles

Wiegman captures the Hesters on
film as they crouch by the colonnade

Hester ducks down, while her husband scrambles towards the pergola. In a blurry pan to the left Wiegman picks up the Bill Newman family sprawled on the ground. He then quickly tilts up to view his own camera car going by his position, while motorcycle cop Haygood also rides past in the foreground. Behind it Camera Car 2 proceeds down Elm Street with a couple of its occupants raising cameras to their faces. Then following a quick blur show-ing a woman wearing sunglasses cowering on the ground, Wiegman stops his se-quence here, and after running down the grassy slope towards another woman, he makes for his car, not wanting to be left behind. "I realized the President's car was not in the area. He had left, and I had no way of knowing he was shot. When I came back down the hill Lem Johns didn't have a ride and I said, 'Come on, get in our car. Here it is,' and he jumped in our car. The driver was confused for just a few seconds. It probably felt like an eternity, because I knew we had to get going to catch up with the President."[39]

Following closely on Wiegman's trail when he jumped out of the car were the two other cameramen. Craven recollects, "I didn't jump out until after we made the turn, and I saw people running up the hill. I saw the Newmans — that's when I started running — when I saw them lying on the ground. It looked like Mr. Newman was digging a hole to bury his son, to protect him with his body. I guess we scared the hell out of that family as we started taking pictures of them. We made pictures of everything that was moving. At this point the motorcade started rolling again, and we ran to our car."[40]

Wiegman pans towards the street, filming Officer Haygood cycling by.

In 1986 Tom Atkins vividly recalled this scene of almost a quarter of a century earlier. "We turned the corner and all hell broke loose. The car came to a stop. We all jumped out. I don't know where I was going or what I was doing. I remember [later] seeing Wiegman's footage — now there's a pro. He ran with his camera running and that footage really shows the feeling of the turmoil. I didn't think to do that. I run to find a scene to shoot and I see that mother and father and kids, and I started to shoot that. I got off very, very little." Up to this point Atkins had taken approximately 1 minute 16 seconds of film of the motorcade. He now made two quick takes lasting for five seconds of film. Atkins's first scene lasts for less than two seconds and is a close-up shot of Mr. and Mrs. Newman on the ground. He quickly spun his lens for a wider angle lens and took a scene of approximately three and one-half seconds showing the Newmans on the ground, while in the background on Elm Street motorcycle cop Haygood heads his 'cycle towards the curb. Atkins's car proceeds down the street and is being run after by Dave Wiegman obviously trying to catch up to the convertible.[41]

Craven believes that he "made some pictures of the President's car underneath the viaduct as it took off," and he can be seen in still pictures aiming his movie camera at the Newmans. As his vehicle passed by his location on the grass, "we ran back and got back into the motorcade. I recall Lem [Johns] running and sort of vaulting from the street over the trunk and us grabbing at him."[42]

Atkins was aware that he had not shot much of the scene, but he was also aware that both Wiegman and Craven were leaving his position. "Out of the corner of my eye, I saw the car start to take off, and I just ran to the car and dove headfirst into the back seat or I'd have been left right there."[43]

The motorcade was now broken up, and not knowing that the vehicles in front were now on their way to Parkland Hospital, the vehicle's driver continued down Elm, under the triple underpass towards Stemmons Freeway and the Trade Mart. Just beyond the underpass, near the ramp leading to the freeway, CBS correspondent Dan Rather was standing holding a vibrant yellow grapefruit bag. Four months after the shooting Rather was interviewed about his role. "Our production crew in the motorcade was going to throw me several reels of exposed film as they passed. I had a cab waiting to rush the film to the KRLD news studios about 3 minutes away for developing. It's a standard procedure we use to get the film on the air faster. The presidential limousine

sped past with several Secret Service cars close behind.   Although I didn't see the
President, I knew something was wrong, so I jumped into my cab and went straight to
KRLD studio."[44]

Atkins films the Newman family lying on the ground

Concerning the ride to the Trade Mart Atkins describes, "I can remember
hanging on for dear life down the freeway at a high rate of speed, not thinking to shoot
[film] or anything.  We pulled into the Trade Mart and got out and ran inside and there
were a lot of people standing around with blank looks on their faces."  Craven remembers, "We got to the Trade Mart where Kennedy was supposed to speak.  No one knew
what was going on.  Agent Johns was on the move.  He got on the back of a three-
wheeled motorcycle and waved us to follow.  That's how our car was the first to the
hospital."  Wiegman, from his position, took some film of the vehicles on their way to
the hospital, including a sequence showing the multi-storied structure coming up on the
left side of the road.  Atkins had run back outside of the Trade Mart and "Just commandeered the first car.  We hailed somebody down, said we were from the White House —
take us to the hospital."[45]

Sometime after the motorcade's arrival at the Parkland emergency entrance, a photographer took this elevated overview, showing the confused knots of humans gathered outside.

Upon the arrival of the vehicles near the Parkland emergency entrance, Wiegman immediately began filming. "I saw the car and saw people going in and I started again filming instinctively, 'I've got to get these people going in.' And I remember the General and Mrs. Lincoln going in. I even took the time to write a caption for the roll, and I put on this the other people who were going in." His film of the arrival shows a station wagon to his front with military aide General Clifton getting out and walking briskly for the entrance. Atkins also shot the same scene in color, showing the parked presidential vehicle, cops and plainclothesmen including the President's personal doctor, Admiral Burkley coming forward, Wiegman filming, and press secretary Kilduff looking quite frazzled. The three movie makers kept taking pictures of the frenzied activities. Craven's impression of the hectic scene includes "the Secret Service cleaning the blood out of the car — the flowers still lying in the back seat — and just chaos until the police figured out what was happening, and then they started to push us off. Senator Yarborough [who was in the Vice-President's vehicle] was crying — he was talking to reporters and really broken up."[46]

For some time few in the growing crowd of reporters, cameramen, and curious citizenry knew just how serious the situation with the President was. Atkins has poignant memories of the hospital scene. "I knew something was wrong. I didn't know that I really thought that anyone had shot the President." The terrible fact fast began to spread, and Atkins continued to make film of the activity. With the professionalism of the documentary film maker's skills, he also took vignette shots including closeups of a discarded bouquet of yellow roses within the Vice-President's convertible, the "Ambulances Only" sign over the emergency entrance, a tight shot of a flashing red dome light of a police car, a view of the upper stories of the hospital tilting down to reveal the commotion around the emergency entrance. Yet while the reflexes of the film maker continued in an almost automatic rhythm, Atkins's mind was racing with other thoughts. "I'm shooting film and I'm crying and I can't see to focus, and I'm telling myself that — you know — I'm having a dream and I'm going to wake up. It was just an incredulous feeling. I just couldn't believe it. Up to that point things hadn't happened like that in our lifetime."[47]

Atkins records newsmen Tom Wicker (left) and Douglas Kiker taking notes outside the hospital.

All three movie men, plus those other photographers now arriving on the scene, kept recording those same pathetic pictures of the outside crowd reacting to the news of the President's being shot and the final realization of his death. Those were the only pictures they were able to take. The story and action inside the hospital was beyond their lenses, and though everyone present was in a fashion part of the story, the photographers couldn't be swept into the high emotions of the moment. Emotions must be checked while they continued with their job. Their inbred training took over, and no matter what private emotional undercurrents swirled within them, the story was just too big to let anything get in the way of their covering it. Many of these cameramen were as shocked, confused and saddened as those around them, but they had the cameras which would convey, better than any reporter's words, what the reality of the scene was. They knew this, and they did their job — no matter how distasteful, disrespectful, or inappropriate it might seem to others or might flash momentarily in their private thoughts.

While some of the crowd did not seem to react to the news, others became very emotional. Some young black women cried hysterically, clutching their pocketbooks; teary children were held close by parents; a scruffy old man in a cap had a distant, forlorn look. And the cameramen danced into position to record the reaction of the emotional ones — pictures the world would see and react to. Says Atkins, "I can remember crying when I heard the announcement. I kept shooting. I shot other people's reactions."

Atkins had the luxury of not needing to worry about getting his film to others, but Craven and Wiegman knew that unless their "take" moved, it couldn't be processed

Tom Craven captures reaction to the death of the President. Rep. Jim Wright cries as does an unidentified woman wearing a scarf.

and telecast, and its immediacy value would be diminished. As Craven put it, "Your main problem right then is when you get film, where the hell do I get rid of it? You're looking for somebody — 'Hey, I've got film!' Anything I had of any value I shipped right there at the hospital." Craven thinks that CBS Reporter Nelson Benton was the one who picked up the film at the hospital.[48]

With his first 100′ roll exposed, Wiegman gave Hoefen the film. "We were to hand that film off the Wee Reiser at the

Trade Mart and he would ship it with the President's speech, as we left in a hurry for the airport. When this all happened half-way there, I had the roll and said to John, 'They want this film in Fort Worth.' He said, 'I'll take it!' We discussed how he would get there as we had no transportation. He went out in the street and hailed a car." On trip assignments Wiegman and Hoefen would typically travel together even when they weren't presently covering a story, ". . . because it's like leaving your wife at a shopping mall — you never do find her again. So we would stay together. I'm glad he did that that day. I know NBC was too."[49]

Finding a phone close by the hospital, Hoefen called in to the NBC affiliate WBAP, and was asked to make a statement over the phone for audio-recording of what he had seen from Camera Car 1. The statement was broadcast over the network at about 1:50 Dallas time. Hoefen reported,

> . . . We had just driven through the downtown section of Dallas through the business area where the President had received a very tumultuous welcome. We were approaching a drive which would put us on the freeway, where we would then drive toward the Trade Mart where the President was to attend a luncheon and make a speech to Dallas citizens. As we turned down this moderate curve here, there was a loud shot. At first we thought it was a cherry bomb by some teenager. Then it was immediately followed by two in (?) three more. Everybody sort of ducked and there were people falling to the ground. We did not know who was shot. Ladies and men both were screaming.

Dave Wiegman, the cameraman in the car in which I was riding immediately jumped out, was making pictures. We did not [know who] was
hurt.[50]

With film in hand, Hoefen then went into the street and stopped the first car
he could and asked for assistance to get to WBAP. According to one later report
Hoefen's volunteer driver made the thirty mile trip to Fort Worth in eighteen minutes.
Back at the hospital Wiegman remembers that later still, "I came out of the hospital and
Reiser was just parked on the curb. He recognized me and I gave him the other roll of
film."[51]

Kilduff told the press to stay together, and following a 1:30 C.S.T. press conference announcing the death of the President, and the President's body being taken away
in an ambulance at about 2:08, the press were herded into a bus to be taken to Love
Field. Many thought they were going there to witness the swearing in of the new President, but as Craven recalls, "When we finally got there, the only thing we got was Air
Force One taxiing. It was all buttoned up." Charles Roberts, a pool reporter present
at the swearing in, described for his colleagues the scene of Johnson's taking the oath.
As the press plane would not leave for a while in order to give reporters time to file
stories, Atkins went into the terminal, bought a newspaper and remembers, "I called my
mother at home in Ohio. I wanted to talk to somebody."[52]

Wiegman was not with the press group. At the hospital he had found an
unoccupied telephone in an upper story office and had taken the opportunity to call
NBC headquarters in New York. "I told them I had given John some film, and the
fellow said, 'Terrific Dave, you're terrific.' And I really felt down because I knew I really
didn't have that much. He was just happy that something was heading to the lab and he
had heard from somebody. So I hung up and went downstairs and that was one of the
biggest shocks." The press area was empty and when Wiegman ran outside, the bus was
nowhere to be seen. "I'm standing there with my camera, and Oh, my gosh, where have
they gone? What's happened? Of course everything ran through my head. The Vice-
President came in — he got sworn in — and I missed the whole thing. It was a terrible
feeling. Up to that time the adrenaline was pumping. I was doing a story." Wiegman
ran into the street and hailed a car. A Mrs. Gonzales and her son stopped, and when
the desperate cameraman told her he had to get to Love Field, he got a ride right up to
where the press plane was parked.[53]

Once the Pan Am press charter took off from Dallas at about 4 o'clock on its
long flight to Washington, many of those aboard, particularly the photographers had
done all they could do for the time being. No Irish wake was held aboard, and little
conversation was even in evidence. Some reporters hammered away at stories in readi-
ness to be filed when the plane landed. Once airborne, Atkins took a brief film sequence of the surrounding emblazoned red cloud blanket. He remembers, "I don't think
I said a word. It was just plain quiet," while Craven echoes, "It was the quietest plane

ride I can ever remember. It was the toughest trip I have ever been on, and I was drained."[54]

Atkins's exposed rolls of film were with him, while Craven and Wiegman's films of the motorcade and the hospital scene had been handed off for development and broadcast by their Dallas affiliates. National television coverage of the assassination story had begun shortly after the shooting, with all three major networks quickly devoting full air time to the developing story, foregoing all regular scheduling and advertisements. As TV is a visual medium, and people expected to see important events almost as they transpired, the network producers craved live hook-ups and film to augment their on-the-air commentators. The Dallas-Fort Worth affiliates knew, as do all news journalists, that speed was of the essence in breaking stories. If a film was not processed and utilized fairly quickly, its value could greatly diminish. Some six months after the assassination KRLD news director Eddie Barker commented concerning the use of films that Friday, "The film was previewed as it was coming out of the processor, and if it was good, we put it on the air." The story was so big that often film was broadcast in unedited versions, so that stations could put on the air, as fast as possible, pictures for a news-craving audience.[55]

In Fort Worth WBAP received the Wiegman film from the hospital, and by about 2½ hours after the shooting, the rough film was out of the processor and ready for a network feed. In New York at about 4:05 Eastern Time anchorman Bill Ryan introduced: ". . . And now for a late report from Fort Worth-Dallas, we go to station WBAP-TV and newsman Charles Murphy." Murphy began a voice-over as the film rolled through its 2 minute and 46 second sequence.

> Here now are late unedited, unscreened films of the shooting scene in Dallas. This is the scene near the Stemmons Expressway — in front — no this is in front of the City Hall in Downtown Dallas, a mile east of the shooting scene. Heavy crowds lined the downtown street to view the presidential party. As in all of the Texas stops, there were many teenagers attracted there by the First Lady and the President. This is Main Street in Dallas. Is this moving west? — This is moving west towards the fatal moment. The motorcade is traveling about 20 to 25 miles per hour. Slowly westward down Main Street in the heart of Dallas. The time about 12:20 during the noon hour. Heavy crowds from downtown offices lining the route. That looks like the School Depository Building on the right, I'm not sure. This, this is the scene of confusion. Something has happened here. The cameraman running towards the scene for the presidential car ahead of him. We caught just a blurred glance of the old School Depository Building from which the sniper fired the shot. This is the reaction from the crowd. All is confusion at the scene. Here, a woman shelters herself. Now racing towards the hospital. . . .

Frames from the Wiegman film

Continuing to describe the scenes at the hospital, Murphy closes at the end of the film clip with, "Later films as they are developed, as they arrive here will be shown." As the film was very jerky and atypical of on-air broadcast quality, Bill Ryan, back in New York felt compelled to explain, "As Murphy pointed out to you there, that was unscreened, which meant that he saw it for the very first time, as you saw it, unedited films of what happened — some of what happened in the motorcade. If I might explain to you that blurry and confusing scene. Obviously what happened when the shots were fired, the cameraman was riding in one of the cars behind the President, very wisely kept his camera running, even as he jumped from the car and ran towards the President's car and then over towards the people who were shielding themselves, ducking down, trying to avoid what was going on. It was the only way the cameraman could have gotten you a picture of what went on. He very wisely took no time to try and align the spring on the camera, or anything else. Just keep it rolling, get as much picture as possible, and get as close as possible to the scene of action. That is what the cameraman did, that is why it looked somewhat unorthodox in terms of what we are used to seeing, and that is why it is such a precious piece of film, because the cameraman thought."[56]

For the remainder of the day and into the next, this remarkable film was periodically rebroadcast, though in a cut-down format with some 13 seconds of Wiegman's quick, jiggling run to the grassy knoll being cut out of the original 37-second-sequence at Dealey Plaza. At about midnight Eastern Time on November 22, White House Correspondent Robert MacNeil narrated an edited series of films of the day's activities, including the now cut Wiegman film. MacNeil reported, "NBC cameraman Dave Wiegman in the car ahead of us takes a passing shot of a building. Then three shots are heard like toy explosions. Wiegman jumps from his car, running towards the President with his camera running."[57]

Many of those who remember watching NBC during the Friday and Saturday coverage can still clearly recall seeing this Wiegman film, one of the only sequences telecast which represented the moments of the assassination and in its unorthodox choppiness, gave viewers the feel of confusion and anxiety. Not until later, when the Muchmore and Nix amateur films were seen by some of the public, and much later still, when the Zapruder film was broadcast in motion picture format, did the public have any real sense of the action of the event. Today with the use of electronic news-gathering and the often overuse of slow motion and freeze-frame videotape, almost instantaneous broadcasting of events is considered the norm. Many can easily recall the startling images of the assassination attempt on President Reagan, the killing of President Sadat of Egypt, or the explosion of the space shuttle *Challenger*. The use and content of the Wiegman film is now more familiar a style to audiences than it was when it was first telecast.

Television news is in the business of using film to tell a story, and no conscious consideration was made to preserve original film in its original form. The Wiegman film had seen edited use before the end of the day. An examination of network use of spot news film clearly shows that various other film clips were edited, spliced, and combined with others to give a coherence as the broadcasters saw it. Little thought was given to the potential historical value of the film itself as source material.[58] Some broadcasters did, however, have the good judgment to videotape their live telecasts.[59]

WBAP had possession of the original Wiegman film, and if normal procedures were followed, the films would eventually be shipped out to NBC in New York. Soon after the assassination NBC sold a copy of the Wiegman film (apparently the edited version) to Hearst Metrotone Newsreel, and Hearst sold broadcast rights of this film to other markets. Indeed, it was the Hearst source through which later researchers were able to obtain the film for study. During the 1978 hearings of the House Select Committee on Assassinations, the Committee staff utilized the film in its study. According to one source, the HSCA located the original film at NBC News in Los Angeles.[60]

NBC made a gift of news film and television tapes of the President Kennedy era to the Kennedy Library in 1967. Copies of the original November 22 through 23, 1963, news coverage are available at the audiovisual department of the library.[61] In 1988 during the twenty-fifth anniversary of the assassination the Arts and Entertainment cable network rebroadcast videotape of the first 4½ hours of the NBC telecast including the original Wiegman assassination clip.

The subsequent use and location of the CBS films taken by Tom Craven on the day of the assassination is even more ambiguous than that of the Wiegman film. In an interview with Craven in 1985, he recalled having taken film at the airport, during the motorcade, and at the hospital including "cleaning the blood out of the car," and of Mrs. Kennedy and the hearse leaving the hospital. He recalls filming the Newmans on the ground at the assassination scene, and remembers that in the car at the time of the shooting, "We thought it was a motorcycle backfire, but after we found out there were shots being fired in the Book Depository, I was hoping for some reason, 'cause I know I was rolling as we made that right turn coming up to the Book Depository — I thought I might have had a flash or a puff of smoke, but it never showed up, because I had a wide angle lens on, and it was so far away, you wouldn't have seen it."[62]

At mid-afternoon Dan Rather, who had raced to KRLD following the turmoil around Dealey Plaza, reported on camera, "In just a moment we hope to have films from the shooting scene just after the shooting occurred by CBS cameraman Tommy Craven, but while we see if the film is ready and can be shown to you, let's switch back to CBS News headquarters in New York."[63]

A short time later Walter Cronkite announced, "We have the first films taken in the motorcade just after the assassination shots were heard." New York switched to Rather in Dallas who did a voice-over as film was shown. "Here is the late President John F. Kennedy and Mrs. Kennedy coming down the ramp at the Dallas Airport. These films were taken slightly less than an hour-and-a-half before President Kennedy was shot and killed in a motorcade in downtown Dallas. The usual receiving line, of course, a number of Dallas dignitaries, and a lady who said that she had waited for sixty-nine years to meet a President. . . . This is part of the motorcade from the Dallas Airport toward the downtown area. Shots taken just before the shooting occurred. This is Dallas's Parkland Hospital where President Kennedy was taken after being mortally wounded. The President reportedly was alive when he reached the hospital but he died a short time after arriving at the hospital. Some efforts were made when the presidential party first arrived at the hospital to keep pictures from being taken. . . ." Additional film clips, some undoubtedly by Craven, were broadcast later that day showing more scenes of the motorcade and at Parkland Hospital.[64]

Craven's film was picked up at the hospital and taken to the CBS affiliate KRLD in Dallas. This writer has not been able to determine just what clips if any were broadcast over the network that day showing the scenes just after the shooting. A query in 1987 to Neil Waldman, director of CBS News Archives Development in New York City, elicited copies of four file cards giving a run-down of film within their archives, summarizing number of feet and camera shots made during the Texas trip with the source listed as "CBS/Craven." Unfortunately upon requesting a study copy of the Dallas segments, it was discovered that the 64 feet of 16mm black-and-white silent film of the arrival of "President and Mrs. Kennedy at Dallas Airport after their arrival from Fort Worth" is missing from the library. The scenes taken of the motorcade from the camera car is not film taken by Craven, but rather film taken by James Underwood of KRLD, filmed from Camera Car 3. Spliced with this motorcade clip are scenes at Parkland and at Dealey Plaza. Mr. Waldman indicated that "I have rechecked our files and still cannot locate the material you are interested in. . . . There is no way to be certain that all the material shot on that day was sent to the New York archives. Some of the material may have remained at KRLD with all the confusion that followed the presidential assassination. It is truly impossible to say if we ever received the material at all."[65]

The press plane ride back to Washington from Dallas on November 22, 1963, was a quiet, somber, private time for most aboard. Arriving in Washington, some of the reporters and cameramen could have a brief respite before covering the next day's events, though many continued to work through the night into the early hours of November 23. Tom Atkins went directly to the White House and remained there until the President's body was brought back to the White House at about 4:30 Eastern Time, Saturday morning. "Next morning I came into the White House, and I was so torn up, I didn't want to film. Not a good trait for a newsreel photographer." Bob Knudsen told

Atkins that Mrs. Kennedy had called saying that she wanted the funeral filmed in its entirety, and this request sent the White House photographers into action. "So I got on the hook and got five or six people, and off we went, and we made a one-hour film of the funeral." With the exception of excerpts of three eulogies delivered at the Capitol rotunda, and scenes at the cemetery, the film was shot without sound. Music was later added to the final product.[66]

Atkins remembers the moment when his emotions caught up to him, at the time he was filming the cortege leaving the White House for Capitol Hill on Sunday. "They had just put the body in the caisson and were driving out of the circular drive at the White House, and I was filming that. As I was looking through the viewfinder, the car with Mrs. Kennedy and little John-John came by. And he was up over the back of the seat and he had this strange look. I saw that and I sat down on the north lawn of the White House and just bawled my eyes out." Atkins also recalled how the events affected White House photographer Cecil Stoughton at the funeral on Monday. "They were going into the church and I saw Cecil Stoughton in my viewfinder. And I saw him just sit down and start to bawl. We've never talked about it."[67]

Atkins had the eight rolls of film he had shot on November 22, plus a number more he had made of the President's activities the day before. The film was sent over to be processed at Eastman Kodak on E Street, and Atkins decided to put together a film of the Texas trip, which he titled, "The Last Two Days." "I was then working with a young sailor who was one of my editors — John McGowan, whose father had been in the film business for years. John did the editing, and the two of us stayed up practically all one night putting the thing together. We got it out fairly quickly."

Virtually nothing has come out in print concerning Atkins and his recollections in official or research publications. In March, 1977 a tabloid publication, *Midnight*, published an article by Robert Sibley about Atkins and his film titled, "JFK Assassination Film No One Wanted To See," with a subtitle, "Three Never-Before Seen Movie Clips That Shattered the Oswald 'Lone Killer' Theory." The article is written in a sensational style typical of tabloid journalism. Claiming that the film was overlooked, "more likely they feared the visual and spoken testimony [of Atkins] would damage this neat conclusion that Lee Harvey Oswald, acting alone, killed the President. If that was their fear, they were right. . . . If the Warren Commission or the police had bothered to interview the movie maker, they would have found a witness of unquestionable integrity who would say the same thing — that the fatal shots were fired from the direction of the grassy knoll." Along with three frames from the Atkins film showing the Newman family on the ground, a sketch showing a bird's-eye view of Dealey Plaza was included with a star in a circle some 240 feet west of the nearest point of the Texas School Book Depository indicating "Commander Atkins believes that the shots fired at President Kennedy came from this direction."[68]

Some eight years after this article appeared, Atkins still bristled at its content. It turns out that the author of the piece had been hired by Atkins during the Johnson Administration as a civilian who worked at the Naval Photo Center, writing scripts for films such as on Mrs. Johnson's beautification project. Atkins describes the tabloid as a "rag," and recalls, "If I could have taken that guy to court and sued him, I would have. The article fabricated. Some people do anything for a dollar."[69] What the article did was combine some twenty-odd sentences of Atkins's quotations blocked into ten short paragraphs packed with a series of half-truths and innuendoes. Using sensational words and unsubstantiated predicates like, "It is entirely plausible," "They undoubtedly knew," "Perhaps that is why," and "It is also possible," the writer created an inaccurate impression. The reader is left with the distinct feeling that the shots came from the grassy knoll, that government investigators knew Atkins's film and testimony were contrary to what they were trying to prove, and therefore refrained from questioning him. The impression is also left that Atkins, being aware of the number of witnesses who had died mysteriously, was not eager to testify.

What Atkins does recall quite clearly is that as his car was traveling down Houston Street towards the Texas School Book Depository the "shots sounded in front of me. I didn't get the sensation that they were from up high. It sounded like in the crowd at my level. I had not even seen the grassy knoll at that point. If they were coming from anywhere, they were coming from that turn. If they had come from the grassy knoll, I don't think they would have been near as loud, because I think the buildings there tended to throw the sound at us."[70]

One of the few points the article brought out which was correct, was the fact that no one interviewed Atkins about his observations. Atkins was not alone, however, in being a cameraman ignored by investigators. Neither Wiegman nor Craven nor the other three in the car with Atkins, nor the five still photographers in the camera car behind theirs, was interviewed or questioned by any governmental agency or investigator. Atkins responds about never being questioned that he, "thought that was kind of weird. The thing is that we are all trained observers. You are trained to notice things that other people don't. It's weird that they wouldn't."[71] One photographer had an interesting response when asked why the motorcade photographers had not been questioned. He said that to officials, the cameramen were there — but they weren't there. They did a job that was somewhat invisible, going with the flow of events around them, but not fully considered to be a part of the events themselves. Although judgment is often much clearer in hindsight and without time and effort deadlines to get in the way, it appears that the investigators of the crime, primarily the FBI and Dallas police did not intensively follow up on potential photographic evidence unless it begged for consideration. The motorcade photographers for the most part simply made their pictures, sent them off, and continued to follow the story back to Washington. And the occupants of the first two camera cars simply did not think that they had witnessed anything that was critical enough to volunteer about. If the investigation had needed their help, they would know where to find them.

While much controversy has swirled around the number and direction of the shots fired that day, Wiegman, who disdains commenting on conjecture, would have told investigators if asked that, "As far as I can remember I heard three shots. I know that they were three like shots. The report was the same on the first one as it was on the third one; equidistant apart like a metronome. The only pathetic thing was that the sound was like in a gymnasium where you don't know where it is coming from. If it were directed we would have all looked up at that window, and if Oswald was indeed there, he would have been caught in the next five minutes. But it didn't have any direction to it, so he lucked out."[72]

In the 1980s Dave Wiegman retired from NBC having been in the film business for 32 years. He has seen many changes in the profession including changes in the technological state-of-the-art every three to five years from the large sound cameras of the mid-1950s to the video mini-cams of today. "When I first went out to Gettysburg with Eisenhower, I had to charter my own airplane to get the film back to Washington. By the time I [retired] there were five to six people with me. It got to be a whole team would go. I saw it go from a very exciting and interesting time to more or less a technical job. During the Kennedy years it was still in the early stages when you had to think on your feet. It was just starting to get big."[73]

Tom Craven remained with CBS until 1974, when for some eight years he did free-lance work. He went back to CBS in 1982. Craven believes that Oswald was the assassin and worked alone, but admits, "You read so many stories over the years — who knows. Our CIA is pretty funny at times, but I have no conclusions." As to his reaction to the death of the President, Craven recalls, "My feelings were very low, I knew this man. When you are covering the White House, you see the President just about every day. When traveling on vacation trips with him, you see him as a regular, every-walk-of-life man. Covering this assignment was just like any other. You get your pictures, but after it's over, you think of what's happened, and then the let-down sets in."[74]

Commenting upon the assassination theories Atkins says, "To be perfectly honest, I've never sat down and read the Warren Commission, and I don't know what exactly it says. I'm not that political-minded. I did my job, tried to stay out of the way, and be as inconspicuous as possible." Atkins remained on at the White House, and his job continued to grow. "By the time I left six years later, I had 23 people working for me. We were making anywhere from a 30- to 45-minute film per week of the official and personal activities of the First Family. We shot the wedding of the Johnson daughters and the trips, beautification [projects] and so on. So the program grew in leaps and bounds." Following his White House tour of duty, Atkins went back to the Photographic Center, working for the Navy Chief of Information, and he made films for Admiral Zumwaldt. Concerning his career, Atkins relates, "I never had a day of sea-duty. I'm first a photographer, second a Navy officer. I never thought of it as a job, and enjoyed every minute of it. The job and promotion just took care of itself." Atkins retired from the Navy as a commander moving to coastal Florida, teaching photography four or five afternoons per week at the Art Institute at Fort Lauderdale.[75]

Though only working at the Kennedy White House for some nine months, Atkins still remembers thinking of himself as a "Kennedy man," even in his service during the Johnson administration. Striking a casual observer as a reflective and sincere man,

Atkins still chokes up at times when remembering November 1963. In a thoughtful moment he recalled one private memory of the President. "Two weeks prior to the day he was buried in Arlington, it was Veterans' Day. And I went with him to the Tomb of the Unknown. He had John-John with him, and I made a little ten-minute film going into the cemetery. John-John gets out and cavorts and plays with the guys with the guns, and they walk over and go through the whole [ceremony]. And I end it with the *Navy Hymn* and a lot of shots at Arlington. It was that day Kennedy made the statement, 'I could spend eternity here.'

"The following Monday I had the finished film and I showed it to him in his office between 11 and 12. He sat there in the rocker, and I stood behind him and the hairdresser came in and was doing his hair. I remember looking at that long hair, and what nice hair he had — as he was watching that film. And the following Monday he was buried at Arlington. Those three Mondays. And to see pictures of the autopsy and what the bullet had done to the hair — I was admiring. Those are things that just stick in your memory."[76]

In a letter written shortly after the twenty-fifth anniversary of the death of President Kennedy, Atkins reminisced, "I guess the wounds of that day will never quite heal. The hospital scene and the caisson leaving the White House still tugs heavily at my emotions. I wish this event had never happened, but it did; and if I had to be somewhere in the world that day, and I did, I'm glad that I was in Dallas. If only I could have done something — anything, to alter the outcome, instead of merely recording it."[77]

## CHAPTER NOTES

1. Gary Paul Gates, *Air Time: The Inside Story of CBS News*, p.5.
2. Raymond Fielding, *The American Newsreel*, p. 5-6, 16, 25.
3. Ibid., p. 37, 49.
4. Ibid., p. 212-214.
5. Ibid., p. 215-219.
6. Ibid., p. 275.
7. Gates, op. cit., p. 55-57, 70-71.
8. Ibid., p. 5; Fielding, op.cit., p.309.
9. John B. Mayo, Jr., *Bulletin From Dallas: The President Is Dead*, p. 19; Richard K. Van Der Karr, *Crisis In Dallas*, p.1. Van Der Karr's 1965 masters thesis is an excellent study of the three Dallas television stations' operations and procedures during November, 1963.
10. Ibid., Mayo, p. 19; Van Der Karr, p. 3-9.
11. Ibid., Mayo, p. 12-21, 139; Van Der Karr, p. 4-5; Telephone interview of Thomas J. Craven, Jr., 5/23/1985.
12. Telephone interview of Craven, 5/23/1985; Questionnaire filled out by Craven, 4/1985.
13. Ibid.
14. Telephone interview of Dave Wiegman, Jr., 3/18/1989.
15. Ibid.

16.    Ibid.
17.    Telephone interview of Craven, 5/23/1985.
18.    Telephone interview of Thomas M. Atkins, 3/19/1986.
19.    Ibid.
20.    Ibid.
21.    Ibid.
22.    Ibid.
23.    Ibid.
24.    Ibid.
25.    Atkins film, roll #5, 11/22/1963.
26.    Telephone interview of Craven, 5/23/1985.
27.    Telephone interview of Atkins, 3/19/1986; Telephone interview of Craven, 5/23/1985; Telephone interview of Wiegman, 3/18/1989; William Manchester, *Death of a President*, p. 130-131.
28.    Hugh Sidey, *John F. Kennedy, President*, (Crest Reprint) p. 389. At about the same time Atkins took his film showing Powers with his camera, White House photographer Cecil Stoughton also snapped a picture of a smiling Powers holding his camera.
29.    *Hearings Before the President's Commission on the Assassination of President Kennedy*, v. 18, p. 753; Hearst news film frame from Dave Hawkins collection (S-535).
30.    Letter, Dave Powers to Trask, 3/28/1989.
31.    Telephone interview of Craven, 5/23/1985.
32.    Telephone interview of Wiegman, 3/18/1989.
33.    Ibid.
34.    Atkins film, roll #5 & 6, 11/22/1963.
35.    Telephone interview of Atkins, 3/19/1986; Telephone interview of Craven, 5/23/1985.
36.    Telephone interview of Wiegman, 3/18/1989.
37.    Audiotape of Westinghouse "Group W" radio program, "Dialogue on Dallas" 12/1963; Telephone interview of Wiegman, 3/18/1989.
38.    Gary Mack, *Coverups!*, 9/1982, p. 2-5; 9/1985, p. 1-2; Letter, Richard Sprague to Robert Cutler, 10/31/1982.
39.    Videotape of NBC television coverage, 11/22/1963 at Kennedy Library (TNN 255-4); Telephone interview of Wiegman, 3/18/1989. The last woman Wiegman filmed at the scene of the shooting has been tentatively identified as Cheryl McKinnon by a caption appearing in *Coverups!*, 7/1984, p.1. A copy of the unedited Wiegman film at the Kennedy Library, and a copy provided the author by permission of NBC News, were both examined.
40.    Telephone interview of Craven, 5/23/1985; Questionnaire filled out by Craven, 4/1985.
41.    Telephone interview of Atkins, 3/19/1986.
42.    Telephone interview of Craven, 5/23/1985.
43.    Telephone interview of Atkins, 3/19/1986.
44.    Mayo, op. cit., p. 130-131.
45.    Telephone interview of Atkins, 3/19/1986; Questionnaire filled out by Craven, 4/1985; Videotape of NBC television coverage, 11/22/1963 at Kennedy Library (TNN 255:5).
46.    Telephone interview of Wiegman, 3/18/1989; Telephone interview of Craven, 5/23/1985.
47.    Telephone interview of Atkins, 3/19/1986; Atkins film, roll #6, 7, 8, 11/22/1963.
48.    Telephone interview of Craven, 5/23/1985.
49.    Telephone interview of Wiegman, 3/18/1989.
50.    Videotape of NBC television coverage, 11/22/1963 at Kennedy Library (TNN 255:2).
51.    James H. Winchester, "TV's Four Days of History," *Readers' Digest*, 4/1964, p. 204J; Telephone interview of Wiegman, 3/18/1989.
52.    Telephone interview of Craven, 5/23/1985; Telephone interview of Atkins, 3/19/1986.

53.     Telephone interview of Wiegman, 3/18/1989.

54.     Questionnaire filled out by Craven, 4/1985; Telephone interview of Atkins, 3/19/1986.

55.     Mayo, op. cit., appendix A.

56.     Videotape of NBC television coverage, 11/22/1963 (TNN 255:4).

57.     Videotape of NBC television coverage, 11/22/1963 (TNN 255:17).

58.     Harold Weisberg, *Photographic Whitewash*, p. 274-275.

59.     Dallas station WFAA went on the air with the story about fifteen minutes after the shooting. After reading an AP bulletin on camera, program director Jay Watson said to one of the station crew, "Bobby lets tape this if you please, particularly the interview of the eyewitness people. It is being taped? — good." The WFAA videotape of its broadcast that day is very dramatic television.

60.     *Coverups!*, 9/1985, p. 2.

61.     *New York Times*, 5/5/1967, p. 78.

62.     Telephone interview of Craven, 5/23/1985.

63.     CBS broadcast transcript, 11/22/1963, p. 54.

64.     Ibid., p. 58-59, 151.

65.     Letter, Neil Waldman to Trask, 7/29/1987. Researcher Richard Sprague claims to have been able to see the Craven film during his research in the 1967-68 period. He indicated that in the Craven sequence he could see a white car parked behind the pergola which vehicle drove away down the Elm Street extension. He was later told that the Craven film was moved to a storage vault in New Jersey, and that access to that vault was not available to him. Further communications to Mr. Waldman by the author concerning the original film's possible location have proved fruitless. At least one sequence of the motorcade taken from Craven's car traveling on Main Street and looking towards the President's car, and a scene at Parkland Hospital appear to be from the Craven film. These two brief clips were shown on *The CBS Evening News with Dan Rather* during a November, 1983 series about the anniversary of the Kennedy assassination.

66.     Telephone interview of Atkins, 3/19/1986.

67.     Ibid.

68.     *Midnight*, 3/1/1977.

69.     Telephone interview of Atkins, 3/19/1986.

70.     Ibid.

71.     Ibid.

72.     Telephone interview of Wiegman, 3/18/1989.

73.     Ibid.

74.     Telephone interview of Craven, 5/23/1985; Questionnaire filled out by Craven, 4/1985.

75.     Telephone interview of Atkins, 3/19/1986.

76.     Ibid.

77.     Letter, Atkins to Trask, 3/2/1989.

CHAPTER 16

# Camera Car 2

Besides the driver, there were five occupants of the second camera car in the Dallas motorcade of November 22, 1963. Whenever the President traveled, his activities and footsteps were shadowed as closely as possible by numerous reporters and photographers. During presidential motorcades and processions, photographic representatives of the national and local press were always assigned cars, usually convertibles for ease of picture-making, which followed closer and had better access to the President's vehicle than the gaggle of press, mostly print people, who followed up typically in press busses far behind in the motorcade convoy. The movie people would occupy one car, while the still photographers, including a representative of each of the two major wire services, would be located in another.

As was customary, the positions of the still and movie car were switched at each new event, to keep equitable the small but sometimes photographically significant distance advantage to the Chief Executive's car. On that Friday morning of November 22, the President had already participated in one motorcade, traveling from the Hotel Texas in Fort Worth to Carswell Air Force Base, where he and his party boarded Air Force One for the short flight to Love Field in Dallas. During the Fort Worth motorcade the still camera car had been in front of the movie car, so in Dallas their positions would be reversed.

The Dallas motorcade, as it actually ran, had the second camera car in which the still photographers rode as the seventh vehicle behind the presidential Lincoln. In this camera car were some of the nation's top news photographers.

Always present at major scheduled news happenings were representatives of the nation's chief news wire services — Associated Press and United Press International. Whereas weekly and daily publications had specific news deadlines, those deadlines usually gave their reporters a margin of flexibility to observe and put their story together. The wire services measured themselves and were only as good as the speed and accuracy it took to report a breaking news story. Newspapers, government agencies, radio and television stations throughout the country subscribed to one or the other or sometimes to both teletype news sources for up-to-the-minute information. Competition between the two wire services was real and constant. A scoop of a major story was a coveted prize, and sending breaking news to one's subscribers and beating out the competition, even by only a few seconds, was a worthy goal. AP and UPI as a matter of course had reporters and cameramen close to the President.  On the Texas trip dean UPI White House reporter Merriman Smith and AP's Jack Bell, whose normal beat was Congress and who had been reassigned for this trip, kept as close as possible to the President.  In the Dallas motorcade they would share space in a telephone car some five vehicles behind and the nearest civilian car to the President's.  When shots were heard, Smith was closest to the car's mobile telephone and grabbing it would quickly send to his bureau a brief report of shots being fired, followed by a struggle of sorts between Bell and Smith over access to the radio phone.

Both wire services also sent along on the Texas trip two veteran Washington-based photographers.  Frank Cancellare was born in Brooklyn, New York, in 1910.  After high school he broke into the news photographer business beginning as a "squeegee boy" in a darkroom for Acme News Photos.  A colleague would later reminisce about Cancellare, "As a young man, Mr. Cancellare elbowed his way into the very front rank of news photographers, and his assignments reflected his skill: the China-Burma-India theater and the making of the Burma Road during World War II, Capitol Hill, the White House under every president from Franklin D. Roosevelt. . . .  His most famous picture was a grinning Harry Truman holding aloft the copy of the *Chicago Daily Tribune* that wrongly proclaimed the Democratic President had been defeated in the 1948 election by Republican Governor Thomas E. Dewey of New York."[1]

Cancellare's famous photo
of President Truman

"Cancy," had begun his photo career using bulky Speed Graphic cameras which had to be reloaded after each picture. The slowness of the process taught an economy in making pictures, and the need to preplan shots when possible. Photographers prior to the motor-driven-camera days used to try and get one good usable overall shot of an event, and when this was "in the bag," they could then wait for an even more dramatic opportunity.  Fiercely competitive as a professional, "Cancy" was also a likable man who willingly gave photo advice to younger colleagues. He enjoyed his job and its challenges, and acquired a number of professional tricks like presetting the focus where a famous or notorious person trying to avoid cameras was about to walk by, and yelling "Hey!" and their name as they went past. Often the technique snagged a memorable shot.  He could sometimes scoop up a singular shot at staged photo opportunities upon getting a good photograph for himself by firmly saying, "Thank you," which often broke up a photo session with "Cancy" having his picture.

By the 1960s Cancellare was seldom using the Speed Graphic cameras, exchanging them for the smaller format cameras with roll film. Yet his background had taught him to make a few good, thought-out pictures, rather than shoot rolls of shots made with the idea that among the many, a few would be usable. He often said to younger colleagues, "The camera doesn't make the picture, the photographer does."[2] White House photographer Cecil Stoughton, who also rode in the Dallas car with Cancellare, later said of him, "He was UPI's best. I was proud to be with him,"[3] while one of Cancellare's professional rivals, Henry Burroughs of AP was at the same time one of Cancellare's best friends.

Associated Press photographer Henry Burroughs was also present in Camera Car 2 in Dallas. Born in August of 1918, in Washington, D.C., and educated at Baltimore Polytechnic Institute, Henry Dashiell Burroughs had joined AP in 1944.[4] Concerning his professional background, Burroughs would later relate, "I covered the White House off and on during the last months of FDR, then was assigned to Paris and Berlin as post-war correspondent covering the Nuremburg trials, the Berlin airlift and other major stories. I returned to Washington in 1949 and covered the White House on a monthly rotation basis with several other AP photographers, covering Truman, Eisenhower, and Kennedy."[5]

Washington-based still and movie cameramen who were assigned to the White House generally worked on a rotation basis, and Burroughs's schedule was typical. For one month he would be the AP staffer assigned to the White House, and before his next White House stint he would do other general assignments, augmenting White House coverage during active news periods or on presidential trips. Wire service photographers didn't process their own film, but would send it in to their bureau to be developed and printed. They would send captions along with the film, but "an editor would look at the film and choose the picture he wanted to use, and then he would write the final formal caption and transmit it on the wirephoto."[6]

Burroughs was the only Washington-based AP photographer on the Texas trip, and he relied on local AP bureau people for support. The local bureau would provide couriers to pick up film and process it locally. In light of the earlier harassment of Adlai Stevenson by right wing pickets in Dallas just weeks before the President's trip, AP city Bureau Chief Bob Johnson had decided to assign his local people to as many spots as possible at Love Field, the Trade Mart where Kennedy was to speak, and along the motorcade route. Peggy Simpson was assigned to the downtown area and instructed to follow the motorcade on foot as best she could and to break away to a phone if heckling was observed. Wirephoto operator and photographer Jim Altgens was stationed with his camera at the corner of Houston and Main Street. For the Kennedy visit, Johnson had four editors at the office, including news photo editor Dave Taylor and night editor Ron Thompson. Extra teletype operators were also on hand.[7]

Accompanying Burroughs, Cancellare, and Stoughton on board the press plane which flew ahead of Air Force One to Love Field so that the press would be there to record the President's arrival, was *LIFE* magazine staff photographer Arthur Burroughs Rickerby. More flexible with deadlines than the wire service reps, Rickerby represented the most important and largest format photo news magazine in history. The name "*LIFE* magazine" was immediately recognizable and respected by the average citizen, and

*LIFE*'s stories and photo layouts of astronauts, warfare, the American scene, and photo essays were popular enough to make the 27-year old magazine a household word.

Arthur Rickerby was a native of New York City, having been born there in March 1921. Receiving a B.S. from Duke University and having served in the Navy during World War II, Rickerby had eventually become a staff photographer for *LIFE* magazine, including work in political and sports coverage. In March, 1963, he had won first prize competition in the White House Photographers' Association competition with a portrait of Senate Minority Leader Everett Dirksen, and had himself been photographed receiving congratulations from President Kennedy.[8] Rickerby had been assigned to cover the Texas trip for *LIFE* magazine, as the trip was seen by many as the first major political sojourn of the President gearing up for the 1964 election. It was also the first political trip taken by Mrs. Kennedy since the death of her child Patrick.

Rickerby generally used 35mm cameras, which was the staple format for *LIFE* magazine, and he was partial to Nikon bodies with an assortment of lenses.[9] He worked both in color and in black-and-white as both types could be used by *LIFE*. *TIME* magazine, *LIFE*'s older sister news publication might also utilize Rickerby's photos, although their format was almost exclusively black-and-white.[10]

Burroughs used two standard, though slightly modified Rolleiflex cameras on the Texas trip, while Cancellare had a Rolleiflex and a Nikon, both cameras on straps around his neck. Both men used black-and-white Tri-X ASA 400 film as color was not useful for wire photo transmissions. Cancellare normally kept his shutter set at 1/250 second with an F8 aperture.[11] The Rolleiflex twin lens reflex camera is a bit more bulky than the 35mm cameras, and does not generally take interchangeable lenses. Many professional photographers liked the "Rollei" however for its fine viewing system and the large negative size which affords crisper enlargements. A reliable and simple camera to operate, the Rollei took 120 negative film on which 12 exposures could be made; each 2¼ inches square. Cancellare had a flash unit attached to his Rolleiflex.

Following the official receiving line, President and Mrs. Kennedy walk towards the fence area.

Landing at Love Field shortly after 11:30, Burroughs discovered that the photographers' cars were farther back from the presidential car than was normally the case, due to the presence of the Vice-President, his follow-up car, and a politician's vehicle behind that. "The advance guys who set up the motorcade were more interested in the politics of the thing. We screamed, of course, as soon as we got off the plane, but it was too late to do anything." Upon the arrival of President and Mrs. Kennedy the photographers recorded yet another presidential arrival, as well as the fairly extemporaneous wending of the President and the First Lady along a waist-high fence separating an exuberant crowd from the First Couple, who shook as many outstretched hands as possible.  More shots were snapped of the couple getting into the gleaming Lincoln convertible, and then it was a rush by the press to their own transportation.

Stoughton got into the rear driver's side of the silver '64 Chevrolet Impala convertible perching on the fold-away convertible boot.  Rickerby, in a light-colored topcoat, and clutching his over-the-shoulder gear bag, sat next to Stoughton, while Burroughs got in the far right side.

To the rear of the still camera car was a third convertible car reserved for local Dallas film and still photographers.  Clint Grant, a staff photographer of the *Dallas Morning News*, went over to this third car, but found it full, whereupon he was invited into Camera Car 2.  He was given space in the middle front seat between the Stetson-clad Department of Public Safety driver and Cancellare.[12]

Born in Nashville, Tennessee, in 1916, Donald Clinton Grant had been offered a press photographer's job with the *Dallas Morning News* in March of 1941.  Called "Clint" by his friends, Grant was offered the job even though the paper had a policy of not hiring relatives of personnel on the payroll. Clint's father, Don, was producing the rotogravure section of the paper, but due to losing their photographers to military service, the paper's hiring policy was slackened. The position never materialized, however, as the younger Grant was drafted into the Army Engineers a month before starting work for the paper.

Bringing his Graflex camera with him to his first military assignment in Missouri, Grant fed to the Dallas paper many pictures of the various local boys going through training. Over a year later, and after three months at officer's school, Grant left with his unit for England aboard the ship *Queen Elizabeth* in July, 1943.  Recalls Grant, "I was never to see a camera again for the remainder of the war." Days after the allied invasion at Normandy, Grant's engineer unit landed in France to begin working on vital supply links including installing pipe lines, storage tanks, and pumping stations.  In late 1945, after receiving five battle stars and the rank of captain, Grant returned to Dallas. So did the other former *Dallas Morning News* staff photographers, and Grant's embryonic job was no longer available.

For four years Grant managed a local photo studio, but when a position finally opened on the paper in 1949, he jumped at the opportunity.  During the next decade Grant covered all phases of press photography, though his best known work was in features, and he developed a reputation as a fine animal and child photographer.  Over the years five of his shots were picked up by *LIFE* magazine, and printed on their popular "Miscellany" page, and he occasionally contributed to *TIME*, *Newsweek*, *Saturday Evening Post*, and other national periodicals.[13]

Grant, like all photographers "worth their salt," had his own set of tricks for catching the right photo.  When trying to capture camera avoiders on film he would sometimes ". . . preset my 4" x 5" Graphic with 135mm lens, pull my slide and pretend not to aim my camera.  Then at the decisive moment, I'd shoot from the hip.  If they objected too strenuously, I would remove the film on the other side of the holder, hand it to him and say, 'no hard feelings?' meanwhile retaining the exposed side. A really good news photographer should be able to shoot many types of photos without putting an eye to the viewfinder and focusing."[14]

Grant used a Speed Graphic until about 1960 when he switched over to a Rolleiflex. The Kennedy tour was his first assignment using a 35mm camera, and Grant carried two Nikon F single lens reflex cameras, one mounted with a 35mm lens and the other with a telephoto 105mm lens. He generally used black-and-white Tri-X film and carried a couple of additional lenses.

Several days prior to the President's Texas trip, Grant had been assigned to fly to Washington to meet with *Dallas Morning News* Washington Bureau Chief Bob Baskin. They were to interview and photograph the Texas congressional delegation for updating file material, and then accompany the presidential party to Texas. Grant also remembers that while in the capital, they did a piece on White House Press Secretary Pierre Salinger.

One of a series of photos Grant
took of the Chamber breakfast

The only Dallas newspaper photographer to make the Texas journey from its origin, Grant accompanied the press corps at the visits to San Antonio and Houston, having been assigned space with the other photographers on the trip. Grant recalls the late arrival of the presidential party to Fort Worth the night of November 21, following a grueling day's schedule. "Much to my chagrin, I had developed diarrhea and had difficulty finding a drug store open. It was after 3:00 [a.m.] before I got to bed." The next morning Grant was up early to shoot the Fort Worth events including the President addressing a friendly crowd in a parking lot, followed by the Chamber of Commerce breakfast. He then accompanied the motorcade to Carswell where he boarded the press plane, taking one photo of the cabin interior. Upon the presidential arrival at Love Field in Dallas, Grant took a number of photos of the airport reception including one sequence of seven frames following the President's walking down the gangway and being greeted by the official party. Working with both his cameras, Grant also took a shot which

Grant then covered the Love Field landing.

showed the President and Mrs. Kennedy, the Vice-President and Mrs. Johnson, and Governor and Mrs. Connally all in one frame.[15]

Grant had just seated himself in Camera Car 2 when the motorcade was off. Henry Burroughs remembers it as a "typical motorcade, a really nice day with a lot of people in the sidewalks," and that he "may have taken a couple of pictures during the motorcade for the record, but nothing very interesting because the President wasn't in the picture. AP wouldn't use a picture of just the crowds, because I know we probably had a photographer somewhere along the line making a parade picture." Rickerby

As the motorcade travels down Main Street, Tom Dillard in Camera Car 3 shoots a picture of the scene including Camera Car 2 in the foreground and Officer Marrion L. Baker on the cycle.

had a fresh roll of Kodak Tri-X black-and-white film in one of his cameras, on which was mounted a wide-angle lens. He had made one exposure of a crowd of people on the street behind a rope barrier as his first shot on the roll.[16]

Grant recalls that "The crowds were much larger than at the other stops and cheered all along the route." Using one of his two Nikons, Grant takes one shot of spectators in the outskirts of the business district with a youth on the trunk of a parked car holding a sign reading "Hi." On his same new roll of film at exposure #6, Grant makes a single shot of the motorcade cars to his front as they travel down Main Street near the Adolphus Hotel. "All the time I was thinking, 'Thank goodness I'll be able to relax.' I knew we were well covered by the rest of our photo staff who would be along the route and at the Trade Mart. I was still feeling lousy." The photo department at the *Dallas Morning News* was run by Tom Dillard who was traveling in Camera Car 3 with the other local press. His staff consisted of seven photographers, all but two of whom were sent out to cover the President's visit. The two not on coverage were back at the paper ready to process film as it was sent back by pre-hired messengers.[17]

After traveling through the downtown district, the head of the motorcade was nearing the freeway that would take them to the scene of the noon luncheon. Some 22 years later Burroughs described his recollection of the events surrounding the assassination scene: "At the time of the shooting the President's car was out of our sight. It was around the bend at the Book Depository. It had already made the turn, and we hadn't. The first notion that I had that something was definitely wrong, was to see looking across the park [Dealey Plaza to his left], to see the Secret Service car disappearing, and there was an agent standing in the back with an automatic weapon of some sort raised. That was very unusual. You never saw them display their weapons at all, so I knew something serious had happened. It wasn't just the local high school drill team firing a salute or something. My recollection was hearing four shots. It went something like this, 'Pow' — and we were sort of frozen — didn't know — brought everybody to attention. There was quite a pause and then there was 'Pow, Pow, Pow,' that's the way I remembered it. The last three were in quick succession. Similar noises, echoing around the buildings. After the first shot somebody said, 'What was that — a Texas salute?' or something like that. But then when the other shots rang out — when I saw the Queen Mary [Secret Service follow-up car] taking off with an agent showing his automatic weapon, I knew that something serious had happened."[18]

Of the same scene Grant remembers "Driving down Main Street, we had just turned onto Houston Street when we heard one shot — pause — two shots in rapid succession. I thought it was someone playing a prank — maybe a kid's cherry bomb. Consequently, I gave it no more thought until we turned onto Elm Street and saw all the people prone on the ground."[19]

Rickerby described the scene to his local Connecticut town newspaper in a telephone interview the next morning. "We heard what sounded like a giant firecracker go off. With that, we saw people diving to the ground, covering up their children, or scurrying up the banks. We saw Secret Service men, running with drawn guns, and thought they were chasing someone. We saw the President's car immediately speed up and take off up a rampway, and figured that something had happened serious enough to get the President out of the area, still not even thinking that he had been shot."[20]

The camera car had by now turned left onto Elm Street, slowing down to a crawl. Three movie cameramen in the first camera car had jumped out of their vehicle heading in the direction to the right of the road where the four Newman family members, husband, wife, and two children, had sprawled to the grass during the shots. Cancellare followed his instinct, and jumped from his position in the front seat of Camera Car 2, and ran towards the direction of the activity.

Shortly before his death in 1985, Cancellare recounted his instinctive movement: "I did not know what had happened. I knew something had been attempted and the police and Secret Service were doing all they could. People were throwing themselves on top of their children to protect them. Police ran their bikes up the bank towards the railroad overpass. I thought they were chasing the culprit, and I think they thought so also. Training and instinct took over at this time. During something like this no two react the same way. If I had made a shot of the man who I thought had done the shooting, I would have been the only one who had got the picture of him. I would have had a beat and a hero to boot. If the others had gotten to the hospital in time to make [pictures] of Kennedy being carried into the hospital, I would have looked stupid and made a poor decision. As it was, it was a stand-off. I probably would make the same decision again — who knows?"[21]

Burroughs remembers hearing four shots. Stoughton and Grant distinctly recall only three; while Rickerby's widow, Wanda, only recalls that "He often stated his disagreement with the number of shots that were reported in the press."[22]   Burroughs continues his recollection: "We came up to the scene of the shooting and people were running all over the place.  Cancellare got out there and there was a policeman running, as I recall, up the hill and Cancy followed him, and we just took off — my feeling was my job was to find the President, not who had done the shooting or whatever, but find out what happened to the President."[23]

Cancellare's first photo of the knoll area

The ground activities of the dark-complexioned and bespectacled Cancellare, after he jumped out of the car, are well documented in the pictures of other photographers. Crossing the sidewalk to the grass forecourt of the north pergola area, Cancy then scurried in a southwesterly direction towards the people lying on the ground near where some cameramen were already filming.  Just north of a metal two-legged Stemmons Freeway sign, Cancellare paused and took a picture of the activity ahead of him.  His photographic negative shows the activity to his southwest, including the grass area in the foreground sloping upwards to his right and upon which are sprawled out near the sidewalk the Newman family of four, three of whom are visible. Closer to Cancellare's position is a woman propped on hands and knees. NBC cameraman Dave Wiegman, wearing a hat, and White House cameraman Tom Atkins are filming the family, while to their right Dallas AP photographer Jim Altgens is beginning to walk in an opposite direction from Cancellare.

In the road two motorcycle cops are riding down Elm Street towards the underpass. These officers are undoubtedly H. B. McLain on the far side and J. W. Courson on the near side. They had been assigned duty on the left side of the motorcade and were located somewhere around vehicles 9 and 12 respectively in the line of parade prior to the shots being fired. On the opposite side of Elm Street a man in a light jacket is seen standing, apparently holding in his hands and close to his chest what appears to be some sort of a sign. Assassination photographic researcher Richard Sprague has written that the sign says, "S. O. B. Jack Kennedy,"[24] although this author has not been able to confirm this by examination of a good quality print. Portions of both Main and Commerce Streets as they enter the underpass are observable in the picture, and 11 vehicles can be counted on Commerce Street, at least some of which are stopped and with three persons out of their vehicles looking towards Elm Street. One man standing adjacent to the concrete column which supports the Main and Commerce Street underpass is James T. Tague. Tague later reported to authorities that he had felt a sting on his face and discovered blood on his cheek, quite possibly as a result of material kicked up from the impact of a bullet fragment hitting a surface. On the embankment behind the railroad tracks, opposite Cancellare's position, and in the background of the picture, is a parking lot filled with cars. At least one assassination buff believes to have located just to the right of a tree near the parking lot what he sees and identifies as ". . . a distinct figure clearly resembling a man holding a rifle-like object."[25] Above the swarm of confused activity a lone bird, its wings flapping in flight, is caught by the lens of Cancellare's Rolleiflex.[26]

As the movie film photographers leave the grass area to get back to their car, Cancellare rushes to position himself for a good shot of the family on the ground. Planting his feet firmly on the ground and crouching to steady his camera, Cancy makes a shot of this dramatic scene. Gail Newman looks at Cancellare while huddling her four-year-old son Billy in her arms. Bill Newman, to Gail's left, has his hands protectively on his two-year-old son Clayton's shoulders, as Clayton, looking bewildered, stares at the photographer. Bill Newman was a 22-year-old electrician going to begin a new job that next week. He and his wife had favored Nixon in the last election, but wanted a chance to see President Kennedy. They had gone out to Love Field for a glimpse of the President and Mrs. Kennedy, unfortunately forgetting their 8mm movie camera at home. Due to the crowds at the airport, they did not see much. The couple then decided to attempt another view on the parade route, and had quickly gone downtown and parked their car in the lot behind the Texas School Book Depository Building and decided on this position as a good one, as it was devoid of crowds. They had been only about 15 feet away from the President's car when the head shot hit him, and seeming to be caught in crossfire, Bill had turned to Gail and yelled, "That's it. Hit the ground." Mr. Newman would later tell researchers that his reaction was not due to hearing a noise behind him but rather from seeing the President's head open up before him. None of the numerous camera people who rapidly turned their attention to the Newmans, and took many quick pictures of their reaction, knew that the President had in fact been shot, but the Newmans knew that fact all too well.[27]

Bill and Gail Newman protect their children.

Cancellare's photo incidentally captured on film the back side of Jim Altgens, now on the sidewalk curb, as well as the feet of spectators on the opposite side of Elm Street. Dignitary Car 2, a convertible carrying congressmen wearing hats and hatless Presidential Assistant Larry O'Brien is seen coming down Elm Street from the left.[28]

Both of these Cancellare photographs would within hours be transmitted over the UPI telephoto circuit to be used in newspapers around the country in late edition Friday and Saturday papers. Captions would include "Looking for Cover," and "Press Children to Ground." As Cancellare was making these dramatic pictures of the Newmans, his ride was passing him by.

From his position in Camera Car 2, Cecil Stoughton took the first in what would be several other photographers' sequences  of grassy knoll pictures of the Newman family. Art Rickerby, using his 35mm camera, turned right and snapped a shot of the

Grant snags a shot from the Camera Car.

five grassy knoll cameramen, just as CBS's Tom Craven began to run off the grass towards the sidewalk. Clint Grant then also turned right to make a shot as Atkins begins to run after Craven, who is now on the sidewalk. AP photographer Jim Altgens, Grant's brother-in-law, is seen on the sidewalk, camera in hand, looking towards Grant who after taking this picture hollered at the photographers, "We'd better get going and catch up with the President." Rickerby wound his camera, turned his torso harder to the right and snapped an additional shot showing Cancellare now quite by himself as Atkins and Wiegman, trying to get back to their car, distance themselves from the Newmans. On the extreme right background of this Rickerby photo, the southwest corner of the Texas School Book Depository looms over the scene.[29]

This second Rickerby photograph was later examined in an attempt to identify one of the two men sitting by the curb at the extreme right of the picture. This man, known to researchers over the years as the "umbrella man," was sporting an open umbrella at the time of the assassination — activity which many found suspicious. In 1978 the House Select Committee on Assassinations released a photographically enhanced blowup of this man taken from the Rickerby photograph as well as other pictures, ". . . in the hopes that citizen recognition . . . might shed light on the assassination. Those recognizing any of the men depicted were asked to contact the Committee by mail."[30] Shortly thereafter the identity of this man in the Rickerby photograph was made, and the self-identified man appeared before the Committee to explain his activity. Mrs. Rickerby recalls that her husband told her that the FBI had made a mural-sized blowup of this picture "in an attempt to find evidence of a second assassin."[31]

The photographers aboard Camera Car 2 didn't want to stay at the scene, but rather wanted to find where the President had gone. The driver, a Texas Ranger from Austin, wasn't sure what to do. Burroughs relates what happened:

> Cecil Stoughton had to really get him to get out of the motorcade. He didn't want to budge. We were yelling at him to get out and

Rickerby takes two frames of activity on the knoll.

to follow the President's car when things stopped. And Cecil pulled out his credentials and really spoke to him in a very authoritative way and got him to move. The President's car had disappeared by the time we got out of the motorcade. So we took off and went to the Trade Mart, and found out immediately that there was no President's car there. It was obvious that they were waiting for him to arrive. At some point [Grant] spotted a friend in the motorcade, and he said to the guy, and the guy just looked at him — the photographer said, "Did they go to Parkland?" And the guy just sort of gave the nod, he couldn't tell, but he stated that that was right, and that's when we went to Parkland.[32]

Grant recalls the sequence of getting to the hospital from a slightly different perspective. "Still not sure the President had been shot, we proceeded with my giving directions to the Trade Mart. We saw no cars, no activity. We stopped and I asked a couple standing at the door if the President was inside. They said they didn't think so." Thinking that the site of the visit might have been changed to Market Hall across the street, Grant told the driver to go there. "We saw a workman and I asked if the President's car had pulled in there. He said a limo with motorcycle escort and sirens, going at a fast rate of speed had passed. I said, 'They're headed for Parkland, let's get going.' We turned to go back to Industrial [the street between the Trade Mart and Market Hall]. Lo and behold here was the whole convoy behind and facing us. Needless to say it was a grand traffic jam for a couple of minutes. Finally getting untangled, we made it quickly to Parkland."[33]

Meanwhile, Cancellare had seen his ride depart. He walked further down Elm Street where a motorcycle cop had left his bike and had run up the embankment by the railroad bridge looking for the culprit. People in the immediate area were streaming across the street and up the embankment, and Cancellare made a picture of 15 spectators peering over the bridge's concrete guardrail and adjoining stockade fence, while the cop in white helmet and black boots stood on the top of the concrete support for a better view. Going around to the parking lot behind the stockade fence, Cancellare took another picture which showed individuals and clusters of people walking without apparent direction among the vehicles and in front of two Missouri-Kansas-Texas passenger cars poised for use by commuting Dallasite businessmen at the end of the workday. Some 57 black and white men, women, and children are identifiable in this photo. Cancellare also made a shot looking towards Elm Street from the grassy knoll area depicting a crowd of people crossing to his side of the street, with the peristyle, the old Court House, the steel construction skeleton of the new County Court House, and the Terminal Annex Post Office Building on Houston Street all visible in the background.[34]

Cancellare could see that newsworthy activity here was dying out, and that the story now was with the President — wherever he was. And he was the only one of his

Officer Haygood stands upon the concrete railroad bridge while other spectators, including NBC correspondent Robert MacNeil (fourth from left looking towards camera), look in various directions.

Washington photographers' circle who was now stuck here. Getting a ride to the police road block on Stemmons Freeway, Cancellare identified himself and shortly met up with local photographer Robert Jackson of the *Dallas Times Herald*, who had also jumped out of the motorcade at Dealey Plaza. The two of them hitched another ride to Parkland Hospital.[35]

Over two decades later Frank Cancellare could still vividly remember the ride to the hospital. "I did not think the President was hit until we were halfway to the hospital, when we stopped to ask directions. A policeman told us the President was hit. From then all the rest of the way to the hospital I got a stomach pain. I had the worst bellyache I ever had in my life on the ride. The pressure was so great."[36] As a citizen, Cancellare was concerned about the condition of his President, and as a news photographer, he was concerned about what spot pictures he might have missed, and that his colleagues might have scooped him.

After having left the Trade Mart complex, Camera Car 2 made for Parkland Hospital. According to Rickerby, ". . . Upon arrival we saw a guard around the President's car. It was then we learned the President and Governor Connally had been shot. We were all shook."[37] Unable to get inside, Rickerby and the other photographers present began taking pictures of the scene. Rickerby used his camera mounted with telephoto and wide-angle lenses to record the outside events around the emergency room entrance. He took some 27 frames depicting among others, the gathering curious crowd, many of them becoming emotional as the events unfolded, plainclothes officers and other

An abandoned vice-presidential car at Parkland

police keeping people back from the President's car, which is shown without, and then with its roof attached to the car body; a shaken Senator Ralph Yarborough speaking with reporters; a Catholic priest; presidential aide General Clifton walking quickly by; and four shots of the interior of the back seat of the Vice-President's convertible, empty except for a bunch of roses lying disheveled on the floor. Likewise Grant and the others took shots of the Vice-President's car. Clicking off at virtually anything that moved, Grant easily shot 29 exposures left in one camera, including several of a man in a suit accompanied by a cop delivering a box thought to contain blood plasma.[38]

Both Burroughs and Stoughton recall taking pictures of officials cleaning out the back seat of the President's vehicle, utilizing a stainless steel bucket. Burroughs explains:

Activity around the emergency area

I took a picture of cleaning out the car, of people crying around the emergency room, the car with the Emergency Entrance sign, [in all] a roll or two of pictures there while we were waiting for some word. A reporter from our office came by, and I gave her the film to take into the office, which she did. Meanwhile, a young man came by, and he said he made a picture of the President's car. He was on top of an overpass, and the car passed under going 90 miles per hour, and he made a picture of Mrs. Kennedy lying on top of the President, and he had the roll of film in his hand. And I said I'd buy it from him — and then I started bargaining with him — there was a UPI reporter that heard this and he got into it. I happened to have some expense money with me, and I said, "I'll give you $100 sight unseen for the roll of film, whatever it is. There may not be anything on it at all, the car going so fast." It was a simple camera of some sort. Anyway, he sold it to me while the UPI guy had to call his office for authorization. I sent that in along with the film I made.[39]

Later in the day Burroughs saw the amateur photographer's picture printed up. "You could just barely discern the figures because there was so much movement, a fast-moving car. I'm not sure if it made the wire. It wasn't really bad." Dallas Associated Press files indicate that four spot photographs by amateurs were acquired that day or later. The names of the photographers were Al Volkland, Don Moorman, David Miller, and Justin Newman. In an effort to discover if these and any other known photographs taken of the President's limousine on its rush to Parkland Hospital were the same as the one Burroughs recalls, photocopies of six pictures were sent to the former AP photographer some 20 years after the events. Burroughs wrote back, "Sorry, none of the photocopies were of the picture I purchased from unknown young man. His picture was made from overpass looking down on presidential limo." This photo has not been able to be identified by this author.[40]

Prior to the official announcement of the death of the President, Cancellare arrived at the hospital. "He was quite unhinged," recalls Burroughs, "because he didn't know what we had done, and he was out of it. It was very competitive and he was as white as a sheet. He was left behind, and when he joined with us, he was highly concerned." The two photographers were good friends, and Burroughs filled Cancellare in concerning what little had transpired. Kennedy had arrived at the hospital at approximately 12:38. Unbeknown to the press, the President was declared dead at 1:00. At 1:27 a Catholic priest in attendance was quoted by news sources to say that Kennedy was dead. The gathered press in the immediate area of the emergency entrance were informed by Assistant Press Secretary Malcolm Kilduff that he

Mrs. Johnson is whisked from Parkland to a waiting automobile by Secret Service agents. Cong. Jack Brooks is in the foreground.

would shortly hold a press conference in a hospital classroom. Unofficial word had been spreading that the President was dead, but no statement had been officially given. It was being held off until President Johnson could leave the hospital.

Johnson's exit from the hospital was swift, most photographers not able to get a clear view of him walking briskly out the door. He was quickly escorted to Chief Curry's car by Agent Rufus Youngblood. One of the local news photographers, Jim Birmingham, had with him a camera with a long telephoto lens which was carried in a holster. Clint Grant recalls, "As Vice-President Johnson passed, the photographer drew his camera out of the holster and Johnson ducked as Birmingham aimed his telephoto. Everyone was real edgy." *Morning News* photographer Bill Winfrey had a similar experience with his 400mm lens with follow focus. "The Secret Service immediately ran

At 1:26 LBJ leaves Parkland accompanied
by Agent Rufus Youngblood (left)
and Cong. Homer Thornberry

up and put guns to my head." They made Winfrey and a colleague lie on the ground as they examined his camera.   Also present outside the hospital emergency entrance was Grant's and Winfrey's colleague at the *Dallas Morning News*, Joe Laird.   Throughout the entire afternoon Laird took rolls of film of the motorcade vehicles, of the reaction of spectators and a series of frames made as a disheveled and sad Mrs. Kennedy leaves the entrance among an entourage of the late President's staff, aides and protectors.[41]

Just before 1:33 hospital classrooms 101-102 quickly filled.  Mack Kilduff had been an Assistant Press Secretary for a year and a half, and the emotion of the situation was extreme.  Recalling the scene only a month after the event, Kilduff remembered:  "I got up there and I thought 'Well, this is really the first press conference on a road trip that I've had to hold,' and I started to say it, and all I could say was, 'Excuse me, let me catch my breath,' and I thought in my mind, 'All right, what am I going to say and how am I going to say it?'  I remember opening my mouth one time and I couldn't say it.  It must have been two or three minutes."  As photographers clicked away, Kilduff finally began his statement, "President John Fitzgerald Kennedy died at approximately 1:00 Central Standard Time today here in Dallas.  He died of a gunshot wound in the brain."[42]

During the announcement Burroughs noticed that, "There wasn't an AP reporter there, and I made a picture of Kilduff, but I was more anxious to get out and get to a phone to get to an AP reporter. Sure enough I ran down the corridor and there was Jack Bell.  He was on the phone, and I came in and said, 'It's the official announcement of the death of the President,' and he handed me the phone and said, 'Dictate it to the office.'  We had it unofficially from a Catholic priest, and strong indications that he was dead, [but] that was the first official statement."[43]

Kilduff announces that the President
died of a gunshot wound in the brain.

Rickerby and Cancellare were in the press room with a few dozen other reporters and photographers as well as government officials and hospital personnel.  Rickerby made nine telephoto exposures of Kilduff's face, the strain of the announcement and events showing obviously in his pained expressions.  Rickerby also clicked off 15 wide-angle pictures of Kilduff standing in front of a chalkboard, fidgeting with an unlit cigarette

Part of a sequence taken by Joe Laird at Parkland includes President Kennedy's party preparing to leave at 2:08. Staff members Mary Gallagher (carrying Mrs. Kennedy's handbag and hat), Evelyn Lincoln, and Pam Turnure enter a car, while Mrs. Kennedy is escorted to the ambulance.

An emotionally taut Kilduff at the press
announcement; Cancellare (wearing
glasses) is in the right background

in his hand, leaning against a table, gesturing with his hands, and drawing attention to the chalkboard with a rough box and x-outline depicting the seating arrangements inside the presidential Lincoln.[44]

Following the press conference Clint Grant radioed his managing editor from a photographer's car asking if he should go back to Washington with the press corps. Told to stay in Dallas, Grant made his way back to Love Field to retrieve his clothes and equipment from the press plane, just after Judge Sarah T.Hughes had come off of Air Force One following her swearing in of President Johnson. He took several pictures of the luggage being off-loaded from the press plane and then returned to the newspaper office to process his film from Fort Worth and Dallas and work on various other photo lab chores. Later that day he also went down to police headquarters and among other photos, shot several of Police Chief Curry at his office desk.[45]

Burroughs and Cancellare had joined up with each other at the press conference. According to Burroughs:

> We looked out the window and saw a car leaving with Jackie Kennedy. We rushed out, and the only place we could think of was Love Field. So we grabbed a taxi and went directly to Love Field. There was a cordon of army around the plane. We just stood on the outside. And all of a sudden the door of the plane opened and out came Cecil Stoughton, and he spotted us, came running over and told me what he had — the swearing-in of the President. We agreed that AP would handle the pooling [of the pictures Stoughton had taken of the swearing-in], and Cecil then managed to get us a police car and a motorcycle escort.
>
> At the downtown AP office within the Dallas News Building, the film was processed and prints were divvied up to send over the wire. Cancellare and Stoughton took off for the UPI office. It was agreed that when Cancellare called Burroughs from UPI they

would then run the picture at the same time. "That's what we did —
I had a hell of a time convincing my boss in New York that we
should wait."[46]

At the Dallas UPI office Cancellare also had his Dealey Plaza pictures developed. At least one and possibly two were sent out almost immediately. A little after
3:00 Eastern Time commentator Frank McGee announced on NBC television, "We
have a still photograph here in the studio that has just moved, and it shows a man
and a woman and what looks like two small children lying on the ground." The TV
camera broadcast the wire service photo of Cancellare's second picture taken near
the scene of the shooting less than an hour and a half earlier.[47]

Burroughs's pictures did not fare as well. Some of Jim Altgens's dramatic
photos of the assassination scene had been sent by wire over the AP network. The
Dallas bureau seethed with activity. Burroughs recalls, "Rolls of film that I made at
Parkland mysteriously disappeared and the AP office never could figure out — there
was so much film and printing and so on going on there — but all those pictures
which were of course secondary at the time — the editor had seen them — but he had
spot pictures of the shooting, and didn't do anything about them. And they disappeared."[48]

Cancellare and Burroughs were able to hitch a Jetstar ride back to Washington with Cecil Stoughton the evening of November 22. Burroughs remembers
"getting in at some ungodly hour and having to go right to work again on what was
happening in Washington." Rickerby stayed at Parkland following the press conference, and made a few more pictures of people clustered around vehicles listening to
car radios. He then boarded the press bus with others. Concerning his return to
Washington Rickerby later reported, "We then went back to the press plane, which
was held up all afternoon because some were filing stories from the scene. We
arrived back in Washington around 8:40 p.m. It was all like a bad dream. We all
hoped it was a dream — that we'd wake up and it would go away — but it didn't.
Riding back on that press plane was like riding in a tomb. I guess that's a poor word
to use, but that's the way it was. All of the press people who had worked with the
President liked him and I, personally, had a great deal of respect and admiration for
him."[49] Many years later Mrs. Rickerby remembers, "I met Arthur in Washington the
next day. He was emotionally exhausted. He went on to cover the funeral at the
church and then he and I went into seclusion at a favorite vacation hideaway in
Gloucester, Massachusetts. I think we both felt that our lives had reached a turning
point. Certainly we were never exactly the same again."[50]

*LIFE* magazine had already locked its November 29 issue, and the presses
had begun their run when the news of the assassination was received. Managing
Editor George Hunt held the run and he and his staff, almost non-stop for the next
48 hours, redesigned the issue to include large sections on the assassination coverage.
Time only allowed for one color photograph to be produced, and the *LIFE* coverage

opened with a full-color closeup of a vibrant President and Mrs. Kennedy at the Love Field arrival.  Opposite that and above an introductory paragraph was placed a black-and-white shot of the Vice-President's car at Parkland with Mrs. Johnson's bouquet of roses strewn in the abandoned vehicle's back seat.  Both these shots had been taken by Rickerby.[51]

Of his reaction to the day's events, Burroughs says in retrospect, "I was in a real state of shock.  We traveled with the idea that it is our job to cover such things like this, we're sort of looking for something every minute.  And here it really happened in spades, and we weren't with him.  It's still a shock, even though it's your job."[52]

Almost twenty-five years after the event Clint Grant would write, "It really didn't hit me until I had wrapped up my day's work.  Then I was stunned, disappointed and embarrassed that it had happened — especially in my home town.  I felt like crawling under a log.  Although I wasn't a great admirer, he was my President and I have great respect for whoever holds the office."[53]

None of the five photographers in Camera Car 2 were ever officially questioned by police or governmental agencies.  Comments Grant, who has seldom spoken of his experiences to researchers, ". . . frankly I'm fed up with writers and armchair quarterbacks 'solving' the Kennedy assassination.  They all have a 'positive' theory with no two alike."[54] These five photographers who had occupied the same car at Dallas continued their successful careers, Arthur Rickerby passing away in August, 1972, and Frank Cancellare in July, 1985.  Henry Burroughs, and Cecil Stoughton were retired by 1980 while Clint Grant semi-retired in 1986 at the age of 71.  He planned to continue working as long as his health permitted.

## CHAPTER NOTES

1.    *Washington Post*, 7/16/1985, p. D8; Questionnaire filled out by Frank Cancellare, 2/1985; Letter, Cancellare to Trask, [3] /1985.
2.    *Washington Post*, op. cit.,p. D8.
3.    Telephone interview of Cecil Stoughton, 7/10/1985.
4.    Questionnaire filled out by Henry Burroughs, 12/1985.
5.    Letter, Henry Burroughs to Trask, [3]/1985.
6.    Telephone interview of Burroughs, 8/21/1985.
7.    Bob Johnson, "Too Busy For Tears," *The AP World*, 8/1972, p.16-17.
8.    Letter, Mrs. Wanda Rickerby to Trask, 3/20/1985; *Danbury* [Conn.] *News Times*, 11/23/1963.
9.    Letter, Mrs. Rickerby to Trask, 3/20/1985.
10.   On November 22, 1963, *TIME* used on page 22 one of the Rickerby black-and-white photos of the Kennedys in San Antonio. In November, 1983 *LIFE* printed one of Rickerby's color photos of the Kennedys arrival at Love Field.
11.   Burroughs questionnaire, 12/1985; Cancellare questionnaire, 2/1985.
12.   Film sequences of the motorcade showing "Camera Car Two" taken by Malcolm Couch and Thomas Atkins, 11/22/1963; Telephone interview of Stoughton, 7/10/1985.
13.   Letter, Clint Grant to Trask, 12/1/1987.
14.   Ibid.

15.     *Dallas Morning News* Reference Department contact sheets #2340, 2344 and 2345 of Clint Grant photos, 11/22/1963; Letter, Grant to Trask, 12/1/1987; 1/6/1988; Grant photo from his personal collection, "At Love Field Landing," 11/22/1963.

16.     Telephone interview of Burroughs, 8/21/1985; Rickerby contact sheet, frame #3A, 11/22/1963.

17.     *Dallas Morning News* Reference Department negatives of Clint Grant #5 and #6, 11/22/1963; Letter, Grant to Trask, 12/1/1987; 1/6/1988.

18.     Telephone interview of Burroughs, 8/21/1985.

19.     Letter, Grant to Trask, 12/1/1987.

20.     *Danbury News Times*, 11/23/1963.

21.     Letter, Cancellare to Trask, [3]/1985; Questionnaire filled out by Cancellare, 2/1985.

22.     Telephone interview of Stoughton, 7/10/1985; Letter, Grant to Trask, 12/1/1987;  Letter, Mrs. Wanda Rickerby to Trask, 3/20/1985.

23.     Telephone interview of Burroughs, 8/21/1985.

24.     Richard E. Sprague, "The Assassination of President John F. Kennedy: The Application of Computers to the Photographic Evidence," *Computers and Automation*, 5/1970, p. 54, 56.

25.     Edgar F. Tatro, "Who's afraid of the grassy knoll south?," *Continuing Inquiry*, 7/22/1981, p.10-11.

26.     Cancellare Dealey Plaza photo sequence #1, 11/22/1963.

27.     John Kirkpatrick, "Caught Up In History," *Dallas Morning News*, 11/22/1986.

28.     Cancellare Dealey Plaza photo sequence #2, 11/22/1963.

29.     Stoughton photo #C420-22, 11/22/1963; Rickerby contact sheet frames #4A, 5A, 11/22/1963; Clint Grant photograph taken from vehicle, 11/22/1963, reprinted in *Coverups!*, 5/1984, p.1; Letter, Grant to Trask, 12/1/1987.

30.     "JFK Slay Panel Seeks 5," *Boston Herald American*, 7/31/1978.

31.     Letter, Mrs. Rickerby to Trask, 3/20/1985.

32.     Telephone interview of Burroughs, 8/21/1985.

33.     Letter, Grant to Trask, 12/1/1987.

34.     The exact number and sequence of photographs taken by Cancellare is not entirely clear. Five photos taken in Dealey Plaza appear to be attributable to Cancellare.

35.     Secret Service report of interview of Robert H. Jackson, file #CO-2-34,030, 12/9/1963.

36.     Letter, Cancellare to Trask, [3]/1985.

37.     *Danbury News Times*, 11/23/1963.

38.     *Dallas Morning News* Reference Department, negatives of Clint Grant roll, frames #7-36, 11/22/1963; Rickerby contact sheet roll 2, #3-23; roll 3, #3A-8A.

39.     Telephone interview of Burroughs, 8/21/1985.

40.     Ibid.; Note reply on Trask letter, 8/27/1985.

41.     Letter, Grant to Trask, 12/1/1987; Letter, Jim Murray to Trask, 11/28/1991; Bill Winfrey remarks at Reporters Remember Conference, 11/20/1993; *Dallas Morning News* Reference Department, Joe Laird photographs and negatives, 11/22/1963.

42.     Audiotape of Westinghouse "Group W" radio program *Dialogue on Dallas*, 12/1963; Film of Kilduff death announcement replayed on last episode of TV series *Call To Glory -JFK*, 1985.

43.     Telephone interview of Burroughs, 8/21/1985.

44.     Rickerby contact sheet roll 1, #6A-11A; roll 2 #24-32; roll 3, #9A-19A.

45.     Letter, Grant to Trask, 12/1/1987; 1/6/1988; *Dallas Morning News*, Reference Department, prints made by Clint Grant, 11/22/1963.

46.     Telephone interview of Burroughs, 8/21/1985.

47.     Videotape of NBC network TV coverage between 2:45-3:45 P.M., 11/22/1963.

48.     Telephone interview of Burroughs, 8/21/1985.

49.     *Danbury News Times*, 11/23/1963.

50.     Letter, Mrs. Rickerby to Trask, 3/20/1985.

51.     *LIFE*, 11/29/1963, p. [22]-23; Loudon Wainwright, *The Great American Magazine*, p.311-316.

52.     Telephone interview of Burroughs, 8/21/1985.

53.     Letter, Grant to Trask, 1/6/1988.

54.     Letter, Grant to Trask, 12/1/1987.

## CHAPTER 17

# Camera Car 3

The local Dallas-Fort Worth television stations had jointly arranged special pool programming in anticipation of the presidential visit to these two Texas cities for Friday, November 22. Channel 5, WBAP, in Fort Worth, was an NBC affiliate with a combined radio and TV news staff of 17. Included was a four-man Dallas team headed by Bureau Chief James Kerr which operated out of the press room at the Dallas County Courthouse. The station had a vehicular fleet including four mobile units equipped with two-way radios, and four remote broadcast trucks which depended upon at-location "on-shore" power hook-ups for picture transmission. Dallas station KRLD included a combined radio and TV news staff of 22. TV News Director Eddie Barker had two assistants, Joe Scott, responsible for editing tasks, and Jim Underwood, assigned to reporting and public relations areas within the department. Its moving equipment included six mobile units and three remote trucks. A portable power generator was available for whatever truck needed an independent power source for remote broadcasts. KRLD was affiliated with the CBS network. ABC's Dallas affiliate was WFAA, Channel 8, which had the smallest news staff of the three stations, and whose staff was separated into distinct radio and TV departments. News Director Robert Walker presided over an eight-man TV news department, assisted by Chief Cameraman Bert Shipp, who handled assignments. Unlike the two other stations which also had fairly distinct "inside" and "outside" men, Walker's team was typically called upon to do tasks referred to as "outside," such as reporting and filming, as well as the inside work of finalizing a story, including editing, writing, and voice-over. Four radio-equipped mobile units and two remote trucks were on call for assignments, including a large, new 1961 vehicle holding six cameras and a 50 kilowatt portable generator.[1]

Given the political importance of the presidential visit to Dallas, each of the networks had made arrangements with their affiliates for late afternoon film feeds to New York. Excerpts of President Kennedy's visit and major address at the Dallas Trade Mart would most likely be used during nationally televised network evening news programs. The Texas visit, which had begun the day before, was a major story in the Lone Star State. The Dallas area stations were likewise mindful of the strong conservative and the right wing elements within the Dallas community. Less than a month earlier, former presidential candidate and present U.S. Ambassador to the U.N. Adlai Stevenson was heckled and hit over the head with a protest sign during his visit to Dallas on U.N. Day. Mindful of the significance of the President's visit, the first official presidential visit to Dallas since 1948, and of the possibility of some sort of incident, all three local stations decided to pool their resources for saturation coverage.

WBAP and the Fort Worth independent commercial station KTVT would set up, televise, and announce the President's morning breakfast and speech at Fort Worth's Hotel Texas, while WFAA would broadcast the events at the presidential party's Love Field airport arrival in Dallas. The Trade Mart speech would be pooled through KRLD, with WFAA supplying the final broadcast and commentary as the President returned to Love Field for his departure on Air Force One. The station responsible for each broadcast event would, through its control room, feed the pictures to the other participating stations, allowing maximum coverage without duplication of effort.[2]

Along with this live on-the-air broadcasting, each station would also augment its coverage with news department cameramen utilizing 16mm black-and-white Bell & Howell silent or Auricon sound cameras. These relatively lightweight cameras would record non-pool events, and be able to film at a closer and more intimate vantage point than the in-place tripod-mounted TV cameras. The resulting film would then be edited by the individual stations for rebroadcast to the network. Such non-pool film would also be used in special re-cap programs planned by several of the stations for airing later Friday night, augmenting the live broadcasts which could be videotaped. The largest concentration of TV news staff was planned for Love Field, as this was considered by news directors to be the most likely place for protests or incidents directed against the President. Almost all of the live local TV and radio narrations of the Fort Worth and Love Field events mentioned the heavy security presence of the United States Secret Service and local police. Some commentators even brought up the subject of assassination. KTVT announcer Ed Herbert, who just prior to the President's arrival at the Fort Worth Chamber of Commerce breakfast, in mentioning the circumstances leading up to the shooting of President William McKinley in 1901, interjected an understatement which would later have poignant overtones saying, ". . . As in many important occasions in the world, no one seemed to sense that anything different was going to happen."[3]

At Love Field, WBAP had Bureau Chief Kerr and cameraman/reporters Robert Welch and Jimmy Darnell on assignment. Both KRLD Assistant News Directors Underwood and Scott, as well as cameraman George Phenix were also there, while WFAA Director Walker narrated his station's pool coverage, assisted by TV technicians, and photographer/reporter Mal Couch. After taking 16mm film of the airport activities, one each of the three stations' news staff was assigned to travel with the President's motorcade in a camera car to the Trade Mart, insuring each representative station's presence to record part of the motorcade and pictures of the Dallas crowds. Still other cameramen were located at key visual locations along the motorcade route who would also record the vehicles passing through the city. Both CBS and NBC also had a reporter and a cameraman arriving with the presidential party who would do filming of their own. WBAP instructed Jimmy Darnell, who would be its representative in the motorcade, that if any incident along the route occurred, Darnell should remain at the scene.

The NBC crew would remain with the presidential party. Darnell had gone to work for WBAP in January 1961 following graduation from college, where he had earned a degree with a double major in journalism and education. His wife Ruth worked as a secretary in the Burglary and Theft Bureau of the Dallas Police Department.[4]

The motorcade quickly formed up when President and Mrs. Kennedy took their seats in their Lincoln convertible. Darnell found his assigned place in a new gray 1964 Chevrolet Impala convertible set aside for the local press and designated as "Camera Car 3," located some eight cars behind the President's. Darnell took up a position in the rear driver's side of the car. He was joined by local newspaper still photographers Bob Jackson and Tom Dillard. The two other Dallas TV cameramen also got into the car which was chauffeured by a Texas Department of Public Safety officer.

James Robert Underwood was an Oklahoma City native, having been born there in 1922. A member of the Marine Corps from 1940 until 1943, he later attended the University of Tulsa and became involved in radio announcing. Stints at Corpus Christi, Texas, and Jacksonville, Florida, radio stations were followed by a job as a TV weatherman at WFAA in Dallas from 1953 to 1954, and an additional four years doing free-lance radio and TV work. His varied experience and willingness to become involved in all aspects of the industry gained Underwood a reputation as a fine utility man able to handle news, weather, and sports. During his career he garnered a large network of people always looking out to give him news tips. In late 1958 Underwood landed a news reporting position at KRLD, and he soon became assistant news director. He also continued to do free-lance television work, and remained an active KRLD reporter who enjoyed doing camera work. After the 1960 Democratic Convention, Underwood had followed vice-presidential candidate Lyndon Johnson to the Hyannisport, Massachusetts, summer home of presidential candidate Kennedy to report on the first post-convention "top gun" strategy meeting of the two candidates. On October 31, 1963, Underwood had been with Wes Wise, who was the only reporter to photograph the U.N. Day verbal assault and placard hitting of Adlai Stevenson by pickets. On Thursday evening, November 21, Underwood and Wise had been requested by the local Secret Service to show them this film and to try and identify from Secret-Service-provided photographs any known extremists who might be a threat to the President. At the airport on November 22 Underwood had been using cumbersome sound-on-film equipment to record the presidential arrival. Switching to a 16mm hand-held camera, he joined Camera Car 3, finding room in the front seat between the driver and Tom Dillard.[5]

The third local TV cameraman to join the car's occupants was Malcolm O. Couch of WFAA. Born in Dallas in 1938, Couch began work at WFAA in 1955, then attended John Brown University from 1957 to 1960, earning a B.A. degree in Social Science. Deciding to continue his education and earn a Master of Theology degree, Couch began attending Dallas Seminary. Couch kept part-time jobs, including serving for a year as executive director at a local Christian camp and work at a film studio, while attending seminary. In March 1962, he returned to WFAA to become a part-time television news cameraman. By late 1963 the 25-year-old Couch was living, along with his expectant wife, in an apartment on Live Oak Street in Dallas.

The motorcade began, and each of the five cameramen aboard the convertible looked for glimpses of the President's vehicle up ahead, as well as good scenes to shoot to document the motorcade and the temperament of the spectators. As the motorcade rolled out of the Love Field environs and closer into the downtown area, the spectators grew in numbers and in enthusiasm. Underwood begins filming from the moment his car moves out, catching in his view two cameramen on the airport tarmac filming him. Brief glimpses are also seen of two TV cameras on elevated positions and three telephone booths marked, "Press Telephones." In all, Underwood takes some 28 separate, mostly quick, sequences of the motorcade as it proceeds out of the airport complex and on its way into Dallas proper. He takes shots to his right, left, forward, and back, primarily of the spectators whose numbers grow as the car gets further into town. Kids and adults show their enthusiasm and often wave at the camera. One man holds a homemade sign which reads, "Goldwater in 1864." Underwood had heard the joke making the rounds during the President's Texas trip that, "JFK is safe in Texas, because You-Know-Who is Vice President." The assistant news director was still on his guard, however, as he knew of the city's strong right-wing sentiment. But the crowds continued to increase, which at one point caused Underwood to comment to his colleagues, "At least they respect the President of the United States. He's got this town in the palm of his hand."[7]

As the caravan neared downtown Dallas, one of a cameraman's worst nightmares occurred for Underwood. "When we turned onto Main Street downtown and headed west toward the scene of where the assassination took place, either the regulator or the main spring in my camera broke and I was without a camera. I knew that we had . . . at least two men on the parade route who were on the street and would be filming the motorcade as we came by and I hoped to exchange my broken camera for one of theirs. . . . At Main and Record one of our men was stationed and I tried to holler at him my camera was broken and I wanted to switch and I started to and there was no point in it because we passed that rapidly." Veteran KRLD cameraman George "Sandy" Sanderson was at the south side of Main Street at Record which was a block east of Houston Street. He had taken some general shots of the awaiting crowd, including men looking out windows in the building east of the County Criminal Courts Building. His uninspired camera work just caught the motorcade as it had passed, so that the sequence shows the rear of the President's and his follow-up car, followed by the Vice-President's car, and his follow-up. The back door on the driver side of the vice-presidential follow-up car is slightly ajar as a means of a possible quick exit for a Secret Service agent. Also captured in this sequence is a quick shot of Underwood's camera car. The last film sequence shows the crowd breaking up after the last vehicle in the caravan has passed.[8]

Mal Couch had begun filming from the camera car at the outskirts of the airport and his eighteen clips taken while in the motorcade and prior to the assassination used up some 1⅔ minutes of film. From his position on the middle of the back seat of the car, Couch had little diversity of subject matter from which to choose. He took shots looking forward at the camera cars to his front with spectators on the sides, or shots looking behind with the trailing cars and busses visible. At times escort motorcycle cop H. B. McLain near the rear driver's side, or cycle officer Marrion Baker near the rear passenger side is visible to Couch's lens. Couch's other filming choice was to take side views of the crowds lining the parade route. The crowds rapidly grow in size and in intensity, so that his later sequence shows throngs of people, many-deep, with various spectators mugging and waving to the camera.[9]

At Dealey Plaza where Houston Street intersects, the motorcade took a right turn, followed after a block north by a very sharp left at Elm Street on its approach to Stemmons Freeway. Upon turning right onto Houston, the large downtown crowds suddenly diminished in size and the motorcade was effectively near the end of public spectator viewing. Testified Couch several months later, "Everyone gave a sigh a [sic] relief that — uh — it was over; and one of the cameramen, I remember, his camera broke and another one was out of film. Everyone was relaxed." At the Houston Street corner Bob Jackson had thrown out a roll of exposed film to a colleague waiting at the corner, and as the film rolled into the gutter, those aboard the camera car watched the comical scene of a reporter scrambling for the film. Couch continued in his testimony, ". . . I remember I was talking and we were laughing and I was looking back to a fellow on my . . . right — I don't know who it was — we were joking. We had just made the turn. And I heard the first shot."[10]

Up ahead the President's vehicle had already turned onto Elm and Camera Car 3 was on Houston in front of the Dallas County Criminal Courts Building some 40 feet northerly of the Main Street corner. Underwood thought the noise to be a giant fire-cracker, while Couch's first reaction was that it sounded like a motorcycle backfire. Darnell described the noise as a backfire from an automobile. In those next seemingly long and uncontrollable seconds, Camera Car 3 continued its forward motion some 160 feet along Houston Street towards the direction of the Texas School Book Depository Building looming to its front left.

When later asked to describe what transpired following the first noise, Couch responded,

> As I recall nothing — there was no particular reaction; uh — nothing unusual. Maybe everybody sort of looked around a little, but didn't think much of it. And — uh — then, in a few seconds, I guess from four-five seconds later, or even less, we heard the second shot. And then we began to look in front of us — in the motorcade in front of us. And, as I recall, I didn't have any particular fears or feelings at the second shot. By the third shot, I felt that it was a rifle. Almost sure it was. And, as I said, the shots or the noises were fairly close together. They were fairly even in sound — and — uh, by then, one could recognize, or if he had heard a high-powered rifle, he would feel

that it was a high-powered rifle. You would get that impression. . . . Uh — as I say, the first shot, I had no particular impressions; but the second shot, I remember turning — several of us turning — and looking ahead of us. It was unusual for a motorcycle to backfire that close together, it seemed like. And after the third shot, Bob Jackson, who was as I recall on my right, yelled something like, 'Look up in the window! There's a rifle!' And I remember glancing up to a window on the far right which at the time impressed me as the sixth or seventh floor and seeing about a foot of rifle being — the barrel brought into the window. I saw no one in that window, — just a quick one-second glance at the barrel.[11]

By the end of the third shot Camera Car 3, some 80 feet from the Book Depository Building, was in the process of making its sharp left turn. As the car arced left, the vehicle in front seemed to hesitate and then stop. The pandemonium of people in the street and sidewalk reacting to the shots was enough for some of the car's occupants to take advantage of their halted vehicle and vault over the side to see what was happening.

Underwood realized the shots were coming from overhead. He saw people falling to the ground in the direction of the underpass, and assumed some of these people had been shot. The newsman was highly agitated. "There I was without a camera; the only thought I had was to get a camera." He leaped over the side of the car, leaving his broken camera behind and ran as fast as he could southerly towards Main Street, remembering he had seen Sanderson at Record and Main Streets. Hearing and seeing the commotion up at the corner of Houston Street, Sanderson had run westerly on Main. Underwood recalls, "I met him just around the corner on Main past Houston and grabbed his camera and said, 'Someone had been shooting at the President.'" Camera in hand, Underwood rushed back to the Elm Street area. "When I got back to the scene, most of the people in the area were running up the grassy slope toward the railway yards just behind the Texas School Book Depository Building. . . . I assumed perhaps who had fired the shots had run in that direction. . . . and I ran up there and took some films and they were running through the railroad yard and they very quickly found nothing and I was having, frankly, a hard time breathing because I had done more running in those few minutes than I am used to doing. I gasped out to a couple people . . . that I thought the shots came from that building [Texas School Book Depository]. . . ."[12]

Returning to the front of the Book Depository Building with others, Underwood began filming in that area for the next ten minutes. His film of the activity around Dealey Plaza includes a shot of people rushing up the stairs leading to the concrete shelter at the north pergola, and two views of the area of the parking lot with railroad cars in the background. At Elm Street Underwood pans his camera from the direction

Activity filmed prior to 12:39 p.m. by a local cameraman adjacent
to the concrete walk on top of the knoll and in the parking area to the rear.

of the street and knoll area right up to the fourth floor of the book Depository. Another clip shows a cop near a cycle with a young black boy later identified as Amos Euins. Underwood heard Euins tell the cop that he had seen a colored man with a rifle lean out of the window of the building. More and varied views of the building and the activity around it including shotgun toting police at the Elm and Houston Streets intersection, a fire truck at Houston Street north of Elm, and another one arriving on Houston Street from the direction of Main, were taken. Underwood also captured on film the escorting of Larry Florer to the first floor car entrance between the Court and Record Buildings. Florer had acted strangely enough to catch the suspicion of spectators and was detained by police. Further indoor film was made in the Sheriff's office of Florer being questioned. From the time Underwood grabbed Sanderson's camera, he had made some 18 film clips.[13]

It had taken Underwood several minutes to get his replacement camera and return to Elm Street. He told Joseph Ball, a Warren Commission staff attorney who interviewed him in April of 1964 that, ". . . There was quite a time lapse between the time the shots were fired and the time anyone checked the building. The main effort was to run to the railroad yards instead of the School Book Depository." Concerning his own recollections of the confused scene in which he found himself, Underwood recounted, "This was a kaleidoscope of things happening. In my business, you need to make a quick appraisal of what is happening if you are going to shoot pictures of it. I was confused and out of breath and unbelieving of what happened."[14]

While still in the courthouse, Underwood phoned KRLD studio, and shortly after 1:00 CST, CBS New York anchor Walter Cronkite switched to an audio report made by Underwood of his observations of what was happening from the scene.

> I was in a car in the presidential caravan about seven cars
> behind the President's car. As we made the turn here at the intersec-
> tion of Elm and Houston I heard first a loud report. It sounded to me

like a giant firecracker. Then in quick succession two more, immediately in front of me. I saw people begin to fall on the grass and run for bushes in a park area here, then police officers ran on the scene and there was a wild general search throughout this entire neighborhood. Finally, one of the officers found a small colored boy who said he saw a man fire from about the fourth window of the School Book Depository Building. Now, a white man only has been escorted from the building. The fire department had earlier come upon the scene with gear and there is a room-to-room search of this building which has two, four, six, eight, nine floors, the building right across the street diagonally from the Dallas County Courthouse. So, evidently, the men, the officers were looking for, or perhaps one of them, has been taken from the building, but now I see police officers running back toward the entrance of the Texas School Book Depository and evidently they are going to continue searching in that building for the would-be assassin of the President. This is Jim Underwood in Dallas. Back to CBS News.[15]

Shortly thereafter Underwood returned to the KRLD studio, and at about that time he received a call that the police had picked up a man who had killed a police officer, and were taking him to the city jail. Underwood had not heard about the Tippit shooting, but on the hunch that it might refer to a Secret Service agent who had reportedly been killed as a result of the assassination, he grabbed a camera and high-tailed it to the police station.

"I reached City Hall in time to film Oswald being brought in, and I rode up in the elevator with him. A police sergeant said, 'We got witnesses that saw him shoot Tippit.' The police tell us whether or not a suspect is good for the charges, and we know how to play the story. But Oswald leaned around and looked straight at me, saying defensively, 'I didn't kill anybody.'"[16]

Underwood had made film of Oswald being brought into the City Hall basement. Normally the shooting of a cop would be a big story, but that Friday was not normal. An officer told Underwood that he did not think the incident was connected with the assassination, and Underwood knew this story would probably get short shrift. Returning with the film to the studio, Underwood shortly got a second call from a homicide officer who told him that this Oswald worked in the Depository Building. The film was now "hot stuff" and was quickly put through the processor in preparation for airing.[17]

Part of Saturday Underwood worked the beat at the County Courthouse area, awaiting the transfer of Oswald to the County Jail. It was during this time that he and Tom Dillard made pictures of the curb near the triple underpass, where a fragment of a bullet appeared to have hit the concrete. (See next chapter.)

Underwood knew Jack Ruby well enough to be on speaking terms with him, though he emphasized in a brief FBI report that, ". . . There had never been any social relationship between himself and Ruby." As to Ruby's presence in the Dallas City Hall basement at the time of Oswald's transfer on Sunday, November 24, Underwood counts it as just a fluke. "He just happened to wander in at the right moment."[18]  Underwood was a real utility man at KRLD, who with his resonant announcer's voice, spoke with ease and articulation. His face and voice were well known to area television viewers. He also kept himself in the news-gathering portion of the business, and enjoyed working his sources and doing film work. Eva L. Grant, the 54-year-old sister of Jack Ruby, contacted Underwood right after Ruby's shooting of Oswald, and by 1:00 Underwood was at her apartment. Later that afternoon he accompanied Grant to City Jail and assisted her through the crush of media. Sharing some of the information he learned from Mrs. Grant in interviews with other reporters, Underwood also garnered for himself and his media organization, exclusive information while being of a little assistance to the shocked Ruby relative.[19]

Underwood remained in the Dallas area as a newsman and later entered public relations. He aided in the later political campaign of Wes Wise, another local newsman, who successfully ran for mayor of Dallas. On September 3, 1983, Underwood died of heart failure from the effects of diabetes at Aransas Pass, Texas, where he had been living for the past five years with his wife Marian.[20]

At the time of the shooting of the President, Underwood was not the only one who jumped out of Camera Car 3. In the back seat Jimmy Darnell also jumped as did still cameraman Tom Dillard from his position in the passenger seat next to Underwood. In two brief FBI reports dealing with Darnell's activities at the time of the shooting, it was typed up that Darnell, ". . . stated he heard the first shot and thought it was a backfire from an automobile. The second shot he thought was a firecracker. He stated, however, after the second shot he realized from the confusion that something had

happened and he jumped out of the car and ran towards the President's car. However, he was unable to see anything and did not get photographs. He said he noticed parents were throwing children to the ground and covering them with their bodies and that he took photographs of this activity."[21]

Darnell films the activity on the north side of Elm Street from across the street.

After jumping from the car Darnell had apparently run down the south side of Elm Street westerly towards the area where he had seen bodies falling. Raising camera to his eyes, Darnell managed to record some 9½ seconds of activity in two film sequences. In the first five-second shot Darnell has pointed his camera across Elm Street as first a car and then a station wagon (the 11th and 12th cars behind the President's vehicle) speeds by from the right. Across Elm Street AP photographer Jim Altgens is looking to his right, apparently waiting for a chance to cross the street. To Altgens's rear can be seen the Newman family on the grass. Bill Newman is on his knees and with his right hand hits the ground three hard whacks venting obvious frustration. A man runs by from camera right down the sidewalk, while a young boy runs down the grassy incline towards the same direction. This view was also made by still photogra-

pher Harry Cabluck from aboard a press bus in the motorcade as it passed by. Just after taking this shot, Darnell shoots a shorter clip as the third bus in the motorcade carrying the "official party" and a black-and-white police cruiser pass in the foreground. Quickly panning to the left, Darnell follows the vehicles as they speed towards the railroad overpass while people dash across the street towards the grassy knoll. This film and other brief clips made by Darnell were shown on NBC, coupled with

As the tail end of the motorcade travels towards the underpass, spectators rush to the knoll area.

other films and narrated by Robert MacNeil as part of a synopsis of the day's events. It was broadcast nationally at about midnight Eastern Time that Friday.[22]

After the motorcade had departed Darnell remained in the Dealey Plaza area for some time, filming and interviewing witnesses, including Jean Hill who along with friend Mary Moorman had witnessed the shooting. At about 1:20 p.m. Dallas time, Tom Whalen of Fort Worth WBAP announced, "WBAP newsman James [sic] Darnell in Dallas on the scene of the presidential shooting — the shooting in which President Kennedy and Governor Connally were shot — has an eyewitness interview with a Mrs. Jean Hill . . . ." Whalen then went on with a taped interview he had made of Hill which was broadcast over the NBC network.[23]

Following his work in the Dealey Plaza area, Darnell went back to Love Field and was able to film the President's coffin being loaded onto Air Force One at about 2:15, taking it from the perimeter of the secure area. Head of Dallas police security for Love Field, Newton Fisher, is said to have confiscated Darnell's film, saying, "That's sacrilegious!" Three film clips shown Friday night on NBC along with the other Darnell shots do show long shots of the ambulance arriving at Air Force One, and might have in fact been Darnell's work.[24]

Darnell, Underwood, and Dillard had jumped out of the car just after the shots. *Dallas Times Herald* still photographer Bob Jackson, who had seen a man shoot from the Book Depository, and Mal Couch, seated next to Jackson, who saw the barrel being withdrawn into the window, remained in the car as it began to move around the corner and down Elm Street towards the triple underpass. Couch only saw about a foot of the barrel, which was pointing at an approximately 45° angle westward down Elm Street. Couch later described what he did next. "Well, I picked up my camera. As I recall, I had it in my hand, but it was down leaning against my legs. And I picked it up and made a quick glance at a setting and raised it to my eye. And you can see from my film that we're just turning the corner. We start the turn and we turn the corner, and you can see people running. . . . After we went, say, 50 to 75 feet on down Elm, we began to hang on because the driver picked up speed. . . . After we got all the way down underneath the three trestles, we finally persuaded the driver — who wasn't too anxious to stop — to stop, and we all jumped out. And I ran, I guess it was about 75 yards or a little more, back up to the School Book Depository and took some sweeping pictures of the crowd standing around. I didn't stay there long."[25]

The 22½ seconds of film made by Couch of the scene along Elm Street taken from the camera car is, along with Dave Wiegman's, the only film sequence made from the motorcade at the time of the shooting. When he first presses his camera trigger, Couch has his lens facing northwesterly. The car has passed in front of the Depository Building and now is some 70 feet from the closest point of the building. In the initial frames one can see the overhead traffic light hanging from a pole at the northeast tip of the sidewalk at the end of the north pergola area. In the background is the west end of the Depository Building and the enclosed driveway and westerly one-story building extension. A crush of spectators are on the sidewalk and street corner of Elm Street Extension. There is much movement, and most people are looking southwesterly down Elm Street. The movement of the crowd shifts generally to the west, including a young boy who skips along the street; though one young woman, seemingly in distress, moves in the opposite direction. Couch's car seems not to be moving. Couch then pans his camera a quick left, and as he does this, a careful observer looking at the sequence over and over again, can pick out a police officer in a white motorcycle helmet jogging northerly to Elm Street Extension. He is observed scooting past the front of a parked car, and running in the direction of the front entrance of the Book Depository. As Couch's camera continues to pan left, a parked cycle is noticed at the curb of the northeast point of Elm Street.[26]

Confusion erupts in front of the Book Depository. While most eyes are focused left, Officer Baker (dark form at gap in crowd onright) sprints to the right towards the building.

Marrion L. Baker was riding motorcycle escort in the motorcade and was located on the passenger side of the vehicles, generally in the location of Camera Car 3. Various films taken by the cameramen of the earlier motorcade often include Baker in their views. Traveling an estimated 5 to 7 miles per hour as he rounded the corner from Main to Houston Street, Baker almost lost his balance, buffeted by the now exposed wind tunneling through Houston Street. Just after straightening his cycle and now some 60 to 80 feet down Houston Street, Baker began hearing shots. He recognized the noise as coming from a high-powered rifle and, "Well, to me, it sounded high and I immediately kind of looked up, and I had a feeling that it came from the building, either right in front of me or of the one across to the right of it. . . . Well, I revved the motorcycle up and I went down to the corner, which would be approximately 180 to 200 feet from the point where we had first started, you know, that we heard the shots." At the sound of the three shots Barker saw pigeons suddenly take flight from the top of the building. Seeing the commotion down Elm Street including people falling and grabbing their children, Baker heard a woman scream, "Oh, they have shot that man!" Deciding to rack his bike at the curb, Baker heard Chief Curry on the radio say to, "Get some men up on that railroad," The cycle cop, however, believed that the shots came from the top of the Book Depository, and he ran to the entrance. Quickly accompanied by building manager Roy Truly, the two trotted to the service elevator on the diagonal corner of the building. Impatient to wait for it, they began up the stairs. From the glass window in the door on the second floor, Baker glimpsed a man walking away at about a 20 foot distance. "I hollered at him at that time and said, 'Come here!' He turned and walked right straight back to me. . .

I turned to Mr. Truly and I says, 'Do you know this man, does he work here?' And he said yes, and I turned immediately and I went on out up the stairs." According to Baker, the man never said a word and didn't change his expression one bit, although Baker had his drawn pistol within three feet of the man. This employee was subsequently identified as Lee Oswald. Baker later was requested to duplicate his movements from the time of the first shot to his stopping Oswald. The time duplicated ranged from between 1 minute 30 seconds to 1 minute 15 seconds. It was also timed as to the possible assassin's route from the sixth floor southeast side to the back stairs and down to the second floor lunch room, leaving time to put down a gun between boxes. That time was calculated at 1 minute 18 to 1 minute 14 seconds.[27]

In his car Couch continues his pan left past Baker's parked cycle, and at about this time his car appears to move forward. Just ahead of Camera Car 3 is Camera Car 2, which is also beginning to move out. Three cameramen are on the back of Camera Car 2, though UPI's Frank Cancellare has already jumped overboard and he and other cameramen from Camera Car 1 can just be discerned in the right background running towards the knoll. In the distance NBC's Dave Wiegman barrels down the knoll incline towards the Newman family. At the left side of Elm Street cycle officer Hollis B. McLain is far down the street followed behind by J. W. Courson, who had been paired opposite Baker in the motorcade. As Couch continues to film this 15-second segment, Clyde A. Haygood, who was on his solo cycle further back in the motorcade adjacent to the first press bus, had sped forward from the right side of the road to the left, avoiding

Baker.  Haygood now appears in Couch's film on the left side of the frame, passing in front of Camera Car 3 and crossing over to the right of Camera Car 2 traveling in the direction of the north side of Elm Street.  On the south side of Elm Street a cop wearing a soft white visor hat and with gun drawn can be seen in the background stepping into the street.

Couch's next film clip is made while his car passes this cop on the left, the cameraman panning left as he travels forward.  Also visible in the background is the north peristyle area and the Post Office Terminal Annex Building to Couch's southeast.  Panning right as the car continues down the street, the film clip shows the triple underpass and the south side of Elm Street as well as part of the car's windshield and the driver's hat.  While panning right

Couch records Baker's parked cycle (right), Camera Car 2 (foreground) and Cycle Officer Haygood (passing in front of car).

and tilting down, it is obvious no one remains in the front seat but the driver.  Re-aiming the camera to his right, Couch catches quick glimpses of the Newman family on the ground with Cancellare taking a picture of them.  AP's Jim Altgens is seen as is White House film maker Tom Atkins, who with his camera visible, is running to the left.  The side of Bob Jackson's face to the right of Couch is also picked up in this scene.  In the final motorcade sequence, Couch's car is further down Elm Street, approaching the underpass.  Cycle Officer Haygood is off his cycle, just beyond the concrete steps leading from Elm Street to the pergola.  A man is running in the street, probably Secret Service Agent Lem Johns who had jumped out of his own vehicle and who now physically vaults

With Bob Jackson's profile visible in the car, Couch films Tom Atkins running down Elm Street.

over the trunk into Camera Car 2, which is beginning to pull out on the left around Camera Car 1.
Atkins is also running for the open passenger door
of the first car, while another man runs down the
sidewalk. Meanwhile Officer Haygood is trying to
right his cycle, which is tipped, and he does so by
physically lifting it as Couch's car passes him by. A
woman can be seen scurrying down the sidewalk.[28]

Jackson and Couch shouted at their driver
to stop at the underpass, and both men ran back to
the knoll area. Couch's first shot here is made on
the sidewalk looking east toward the north peristyle
from the parked cycle location where numerous
people are now milling around. A second view is
taken from the top of the knoll steps where a large
crowd of over 60 people are seen, including many
walking down the steps to the street, and others
crossing the street.

When later asked why Couch did not take
pictures of the School Book Depository Building,
he explained, "Well, ah — as best I can recall, the
excitement on the ground of people running and
policemen 'revving' up their motorcycles — and I
have a real nice shot of a policeman running towards me with his pistol drawn — the activity on
the ground kept my attention. The reason I did
not stay and take pictures of the Depository Building — which I had originally intended to do when I
got out of the motorcade — was that — another
cameraman from our station, A. J. L'Hoste . . . he
came running up and when he ran up, why I said,

With the knoll stockade fence in the
background, Couch records Haygood
stabilizing his cycle before running up
the slope.

'You stay here and get shots of the building and go inside — and I'm going to go back —
I'm going to follow the President.'" Couch and one or two other photographers stopped
a car on Elm Street driven by a high-school-aged boy and asked him to take them up
Stemmons Freeway. Seated on the right side of this sedan, Couch took more film
looking out the window at people on the curb as they step back. The underpass is in the
distance. A second clip looks back at a view of the parked cycle, the knoll and the west
side of the School Book Depository in the background as the car travels away from the
scene. Stopped at a police roadblock just after entry onto the freeway, Couch takes
three quick shots of activity there. At the roadblock Couch links up with UPI's Frank
Cancellare; and the photographers, upon identifying themselves as press, were allowed
to hitch-hike an additional ride to Parkland Hospital. At the hospital Couch took

numerous other films of activities there and the crowd's reaction to the events.[29]

A. J. L'Hoste was news editor at WFAA-TV, and during the Friday presidential visit, was assigned film coordination. He also was to film the procession in the downtown area. He chose a location on the south side of Main Street, nearly opposite Hotel Maurice, at 909 Main Street, some four blocks east of Houston Street. From this position, L'Hoste took some pre-parade shots of the gathering spectators, many sitting at the curb, and all who looked to be enjoying the beautiful day and anticipating viewing the President and the First Lady. As the procession made its way down a bunting-festooned Main Street, L'Hoste took a long shot of their approach, followed by a panning view first of the five escort cycles, then the pilot car, and finally the presidential vehicle on whose rear bumper Mrs. Kennedy's Secret Service Agent, Clint Hill, can be seen crouching. He also shot a quick view of a bus marked "OFFICIAL PARTY."

In this Jim Murray photo, A. J. L'Hoste (left) films Sheriff Decker outside the Book Depository.

Learning of the incident in Dealey Plaza a few minutes later, L'Hoste quickly made his way up Main Street. Crossing Houston but still on Main, within 7 or 8 minutes of the shooting, he begins to take film looking northerly towards the grassy knoll area. Soon he chanced to meet Couch who asked him to cover the Depository area as Couch wanted to get back to the presidential party. L'Hoste remained on the scene until about 3:00 p.m., and among the sequences he recorded were heavy police activity around the Depository Building, including 3-wheel cycles and cruisers arriving in the area, cops toting long guns, a man in a hard hat being escorted by an official, Sheriff Bill Decker giving an interview, Larry Florer being walked away, and witnesses including Danny Arce and Bonny Ray Williams being brought to and put into a vehicle. By about 3:30 the film had been returned to the station, processed, and broadcast once and then almost immediately repeated with cameraman Ron Reiland giving a narration.[30]

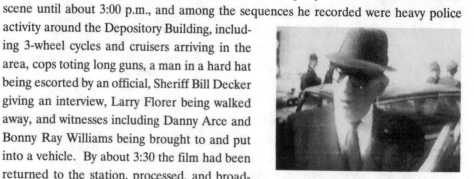

L'Hoste's camera view of the same scene

Mal Couch had traveled to Parkland Hospital. He had told many there of his having seen a gun barrel in the Texas School Book Depository and his observation was passed on to the public. Ron Jenkins radioing from his KBOX mobile unit at Parkland reported, ". . . And a Dallas newsman Mal Couch said he was riding shortly behind the President in the parade. He said after the shots were fired he happened to look up at about the fifth or sixth floor of the Texas School Book Depository. He said he saw the rifle being pulled back in." The report got onto the wire services as around 1:55 Dallas time NBC New York newscaster Merrill Miller announced, ". . . We also have two eyewitness reports from the wire services. One eyewitness reporter, a television reporter named Mal Couch said he saw a gun emerging from the window of a warehouse." Then around 2:00 Couch's own news director, Bob Walker, also mentioned, ". . . Our WFAA-TV reporter Mal Couch saw the gun emerge from the upper story of a warehouse,

As a father and children at Parkland react to the news of the death of President Kennedy, a somber Mal Couch (with camera) pauses before continuing with his job.

which has turned out to be the second floor of the Texas Book Depository, which is a familiar sight." *New York Times* reporter Tom Wicker was at Parkland and at the time he made note of what Couch said, writing years after the event that, "A local television reporter, Mel Crouch [sic], told us he had seen a rifle being withdrawn from the corner fifth — or sixth floor window of the Texas School Book Depository. Instinct again — Crouch sounded right, positive, though none of us knew him. We believed it and it was right." Though these fragmentary reports indicated some factual errors — Couch's name, emerging rather than withdrawing, and the floor number — the basic fact of Couch's seeing the weapon was quickly reported.[31]

Following the President's death announcement, a majority of the visiting press boarded a bus for Love Field, and Couch apparently went along arriving just as Air Force One took off back for Washington. Travis Linn was sent from WFAA out to Love

Field to pick up Couch's film, which was brought back to the studio for processing.[32] Friday evening the Couch film was aired as part of an editing job done by Bert Shipp and incorporated into a running segment of spliced films titled, "The Last Hours of President Kennedy." It was re-broadcast at later intervals, including Saturday morning with voice-over narration done by NBC's Bob Clark.

After leaving Love Field Jimmy Darnell reported to the Dallas Police Department and remained on duty there into the early morning hours of Saturday. "I filmed Oswald when they brought him into the 'show up' room," recalls Darnell of Oswald's brief exposition to the hoards of press at an assembly room late Friday night. Darnell's wife had earlier that day been temporarily reassigned from her secretarial position with the Burglary and Theft office into Chief Curry's office to help answer the deluge of phone calls from all over the world. Jimmy Darnell was off-duty on Saturday and on-duty on Sunday at Parkland Hospital to catch up on Governor Connally's condition. Darnell was present to film Oswald being brought in following his being shot by Jack Ruby.[33]

The film work done by the various local and national cameramen on the scene in Dallas was in great demand for telecasting by the local stations and the networks. This film was looked upon merely as a tool for getting visuals out to TV viewers. The historical or investigative value of the films, if even considered, took a subservient role to its immediate story-telling value. Thereafter, much of the work of the various film makers was chopped up, edited, and spliced to visually tell the story the film editors were looking to tell. Some of the early films were deemed so newsworthy to the visually hungry stations that they were broadcast without editing. If the studio was videotaping its broadcasts, there exists a complete, though inferior, surviving copy of some of these early film sequences. Much "bad" film (under- or over-exposed or choppy sequences) was edited out and discarded, and the authorship and time sequences were often helplessly muddied. Today most of the original 16mm prints of the work of Darnell, Couch, Underwood, Sanderson, L'Hoste and the other cameramen are broken up at best, mislaid, unaccounted for, or completely lost at worst. None of their work was ever seriously collected or used in the FBI, Warren Commission, or HSCA investigations.

## CHAPTER NOTES

1.  Richard K. Van Der Karr, *Crisis in Dallas*, p. 2-8; John B. Mayo, Jr., *Bulletin From Dallas: The President is Dead*, p. 143.
2.  Van Der Karr, op. cit., p. 10-13.
3.  Ibid.; WFAA-TV, *The Kennedy Tapes*, 11/19/1983.
4.  Van Der Karr, op. cit., p. 13, 81-82; Letter, Jimmy Darnell to Trask, 12/17/1993.
5.  Ibid., p. 12; *Hearings Before the President's Commission on the Assassination of President Kennedy*, v. 6, p. 168; "Jim Underwood" [obituary] *Fort Worth Star Telegram*, 9/6/1983; Texas Department of Health Certificate of Death, Jim Underwood, state file # 79606.
6.  *Hearings*, op. cit., v. 6, p. 153-154.
7.  Mayo, op. cit., p. 135; Underwood/Sanderson 16 mm film, 11/22/1963. A copy of this film was obtained by the author in 1987 through the CBS News Archives Development Department. The

film's CBS index assignment number is 178,876. It is attributed to "CBS/Craven" and described as a "16 mm, silent, b&w film." The film is not, however, that taken by Tom Craven, but rather the film made by Jim Underwood, as can be seen by its content and the location of the cameraman in Camera Car 3. Also spliced into this sequence are shots taken by George Sanderson from a stationary position at Main & Record Streets, as well as film taken at the Texas School Book Depository by Underwood after getting the camera from Sanderson. It would appear that the original film or a copy of it was sent on to New York by KRLD, and subsequently misidentified in the CBS film index.

8.   Ibid.; *Hearings*, op. cit., v. 6, p. 168.
9.   Couch film, 11/22/1963, from WFAA-TV, *The Kennedy Tapes*, 11/19-21/1983.
10.  *Hearings*, op. cit., v. 6., p. 155-156.
11.  Ibid., v. 6, p. 156-157.
12.  Ibid., v. 6, p. 169-170.
13.  Underwood film, op. cit.
14.  *Hearings*, op. cit., v. 6, p. 170-171.
15.  CBS Broadcast Transcripts, 11/22/1963, p. 13-14.
16.  Mayo, op. cit., p. 137.
17.  Ibid.
18.  FBI report by agent John T. McMurrer, C.R. 105, 12/18/1963; Mayo, op. cit., p. 138.
19.  WFAA-TV., op. cit.
20.  Certificate of Death, op. cit.
21.  FBI report by agents Richard E. Harrison & George W. Carlson, 11/29/1963, obtained by Trask through FOIA request # 277,779, 11/1986.
22.  NBC telecast, 11/22/1963, from Kennedy Library videotape copy, TNN-255 #17.
23.  Ibid., TNN-255-R1.
24.  Ibid., TNN-255 #17; Gary Mack, ed., *Coverups!*, 3/1986, p. 8.
25.  *Hearings*, op. cit., v. 6, p. 157-158.
26.  Couch film, op. cit.
27.  *Hearings*, op. cit., v. 3, p. 241-254, 266-269.
28.  Couch film, op. cit.
29.  Ibid.; *Hearings*, op. cit., v. 6, p. 159; U. S. Secret Service report by SA Elmer W. Moore, file # CO-2-34,030, C.R. 87, 12/9/1963.
30.  Mayo, op. cit., p. 82; "Interview with L'Hoste" & F25A, undated [ca. 1967] Georgetown University Library, Richard Sprague collection; L'Hoste film, WFAA-TV, op. cit. This film sequence, aired about 3:24 p.m. CST, is identified as being made by L'Hoste. Four clips, however, appear more logically to have been made by Couch. Their subject matter appears to be from Couch's recollections of items shot including a clip of the roadblock onto Stemmons Freeway and a telephoto shot of the west side of the Book Depository (see *Hearings*, v. 6, p. 159.) Several photos taken by Jim Murray include L'Hoste in the frame, including roll 1, #34, and roll 2, #8 & #9.
31.  Colpix Record, "Four Days That Shocked the World"; NBC telecast, op. cit., TNN 255 R2R3; WFAA-TV, op. cit.; Tom Wicker, *On Press*, p. 117.
32.  Log of audio tapes with notations at the Kennedy Library, PKA 6-3, 47:45.
33.  Letter, Darnell to Trask, op. cit.

## CHAPTER 18

# Dillard and Jackson

Though dissimilar in age, experience, background, and style, photographers Tom Dillard and Bob Jackson would share on the weekend of November 22, 1963, important and troubling experiences centering around the death of the President of the United States. And both these men would, in the pursuit of their craft, produce important visual images which would become burned into the American psyche. Tom Dillard, who worked as chief photographer for the *Dallas Morning News*, was perhaps the dean of the Dallas news photographers; while 29-year-old Robert Jackson, a staff photographer for only some three years, worked for the other major Dallas-area daily, the *Dallas Times Herald*.

Thomas Clinton Dillard was born in Fort Worth, Texas, October 26, 1914. In 1929 at the tender age of 14, young Tom went to work at the premier Fort Worth newspaper, the *Star-Telegram*, as a copy boy. Remaining in that position, he also eventually took on some sports and market writing tasks. After working there six years, Dillard now as a young man finally told the manager that he was tired being a copy boy, and asked for a chance to work within any other area of the paper. If he failed after a two weeks' try, he promised he would quit. The manager told Dillard that a photographer was needed, and although Dillard "didn't know anything about photography," he quickly applied himself and found the job to his liking. Dillard began his new photographic career in the days of the bulky Speed Graphic cameras, popping flash bulbs and heavy tripods. Dillard's career was set. "I became the fair-haired boy of society and sports, and became the star photographer on the *Star-Telegram*."

Although the Speed Graphic camera's large-format negative was the universally preferred camera for newspaper work prior to World War II, Dillard and others had begun experimenting with the so-called "miniature" 35mm cameras. While in Chicago in the 1930s covering a Golden Gloves boxing match, Dillard met a photographer who used 35mm exclusively, and the Texan was impressed with its results of capturing fast, live action. Back at the *Star-Telegram*, Dillard began occasionally working with a miniature Zeiss and did a lot of experimenting, trying to get an acceptable fine-grain film. He recalls, "We had a hell of a time. Nothing worked until Tri-X film." A small camera was easy to manage, and with the use of roll film, a photographer could get off many more shots than with having to change film plates after each exposure. Yet the slow speed of the film and the small size of the negative was considered just not as acceptable for newspaper purposes as the large format camera negatives. Out of necessity the large format cameras required these pre-World War II newspaper photographers to set up picture possibilities in their minds before taking them, or risk missing the shot completely.

During a visit by President Franklin Roosevelt to Fort Worth in the 1930s, the cameramen were aware that photographers of the President were usually told precisely when they could make their photos and after a few seconds they would be told to stop shooting. Dillard was ready. Roosevelt was on the back platform of a train and, "I was always very proud of the fact that I think I got four shots with the Speed Graphic including changing holders before they said 'stop.' That camera was an extension of my arm." This experience of making every shot count was typical of the 1930s generation of news photographers who would work into the 1950s and 1960s when smaller format cameras became the acceptable standard. "We were of the Speed Graphic single shot school — me particularly. I always shot what I saw. I composed pictures and I never shot hoping I'd get one. I always saw what I was shooting."[1]

When the war came along in 1941, Dillard attended Officer Candidate School in the Military and Air University eventually attaining the rank of lieutenant colonel. Assigned in 1944 as a major to the China-Burma-India area of operations, Dillard was an executive officer in a P.R. position. That's where he first met Frank Cancellare who, in Dallas 19 years later on November 22 would be the UPI photographer assigned to the presidential motorcade. It was while Dillard was in the C.B.I. theater that he picked up a small Leica F 35mm camera which he used and easily carried around in his pocket during the rest of the war.[2]

Dillard was scheduled to teach at the Air University, but then the war ended. As he recalls, "The *Dallas News* wanted me. They hired my wife and figured I'd follow." He had met his future wife when they had both worked at the *Star-Telegram*. "She was a much better newspaper man than I, and became the women's editor." After the war, however, Dillard wasn't ready to go back to a newspaper job quite yet. He obtained a position with the Veterans Administration, but after six months behind a desk discovered he couldn't stand government work. After teaching public relations at the Air University for a year, in 1947 Dillard finally settled into work at the *Dallas Morning News*.[3]

By 1963 Dillard managed the *Dallas Morning News* photo department as chief photographer. Besides managing and doing photographic work himself, Dillard also wrote the paper's aviation column. There were 12 people in his department, and although it was not unusual for some to still use Speed Graphic cameras, the transition to the smaller cameras was in full swing. "We were getting into the reflex cameras and were using Yashicas a lot as well as Nikons and the Mamiyaflex. The camera we issued our people was the Mamiyaflex with two or three lenses. A lot of people were also bringing their own 35mm cameras." The Mamiyaflex was a twin-lens reflex camera which allowed interchangeable lenses and utilized 120 film. It was a less expensive Japanese version of the Rolleiflex. Speaking of the cameras in use in 1963, Dillard explains, "By then many had gone to the Mami. The Yashica was cheap and was like a Rollei. It didn't hold up as long, but it was really quality. Mami's problem was that when you changed lenses you raised the thing up to block out the film so you wouldn't expose it. A lot of people left the thing up. I settled on a Nikon, but I also liked the Leica M1. I never liked reflex cameras for shooting flash because you couldn't see the flash hitting your subject in the eyeballs. That's your old photographer who knows when their eyes were open. I'd shut my eyes and see the picture that I shot. It was imprinted on my optic nerve. That's why I loved the Leicas for inside flash. I'd see the flash hit them in the eyes." Concerning issuing photo assignments Dillard recollects, "I had a log book. Paper assignment sheets were sent back to me from every department, and I assigned them to various members of the staff. I didn't instigate coverage. The *Dallas News* and I always considered it highly ineffective to go out and shoot everything that moved and then let the editor look at it. My theory was that as far as staff and costs were concerned, the most effective system was to know what you wanted to cover and then go cover it."[4]

Costs were always a concern to the paper, and Dillard recalls the pay scale for the staff photographers wasn't very high and materials always seemed in short supply. Staff photographer Clint Grant describes the 1963 photo department as being "just adequate" and with very limited equipment. "We were just beginning to use 35mm cameras and had few extra lenses. Little color was used as it took so long to process, get separation prints, then send it to the engraver on the other side of town, then back to our composing room in a couple of hours or so. We were just not ready for spot news color."[5]

According to Dillard each photographer usually did his own processing, with the lab men picking up the slack. Lab men were typically photographers who, on a rotation schedule, were assigned to this least favorite departmental chore. Much of their work was making on-demand print orders for the general public. Dillard also looked the other way allowing his staff personal access to the photo lab for their own work, as he felt their low salary justified some latitude. Concerning job security at the paper, Dillard noted, "We didn't fire people much. You had a job for life pretty much if you didn't hit the managing editor in the mouth. I had two men, however, who were so inept as photographers, that I eventually made them lab men."[6]

Robert Hill Jackson was born in Dallas on April 8, 1934. Jackson was an only child from a family with an affluent background, his father being an executive with the Dallas Savings and Loan, and his mother active in church affairs. Having a talent for drawing as a child, Jackson first discovered the world of photography after receiving a gift of a Baby Brownie Special. He attended Highland Park High School followed by Southern Methodist University where he studied business. He left in 1957, just 8 hours short of a degree. Engaging in free-lance photography, including much work with sports car racing, Jackson in October of 1958 joined the army on a six-month active duty plan through his local National Guard unit. In the army Jackson served as a photographer and picked up much on-the-job training. Following his active tour of duty, Jackson remained in the Guard, re-enlisting four years later while at the same time pursuing free-lance work.  In August of 1960 he was hired by the *Dallas Times Herald* as a staff photographer.

Jackson had married his childhood sweetheart, Margaret, and by November 1963 they had a one-year-old daughter and a new home on Sperry Street near White Rock Lake, some four miles northeast of downtown Dallas and the *Times Herald* building. Having accumulated some $4,000 worth of cameras, Jackson was described by colleagues as a quiet person with a very professional attitude.  Jackson was known not so much as a hard news photographer of the old school, but rather became noted as an exceptional fashion and society photographer.[7]

On November 22, 1963, Dillard had arrived at the *Morning News* office early to check on the day's heavy photographic assignments for the coverage of President Kennedy's visit to the city.  Around 10 a.m. he traveled to Love Field where the various other local press and media were gathering in anticipation of the arrival of Air Force One.  Bob Jackson also arrived there with other *Times Herald* photographers, including chief photographer John Maziotta.  Jackson had been assigned to shoot the airport arrival and then to ride in the motorcade in anticipation of any other possible newsworthy photo opportunities.  As the *Times Herald* was an afternoon paper, any pictures he took would have to be sent back to the office as fast as possible to make it into the late Friday edition.  By pre-arrangement Jackson would toss his most recent film from his vehicle within the motorcade to court reporter James Featherston, who would be located on the corner of Main and Houston Streets, near the very end of the downtown portion of the motorcade.  The film drop-off point was fairly close to the *Times Herald* office, and Featherston could quickly courier it back for processing and possible use in the 2 star edition, which would lock up at 1:15 p.m.[8]

For the Dallas motorcade the President would be using the custom built 1961, 21-foot long Lincoln Continental, a 7-passenger, 4-door drop-top convertible sedan equipped with removable, steel and transparent plastic roof panels. Built by Ford Advanced Vehicles from an initial stock Lincoln, the car cost $200,000 and was leased to the government for $500 per year.  It featured an hydraulically operated rear seat, four

Interior view of the presidential Lincoln

retractable side steps for agents as well as rear bumper steps, two radio-phones, and Firestone bullet-resistant tires.  Also in use would be one of two 1956 Cadillac touring sedans with top down, occupied by the Secret Service as a follow-up car and designated SS679X.  Both these vehicles had been flown ahead to Texas on an Air Force C130 from

Washington the day before.  After having been used in an earlier reception, they had been flown to Love Field arriving there around 6 p.m. Thursday evening and stored at the Main Terminal Building's underground garage.  At 11 a.m. on Friday the vehicles had been checked over and washed.  The Secret Service advance men were instructed not to place the bubble-top on the President's vehicle, as the earlier inclement weather was rapidly clearing.  The two cars were then driven out onto the tarmac near the landing point of Air Force One.[9]

Sign holders at Love Field

Awaiting the arrival of the presidential party, Dillard, "Made some pictures of a sign critical of the President, but everything was pretty open.  I was wandering around and shot pictures of the inside of the car he was going to use for reference purposes.  There was really nothing to do waiting out there for him to arrive."  The picture Dillard made of the protestor's sign included a group of mostly young people standing behind a chain-link fence, many smiling and good naturedly raising their homemade signs welcoming JFK in the name of the grass-roots Democrats towards the anti-Kennedy sign. The protest sign read, "HELP JFK STAMP OUT DEMOCRACY."[10]

Upon the President's arrival at 11:40, Dillard recollects, "From the minute they got out from the airplane I was shooting as fast as I could shoot.  It was very pleasant and he was into the crowd."  Dillard, wearing his light colored London Fog coat and sporting a favorite cap, had two cameras with him attached to straps around his neck — his old and small Leica F with a wide angle 28mm lens and a 35mm Yashica.  "I had a 100mm lens on the Yashica.  It didn't have an automatic shutter.  You had to raise the mirror, open the lens, focus, close the lens down and shoot it. When the President got off the plane I shot a whole bunch of pictures of him with the damn thing wide open. We all have done those things at times."

One of Dillard's photos of the airport scene includes the President and Mrs. Kennedy being greeted by a member of the official greeting party and trailed by Secret Service agents, including Special Agent-in-Charge Roy H. Kellerman.  Presidential driver William Greer is seen speaking with a Dallas Police officer in front of the Lincoln convertible.  In another photo which Dillard recalls making with "the 28mm held over my head," he captures the President and First Lady seated in their car still greeting people, and with the follow-up car right behind them and airfield personnel and Air Force One and Two in the background.  Numerous other photographers and cameramen like Dillard were working the arrival.  Jackson also had two cameras with him. One of his photos of the President and Mrs. Kennedy arriving just at the bottom of the gangway and being received by Mayor and Mrs. Earle Cabell would be used in cropped form in the Saturday issue of the *Times Herald*.[11]

A *Morning News* photographer makes a photo of the vehicle ready to leave. Agent Clint Hill is seen at far left.

Once the President was in his car, the reporters, photographers, and presidential staff scrambled for their assigned motorcade seats. Recalls Dillard, "The sad thing news-wise was the custom always was that a selected group of press people — photographers — were to ride a flat-bed truck in front of the President. That was standard procedure in all presidential parades. I was one of the selected photographers. I was the head man at my paper and a pretty good photographer, and was going to be one of the key photographers. I had a ticket for the luncheon. It was understood the flatbed was going to be there. But at the last moment it was canceled. We bounced around and ended up on one of those Chevrolet convertibles." Dillard and Jackson, who knew each other quite well, both got into the third camera car in the motorcade, which was the eighth car behind the President's. A Texas Department of Public Safety driver was assigned to this car which also carried local Dallas TV 16mm cameramen Jim Underwood, Malcolm Couch, and Jimmy Darnell. Dillard took the front right passenger seat while Jackson was right behind him in the right back seat, sitting not on the seat itself but on the top of the back seat for a better view.

The motorcade through Dallas was well received. "We rode in and shot what we could," explained Dillard, "and I watched rooftops and everything like that, and everyone was so glad to see him. I'm sure it was a very pleasant thing for the President." On at least one occasion, the motorcade stopped, and Dillard jumped out of his car to run out and perhaps get a general interest shot, but the cars resumed traveling before he could get up to the President. "On the whole ride, I had been watching the tops of buildings and watching for any signs of anything unusual which, of course, was a newsman's chore on

In Camera Car 3 Bob Jackson, with telephoto lens, looks up at the buildings on Main Street. Standing in front of Jackson is Tom Dillard in his London Fog coat.

a parade like that. We were all, as any news photographer is, rather tense when he is covering a presidential or an affair of that sort and he is trying to get whatever pictures possible and watching for every possibility . . . ." A fresh roll of Tri-X in his camera with

Early in the motorcade Dillard shoots
a contemptuous protest sign.

the wide angle lens, Dillard shot one photo of a man near the National Motor Club holding a sign bound to have been seen by the dignitaries. One of the few negative signs seen during the ride, the sign proclaimed, "Because of high regard for the presidency I hold you JFK and your blind socialism in complete contempt." Jackson later would relate, ". . . Because of the photographers in the car ahead of us who were sitting up on the back of the seat just like we were, we did

not have a clear view of the car at all times." When finally arriving in the downtown district, Dillard made four 28mm shots, holding the camera above his head, of the procession traveling down Main Street near the Adolphus Hotel. The crowds of spectators are eight to twelve deep, creating a very reduced one-lane passageway through the

street. Up ahead, a good block away, one can just pick out the President's car. Turning around in his seat, Dillard faces to the rear and shoots one last shot in the sequence looking back towards Dignitary Car 1 and the three other cars in front of the first bus. This was the last picture Dillard expected to take prior to the Trade Mart stop.[12]

At the intersection of Main and Houston Streets the motorcade was to turn right and travel northerly a short block and then take a sharp left at Elm Street. This

From Camera Car 3 Dillard photographs the motorcade vehicles trailing him on Main Street. The car in the foreground will be the one he jumps upon later on Elm Street.

area adjacent to Dealey Plaza would be the end of the heavy spectator viewing and the cars would be at the Trade Mart within five minutes. It was at the corner of Main and Houston that Jackson was to toss out his exposed film to the courier. As Dillard commented, "The thing was all over pretty much by then, and the cars' occupants were more or less relaxed, assuming that picture possibilities would be minimal as the motorcade would speed up en route to the Trade Mart." Jackson removed the film from one of his cameras, and as his convertible turned the right hand corner onto Houston, he spied reporter James Featherston and tossed the exposed roll of film towards him. The thrown film was caught in the cross-street wind and rolled into the street, and as Featherston scurried along the curb to retrieve it, all the photographers on board Camera Car 3, looking to their extreme right, laughed at the comedic sight. Jackson later testified, ". . . As I threw it out the wind blew it, caught it and blew it out into the street, and our reporter chased it out into the street and the photographers in our car, one of the photographers, was a TV cameraman whom I do not recall his name, and he was joking about the film being thrown out and he was shooting my picture of throwing the film out. . . . Well, as our reporter chased the film out into the street, we all looked back at him and were laughing, and it was approximately that time that we heard the first shot, and we had already rounded the corner, of course, when we heard the first shot. We were approximately almost half a block on Houston Street."[13]

Twenty-three years after the event, Tom Dillard still vividly recalled the scene: "It was a very bright, crisp day. And a shot sounded. I said, 'My God, they're throwing torpedoes at him.' Why I said 'torpedoes' I don't know. We called them 'nigger chasers' back when I was a kid. Then another shot fired and I said, 'My God, they're shooting at him.' And we were stopped pretty much, and then we were just creeping along." In testimony in 1964 Dillard reported what next transpired. "Well, after the third shot I know my comment was, 'They killed him.' I don't know why I said that, but Jackson — there was some running comment about what can we do or where is it coming from, and we were all looking. We had an absolutely perfect view of the School Depository from our position in the open car, and Bob Jackson said, 'There's a rifle barrel up there.' I said, 'Where?' I had my camera ready. He said, 'It's in that open window.' Of course, there were several open windows, and I scanned the building . . . and at the same time I brought my camera up and I was looking for the window. Now, this was after the third shot, and Jackson said, 'There's a rifle barrel up there,' and then he said it was the second from the top in the right-hand side, and I swung to it, and there was two figures below . . . ."[14]

In a by-line article in Saturday's *Times Herald*, Jackson wrote of the scene of the day before. "As I looked up to the window above, I saw a rifle being pulled back in the window. It might have been resting on the window sill. I didn't see a man. I didn't even see if it had a scope on it. . . . He [the gunman] had about a 45-degree angle from the building to the President's car. I looked to my left and I could see both cars speeding off, the President's car and the car behind him carrying the Vice-President. They disappeared under the underpass. Then I could see a colored family covering up their child on the grass. A policeman was down on his knee. I couldn't tell if he were hit. I thought the child was dead or something. Then the Negro parents picked up the boy and ran. As soon as I saw the rifle, I knew someone was trying to kill them, but it never entered my mind that he could be dead."[15]

Jackson later gave dramatic testimony in Washington, D.C., before the Warren Commission as to what he saw.

> And as we heard the first shot, I believe it was Tom Dillard from *Dallas News* who made some remark as to that sounding like a firecracker, . . . and before he actually finished the sentence, we heard the other two shots. Then we realized or thought it was gunfire, and then we could not at that point see the President's car. We were still moving slowly, and after the third shot the second two shots seemed much closer together than the first shot, than they were to the first shot. Then after the last shot, I guess all of us were just looking all around and I just looked straight up ahead of me which would have been looking at the School Book Depository and I noticed two Negro men in a window straining to see directly above them, and my eyes followed right on up to the window above them and I saw the rifle or what looked like a rifle approximately half of the weapon, I guess I saw, and just as I looked at it, it was drawn fairly slowly back into the building, and I saw no one in the window with it. . . . I said, "There is a gun," or it came from that window. I tried to point it out. But by the time the other people looked up, of course, it was gone, and about that time we were beginning to turn the corner.

In further testimony Jackson related that prior to the shooting his car was traveling not over 15 miles per hour. He recalled that the three shots he heard lasted some 5 to 8 seconds, and that though he did not see a telescopic sight on the gun, he saw some 8 to 10 inches of the stock, the barrel pointing west to his left and directly down the street. He also observed corrugated boxes stacked at the left of the open window, as high as the window was open. Jackson had his just-emptied camera with the telephoto lens in his lap and another camera on a strap around his neck, but as he later wrote, "It happened too fast, then, for me to get a photo of it."[16]

Before a Warren Commission lawyer in 1964, Dillard stated about the gunshots, "We were getting a sort of reverberation which made it difficult to pinpoint the actual direction, but my feeling was that it was coming into my face and, that I was facing north towards the School Depository — I might add that I very definitely smelled gunpowder when the car moved up at the corner." Dillard, years later, had vivid recollections of the incident. When asked by the author about the number of shots, he slowly and emphatically replied, "As distinct as I know I'm talking to you, I'm as convinced that there were three clear shots. I shot high-powered rifles all my life, bolt action rifles.

Right now that's my hobby. I shoot silhouettes. So there is no question of my being an expert witness as far as gunfire is concerned. The spacings [of the shots] were such that could be duplicated with one familiar with a bolt-action rifle. I thought they were fairly evenly spaced. I remember that gunpowder smell quite well. I said, 'My God, I smell gunpowder.' It was clear, crisp, fresh air. Gunpowder is not an unpleasant odor. It's not pervasive particularly, but you can smell it." Dillard also once remarked in a letter to another researcher concerning one person being able to fire the shots in the time sequence he recalled that, "I was positive at the time that there was plenty of time to get off three shots."[17]

As the Chevy convertible slowed down to a crawl with the School Book Depository looming in front of it, Dillard, in the midst of all the sudden confusion, reacted like the old-time pro that he was. His two cameras were on straps around his neck and loaded with Tri-X film, the shutters at a 1/500 second speed and the lenses at F-16 or F-11. Reacting to Jackson's words about the gun location, Dillard put his Leica to his eye and clicked off a shot. "I had my camera in my hand. I'm sure I shot it with the 28 [mm lens] first, and it's fairly well centered. Jackson said something like upper right hand corner, two down from the top, or whatever he said. By that time I had it dead centered. I'm sure the first picture is maybe a few seconds after the last shot." Dillard then grabbed his Yashica mounted with a 100mm lens and took a close-up photo of the window.[18]

Dillard's two photographs are sharp and well executed. To a casual observer they might be assumed to be architectural photographs made to record an overview and then a detail shot of the old building with its brick-patterned facade. The seven-story building with basement and a street address at 411 Elm Street was built in 1901 by the Southern Rock Island Plow Company to replace a five-story building which had burned down that same year. Of masonry load-bearing walls with heavy timber column and beam construction, this warehouse-type structure was said to be modeled after company buildings in Rock Island, Illinois. When completed it was locally described as "one of the most modern and thoroughly equipped houses in the South or West," and its architectural style is referred to as Commercial Romanesque Revival. The facade was made up of common, probably locally made salmon-red brick, while the paired double-hung windows were set in a structural masonry arch. An over-tall first floor is the result of the interior floor level being a number of feet above the outside street level. On the Elm Street first floor face, decorative masonry cutouts form the in-fill between six brick pediments of the main entrance. Six brick monumental pediments rise from the second to the sixth floor and are paired to form into five brick arches, while the two opposite side banks of windows are headed at the sixth floor with decorative horizontal brick banding. The seventh floor is set off from the bottom floors by masonry and brick dentil work, and its seven pair of double windows are taller than those below and flanked by sets of thin double brick pilasters. The roof is delineated by a wide cornice including octagon-shaped louvered vents.

Dillard's Leica 28mm view of the Book Depository, taken moments following the last rifle shot

In 1939 Dallas businessman D. H. Byrd purchased the building. Over the years he leased it to a variety of companies, including John Sexton and Company, and Binyon O'Keefe Storage Company. By 1963 the building was being rented by the Texas School Book Depository. This private corporation served as an agent for a number of school book publishers, including its biggest account, Scott-Foresman and Company. Space was available to publishers who desired Texas offices while the bulk of the building and business was concerned with collecting, inventorying, shipping, and doing the book-keeping for the various publishers' books to be used principally in Texas school districts. Publishers' stock was located in the basement, first, and fourth through seventh floors. It was through this company that Lee Harvey Oswald applied for a job on October 15, 1963, and was hired at $1.25 an hour by Superintendent Roy S. Truly to fill book orders.

In 1963 one could see on top of the roof a flagpole set on the front southeast corner together with a large Hertz advertisement sign kitty-cornered on the building. The sign displayed a lighted sequence with a timed cycle which alternately flashed the time of day and the temperature. The sign was strapped and bolted to the roof through the wood columns below, which during windy days rocked the building. A long narrow metal fire escape was attached to the building on its east side.[19]

At a point on Houston Street about 60 feet from the southeasterly corner of the Depository, Dillard had taken his wide-angle shot of the upper portion of the building. His negative was frame #8 on the roll, and the lens's wide-angle view took in the entire roof facade including the flagpole and a portion of the Hertz sign, and almost the entire seventh floor. As one examines the picture's content from the top floor down, increasing portions of the westerly end of each floor are missing from the photo as Dillard was not concentrating on the entire facade, but rather on that portion pointed out by Jackson. At the lower edge of the photo, one can just discern the top brick archwork of several second floor windows.

Of the five double sets of windows visible on the third floor, all containing venetian blinds, the third window from the east side reveals a man wearing a suit who is looking out of the closed window. Stephen F. Wilson, a publishing company officer, watched the motorcade from the company's main office. He had raised the blinds, but the window remained closed as it was secured with screws due to the room's being air conditioned. Wilson later stated, "The three shots were fired within a matter of less than five seconds. The shots sounded to me like rifle shots. At the time it seemed shots came from the west end of the building or from the colonnade located on Elm Street across from the west end of our building. The shots really did not sound like they came from above me." Having just a year earlier suffered a heart attack, Wilson had decided to forego the possible jostling of the parade spectators below, and instead sat in a chair watching the motorcade through his window. Just before the shots were fired, Miss Doris Burns, who worked on the same floor, but had no desire to see the President go by her place of employment, was listening to the radio. As it was broadcast that the President's car was turning onto Houston Street, she decided to go and look out a window. As she was walking she heard one report. Her timing was off, and as she entered Mr. Wilson's office, he exclaimed, "Oh, my God, there's been a shooting." Burns asked, "Has the President already passed?" Wilson, watching the confusion below answered, "Yes," and Burns turned back out of the office with the comment, "Well, I hope nobody got hurt." Wilson watched from the window for quite some time until his workers returned to the office. He then had to lie down for a time as he was feeling so upset about the shooting.[20]

Dillard's wide angle photo also captured activity on the building's fourth floor. At least eight employees of book publisher Scott-Foresman and Company watched the motorcade from windows on that floor. Dorothy Garner looked out of the fifth window from the east while Elsie Dorman viewed from the adjacent sixth window. Co-workers Victoria Adams and Sandra Styles shared the view from these double windows. Mrs. Dorman was a 57-year-old native of Pembroke, Maine, who had married aircraft mechanic John T. Dorman in Boston in the late 1920s. The couple had moved to Dallas in 1951, where Mrs. Dorman continued to work for Scott-Foresman as a secretary, having joined the company in 1946. In a sworn statement to the FBI months after the shooting Mrs. Dorman related, "On November 22, 1963, I went to a window near my desk to view and photograph the presidential motorcade as it passed along Houston and

Elm Streets. I was using my husband's camera and was not too familiar with its operation. As the motorcade turned on to Houston Street from Main Street, I started taking photographs. I was seated on the floor with the camera in the window. The window was raised. I continued taking photographs, but as the motorcade turned from Houston Street to Elm Street, I became excited and did not get any more photographs. I was at this window attempting to photograph the motorcade when I heard a noise like gun shots. I did not see Lee Harvey Oswald and have no recollection of having seen him." In an earlier and briefer FBI interview, Mrs. Dorman indicated, "She felt that these shots were coming from the area of the Records Building," which was the building diagonally southeast of her position, on the corner of Elm and Houston Streets. Incredibly the FBI did not pick up on Mrs. Dorman's having made a movie from a window within the Book Depository Building at the time of the assassination. No evidence has come to light to indicate that they looked at nor requested a copy of the film which more closely than any others would replicate the view of a possible sixth floor assassin — an example of incredible incompetence on the part of the investigation. It wasn't until 1967 when *LIFE* magazine published three frames of the film that its existence became generally known. The *LIFE* editors noted that during the summer of 1967 they learned of Elsie Dorman and her movie which she kept in a closet, never showing it to anyone.[21]

Dorman's view of the Lincoln
on Houston Street

The elevated view of her camera picked up the President's vehicle just after it turned onto Houston Street, and as the Vice-President's convertible is into its turn. The film is choppy, the panning erratic, and the camera appears to have had a telephoto lens. Researcher Richard Sprague, who in 1967 visited the Dormans and saw the movie, recalls, "The movie starts with JFK just after rounding the turn at Houston and Main. She continued until well after the last shot, but missed JFK because of the trees. She also aimed her camera too high, and caught mostly trees. . . . You can see the top of Mayor Cabell's head as he goes by." Mrs. Dorman told Sprague she had stopped filming when the President's car was right below her window and that when she resumed filming, she aimed the camera by peering over the viewfinder, so she could see the President. Sprague describes the film as containing two sequences with an approximate total of 400 frames. The final sequence in the Dorman film is an erratic one in which spectators on the southwest corner of Elm and Houston Streets are seen as she then pans left onto Houston Street to reveal motorcycle cop Hollis B. McLain beginning to make the sharp left turn on to Elm Street moments after the third shot has hit the President in the head, some 240 feet westerly on Elm Street. After serving Scott-Foresman for 25 years, Mrs. Dorman retired in 1971. She survived her husband some six years, dying in 1983. By the mid 1980s, the film, reported broken in two places, was in the possession of son John, a Tenneco oil executive.[22]

In Dillard's wide angle photo, the fourth floor's fifth window and half-opened lower sash sixth window does not reveal obviously identifiable human bodies, although there are at least two images visible. Vickie Adams testified that within seconds after the last shot both she and Sandra Styles had run to the back stairs wanting to get down to ground level and find out what was happening, particularly on the west side.[23]

The next set of westerly windows on the fourth floor records what appears to be an elderly lady in a long dress peering out of the window with her right hand raised. Some have erroneously identified this woman as Elsie Dorman, believing that her testimony concerning her filming while sitting on the floor and through an open window was incorrect. Dorman and her co-workers' statements show clearly that she was filming from the adjacent open window. The older woman standing at the window is undoubtedly 66-year-old Ruth Nelson, who along with Yola Hopson, watched the motorcade from this specifically identified pair of windows in the middle of the building.[24] Finally, on the fourth floor, at the second from last set of windows, one of the windows is opened all the way up from the bottom sash, wherein stands a buxom young woman looking in a westerly direction. Although unidentified, she might be Betty Foster or Mary Hollies, as these two women deposed that they were in the fourth floor stock room from where they also viewed the motorcade and shooting.[25]

The fifth floor was also occupied by persons watching the motorcade. Street-level witnesses would later remember seeing them prominently in the open east-end windows of the Elm Street facade. Harold Norman, a 26-year-old order filler, and James Jarman, Jr., a 34-year-old checker, were both employees of the Texas School Book Depository. Both had seen co-worker Lee Oswald on that Friday morning, Jarman answering Oswald's query about the President's supposed to be passing the building that morning from the direction of Houston Street. Around noon the two young black men had briefly gone out to Elm Street to see the procession, but shortly before it arrived, they opted to view it from an upper story of the building. Norman positioned himself on the eastern-most window of the fifth floor and "Junior" as he was called, at the fourth window from the east. Just prior to the pass-by, the two were joined by Bonnie Ray Williams, who normally worked at the other Dallas Book Depository Building, but was temporarily here at Elm Street to help lay a new plywood floor on the fifth and sixth floors. Williams knew Oswald only by sight, and when he and others had kicked off for lunch, he later related that Oswald called down for the co-workers to send the elevator back up. After washing up for lunch, Williams had taken his paper bag lunch consisting of a chicken sandwich and a bag of Fritos and a bottle of Dr. Pepper back to the sixth floor. He ate lunch around the third or fourth set of windows surrounded by stacks of book boxes. He left his trash by the window and ended up joining Norman and Jarman on the fifth floor at the second window from the east side. Later, Williams's lunch leavings would be discovered by the police and identified as possible remains from a lunch casually eaten by the lurking assassin. Later that same afternoon pictures of police

Allen photo of detective
carrying out the bottle and bag
(covered with fingerprint powder)
and a cigarette wrapper

detectives carefully carrying the lunch debris out of the building would be made by various photographers including Dallas's Willie Allen and Forth Worth *Star-Telegram* photographer George Smith.[26]

The faces of Norman, Jarman and Williams were captured in Dillard's first photo as they peered from the fully open bottom sash windows of the fifth floor. According to testimony by Williams, within a minute after the last shot was fired the three had left these windows. In testimony before the Warren Commission, Williams in answer to questions of attorney Joseph A. Ball, stated about his experiences while at the window:

After the President's car had passed my window, the last thing I remember seeing him do was, you know — it seemed to me he had a habit of pushing his hair back. I assumed he was brushing his hair back. . . . And then the thing thathappened then was a loud shot —first I thought they were saluting the President, somebody — even maybe a motorcycle backfire. The first shot — there was two shots rather close together. The second and the third shot was closer together than the first shot and the second shot, as I remember. . . .

Well, the first shot — I really did not pay any attention to it, because I did not know what was happening. The second shot, it sounded like it was right in the building, the second and third shot. And it sounded — it even shook the building, the side we were on. Cement fell on my head. . . . Cement, gravel, dirt, or something, from the old building, because it shook the windows and everything. Harold was sitting next to me, and he said it came right from over our head. . . . My exact words were, "No bull shit." And we jumped up. . . . [Norman] said it came directly over our heads. "I can even hear the shell being ejected from the gun hitting the floor. . . .

I think Jarman, he — I think he moved before any of us. He moved towards us, and he said, "Man, somebody is shooting at the President." And I think I said again, "No bull shit." And then we all kind of got excited. . . .

We saw the policemen and people running, scared, running — there are some tracks on the west side of the building, railroad tracks.

They were running towards that way. And we thought maybe — well, to ourself, we know the shots practically came from over our head. But since everybody was running, you know, to the west side of the building, towards the railroad tracks, we assumed maybe somebody was down there.[27]

When asked by then congressman and Commission member Gerald R. Ford why the trio hadn't gone up to the sixth floor, Williams responded, "I really don't know. We just never did think about it. And after we had made this last stop, James Jarman said, 'Maybe we'd better get the hell out of here.' And so we just ran down to the fourth floor, and came on down. We never did think about it, going up to the sixth floor. Maybe it was just because we were frightened."

In 1993, a day shy of the 30th anniversary of the assassination, this author had the opportunity to speak with Norman at the base of the former Texas School Book Depository. He recalled the events of three decades earlier: "I heard the first shot when the motorcade came by. It looked like the President slumped. I heard two more shots. Just above me I could hear the [shell] hulls hitting the floor, and I heard the bolt action on the rifle being pushed back and forward. The rhythm of the shots were like 'boom! click, click; boom! click, click; boom!'"[28]

In the first Dillard photo, the sixth floor easternmost window is empty of any human figure. Dillard, though fast on his shutter trigger, had not captured what Jackson had seen. The first window is raised so the bottom sash is halfway open. To the left and right of the window's mid-line one can note objects caught in the light of the noon sun which appear to be cardboard boxes.

Now sure of where to shoot his picture, Dillard quickly switched to his Yashica mounted with the telephoto lens. As his car was still virtually stopped dead in the street below, Dillard snaps a well executed, clear focused shot. It was frame #24 on the roll in the Yashica. The sunlight reflects on the window glass of one of the fifth floor sash and each individual brick and their combined decorative patterns are clearly delineated. The center of the photograph includes the east side fifth and sixth floor double windows. Harold Norman, slightly inside the room, seems to be peering in Dillard's direction. To Norman's right Williams, leaning further forward, is caught in the sun looking to his right down toward lower Elm Street. The open sixth floor window above the two still does not reveal any person, though the boxes, one with its corner facing the outside, are more easily identifiable than in Dillard's previous picture. Dillard's two shots were technically well executed and in the finest tradition of spot news photographs. What he captured, however was an unexciting photograph of the scene after the fact. If the probable assassin had lingered a second or two longer in the window, or Dillard had been able to shoot even faster than he actually did, this photograph could have been the most important photo taken that weekend, solving many later debated and unresolved questions. And Dillard most probably would have gotten for himself a Pulitzer Prize in

Dillard's Yashica telephoto view of the fifth and sixth floor corner windows

photography.  Some assassination critics would later claim that Dillard had in fact shot a picture of what the window would have looked like five, ten, thirty, or even sixty seconds earlier — simply an empty window.  Yet, as Dillard would later incredulously comment about those critics, "There are still questions of whether the bullets came from that window, aren't there?  Hell, the gun was there, the empties were there, the angle was right, Bob saw him poking the gun out the window.  God, Almighty, what more do they want to know?  I can't understand people."[29]

Dillard, however, was not the only person who photographed the upper stories of the School Book Depository right after the shooting.  A curiously intriguing and somewhat obscure photographer took another picture less than half a minute after Dillard's from a position only some 100 feet from the building at the southeast corner of Elm and Houston Streets. There are very few references to James Powell and his picture within the Commission records, and that which is included is fragmentary and somewhat contradictory. James W. Powell was a Special Agent of Region II, 112th INTC, Army Intelligence Corps, which had offices at 912 Rio Grande Building in Dallas. The official role of Army Intelligence in the visit of President Kennedy to Dallas is unclear.  Along with other protective service people, one of the occupants of the motorcade's pilot car was Lieutenant Colonel George Whitmeyer, U. S. Army Dallas Sub-Action Commander.  Powell is silent in his brief post-assassination interviews as to

Slide view of the Depository Building made by James Powell

his official role that day, if any, and of just where precisely he was at the time of the shooting. In an FBI report dated January 3, 1964, it is stated that, "Powell was approximately one-half block east of the intersection of Elm and Houston, and the presidential motorcade had already turned west on Elm, when he heard two shots and possibly a third fired at President Kennedy. He then ran to the southeast corner of Elm and Houston Street intersection and, seeing some people pointing to the Texas School Book Depository Building, he took a picture." In a Secret Service report of an interview of January 28, 1964, the statement is made that, "Mr. Powell was interviewed relative to his location at the time of the assassination and his actions subsequent to the assassination. Mr. Powell stated that he had been watching the parade from a position near the corner of Houston and Elm Streets, the site of the assassination. Mr. Powell stated further that he heard the shots and then joined a group of Sheriff's Deputies, who were heading towards the rear of the Texas School Book Depository on the basis of the information that the assassin had shot from the railroad yards."[30]

Was Powell watching the motorcade at the corner of Elm and Houston, and as soon as the President's vehicle passed him, but was not out of sight, did he quickly start walking easterly, or was he in fact watching from the corner itself? A photograph taken by AP's Jim Altgens of the presidential vehicle on Houston Street does show a young man at the northeast corner of Houston and Elm Street wearing an Army uniform with what appears to be a private's single stripe on his tunic. Only one of his hands can be seen and it does not hold any object like a camera. The soldier appears to be with a woman. It is not known if Powell was in uniform, though military personnel often were not uniformed when in sensitive situations. No mention is made of Powell wearing a uniform that day.[31]

From his FBI interview we know Powell had with him a Minolta 35mm camera loaded with Kodachrome X slide film with an ASA of 64. The shutter was set at 1/25th of a second focused on infinity and set at F-11, and his picture was taken approximately 30 seconds after the last shot.[32]   No mention is made of other photographs taken by him at the time, although it would seem logical that if Powell was at the scene of the motorcade with a camera, he would take pictures of the event. If he were not viewing the motorcade, but located one-half block away, why wouldn't he bother to watch the motorcade, and why did he have a camera with him?  The impression one has when reading these sketchy interviews is that either purposefully or not, Powell's actions, location, and photos taken are not candidly revealed. Neither the Secret Service nor the FBI seemed to bother following up with the obvious question of whether or not Powell had other pictures taken before or after the shooting.

The Powell color photograph which finally found its way into the record, shows portions of windows of the second floor as well as windows of the upper five floors, including some on the west side not included in the Dillard wide-angle photograph. Two additional windows on this west end of the sixth floor are recorded as open along with the three seen in the Dillard shot. An open window at the west end of the fifth floor is also visible. The young woman on the fourth floor window peering out in a westerly direction, and Bonnie Williams on the fifth floor, are still both in place as in Dillard's photo. From Powell's testimony and a physical examination of the site viewed by this author utilizing an uncropped print of the Powell photograph, it is clear that his picture was taken at the Houston and Elm Street southeastern curb.[33]

Examining the interviews of Powell, it would appear that following the shots and his making the picture, Powell followed Sheriff's Deputies to the rear of the Depository near the railroad yards and, "worked with the Sheriff's Deputies" for some six to eight minutes. He questioned a man near the entrance of the Depository who he believes was a beer company employee whom the police took under control for questioning. Upon entering the front door of the building, Powell observed WFAA-TV reporter Pierce Allman using a phone in the lobby and another man with Allman. Powell wanted to use the phone to call his office, and according to one researcher's information, he ordered the man to hang up the phone so he could use it. On entering the building Powell did not meet anyone, nor was he called upon to identify himself. He remained long enough however to be "trapped inside . . . after the Depository doors had been sealed." In the Secret Service report it states, "Mr. Powell has submitted a report of his activities immediately subsequent to the assassination of the President and states that his report will be available to this office upon request." Although this report may be the earlier

FBI interview report, it sounds like a report filed with the Army, and if so, this is not presently in the public record.[34]

We might presume Powell's film belonged to him personally as he had it developed at the Cardinal Card and Camera Store in Dallas, and although ". . . he could not see anything otherwise significant in this picture" other than the Negro male on the fifth floor, he apparently turned it over to Lt. Col. E. E. Boyd who, in turn, made the transparency available to the FBI.[35]

This photograph first came to public light in black-and-white form in 1976 and was first published in the Gary Shaw book *Cover-Up*. Yet in 1977 FBI director Clarence M. Kelly was informing researchers that the photographs, ". . . were only available to the FBI temporarily. The photographs have been returned to the Army Intelligence Corps." Freedom of Information Act requests in the mid-1980s to the FBI have resulted in color, and black-and-white copies being made available, though print copies of this photograph are invariably cropped.[36]

During the congressional House Select Committee on Assassinations investigation in 1977-1978, both the original two Dillard negatives and a copy of the Powell transparency were examined by the photographic panel looking for evidence of a gunman. The panel, through outside contracted reports prepared by the Rochester Institute of Technology and the Stanford Research Institute, Inc., showed that by analysis of shadows these photos were taken at approximately the same time though Dillard's two were made first. Through photographic enhancement and utilizing photo-optical and photo-chemical techniques and autoradiographic enhancement, details within the Dillard negatives were made visible in the underexposed regions of the photographs in the area of the interior of the windows. The major item revealed from this process was a circular light fixture including a light bulb hanging from the ceiling of the fifth-floor room. In none of the three photographs examined were there any signs of a human face or form in the open sixth floor or adjacent window. Through what was described as a simple "trigonometric calculation" it was noted in the photographic report that concerning the placement of boxes in the sixth-floor corner window, ". . . the additional boxes visible in the Powell photograph were moved during the interval between the Dillard and Powell photographs." Thus if the report were accurate, following the last shot, someone had moved some of the boxes into a different pattern within less than a half of a minute of the shots. Subsequent examinations of these photos, the box locations and sunlight patterns would indicate that there is no inconsistency.[37]

SRI International had been the firm which had submitted a proposal to the House Select Committee for the autoradiographic intensification of the important Dillard negatives. It was assumed that by means of state-of-the-art enhancement information possibly hidden within the negatives could be revealed. Costing the Committee over $5,000 for the study, SRI noted that the proposed non-destructive radioactivity procedure had been used in thousands of cases, with the negatives returned in their original state with no measurable alteration of their image quality. Dillard, who had custody of the original negatives, cooperated by turning over twelve of his original negatives, four of which were eventually processed.

SRI was careful to note, however, that it would not accept liability in the event of inadvertent image degradation during the project. The early fall 1978 study resulted in the findings mentioned above. Unfortunately, the negatives, particularly frame 24, were irreparably damaged. In a letter to the Committee, the SRI radiation physics manager explained how the frames had been "radiochemically toned, autoradiographed, and the I-125 isotope removed." During the removal of the isotope, frame 24, ". . . became detached from the agitation apparatus and the gelatine was abraded during the time it was freely agitated without support." Reiterating that the procedure is non-destructive, blame for the damage done was placed upon the malfunction of the equipment. Apologies and regrets were extended to the Committee and Dillard. Committee independent consultant Robert Groden was asked to comment upon the damage. He found that negative #8 had also been damaged by a coating not originally present, but now evident on its emulsion face. The image itself was in poor condition, showing the effects of reticulation, and having the appearance of small cross-hatchings running through the image area. Negative #24 suffered from this problem as well. Compound-

Irreparable damage done to the Dillard negative frame #24 during the course of the SRI study

ing that damage was the fact that part of the negative area appeared to have had its emulsion rubbed off from the film base. To a lay person, the negative looks deplorable — the emulsion of part of the image having the appearance of having melted and oozed down into a frozen taffy-like pool below. The left side of the so-called sniper's double window is badly affected, though the lower portion of the sniper's window itself escaped the most serious damage. The entire negative also has a worn and crackled look.

By early 1979 Dillard was sent back his damaged goods, together with copies of the SRI report and letter and the Groden comments. Chief Counsel Blakey lamely wrote Dillard that the Committee was assured the process was non-destructive and regretted the damage to Dillard's property. These two historically significant frames had been irreversibly harmed by experts.[38]

We had left Dillard on November 22 still seated in the third camera car. After making a quick shot of the building with each of his cameras, the photographer instinctively jumped out from the front right side of the motionless convertible. "I wasn't doing any good sitting there. I wanted to get out there where I could see something. . . . I dashed down to the corner and looked down, and there were people lying on the ground. And I shot a picture there as his car was racing on up getting out of there. . . . It's just a shot kind of into the sun, into the light. I think the car in my picture may be the Mayor's car. The first thing I did when I got to where I could see something, I shot a picture. What you do always — what I always tell news photographers is, 'For Christ sake, when you come up on a fire or a scene — shoot a picture, the first thing you see, shoot it. Then move in for close ups. Shoot the overall picture first when you get there. Start shooting from the first sight of any major news event — shoot.'"[39]

Following the assassination, Dillard captures the Camera Cars on Elm Street.

Dillard's running shot, frame #25 of his roll in the Yashica camera mounted with a telephoto lens, shows the triple underpass in the background including parts of the Elm and Commerce Streets tunnel and all of the Main Street tunnel entrance. On the extreme left of the photo, spectator James Tague is seen standing near the vertical abutment column which straddles the Main and Commerce entrances. Atop the bridge are some 11 men, most in hats, some wearing railroad engineer caps, most looking down at the action below. Camera Car 2, having passed the first camera car, is just ready to approach the shadow of the tunnel. Camera Car 1, now the second in line, is in the middle of the frame and in the middle of the street. Its brake lights are on. All the car occupants, including cameramen Dave Wiegman and Tom Craven are looking hard to their right, two with outstretched hands, as a fast-running White House cameraman Tom

Atkins approaches the car to attempt a pick up.  In the foreground, partly out of the frame, Camera Car 3, with Bob Jackson looking to his right, makes its way down the street, beginning to veer left to avoid and pass the other vehicle.

In his Warren Commission testimony, Dillard declared what he did next.  "Well, I made a picture of the cars moving into the sun under the underpass, somebody chasing the car, and I looked at the situation in that area and saw absolutely nothing of the presidential car or anything that appeared worth photographing to me at the time. . . . Another car, Chevrolet convertible, of the party came by with, I assume, dignitaries in it and I jumped on the back of it and we started — I told them, of course, who, who I was and we started out Stemmons Expressway toward the Trade Mart and I explained to them what I knew and tried to hold onto the back of the car at a rather high speed."[40]

The car the 49-year-old photographer jumped onto was a dignitary car directly behind Camera Car 3 and containing Texas Congressmen as well as presidential Assistant for Congressional Affairs, Lawrence O'Brien.  O'Brien recalled Dillard's thumping himself onto the back of the car which on the Expressway traveled some 60 to 70 miles per hour. O'Brien's recollections of Dillard's actions is slightly different from the cameraman's.  "And a photographer jumped on the trunk of our car, it was a convertible, holding on to the edge of the seat, and pounding his fist on the trunk, and obviously in a most excited state.  We did not get anything coherent from him. I do not think we really attempted to because at that point, as he hung on to our car, obviously to try and keep up with the motorcade himself, our car moved out with great speed."[41]

Earlier, Camera Car 3 occupants Underwood and Darnell had also jumped out of the car just after Dillard.   Bob Jackson and Channel 8 TV cameraman Malcolm Couch remained in the car until it passed under the railroad bridge.  As the car reached

Arriving at Parkland, Dillard first took several establishing shots, his first pictures since at the site of the assassination.  With his Yashica he recorded cameramen, including Wiegman and Atkins, at right.  Near the follow-up car DPS drivers, several cycle cops, and a Secret Service agent are visible.  The wide-angle view shows the President's car in the ambulance bay, the cameramen shooting Press Assistant Kilduff, while cycle cops at left receive instructions.

the curve approaching Stemmons Freeway, the driver finally slowed down so these last two photographers could also jump out. They ran back to the area of the shooting and from there into the parking area west of the Depository Building. Tarrying there forsome minutes, the two decided that nothing newsworthy was occurring and that they should get to the President. They hitched a ride to the Freeway where they were briefly stopped at a roadblock. Arriving at the Trade Mart, Jackson learned that the President had apparently gone to Parkland Hospital, and he and UPI photographer Frank Cancellare hitched another ride. Arriving at the hospital, Jackson took his first photographs since before the incident.[42]

Dillard preceded Jackson to the hospital and began making pictures of the confused scene where remnants of the motorcade continued to arrive and were mixing in with curious hospital employees and an ever-growing crowd of spectators. "There I photographed everything. I photographed the car [Vice-President's convertible] with the roses in it down on the floor. I tried to get something that told the story. Yellow roses on the floor of the car. I photographed the President's car with the top down and all, and then they came along and put the top up.

I tried to photograph people around there, and nobody knew nothing. A sick feeling." Dillard remained at Parkland quite a while. When the crowd learned that the President was dead, Dillard remembers, "I was trying to get pictures of reaction around the hospital. People standing around crying."[43]

The remainder of the day blurs in Dillard's memory. Returning back to the *Morning News* building, he developed and printed up his photographic take of the day and tried to coordinate the photo coverage of this hectic and confusing news event. All Friday night Dillard stayed up working along with police reporter Harry McCormick. Dillard learned of the existence of a film made

One of a five-shot sequence made by Dillard at Parkland of press gathered around two young men. The youth with a 35mm camera is identified on one print as "Boy who shot pix of Pres. & Jackie right after shooting." This is possibly the event recalled by AP photographer Henry Burroughs. Could this be Al Volkland?

of the assassination by local businessman Abraham Zapruder, and he attempted to obtain print rights to some of the frames when he discovered that other news agencies were pressing Zapruder to sell his film. "I was trying to get a print of the Zapruder film at the lab. I was trying to con Zapruder into telling him if I ran a black-and-white in the *News*, it would make his film much more salable." By the next day *LIFE* magazine had purchased rights to the Zapruder film. Dillard had years earlier worked as a stringer for *LIFE* covering Texas events and "had a lot of stuff published in *LIFE* magazine." He was not happy at how the magazine always had the money and clout to get its way. "People jump through their assholes when the word '*LIFE*' was mentioned. They would do anything. But you couldn't get the whole school turned out for a school picture. You did what you could. Although it may sound like sour grapes, I could do in 1/10th of the time with 1/100th of the film what they did. And get a better picture than they did."[44]  To say the least, Dillard was unimpressed by much of *LIFE*'s mythical camera work and resented *LIFE*'s power over the American psyche.

Beginning that Friday afternoon the onslaught of the out-of-town press was tremendous. National and international photographers, commentators, and reporters poured into Dallas from airports around the country and the world. Dillard recalls the pressures exerted on his newspaper as it tried to be cooperative. *Dallas Morning News* owner Joe Dealey let it be known his staff would be helpful, including allowing outside press to order and obtain photo prints from his newspaper for a $1.50 lab fee. Bemoans Dillard, "We were tired, and didn't like printing pictures for somebody else. Dealey had turned them loose in our [photo] library and they stole all the prints — any pictures they could. We practically turned everything over to the sons of bitches. They were frantic." *Morning News* photographer Clint Grant, whom Dillard recalls as a great animal, kid, and feature photographer as well as a fine and kind gentleman, also described the virtual rape done to the photo department. ". . . The visiting press, who were given free access to our photo and print files immediately after the shooting, robbed us blind. They just cleared out our files on anyone the least involved." Protecting his own negatives from the onslaught, Dillard kept his film unfiled in a box within his locked desk drawer. By the 1990s the assassination-related photographs were stored in the lateral reference files with other Kennedy related photographs and within the room containing the paper's photograph collection. The assassination materials include various 8" x 10" prints, contact sheets and negatives. Gaps in each category are present, however, and many negatives are either missing or mislaid.[45]

Bob Jackson also remained busy Friday into Saturday. In the final edition of the Friday evening *Dallas Times Herald*, the first page news story mentions Jackson having heard three shots and seeing the assassin's rifle being drawn back into the window. The Saturday edition included a Jackson photo of the President and Mrs. Kennedy being greeted on the gangway at Love Field by Mayor Earle Cabell as well as a by-line article recounting Jackson's experiences of the day before.[46]

Dillard and Jim Underwood, another occupant of Camera Car 3, would together make one other series of pictures which have a bearing on the presidential assassination story, although these pictures were not taken until Saturday, November 23. During the afternoon of November 22, while Underwood was still in Dealey Plaza following up on the shooting story, he had been shown by a deputy sheriff a mark on the curbing at the south side of Main Street about 20 feet from the underpass entrance. The mark was white, fresh, and appeared to be a smear adhering to the curb, though not having chipped the cement itself. It was speculated that this could have been caused by a bullet striking the curb.

The following day with Oswald in custody at the city jail, newsmen had been staking out the building awaiting Oswald's infrequent appearances in the corridors in between interrogations. Other reporters were stationed at the county jail on Houston Street awaiting Oswald's probable transfer to this more secure location. Dillard was hanging around Sheriff Bill Decker's office at the County Criminal Courts Building waiting for the expected Oswald transfer. Also there was

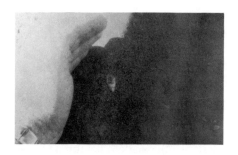

A frame from Underwood's sequence showing the splotch on the curb

Underwood, who while being assistant news director of KRLD also performed camera work. Underwood later stated, "I was bored just waiting there, so I asked one of the deputies if I had time to go across the street. He said I did. We worked together that way. If he knows the prisoner is coming, he will say 'better stick around,' or he will tell

From the site of the mark, Underwood points his camera towards its possible origin.

me, 'you've got about an hour,' and I know I can trust him. The press has very close relations with all of the law enforcement agencies in Dallas." Seeing Dillard, Underwood told him where he was going, and the two walked to the location of the smear on the curb which was some 500 feet from the county jail. They both had no trouble finding the fresh mark on the curb. Although Underwood was not sure whether it was a bullet mark, he decided to film it with his 16mm camera in the event that at

a later date it could be pertinent or proved to have been actually caused by a bullet. Dillard later remarked to a researcher, "It couldn't have been a jacketed bullet, because there was no copper on the curb. The only evidence was a lead smear on the rounded edge of the curb." With Dillard cupping his hand over the mark so it wouldn't be washed out on film due to the bright sun, Underwood squatted down in the gutter and took a close-up film sequence. As a point of reference he then used a wide-angle lens and placing the handle of his camera on the curb near the mark, he pointed the camera towards the Texas School Book Depository and made a low-level sequence showing the Depository Building in the background. Dillard was using a 35mm camera that Saturday. Giving Underwood his Cross pen, Underwood pointed to the spot while Dillard, with a fresh roll of Tri-X in his camera, made three almost identical shots of it. As to its publication, Dillard remembers, "We used it in the paper several days later, but nobody paid attention to it."[47]

This information might never have been brought to the attention of the Warren Commission had it not been for a chance meeting between Dillard and U.S. Attorney

Barefoot Sanders. "I was at a cocktail party months later and Barefoot Sanders was there and I mentioned the bullet mark." On June 9, 1964, the U.S. Attorney wrote to the Commission's General Counsel J. Lee Rankin enclosing a Dillard photo and mentioning that Dillard said of the curb that, ". . . It looked like a piece of lead had struck it." The Dallas FBI had also deposed Underwood on June 15, and by early July Rankin formally requested FBI Director Hoover to investigate the mark including tracing the trajectory of a possible bullet from the Depository Building's sixth-floor corner window to the curb, analyzing the mark to determine if it were possibly created by a bullet, and determining if the Dillard and Underwood pictures were of the same curb site. Hoover, in turn, instructed the Dallas agent-in-charge to follow through on the request, including removal of a section of the curb for laboratory examination. A detailed report resulted utilizing

Dillard makes three frames of the mark.

interviews and site visits with both Dillard and Underwood. The general area of the curb was located using the witnesses and the photographic information. No nick or break in the concrete was observed, nor any mark similar to the one photographed. It was speculated that the mark itself might have washed off due to numerous rains and street cleaning machines being used in the area on a fairly regular basis. On August 5, 1964, a section of the curb was removed under the direction of Washington Special Agent Lyndal Shaneyfelt, who was successful in locating a mark. The chunk of concrete was then transported back to the FBI lab in Washington.[48]

The laboratory report findings submitted to the Warren Commission indicated that the mark was located 23 feet 4 inches from the abutment of the triple underpass. "Small foreign metal smears were found adhering to the curbing section within the area of the mark. These metal smears were spectrographically determined to be essentially lead with a trace of antimony. No copper was found. The lead could have originated from the lead core of a mutilated metal jacket bullet such as the type of bullet loaded into 6.5mm Mannlicher-Carcano cartridges or from some other source having the same composition." The report went on to state that the mark could not have been the result of a direct hit by an unmutilated full metal jacket bullet. If such a direct hit had taken place, damage to the curb would have been more extensive. No chipping occurred on the curb, while the smear splayed out in a fan-like pattern. The lead object that struck the curb was also moving in a general direction away from the Book Depository. It could not be determined if the smear were from a fragment of a bullet that had hit there after striking the President's head or if it were a fragment of a shot that missed the President's car altogether.[49]

Circumstantial evidence seemed to corroborate that the curb smear was associated with the assassination, especially when coupled with another nearby incident. Thirty-seven-year-old James Thomas Tague, a car salesman, was traveling easterly on Commerce Street a little before 12:30 p.m. November 22 on his way to pick up his girlfriend for lunch. As he approached the triple underpass into Dealey Plaza cars in the left lane in front of him were stopped forcing him to do likewise. His car was just sticking out from underneath the Commerce Street underpass. As other traffic was also stopping, and activity could be seen ahead of him to his front left, Tague got out of his car and stood about 3 or 4 feet from the abutment between Commerce and Main Streets to catch a glimpse of what he now realized was the President's motorcade traveling through Dallas. He had arrived less than a minute ahead of the President's car. Tague heard a loud firecracker-like noise followed by two more shots, and realized that someone was shooting. Following the third shot, he claims to have ducked behind the bridge abutment. About three minutes later, after the motorcade had quickly disappeared and while people were streaming into the area and still trying to figure out what happened, Tague walked over to the north side of Elm Street. One man Tague overheard said that it looked like the President's head had just exploded, while a patrolman mentioned that, "Well, I saw something fly off back on the street." A deputy sheriff and Tague went back to the vicinity of the southern end of the triple underpass and Tague mentioned to him, "Well, you know, I recall something stinging me on the face while I was standing down there." The officer looked at Tague and commented that there was blood on his cheek. Tague touched his left cheek and saw a couple drops of blood on his finger. They walked to where Tague was standing and about 10 feet away the deputy brought his attention to a fresh mark on the curb. Looking back in a northerly direction, the men saw the Book Depository Building with its open windows in clear view, and someone commented, "maybe that is where the shots came from." The deputy ran back to alert other officers.[50]

In testimony given in late July 1964 before Wesley Liebeler, an assistant counsel of the Warren Commission, Tague indicated that he had heard the first noise and that at some time during the second or third shot he felt a slight sting to his cheek. Not making any connection, he ignored it, consumed by what was transpiring in front of him. Tague guessed that this sting to his face probably occurred at the second or third shot, and when pressed for an opinion, thought it might have happened at the second shot. Tague's chance timing onto the scene of the assassination was amazing. ". . . I just stopped, got out of my car, and here came the motorcade. I just happened on the scene." Following the shots, Tague noticed that the Hertz sign on top of the Book Depository Building read 12:29. Independently, without recalling Tague's name, Deputy Sheriff Eddie R. Walthers corroborated all the important aspects of the civilian's testimony, when Walthers gave his own testimony to Counselor Liebeler. Walthers stated that following the shooting he was looking in the grass for an indication of a bullet strike and that a man, ". . . came up to me and asked me, he said, 'Are you looking to see where some bullets may have struck?' and I said, 'Yes.' He says, 'I was standing over by the bank here, right there where my car is parked when those shots happened,' and he said, 'I don't know where they came from or if they were shots, but something struck me on the face,' and he said, 'It didn't make any scratch or cut and it just was a sting,' and so I had him show me right where he was standing and I started to search in that immediate area and found a place on the curb there in the Main Street lane there close to the underpass where a projectile had struck that curb." To Walthers it was most obvious that the projectile either came from the School Book Depository or from the Dal-Tex Building due to the angle with which it struck the curb. He alerted another deputy to the fact by saying, ". . . 'From the looks of it, it's probably going to be in the School Book Building,' and immediately then everybody started surrounding the School Book Building. . . ." Walthers described the mark to Liebeler saying, "Yes; it was a fresh ricochet mark. I have seen them and I have noticed it for the next 2 or 3 days as it got grayer and grayer and grayer as it aged."[51]

Tague (at extreme right) listens to
Charles Brehm in this Willie Allen photo.

Besides Tague being seen in one of Dillard's photos, a photograph made by UPI's Frank Cancellare taken moments after the shooting from on the "grassy knoll" looking southerly shows Tague in the background standing by the abutment. A photograph made by *Dallas Times Herald* photographer William Allen, taken a few minutes later and showing the gathering throng at the street by the foot of the "grassy knoll" pergola, portrays witness Charles Brehm who had seen the shot hit the President in the head. Brehm is talking and motioning to a nearby reporter while on the extreme right, listening to the conversation, is Tague with what looks to be a scratch on his left cheek.[52]

The lateness of this curb evidence being discovered and followed up by the Commission precluded its being fully analyzed by Warren Commission Counsel Arlen Specter, who was responsible for that section of the final report concerning the basic facts of the assassination. Specter had submitted his draft report by June 1. The new evidence which to some might suggest a possible fourth and last shot, especially if the trajectory of the shot were straight from the Book Depository, had no opportunity of being properly weighed in Specter's chapter. At the least it was an important piece of evidence which should not have been given short shrift. A pick-up paragraph was inserted in the final report mentioning the mark but indicating, "Under the circumstances it might have come from the bullet which hit the President's head, or it might have been the product of the fragmentation of the missed shot upon hitting some other object in the area." Edward Epstein in his 1966 book *Inquest*, which delved into the procedures followed by the Warren Commission, noted a failure on the part of the Commission itself to follow through with such lingering questions. He noted that the investigation of the assassination's basic facts tended to center upon the more prominent problems. The Commission had neither the staff nor the time necessary to delve into problems of a more nebulous nature. Thus, according to Epstein, "while known facts were substantiated, unknown facts were left unknown." In 1967 Josiah Thompson in his book segment dealing with "Answered and Unanswered Questions," after reviewing the evidence concerning the curb, was persuaded that the soundest theory was that a bullet fragment resulting from the head shot was the cause of the mark on the curb. He acknowledged, however, that 270 feet was a long distance for such a fragment to travel.[53]

Bob Jackson's photographic "day of destiny" had not been the Friday of the assassination of President Kennedy. As he later wrote, "I was in the motorcade when the shot[s] were fired at Kennedy and I saw the rifle being pulled back in the window. . . . It happened too fast, then, for me to get a photo of it." Sunday, however, he would redeem any feelings of professional guilt. Sunday was the day of the transfer of Oswald from the city to the county jail, a trip Oswald would never complete. Jackson's being there, however, was a matter of good luck for him. William Allen relates that photographer "Eamon Kennedy was assigned to city hall and Bob Jackson to the county jail. Eamon was a real enterprising kind of guy and he said if anything happens, it's going to happen at the County Court House. He talked Bob Jackson into trading assignment locations with him."[54]

The press, eventually consisting of some 40 or so reporters, still, movie, and TV cameramen, had been standing around the basement of the Dallas Municipal Building, located between Main and Commerce Streets, for a good part of the morning. They were all awaiting the transfer of Oswald from the upper floor by elevator into the basement. From there he would be placed into an unmarked police car for a quick ride to the more secure county jail on Houston Street, where crowds and more press awaited his arrival. As Oswald continued to be interrogated upstairs, the transfer time kept getting shoved back. Tom Dillard, home now for some rest, had assigned Jack Beers to the basement transfer. Beers was one of the *Morning News*'s top sports photographers and a very meticulous person. Considered by Dillard as not the best feature man, he was nonetheless an excellent news photographer, and what Dillard called "a sure news shot." Beers was friendly with many police officers and on occasion enjoyed riding in squad cars during free time. He also happened to know a local night club operator and police "hanger-on" named Jack Ruby. Beers had done an assignment a year earlier taking a series of photographs of some of Ruby's strippers. Sunday, November 24, Beers had a Mamiyaflex with a 65mm lens and flash attachment. He arrived in the basement at around 9 a.m. and by about 11:20 had secured a perch on the top of a two-pipe railing alongside a television camera's position. In this cramped space with limited photographic views, Beers decided to attempt one clear photo of Oswald as he would be brought down the corridor after alighting from the elevator. Beers' position on the railing would allow him to shoot over the heads of other newsmen present.[55]

Bob Jackson was also there. Jackson had seen Jack Ruby only once before when Ruby visited the paper's photo department with a stripper who as part of her act danced with a snake. The night club operator had been doing one of his not infrequent publicity gimmicks trying to drum up print interest for his clubs. Today at the police station Jackson had a 35mm Nikon S3 range finder mounted with a wide angle 35mm lens. His camera was loaded with Tri-X black-and-white film and Jackson made some pictures in the basement area, including two frames of Sergeant James A. Putnam holding up Oswald's booking slip. He also made a series of shots of the car ramp leading up to Commerce Street with an armored truck at the head of the ramp, its back door open. He changed film after the 16th exposure, wanting a fresh full roll in his camera for the transfer. He knew he must position himself for the best photo and make sure he could snag at least one good shot. Prefocusing his camera to a spot where he was sure Oswald would cross, Jackson planned then to move parallel to the parked cars, getting several more pictures as Oswald was led to his vehicle.[56]

Though now indelibly etched into the minds of the millions who witnessed the shooting on television or through newspaper photographs, and seen and re-seen as the most famous public execution in history, the unexpected killing of Oswald was an additional unbelievable shock to a seemingly numbing series of events during that 1963 weekend. Probably the most famous of any modern spot news event, the shooting was recorded by the media in phenomenally successful fashion and excruciating detail. Nationally only NBC broadcast the shooting live, but coverage was picked up within moments by the other two networks. Some ten minutes after the shooting, NBC broadcast the incident in slow motion and stop action. This "instant replay" was a relatively new television technique used at the time, but in years to come would become a universally familiar and often over-used device. Yet for all the drama and confusion captured by television and motion picture film, the still photographs were what best lent themselves to displaying the shock of the event itself. Through the camera work of Jackson and Beers, this key incident, the results of which would lead to much of the obscuring of truth, the creation of such fundamental doubt, and a generation of pessimism, was captured on film as a moment frozen in time forever. Their lenses captured all of the reality of the event within their range, including both the killer and victim. How unlike the numerous questions and mysteries which surrounded the limited field of view of the camera lenses at the time of the President's assassination.[57]

The first of the two soon to be historic photographs taken at the time of the shooting was made by Beers. At 11:21 a.m. the elevator door to the basement opened and Oswald, handcuffed and flanked by two Dallas detectives, was escorted down a corridor, past the booking office, and out towards the awaiting vehicles and crowd. Cameras whirled and clicked and some of the newsmen hollered out questions. Beers recalls:

Jack Beers captures on film Ruby shooting Oswald.

I put my twin-lens reflex camera to my eye, looking through the open viewfinder. I followed Oswald and his guards in that way, waiting for a clear and closer view of him. . . . Then just as he came into a new area which gave me an unobstructed view for my higher position, I saw a rather sudden movement below me and to my right. My eyes were glued to the viewfinder. My impulsive first thought was that it was a cameraman moving out into a position which might obstruct my view. He was probably six feet away, to my right and below me. . . . Just in that fraction of a second, the second I had observed the man's movement, I tripped the shutter of my camera. I had started to take a picture an instant before that, but the distraction of the man's movement caused me to delay a fraction of a second. In that same second a man's falsetto voice screamed, 'You son of a bitch!' I made the picture with the thought foremost in my mind to get my picture before my view was obstructed. I had no idea the man was about to shoot Oswald. I was still looking into the viewfinder when the curse ended and the shot rang out, like putting a period quickly at the end of a sentence.

Following its processing back at the news lab, the Beers photo was quickly put out as an AP wirephoto with credit to the photographer and a copyright listing to the *Dallas Morning News*.[58]

The Beers photo is flawless. It shows a rushing Jack Ruby with an extended hand clasping a gun and quickly closing in on Oswald. Walking past a gauntlet of police with reporters mixed among them rather than being held behind the railing, as was supposed to be the case, Oswald and his two side escorts are unaware of Ruby's approach. At right, NBC reporter Tom Petit, wearing glasses and holding a mike, is in a front row position. To Petit's left, WNEW radio reporter Ike Pappas, who had just rushed down from the floor where Oswald entered the elevator, thrusts his tape recorder mike towards Oswald asking, "Do you have anything to say in your defense?" In the finest tradition of spot news photography, this photo would have likely garnered Beers a Pulitzer Prize for photography if Jackson had not taken his picture a split second later. Some local photographers would wryly comment that because Beers was so good and fast in a tight situation, he had taken the perfectly thought-out picture and that by luck Jackson's chance shot happened to turn out the better photo. No matter, as the Beers picture was a technically pure and dramatic one which would be one of the handful of historic pictures that would often be used in history books telling the story of the weekend's traumatic events. Jackson later confessed concerning the Beers shot that after returning to his paper and prior to knowing what he had on his roll, "The first thing I saw [was] an Associated Press photo which showed Ruby pointing a gun at Oswald. It was a great shot, and I didn't think I had anything as good."[59]

Jackson had gotten off one photo of a uniformed police officer leading the prisoner down the corridor, but Oswald was obscured. At the time of the shooting Jackson was in a position on the Commerce Street side of the ramp partially behind and leaning against the fender of a parked police car and to the left of Beers. "I was busy watching a point I had picked out to focus on for my pictures. Then I noticed the movement of a body to my right. . . . I didn't realize what he was doing. I was concentrating on getting a picture of Oswald, a clear face shot. . . . As this body to my right kept moving, I became worried about missing the picture of Oswald I was attempting to take. The closer he got, the more I knew I would have to shoot the picture sooner than I expected or lose it altogether. I took my picture just as Ruby shot, but I can't recall whether it was exactly at the time or a split second afterward."[60]  The flash unit Jackson was using on his camera took some moments to recycle, but now seeing the turn of events, Jackson clicked off another shot, hoping the TV's kleig lights might fill in the scene for him.

Just after the shot sounded, voices screamed and Ruby was rushed, subdued, and quickly taken out of the area. In the first moments of panic Oswald was removed by officers back to the booking office. Most of the photographers continued to make pictures of the activity, burying their own panic in work. In the crush of the excitement jittery cops were shoving the press back, while cars were moved and an ambulance was brought in. Oswald's ashen face and limp body was gurneyed head first into an ambulance as photographers clicked away. The basement was sealed off for a time, and many remained there until Police Chief Curry announced that Oswald was dead a little after 2:00 Central Standard Time.

Prior to Oswald's transfer, Tom Dillard was at home trying to get some rest. Yet he was starting to feel fidgety. "Sunday I was at home looking at television and all that damn bunch of TV cameras making a production of moving Oswald. I began to get nervous. I didn't like it. It was just bad. I got up and dressed and was just getting ready to leave for the office." Seeing the shooting on TV, Dillard "got to the police station pretty quickly. I was talking to Bob Jackson, and Bob didn't know what to do. He told me he had shot a picture with his flash of their coming out. Those flashes didn't recycle quickly enough. He thought his second shot was when the shooting took place and the flash didn't go, though they had television lights down there. And he didn't know if he should push it [the developing formula] or not. And he said, 'Damn it, the flash picture is not the picture I want. The picture of the shooting is my second shot.' He was the competition, but a friend, too. I said, 'If you push it, you know your flash is going to be bad, and I believe I'd go with it like it is.' And he did, and sure enough the flash shot was the shot of the actual shooting. And my man Beers who's a newsman and a great sports photographer, saw the action and shot first. His first picture was of Ruby sticking the gun at him — which cost him the Pulitzer Prize."[61]

Jackson arrived back at the *Times Herald*. As Willie Allen remembers, "He ran into the paper and he was just shaking." He told his chief that he thought he had taken his photo of Oswald a moment too early. He did not push the development, and in so doing, the non-flash picture was too dark. His best picture, however, was preserved. "Not until I processed my film in the darkroom did I realize I had snapped a picture of the actual shooting. Looking at the wet negative I still didn't realize what I had taken. I noticed the position of a police officer standing next to Oswald but thought he was reacting to seeing the gun. Then when I looked in the enlarger, the realization came that I had taken the photo of the actual shooting. I had been hungry, my nerves were on edge and my head ached, but I felt good. It made me feel that I had made up for what pictures I had missed when President Kennedy was assassinated."[62]

Bob Jackson's Pulitzer Prize-winning photo

Allen recalls looking at the dramatic picture and exclaiming, "Oh, my God!" "The first thing we did was make a 4" x 5" copy negative of it, put it into the vault and start making copies." Quickly marked "Copyright 1963, The Dallas Times Herald and Photographer Bob Jackson," the photo was sent out as a UPI telephoto and picked up by hundreds of newspapers. In its Monday afternoon edition, the *Times Herald* included a massive front-page reproduction of the photo. Below, in a box caption, the paper justifiably declared that "Photographer Jackson has recorded for history one of its most bizarre and dramatic moments." Most papers cropped the photo to include the dramatic action in the center of the print where Oswald, mouth open in a moan, his eyes closed to slits, brings his hands to his chest as he begins to crumple. The black pullover sweater, now with a hole in it, had minutes before been put on by Oswald in an interrogation room. Offered one of two sweaters, he had requested the black one. Wearing a white Stetson and a new white suit, Detective James R. Leavelle, escorting Oswald on his left, leans backward in surprise while beginning instinctively to tug Oswald away, grasping him at his belt. Escort Detective L. C. Graves's face and body are all but obscured by the burly onrushing Jack Ruby who, with clenched left hand and his right hand still pointing the just-fired snubnose revolver, is in low and close to his victim.[63]

A few papers, including the *Scranton [PA] Tribune,* carried the near full Jackson print on its front page over a caption, "DRAMATIC PHOTO SHOWS OSWALD BEING SLAIN. THIS IS THE COMPLETE NEGATIVE OF DRAMATIC SCENE CAPTURED BY DALLAS TIMES-HERALD STAFF PHOTOGRA-PHER BOB JACKSON AS JACK RUBY FATALLY SHOT LEE HARVEY

OSWALD, ACCUSED ASSASSIN OF PRESIDENT KENNEDY. . . ." The full negative showed police Captain Will Fritz, chief of the homicide investigation, on the extreme left seemingly oblivious to the action behind him. Meanwhile on the right a couple of newsmen, including NBC's Tom Pettit, hold microphones in their hand. In the background one uniformed white-hatted cop has an expression of horrified surprise on his face, he being the only one seen to be so quickly reacting to what was occurring.[64]

It came as no surprise that the assassination story would be the principal news story of 1963, and when the Pulitzer Prizes for 1963 were announced in early May, Merriman Smith, UPI's dean reporter, whose coverage of the shooting began while he was riding in the motorcade, won the prize for national reporting. Under the News Photography category, Bob Jackson won the Pulitzer. In an interview for the Pulitzer announcement, Jackson said concerning his photo, "I thought I had something, but I was afraid I might have got the picture just too soon — I do that sometimes."[65]

Jackson remained with the *Times Herald* until 1974 with the exception of a brief stint in 1968-69 with the *Denver Post*. Working free-lance until 1970, in that year he joined the Colorado Springs *Gazette Telegraph*. With few exceptions Jackson is publicly quiet about his role in the story of the assassination. As to the idea of a conspiracy, Jackson says, "I think the critics are groping. I heard three shots and saw the rifle. Those are facts to me."[66]

Tom Dillard believes that, "The greatest picture I made of the whole story was of the police chief [Jesse Curry] surrounded by microphones framed all around his face. And he is announcing that Oswald has been killed. You talk about a broken man. He had done that [the public transfer] for national television. Those bastards had the power."[67]

Dillard remained with the *Morning News* until 1977 when he retired to Henderson County, Texas. He has a pistol range in his back yard and confesses happily and emphatically that nowadays, "I never touch a camera." Dillard recalls that November 22, 1963, was professionally "a most frustrating day for photographers." His opinion of the House Select Committee on Assassination's investigation is strong. He explains that they requested his photographs, kept them for a long time and ruined several key negatives. He states that the congressional investigation, "was a nauseating boondoggle if I ever saw one." Concerning various theories which have arisen over the years, Dillard calls the idea of the three tramps found in the railroad yard and photographed by Beers and Allen being involved in the shooting as "a ridiculous bunch of crap." Still with strong opinions and a keen newsman's remembrance of what he did see, Dillard does not completely rule out all possibilities of conspiracy. "I was pestered so much and I'm so heartsick about the whole thing. I've been interviewed many, many times. I've given very careful and factual answers to everything and they always would generally come out as very strange, twistings of the truth with the people writing about the mysterious things. . . . I don't trust the majority of people who talk to me because practically everyone seems to have preconceived ideas about what happened. And they damn sure weren't there. But they surely had certain fixed ideas that they know exactly what happened. I know what happened, but I don't know if it were a conspiracy or whether we had him killed, or Cuba had him killed — who had him killed or what happened. I just know what happened while I was there. I only say that I would bet my life that a man, and I'd bet a lot of money that it was Oswald, shot that old 6.5mm Carcano war surplus gun from the Book Depository three times. I wouldn't say that there was not another man around prepared to. Whatever else happened, who knows? I certainly don't."[68]

## CHAPTER NOTES

1.    Telephone interview of Tom C. Dillard, 2/21/1986.

2.    Ibid.; Questionnaire filled out by Dillard, 10/25/1985.

3.    Ibid.

4.    Ibid.

5.    Letter, Clint Grant to Trask, 1/6/1988.

6.    Telephone interview of Dillard, 2/21/1986.

7.    Ibid.; *New York Times*, 5/5/1964, p. 39; Interview of James W. Altgens, 11/22/1985; *Hearings Before the President's Commission on the Assassination of President Kennedy*, v. 2, p. 155-156; Marianne Fulton, *Eyes of Time*, p. 306.

8.    *Hearings*, op. cit., v. 2, p. 156-158; Photo files of the *Dallas Times Herald*, folder JFK #9, "Listing for  Friday Schedule," 11/22/1963.

9.    *Hearings*, op. cit., v. 18, p. 724, 761-762.

10.   Telephone interview of Dillard, 2/21/1986; *Dallas Morning News* Reference Library, Dillard photographic print, 11/22/1963.

11.   Ibid.; *Hearings*, op. cit., v.2, p. 156-158;  *Dallas Times Herald*, 11/23/1963, p. A-3.

12.   Telephone interview of Dillard, 2/21/1986; *Hearings*, op. cit., v. 6, p. 164; *Dallas Morning News* Kennedy Supplement, 11/20/1983, p. 15; *Dallas Morning News* Reference Library, Dillard negatives #2-7, 11/22/1963.

13.   Telephone interview of Dillard, 2/21/1986; Secret Service Report on Robert Jackson made by SA Elmer W. Moore, CR 87, 12/9/1963; *Hearings*, op. cit., v. 2, p. 158.

14.   Telephone interview of Dillard, 2/21/1986; *Hearings*, op. cit., v. 6, p. 164.

15.   *Dallas Times Herald*, "Lensman Heard Shots, Saw Gun," 11/23/1963.

16.   Secret Service Report, op. cit.; *Dallas Times Herald*, 11/25/1963; *Hearings*, op. cit., v. 2, p. 158-165.

17.   Telephone interview of Dillard, 2/21/1986; Letter, Tom Dillard to Robert B. Cutler, 2/16/1971.

18.   Telephone interview of Dillard, 2/21/1986; Dillard questionnaire, op. cit.

19.   Texas Historical Commission Marker, 1981, located at 411 Elm Street, Dallas, Texas; Shirley W. Caldwell, "The Dallas County Administration Building," Typescript # 6148, p. 1-6; *Hearings*, op. cit., v. 3, p. 213-215.

20.   *Dallas Morning News* Reference Library, Dillard negative #8, 11/22/1963; Print of Dillard Depository photo #8, 11/22/1963; *Hearings*, op. cit., v. 6, p. 397-399, v. 22, p. 684-686.

21.   *LIFE*, 11/24/1967, p. 3 [88]; Harold Weisberg, *Photographic Whitewash*, p. 177; *Dallas Morning News*, "Dorman obituary," 11/1/1983; *Dallas Times Herald*, Dorman obituary, 11/1/1983; *Hearings*, op. cit., v.22, p. 644.

22.   Letter, Richard Sprague to Robert B. Cutler, 11/28/1971; *Grassy Knoll Gazette*, 4/1982, p. 85; Richard Sprague, "Twelve sets of important photographs of the assassination of President Kennedy," Typescript article, 3/1971, p. 14; *Appendix to Hearings Before the Select Committee on*

*Assassinations*, v. 1, p. 706-719; *Coverups!*, 11/1983, p. 4. Examination of a plan of Dealey Plaza with approximate locations of the motorcade vehicles noted at the time of the fatal head shot would appear to confirm motorcycle officer McLain's having just reached the corner of Elm and Houston street at that point in time.

23.   *Hearings*, op. cit., v. 6, p. 386 & v. 22, p. 632, 644, 648, 676.

24.   Ibid., v. 22, p. 653, 665.

25.   Ibid., v. 22, p. 647, 652.

26.   Ibid., v. 3, p. 161-177, 186-194, 199-208 & v. 22, p. 655, 666, 681. One of the Allen photos would be published in the UPI book *Four Days* (p.29) with the incorrect caption, "A lunch bag and pop bottle, held here by a Dallas police technician, and three spent shell casings were found by the sixth-floor window. The sniper had dined on fried chicken and pop while waiting patiently to shoot the President."

27.   Ibid., v. 3, p. 175-177.

28.   Interview with Harold Norman, 11/21/1993.

29.   *Dallas Morning News* Reference Library, Dillard negative #24, 11/22/1963; Print of Dillard Depository photo #24, 11/22/1963; Telephone interview of Dillard, 2/21/1986.

30.   FBI interview of James W. Powell by George T. Binney, CD 354, 1/3/1964; Josiah Thompson, *Six Seconds in Dallas*, p. 312-313.

31.   James W. Altgens photograph #5, 11/22/1963.

32.   FBI interview of Lt. Col. E. E. Boyd by S.A. Wallace R. Heitman, CD 206, 1/2/1964; FBI interview of Powell, op. cit.

33.   James W. Powell Depository photograph, 11/22/1963, obtained through FOIA request; Author's visit to Dealey Plaza, 11/22/1985.

34.   Jim Marrs, *Crossfire*, p. 309; Secret Service investigation by S.A. Roger C. Warner, CD 354, 2/3/1964, reproduced in Thompson, op. cit., p. 313; FBI interview of Powell, op. cit. In testimony given the Warren Commission by Dallas police detective V.J. Brian, he makes mention that following a search of the Depository Building, at about 2:00 p.m. Dallas police Lt. Revill, a supervisor in criminal intelligence, brought Brian and other detectives back to the city hall. Also in the car was one man Revill knew and who Brian believed to be some type of military agent. "I don't remember whether he was a CIC agent or a CID or OSI, he was some type of, as I recall, Army Intelligence man." The agent was dropped off around Field Street. It is unclear if this man was Powell, though if so, he remained at the shooting scene and probably in the building while it was carefully searched. (*Hearings*, op. cit. v. 5, p. 48-49, 57)

35.   FBI interview of Boyd, op. cit.; FBI interview of Powell, op. cit.; FBI [memorandum] DL100-10461 / RPG:eah regarding FBI laboratory furnishing information regarding Powell transparency on 1/8/1964.

36.   J. Gary Shaw, *Cover-Up*, p. 31; Letter, Clarence M. Kelley to Robert B. Cutler, 3/23/1977; Trask FOIA request 247,656, 5/1984; 274,209, 10/1986; 295,678, 2/1988. It took three separate, time-consuming requests from this author before being able to obtain an uncropped black-and-white copy of this picture.

37.   *Appendix to Hearings*, op. cit., v. 6, p. 110-115, 133-135.

38.   *SRI International Research Proposal No. PYU-78-061*, R. R. Pettijohn, 3/3/1978, p. 1, 5, 7, 15; letter, Richard R. Pettijohn to Ms. Jane Downey, Select Committee on Assassinations, 10/27/1978; Letter, Robert J. Groden to Jane Downey, 2/25/1979, p. 1-2; Letter, G. Robert Blakey to Tom Dillard, 3/30/1979, p. 1-2; *Appendix to Hearings*, op. cit., v. 6, p. 309-310, 313; *Dallas Morning News* Reference Department, Dillard negatives #21-26, 2-12, 14-25, 11/22/1963.

39.   Telephone interview of Dillard, 2/21/1986.

40.   *Hearings*, op. cit., v. 6, p. 165.

41.   Ibid., v. 7, p. 465

42. Secret Service Report on Jackson, op. cit.
43. Telephone interview of Dillard, 2/21/1986; *Dallas Morning News* Reference Department, Dillard negatives #9-25, 11/22/1963.
44. Ibid.
45. Ibid.; Letter, Clint Grant to Trask, 12/1/1987; Visit to *Dallas Morning News* Reference Department in 1991 and 1992.
46. *Dallas Times Herald*, 11/22/1963, p. 1, & 11/23/1963, p. A5 and A8.
47. Telephone interview of Dillard, 2/21/1986; John B. Mayo Jr., *Bulletin From Dallas: The President is Dead*, p. 136; *Hearings*, op. cit., v. 21, p. 472-474; Thompson, op. cit., p. 231; FBI interview of James Underwood made by SA Ivan D. Lee, CR 1245, 6/15/1964; *Dallas Morning News* Reference Department, Dillard negatives #1-3, 11/23/1963.
48. Telephone interview of Dillard, 2/21/1986; Letter, Barefoot Sanders to J. Lee Rankin, 6/9/1964; Letter, J. Lee Rankin to J. Edgar Hoover, 7/7/1964; Airtel, J. Edgar Hoover to SAC, Dallas, 7/13/1964; *Hearings* op. cit., v.21, p. 472-474 & v. 15, p. 698 & 700.
49. Letter, J. Edgar Hoover to J. Lee Rankin, CD 1383, 8/12/1964, p. 1-3; *Hearings*, op. cit., v. 15, p. 700-701.
50. *Hearings*, op. cit., v. 7, p. 552-554.
51. Ibid., v. 7, p.546-550, 555-558.
52. Frank Cancellare photograph #1 taken at Grassy Knoll, 11/22/1963; William Allen photograph of crowd at Grassy Knoll with Charles Brehm being interviewed, 11/22/1963.
53. Edward Jay Epstein, *Inquest*, p. 80-83; Thompson, op. cit., p. 230-233.
54. *Dallas Times Herald*, "Lensman Tells of Big Moment," 11/25/1963; Telephone interview of William Allen, 1/20/1987.
55. FBI memorandum to SAC, Dallas, from SA James C. Kennedy regarding photos taken by Jack Beers, 12/4/1963; FBI interview report by James C. Kennedy and Will Hayden Griffin of Ira Jefferson Beers, p.2, 12/4/1963; *Dallas Morning News*, "Front Page Photo Tells Grim Story," 11/25/1963, section 1-3.
56. Sheryle and John Leekley, *Moments: The Pulitzer Prize Photographs*, p. 56; *American Photographer*, 12/1981, p. 88-89.
57. *There Was A President*, p. 90-99.
58. *Dallas Morning News*, 11/25/1963 op. cit.
59. *Dallas Times Herald*, "Lensman Tells of Big Moment — Historic Photo," 11/25/1963, p. 46-A.
60. Ibid.
61. Telephone interview of Dillard, 2/21/1986.
62. *Dallas Times Herald*, "Lensman Tells. . . ," op. cit.;Telephone interview of William Allen, 1/20/1987.
63. *Dallas Times Herald*, 11/25/1963, p. 1; Fulton, op. cit., p. 207; *Hearings*, op. cit., v. 7, p. 300-301.
64. *The Scranton Tribune*, 11/25/1963, p. 1; *American Photographer*, op. cit., p. 88.
65. *New York Times*, op. cit.
66. Fulton, op. cit., p. 306; Conversation with Robert Jackson, 11/19/1993.
67. Telephone interview of Dillard, 2/21/1986; A cropped version of this Dillard photo appeared in Jesse Curry's *JFK Assassination File*, on p. 80.
68. Telephone interview of Dillard, 2/21/1986; Conversation with Tom Dillard, 11/19/1993.

# PART FOUR

# AFTER THE SHOTS

Minutes after the shots, investigators begin to try to find evidence.

Only able to stare at the President's car ahead, the Secret Service agents in their follow-up car are now forever unable to protect their charge. Aide and friend Kenny O'Donnell (sitting behind driver) makes what looks like the sign of the cross with his fingers to his forehead.

## CHAPTER 19

# Beyond the Underpass

The triple underpass, with its railroad bed above, was a physical dividing line between the multi-storied downtown Dallas buildings to the east and the system of elevated entrance and exit ramps leading to the highway system and points beyond. Not "pedestrian friendly," the land west of the underpass leading to Stemmons Freeway was the environment of accelerating or decelerating vehicles. The concrete underpass was a Dallas landmark. Three of the city's major arteries, Elm, Main, and Commerce Streets, as well as two sidewalks pierced under this multiple track railroad bridge. Though to vehicular travelers the tunnel appeared well maintained, to a pedestrian treading on its sidewalk there would be a faint though permeating whiff of urine mixed with the sooty ambience of an area adjacent to an active train yard. A plaque attached to an underpass wall would proclaim to those who took the time to read it: "Union Terminal Co. Underpass Built In 1936 By Texas Highway Department. Austin Road and Bridge Company, Contractors."[1]

Under normal circumstances few walkers would venture to the highway side of the underpass. On November 22, however, a small group of people were gathered there before 12:30 p.m. awaiting a fleeting view of President Kennedy and his entourage as it made its way up the ramp to Stemmons Freeway and the Trade Mart beyond. The male-dominated group of spectators who situated themselves on the north side of the entrance ramp included several who had stopped and gotten out of their cars to see the goings-on, as well as several who had purposely chosen this location.

Thirty-five-year-old Dallas resident Jack Daniel had decided to take his sons downtown to see the President. One son was celebrating his ninth birthday on November 22, and Daniel specifically picked the spot west of the underpass away from the crowds so that if the President saw them there, he would hopefully notice and wave just to them and not towards an amorphous crowd. Daniel brought with him his 8mm movie camera loaded with color film, and positioned himself several feet behind the boys so that they would be included in the foreground of his film as the President's car approached.[2]

Also in this vicinity was 31-year-old Mel McIntire. McIntire was a professional photographer working for a commercial studio, Squire Haskins, on Commerce Street. Recalls McIntire, "I was returning from a shoot and southbound on Stemmons with a fellow photographer, Bob Tenny. Listening to the radio, I realized that the motorcade was coming through.  It was a spur-of-the-moment decision to stop and park on the side of the freeway and walk down to that ramp. I took the camera down with me, not really caring if I got a photo." His camera was a Rolleiflex f3.5 and was loaded with 120 black-and-white film.  Positioning himself on the side curb of the entrance ramp closest to the freeway, McIntire would have a view of the President's car beginning from the underpass itself.  It would then travel right in front of him and up the ramp.[3]

In their location west of the underpass, these spectators did not have the benefit of seeing and experiencing the tumult and crowd reaction which preceded the motorcade. One of hundreds of spectators situated nearby but on the east side of the underpass and who saw the motorcade from a bird's eye view, was Patsy Paschall.  Mrs. Clyde W. Paschall, Jr., was a young court clerk who with movie camera in hand took some film of the procession from an upper story Main Street window of the old Court House, located at the corner of Main and Houston Streets.  After the President's car passed her position, she had stopped filming, but upon hearing shots, she pointed her lens towards the Houston and Main Street corner with Dealey Plaza and the underpass seen in the film's background.  On her film clip she picked up the President's car and follow-up vehicle rushing into the shadows of the underpass, quickly gaining on the lead car which is veering toward the left.[4]

After the passage of almost a week, the Paschall film was taken by attorney-friend Fred Bruner to Dynacolor Corp. on Halifax Street to be developed.  Told that any film of the assassination might be of interest to the FBI, Bruner immediately made contact with Agent Robert M. Barrett, who came over to the film lab.  The agent requested to borrow the film.  Bruner agreed to hand it over for use only in the investigation and Barrett gave the attorney a receipt.  Several weeks later Barrett returned the film stating that it was of no evidentiary value, but commenting that he had noted that he saw himself in some of the film which had been taken of the Plaza after the incident. On behalf of Mrs. Paschall, Attorney Bruner attempted to sell rights of the film to the media, and in 1967, when *LIFE* magazine was publicly on the lookout for assassination-related films, this reel was brought to their attention.  Subsequently in a November issue of *LIFE*, a single frame from this movie, along with a picture of Paschall, was published.[5]

In the Paschall segment of the film taken right after the assassination, the President's vehicle was just behind Chief Curry's lead car as both entered the triple underpass from the east.  By the time they emerged from under the bridge, the President's Lincoln had overtaken the white Ford sedan.  The view now seen by Daniel and McIntire and the approximately ten others on the west side of the underpass was unexpected. Jack Daniel would later comment that he had heard three shots and knew that something was wrong.  The cars emerging from the underpass speed towards his position as two of the boys wave furiously attempting to get the President's attention.  The ten-seconds of  film made by Daniel includes 176 frames which, when examined not in real time, but in slow-motion and stop-action, show a confusing sight.  The President's Lincoln, with hood flags flapping and alternating red lights flashing on the car's bumper, approaches Daniel's position.  The car has now passed Chief Curry's, which is seen at far right. There are several other cars and at least one motorcycle behind. Daniel pans right as the President's car passes parallel to him. One sees a blurry vision in the foreground in which only the American flag on the right hood and a bulky image of Agent Clint Hill on the trunk can be picked out by a discerning eye.[6]

Mel McIntire captures a fleeting moment.

Meanwhile McIntire, at his position further back from the underpass, points his camera at the approaching vehicles and clicks off an exposure. His shutter is set fast enough so that he captures the view frozen in time with little blurring or distortion, even though the vehicles are rushing towards him. His photographic image is quite dramatic. In the foreground are three motorcycle cops directing their two-wheeled Harley-Davidson cycles up towards the access road. To camera left is seen a small street sign reading, "Stemmons Fwy." The cycle officers' expressions belie the terrible event behind them, and judging from their faces they seem oblivious to concern. It looks like they are just cruising. Officer W. G. Lumpkin, riding the middle cycle, appears laid-back. His left hand rests on his leg rather than on the cycle controls. Sergeant Starvis Ellis is to camera right, his stripes of rank visible on his left arm. The 13 all-male spectators on the north side of the road and three men visible on the south curb are paying no mind to the cycle officers. They all have their bodies and heads directed towards the cluster of cars obviously racing down the street towards them. Out front is the President's limousine, and to its side and slightly behind is the Curry lead car. Behind the presidential

Lincoln is the follow-up car with several agents leaning into the car, though standing on the running board platform. In the car the barrel of a long weapon is pointed to the sky. One can just make out the top of the light colored vice-presidential follow-up car behind the President's follow-up vehicle, the Vice-President's car itself obscured from view between these two. The Lincoln is almost parallel to the Daniel position on the curb's edge, and two of the Daniel boys are seen waving at the car. Under the bridge the silhouettes of two police motorcycles can be made out, probably ridden by Billy Joe Martin, on the right side with lights flashing, and James M. Chaney, further back and at the left side of the Elm Street tunnel. These two men were part of the four-man motorcycle escort just to the rear of the President's car when the shots were fired.

A large billboard located to the north of Elm Street and in front of the railroad embankment advertises, "Old Charter Kentucky's Finest Bourbon," with the smiling face of a tuxedo-clad man offering a glass of the seven-year-old aged liquor, while holding tray with bottles and glasses. Just beyond the railroad embankment at left is one of the railroad passenger cars set on a spur awaiting the afternoon commute. Also seen is just the top of the roof of one of the concrete shelters of the north peristyle by the grassy knoll. In the photo's background is a row of tall buildings, including a full view of the Texas School Book Depository Building with its name in gigantic letters displayed at the cornice line on the west elevation of the building. A sixth-floor window on this slide closest to the southwest corner is half opened. On top of the building the immense but somehow appropriately scaled Hertz Rent-a-Car sign has its time and temperature sign on the time sequence. It displays "12:30," a chance benchmark notation for the precise time when American history changed forever. Also seen in the cityscape are other of the multi-story commercial and governmental buildings on and around Houston Street, while in the extreme background, jutting far into the sky, are the steel frames of buildings of the new Dallas under construction. In the Elm Street gutter and pooled near the Stemmons Freeway sign, water meanders to a catch basin, the remnants of an earlier morning rain shower. The noontime sun is now in stark evidence, with crisp shadows trailing from all objects. Rich in pedantic detail, and superficially belying its important subject matter, this photograph has a haunting contradiction to it.[7]

Moments later McIntire made an additional shot. Turning just slightly to the left, he was not quick enough to photograph the President's Lincoln as it sped by, but did manage to get a slightly blurred photo of the President's follow-up car. From left, Secret Service Agents John D. Ready, Paul E. Landis, and William McIntyre are hugging onto the car and looking forward as they ride the running board. ASAIC Emory P. Roberts, in the front passenger seat, has his radio microphone to his mouth. The spectators visible in the background are looking in the direction of the car, probably not quite sure what they are witnessing.The Hertz sign on the Book Depository now shows a mild temperature of 66°.[8]

Later still McIntire, returning to his car up on Stemmons Freeway near the Continental Avenue exit ramp, snapped off his third photo. The police had set up a temporary road block. Taking the picture in a northeasterly direction with the Texas

School Book Depository warehouse and the Sunshine Biscuit Company on Munger Street in the background beyond the railroad abutment, the photo shows several Dallas police officers and motorcycle cops near parked cycle #333. Civilian dressed men, including two holding 16mm turret cameras and one also having an audio tape recorder, are also on hand. McIntire was annoyed that the motorcade had driven by so fast. Neither he nor Tenny had heard the shots, and it was not until they were driving on to their office that they learned of the shooting.[9]

Vehicles speeding on Stemmons with Dealey Plaza buildings evident in the background

Once the presidential car had turned up the entrance ramp off Elm, it quickly merged onto the Stemmons Freeway traveling north on Route 35E towards Parkland Hospital. Not too far from McIntire's initial position Al Volkland had stopped on the freeway. Carrying a camera, he caught sight of the fast-approaching cluster of vehicles. He made a photo of the President's car with the follow-up car traveling close behind. Agent Clint Hill is situated partially on the trunk of the President's limousine with his hands spread out. In the follow-up car the agents have by now climbed into the vehicle from their precarious running board location. Agent George W. Hickey, Jr., can be seen holding the AR15-.223 automatic rifle. A line of parked cars are near the railroad embankment, and on the side opposite the embankment the railroad switching tower, the rear and east side of the School Book Depository Building, and the Post Office Terminal Annex Building are in view.[10]

Several minutes later as the presidential limousine rushed past the Dallas Trade Mart, Justin Newman made a quick photo using an inexpensive camera. Newman tracked the car itself with his camera so that the background of the photo exhibits a blurry image of spectators and a building. He did capture the rear portion of the limousine, and the photo shows Clint Hill with his right leg still outside on the trunk of the car while his left leg is on the rear seat among the jumble of bodies. Mrs. Connally is seen as she cradles the viciously wounded governor, while the front wheel of an escort motorcycle is just visible behind the car.[11]

The Dallas Trade Mart had been the scheduled location for President Kennedy's luncheon address. Though the many local and national press traveling within the motorcade would report this newsworthy speech, arriving at the site with the President, other reporters and cameramen were already there having previously staked out spots for good coverage. Bert N. Shipp, the energetic Assistant News Director and chief cameraman for WFAA-TV, had arrived at the Trade Mart early to take pick-up shots of the pre-arrival activities there. With his spring-wound 16mm camera, Shipp had made exterior shots of a group of protestors, several carrying signs including one reading "Hail Caesar." One clip shows a police officer directing several of the protestors across the street to keep them isolated from the arrival area. Shortly after 12:30 Shipp heard approaching sirens and decided to position himself by the main entrance to film President Kennedy arriving in his automobile. "As I saw the cars approach, I thought 'boy, they are going fast—they're going to miss the turn-off and have to backtrack.' It seemed strange that I couldn't see anybody in the car, just a foot sticking up in the air in the back of the President's limousine." Realizing something was wrong, the cameraman managed to take a quick view of the vehicles traveling up the incline in the distance. The crowd of expectant spectators appear undirected, while several run towards the street and a police cruiser and motorcycle take off.[12]

Chief Curry at Parkland Hospital

Running to the back of the Trade Mart, Shipp found an officer who told him that the President had been "hit." The cameraman hitched a ride with a police juvenile officer in an unmarked squad car to Parkland Hospital, leaving in the same small convoy as several homicide detectives. Upon approaching Parkland, Shipp immediately began filming. His clips include views of the motorcade cars parked helter-skelter in the entrance drive to the emergency room, Chief Curry, an obviously upset Senator Ralph Yarborough and Congressman Jim Wright, a view of the interior of the Vice-President's convertible, several women White House staff members entering the emergency area, and a view of the presidential Lincoln being fitted with its roof sections. While briefly inside the hospital attempting to find an open phone to call the station, Shipp asked an orderly in the hospital's blood bank of Kennedy's condition. The orderly stated, "He's gone."[13]

After remaining at Parkland for some 20 minutes, Shipp commandeered a car driven frustratingly slowly by a Parkland janitor. Shipp, believing himself the only local cameraman at the scene, wanted to get back to the station to process and air his film. By 1:15 Shipp was at the station and briefly described on air what he had seen, and commented that they would quickly develop the film. At about 1:50 Shipp proceeded to give a running commentary as the first post-assassination film was broadcast unedited over Dallas television. The transmission was also picked up and broadcast nationally by ABC.[14]

Back at the WFAA newsroom Shipp (center) describes what he saw to Program Director Jay Watson (right).

Of the grouping of post-assassination amateur still photographs taken after the motorcade traveled through the triple underpass, only the Volkland photo quickly came into public notice. Volkland apparently contacted the *Dallas Times Herald*. By early Saturday morning AP had the photo and was wiring it to its subscribers. The wirephoto code indicated it was obtained through the *Times Herald* and the caption, written at 5:00 a.m. by Richard H. Strobel, began with the words, "KENNEDY SPED TO HOSPITAL." The *Times Herald* also used the picture in their Saturday edition over a caption, "President's Car Speeds Down Freeway Toward Hospital. Photo by Al Volkland."[15]

A year later, at the time of the first anniversary of President Kennedy's death, AP acquired the Newman photo. The resulting wirephoto sent out to subscribers in 1964 included in the caption how it was obtained. "This photo was made by Justin Newman, an amateur photographer with a cheap camera. He sent film to drug store finishing service about week after assassination and this picture wasn't printed because of movement. Newman got curious and had print made today by a friend."[16]

The Daniel film surfaced during the final days of the House Select Committee on Assassinations investigation in 1978. One of Daniel's sons, who at that time lived in Colorado, mentioned to a colleague of his ninth birthday outing to see the President, and was urged to contact federal authorities about this film. Another son made the contact and the House Select Committee called the father on December 28, 1976, stating their interest in the film. Mr. Daniel thereupon sent a copy of it to Washington. It was initially used to attempt to identify what motorcycle officer might have been in the Plaza at a time to have had his microphone stuck open, causing part of the assassination to have been recorded as part of the police department radio transmissions. Realizing that he might have a film that could be monetarily valuable and wanting to protect its use, Daniel acquired the services of Attorney John Sigalos of Sigalos and Levine, who also represented the assassination images taken by Charles L. Bronson. Under a copyright notice one frame from the Daniel film was included in the exhibit volumes of the House Select Committee's report in relation to the motorcycle question. Since only one cycle was observed in the Daniel film, which was identified as belonging to B. J. Martin, it was felt at the time that this buttressed the idea that the stuck microphone could belong to H. B. McLain.[17]

McIntire joined the staff of the *Dallas Times Herald* in February 1964 and remained with the paper until its demise in December 1991. It was not until 1983 that the two McIntire photos taken at the Elm Street off-ramp came to light. These two views were published as part of the paper's 20th anniversary remembrance. McIntire had never done anything with his pictures. As he did not see any particular value in them, he was surprised that people were interested. Researcher Gary Mack shortly thereafter reproduced these two pictures in his newsletter *Coverups!*. Subsequent to the cessation of the *Times Herald,* McIntire took a position with a small newspaper north of Dallas.[18]

The Newman photo of the President's car near the Trade Mart

## CHAPTER NOTES

1.    Plaque at triple underpass.

2.    Kit Miniclier, "Lone Police Cycle Shown In Film," *The Denver Post*, 2/8/1979; "Technology Enhances Daniel Movie," *The Denver Post*, 2/9/1979.

3.    Letter, Gary Mack to Trask, 12/14/1984, 3/1/1985; *Dallas Morning News*, 11/20/1983, p. 8; Letter, Mel McIntire to Trask, 11/26/1993.

4.    Patsy Paschall film, 11/22/1963; *LIFE*, 11/24/1967, p. [94]. Also incidentally included on Paschall's film was a view of part of the now breaking up motorcade on Elm, including Camera Car 2 being overtaken by Camera Car 3 and followed by three dignitary cars, a station wagon, and the first White House press bus. Meanwhile in the same scene, but closer to the camera position on Main Street, the rear of the motorcade is turning right onto Houston. The second White House press bus is followed by two dark sedans, a light-colored sedan carrying Signal Corps representatives, a dark sedan with light top, and the "official party" bus trailed by a Dallas police car.

5.    Teletype, To: Director, Attention Assistant Director A. Rosen, From: Dallas file #62-109060-5881, 10/16/1967; *LIFE*, op. cit. Agent Barrett, who reported to have arrived in Dealey Plaza about 1:00, is the agent several researchers contend was the man photographed by Jim Murray and William Allen looking over and probing the ground near the sewer cover adjacent to Elm Street just minutes after the assassination. From several other photos including one taken by Allen the person thought to be Agent Barrett may simply have been a civilian.

6.    Daniel film, 11/22/1963; Miniclier, op. cit.; *Appendix to Hearings Before the Select Committee on Assassinations*, v. 5, p. 719.

7.    Mel McIntire photo #1, 11/22/1963; Letter, W. G. Lumpkin to Trask, 11/16/1992.

8.    Mel McIntire photo #2, 11/22/1963.

9.    Mel McIntire photo #3, 11/22/1963; Letter, McIntire to Trask, Op. cit.

10.   Al Volkland photo, 11/22/1963.

11.   Justin Newman photo, 11/22/1963.

12.   Telephone interview with Bert N. Shipp, 3/22/1986; WFAA Videotape of Shipp film, 11/22/1963.

13.   Ibid.; John B. Mayo, Jr., *Bulletin From Dallas: The President is Dead*, p. 142.

14.   Richard Van Der Karr, "Crisis in Dallas," p. 19-20.

15.   *Dallas Times Herald*, 11/23/1963, p. A-3; AP Wirephoto (DN1) Dallas, Tex., RHS70500T-H-CKR, 11/23/1963.

16.   AP Wirephoto (DN4-Nov. 20, 1964) (CEL 62219STR).

17.   *Appendix*, op. cit., v. 5, p. 719; Miniclier, op. cit.; Gary Mack, "Jack Daniel Film West of Triple Underpass," *The Continuing Inquiry*, 2/22/1980, p. 6; Gary Mack, "Unlocking HSCA Evidence," *The Continuing Inquiry*, 3/22/1981, p. 1. However, the McIntire photo showed two cycles traveling under the underpass.

18.   *Dallas Times Herald*, 11/20/1983, p. 8; *Coverups!*, 11/1983, p. 1-2; Letter, Mack to Trask, 12/14/1984, op. cit; Letter, McIntire to Trask, Op. cit.

## CHAPTER 20

# The Student

One of the youngest photographers to capture on film part of the story of the presidential assassination was a Dallas native and high school honors student. David Robert Miller was a 17-year-old junior attending Hillcrest High School, located some eight miles north of downtown Dallas. An avid camera buff who was encouraged in his interest while attending Dallas's St. Thomas Aquinas School, Miller joined the high school camera club in 1962 during his first year at Hillcrest. By the fall of 1963 Miller was the club's secretary-treasurer, as well as a photographer on the staff of the *Panther*, the annual yearbook.[1]

The visit and motorcade route to be taken by President Kennedy through Dallas on November 22 to a speaking engagement at the Trade Mart had been prominent news in the local press and on television, and Miller was caught up in the excitement of the possibility getting a few photographs. Miller wrote of the event some 22 years later, "I had left school that day to photograph the visit of President Kennedy, which we thought might have been worth including in pictorial fashion in the publication of that year's Hillcrest yearbook. Since the route of the presidential motorcade had been well published in the newspaper, I had an opportunity to plan ahead. . . ."[2]

Miller brought with him his own Anscoset automatic 35mm camera loaded with Plus-X black-and-white film with an ASA rating of 125. In the late morning he drove over to a likely position on the motorcade route at Lemmon Avenue. He had it in mind to take a few pictures at this location, and then quickly get back to his car. A shortcut auto ride of a little more than a mile southeasterly across town would get him to a position on Interstate 35 for a second chance for more pictures of the motorcade. Miller figured he had the time to get to this new position since the motorcade route would snake in a clockwise movement through the downtown area before reaching the entrance to I-35 for its trip to the Trade Mart.

At approximately 11:40 CST, Air Force One touched down at Dallas's Love Air Field, and at 11:55 the presidential procession commenced. The motorcade, preceded by a lead car and motorcycles, included over 20 vehicles carrying the official party of government officials, the traveling press and photographers, congressmen, and invited guests packed into assorted convertibles and busses. Traveling out of the airport complex and turning left onto Mockingbird Lane, the motorcade continued a short distance until making a right at Lemmon Avenue. As the motorcade traveled further from the airport environs, the crowd of spectators grew in size and in enthusiasm.

A *Times Herald* staff member was in this area gathering local color observations for possible insertion into the newspaper's last afternoon edition. His reporter notes described the scene. "Thousands lined up along Lemmon as far as could see at Oak Lawn. No sign of demonstrators. No hostile placards. Very enthusiastic crowd. Screams of greeting as the President went by. Many school children. Many Catholic nuns. Perhaps from Holy Trinity nearby. Ten-15 deep crowds on Lemmon. They began gathering before 10:30 a.m."[3]

Miller had taken up a position on the west side of Lemmon Avenue not far from Oak Lawn Street. He would later remember, "On Lemmon Avenue, the motorcade proceeded at a very slow pace, the President and his wife, and Governor Connally of Texas, all waving at the crowd. I vaguely recall that a Catholic school in the nearby area had allowed its children to assemble along the curb for a better look at the President, and both he and Mrs. Kennedy spent a great deal of attention waving at these children."

The first of the two photos Miller took at this location was snapped as the presidential limousine is coming towards his position. On both sides of the street a good number of spectators, including many school-age children, line the curb and wave and applaud as the vehicle approaches. President Kennedy can be seen in the back seat on Miller's side of the street, and a line of vehicles, including the Secret Service follow-up car directly behind, and a press bus in the distance can be discerned. From the camera's apparent elevated view

The motorcade on Lemmon Ave.

in relation to the spectators in the foreground, Miller was either standing on something or held his camera above his head.[4]

After the President's limousine passed Miller's location, the high-schooler quickly got to his car and through pre-planning worthy of a professional photojournalist, he drove to a second location on Stemmons Freeway. Across the street from Miller's new position was the Corham Art Flower Company at 1645 Stemmons, while to his right was an S & H Green Stamps store. A short distance from here was the P.C. Cobb Stadium, used for area high school athletic events.[5]

While Miller was stationing himself at his new location, about 1½ miles back in the motorcade gunshots had been fired at the presidential car while it was winding its way through Dealey Plaza. Now with sirens wailing, the limousine and Secret Service follow-up car and a few motorcycles were racing along Stemmons. Their destination had suddenly changed from the Trade Mart to nearby Parkland Memorial Hospital. An assassin's bullet had found its mark. Miller and the few other spectators at his location were unaware of the new situation. What they saw was a fast-approaching group of vehicles. "I assumed that the motorcade must be behind schedule, and was trying to make up extra time by moving quickly along the large highway. I could see ahead of time that the speed at which the motorcade was traveling was not going to give me a lot of time to work with, so I sighted through my camera and began snapping off shots as fast as possible and panned with the action as the President passed. The entire scene went so fast that I did not realize that the President had been shot, nor that I had pictures showing him in his current condition."

The limousine on Stemmons Freeway

It is unclear how many photos Miller was able to click off or how much detail they revealed. David's father does not recall ever seeing any other photos taken on Stemmons other than ". . . the famous one with the foot sticking out of the car." That picture was taken at the moment the car was parallel to Miller's position. It is a dramatic shot in the best tradition of spot-news photos. The presidential limousine is in the center of the frame obviously traveling fast as both the American and presidential flags are caught fully extended in the wind. Slightly blurred in the right foreground and on the left background of the frame, two Dallas motorcycle cops, part of the motorcade escort, are traveling with the car. In the front passenger side of the Lincoln, Agent Roy Kellerman is looking behind to his left at the jumble of bodies in the back seat. What appears to be the head of Mrs. Connally is visible in the jump seat area. After her husband was shot through the back and chest, she cradled him in her lap as the Lincoln sped to the hospital. A portion of the First Lady's body can also be glimpsed, as she lay protectively over the body of her husband, whose torso and ghastly head wound is hidden from view.

Towering over the scene and in an awkward position with little room to maneuver is Clint Hill, Mrs. Kennedy's assigned Secret Service agent. Hill had been standing on the left front running board of the open Cadillac follow-up car right behind the President's vehicle when the shots were fired. He almost instantaneously began running for the Lincoln in order to protect his charge, but before he could get to the grip handle on the trunk of the car, another bullet had crashed through the skull of the President. Hill had finally jumped onto the back platform of the car, and pushed Mrs. Kennedy back into her seat as she tried to scurry onto the trunk to retrieve a portion of her husband's skull. At first hanging onto the trunk as the Lincoln accelerated to follow the lead car to the hospital, Hill finally managed to get into the back seat amid the bodies and the gore. Yet the cramped space forced him to leave his foot hooked over the right side of the car. At the time Miller took this picture neither Miller nor the sprinkling of spectators seen across the street watching the car pass knew that shots had been fired. The human eye could not grasp in real time what the photographic image would reveal on later careful examination. And of all the people rushing with the convoy to the hospital, few if anyone, besides Hill himself, realized that the President had in fact not survived an attack by an assassin.[6]

Miller walked back to his car not realizing what he had just witnessed. His oblivion to the tragedy was short-lived, however. "After returning to the car to go back to school, the radio was already buzzing the unsubstantiated reports that the President had either been shot or shot at. By the time I made my way back across to school, it was obvious that the President had been shot, and was in serious condition. As I recall, he died some time after I was back in school, the radio broadcast by this time having been patched on to the P. A. system throughout the entire school so all of us could listen. Realizing that I must have had some pictures which might be valuable, I immediately went to the school dark room where I processed the film. I printed a couple of pictures of those which seemed to be the most interesting and made a phone call to the *Dallas Morning News* to see if they would be interested in purchasing the picture." Miller was told by a man at the City Desk that they would indeed be interested in taking a look at his photos, and to come down.

In the evening David, accompanied by his father Robert E. Miller, traveled the approximately nine miles from their home at Kenny Lane to the *News* building. After looking over Miller's negatives, staff members ushered him into the paper's dark room area and made a copy of the negative which appeared of most interest. Tom Dillard, chief photographer for the *Dallas Morning News*, remembers the event, though not Miller by name. "I had a kid that shot pictures of the President's car riding down the expressway with the President rolled over on the side and his wife holding him. And I got those pictures from him. A guy tried to con him out of those — steal them from him. I paid the young man for the pictures. I got the film and developed it and printed it for him, I think. The pictures were made with a cheap camera of some kind. They were pretty good pictures as I remember. I think we ran it a couple of days later."   Miller was told that they would like to use the photo and that he could either receive a $5 fee or the caption could include some information about the photographer.  Miller opted for a photo credit, and on Sunday the *Morning News* ran the photo under the caption, "Horror and fear in the presidential death car."  A white arrow pointed to what the caption described as President Kennedy's foot hanging "limply over the side of the speeding death car. . . ." Crediting David Miller as the photographer, the caption also mentioned that it was taken as the limousine was traveling towards the Oak Lawn exit on Stemmons Freeway.[7]

> Upon exiting the *Dallas Morning News* building and obviously having some photographs in my possession, I was  besieged by many reporters from various news agencies and magazine publications around the world, hungry to get their hands on whatever I had.  I sold several copies of pictures I had made to various individuals who were willing to pay cash, and arranged with one individual who was a French reporter from Paris to meet at his hotel the next day to bring him more pictures.
>
> I went home that evening and printed more copies of the various pictures I had taken, to have ready for the Saturday morning meeting at the Statler Hilton Hotel.  Saturday morning, I proceeded to the Statler Hilton, met with this individual, and transferred him the pictures.  By the time I returned home that afternoon, I had received a phone call from a reporter at the Associated Press who was interested in purchasing rights for distribution of some of my photographs by wire across the U.S. to  subscriber newspapers. After a discussion with him over the phone, I then returned back to downtown Dallas to the Associated Press for the signing of a contract giving AP the exclusive rights to distribution by wire of one of my photographs across the U.S.

The Associated Press was the major wire service used by the *Dallas Morning News*. Tom Dillard explains how that association worked.  "AP was supposed to pay the paper for special stuff, a standard $5 fee if they picked up one of our pictures.  AP has access to anything made in your town on your time.  But if you go out of your area, and shoot a picture, then AP can't demand it.  They also can't ship your picture before you run it, because they could get it as soon as we shot it and get it in AP, and, hell, the opposition could get it."[8]  As the Miller photo was not the property of the *Morning News* save for an apparent "one time use," AP, when they knew about the photo, had to make their own arrangement with Miller.  They were, however, under no obligation to hold off sending the picture over their wire until after it was published in the Dallas paper.

Purchasing rights to Miller's dramatic view of the presidential vehicle with the Corham Building behind it, AP made extensive use of this photo, sending it out over their photo drum to all their wirephoto subscribers on Saturday, November 23. The news photo editor included as a caption for this picture, "(DN14) DALLAS, Tex., Nov. 23 — Assassination Scene — This picture, made moments after President Kennedy was shot in Dallas yesterday, shows his limousine speeding towards Parkland Hospital. White arrow points to Kennedy's foot protruding over side of car. Black arrow points to Mrs. John Connally, wife of Texas's governor, ducking bullets. Connally is visible just to the right of the Secret Service man leaning over back. Picture was made by amateur photographer David Miller. (AP Wirephoto)." In 1984 AP corrected this caption by including on subsequent captions that it was Secret Service Agent Clint Hill's foot, which was protruding from the car.[9]

Besides use of the photograph being picked up in numerous newspapers, the picture was also reproduced as part of the assassination coverage in the November 29 issue of *Time* magazine over a caption reading "A MOMENT AFTER THE PRESIDENT WAS FELLED," and including a credit line "David Miller-AP."[10]

Miller believes that the French gentleman to whom he sold pictures on November 23 later wrote a book on the assassination. The book to which Miller refers is a European-published volume titled, *Red Roses from Texas* credited to Nerin E. Gun. The 208-page volume is described in its introduction as, "A timely document that sets the scene for the tragic events of that November afternoon and enables us to view the great American tragedy in broader perspective." A curious book, it was published in 1964 and should be read with a great amount of caution. American culture and reality are commented upon through a European mindset, and translated terms come out somewhat askew, as "Minister of Defense" being used instead of "Secretary of Defense." The author takes information gathered from various sources and puts it together so that it reads as fact, but often does not hit the mark. Time and again, half-truths or simply made-up information is substituted for basic facts.

According to Gun, "David Miller a seventeen-year-old cashier at a nearby supermarket, had finished work, and taken along his new instantprint camera, meaning to use it this same afternoon for the first time. He saw the procession near the Neiman-Marcus crossing, but decided to take his pictures further along, where it was more open, with no skyscrapers to shadow his subject."[11] Describing the shooting scene as if Miller were present, the author writes:

> It was twelve-thirty exactly as the blue Lincoln turned the corner. David Miller took his photograph, but having noted that just at that moment Kennedy and his wife were looking the opposite way, he decided to run round the Texas Book Depository Building in order to get another picture when the car reached the motorway.
>     . . . So it came about that he saw a car with the American flag and a blue and gold pennant come tearing along flanked by police

motor cyclists. Without proper view-finding, he levelled his camera and took a photograph which must be the most striking of all the pictures taken that day.

It shows the policeman, Hill, standing in the back of the car trying to calm Jacqueline and telling her to keep her head down (there could well have been other attempts, or accomplices further along the route). Mrs. Connally is huddled up in the bottom of the car, covering her unconscious husband. The President's body is lying on the back seat, but one of his feet remains caught on the top of the car. Another Secret Service man, sitting next to the chauffeur, has turned round to see what is going on, and cannot believe his own eyes.

Young Miller did not know until later that he was the last person in the world to photograph Kennedy — at least, his foot. When he developed the film, he could not make it out; his father then told him about the assassination.[12]

As a result of Gun's book Miller received a call in 1964 from Washington from a member of the Warren Commission staff. He was inquiring if Miller had actually witnessed the assassination. "Once the Warren Commission investigator realized that I was actually several miles down the road from Dealey Plaza when I took that picture, he dropped the conversation at that point."

The Miller Stemmons Freeway photograph has also been the subject of speculation by some amateur assassination buffs. One of these researchers noticed that on top of a building across from Miller was the form of a man with a rifle-shaped object. The figure is on the roof of one of the buildings in the background of the photograph at a location on the print just above the flapping American flag. A Dallas police radio dispatcher broadcasting on Channel 1 made mention at 2:20 that day that, "There is a subject on this overpass carrying a rifle — railroad tracks, Cobb Stadium. Can you see him?" Other and more ambiguous dispatch messages were made, but no suspect was apprehended. Some independent buffs who believe that the assassination was a well-planned conspiracy speculate that a back-up kill site was set up at the Cobb Stadium area along the motorcade route.[13] This is broad speculation, as close visual examination of this small object in the Miller photograph can just as clearly make out a witch on a broom as any other animate object.

David Miller eventually became North American Sales Manager for Fairchild in its semi-conductor division, and his career took him to residency in Houston, Boston, and finally California where in the mid-1980s he met his future wife, Denise. Miller retained his interest in photography throughout his life. As his wife remembers, "He took pictures every day. We have boxes and boxes of pictures." He had never mentioned the November 22, 1963, photos to Denise until 1987 during the 25th anniversary of the assassination when he dug them out and showed them to her. The Millers and their young daughter, Elizabeth, moved back to the Dallas area in 1987.  In January 1988 Mr. Miller passed away.[14]

Concerning his reaction to the events he witnessed in Dallas as a high schooler, Miller wrote in 1985, " Since I was only in my teens at the time, and was not a profound follower of politics of the day, the assassination had no material effect on me.  I was, of course, sad to see that this sort of thing could have happened to our President, as I had admired Kennedy during his term in office.  As I look back today over the history of our country and the politics which have ensued since that event, I suspect that the assassination has had a fairly large effect on me.  However, no more so or less than most historical events which take place outside of our own control."

## CHAPTER NOTES

1.    *Hillcrest High School Yearbook*, 1965, p. 105; Letter, Denise M. Miller to Trask, 6/1989.

2.    Letter, David R. Miller to Trask, 3/8/1985.  The events as described by Miller are all in quotes and taken from this letter unless specifically noted.

3.    Photocopies of typescripts of *Dallas Times Herald* reporters' notes attributed to "Bates," 11/22/1963 within photograph files, JFK file # 9, A. H. Belo Corporation.

4.    Miller Lemmon Avenue photograph, 11/22/1963.

5.    Gary Mack, *Coverups!*, 7/1984, p. 3, 8.

6.    Miller Stemmons Freeway photograph, 11/22/1963.

7.    Letter, Robert E. Miller to Trask, 10/20/1992; Telephone interview of Tom Dillard, 2/21/1986; *Dallas Morning News*, p.1-11,  11/24/1963.  Dillard's recounting of this event could also have been something that happened at the hospital with another kid, though Dillard believes it occurred later that day at the *News*.

8.    Telephone interview of Dillard, op. cit.

9.    AP Wirephoto, DN14, 11/23/1963.  According to AP, "Hill made the correction when checked by the Miami News in connection with the recent anniversary of President Kennedy's death in Dallas."

10.    *Time*, 11/29/1963, p. 23.

11.    Nerin E. Gun, *Red Roses From Texas*, p. 15.

12.    Ibid., p. 22, 112-113.

13.    *Coverups!*, op. cit., p. 2-3.

14.    Letter, Denise Miller to Trask, 6/1989; Telephone interview of Denise Miller, 6/12/1989.

## CHAPTER 21

# The Free-Lancer

Free-lance photographer and film maker Jim Murray had not expected to take any pictures of the President's visit to Dallas on the 22nd of November. Indeed, his viewing of the motorcade and the President was not a matter of pre-planning, but rather that of casual timing. Murray never did take any pictures of the fateful motorcade, but because of his chance proximity to the scene of the assassination, he did in fact record more photographic frames of the confused aftermath at Dealey Plaza than any other photographer that day.

In 1963 Jim Murray was a 34-year-old husband and father of two children. Born in Rockford, Illinois, on September 9, 1929, Murray had moved to Texas as a teenager. He had attended the Universities of Missouri, Houston, and Arizona, and graduated in 1954 from Southern Methodist University in Dallas with a degree in journalism. Possessing a casual interest in photography, Murray learned to work in both still and motion picture formats after going to work in the Dallas bureau of Fort Worth television station WBAP. From 1955 to 1960 he worked out of the press room of the Dallas County Criminal Courts Building, across Houston Street from Dealey Plaza. Around

Jim Murray interviewing
Senator Kennedy in 1957

Thanksgiving time in 1957, WBAP Channel 5 assigned Murray to interview the junior senator from Massachusetts when John Kennedy was traveling through Dallas. Having been nominated and considered as a serious contender for the vice-presidential slot at the 1956 Democratic party convention, the youthful Kennedy was a rising star within the nation's political scene. Performing all the film interview tasks himself, Murray set up his camera equipment and placed Kennedy in a bench seat at the American Airlines airport lounge. He then sat down himself with microphone in hand and conducted the interview, reaching out to the camera several times to adjust the lens. Murray questioned the senator about his political future, asking if he would accept a draft at the 1960 convention. He also inquired if Kennedy believed his youthfulness was an asset or liability. Kennedy responded that his immediate political future was to run for re-election to the Senate in 1958, and that whatever asset or liability youth is, time has a way of dealing with it. In September during the 1960 presidential campaign, Murray again filmed the now presidential candidate when he toured the San Antonio area.[1]

Murray had moved the 270 miles to San Antonio in August, 1960, first employed as assistant news director for KENS-TV, and later working as a free-lancer, doing magazine still photography as well as motion picture assignments. Around the beginning of November 1963, the Murrays had moved back to Dallas where business prospects for a free-lancer were brighter. On Saturday, November 23, Jim was scheduled to film a Southern Methodist University football game for Dallas television station WFAA, highlights of which would be packaged for a day-after broadcast. Deciding to check out the station's film equipment in preparation for the next day, Murray went in the late morning of November 22 to WFAA, located at Communications Center only a few blocks southeast of Dealey Plaza. He arrived there at about the time President Kennedy was landing at Love Field, and watched some of the live airport coverage on a monitor at the station.

As Murray had no assignment to cover the President's visit, and knew that the event would be thoroughly covered by the local and national press, a saleable free-lance photo seemed a remote possibility. Ironically, had he been on an "assignment," he likely would have been somewhere other than near Dealey Plaza, which was at the tag end of the downtown motorcade route. The best photo opportunities would have been elsewhere. He didn't think there was any point in making personal snapshots of the arrival and motorcade, and a brief glimpse of Kennedy in a parade was not a high priority.[2]

Murray was, however, an unqualified "supporter" of the President, and although he would not go out of his way to see the motorcade, he was close to where it was scheduled to pass by. The County Sheriff's office was located at the Dallas County Criminal Courts Building on the northeast corner of Houston and Main Streets. The County Press Room was in this building, and Murray had worked out of this room for some five years prior to his move to San Antonio. As he knew most of the local reporters as well as people in the Sheriff's office, Murray decided it would be an opportune time to renew old acquaintances and incidently get a chance to see the motorcade.

Driving to the Plaza area, Murray noted that the parking spaces on the main streets were off-limits due to the motorcade route. He found a space on Houston Street by the rear loading dock of the Texas Book Depository Building, parking probably illegally, but figuring that the police would be too busy working the parade to write up parking tickets on streets off the parade route. In the trunk of his 1959 Ford, Murray had left his two Asahi Pentax 35mm cameras. The black-bodied cameras were relatively new, having been purchased by mail from Hong Kong in 1961. In retrospect, Murray regrets not thinking to carry his cameras with him. There was an undercurrent of uneasiness about the President's visit. Dallas was a hotbed of right-wing politics, and city officials had gone out of their way to urge citizens to refrain from any embarrassing incident that would mar the Kennedy visit.  But that the President could be murdered on a downtown street was simply beyond comprehension.[3]

While at the Sheriff's office, Murray remembers engaging in conversation about the day's events.  A woman remarked how nice it was that the weather was now so good that they could take the bubble-top off of the presidential Lincoln.  Murray, like scores of others on the scene that day, noticed the man on Houston Street who went into a seizure, and the commotion it generated a few minutes prior to the motorcade's arrival. He watched the motorcade through windows on the first floor of the Criminal Courts Building, first from the corner window facing on Main Street, and then as the cars turned on to Houston Street, switching his view to the west-facing windows.  As the Lincoln passed under Murray's window, he recalls observing Mrs. Kennedy leaning towards the President.  A frown on her face, she made a brief and private comment to her husband, before resuming her smiles to the cheering crowd.  Murray remembers thinking it appeared that for the First Lady, motorcades were not a pleasure — just a tiresome duty.

> I watched the vehicles till they turned back down [Elm] towards the triple underpass, and at that point they were very quickly lost to my line of sight behind that cement grillwork on the Plaza.  They were then out of my sight and I heard what I didn't recognize as gunshots. . . .  What I heard were three reports, and there was a longer pause between the first and second than the second and third.  And at the same time, or immediately afterwards, I saw running up the embankment, the infamous "grassy slope," what I think were teenagers. And I thought,  "Teenagers have thrown firecrackers at the motorcade — Dallas has got more egg on its face."

Being a photographic free-lancer aware of a potential transitory though saleable spot news photo, Murray figured if he acted fast, he might make a picture at the scene which could be captioned something like, " Teenagers Collared by Cops."  Running out the back door of the Sheriff's Department, Murray raced to his car and opened up the trunk. "I had a roll of Kodachrome in at least one of my cameras, and a roll of Kodachrome was several dollars which I couldn't afford to waste; and if you were thinking in terms of a news photo that would more quickly run on a wire service, Kodachrome [color] was not very useful because it couldn't be processed quickly.  So I swapped out, rolled it back and put black & white film in both cameras.  Again, I was not thinking in terms of the biggest news story I would ever cover.  The murder of a President within earshot was simply unimaginable."

The teenagers Murray saw were undoubtedly two boys who were standing on the north side of Elm Street near the Chism family, watching the procession, and who, when the shots were fired, ran up the incline to the northeast concrete shelter.  Shortly thereafter, they ran down the slope in a southwesterly direction and were captured, together with another running youth, in several photographs taken by Harry Cabluck from aboard a press bus in the motorcade.[4]

Murray estimates it took him about three minutes after hearing the three reports to get to his car and prepare his cameras. With the two cameras around his neck, he quickly moved to the Elm and Houston street corner near the Book Depository's front entrance. "The first thing that attracted my attention was a couple of black women

Murray takes his first photo near the corner of Elm and Houston Streets.

holding on to each other, sobbing. It was obviously a scene worth shooting, but it struck me as hysterical; an overwrought response to what I still believed was a minor incident involving teenagers and firecrackers. The crowd seemed stunned and milled around without direction. There was no visible focus to the activity." A problem arose trying to snap this shot. In three of Murray's first four pictures, his camera jammed with the shutter open due to a mismated 55mm automatic lens. The frames were completely over-exposed. The first good exposure shows the two black women clutching one another, one crying and the other holding a portable radio. The scene indicates confusion. Ten other spectators, including a cop and two men in hard-hats, are looking in various directions. A black woman on the right of the frame has a troubled look and is gazing toward Murray with her right hand caressing her chin. Another woman in the left background also has a hand to her face. Murray snapped this shot near the north finger of land adjacent to Elm Street and Elm Street Extension. To the rear can be seen the two bottom floors of the Dal-Tex Building. Josiah Thompson, in his 1967 book *Six Seconds in Dallas*, reproduced three of Murray's photographs, including a cropped version of this one, identifying one of the hard-hat men as Howard Brennan. He is looking up, ". . . at the Depository window where minutes before he had seen an assassin take his last shot."[5] Brennan had been sitting on the concrete retaining wall by the north reflecting pool and was facing the Book Depository. Shortly after this photo was taken Brennan told officer William Barnett, also visible in the photo, that he had seen the assassin fire from the sixth-story corner window.

Murray's next frame shows another blank, and it was at this point that he switched lenses to a 35mm wide-angle lens. "I sort of worked my way off that corner,

As one cop looks over the area from the top of a railroad car, other people walk among the parked cars.

down toward the site of the grassy knoll, and the news became worse at every step." Moving westerly along the dirt Elm Street Extension road into the railroad parking area, Murray squeezed off two pictures, the first including in its view the north tower of the Union Terminal Railroad. The second shot was made to the rear of the north pergola, near a parking curb made up of railroad ties. It included the open-grid metal railroad signal tower in the background. In the foreground of both pictures are parked cars and numerous people milling around, many looking at the ground. A number of these people had run up the knoll facing Elm Street seeking the assassin's location. All this activity and tramping around only made a search for potential clues nearly impossible.

Turning easterly, Murray then made a picture of the Elm Street Extension road with part of the front and west side of the Book Depository visible to the left. A large crowd is gathered in front of a paneled truck, while others are walking back towards the Depository. Photographic researcher Richard Sprague later identified the Dallas

Witnesses Amos Euins and Hugh Betzner are among those wandering around the parking lot area.

police officer standing near the parked police cruiser at the left as Elvin M. Perdue, with Sam Webster behind him.[6] Knowing some of the law officers who were in the crowd, Murray soon learned more facts that something terrible had occurred. "It wasn't until I worked my way west on the Elm Street Extension, behind the grassy knoll, talking to witnesses, that the enormity of the event began to hit home, one fact at a time.

"Yes, there were gunshots!"

"Yes, the President was hit!"

"Yes, he was hit bad!"

Murray describes his next 20 minutes or so as "walking around in a daze that this could have happened," and "shooting randomly without any specific direction." Any time that afternoon that he saw activity, he made a picture. He left the railroad yard area and traveled southerly to the area of the grassy knoll. Taking four additional pictures

An easterly view up the dirt Elm Street Extension towards the front door of the Depository Building

of more clusters of people, Murray also captured on some of these negatives the seeming impropriety of traffic now reusing Elm Street for its intended mundane purpose, where only minutes before on this same location American history had been unalterably changed.

People cluster about near the sidewalk on the north side of Elm Street.

Seeing activity on the south side of Elm Street, Murray then crossed over to the triangle of land between Elm and Main Streets. Taking a shot towards the grassy knoll and pergola area, Murray at about this time probably used his second camera for the first time. Loaded with the same type 36 exposure Plus-X black-and-white film as his first camera, this second camera was mounted with either his 85 or 105mm telephoto lens. Murray took a frame looking towards the triple underpass, upon which can be seen a few spectators, and then he shot an additional view of the crowd at the base of the knoll.

Looking back towards the knoll

Murray next directed his attention to activity near a round metal "City of Dallas" storm sewer cover at the south curb of Elm Street.    Crouching down slightly, Murray photographed a bent-down patrolman J.D. Foster pointing in the general direction of the Book Depository, the front of which can be seen in the background, including the Hertz sign on its roof with a lighted time-and-temperature indicator, which reads "12:39."

Deputy Sheriff Eddy Raymond "Buddy" Walthers is looking towards where Foster is pointing, while a man with a light jacket and plaid shirt, who does not appear from his dress to be a law officer, peers towards the camera lens. This civilian may in fact be a spectator who held up some type of sign during the motorcade, and who can be seen in the Zapruder film and a Cancellare photo, close to this present location.

Nine minutes ago, upon hearing gunshots, Walthers from his position at the corner of Houston and Main Streets, had run to the railroad yard. He had just moments ago crossed to this location, ". . . looking at the grass to see if some shots had been fired and some of them might had chugged into this turf here and it would give an indication . . . if they were shots and not just blanks or something. . . ."[7]

Officer Foster had been stationed on top of the triple underpass. Witnessing the shooting, he believed the shots to have come from the vicinity up around Elm and Houston Streets and had moved ". . . down the roadway there, down to see if I could find where any of the shots hit."[8]

Between 12:39 and 12:40 Murray took a series of seven photos of the activity here [roll 1, #13-19], including Walthers lighting a cigarette, and then stooping over and feeling in the grass. Another man with sandy hair and dressed in a suit is also visible in two frames bending over and probing the area with his left hand. Later, critics of the Warren Commission claimed that a spent bullet had been recovered at this time, citing the interpretation of photographic blow-ups of these Murray prints, as well as a similar series of photos made about the same time by *Dallas Times Herald* photographer William Allen. An article in the December 1963 *New Republic* by Richard Dudman also reported that a police inspector had told Dudman that upon entering the area at the side of the street where the President had been shot, they had ". . . found another bullet in the grass."[9]

In his testimony before a lawyer representing the Warren Commission, Officer Foster stated that they "found where one shot had hit the turf there at the location." He indicated that the bullet hit the turf at the concrete corner of the manhole cover and ricocheted out. Years later when asked by a researcher if he had observed the plainclothesman at the scene, ". . . picking up a bullet and putting it in his pocket or anything like that," Foster replied, "No sir."[10]

The similarities between the Murray and Allen sequence have caused some confusion among researchers as to whose photos are whose. Many researchers have treated the two sequences

Nine minutes after the assassination, officials gather near a sewer cover as Officer Foster points towards the Depository Building in the first picture of this Murray photo sequence.

as made by the same person. The Murray and Allen series of pictures indicates interest on the part of the officers at a spot about three feet to the west of the rectangular concrete frame surrounding the manhole. An examination of first generation prints from the original Murray negatives show an area in the turf darker than the surrounding grass. When the question of a possible "slug in the grass" became a point touted by New Orleans District Attorney Jim Garrison during his investigation into the Kennedy Assassination in 1967, Murray was curious enough to make blow-up prints from some of his negatives. The Murray photo shows no identifiable bullet. When asked 22 years later about his thoughts as to what he was seeing while taking this group of photos, Murray stated, "At the time I was photographing, my honest opinion was that it looked like there had been heel marks, and something like a spiked heel had come out of the

dirt and created a little mound of damp earth. I certainly didn't see any bullets or anything. The later speculation, and I'm willing to believe it, is that the mound was brain matter from Kennedy's skull. It could well have been tissue. It was dark — muddy color — nothing to suggest brains or blood." The photos themselves are too inconclusive to be able to tell us what, if anything, was picked up off of the ground.

The unknown man dressed in a suit has been tentatively identified by some recent researchers as Dallas FBI Agent Robert M. Barrett. Later that afternoon Barrett is known to have been at the site of the Tippit shooting and also assisted in the apprehension of Oswald at the Texas Theater. Many have made an issue that in the last and only horizontal Murray view of this scene, this man appears to be putting something in his left pocket. Perhaps he did, though in the previous frame two civilians also have hands in their own pockets. Jim Garrison in his 1988 book *On the Trail of the Assassins* contends that Walthers ". . . is shown looking down at a bullet while a neatly dressed blond man is reaching down to pick it up. The unidentified blond man was wearing the plastic radio receiver clipped to his ear lobe." In Murray's clear, sharply focused photo, however, such an alleged receiver is completely invisible and clearly not present! For the next several hours a police presence was always kept at this sewer cover site, and the Dallas Police Department took several photographs of this location.[11]

An ancillary use of the Murray and Allen photos was made by critics Richard Sprague and Gary Shaw, trying to correlate the testimony of Deputy Sheriff Roger Craig. The 27-year-old Craig had testified that following the gunshots, he had run down to this general area, and at around one o'clock, had observed a man running westerly down the grassy knoll. A Rambler station wagon, driven slowly, came parallel to the man, stopped, and the man jumped into the car. Later that day at police headquarters, Craig identified this running man as Lee Harvey Oswald. Investigators chose not to believe Craig's account, while many critics of the government made Craig a darling of their cause, the implication in his testimony being that Oswald had help and there was thus a conspiracy. Subsequently, Craig's relations with the Sheriff's Department soured and his credibility in this and other related matters suffered as he spoke out on various controversies dealing with the assassination. Fired as a deputy in 1967, Craig for a time was involved in the Garrison investigation. After numerous personal problems and some perceived at-

Murray's last photo in the "sewer cover" sequence is this horizontal shot.

tempts upon his life, Craig shot himself to death in 1975.

Sprague and others have identified a man they say to be Craig in some of the Murray photographs, and in the Allen and Murray photo sequence they have located a Rambler station wagon at 12:40 driving down Elm with a person whom they identify as Craig looking up Elm Street in that general direction.[12]

A panoramic view of the north Plaza area

Murray, after taking the sequence of seven pictures near the sewer cover, traveled to the southwest embankment of the triple underpass and made a horizontal and then a vertical panoramic exposure of traffic on Elm, Main, and Commerce Streets, with the Book Depository, Dal-Tex, and County Records Buildings in the backdrop. The Hertz sign atop the Book Depository was on its temperature cycle and recorded a mild 66-degree temperature.

Realizing the enormity of the event, and the fact that he was at an important location with cameras, Murray, about 20 minutes after the shooting had occurred, found a phone and called Patsy Swank, a local part-time *LIFE* magazine correspondent. Swank confirmed a photo assignment for Murray and told him to be on the lookout for amateurs who had photographed the assassination.[13]

By now activity within the Plaza was centering around the front entrance of the Book Depository, and Murray walked up there and began making pictures of this area. His first two pictures in this sequence are vertical exposures of the Depository front entrance, showing a portion of all seven floors, including the sixth floor corner window, where he later learned that Oswald was alleged to have fired his shots at the President.

Concerning his use of two cameras that day, Murray much later explained that he would use the telephoto lens only if he saw something that demanded a closer lens,

Activity has focused on the Depository Building as Murray photographs its facade and main entrance.

but that in newsworthy situations like this, ". . . you probably rely on your wide-angle lens more." Murray now clicked off a number of shots at the Depository. On his camera mounted with the wide-angle lens, he recorded two exposures of the crowd at the building's entrance as well as a young black boy in the back seat of a police vehicle. The boy was 15-year-old Amos Lee Euins. At about 12:36 Sergeant D. V. Harkness had located Euins near the Elm Street Extension by the railroad parking lot. Euins can be seen in this area in Murray's third photo taken of this area when he had earlier been there. The boy told the sergeant that the shots had come from the corner window under the Book Depository Building's ledge. He later told investigators, "From where I was standing I could look across the street and see a large red brick building. . . . I heard a shot. I started looking around and then

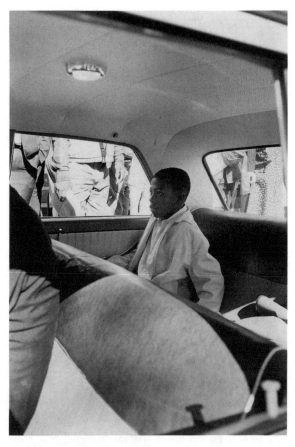

Amos Euins in protective custody

I looked up in the red brick building. I saw a man in a window with a gun and I saw him shoot twice. He then stepped back behind some boxes." According to Harkness, "After I took his name and address and put this information on the radio, I then took him on the back of my three-wheel motorcycle and put him in inspector Sawyer's car." Inspector of Police J. Herbert Sawyer had arrived at the Depository front entrance shortly after 12:34. Following a quick perusal of the interior of the building, the inspector instructed officers not to allow anyone in or out. He then set up a command post near the entrance.[14]

Murray made two shots looking east on Elm and Houston Streets showing a cruiser and motorcycles traveling down Houston to the Depository. KRLD television cameraman George "Sandy" Sanderson is also seen taking film of the street activity. Murray then walked up Houston where he made two additional shots, including a view showing most of the front of the Depository Building. By this time the crowd in front of the Depository was being cleared out to the opposite side of Elm Street, and Murray finished his roll of 36 exposures taking shots of uniformed police, some holding shotguns, with the Depository sighted as an overpowering backdrop to his photographic composition.

Brennan (in hard hat) at entrance of the Depository Building

Concurrently with his use of the first camera, Murray also was using his second camera mounted with the moderate telephoto lens. Among the cluster of photos Murray made, one can observe Howard Brennan in a series of three exposures shot of the front of the Book Depository. Following the shooting Brennan had told police officer Barnett what he had seen. He was brought to the front entrance but refused to enter the building and remained on the steps where he gave a description of the man he had seen in the window. He later related, ". . . I was confronted by a television reporter and cameraman. They wanted to interview me and find out what I knew about the shooting. I did not want to talk to him and I certainly did not want my picture broadcast. If there were more people involved than the young man I had seen, then showing me on television as an eyewitness would be like hanging a target over my heart for someone to shoot at. He kept asking 'Who are you, what do you know about the shooting of the President?' I turned my back on him without answering. He continued to try to get me to talk even though I moved away from him. Finally I said 'I don't know anything.'"[15] Murray's photos show both cameraman Don Cook of KTVT and Walter Evans of KRLD radio on the steps near Brennan.

Other pictures in this second camera sequence include two exposures of Sheriff Bill Decker giving an interview while being filmed by Channel 8's A. J. L'Hoste, three women on the fire escape of the Dal-Tex Building, and two frames showing Sergeant Gerald Hill yelling out of a sixth floor window at around 1:00 just after spent shells had been located under the corner window to which he is pointing. Four additional pictures are made of a group of cops poised with shotguns and located at the Houston & Elm Street intersection. His first 36-exposure roll of Plus-X film used-up, Murray had inserted a fresh 20-exposure roll into his first camera with the wide angle lens, and took four more exposures of activities around Houston and Elm Streets. Frames #4 & #5 show cops on the east side of Houston Street beginning to set up a rope line to keep spectators back. At about 12:54 a broadcast had gone over police radio Channel 2 requesting a Fire Department Rescue Unit to respond with rope, the paneled vehicle arriving on location shortly thereafter.

Cops with pump shotguns on Houston Street with the Dal-Tex Building in the background

While making the phone call to Swank, Murray had apparently missed the arrest of a seemingly intoxicated Larry Florer near the Elm and Houston corner sometime after 1:00 p.m. He now went into the Sheriff's office and recorded with both his cameras Florer seated in the office. Other witnesses there and seen in his photos include Charles Brehm and Hugh Betzner. At about this time he made contact with an amateur photographer who was at the shooting scene named Mary Moorman. Moorman took an important Polaroid picture at the time the President was shot in the head. Murray tried to get the picture committed for *LIFE* magazine, but it was already locked up by UPI. Murray took a picture of Moorman, showing her talking on the phone while she held a bottle of Coke in her other hand.

Murray was now fast running out of film, and would be in trouble if something important broke. Reluctantly, he decided it better to leave for a short time to get more film, rather than be caught on the spot without a means of recording possible important activity. Thus, at about 1:15, Murray walked back down Houston to Elm, shooting off several frames with both cameras. Two frames include cops on Houston with the Dal-Tex building in the background. Chalked on the building wall is a graffiti message reading, "If you want to live longer stay off the highways." Murray caught a passing taxi and went down to the Elko camera store at Main & Akard Streets. The cab driver had not heard about the shooting; and as Murray told him the news, the driver turned around and Murray made a reaction shot with his wide-angle lens. At Elko Murray picked up a supply of black-and-white film, switching to a higher speed, Tri-X, with an ASA of 400, rather than the ASA of 125 of the Plus-X film. This would give him more flexibility in shooting interiors.

Returning to the Sheriff's office at about 1:30, Murray finished up his two rolls in the cameras with additional shots of the office with witnesses and others sitting around. Reloading with fresh Tri-X film, Murray then left the building for the corner of Elm and Houston, where with his telephoto lens he made three exposures of Elm Street looking towards the underpass. Shortly after returning to the Plaza, Murray ran into Duane Robinson, a photographer friend who worked out of the Kincaid Photo Studio Service at Routh Street, a local gathering place for professional photographers. Murray gave Robinson his first two rolls of film, as well as his recent third roll on which there were 14 only exposures, Murray pulling it from the camera early to expedite processing. Robinson brought the three rolls to Kincaid's to be quickly processed and then to have contact prints made of each roll.[16]

Now becoming aware that the assassin's position had been supposedly discovered in an upper-story corner window of the Texas School Book Depository Building, Murray took two pictures with his telephoto lens of the front west end of the building, followed by five additional exposures of activity on the street level, and then eight pictures of the upper front east side of the building. In these photos showing the sixth floor corner window, activity is evident. A member of the crime scene section of the police department can be observed through the window examining this area. Murray then ". . . roamed around the fringes of Dealey Plaza looking for amateur photos and shooting a few myself." He made a few shots from an upper window of the Terminal Annex Post Office on Houston Street which overlooks the entire Plaza area from the south.

By now the shocking announcement of the death of the President had been made, and Murray, though still somewhat dazed by the events, decided that he should begin to round out his photo take with other locations, as he had pretty much covered all that could be shot at this location, and since he could not get into the Depository Building itself. All told, Murray had made just under 100 exposures at Dealey Plaza between approximately 12:33 and 1:45 p.m.

Finishing up his Plaza photos with views of the area
from the Post Office, Murray then went to Parkland.

Murray hitched a ride to Parkland Hospital with another newsman and made four exposures there, the only action at the hospital being in a makeshift press room in a hospital classroom set up for reports on the condition of Governor Connally. Murray then went over to the Trade Mart where the President was to have spoken, making shots of the dining room, deserted save for a few workmen, and the head table with food and china now set up for no one. At some point during the afternoon, Murray took a series of exposures of a flyer which had been circulated earlier in the day by right wing sympathizers. The flyer was made to look like a criminal reward poster including a profile and front face picture of Kennedy with the heading: "Wanted For Treason."

Concerning his activities of the afternoon, Murray wrote some twenty-three years later, after having reviewed his contact prints:

> The afternoon was pretty much a blur. Like most everyone, I was in a state of shock. Operating independently as a free-lancer, I didn't have the news organization backup to keep me pointed everywhere the events were breaking. I had left my car downtown and hopped rides with other photographers and newsmen. One stop was at the KRLD-TV newsroom. The enormity of the Kennedy murder was sinking in. One veteran newsman was crying as he sorted through the chaotic reports coming in. While I was at KRLD, the police monitor reported the shooting of a patrolman in Oak Cliff. But at the time there was no known link to the Kennedy assassination.
>
> It was late afternoon when I went back to my car and then on to Kincaid's. My first three rolls had been processed and contacted. I put my name on them and gave them, plus the next three unprocessed rolls to Shel Hershorn who was gathering stuff for shipment to *LIFE*. Shel was a Dallas free-lancer who did a lot of *LIFE* work through Black Star. He got back to Dallas from an out-of-town assignment late in the day. Normally, film shot for *LIFE* goes to the New York editorial offices, but that day, with the magazine on deadline, Kennedy film was being sent directly to Chicago, where the magazine was printed.
>
> By evening, *LIFE* had set up headquarters at the Adolphus Hotel. I checked in there and was sent to Parkland where Connally was. No access, so I went to police headquarters and spent the next several hours in that incredible melee while Oswald was shunted back and forth between cell and the homicide office.

A deserted Trade Mart

Oswald leaving the Homicide Office

"The crush of newsmen outside the Homicide office was a madhouse — like a feeding frenzy. By evening the national and foreign press had arrived. Oswald was being held on the fourth floor, and homicide was on the third floor. He would be taken back and forth through this incredible mass of photographers. We all just waited there in just this packed little sardine-like group. There was a photographer from the [New York] *Daily News* that was an asthmatic, and he had come down there with a Hasselblad with a sports finder. It was the only thing he had. He had been covering some sports event, and they said 'get on a plane and get to Dallas.' We were packed in so tightly that he was having an asthma attack, and he couldn't even fall out. It was just ghastly."[17]

The crush of newsmen

Murray had shot at least one sequence of Oswald being brought through the corridor, but his view was not clear, and he knew he probably did not have a very good shot. Prior to midnight he learned about another possibility of capturing the alleged assassin on film.

The Accused

As we pushed and jockeyed for position in the hall outside the Homicide office, newsmen were clamoring for a chance to question Oswald and to get a better look at him than they had been getting as he was hustled to and from his cell.  The authorities yielded to the media pressure, and took him to a basement line-up room late that night.

> I knew my way around the building and went down a back way to the line-up room. There was a terrible crush of newsmen down there too, so I climbed up on a cabinet and waited for Oswald to come past. I shot a picture as he and his escort came under me. He was ringed by detectives with these typical western hats that Texas lawmen favor. Oswald looked up with a sort of sullen and quizzical look, as if to say: "What the hell are you doing up there?"[18]

This is undoubtedly the best known of Murray's pictures taken that day as *LIFE* magazine published it on page 38 of their November 29 issue with an incorrect caption reading "Ninety minutes after President was shot, detectives wearing ten-gallon hats hustle Oswald into Dallas Police Headquarters. 'I didn't kill anybody,' he insists." An extreme blow-up of Oswald's face, copied directly from the image on the page in *LIFE* magazine, was used on the dust jacket and paperback cover of the book, *Portrait of the Assassin*, first published in 1965. This pro-Commission volume was written by one of its members, Gerald R. Ford, a member in the House of Representatives, and a future President of the United States.[19]

After leaving the police station early that Saturday morning, Murray dropped off his film. He found himself driving around aimlessly, listening to radio reports. "For the first time that day, I had nothing to do, and I finally shed my first tears. I stopped at a friend's house. All of the people gathered knew that Kennedy's death had changed our city and the whole world. But I don't think any of us realized how profoundly it would change things."

Those who watched the activities at the Dallas police headquarters via the frequent television reports of that weekend can vividly remember the crush of activity and seeming circus side-show atmosphere which was later almost universally condemned. Murray, a local observer and critic of the Dallas scene, gives a little insight into the factors that brought this about:

> The city has taken lots of lumps for the lax security. Having been very critical of the Dallas political scene in the 50s and early 60s, I now find myself in the odd position of defending Dallas against critics who haven't always made the distinction between sinister motives and just plain stupidity. When the roof fell in, Dallas authorities were simply unprepared to deal with the enormity of it.
>
> You had to have been a newsman in Dallas in the pre-assassination years to understand how the authorities perceived the media. I daresay it was different from any U.S. city — at least those cities with a "watch dog" press.

There was a cozy, basically unhealthy relationship between ownership of the papers and the municipal government. They were members of the same "club." The authorities had no reason to keep the press at arm's length, because they knew that negative stories, dug up by street reporters, seldom found their way into the papers. Consequently, they were conditioned to let the press have its way — even when it came to protecting a suspected presidential assassin. Aside from fighting off other newsmen, my access to Oswald was never challenged at the City jail.

This "kid gloves" treatment of the press was a critical factor in what occurred after the Kennedy assassination. In effect the authorities let the news organizations set the ground rules for coverage of Oswald. I was standing next to Police Chief Jesse Curry and District Attorney Henry Wade outside the Homicide office that Friday night. From overhearing their conversation, it was evident they were caving in to media pressure by bringing Oswald down to the basement "press conference." They were anxious to show that Oswald wasn't being mistreated. They forgot security concerns.

I believe to this day, that misjudgments in handling the press — and not a "plot" — were responsible for Oswald's murder. It's not surprising that a "hanger-on" like Ruby could get in the Police Station. The basement should have been sealed off from everyone — including the media. We would have howled, but Oswald would have lived to stand trial. And when he was killed it was much more damaging to the national psyche than the death of a president.[20]

After the use of his photographs by *LIFE* magazine, Murray had his whole series of negatives sent to Black Star in New York. A photo agency for use by authors, magazines, and the like, the Black Star would sell reprint rights of their client photographers and give sixty percent of the proceeds to the photographer. A number of Murray's pictures were used by European magazines. There have been other uses without payment or permission. Murray was not pleased with how he saw some of his photos being used. In 1967, Josiah Thompson's book *Six Seconds in Dallas* was published, and it included legitimate purchases of three of Murray's photos.[21]

Utilizing a Murray photo, together with a frame from the Robert Hughes amateur film taken at the corner of Main and Houston Streets, the caption in Thompson's book contended, concerning the Murray photograph that "this photo of the Depository windows, taken only moments after the assassination by Dallas photographer Jim Murray, shows boxes much lower in the window than the figure apparent in the Hughes film."[22] Thompson's contention was that there was a figure visible in the Hughes film in the window next to the supposed assassin's window, and the figure had disappeared in Murray's picture. Murray says he was "appalled" by Thompson's interpretation of his photograph and told this author:

> The book says my photo was taken "only moments" after the assassination, and was taken "not far" from the Main & Houston intersection where the Hughes film was shot. Thompson was wrong on both counts, and careful research would have borne this out.
>
> My photo was taken at least 10 minutes after the assassination, and from the intersection of Elm & Houston — a more acute angle to the Depository Building than Hughes's 8mm film, which would account for the fact that whatever "mysterious" object showed in the window in the Hughes film could not be seen in mine. In other words, my photo was misinterpreted to support an unproven theory.
>
> And I thought that if a researcher who has academic credentials like Thompson had, could be so careless about finding out exactly from where and when a picture was taken, and jump to this conclusion that had no basis in fact, then I didn't have enough control over the photographs. You couldn't expect Black Star to get a pledge from everybody who used them that they weren't going to come to wild conclusions. In short, I took them back because I couldn't control their misuse. It's been very disturbing to me some of the fantasies that have arisen out of this — I don't know the answer, but I know that a lot of the conspiracy theories just don't hold water. I did not want my photographs to be misused to distort the story to add fuel.[23]

Jim Murray took back possession of his original 1963 negatives, which for a period during the Jim Garrison controversy concerning the bullet in the grass, he kept in a security box. Remaining in Dallas, Murray broadened his business to include work in film documentaries. Over the years he has been contacted by a few dozen Kennedy researchers, including Richard Sprague. While admitting to a fascination of the subject of November 22, 1963, Murray has found it bothersome to deal with many of the so-called researchers, and became selective about with whom he speaks. It was, therefore, a treat for this author to have first met Murray in November 1985 and be invited late one night to Murray's office, filled with equipment, books, paraphernalia, and pictures. Located in an elderly commercial building only a few blocks from Dealey Plaza, the office gave one the feeling of an inner sanctum filled with comfortable clutter. Murray was careful and articulate when conversing about the assassination, not wanting his words to be misconstrued.

Murray strikes one as having thought about the 1963 events and its aftermath not only from the narrow viewpoint of a witness to some of those events, but as one trying to understand the event's full impact. He is a photographer of the events who speaks about the assassination photographs with a critical eye. Concerning the critics who have used photographs to aid their theories, Murray comments: "You can read just about anything you want to in a photograph. I have never found anything in any of my photographs that supports any of the conspiracy theories that I have heard. . . . I have shown prints to people who have pored over them with magnifying glasses, and have found everybody but the risen Elvis lurking in the shadows."

Murray remained active with a myriad of film projects including a major film documentary about sculptor Henry Moore. In 1989 Jim was struck down by a severe stroke, losing much of the function of his right side. With strong resolve and support from family and colleagues, he fought the debilitation while with the assistance of younger associates, he recorded his physical struggle and progress on video. Though partially impaired, Murray made remarkable strides, and in spite of his difficulties, remained vibrant working his craft.

Reflecting upon the Kennedy assassination of 1963 and its place in contemporary society, Murray comments:

> We might have recovered from Kennedy's assassination. Oswald's murder was even more traumatic. I think many people would rather believe it *was* a conspiracy, than live with unanswerable questions that arose from that awful weekend. It shattered all our lives, and we keep looking for some sort of *logic* to explain it. Our minds rebel against senseless events and try to give them some order — something that will tie up the loose ends into a neat package. We're really not so different from primitive tribes who believe a bolt of lightning *must* have been an event planned by someone all-powerful.
>
> Obviously, no single person can disprove all the fictions that have worked their way into the Assassination Folklore. But, thanks to my photos, I've had a unique opportunity to see how so-called "researchers" will bend the truth when there's a buck to be made. They're corrupting History, and it's shameful.
>
> I don't accept all the Warren Commission details, but I think their main conclusion was basically correct. For those who care enough to examine it, Oswald left a trail of irrational, violent behavior since he was a child. We'll probably never find answers that cover all the unknowables. But there have been many who have built profitable careers exploiting the doubts that exist. In this Talk Show culture, facts don't stand much of a chance against lies — or a 40-million dollar film budget.
>
> Lately I've decided that a person's response to the Kennedy assassination theories is a good litmus test of their judgment on other matters. It's like we're being asked to choose our own paranoia. Depending on which book you read last, it was either the Mafia or the

Military Industrial complex or the CIA — or was it pro-Castro Cubans or anti-Castro Cubans. Who's next?

Meanwhile, the most reasonable thesis is being buried under all the lies. And *History* is the big loser.[24]

## CHAPTER NOTES

1.     Murray interviews, 11/22/1985; 10/24/1992; Letter, Murray to Trask, 10/19/1992; Copy of WBAP-TV film and out-takes in the possession of Murray. Unless specifically noted, all other information in this chapter is taken from these Murray interviews and the letter of 10/19/1992.

2.     Letter, Murray to Trask, 8/6/1986.

3.     Murray telephone interview, 3/27/1986.

4.     Harry Cabluck press bus photographs numbers 1-2, 11/22/1963.

5.     Murray photographs, roll 1, #1-3, 11/22/1963; Josiah Thompson, *Six Seconds in Dallas*, p. 135.

6.     Murray photographs, roll 1, #4-7, 11/22/1963; Notes on reverse of oversize print of Murray photograph roll 1, #7, located within the Richard Sprague collection, Western New England College, Springfield, Massachusetts. Subsequent photo descriptions come from an examination of eight contact sheets obtained from Murray of his photo take of 11/22/1963. Frame numbers will not be specifically mentioned unless they are particularly noteworthy.

7.     *Hearings Before the President's Commission on the Assassination of President Kennedy*, v. 7, p. 546.

8.     Ibid., v. 6, p. 252.

9.     J. Gary Shaw, *Cover-up*, p. 72. Hugh Betzner, Jr, seen at left in roll 1, #17-18 later deposed at the Sheriff's office that, "These police officers and the man in plain clothes were digging around in the dirt as if they were looking for a bullet." (*Hearings*, v. 24, p. 200). Betzner is also photographed by Murray at the Sheriff's office in roll 3, #15.

10.    *Hearings*, op. cit., v. 6, p. 252; Mark A. Oakes, *Eyewitness Video Tape*, Foster interview, 7/9/1991.

11.    Ibid., v. 5, p. 111-112; v. 26, p. 497; Mark Oakes, "On the Trail of the Mystery FBI Man," *Dateline: Dallas*, Winter 1993, p. 31-32; Todd Vaughan interview, 10/24/1992; Jim Garrison, *On the Trail of the Assassins*, p. 209; Murray photographs, roll 1, #16, 17, 19, 11/22/1963.

12.    *Cover-up*, op. cit., p. 14-18, 26-28.

13.    Letter, Murray to Trask, 4/1/1986; Murray believes he left to call Swank sometime around roll 1, #21-22.

14.    *Hearings*, v. 7, p. 310-313, 315-320; v. 16, p. 963.

15.    Howard L. Brennan, *Eyewitness To History*, p. 17.

16.    Letter, Murray to Trask, 4/1/1986.

17.    Ibid.

18     Letter, Murray to Trask, 7/11/1993.

19.    *LIFE*, November 29, 1963, p. 3, 38; Gerald R. Ford, *Portrait of the Assassin*, dust jacket.

20.    Letter, 7/11/1993.

21.    *Six Seconds*, p. 125, 135, 246.

22.    Ibid., p. 246.

23.    Letter, 7/11/1993; Letter, Murray to Trask, 8/15/1993.

24.    Ibid.

## CHAPTER 22

# The Sixth Floor: Evidence From Within

Following the brief but deadly brutal gunshots on Elm Street at about 12:30 p.m., scores of people who had been watching the motorcade and were within earshot of the gun blasts quickly radiated to this location. Many of those who converged into the Plaza were police or other peace officers who, on their own volition or by command of superiors, raced to the scene of the crime. So eventually did dozens of members of the working press and media free-lancers. Soon the area encompassing the triple underpass and the Texas School Book Depository was saturated with photographers, reporters, and film makers on the prowl for anything that might explain or add to the unraveling story. The Dealey Plaza area, a local pocket of landscaped greenery poised at the outskirts of the city in close proximity to the shabby commercial warehouses and active railroad yards, would never again be the same. From that half hour past noon on November 22 forever into the future, a day would not pass without travelers from afar seeking out this site for taking souvenir pictures and pondering the sadness and mysteries of this area.

As years passed, those who were either riding in the fateful motorcade or simply watching the procession pass by, would feel, even if they found it difficult to express in words, a certain kinship to history — a special and finite membership among those who were there when "The Man" was cut down. They had been there when an era of our nation's history unalterably turned a corner. They had seen the sights, smelled the air of the day, and felt the Texas sun at that point of time which changed so much in our nation's life.

The professional press and photographers from among this membership, even if they had experienced, recorded or reported little of the first-hand event itself, would always carry with them that invisible badge of the veteran who had been there as witness to and recorder of the seminal news event of their time. Several photographers, though not at Dealey Plaza to hear the echoes of the assassin's shots, would nonetheless arrive there soon after to record scenes around and in the Texas School Book Depository, all which would importantly document the aftermath of the crime.

In the confused melee following the shots fired at the President, scores of spectators who had watched the motorcade pass their position on Houston and Main Streets began streaming towards the north end of Dealey Plaza. A number of these sprinters were deputy sheriffs who had been standing in front of the Criminal Courts

Building at 505 Main Street. Several, including Deputies Eugene Boone, Ralph Walters, Allan Sweatt, John Wiseman, Luke Mooney, and Deputy Constable Seymour Weitzman, upon hearing three distinct shots, raced to the northern side of Elm Street. They converged upon the area of the grassy slope and concrete pergola, through to the extensive parking area, and onto the railroad yard beyond. After a few minutes of unfocused, futile searching, some of these men had their attention diverted to the Texas School Book Depository. As precious minutes passed during which employees and workers traipsed in and out of this building, various law enforcement officers were picking up fragmentary pieces of information that shots may have come from that location. With no specific orders and little understanding of exactly what had occurred, those initially few law men on the scene attempted to get a hold on the situation. Five-year veteran Dallas County Deputy Sheriff Luke Mooney, whose job was with the Civil Writ and Execution Department, approached the building at its rear entrance accompanied by two other deputies. Closing an open security gate and instructing a civilian present to keep it closed until another officer arrived, the deputies entered the open back door, closing it behind them. Deputies Webster and Vickery took off for the stairway, while Moody decided to use the freight elevator, all intending to get to the upper floors to conduct a search.[1]

Thirty-year-old Welcome Eugene Barnett, an 8½-year veteran Dallas Police Department officer, had along with two other Traffic Division men, originally been assigned traffic and crowd control at the Elm and Houston Streets intersection. Standing under the looming seven-story School Book Depository near the Elm Street Extension road on the northwest corner of the intersection, Barnett watched as the President's car passed just a few feet from him. "When the first shot was fired, I thought it was a firecracker, and I looked across the street. . . . but none of the people moved or took any action, whereas they would have if a firecracker went off. And when the second shot was fired, it sounded high. . . . And I looked at the building and I saw nothing in the windows. In fact, I couldn't even see any windows at the time. . . . I was standing too close, was the reason. And I looked back again at the crowd, and the third shot was fired. And I looked up again, and I decided it had to be on top of that building. To me it was the only place the sound could be coming from."[2]

Deciding that a possible culprit located on the roof would attempt a getaway down the fire escape, Barnett ran northerly down Houston Street, scanning the east fire escape and checking to see if there was another iron grill exit on the back side of the building. Arriving at the rear he saw other officers searching in the railroad area. As the building had only the one fire escape, and Barnett thought he was the only man watching the building, he returned toward the front to check that area while keeping an eye on the side fire escape. According to the officer, about 2½ minutes had elapsed since the last shot had been fired. Approached by a police sergeant asking the name of the building, Barnett ran to the front to note "Texas School Book Depository" on a sign over the entrance. He also noticed that at this entrance, "There were people going in and out at that time." Shortly thereafter Howard Brennan approached Barnett exclaiming that he had seen a man with a rifle in a window of this building. Barnett, giving up his rooftop fire escape theory, rushed again to the front entrance, halting any further exodus from the building while keeping the witness, Brennan, with him. The sergeant and Barnett then dashed off to the rear entrance to make sure it was covered. Within 15 minutes of the last shot, another of the original intersection cops, Joe

Officers Barnett (left) and Smith guard the Depository Building entrance.

Marshall Smith, reported to the front steps of the glass entry door to take up a guard position with Barnett. The two remained there until finally relieved around three o'clock. Not too long after Barnett began guarding the entrance, three-wheel motorcycle cop Thomas A. Hutson arrived. He had heard the incident broadcast over his cycle's radio from a position on Main and Ervay Streets. "I pulled up in front of the Texas School Book Depository and got off my motorcycle and took a position up on the sidewalk in front of the main entrance. . . . I stopped people and screened them from trying to enter, and prevented anyone from leaving if he got through the other two officers."[3]

The sequence of the shifting of attention from the underpass and knoll area at around 12:30 to the Book Depository beginning at about 12:35 can best be reconstructed by using the photo sequence made by free-lance photographer Jim Murray (previous chapter) when after 12:40, seeing the flow of events, Murray began to concentrate his photo coverage towards the area around the Depository entrance. This heightened activity around the building is also displayed by listening to the early police broadcasts.

The day of the presidential visit, the Dallas Police Department was using their regular police radio Channel 1 for normal police business, while the second channel (Channel 2) was used as the motorcade security channel. Police Chief Jesse Curry's motorcade lead car broadcast the vehicles' progress on Channel 2 which was in turn monitored by other motorcycle and police vehicles and parade security. Just after a 12:30 time check recorded on the voice-activated Channel 2 Gray Audiograph flat disk recorder, and immediately following the shots on Elm Street, Curry broadcasts over the radio: "We're going to the hospital, officers. Go to the hospital — Parkland Hospital. Have 'em stand by. Get men on top that there over-underpass. See what happened up there. Go up to the overpass." County Sheriff Bill Decker, riding in the same vehicle, and knowing that his Sheriff's Department was close by with many of his men watching the parade, used Curry's mike. He tells the police dispatcher, "Advise my department for all men available back there, back behind there is the jail and up on the railroad right of way there. I'm sure it's going to take some time for you to get your men in there, pull every one of my men in there." The dispatcher, designated by call number "531" says to the lead car, which is now racing with the President's vehicle towards Parkland Hospital, "Repeat One, I didn't quite understand all of it." Decker orders, "Have Station 5 [Sheriff's Department] to move all men available out of my department back into the railroad yards there in an effort to try to determine just what and when it happened down there, and hold everything secure until the homicide and other investigators should get there." The lead car was just about to enter the triple underpass on Elm when the shooting incident occurred, and its occupants assumed from the people they observed on top of the underpass, that that was from where the problem was emanating. For those who heard this broadcast, or saw spectators fall to the ground near the steps leading from the sidewalk to the plaza's north pergola, this area first attracted their attention.[4]

Approximately five minutes after the shots, solo motorcycle officer Bobby W. Hargis, designated by call number "136," calls in to dispatch. Hargis had been one of the four cycle escorts flanking the President's car. When the bullet struck the President in the head, ". . . It seemed like his head exploded, and I was splattered with blood and brain, and kind of a bloody water. It wasn't really blood. And at that time the presidential car slowed down. I heard somebody say, 'Get going!'" As the President's limousine leaped forward, Hargis braked his cycle, racked it, leaped off, and ran to the north side of the curb. "I ran across the street looking over towards the railroad overpass and I remembered seeing people scattering and running and then I looked . . . over to the Texas School Book Depository Building, and no one that was standing at the base of the building was — seemed to be looking up at the building or anything like they knew where the shots were coming from." Seeing nothing, Hargis got on his cycle, proceeded to the other side of the underpass to look there and finally rode back to the Depository Building. It was there that he radioed to dispatch: "A passer-by standing at the Texas School Book Depository stated the shots came from that building."[5]

Within moments another cyclist called in a report. Clyde A. Haygood had been cruising further back in the motorcade on the right side near the first press bus, some 13 vehicles behind the President's limousine. On Main Street just approaching Houston, Haygood had heard three shots and shifting down to lower gear, traveled to Elm Street where he saw people on the ground and several others heading back toward the railroad yard. Pulling over and dismounting from his cycle at the north curb, the officer ran up to the north end of the railroad overpass, by a wooden stockade fence. Peering over the fence, but seeing nothing sinister, he returned to his cycle location. He then spoke with several witnesses there, including James Tague, who had been slightly cut on his left cheek by a piece of concrete, possibly from a ricocheted shot. Another man said the shots had come from the Depository. Taking mike in hand, Haygood alerted dispatch identifying himself by call number "142." "Just talking to a guy here at the scene of this — where these shots was fired at, and he said that he was sitting here close to it and the best he could tell it came from this Texas School Book, this Depository Building here with that Hertz Rent-A-Car sign on top." Haygood subsequently reported to the rear of the Depository Building and later assisted in the search of the sixth floor, being present when evidence was located.[6]

At 12:36 Sergeant D. V. Harkness, call number "260," after waiting to get free air time reported in, "I have a witness that says it come from the fifth floor of the, uh Texas Depository Book Store at Houston and Elm. I have him with me now, we're going to seal off the building." Assigned to supervise traffic officers from Main and Field to Elm and Houston Streets, Harkness at Main and Houston, upon hearing three shots, ran to his three-wheel cycle and rode west on Main Street, " . . . to observe the area between the railroad tracks and industrial." Attempting to see if anyone was fleeing from the area, upon seeing no one, Harkness rode to the Depository and to the Elm Street extension area. "I found a little colored boy, Amos Euins, who told me he saw the shots come from the building." Fifteen-year-old Euins told Harkness he saw the shots come from the corner window under the ledge, being the sixth floor. Harkness in his haste counted this as the fifth floor.[7]

Deputy Sheriff John Wiseman had run over to the knoll area from Main Street when he saw a man named Hester on the grass. "This man laying on the grass said the shots came from the building and he was pointing to the old Sexton Building [Texas School Book Depository]. I talked to a Marilyn Sitzman . . . who said her boss Abraham Zaprutes [sic ] . . . had movies of the shooting. She said the shots came from that way and she pointed also to the old Sexton Building. I ran at once to the Sexton building and went in."[8]

At about 12:37 call number "22" commands: "Get some men up there to cover this building, this Texas School Book Depository. It is believed the shot come from that, as you're facing it on, uh, Elm Street looking toward the building, it would be your upper right hand corner, there at the second window from the end." Cycle officer E. D. Brewer, who was a member of the lead cycles and had broken off from the motorcade to secure the Stemmons Freeway exit for the presidential party, heard of the shooting on his radio, whereupon he proceeded towards the Book Depository going east on Elm Street the wrong way. A man signaled for Brewer to stop. The man's information was radioed to dispatch at 12:38 by Brewer. "We have a man here who said he saw him pull the weapon back through the window off of the second floor on the southeast corner of that Depository Building." Asked by dispatch if "137" had the building covered off, Brewer said he was ¾ of a block away. Dispatch told him to "Report on down there," and Brewer ten-foured, indicating he would leave the witness there.

It is now unclear who this informant was (possibly TV cameraman Mal Couch who was on foot in this area for a little time) or if the reference to the second floor actually meant second floor from the top. Brewer subsequently assisted in the building search, and along with Haygood was on the sixth floor when evidence was located.[9]

By 12:40 it was reported that about 15 sheriff's deputies and half a dozen city policemen were at the Depository, and at about 12:43 both Channel 1 and Channel 2 dispatchers were instructing units to report Code 3 [Emergency] to Elm and Houston Streets with caution, as they were attempting to seal off the building until it could be searched for possible suspects.  Shortly thereafter, a description as provided by witness Howard Brennan, was broadcast.  All squads were to be on the lookout for an unknown white male, approximately 30 years of age, 165 pounds, slender build, armed with what is thought to be a 30-30 rifle.[10]

Among the gathering crowd around the School Book Depository was a TV cameraman based in Forth Worth.  Donald Cook was a cameraman-reporter from the only independent commercial TV station in the Dallas-Fort Worth broadcasting market — KTVT.  News Director Ed Herbert had assigned Cook to record pickup shots of the motorcade in Dallas.  Cook, with his 16mm springwind movie camera loaded with black and white film, had originally positioned himself on the Main Street sidewalk in front of the Criminal Courts Building near the Houston Street intersection and just opposite the brownstone "Old Red" County Court Building.

Mingling with sheriff's deputies who had come out of their building to view the motorcade, Cook poised his camera to take a panning shot from left to right as the President's sleek car passed his position.  He began the short film clip as the presidential vehicle just approached the east boundary of the old court house lot.  As Cook smoothly and professionally panned his camera, the President and Mrs. Kennedy acknowledged the responding crowd.  The follow-up car and the police motorcycles follow close behind, as the two Secret Service agents on the car's right running board are clearly seen with their heads and eyes cocked upwards at the tall buildings flanking Main Street.  As the President's car reached the intersection, Cook released his shutter button.  He then rushed up to the corner himself and watched as Kennedy's vehicle traveled down Houston to Elm Street.  At that point Cook turned back and started to the Main Street entrance of the Sheriff's office.  Hearing shots, Cook, along with numerous deputies in the area,  spirited toward Elm Street, glimpsing what he thought to be the President's Lincoln darting under the triple underpass just visible to his left.  Cook recalls beginning to film the confusion, including shooting a cop with drawn revolver and people on the Elm Street sidelines.  Running into the parking area to the west of the Depository, the cameraman filmed  activity there as more and more people streamed into the dirt lot.  Other sequences he filmed included looking east up Elm Street Extension toward the entrance of the Depository.  For a good part of the next hour Cook remained in the area attempting to get the story of what had occurred and filming any possible related activity.  In several still photographs made by Jim Murray, Cook is visible on the front steps of the Book Depository, his camera in hand. (See photo on page 502.)  His rectangular identification badge given to the press who covered the President's visit was pinned to his sports jacket.  Cook attempted to get information from Howard Brennan, who was also on the open foyer steps leading into the Book Depository.  Brennan, in a workman's hard hat, had seen someone shoot from an upper story window.  He had been temporarily placed here. Brennan, who had ambivalent feelings about this situation, did not want to have anything to do with reporters, and he attempted to ignore Cook's questions and lens.[11]

Within 15 minutes of the shooting, the police investigation centered on the Book Depository area. The crowd of spectators who had congregated in a confused cluster of humanity around the building's front entrance were being scooted out of the immediate area, and an ever larger force of police were arriving by cycle and squad car. By around 12:50 Sergeant S. Q. Bellah requested rope for erecting barricade lines, as a large crowd of spectators was inundating the area. At 12:54 dispatch related that they were sending a fire department rescue unit equipped with a large supply of rope to that location. Both a red fire truck and a light-colored Dallas Rescue Service panel truck responded and rope containment lines were set up along positions on Elm and Houston Streets.[12]

By approximately 1:00 the crowd is kept back from the front of the building, though not yet behind rope barricades. A large police presence is now on hand and the building is being searched.

Setting up a Houston St. rope barricade

Though various other press, including cameramen Jimmy Darnell of WBAP, A. J. L'Hoste of WFAA and George Sanderson of KRLD were evident on the scene with their cameras along with Don Cook, their film work was relegated to exterior views of the building and the unfolding, increased activity around it. Neither they nor any still photographer managed to get into the Depository and take any photos. Instead it was by a chance of timing and situation, the luck of which all newsmen are aware, that a cameraman with Dallas's Channel 8, WFAA news team got inside. He had missed assignment to the Dallas motorcade and events, yet happened to be the only person, other than police photographers, who took any film of the inside of the Depository as the criminal evidence was being found and processed. His luck would hold through to events on Sunday.

Tom Alyea was a native of Enid, Oklahoma. In his early 30s and with crew-cut hair and dark-rimmed glasses, Alyea had worked as a cameraman-reporter for Dallas station WFAA, an affiliate of the ABC network for the last 2½ years. The TV news department was non-union and smaller than the two other major area station staffs at KRLD and WBAP. The eight-man news team was headed by Director Bob Walker with assistant Bert Shipp taking care of assignments. All staff were expected to be able to perform camera work, reporting, writing, processing, and editing.[13]

The evening of November 21 and morning of November 22 Alyea and Ray John had been assigned to film the President's arrival and activities in Fort Worth. While on assignment there and in and around Hotel Texas, Alyea's camera had broken down and he had been forced to borrow one there, returning it prior to his trip back to Dallas. The men took the WFAA news station wagon via the Route 20 turnpike from Fort Worth into Dallas with John driving. The afternoon would be spent at the station processing and working up the Fort Worth film coverage for use on the evening news. Arriving in Dallas shortly after 12:30 and traveling east on Commerce Street within the Dealey Plaza area, John was preparing to make a right onto Houston Street to the WFAA station on Young Street. The newsmen had both the car's radio as well as the police band radios turned on. Not cognizant of the fact that they were only several hundred feet south of Elm Street when the remnants of the presidential motorcade was passing by, the men were halted at a traffic light some eight car lengths from Houston Street. Alyea would later recall to an interviewer what next transpired. "We sat there listening to the parade coverage on the radio. I didn't even think to look across Dealey Plaza to the Depository. The first indication that anything had gone wrong came when we heard a voice on the police radio. It gave an unusual alert — 'All units on Stemmons and Industrial, Code 3, Parkland.'"[14] Not associating the initial call with the President at first, the call was repeated, and within about 20 seconds the men heard the WFAA commercial radio announcer, John Allen, break in with the statement that shots had been fired at the President near Houston and Elm. "We were still waiting for the traffic light to change; suddenly, I realized where I was. . . . I grabbed Ray's camera, told him to take the other film on to the station, and I took off across Dealey Plaza for the Houston and Elm intersection. I filmed while running and, assuming that the shots came from the ground, I looked around and began shooting."[15]

The camera Alyea grabbed was a Bell & Howell 70 DR 16mm camera loaded with black and white film. It was an old camera and had a history of losing the film loop when being operated. Alyea also grabbed three extra cans of film along with the emergency roll he always carried in a back pocket. All told, Alyea had 500 feet of unprocessed film available to him. "I raced across Commerce and Main Street dodging traffic. On the far side of Elm I saw people rushing around. I had begun filming on the way as I crossed Main. As I was filming I was looking for police. They were not around. Some people were running towards the railroad tracks while others towards the monument area. I thought, 'There's nothing going on here,' and I went up to Elm and Houston." Not knowing anything about the incident, and seeing little direct activity around the intersection, Alyea did notice several cops and one man looking up at the Depository Building. He filmed the entrance, and as six or seven plainclothesmen rushed in through the double entry door, Alyea followed unchallenged with *Dallas Morning News* reporter Kent Biffle directly behind him. As they got in, Alyea heard a fellow say, "Shut the door! Lock it — no one in, no one out."[16]

It would appear that Alyea arrived at the Depository some time between 12:34 and 12:36, when there was still much confusion in front of the building and prior to the large scale uniformed police response to the police dispatch orders. Various officers, primarily plainclothes deputies, were in the building looking for a culprit or evidence. The search at this time was uncoordinated with people scattered on and scurrying among

floors, looking for anything out of place. Deputy Luke Mooney had first made a cursory examination of the second floor, then took the stairs up meeting other officers coming down. He stopped at the sixth floor, criss-crossing it and checking the fire escape. He then went up to the seventh floor, looking there for a time along with officers Webster and Vickery. They peered into the stairway leading into the attic, but it was pitch black and they decided to wait for flood lights which someone was supposed to procure. Mooney then decided to go back down to the

Luke Mooney (in hat) conferring with others in the School Book Depository

sixth floor. "At that time, some news reporter, or press, I don't know who he was —he was coming up with a camera. Of course he wasn't taking any pictures. He was just looking, too, I assume. So I went back down ahead of officers Vickery and Webster. They came in behind me down to the sixth floor."[17]

Interviewed by media researcher Richard Van Der Karr in 1964, Alyea graphically described his experience in the building. "I thought that there would be a gunfight, and I wanted to film it. First, we went to the fifth floor; no one seemed sure of from where the shots had come. We then went to the sixth and seventh floors. . . . I filmed them looking for the suspect. I was sure they would find the man, and I wanted to record the gunfight. I kept hoping that, if a battle did break out, it would be near enough to the windows so that my film would be adequately exposed. . . . The most interesting filming I did was concerned with the search for the gunman. . . . men crawled over and between huge piles of boxes. They climbed up to the ceiling air ducts and similar places where a man might hide. The mood was so tense that, if someone had dropped a book, I'm sure that fifteen bullets would have been shot in the direction of the sound."[18]

John W. Fritz, Captain in charge of the Dallas Police Department Homicide and Robbery Bureau was waiting at the Trade Mart when he heard of the shooting. Along with two detectives he sped over to Parkland Hospital. He only stayed there a moment,

Using portable lights, men search among the warehouse clutter.

however, requesting of Chief Curry permission to report to the crime scene. Driving Sheriff Bill Decker back with him, the officers arrived at the Book Depository at about 12:58. Decker remained outside while the police officials went in, now knowing from radio reports broadcast on their way to the scene that shots were apparently fired from this building. Attempting to tighten up the situation, and not sure if the building had been fully secured, Fritz ordered it sealed. Believing the culprit possibly to be inside, Fritz and his companions ". . . took our shotguns and immediately entered the building and secured the building to see if we could find him." While some officers began on the ground floor, others went to the top, both groups working towards the center, all the while other scattered officers also working the building on their own.[19]

Plainclothes Sergeant Gerald L. Hill heard of the shooting at City Hall, and arrived at the School Book Depository just ahead of Fritz. Asking if it was okay to go in and "shake it down," he entered with Fritz, and went to the seventh floor, and then the sixth at the time Deputy Mooney arrived there his second time. Searching the sixth floor again, Moody made a discovery. "I went straight across to

A police photo of the sixth floor, looking towards the piled boxes in front of the southeast corner window, where Mooney discovered the shell casings

the southeast corner of the building and I saw all these high boxes. Of course they were stacked all the way around over there, and I squeezed between two. And the minute I squeezed between these two stacks of boxes, I had to turn myself sideways to get in there — that is when I saw the expended shells and the boxes that were stacked up looked to be a rest for the weapon."[20]

Leaning out the partially open sixth floor corner window, Mooney called below that he had found the firing location. Hill heard Mooney holler his discovery and saw that book cartons had been stacked, "in sort of a three-sided shield, that would have concealed from general view . . . anyone who was in a sitting or crouched position between them and the window. In front of this window and to the left or east corner of the window, there were two boxes, cardboard boxes that had the words 'Roller Books,' on them." Three spent shells were on the floor near the baseboard. Asking the deputy to guard the scene, Hill went to the next pair of windows to the west. He opened the bottom moveable sash of the east side of the arch shaped window pair, and seeing Sheriff Decker and others below, hollered to them to send up the crime lab people. He motioned with his arm towards the adjacent pair of windows. Several photographers, including Jim Murray, took pictures of Hill as he leaned out the window. Not knowing if he had been understood, Hill decided to go down to the street to make sure the lab people were en route. He met Fritz on his way down, informing him of the location. As Hill reached the front entrance, he saw Lt. John C. Day of the Crime Scene Search Section just arriving, and told him of the discovery. Shortly thereafter a fire truck arrived at Houston Street, and a number of firefighters also went into the building to assist where they could.[21]

Sergeant Hill leaning out a sixth floor window, pointing to the corner window where shell casings were found

Deputy Mooney thought the shell casings were found around 1:00 p.m., while Homicide Detective Richard Sims, accompanying Fritz that afternoon, recalled the hulls having been found about 1:15. A photograph showing the Book Depository with the window Sergeant Hill had opened shortly after the bullet hulls were found also includes the Hertz sign on the roof. It shows the time as 1:05. Thus the discovery of the hulls took place prior to 1:05. At 1:11 Inspector J. H. Sawyer, who had been the first officer on the scene at Elm and Houston Streets to coordinate police activity, called in to radio dispatch from outside the building. "On the third [sic] floor of this book company down here, we found empty rifle hulls and it looked like the man had been here for some time. We are checking it out now."[22]

The inviolate physical condition and location of the hulls and shooting area prior to the time of the arrival of the crime scene men was much belabored in later testimony before the Warren Commission. Mooney testified, " . . . I didn't lay my hands on anything because I wanted to save every evidence we could for fingerprints." Hill told of instructing the deputy, " . . . to guard the scene, not let anybody touch anything . . . ."

Captain Fritz later signed an affidavit stating, "When the officers called me to this window, I asked them not to move the shells nor touch them until Lt. Day of the Dallas Police Department could make [a] picture of the hulls showing where they had fell after being ejected from the rifle." He testified to the Commission, "I told them not to move the cartridges, not to touch anything until we could get the crime lab to take pictures of them just as they were lying there and I left an officer assigned there to see that that was done, and the crime lab came almost immediately, and took pictures, and dusted shelfs [sic] for prints." Homicide Detectives Leslie D. Montgomery and Marvin Johnson arrived at the window location after its discovery and were told by Fritz to "preserve the scene." Johnson stated to the question of whether anything had been moved prior to photographing the scene, "No, sir; as far as I know, they hadn't been moved. They weren't supposed to have been, and that was our job to keep them out of there, and nobody came in there, I am pretty sure." In recent years Tom Alyea recounts that "The local police were very helpful in assisting me in recording these historical events. Capt. Fritz even picked up the scattered shell casing from behind the barricade and held them in his hand for me to get a close up." If correct, this may have been at a point following their being photographed and dusted. If not, it violated all concept of police scene documentation. This particular film scene is unfamiliar to the author.[23]

Lieutenant John Carl Day was a 23-year veteran of the police force with 15 years experience in fingerprint identification and 6 years assigned to the Criminal Scene Search Section of the Dallas Police Department Identification Bureau. He had arrived in front of the Depository at about 1:12. Accompanying him was Detective Robert Lee Studebaker, a 9-year veteran of the department who had only been assigned to the search section since October. As the newest member of the ID Bureau, Studebaker was expected to do much of the grunt work as he learned the procedures. The two arrived in a department station wagon which contained their specialized equipment, including 4 x 5 Speed Graphic camera, fingerprint kits, and containers. It was the responsibility of this section, of which Day had immediate supervision, to go over the crime scene and to assist in the investigation by photographing the scene and related objects, checking for latent fingerprints and collecting any potential evidence.[24]

On Elm Street these two investigators were told by Inspector Sawyer to report to the sixth floor. Upon arrival via the elevators, they walked over to the southeast corner and immediately took photographs of the shell casings as they had originally fallen. According to both men, the photos were made prior to any movement of the casings or of the stacked cardboard boxes. The first photo taken was made by Studebaker from a westerly direction looking eastward at the floor, with the lower portion of the double windows in view. Through the window one can observe spectators standing on the eastern Houston Street sidewalk. Several cars, a fire truck, and the light-colored Dallas Rescue Service panel truck with its dark-colored hood are parked in the street. On the oily and grimy floor are two spent rifle hulls close to the base of the south wall. Another lies near a box and is just visible on the lower edge of the photographic frame. Boxes, at least four high, are on the left foreground and others at camera right. The

Crime scene photo showing location of the carton on the window ledge, as well as
all three shell casings. In most reproductions of this photo, the casing on the lower edge of
the photo in the shadow of the box at bottom middle is typically cropped out.

partially open window sash of the next easterly window includes on its brickwork and just
touching the wood sill, a small cardboard box resting on the inside ledge. Studebaker
shoots two negatives of this scene. Due to the surrounding stacks of boxes, the location
is cramped. The photographer is forced to take a less than ideal shot of the scene,
"without getting up on everything and messing everything up. This is exactly before
anything was ever moved or picked up." The photos are nearly identical except for a
slight change of the camera's aperture. As was Day's practice, two photos were typically
taken of each scene to assure at least one would come out correctly exposed.[25]

A second set of double photos is made of the scene by Day and Studebaker,
who squeeze into the east side and shoot looking down to the floor in a westerly direction. All three casings are observable, the third westerly of the other two, further away

A second view of the location of the shell casings, one made by Day and the other by Studebaker. The top photo is made from the original police negative, while the lower photo, provided to the FBI, is a later generation copy with loss of photographic detail. Circles locate casings.

from the wall and resting near a stack of boxes. The box leaning on the sill is in the lower foreground and can be seen in this photo resting against the side of the higher of two other boxes stacked up from the floor.[26]

The men had only one camera between them, and took turns photographing, doubling up on each exposure. At least two other photos were taken by Studebaker from the inside of the sixth floor's easternmost aisle, looking south toward the southeast corner and at the wall of boxes which hid the floor area in front of the corner double window. One photo was made from the north end of the floor, while the other about half-way down. In this second view, metal fingerprint investigation boxes are seen at camera right, sitting on top of stacked book boxes.[27]

The photos shot, Homicide Detective Richard M. Sims picked up the shells by their ends and gave them to Day, who then processed each one by applying black powder. No prints were found. According to Studebaker, seven pounds of pressure must be exerted to an object to leave latent fingerprints. A fingerprint results from the moisture in the pores of one's skin leaving an impression of the finger on an object. These prints are generally invisible unless a powder is applied to the object to allow it to "lift off" or visibly stand out from the object. For best results various types of powders are used for different kinds of objects. Latent prints will eventually become too old to be "seen," even with the best powders. When a print (prints can be left from any part of the underhand) is lifted, it is general procedure to tape over it with clear masking tape to preserve the image and to be able to photograph it.[28]

The three shells were 6.5mm and after they were dusted for prints, Day gave them to Detective Sims. Sims placed the shells in an evidence envelope and marked the envelope with his initials, the date and the time, which was now 1:23 p.m.[29]

Photo by Studebaker looking towards the southeast corner and the wall of boxes. Note fingerprint kits on top of book cartons at right.

Photo showing the Dr. Pepper bottle where police say they found it on the sixth floor

While the shells were being given a close examination by Day in the cramped aisle by the window, Studebaker took two additional photos of some items located two aisles further west. On the front or the south side of the building, some three aisles from the east wall, a paper lunch bag and an empty Dr. Pepper soda bottle had been found close to the front windows and near a two-wheeled book carton truck. Detective Marvin Johnson had been assigned to this location to preserve the scene. Studebaker took one photo facing south which included in his view boxes, the bottle, book truck, double windows, and what he described as "a little ole brown sack" near the truck. The bag contained chicken bones wrapped up and put into the bag as well as "a little piece of Fritos" [corn chip]; also found in the bag. Though Johnson and several others would later describe chicken bones on top of a box, Studebaker could not recall seeing such a thing. He stated that it ought to be there in his pictures if that were the case. Fritz would later comment that there was such old trash as this at various locations throughout the building. A second photo of the pop bottle and boxes taken from an easterly direction was also made. For a time it was assumed that this lunch trash was associated with the sixth floor shooter who had

eaten a noon meal prior to the assassination.  Later it was learned that the lunch belonged to Bonnie Ray Williams, who had eaten and then left the trash here to join
several co-workers on the fifth floor to view the motorcade.[30]

One other object, besides the three rifle hulls, was discovered on the floor near
the southeast corner.  Detectives Johnson and Montgomery and crime scene officers
Studebaker and Day all later testified to the presence of a handmade brown paper sack,
measuring some 38" x 8" and put  together by means of 3" tape.  The sack was found
folded on the floor with the fold next to the two floor-to-ceiling pipes at the southeast
corner.  It lay perpendicular to a carton of books, just inches to the east of the three
stacked boxes adjacent to the half-open window.  No photos were made of the sack as
found.  The first documented photos of it are made by members of the press when
Detective Montgomery is photographed carrying it out of the building later that afternoon.  Why it was not photographed in place is not explained in later police testimony.
Perhaps it was a lapse of procedures for what at the time was considered a less important
piece of evidence compared to what else was being recovered.  Or perhaps the one police
camera was unavailable, being used at the rifle location.  Studebaker told of picking it up
and dusting it for prints, indicating he found smudges and a partial print, but nothing
useful for identification purposes.  Montgomery at first indicated in his testimony that he
picked the sack up, but quickly added it was not until it had been examined by Studebaker.  Detective Johnson says of the incident, ". . . My partner picked it up and
unfolded it and it appeared to be about the same shape as a rifle case would be. In other
words, he made the remark that that was what he [the assassin] probably brought it in."[31]

Though Day spoke of it being found, and wrote an identification on the sack,
"Found next to the sixth floor window gun fired from.  May have been used to carry
gun," this ID was probably not written until later at police headquarters.  By the end of
the day, however, similar samples of the type of paper and tape was gathered from the
first floor Book Depository shipping room, indicating this was the place of origin for the
materials used in putting the sack together.  Through subsequent investigation, the
Warren Commission believed that this sack had been made by Lee Harvey Oswald as a
container for his broken-down Mannlicher-Carcano rifle.  They concluded that the rifle
had been retrieved on November 21 at its place of storage at the Paine house in Irving,
Texas, where his wife was living.  Describing the package as containing curtain rods,
Oswald had, the Commission concluded, brought the concealed, broken-down rifle in this
package to work on November 22.  He subsequently is believed to have hidden by the
boxes at the southeast corner, assembled the rifle, and discarded the sack shortly before
he shot the President.  Except for the dusting powder applied to its exterior by Studebaker at the scene, Day was not allowed time to further examine its exterior or interior
prior to being ordered to ship this and much of the other physical evidence found at the
site to the FBI lab in Washington the  night of November 22.  At the Washington
laboratory the sack was examined utilizing silver nitrates, and a latent right palm print
near the wrist, and a left index fingerprint of Oswald's was identified by the federal
technicians.  Through observations and physical tests made comparing the sack to the

samples taken from the shipping department, it was determined the materials were the same.[32]

At just about the time Sims and Day were putting the spent rifle casings in the evidence envelope, they and Studebaker were summoned to the northwest corner of the building where a rifle had been spotted hidden among boxes. Though Studebaker would soon be released to return to the southeast corner to process the pop bottle and the stacked boxes for prints, the senior, more experienced Day would remain with the rifle — the most important piece of evidence. Studebaker, with limited crime scene experience consisting of on-the-job training since October 1, did not retrieve the one camera, nor was he instructed to do so in order to photograph the sack or take a full view of the three stacked boxes at the southeast corner window before they were moved.[33]

WFAA cameraman Alyea had been taking scenes on the fifth and sixth floors as detectives and deputies combed the area. In one scene a plainclothes detective, shotgun in hand, bends out of a half-open fifth floor southwest window speaking to officers in the street below. Other scenes show the active search and probing on top of stacks of boxes by men using portable lights. Some feel around large ceiling beams, while others push aside and look over stacked boxes.[34]

Deputy Eugene Boone had taken assassination witness Hugh Betzner back to the Sheriff's office. While there Boone fell in with some other deputies who were fetching heavy duty battery flashlights to use in the search of the Depository. Returning with them and their flashlights to the sixth floor of the Depository, Boone aided in the

shakedown of the floor. "And as I got to the west wall, there were a row of windows there, and a slight space between some boxes and the wall. I squeezed through them. When I did — I had my light in my hand. I was slinging it around on the floor, and I caught a glimpse of the rifle, stuffed down between two rows of boxes with another box or so pulled over the top of it. And I hollered that the rifle was here."[35]

On the floor just to the right of the window is the area where the rifle was discovered.

Deputy Constable Weitzman was nearby also searching the immediate area. ". . . I was on the floor looking under the flat and the same time he [Boone] was looking on the topside and we saw the gun, I would say, simultaneously and I said, 'There it is,' and he started hollering, 'We got it.'" Well concealed, the gun's location had been superficially searched several times before the two men finally spied it. Not touching anything, Weitzman remembered, "We made a man-tight barricade until the crime lab came up and removed the gun itself." Boone noted the time by his watch as being 1:22 p.m., while Weitzman, glancing at the weapon, though not able to clearly examine it, thought it to be a 7.65 Mauser bolt-action rifle.[36]

Lt. Day makes one of several photos of the rifle in its discovered position.

From atop an adjacent stack of six box cartons, in good light one could see about 5 inches of the gun stock as well as the barrel end of the rifle as it lay propped in a manner so the trigger guard area faced the floor. Desiring to get photos of the rifle as discovered, Day, who had quickly arrived, climbed upon the cartons and took two flash exposures with the Speed Graphic while kneeling. Then to assure at least one of the photos would come out with the correct exposure, Day had Studebaker climb up and take two additional exposures of his own of the same scene. Day later explained the photos were, "Identical shots, we just made both to be sure that one of us made it, and it would be in focus." The only difference between the two photo sets is that in the Studebaker shots a black blotch is evidence in the entire lower right corner, being Studebaker's knees, which got in the shot as he took it from a kneeling position.[37]

By now most everyone on the sixth floor had congregated in the area around the discovered rifle. Deputy Boone later described how, "There was some newsman up there right behind Officer Whitman [Weitzman] and myself who took movie film of it, too." Luckily for himself as well as for the historic record, Alyea was there. He counted it fortunate that the rifle had been hidden near an outside wall of the building so that the windows allowed light into what in the middle area of the floor would have been too dark for him to record on film. Pointing his 16mm camera up at Studebaker hunched on boxes and looking through his own camera, Alyea captured the detective in his horn-rimmed glasses and short-brimmed dark hat taking one of his police crime scene photos. With little light to record the scene, Alyea opened his lens all the way and set his exposure from 24 to 12 frames per second. As he began taking footage of the rifle on the floor and Fritz standing near it, someone (whom Alyea believed at the time to be a Secret Service agent) ordered him to stop taking pictures and return to the first floor. Alyea asked a deputy if he would take the camera and make the picture. "Damn right, give me the camera. Let that ____ try to take it away from me." According to Alyea, the "agent" did not have the authority to interfere with the local investigators. He got the message and Alyea continued to make pictures, though avoiding this man whenever possible. Earlier Alyea had problems with this same man, who had ordered him to leave. "After each order to vacate the floor I would walk toward the stairway as if complying, then dally a bit until the group moved on. Circling back to rejoin the perimeter took some stealth and I made certain there were piles of boxes or other objects between me and the uncooperative agent. . . . Much of my shooting of the search team crawling over the boxes, checking dumb waiters and examining possible hiding places was done by turning my back on Mr. 'Grumpy' and shooting from my waist or hip without looking through the view finder. When he was out of sight, I would frame it properly by utilizing the view finder."[38]

With two important but separate areas on the sixth floor containing potentially critical evidence, Day stayed with the rifle. As the bullet hulls were already safely photographed and secured, Day instructed Studebaker to finish up fully examining the southeast corner area. It was about this time that word reached the 6th floor that the President was dead. Remembers Alyea, "It stunned all of us, regardless of our politics, and casual conversation stopped. . . . we stared at the butt of the rifle. It was different now, we were looking at the weapon that killed our President." Lieutenant Day later described his activities to the Warren Commission in regard to retrieving the rifle. "Captain Fritz was present. After we got the photographs I asked him if he was ready for me to pick it up, and he said yes. I picked the gun up by the wooden stock. I noted that the stock was too rough  apparently to take fingerprints, so I picked it up. . . ."[39]

Alyea was right on the spot with the camera poised. Day was out of his coat and wearing a short-sleeved shirt and bow tie. His service revolver was exposed in a clip on the left side of his waist belt. As he crouched down to pluck the rifle from its hiding place, Alyea pressed his shutter release button. Attached to the rifle was a peculiar sling which years later would be identified as a jerry-rigged strap using a shoulder harness from an old-style U.S. Air Force pistol holder.[40] Day now utilized this sling by grabbing it at opposite ends of the rifle. He lifted the weapon up from among the boxes, not having to move any of the boxes to retrieve it. Situated to the west of Day with the building window to his back, Alyea positioned himself so he would not be filming into backlight, but with the daylight washing onto Day and the rifle. For several moments Alyea's position in relation to Day obscured much of the rifle. As Day straightens his body and the camera

Day picks up the rifle by its strap.

tilts up and pans slightly right, Will Fritz is seen in the frame motioning to take hold of the gun. The next view Alyea films is a clear shot of the rifle in a vertical plane as Day grasps it by the sling, holding it away from his body and rotating it to reveal the scope and main housing area. The rifle bolt, though in a forward position, appears not to be fully turned down in a locked position, but is sticking out perpendicular to the stock. From these clear frames a comparison between this rifle and illustrations of Mannlicher-Carcanos show it to be one and the same. Day begins to hand the weapon off in Fritz's direction. Fritz in the background facing Alyea, and with a handkerchief in his hand, takes hold of the gun as both men closely examine it. Rotating it from the butt end up and around to the barrel side up so it is pointing towards the ceiling, the two investigators comment about what they observe. Day takes out a pocket magnifying glass and looks at the bolt, while Fritz points. All told, Alyea filmed some 40-plus seconds worth of this sequence.[41]

Fritz and Day examine the bolt area.

Day in his later Warren Commission testimony told what next transpired. ". . . Captain Fritz opened the bolt as I held the gun. A live round fell to the floor. . . . The only part that Captain Fritz touched was the round nob [sic]. I looked at it through a glass and decided there was not a print there, and it would be safe for him to open the bolt."[42] Upon first glance of the weapon in its hiding position, Deputy Boone and several others had made a casual guess that the shape and style of the gun resembled a 7.65 Mauser rifle. This early, casually made description in various forms was reported in the rumor mill and broadcast on some radio and television stations. During the late afternoon and evening of November 22 Dallas station WFAA would variously describe the rifle as a "German Mauser" found on the sixth floor, a 6.5 "Argentine Mauser" with a four-power scope and a 7.65 "Mauser" found on the fifth floor stairway. Some of these reports were attributed to the Dallas Sheriff's office.[43]

Unlike Boone's preliminary remark, Fritz and Day now actually handled and examined the rifle. Among other markings on the metal parts of the rifle, they could read the stamp impressions of the serial number "C2766"; the barrel calibre "CAL 6.5"; date of manufacture "1940"; and the words "MADE IN ITALY." To them there was no controversy. Stated Fritz, "I heard all kinds of reports about that rifle. They called it most everything. . . . You can read on the rifle what it was and you could also see on the cartridge what calibre it was." Day recalled being asked later by the press if the weapon was a Mauser or a .30-06. Although he knew perfectly well its 6.5 calibre and Italian origin, refreshingly he was one of the few police officers that day not to freely give out thoughts, opinions or interviews that might possibly jeopardize the case. "It wasn't my place to give them that information. I didn't know whether they [investigators] wanted it out yet or not."[44]

Day kept physical custody of the rifle from the time it was picked up from among the boxes, through photographing it and having a description of it typed up at headquarters that night, until temporary custody of it was given up to the FBI for their tests in Washington.

After having picked up the rifle, Day carefully removed from the floor the live round that Fritz had ejected from the weapon. Holding it by its two end points, he noted the 6.5mm bullet had parallel sides and a round nose, was a full-metal jacketed bullet with a brass hull, measuring just a hair under 3" in length. As Day brushed the round with black fingerprint powder, Alyea filmed part of the process. No prints were found by Day, who then turned his attention to the rifle. "I put fingerprint powder on the side of the rifle over the magazine housing. I noticed it was rather rough. I also noticed there were traces of two prints visible. I told Captain Fritz it was too rough to do there, it should go to the office where I would have better facilities for trying to work with the fingerprints." Day later had 5 photos made at police headquarters of the two latent fingerprints found on the left side of the trigger housing. The photos were made with light shining from different directions to allow for better contrast. During the Warren Commission hearings, Day testified that although he could not exclude all possibilities of whose prints they were, he thought they were Oswald's. The identity was not conclusive, however, and neither could the FBI make a definitive identification. In 1993 the PBS program *Frontline* revealed a study they had requested fingerprint expert Vincent J. Scalice to conduct using these 5 pictures. Scalice, who had worked on the HSCA panel in 1978, noted all these photos were not available back then and that by using different enhanced techniques with each photo, he was able to identify sufficient characteristics on the prints for a positive identification. His conclusion was that ". . . the developed latent prints are the fingerprints of Lee Harvey Oswald's right middle finger and right ring finger."[45]

In the Book Depository Alyea had also filmed scenes of Day working with his powder and brush. He first dusted the barrel area to the front of the cheap scope mounted on top of the rifle, and then dusted back and forth in quick flicks of his wrist the left rear part of the scope itself. "I had a ring-side position," recalls Alyea, "with plenty of light to film Lt. Day meticulously going over the rifle

A frame from Alyea's film showing Day dusting the weapon

with his black powder and little dusting brush." Putting on his jacket and hat, Day, keeping firm possession of the rifle, took the elevator down to the ground floor, and walked out the door of the Book Depository. Pausing briefly at the doorway, he traveled down the sidewalk towards his vehicle accompanied by a plainclothes officer. Day was quickly trailed by a gaggle of waiting press and photographers who made quick shots of the removal of this very dramatic evidence. Day took the rifle to his office and locked it up in a box until he had more time to carefully examine it. He returned to the Depository Building prior to 3:00.[46]

About the time that Fritz and Day were finishing up with examining the rifle on the sixth floor, Roy S. Truly, Superintendent of the Book Depository Building told Fritz that one of his approximately 15 employees was unaccounted for. He gave Fritz the name of Lee Harvey Oswald together with the Irving address and phone number that they had on file for Oswald. Fritz thereupon left the building to follow up on this information.[47]

After the discovery and photographic record had been made of the hidden location of the rifle, Studebaker had left Day processing the weapon for evidence. He returned to the southeast corner of the floor to continue working up the evidence there.

Alyea could see he was the only news cameraman present. "This had gone beyond getting a news scoop on the competition, this was recording history and I was uncomfortable with the thought that I was the only one to record it." For the time being he was also a captive in this sealed-off building. The tension of earlier minutes, when it was still thought that the shooter or shooters could be hiding in the building, had now passed. Though wanting to get his exclusive film out for broadcast, Alyea kept as low a profile as possible so he could remain present around the intense police activity. Most of the officers present knew he was a reporter, yet he did not want to make himself too obvious, fearing someone might again question his presence or feel forced to take action about his being there. Alyea realized that his position there required him to act contrarily to the role of the inquisitive reporter, remaining as inconspicuous and making as much film as possible, all the while listening carefully to what was being said by those around him.

This poor reproduction frame from the original film sequence shows the boxes by the window in their original configuration.

Alyea roamed the floor taking whatever shots of activity he found. A quick close-up clip of the paper lunch bag on the two-wheeled box truck was followed by a view looking into the stacked box section of the southeast corner of the sixth floor. This one scene is the best preserved evidence of how the three boxes were stacked next to the half-opened window at the place where an assassin had fired shots at the President.

The police investigators failed to make overview still shots of this area prior to the boxes being moved around and examined for prints. Subsequent police reconstructions of the scene made on November 25 for photo documentation were perhaps close to the original, but still a reconstruction. Though Alyea was not permitted to get into this enclosure area, he did manage to shoot it, peering in between two sets of stacked boxes parallel and perpendicular to the front wall. He filmed it looking from the northwest into the space. Though the original film sequences are somewhat difficult to reconstruct, from Alyea's recollections and film clips themselves, it appears that Alyea had also made shots of this area prior to the discovery of the rifle. With plainclothes officers looking around and a motorcycle cop also evident in the film, Alyea had ". . . shot the location from several angles including the view the gunman had of the street below."[48]

From these Alyea film segments, together with the copies of the full frames of the photos made by the police of the shell casings lying on the floor, as well as the testimony of Day and Studebaker, we can develop a fairly specific placement of these boxes. A carton with large letters reading "BOOKS" printed on its side and measuring 18" x 12" x 14" was set near the window. On top of this larger box was a carton measuring approximately 13" x 9" x 8" and marked "10 ROLLING READERS." It contained not text books, but light blocks used as reading aids, and was placed with the side which faced the camera sticking out slightly further than the bottom box. Resting primarily on top of the six-course, one-brick-thick face wall below the window, and just touching at its southeast corner the wooden window sill, was another "10 ROLLING READERS" carton leaning against the other "ROLLING READERS" box for support. This second box tilted down into the room, was positioned lower than the first "READERS" carton it rested against, and set on its side. These two small cartons had been deliberately moved here from their original location on a stack several aisles to the west of this floor bay. Not within the picture frame was another "BOOKS" box set on the floor with its long side parallel to the front wall. According to testimony, the longish homemade paper sack was on the floor beside this box.

The significance of the layout of the scene was clear to those investigators present. Someone had taken advantage of stacks of books near the southeast corner, strategically adding to the collection of cartons, thus creating privacy from scanning eyes elsewhere on the floor. The single box on the floor near the corner wall pipes was a perfect seat for someone who wanted to peer out the window and remain as inconspicuous as possible to the gaze of people down below at street level. The purposefully piled three cartons adjacent to the window was, in Studebaker's opinion, "a good gunrest." Alyea would later write that "The positioning of these boxes was obvious, they had been used as a rifle rest for the gunman." It afforded an assassin with a comfortable, steady support for himself and a long gun so that he could fire in what is commonly called by marksmen a "bench-rest" position, not needing to raise above the sill and with feet on the floor. This position also gave the shooter as little exposure as possible.[49] Studebaker, upon his

Studebaker examining the Dr. Pepper bottle

returning to this side of the building, had first examined the paper lunch bag and then the glass Dr. Pepper bottle. Alyea films as Studebaker, processing kit nearby, dusts the bottle and then picks it up by the base and neck to examine it for latent prints. None was found.

A cameraman using a telephoto lens makes a shot of the sixth floor window as Studebaker examines the boxes for evidence.

It now became the task to check the primary boxes in the southeast corner for prints. Studebaker applied black finger-print powder to each of the four principal boxes. The dark pow-der gave each box a dirty, smudged appear-ance in subsequent photographs made of the scene. As the pro-cessing with black powder was done on each carton stacked near the window, it was moved to allow work to be done on the next. As Day testified, "They had simply been moved in the processing for prints. They weren't put back in any particular order."[50]

Now stacked one on top of the other, and at a different angle from the one below, this realignment of stacked boxes was later photographed by both the police camera and subsequent press representatives allowed into the scene. This view is what was universally reproduced in newspapers the world over, with most people assuming it to be the way the now-termed "sniper's nest" had been set up by the assassin. Many later critics of the investigation, misunderstanding the chronology of police evidence processing in the corner, found a confusion of several photographed versions of the so-called "sniper's nest." They saw in it an apparent manipulation of evidence. Several pointed out that the three-tier boxes were too high to allow a sniper to shoot out of a half-opened bottom window sash, thinking they had found a fatal flaw in the govern-ment's supposed evidence. They simply were misunderstanding the photographic evidence. Alyea's film of the area prior to its being disrupted by the police looking for fingerprints, is thus an important corroboration of the less-than-complete police photo documentation of the scene and the officers' verbal description of the scene itself.[51]

Fingerprint evidence was developed by the Dallas Police and independently by the FBI, who conducted their own examination of the physical evidence. The paper sack, found but not photographed at the scene, was discovered by the FBI to include a left index finger and right palm print of Lee Oswald. The carton, assumed to have been used as a seat by the window, was authenticated by Lieutenant Day to contain a palm print on its top edge on the side closest to the window. Day would later recall how he realized the importance of the palm print on the box. It was clear, fresh and unsmudged. The person who had made it had his hand there long enough for a fine impression to develop. Unlike those on other boxes, it was not at a position where it would have been created by persons randomly moving boxes, but was in a spot consistent with sitting and looking out the window. Day and the FBI positively identified the palm print as being Oswald's. Also found was a left palm print and a right index fingerprint of Oswald's on opposite ends of the top of the "ROLLING READERS" box, which was on top of the larger "BOOKS" box by the window. Of other fingerprints developed on these boxes by the FBI, the rest were of investigators who handled the evidence, none identified as being left by any of the other twelve warehouse employees who might have, in the course of their work, handled the boxes. This evidence alone could not be conclusive that Oswald was the assassin, but was of probative value concluding that Oswald was at this area as set up. An exact time frame could not be established, however, as is the case with all fingerprint evidence. Prior to giving up possession of the rifle to the FBI on Friday night, Day had also lifted a palm print on the underside of the gun barrel, which normally would be unexposed and covered by the wood stock, except when the weapon was broken down. He lifted the print by means of adhesive tape. This lifting was so complete as to remove all traces of the print on the barrel. The print was subsequently identified as that of Oswald.[52]

Once Day returned to the Depository after securing the rifle in his office, he took several photos of the School Book Depository Building from Houston and from Elm Street some time after 3:00 p.m. He also took a photo from the southeast corner window at about 3:15, looking towards Houston Street, towards where he assumed the assassin had fired, shooting a second view about 15 or 20 minutes later, looking down Elm Street, when he learned the direction from where the President had been hit. Members of the crime scene crew would stay at the Depository into the evening.[53]

Alyea had some great and undoubtedly exclusive film. Yet he was unable to leave the building with it, not even when Day left with the rifle. Managing to get to a telephone within the building, the cameraman called WFAA and requested someone to get to him and exchange exposed film for a fresh can. Photographer-reporter Ron Reiland arrived, but was unable to get in to exchange with Alyea. "I signaled Ron to throw the new film to me and I threw my film to him. He took off, but the officer couldn't leave his post to chase him, so, I got my film back to the station."[54]

Back at the television station film was being processed as quickly as it arrived, most of it being broadcast unedited. Sometime after 3:15 the first of the Alyea film was telecast. Assistant News Director Bert Shipp introduced as the film was screened — "Tom Alyea, one of our reporters-photographers, shot this film. He has just now managed to get out of the building because of the close security around it. . . . This is the first time we have even seen the film." The 1 minute, 45 second sequence is not the first Alyea took, as it shows the already discovered rifle being dusted as well as 15 other short sequences including the "sniper's nest" scene. A short time later a 25-second additional segment looking from the inside first floor entrance through the closed door at the two cops on the steps is also projected. Commentator Jay Watson explained to

Alyea takes a view of the police
and cameramen on the street below.

his viewers how this film was thrown out one of the windows and was developed during the last 10 or 15 minutes. All told, WFAA broadcast Alyea's films on Friday on some 5 separate occasions. Not including replays of the same film, some 34 scenes were shown, including v i e w s   o f   t h e police on the street below and crowds of spectators corralled on the opposite side of Elm Street near the reflecting pool area. The total non-repeated film amounted to 4 minutes and 12 seconds. A 1964 David Wolper documentary film included 5 other short clips by Alyea not seen on the WFAA telecasts of 1963. These clips, showing further searching in the Book Depository, amounted to an additional 14 seconds of film. A still later televised series, *The Men Who Killed Kenendy*, included additional Alyea film. Among these three sources are a total of 54 separate film clips of approximately 5 minutes 26½ seconds duration, all identifiable to Alyea. The clips include several other views of the southeast corner of the sixth floor and views of the rifle prior to its being picked up by Day.[55]

Alyea shot all of his film amounting to some 500 feet. At the station this precious film was not looked upon as historical documentation or even of possible investigative use. It was part of the news package and would be edited, cut up, and shown with only the concern of telling a breaking news story. Alyea incredulously remembers, "The news director had a bunch of it burned and I said, 'Bob, don't burn anything — this is history, we don't know what's on there.' He said if we can't use it on the news get it out of here." So much film was piling up in the cramped editing room floor that the next day much of it was destroyed. Alyea recalls that in between assignments he would come in to have his new film processed, and while there would pick up some of his discarded film, spin it on a reel and take it. He retains some of these clips, but bemoans the loss of other potentially historic film, "I could have shot Oswald coming out — could have shown someone else coming out." In April 1964 WFAA furnished to the FBI, upon its request, a dub of all the segments which survived and could be identified as being Alyea's.[56]

Alyea would film one final dramatic, though post-shooting event. Scheduled on Sunday to cover a news conference given by Mrs. John Connally at Parkland Hospital, the gathered press learned by a phone call to the press room that Oswald had been shot. Many took off for the Baylor or Methodist hospitals which were located closer to the city jail. Alyea and others, on a hunch, ran to Parkland's emergency entrance. His camera

Alyea and several other cameramen and photographers were on hand to
capture Oswald's arrival at Parkland Hospital on Sunday, November 24.

is running as a police cruiser rounds the circular drive followed by an ambulance which
stops and, as a cop motions with his hand, the vehicle backs under the canopy. Oswald's
stretcher is removed from the back of the ambulance amid much pandemonium.  Attempting to follow the gurney into the emergency room and down the corridor, Alyea
recalled, ". . . the officers forced a human wall across the hallway and refused to let us
pass." In the crowded corridor Alyea could not see in front of him. Another cameraman,
Bob Welch of WBAP, had a light attached to his camera, and Alyea  told him to shine
his light over the cops' heads.  As he did this, Alyea using that man's light, held his
camera as high as possible and pushed his film button.  "I couldn't see what I was
shooting."  His film includes Oswald being wheeled down the hall.  "I had filmed that,
as well as the doctors rushing from the emergency room to take Oswald from the police,
and I hadn't even been sure that I'd gotten anything. It was a real stroke of luck."[57]

While Alyea had been inside the Book Depository on Friday afternoon, one of
the newly arriving television cameramen was Daniel Owens.  Owens was on the four-
cameraman news staff of Fort Worth's WBAP television station.  During the 1960
presidential election campaign, Dan had made a local news splash, being the only area
newsman to have journeyed up to Hyannisport, Massachusetts, to cover a major Kennedy-Johnson campaign strategy meeting.  He had brought back locally exclusive sound
film of the event. Owens had arrived at the Plaza scene during the initial confusion, but
after the investigation had begun concentrating on the Book Depository itself.  He filmed

much of the front entrance area activity and can be seen in other photographers' shots wearing an open-front sweater with no tie and plaid pants. Filming Day removing the rifle from the building, Owens also was one of the press who accompanied the police up to the sixth floor later that afternoon and made film of the places where evidence had been recovered.[58]

Two still photographers also on the scene, who had covered the President's early Friday activities, did not possess the chance luck that Alyea had fallen into to end up as early as he in the Book Depository. Nonetheless, their coverage on the outside and later on the inside of the building would be important to the visual record of the story that day.

Known as "Jack" to almost all his friends and acquaintances, Ira Jefferson Beers, Jr., was a well known and accomplished 40-year-old professional photographer who had worked at his craft over half of his life. One of ten photographers on the *Dallas Morning News* staff, Beers had been working for the paper for over 14 years. Taking on free-lance jobs on occasion for extra income, Beers in 1962 assisted *Morning News* staff writer Dale E. Basye with a fluff piece he was putting together on speculation for a girlie magazine named *Adam*. The article, titled "Cool School," was to feature a supposed strip-tease school for amateurs conducted under the auspices of Dallas night club owner Jack Ruby. Beers thought the article to be "purely a promotional scheme" on the part of Ruby, as the "amateurs" were already in Ruby's employ. The training was just a charade used as an angle to sell the story. Still the money was real and Beers spent a summer afternoon at Ruby's Carousel Club in Dallas taking some 11 rolls of 120 film of young women in various stages of undress. The article ran in the December 1962 issue of *Adam* along with several of Beers's photographs, and thereafter the photographer came into contact with Ruby on several occasions.[59]

On November 22, 1963, Beers had no thoughts of the self-promoting local night club operator, especially since his major task of the day was assisting in the coverage of the President in Dallas. By Sunday afternoon, when Beers would be on hand to spectacularly film a gun-toting Ruby rushing in to kill the purported assassin of the President in the basement of the Dallas Police Department, the local photographer would forever have his name associated with Ruby and Oswald. On Friday, however, Beers, like dozens of other newsmen, was just performing his job, photographing a presidential visit.

*Morning News* chief photographer Tom Dillard had assigned Beers, along with Dillard himself, to cover the arrival of the presidential party at Love Airfield. Like many other photographers present, Beers obtained filler shots of the enthusiastic local crowd waiting in anticipation of the arrival of Air Force One. The photographer's preferred camera was a twin-lens reflex camera which gave a large format 120 negative. The paper provided its photographers with the Japanese Mamiyaflex which was a less expensive version of the Hasselblad. A 12-shot pack was the typical setup with the camera.

Once the President and Mrs. Kennedy had arrived, Beers was able to get some shots of them speaking to those in the official reception line with Air Force One in the background. When President Kennedy veered off to the fence area to greet the enthusiastic spectators, Beers also captured some of these human interest scenes on film.

*Morning News* photographer Clint Grant was also on hand at Love Field, having covered the presidential visit from its origin in Washington. Dillard had also assigned a fourth photographer to the airport. At the time Doris Jacoby was the paper's women's photographer. Not often called in to cover spot news, she was an excellent choice for the occasion. Originally from Germany, Jacoby had lived and worked in New York for a time. Possessing a graduate degree in photography, she was at home in the darkroom, and the envy of some of her co-workers for the quality of the work she produced. She would later be described both by Dillard and Associated Press's Jim Altgens using the same words — "a master photographer."[60]

Assigned to cover the arrival and make pictures of the activity of the First Lady, Jacoby used a Hasselblad loaded with black-and-white 120 film. The two rolls consisting of some 21 frames of large format negatives which she made are almost all well composed. They were consistently of a high quality that would leave a photo editor in a quandary as to which to use. We see Mrs. Kennedy, often with the President in the background, radiating smiles and interest whether greeting important local people in the official receiving line, such as the elderly Annie Dunbar, seated in a wheelchair, or a crowd of excited teenagers jumping up and down at the chain-link fence area.[61]

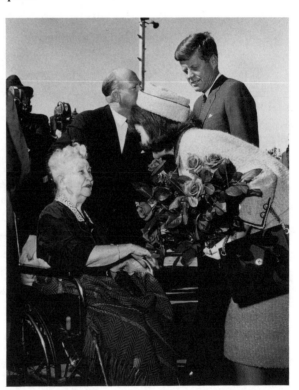

Mrs. Kennedy greets 85-year-old Annie Dunbar at the airport reception in this Doris Jacoby photo.

Once the presidential party had departed the airport tarmac area, Jack Beers drove back to the *Morning News* building with his morning photo take. "I was in my photo lab in the process of finishing films of the arrival at Love Field, and a lab man who works with us told me that the President had been shot, and I immediately thought he was making some sort of joke, and I continued to turn out my picture of his arrival at Love Field. And I told the fellow, 'Well, go ahead with your joke.' And he said, 'No; that is right, the President has been shot.' And he just turned around and walked out. And I still didn't believe him.

In a few minutes our intercom between the City Desk came on and I was told to report to the Texas School Book Depository Building, that they thought they had the man that shot the President in the corner there."[62]

Stunned by the news, which nonetheless did not quite sink in, Beers said, "Okay." Yet he kept standing there working on his prints. Several minutes later the city editor came in and hollered, "Get the hell out and go over to the Depository." It was now some 20 minutes since the assassination had occurred.

Several blocks closer to the Depository, at the *Dallas Times Herald* newspaper office, another photographer working in a darkroom also heard of the shooting. William Gaston Allen was a native of Little Rock, Arkansas, having been born there on April 19, 1936. He had received his undergraduate degree from Henderson University in Arkansas, and later worked towards his master's at North Texas University. Always interested in photography, Allen had earned his way through college doing photo work.[63]

As a young man of 20, Allen had begun work as a photographer with the *Arkansas Gazette* in 1956. He covered the Little Rock Central High School integration crisis in 1957. In 1960 he secured a job with the United Press International wire service and was assigned as a photographer at the  Democratic National Convention in Los Angeles, where Senators Kennedy and Johnson were nominated President and Vice-President on the Democratic ticket. Allen then moved to Austin, Texas, for a year and then was assigned to Dallas. The *Dallas Times Herald* had a contractual agreement with UPI. The wire service provided the daily newspaper with two photographers to the staff who could feed photos to the local paper while still working for UPI. Allen and Darryle Heikes were the two UPI staffers within the eight-man photo department under John Maziotta. The paper worked on a three-shift system, referred to as "tricks." According to Allen, as the *Times Herald* was "an afternoon paper, the latest trick was from 1:00 to 10:00 at night. The rest of us either came in at 8:00 and worked till 5:00 or 10:00 and worked till 7:00. You processed your own prints and then we had a photo editor who was not a photographer to whom we gave the photos."[64]

UPI provided the staff with inexpensive twin-lens Yashica cameras rather than the more expensive Hasselblad. The theory was that since the cameras were always being banged around carelessly by the staff photographers, when they broke they were cheaper to throw away rather than attempting to repair them. Most staff augmented the assigned cameras with cameras of their own. Allen preferred 35mm SLRs. He also had 35mm cameras available to him through the newspaper, and particularly remembers using Nikon Fs. Often he would go on assignment with a Nikon mounted with a wide-angle 35mm lens, a wider 24mm lens on a Leica Rangefinder camera, and an 85mm telephoto on a Nikon F. A gear bag would contain other lenses, extra film, and paraphernalia.[65]

The *Times Herald* photo assignments for the President's visit on November 22 had Allen as their only photographer at Fort Worth to cover the President's early morning activities prior to his flight to Dallas. Allen relates, "I was to go to Fort Worth that morning and cover the President. I was to come back to Dallas with the photos for the early editions, not only for the *Times Herald*, but also for the wire service. I had a kind of double assignment that morning. Then I was supposed to pick the President up down on the parade route, and go with him to his speech at the Trade Mart, then just stay with him from there to the airport."[66]

Having returned to Dallas and the *Times Herald* building from Fort Worth, "I was in the darkroom printing my photos when a call over the police radio said there had been a homicide at the triple underpass. Our office was only a block away, so I just ran down there because that is basically where I was to pick up the motorcade, anyway."[67] Allen believes he reached Dealey Plaza in time to see one of the press busses in the motorcade just leaving. Not knowing quite what had occurred, he stayed in the area trying to figure it out, while looking for photo opportunities with his camera. Initially Allen seems to have been drawn down Elm Street, where there was activity on both sides of the road. He saw a small group of people, including a uniformed cop and a photographer near a sewer cover on the south side of the street.

Photographer Jim Murray had already been there for over a minute, and at 12:39 had shot off four quick pictures as Officer Foster and Deputy Sheriff Walthers looked around the area and Walthers probed the ground. At about 12:40 Murray and now Allen, just slightly to Murray's right, watched in their view finders as a man dressed in civilian clothes bent down and probed a darker area of the ground with his left hand. With the Texas School Book Depository in the background and both photographers close by the curb where traffic was approaching towards their direction, first Allen and then, within a split second, Murray made an exposure. Moments later Allen took another picture as the civilian clad man stands up, his left hand cupped and his head facing up the street.[68]

Allen photographs activity near the metal storm sewer cover.

What were the cameramen shooting? Murray's recollection is found in the previous chapter. According to Allen in an interview over 20 years later, "It was my understanding that they were looking for either bullets or something like that, fragments of bullets or fragments of something. I didn't see them hold up a bullet and say, 'Hey, here's a bullet,' because I'm sure I would have photographed it if they picked up something like that. I do recall them talking about a chip in the curb, but I don't recall, in fact I know I didn't see a bullet. I know I would have photographed it if they picked a bullet up. But I don't recall them picking up and holding anything up and saying, 'We got to keep this for evidence,' because I was standing right there with them the whole time."[69] Turning his attention to the other side of Elm Street, and towards a cluster of people near the sidewalk, Allen made a shot of the scene. He then crossed the street to the group of people at the sidewalk.

Using both his wide angle and telephoto mounted cameras, Allen made nine exposures at this location, including a series focused on a man with a receding hair line who is wearing a zipped up light colored windbreaker jacket. He was the center of attraction to those gathered around him. Charles F. Brehm had brought his 5-year-old son Joe with him to see the presidential motorcade. They had arrived at the Houston-Main Street area about a quarter of an hour prior to the scheduled motorcade time. Taking up a position at the northwest corner of the intersection, they watched and waved as the President's car had rounded Main Street onto Houston. Wanting another chance to view the President, Brehm picked up his son and ran diagonally down the grass infield area west of Houston Street to a position right on the curb south of Elm Street.[70]

In one of several emotional interviews recorded on audiotape that day, Brehm described what he had observed. "I happened to be about 15 feet away from the President when the first shot hit him. There is some discussion now as to whether there was one or two shots that hit him, but the first shot rang out and I was positive when I saw the look on his face and saw him grab his chest and saw the reaction of his wife, that he had been shot. And just at that time, which was probably a few seconds later, the second shot rang out and he just absolutely went down in the seat of the car. . . . But the only thing that I did witness, and something I'm sorry I did witness, very honestly, was the look on his face when that shot hit and the look again on him and his wife's face when the shots started to ring out, and it was very obvious that he was hit."[71]

In an interview three days later with FBI agents, Brehm told them of noticing that at the first shot President Kennedy "seemed to stiffen and come to a pause when another shot sounded and the President appeared to be badly hit in the head." When hit the second time, the President's hair had flown up, there was blood on his face, and he rolled over to the side, ". . . as Mrs. Kennedy was apparently pulling him in that direction." Brehm also told the agents that with his military experience and familiarity with bolt-action rifles, it was his opinion that the three shots had been fired, "just about as quickly as an individual can maneuver a bolt-action rifle, take aim, and fire three shots." Brehm also stated it was apparent to him that the shots had come from one of the two buildings at the corner of Elm and Houston Streets.[72]

In a conversation with this author many years later, Mr. Brehm was still clear and unchanging as to what he had witnessed. He vividly described hearing the sound of the bullets whiz through the air, a sound he recalled from his military days, and the fear he experienced realizing his son was in harm's way. He violently pulled the little boy to the ground.[73]

In two of Allen's photos (see photo on page 460) Brehm is talking and gesturing with his right hand, while a reporter with note pad in hand records some of his comments, including the words, "wife grabbed him."[74] In the Brehm interview with the FBI he told them that following the shooting, many people had gathered around him and asked him questions, and that he answered questions of the police and reporters to the best of his knowledge and recollections. A short while later he was brought up to thefront of the Texas School Book Depository Building and then escorted with several

other witnesses to the sheriff's office where he re
mained for about 2 hours.[75]

Included in the background of one of
these Allen photos are both the Texas School
Book Depository and Dal-Tex Buildings, while in
the foreground on the right side of the frame
among the group listening to Brehm is James
Tague. Tague had been standing near the concrete
underpass and was hit in the face by something
during the assassination. The Allen photo seems
to show a mark on Tague's left cheek. In his
testimony before the Warren Commission, Tague
spoke of Brehm, though not recalling his name,
commenting of him that he was ". . . very excited
saying he was watching the President and it
seemed like his head [the President's] just exploded."[76]

Also within the same photo, but on the

This Allen photo shows Brehm (light-
colored jacket) being interviewed. In the
background (wearing a hat) is a man identified in this and in another photo as Eugene Brading.

left side further back from Brehm and Tague, is a
man in a light-colored trench coat wearing a hat with a distinctive band. This man's
picture was later identified by Dallas Chief Criminal Deputy Allan Sweatt and another
deputy who had assisted in processing witnesses that day, as being Jim Braden. Braden
was picked up by police sometime after this Allen photo was taken. He had been
pointed out by a Dal-Tex elevator operator who noticed the stranger in the building
getting off the elevator at the ground floor. Braden was taken to the sheriff's office.
Producing a California license, he identified himself as 49 years old and from California.
He stated he was in Dallas on oil business and explained that while walking down Elm
Street trying to hail a cab he heard people talking about the President being shot.
Walking up to the Dal-Tex Building, he went inside looking for a telephone. Unsuc-
cessful in making his call, he was then detained as he left the building. Following a brief
stay and his signing of a deposition at the sheriff's office, Braden was allowed to go his
way.[77]

Braden was in reality Eugene Hale Brading, a career crook with a multi-page
rap sheet including charges of burglary, vagrancy, mail fraud, shoplifting and embezzling,
dating as far back as 1934. Referred to by an acquaintance as "amoral to the core,"
Brading had served part of a 12-year sentence for mail fraud and conspiracy, having been
released in 1959. Any out-of-state travel had to be approved by the U.S. Parole Board,
and in September 1963 Brading had received permission to travel to Texas, "to discuss
business . . . with Tidewater Oil Company." That same month he had been allowed to
obtain a change-of-name on his California motor vehicles license to "Jim Braden" for
"business reasons." Former Dallas investigative reporter Earl Golz, among others, had
traced the shadowy past of this known felon who had ties to many Mafia-connected

individuals and who had been at the scene of this presidential assassination. Speculation by some is that Brading was involved in some "shady deal in Dallas unconnected with the assassination." His presence in Dealey Plaza and his being detained by authorities, in light of his past difficulties, necessitated his being careful with telling the full truth. He had in fact reported as Brading to a Dallas probation office on November 21. According to Golz, an FBI agent who was involved in post-assassination developments told the reporter, "We found absolutely nothing whatsoever that connects this guy with the assassination." Speculation among some assassination researchers concerning his possible role abounds, however. Golz reported that some believe " . . . his role in Dealey Plaza may have been one of the Mob's observers and bag man."[78]

The situation in the Plaza during the first 15 minutes following the shooting was still very confused and unfocused. Activity was intensifying at the front of the Depository Building, and Allen made his way up there. "We just ran into the building, because we thought that's where something happened. Initially there were only three or four of us there. . . . It seems like initially I remember running in the front door and people being everywhere, so I think I was asking somebody who I thought worked there what was going on. There was confusion. By that time there were sirens, it was even before all the police had arrived." Allen remained inside only a brief time, as he was forced out, after being checked by authorities. From this point on Allen stayed around the building.[79]

Allen would eventually take some six rolls of 20-exposure black and white Tri-X film, shooting just shy of 100 frames of the activity in and around Dealey Plaza. Though he had not taken any pictures inside the Depository, now outside, "I just shot everything that moved around there for a while. I did several exteriors of the building, policemen leaning out windows, cops with shotguns looking up at windows, and pictures of people being interviewed." Allen believes he was the only photographer on site from UPI or the *Times Herald*. "I guess by that time I became a UPI employee again. Every time I thought I had a photograph, I would call and a runner would pick my film up and take it to UPI, and in turn they would make prints and take them down to the *Times Herald*. Once I got on site, I didn't coordinate with the *Times Herald* at all." Though the negatives technically belonged to the newspaper, the wire service wanted to get material out as fast as possible. Several of Allen's photos were sent that afternoon to all UPI subscribers. Negatives were often printed still wet with wash time only several minutes, and chemical residue of the fixative still on them. Allen remembers the most pressing business at hand was to make the pictures and get several newsworthy ones out fast with little regard that "Good God, we'd better make a record of all these."[80]

Many of the photos taken around the Book Depository were similar in content and shooting location to those being taken by Jim Murray. Both men took photos of cops toting shotguns on Houston Street looking up at the building, and of Sergeant Hill motioning out of a sixth-floor window shortly before 1:05 p.m. when the shell casings were discovered.[81]

Foraging for other potentially newsworthy shots, some time close to 1:00 p.m., Allen caught sight of a pudgy young man with horn-rimmed glasses being held and examined by two uniformed cops. The detainee was dressed in a raincoat under which he wore a coat and tie. His actions seemed a bit erratic, as if he had been drinking. Allen made two shots of the scene, while other photographers and cameramen also recorded him being whisked away by plainclothes officers who walked briskly on both sides of him. All three, with heads hunkered down, made

Larry Florer is detained by police.

their way to the enclosed driveway beside the Dallas County Criminal Courts Building on Houston Street.

The *Dallas Times Herald* described the incident in its November 22 final edition. "Patrolman W.E. Barker [Barnett] saw workers in the Texas School Book Depository pecking on a window from the third floor and pointing to a man wearing horn-rimmed glasses, a plaid coat and raincoat. The officer immediately arrested the man for questioning and placed him in a room full of witnesses in Sheriff Bill Decker's office across the street from the Depository. With the young man protesting, the crowd all along the way jeered at him as he was escorted across the street. One woman said to the man: 'I hope you die.' Another screamed hysterically, 'Is that the man? Is that him?' An unidentified photographer shot a picture of the arrested man and then said bitterly, 'I hope you burn.'"[82]

The man "under arrest" turned out to be 23-year-old Larry Florer, who was brought to the Sheriff's office where he remained with various other witnesses also detained. Sitting in a chair and appearing uncomfortable in his situation, Florer became the unwitting subject of several photographers, including Allen.

Florer was in fact not under arrest. He eventually gave and signed a voluntary statement. After several hours of being "voluntarily" detained, Florer was allowed to leave. His statement indicated that he and a friend had seen the motorcade at Poydras Street, after which they visited a Bar-B-Q on Pacific Street. While there they heard about the shooting. Florer walked down the railroad tracks to Houston Street and after observing the police activity around the Book Depository from the east side of Houston, he decided to make a phone call. A woman told him there was a pay phone on the third floor of the County Records Building, and he went into the building and took the elevator. Speaking to a woman at what he thought was an information desk, Florer was unable to obtain the use of a phone. Remaining by the desk, Florer was approached by a man who asked what he wanted and told him that he could not use the phone. Florer returned to the elevator and back into the street. His actions apparently struck the man in the building as being suspicious. The man went to a Houston Street window and motioned to officers below that the man leaving was a stranger in the building. Thereupon, two officers approached and detained Florer.[83]

The spectators jeering at Florer while he was being escorted by police was not unique. Some spectators assumed that anyone being detained or escorted by the police must be involved in the incident. Charles Brehm could recall years later the unfounded and vicious comments yelled at him by some people who assumed he was a captured criminal, when he and his five-year-old son were temporarily placed in a squad car on Elm Street. Brehm was nervous for the safety of both himself and his son.[84]

It was most likely some time after 1:00 and nearer 1:15 when Jack Beers arrived by car from the *Morning News* office and parked on Main Street across from the County

One of the first photos Beers made at Elm Street

Jail. He grabbed his camera and walked towards the Book Depository. "As I arrived, there was quite a crowd of people gathered around the building, and so some officers brought a disheveled looking man from the building, and I thought this probably was the person, so I ran over and made a picture and then went over to the building. This time the building was sealed off and no one was allowed to enter. I remained at the School Book Depository for two or three minutes, and I heard the report that an officer had been shot on Oak Cliff. I ran back to my car . . . and notified our office by two-way radio that there was a report of a shooting, that a police officer had been involved, and asked them if they had any information, or if this would probably be linked to the President's assassination, and they had no information. I checked the police dispatcher, and the dispatcher didn't have enough information to tell us, so I was told to remain at the Texas School Book Depository, which I did until some time quite late in the afternoon, at the time the police had finished their investigation there at the building. . . ."[85]

The Beers photo of the "disheveled looking man" is most probably one showing an elderly white-haired man in an over-large coat-jacket, baggy pants, and a tie, seemingly being escorted by a police officer with three others close by. The School Book entrance is in the background of the photo and was taken after the spectators had been moved back beyond the entrance and Elm Street itself. A man in a hat, identified by many researchers as Assistant District Attorney William Alexander, is reaching as to open the rear door of a squad car. At 1:18 a citizen had broken into the police radio channel with a report that an officer at his location had been shot. The shooting in the Oak Cliff district of Dallas turned out to be that of Dallas police officer J. D. Tippit. Shortly thereafter Alexander and others at the Book Depository scene left for this new shooting scene. Thus this picture seems to conform to Beers's testimony relating to the close proximity of taking his first picture and the general 1:30 time frame when it became common knowledge in the Plaza area that a cop had been shot elsewhere in Dallas.

Beers, Allen and other still and movie photographers continued to take pictures of any activity in the area. They observed several men being escorted by a cop with a pump shotgun carried at port arms and a motorcycle cop in his distinctive white helmet. As these men walked from the front of the Depository to a cruiser parked down Elm Street, both Allen and Beers shot this activity, with Beers taking a close-up photo of two of the men as they sat in the cruiser's back seat. The black man with moustache is captured on film with his eyes closed and a blemish mark on his forehead visible above his left eye. He is Bonnie Ray Williams, one of the three Depository workers who an hour earlier had been watching the motorcade from open windows on the building's fifth floor, and had heard what they believed to be a rifle firing on the floor above them. Another Depository worker, Danny Garcia Arce, is sitting next to Williams. Arce watched the motorcade from street level and believed that the three shots he had heard had come from ". . . the direction of the railroad tracks near the parking lot at the west end of the Depository

Two Depository workers placed in a cruiser on Elm Street, ready to be transported to make a statement

Building." These two, along with other Depository employees, were taken down to police headquarters to give statements and to assist in the investigation.[86]

Some time close to 1:45, Lieutenant Day left the Book Depository's front door carrying the rifle discovered on the sixth floor. Photographers swarmed around Day as he walked to Houston Street and crossed the street over to its east side and proceeded a short distance easterly on Elm Street to his vehicle. Day held the weapon by its strap and away from his body, attempting to touch it as little as possible to preserve any potential evidence on the rifle itself. The significance of the scene and the clear view of the presumed assassination weapon was not lost on any of the photographers. Allen took eight exposures while Beers shot at least three. By early evening the wire services would be circulating photos of this dramatic scene. Several of these photos clearly show the end of an ammunition clip protruding from the bottom of the rifle. The brass clip held up to 6 rounds. When the final round was bolted into the rifle chamber, the clip was supposed to fall out from the bottom of its chamber. The clip, however, had a propensity to catch and not fall out. The base of the clip is marked:"SMI" and "952." FBI expert Robert A. Frazier, in his Warren Commission testimony was unfamiliar with the significance of the markings, stating that they could be part of a manufacturer's code.

Day carries the rifle from the building to his car for transport to Police Headquarters. On the sidewalk in front of the Dal-Tex Building, Day is trailed by WBAP cameraman Dan Owens.

This author has a box of 6.5mm ammunition in which each of three clips contains the identical markings. The box is printed in part with the information: "Soc. Metallurgica Italiana" and "Partita No. 1A/1/1952." This is the probable origin of the clip markings.[87]

Fort Worth photographer George Smith arrived at the Dealey Plaza area shortly before 2:15. Some time after 2:19 Smith, Beers, and Allen took a series of photographs of three "tramps" being escorted by the police. Beers took two photos with a clear view of each of the three men as they made a right turn by the Depository front door, crossed Elm, and skirted the sidewalk by the north end of the reflecting pool. Allen also took up a position to photograph them, getting off three frames as they crossed to the east side of Houston Street and were traveling towards the Criminal Courts Building. (See also Chapter 14.)

Over 23 years later Allen told what he remembered of the incident. "The best I recall, I was standing on the corner and saw the cops coming down the side of the School Book Depository, and they were on each side of these guys. And when you see a cop walking down the street with somebody in tow, you're going to photograph them. And then they took them into the County Jail. 'Course I didn't get any names and I couldn't get anybody to identify them or tell me who they were. I even tried later to find out who they were. That's one of the reasons we never did run the photograph, because we didn't know if they had been charged or who they were. I just remember them coming down the street and I happened to be standing there, so I think I probably made two or three exposures, that's about all I did."[88]

Also photographed by several still photographers around this time were close-up shots of uniformed officers W. E. Barnett and J. M. Smith standing guard in front of the glass door entrance to the Book Depository. (See photo, page 515.) Within a short time other photos were made of Homicide Detectives Montgomery and Johnson pausing at

Two of three photos taken by Allen of the tramps being escorted to the Criminal Courts Building. Officer Bass leads them across Elm St. (top) while Officer Wise (bottom) trails them as they cross Houston St.

the building's front entrance. Montgomery had possession of the long homemade bag found by the sixth floor corner window, while Johnson carried the empty Dr. Pepper bottle and the lunch bag found a number of feet further to the west. They were being brought back to the police crime lab for further examination.[89]

The paper sack, purportedly used by Oswald to transport his rifle, is carried out of the building by Det. Montgomery. Detective Johnson is seen holding the Dr. Pepper bottle in this Allen photo.

Between 2:30 and 3:00 things were quieting down in the building. Outside curious spectators had been relegated to a second and more distant police line up on Houston and Main Streets. All occupants of the Depository had been checked and allowed to leave, and the police who had taken over full responsibility from the first-to-arrive Sheriff's Department, had searched and secured all floors. The Crime Scene Section was still working on the sixth floor and Lieutenant Day arrived back to the area to take more document photographs, but now was mainly performing wrap-up chores. Yet with the exception of WFAA radio reporter Pierce M. Allman, *Dallas Morning News* reporter Kent Biffle and cameraman Tom Alyea, who had been in the building during the early search, no other media representatives had been able to gain access. The press's desire to see the sixth floor scene was keen and the Dallas authorities, never having an adversarial relationship with the local press, wanted to be at least partially cooperative. Deputy Police Chief George L. Lumpkin instructed officers to have those press still on scene to assemble as a group by the front entrance. The fairly small group still present included Beers, Allen, Smith, Owens, and several other reporters including Darwin Payne. They were escorted as a group to the sixth floor, where they were allowed to look and to take photographs.[90]

Allen recalls, "There were three or four of us that went up to the sixth floor with the police. As we got off the freight elevator on the sixth floor it was an oily, old building. Where they found the rifle was to the right, behind some boxes. It was real dark in there. They took us over to the window and showed us where the boxes were stacked. That's when I got the shot of the boxes and looking out the window."[91]

Beers in 1964 spoke of his recollections: "And upon going in the building, I photographed the area where the rifle was found. I photographed the area around the window from which the assassin was supposedly seated, and I moved into that area and made a picture from the window, supposedly the window from which the bullets were fired, that showed a little corner of the boxes, on which the rifle possibly rested. It shows the street down below where the automobile was traveling when the President was killed."[92]

With Day obliging the photographers, they took photos of the area near the stairs at the north-west side of the sixth

Photo of the sixth floor corner area. This was taken late in the afternoon, after the rifle casings had been picked up and the three boxes by the window had been dusted and moved.

floor where the rifle had been found. Day pointed to the area behind stacks of boxes for the cameras. By the southeast corner the press were allowed to peer and then, one by one, step into the area where the shell hulls had been found. Studebaker had earlier dusted several of the boxes for prints, and as he would later testify to the Warren Commission, the three boxes by the window from which he believed the assassin had rested his weapon, were not now in their original positions. They had been moved during the dusting.[93] Pictures were taken of the three boxes stacked one on top of the other. With their quick publication in the media by the end of the day, and with no explanation of their not being in the original positions, most who saw them assumed they were in this position at the time of the assassination. Others, with a mind-set towards conspiracy and police complicity, eventually saw the movements and differing versions of the stack of boxes to be proof of their presumptions. Another view shot by all present was a view from the boxes through the window to Elm Street below. These views would become familiar to millions of Americans as an authentic view the assassin had of Elm Street, with an easily imagined presidential vehicle on the street below. Though not meant to, these late afternoon photos made of the southeast corner of the sixth floor, helped to muddle the facts of the shooting scene rather than exhibit how it was when actually discovered.

The photographers' view of the sixth floor corner window showed traffic using Elm Street. Police vehicles still at the scene on Elm and Main had been moved onto the sidewalk or the grass infield area. The manhole sewer cover near the curb at the south side of Elm Street was still being watched over by Officer Foster, and was a scene of interest to curious civilians. The railroad was still using the triple overpass, freight trains passing over the bridge on a regular basis.[94]

One of a group of similar views of the "assassin's window" taken
late on the afternoon of November 22 by various news photographers

Following the photo opportunity on the sixth floor, the press were taken down to the first floor where Building Superintendent Roy S. Truly was briefly made available to them for questions. Escorted out the building, the press dispersed, the building was locked, and the Crime Scene Section continued its work. Beers returned to the *Morning News* and developed his take, several being selected to be sent out by Associated Press in the early evening hours. Allen remained at the Plaza until dark.

As described in Chapter 18, Jack Beers's most famous assassination-related photograph was taken on Sunday, November 24. In the basement of City Hall, Beers captured on film the dramatic scene of the shooting of accused assassin Lee Oswald by night club operator Jack Ruby. This same Ruby was the man in whose strip club Beers a little more than a year earlier had shot a day-long free-lance photo layout. Willie Allen was not on assignment with the *Times Herald* the day of the Oswald shooting, and UPI had requested he do general street coverage. At the time of the incident, Allen was in a cafe and saw the event on television. He ran back to the *Times Herald* to help where he could and assisted in processing incoming film including the startling photo of the shooting taken by *Times Herald* photographer Bob Jackson. Allen's reaction to the print when he held it up to inspection was, "Oh, my God!" As for the man who shot Oswald, Allen mentions, "I didn't know Ruby well, but I did know him. He used to hang around our office a lot."[95]

And what of the historically significant photos taken on Friday by Beers and Allen? Beers later told investigators that the *Dallas Morning News* planned to keep all of the assassination-related negatives in the paper's permanent file, though separate from the run-of-the-mill negatives. In 1964 Robert B. Denson, the chief Dallas investigator for the Ruby trial defense team, published a booklet entitled *Destiny in Dallas, On-the-Scene Story in Pictures*. Included in the booklet were a number of Beers's photographs identified with the initials "JB." Though many photos were of events after the November 22 activities around the Book Depository, several otherwise unavailable pictures were published, as was Beers's description of taking the photo of the Oswald murder.[96] Beers died in February 1975. The *Dallas Morning News*, having had a bad experience with their photo archives being scavenged by press colleagues the weekend of November 22, and not wanting to assist in feeding further developing assassination buffs with their many theories, had much earlier closed its photo collection to the public. By the 1990s the *Dallas Morning News* only had within its collection a small group of 8" x 10" prints identified as being made by Beers. None of his original negatives are with the photo files. According to various sources, Mrs. Christine Beers, widow of Jack, had possession of her husband's assassination-related negatives.

On November 24, 1963, right after the Oswald shooting, Homicide and Robbery Division Detective Guy F. Rose obtained a search warrant for Jack Ruby's residence at the Marsala Place Apartments. Around 1:00 p.m. he and two other detectives served the warrant to the owner at the apartment complex. Due to a misidentification of the apartment number, Judge Joe B. Brown, Jr., was requested to come over to correct the error in the warrant, whereupon they were able to gain entry. The detective searched the rooms until about 2:00 looking through the clutter, though attempting to return items to their original positions. No photographs were made at the scene.[97]

Though the apartment was supposed to be unavailable to anyone else, Willie Allen craftily obtained access and made at least two photos of Ruby's bedroom. During the subsequent Ruby murder trial, the defense made a point of noting that Ruby, shortly after the shooting, claimed that he had done the deed after seeing a heartbreaking letter published in a local newspaper addressed to President Kennedy's young child Caroline. He also said he read that Mrs. Kennedy might have to return to Dallas for the Oswald trial. According to Ruby in a later statement, " . . . Suddenly the feeling, the emotional feeling came within me that someone owed this debt to our beloved President to save her the ordeal of coming back. I don't know why that came through my mind." In Allen's photo-to of Ruby's bedroom, a copy of the Sunday morning *Dallas Times Herald* is seen at the foot of Ruby's dishev-

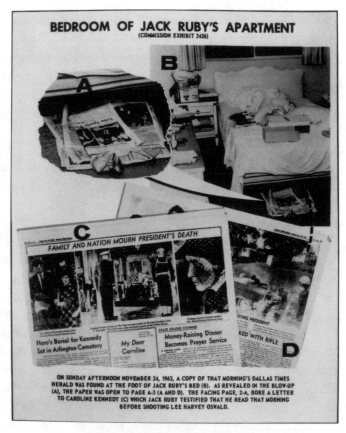

**BEDROOM OF JACK RUBY'S APARTMENT**
(COMMISSION EXHIBIT 2426)

FAMILY AND NATION MOURN PRESIDENT'S DEATH

Hero's Burial for Kennedy Set in Arlington Cemetery

My Dear Caroline

Money-Raising Dinner Becomes Prayer Service

ON SUNDAY AFTERNOON NOVEMBER 24, 1963, A COPY OF THAT MORNING'S DALLAS TIMES HERALD WAS FOUND AT THE FOOT OF JACK RUBY'S BED (B). AS REVEALED IN THE BLOW-UP (A), THE PAPER WAS OPEN TO PAGE A-3 (A AND D). THE FACING PAGE, 2-A, BORE A LETTER TO CAROLINE KENNEDY (C) WHICH JACK RUBY TESTIFIED THAT HE READ THAT MORNING BEFORE SHOOTING LEE HARVEY OSWALD.

Warren Commission exhibit utilizing an Allen photograph of Jack Ruby's bedroom

eled and cluttered bed with the paper open to page A-3. The facing page included the letter to Caroline Kennedy.[98]

Allen's photographic take of Friday, November 22, though sent to and used by UPI, technically belonged to the *Times Herald*, and Allen believes all the negatives ended up back with the newspaper. Often on a breaking news event, the photo lab was most concerned to get the negatives and prints made, the negatives still being wet when printed. Allen thinks that all the assassination-related photos and negatives were collected together by the paper. After several months he does not recall seeing the negatives again, though proof sheets were still around. By mid-1964 Allen had left the *Times Herald* assignment, though without any negatives or prints of his work of November 22, 1963.[99]

In 1967 assassination researcher Richard Sprague was allowed to view proof sheets of negatives identified as being shot by Allen. Twelve were ordered and purchased by Sprague, after which chief photographer John Maziotta, following many requests and potential controversy, decided to disallow any further public access to the paper's assassination photo collection.

A majority of Allen's Dealey Plaza negatives were transferred from the *Dallas Times Herald* to the collections of the Dallas County Historical Foundation prior to the paper's demise in 1991. The *Dallas Times Herald* assets were purchased by the parent company of the *Dallas Morning News* and the assassination photo files, replete of negatives and chiefly consisting of clippings and 8" x 10" prints, were donated to the Dallas Public Library in 1992.[100]

By the late 1980s Allen was living and working in Little Rock, Arkansas. Concerning the events of November 1963 he comments, "I've read all of the books and there's an awful lot of evidence that was not brought out as well as a lack at the time of an intensive investigation. There's just a lot of things that will never be answered. I think my gut feeling will be that there would have to be an awful lot more than just one guy that could accomplish all that Oswald did."[101]

Tom Alyea covered the Ruby trial for WFAA and also filmed a day in the life of Marina Oswald, the accused assassin's Russian-born wife. In 1966 he moved to Lafayette, Louisiana, beginning his own news service operation and publishing a bulletin relating to the oil and gas industry. Following the 1983 oil price depression, Alyea moved to Oklahoma. An avid cartoonist with a flair for teaching, Alyea, known to his audience as "Toma," produced several successful children's tapes on learning to make cartoons. It has only been in recent years that he has become aware of all the misinformation concerning the assassination and now he believes it important to help correct some of the factual errors.[102]

## CHAPTER NOTES

1.     *Hearings Before the President's Commission on the Assassination of President Kennedy*, v. 3, p. 281-283, 291-292; v. 7, p. 105-107; v. 19, p. 505, 531, 535.

2.     Ibid., v. 7, p. 539-542.

3.     Ibid., v. 7, p. 27-28, 536-543. In the first photo of the series taken by Jim Murray in Dealey Plaza, officer Barnett can be seen in the background near his original Houston Street position. To camera left Howard Brennan is seen looking up at the building, probably only moments before he told the officer what he had witnessed (Murray photographs, 11/22/1963, roll 1, #3). In later Murray photos, by around 12:40 p.m. a large crowd has begun to congregate around the front entrance of the School Book Depository, and both Barnett and Smith are clearly seen in position at the door prior to 1:00 (roll 1, # 19-27). Shortly thereafter, with the arrival of more motorcycles and cruisers, the front entrance is cleared of most civilian spectators who are forced back to the south side of Elm at the corner of Houston Street.

4.     Audio tape of Dallas Police Department transmissions, 11/22/1963, as provided by Stephan N. Barber, and transcribed by Trask.

5.     Ibid.; *Hearings*, op. cit., v. 6, p. 294-296.

6.     Ibid., v. 6, p. 297-300; Audio tape, op. cit.

7.     Ibid.; *Hearings*, op. cit., v. 6, p. 309-313.

8.     Ibid., v. 19, p. 535.

9.     Audio tape, op. cit.; *Hearings*, op. cit., v. 6, p. 303-305.

10.    Ibid., v. 17, p. 369, 371, 397-398, 464.

11.    Richard E. Sprague notes on his interview with Don Cook, Richard Sprague Papers, Special Collections Division, Georgetown University Library, file B3, F21; Jim Murray photographs,

11/22/1963, roll 1, # 22-23, roll 2, # 5-7; Richard E. Sprague typescript article, "The American News Media and the Kennedy Assassination," p. 26. Later sequences filmed by Cook included Brennan, Charles Brehm and several other witnesses being gathered together and walked over to the sheriff's office, as well as Larry Florer later being escorted to the same place. Pioneer assassination photo researcher Sprague had located and interviewed Cook in 1967, and except for several film excerpts used by Fox Movietone, most of Cook's coverage has not been seen by the public. KTTV, which had participated in the early pool coverage of the President's visit, requested and was given permission to broadcast the Fort Worth NBC affiliate station WBAP coverage of the afternoon's events. According to a latter inquiry by Sprague to KTVT, Cook's footage of that day had ended up "on the cutting room floor."

12.    Murray photos, op. cit., roll 3, # 4-5.

13.    Telephone interview of Bert Shipp, 3/22/1986; Interviews with Tom Alyea, 11/20 and 11/21/1993.

14.    Richard K. Van Der Karr, "How Dallas TV Stations Covered Kennedy Shooting," *Journalism Quarterly*, 1965, v. 42, p. 64. It is unclear what broadcast Alyea heard. If he was monitoring the regular police channel 1, at about 12:36 he would have heard instructions for police to cut off all traffic for an ambulance going to Parkland "Code 3," followed by an attention to all emergency equipment not to use Industrial Blvd. If he were listening to channel 2, he would not have heard a code 3, but at 12:30 would have heard Chief Curry say, "Go to the hospital — Parkland Hospital — Have them stand by," followed by a statement that it appeared the President had been hit and, "Just go onto Parkland Hospital with me."

15.    Harold Weisberg, *Photographic Whitewash*, p. 274; Richard K. Van Der Karr, *Crisis in Dallas*, p. 21.

16.    Weisberg, op. cit., p. 274; Interview with Alyea, 11/21/1993; Talk by Alyea at "Reporters Remember" Conference, Dallas, 11/20/1993.

17.    *Hearings*, op. cit., v. 3, p. 283-284.

18.    *Crisis*, op. cit., p. 22.

19.    *Hearings*, op. cit., v. 4, p. 203-205; v. 7, p. 158-161.

20.    Ibid., v. 3, p. 284; v. 7, p. 45-46.

21.    Ibid., v. 3, p. 285; v. 7, p. 46-47; v. 19, p. 506; Murray photos, op. cit., roll 2, # 10-11.

22.    *Hearings*, op. cit., v. 3, p. 285; v. 7, p. 162; Audio tape, op. cit.; Unattributed photograph of Texas School Book Depository, 11/22/1963, from Richard E. Sprague photographic collection, Western New England College Library.

23.    *Hearings*, op. cit., v. 3, p. 284; v. 4, p. 205; v. 7, p. 46, 101-103, 403-404; *JFK Facts Update, Preview Edition*, p. [5].

24.    Ibid., v. 4, p. 249-250; v. 7, p. 137-138.

25.    Ibid., v. 7, p. 139; v. 17, p. 499. These pictures as reproduced in the exhibits of the Warren Commission invariably crop out the hull located near the bottom of the photographic image. The pictures of the crime scene provided to the Warren Commission by the Dallas Police Department were not the best quality. According to one police source, they were copies of photographs rather than prints provided from original negatives.

26.    Ibid., v. 4, p. 250-251; v. 7, p. 138; v. 17, p. 221; v. 21, p. 643.

27.    Ibid., v. 4, p. 265; v. 17, p. 504-505.

28.    Ibid., v. 4, p. 253; v. 7, p. 137-139.

29.    Ibid., v. 4, p. 256.

30.    Ibid., v. 3, p. 169; v. 7, p. 146-147; v. 21, p. 648. Tom Alyea believes that a bag containing old chicken bones from a meal two or three days earlier, and a pop bottle were located on the fifth floor. He recalls an officer poking the sack with his foot and Alyea's making film of it. He thinks that after the search was completed, these items were brought to the sixth floor for examination. Employee Williams was quite clear in his description of eating his lunch on the sixth floor, the nearby book truck, etc. Police photos of the scene also confirm these were

located when photographed on the sixth floor. Were there two sacks and bottles nearby? Is Alyea correct and are the others incorrect? (*JFK Facts*, op. cit., p. [6].)

31.  Ibid., v. 4, p. 266-268; v. 7, p. 97,104,143-145.

32.  *Report of the President's Commission on the Assassination of President John F. Kennedy*, p.135-136.

33.  *Hearings*, op. cit., v. 7, p. 137,141.

34.  Tom Alyea film sequence, 11/22/1963.

35.  *Hearings*, op. cit., v. 3, p. 292-293; v. 19, p. 505-506.

36.  Ibid., v. 3, p. 294; v. 7, p. 107-109.

37.  Ibid., v. 4, p. 257-258; v. 7, p. 140; v. 17, p. 501; v. 21, p. 645.

38.  Ibid., v. 3, p. 294; Alyea film sequence; *JFK Facts*, op. cit., p. [3, 5]; Tom Alyea, *The JFK Conspiracy HOAX* [unpublished manuscript] p. 29-30, 33. Like so many others that afternoon, Alyea referred to Secret Service men as being at the scene. During the early stages of the search, the majority of the plainclothes officers were sheriff's deputies who had been very close to the crime scene. Later when the Dallas Police Department's presence arrived in force, they took over the investigation. The detectives, including the Crime Scene Search team, all wore civilian clothes. As there were not Secret Service agents in the Depository at this point, and even the assassination conspiracy critics would not presume those in the building were phoney agents, Alyea and others brushed the plainclothes peace officers with the broad though erroneous term of "Secret Service agents." Some DPD plainclothes officers were in fact members of the department's "Special Services" which was a bureau performing investigations in the areas of vice, narcotics and undercover work. There were other possible federal representatives at the location within a short time including FBI agents and James Powell.

39.  Ibid., p. 34; *Hearings*, op. cit., v. 4, p. 258.

40.  John K. Lattimer, *Kennedy and Lincoln*, p. 297.

41.  Alyea film sequence.

42.  *Hearings*, op. cit., v. 4, p. 258.

43.  WFAA telecast, afternoon of 11/22/1963.

44.  *Hearings*, op. cit., v. 4, p. 206,260. Many people describe rifles with such a side bolt action as "Mauser" type weapons, from the earliest and most well known of the bolt action type rifles. The 6.5mm Mannlicher-Carcano is designated as model "91/38" to distinguish it from an earlier and similar outer barrel sized model "38" which possesses an inner barrel size of 7.35mm.

45.  Ibid., v. 4, p. 256; Weisberg, op. cit., p. 274; Gary Savage, *JFK First Day Evidence*, p. 101-107, 119-120.

46.  Alyea film sequence; *The JFK Conspiracy HOAX*, op. cit., p. 34; *Hearings*, op. cit., v. 4, p. 264.

47.  Ibid., v. 4, p. 206.

48.  Alyea film sequence; *The JFK Conspiracy HOAX*, op. cit., p. 30.

49.  *Hearings*, op. cit., v. 7, p. 141, 149; *The JFK Conspiracy HOAX*, op. cit., p. 30. One day short of the thirtieth anniversary of the assassination, the author observed between 12:00 and 12:30 p.m. the play of sunlight through the sixth floor corner window of the reconstructed "sniper's nest" in the former Book Depository. The clear sky afforded a bright, vibrant, washing light through the window which fell upon the three boxes resting by the windows and which would vividly shine upon a person crouched parallel to the window as if to get off a shot at a vehicle coming down Houston Street. The closeness of the wall of boxes parallel to the window would also have made it difficult for an adult to fit within the open space to aim down Houston. It is evident, however, that a person sitting on the box slightly east of the window would have been out of direct sunlight and window exposure. It was a protected position. Though the setup of the "Sixth Floor Exhibit" is a reconstruction, it did give this author a personal insight not noticed on previous visits at other times of the year or during other weather conditions.

50.  Ibid., v. 4, p. 265.

51.  Alyea film sequence. Critic Richard E. Sprague in a 1982 article titled, "More Evidence of the Framing of Lee Harvey Oswald" attempted to show that the three tier group of boxes was the

original set-up and that it was not until November 25 that the investigators "designed" the government's later version of the "nest." Sprague did not take into account the correct timing of the Alyea film.

52.  *Report*, op. cit., p. 122-124, 138-141, 565-566; *Hearings*, op. cit., v. 4, p. 269-271; v. 7, p. 145.

53.  Ibid., v. 4, p. 264-265, 275; v. 17, p. 504-505, 512-513.

54.  Van Der Karr, *Crisis*, op. cit., p. 22-23. Alyea has also spoken about initially throwing two cans of film out of a 5th floor window to WFAA cameraman A. J. L'Hoste (*The JFK Conspiracy HOAX*, p. 31-32).

55.  Alyea film sequence, WFAA-TV, 11/22-23/1963; *Four Days in November*, Wolper Productions released by United Artists, 1964; *The Men Who Killed Kennedy*, Nigel Turner, Central Independent Television, 1989.

56.  Interview with Tom Alyea, 11/20/1993; Weisberg, op. cit., p. 274-275. A careful examination of the broadcast film was made by this author. The Day and Studebaker testimony, the Alyea interviews, as well as problems with a film loupe seen as a shaking during broadcasting, all fit in to allow an understanding of the general chronology of the film sequence.

57.  *Crisis*, op. cit., p. 38-39; Alyea film sequence broadcast over WFAA TV, 11/24/1963.

58.  Sprague, "American News Media," op. cit., p. 15; Owens is seen in Murray photos, op. cit., roll 1, #34, and in a Jack Beers photo of Day beginning to cross Houston Street with the rifle.

59.  *Hearings*, op. cit., v. 13, p. 110-111; Memorandum, To:SAC Dallas, From: SA James C. Kennedy, Subject: Jack L. Ruby, file #44-1637-1324, 12/4/1963; "11 sheets of photos taken by Beers at Jack Ruby's"; FBI interview of Dale E. Basye by SA Jack Peden, 12/18/1963, all from Trask FOIA request #288,781, 3/1988.

60.  Interview with James Altgens, 10/23/1992; Telephone interview with Tom Dillard, 2/21/1986.

61.  *Dallas Morning News*, Kennedy photo and negative file, envelope "President & Jackie arrival at airport, 11/22/1963."

62.  *Hearings*, op. cit., v. 13, p. 104-105.

63.  Telephone interview with William Allen, 1/20/1987.

64.  Ibid.

65.  Ibid.

66.  Ibid. In the *Times Herald* evening edition on November 22, a three-column front page photo of the President and First Lady greeting the crowd at Love Field is credited as a staff photo taken by Allen. Allen did not take the photo, and thinks that one of his similar Fort Worth pictures had run in the same space in an earlier edition. When the later edition used new photos, they didn't have time to correct the credit line. It was Eamon Kennedy who was at Love Field and who took the picture used on the late edition front page.

67.  Ibid.

68.  Murray photos, op. cit., roll 1, #13-17; William Allen photographs, 11/22/1963, roll 1, # 3-4. The Allen photo numbers are taken from the number system assigned by Richard Sprague, as listed in an article in *Computers and Automation* in May 1970. Sprague constituted this list of Allen photos by frame number from an examination of contact sheets. Each frame included a brief description. Most of these Allen negatives, including several sequences not noted by Sprague, are now in custody of the Dallas County Historical Foundation, which was given rights to them from the now defunct *Dallas Times Herald*. This author examined the contents in 1993.

69.  Telephone interview with Allen, op. cit. On November 23 UPI sent to its subscribers a cropped version of Allen's photo which showed the man bending down with his hand cupped. The caption read in part, "Police search ground in area where President Kennedy was shot and killed 11/22 for a bullet believed to have lodged in the earth." (UPI Telephoto DAP112305)

70.  *Hearings*, op. cit., v. 22, p 837.

71.  Colpix Record, *The Actual Voices and Events of Four Days That Shocked The World*, side 1, Colpix Records, CP2500.

72.  *Hearings*, op. cit.

73.     Conversation in Dallas with Charles Brehm, 10/22/1992.

74.     Allen photos, op. cit., roll 1, # 6-7.

75.     *Hearings*, op. cit.

76.     Ibid., v. 7, p. 553.

77.     Earl Golz, "Eugene Hale Brading; Suspect," in Penn Jones, Jr., *Forgive My Grief IV*, p. 124.

78.     Ibid., p. 123-124, 127-130.

79.     Telephone interview with Allen, op. cit.

80.     Ibid.; Examination of 17 contact sheets of *Dallas Times Herald* now in custody of the Dallas County Historical Foundation. In a typescript copy of one unattributed *Times Herald* reporter's notes made at Dealey Plaza on Nov. 22 is a mention: "Willie Allen wants another photographer there." (*Dallas Times Herald* photo archives)

81.     Allen photos, op. cit., roll 2, # 14-16; Murray photos, op. cit., roll 2, # 10-16.

82.     *Dallas Times Herald*, final edition, 11/22/1963, p. 19.

83.     *Hearings*, op. cit., v. 19, p. 476.

84.     Conversation with Brehm, op. cit.

85.     *Hearings*, op. cit., v. 13, p. 105.

86.     Ibid., v. 3, p. 182; v. 22, p. 634; Allen photos, op. cit., roll 5, # 8-10; Beers photographs within the collection of the *Dallas Morning News* photo archives.

87.     Ibid.; Allen photos, op. cit., roll 5, # 11-18; *Hearings*, op. cit., v. 3, p. 398; *Appendix to Hearings Before the Select Committee on Assassinations*, v. 7, p. 365; Box of cartridges in possession of author.

88.     Ibid., roll 3, # 14-15; J. Gary Shaw, *Cover-up*, p. 83-84; Telephone interview with Allen, op. cit. For a more detailed discussion of the "Tramps" and subsequent interest in them, see Chapter 14 on the *Fort Worth Star-Telegram* photographers.

89.     *Hearings*, op. cit., v. 13, p. 105.

90.     Ibid., v. 21, p. 582.

91.     Telephone interview with Allen, op. cit.

92.     *Hearings*, op. cit., v. 13, p. 105.

93.     Ibid., v. 4, p. 265.

94.     *Fort Worth Star-Telegram* contact sheet "40" taken by Smith; Allen photos, op. cit., roll 4, # 14-19; Beers photos, op. cit. Though the Book Depository was said to be sealed off to non-officials during the weekend of Nov. 22-24, several photographers gained entry on Saturday and Sunday. Thirty-three year old photographer Flip Schulke was a well known free-lancer whose work had been published far and wide. His photojournalistic work on the civil rights movement and his developing association with Dr. Martin Luther King, Jr., would securely place him as an important chronologist of this turbulent time in American social history. Schulke often worked through the well known New York photo sales agency, Black Star. Arriving in Dallas sometime on Saturday, Schulke was able to make several shots of the Depository's sixth floor corner window including the stack of three boxes near the window. *LIFE* magazine picked up from Black Star one of these images and ran almost a full page copy of it in their Nov. 29, 1963, issue on page 32 H above a heading "Death Found Him From This Window." Part of the caption read, "This photograph was made a day later to recreate the scene." The view was virtually identical to those made by Beers and Allen.

95.     Telephone interview with Allen, op. cit.

96.     R. B. Denson, *Destiny in Dallas, On-The-Scene Story in Pictures*, p. 1-19.

97.     FBI statement by J. C. Day & Guy F. Rose reported by SA Raymond P. Yelchak, File DL44-1639, 7/20/1964 & 7/24/1964; FBI statement of Mrs. Doris Warner reported by SA Yelchak and James W. Swinford, 7/24/1964, all through Trask FOIA request # 288,781, 1/25/1988.

98.     FBI statement by John Maziotta reported by SA Raymond P. Yelchak, 7/21/1964, Ibid.; *Report*, op. cit., p. 355; *Hearings*, op. cit., v. 25, p.525.

99.     Telephone interview with Allen, op. cit.

100.     Sprague, "American News Media," op. cit., p. 24; Examination of *Times Herald* collection by Trask at A. H. Belo Corp.,Dallas, 10/21/1992; Letter, Cheryl Price, Dallas County Historical Foundation to Trask, 11/2/1993.

101.     Telephone interview with Allen, op. cit.

102.     *JFK Facts*, op. cit., p. [5, 7, 9]; Interview with Tom Alyea, 11/21/1993.

Around 3 o'clock Lt. Day took a Speed Graphic view of the School Book Depository and the surrounding streetscape. In the foreground is the storm sewer cover and Day's crime scene kit.

## CHAPTER 23

# Dallas Cinema Associates

Almost since the inception of practical photography with the introduction of the daguerreotype in 1839, Americans have been enthusiastic collectors of the visual image, particularly of images of themselves and of their families. Yet the first few generations of photographic consumers had to rely principally upon professional photographers who had both the expertise and the cumbersome equipment needed for quality work. This all changed in 1889 with the introduction of the Kodak box camera, which allowed anyone to simply point the camera and press the shutter release. The company would then upon receipt of the camera do all necessary processing. From that time on, with the continual advancement of cameras and film, the amateur photographer became a voracious consumer who, by 1961, was using some 40 million cameras to shoot over 2 billion black-and-white photographs per year.[1]

Motion picture film had trailed the development of photography by some 50 years when, in the late 1880s Thomas Alva Edison and others exhibited and then continued to perfect its practicality. Although at the end of the 19th century equipment was available for amateur movie makers, it would not be until the middle of the 1920s when, with the development of safety film rather than the highly volatile nitrate film, movie making began to achieve a more general popularity. First utilized was a black-and-white 16mm film format. By the late 1930s safety film in a smaller 8mm size and the introduction of easy-to-use movie cameras, created a new non-commercial film system geared specifically to the amateur home movie makers.

The popularity of 8mm home movies exploded following World War II into the 1950s and 1960s. Simple to use, yet more sophisticated cameras were introduced almost yearly, with zoom lenses replacing 3-lens turret cameras, magazine loading beginning to compete with spool-loading models, and electric eyes replacing hand-held light meters or guesswork. These changes, while often compromising slightly on the resulting film quality by allowing the equipment to cut corners rather than necessitating an intelligent amateur doing the task, nevertheless, were viewed as progress. They almost always resulted in a product very acceptable to the amateur.

By 1963 numerous companies, some quite old and some just getting into the 8mm camera market, gave the consumer a wide choice of equipment. Bell & Howell of Chicago, and Eastman Kodak of Rochester, New York, competed with such other American companies as Keystone of Boston, Revere from Chicago, and Argus of Ann

Arbor, Michigan. Other models in manufacture included Bolex by Paillard Products of New York, Wollensak Optical Company of Ann Arbor, and DeJur Ansco Corporation of Long Island City. Canon, Konica and Yashica of Japan were also making strong inroads in the United States 8mm market.[2]

Besides less expensive, older model, second-hand 8mm cameras lined up in the windows of hundreds of photo dealers across the country, new models coming out yearly were available at a variety of suggested dealer list prices. Top-of-the-line models such as the Bell & Howell Zoomatic Director's Series retailed for $210, while a simple one-lens camera could be purchased for about $60.[3]

By the early 1960s the 8mm electric eye camera was the most popular type and size for use for home movies, and the preferred film was Kodachrome II. With an ASA rating for daylight use of 25, this film was 2½ times greater in speed and had a better sharpness than that of the regular Kodachrome. Kodachrome II Type A Tungsten, available for indoor, flood-light use, was rated ASA 40. Kodachrome II tested in *Consumer Reports* as substantially better than all other films tested. Retailing for a suggested $2.65 and a suggested Kodak developing cost of $1.85 also made the 25-foot double 8mm roll film more expensive than most other films. Some serious amateurs, as well as those trying to save money, could also use Ansco Moviechrome 8 film with an ASA of 20, Technicolor film with an ASA of 25, Sears, Roebuck's Tower film with an ASA of 10, or Dynachrome.[4]

Dallas, Texas, had its share of 8mm movie camera buffs, some of whom liked to talk about the technical aspects of their photography, shared information and belonged to camera clubs such as the Camera Guild of Texas, and the Dallas 8mm Movie Club. The city had numerous photo supply stores and vendors, including the large retail outlets of Sears, Roebuck & Co., and Montgomery Ward & Co., and the local Sanger-Harris Department Stores, all of which included well-stocked camera shops. Smaller, independent stores, including Glendale Camera Shop and Kincaid Photo Service, sold photographic films and cameras, and processing could be ordered through any of these outlets, plus numerous drug and department stores. There were also several large photo processing laboratories, including Fox Film Studio, Color Photo Inc., and Eastman Kodak.

With news of the coming of President Kennedy to Dallas's Love Field, and a noontime motorcade through the downtown area to a scheduled luncheon at the Trade Mart, scores of 8mm movie enthusiasts decided that such an event as this would be worth filming, and would be a fine addition to their reels of family events, local happenings, and vacation remembrances.

Irving Gewertz lived in Dallas with his wife Anita and their 14-year-old high school sophomore son Martin Anson Gewertz. A 40-year-old architect with Roscoe DeWitt, Architect, on Cedar Springs Road, Gewertz owned a Bell & Howell 8mm Model 416 camera with electric eye. Recently the electric eye had not been working properly, and Gewertz brought it in to the Sanger-Harris camera department at Main and Lamar Streets to have it checked out. Deputy manager Bryant Boren, who had sold the camera to Gewertz, looked it over and not finding anything obviously wrong with it, advised Gewertz to try another roll of film, and that if it still gave difficulty, Boren would send it out for repairs. Learning of the President's visit to Dallas, and that the motorcade would travel right by Gewertz's office, the family decided to watch and film the motorcade from that location on November 22. Martin was allowed to miss school, and he and his mother met Mr. Gewertz a little before noon that Friday. In the office they listened to the motorcade's progress until about 12:05, when they walked outside and took up positions on the north side of Cedar Springs Road at #2025.

About 12:20 the motorcade was in view, and Martin, who had custody of the family camera, attempted to take some movies. Irving saw his son shaking and banging the camera in frustration. By the time the President's vehicle had gone past, Martin had only been able to get a short sequence as it disappeared on Harwood Street. Martin was upset with the camera and the situation; and his parents, seeing the disappointment, told him to get into the car and they would quickly go to the Trade Mart, where he might get another chance to take movies.

The trio got as far as the service road opposite the Trade Mart, and just after they arrived, they watched as the President's limousine came at a high rate of speed up Stemmons Freeway with lights flashing and sirens wailing. Mrs. Gewertz saw a man lying over the back of the President's car, who was pounding the trunk of the car with his fist as the car passed their position. Not prepared for such a sudden and fast ride-by, Martin apparently took some film of a few of

One of the motorcade convertibles rushing down the Freeway near the Trade Mart

the later motorcade cars rushing by on the freeway above, followed by a short clip of two of the motorcade busses. Listening to their car radio, the Gewertzes discovered that the President had been shot and was taken to Parkland Hospital. The three drove to the hospital area and observed much commotion. Around 2:00 Mrs. Gewertz told her son to film an ambulance as it was leaving the hospital, which scene they later learned was of the body of President Kennedy being taken from the hospital back to Love Field. The next day the three visited the site of the assassination and took movies of the spectators and floral tributes gathered there.[5]

Within a short time Mr. and Mrs. Gewertz took the film they had made the week of November 22 to the Sanger-Harris Department Store, and complained to manager Boren that the camera had not operated properly. They were bitter that their son had missed some historic film of the motorcade because they had taken Boren's advice about the camera. Boren suggested that, as he knew of several people who had taken sequences of the motorcade and had processed their film at the store, he would attempt to obtain copies of these so that the Gewertzes could have a record of it. Boren

Frame from a second sequence, probably made
by Martin Gewertz, showing the two press
busses on the road to the Trade Mart.

had himself, with fellow employee Richard Stewart, viewed the motorcade. At the time Stewart was learning the operation of a Bolex camera from Boren and had taken a few feet of the motorcade. Boren subsequently gained possession of this film and gave a copy to Gewertz. Boren also contacted Clarence Hays, who had likewise taken film of the procession and had it developed through Sanger-Harris. Being informed about Mr. Hays, Mrs. Gewertz took it upon herself to visit Hays and his wife Frances, and view his film. Mrs. Hays became particularly interested in the possibility of gathering other sequences from other amateurs.[6]

The original intention of obtaining a few sequences by the Gewertzes soon developed into the gathering of a number of film clips which could be swapped and shared by the various movie makers. Mrs. Gewertz had the idea of not just relying upon those film makers Boren discovered through the department store, but to take the initiative of telephoning residences and businesses along the motorcade route to find other possible film sources. Both Mrs. Gewertz and Mrs. Hays began pursuing this objective. From December 1963 to early January 1964, Gewertz and Hays telephoned and visited numerous places looking for film. Their persistence bore fruit. Irving Gewertz's friend George Kincaid, owner of a popular still photo print service, had himself taken an 8mm film clip of the procession and gave his movie to Gewertz, releasing all rights to it. Gewertz and Hays also located five other film makers who were willing to share their movies. One of them was Albert Bunnell, a purchasing agent for Cambell-Taggart Associated Bakeries, who in turn was able to provide Gewertz with three other names of men who had film, including one co-worker and two fellows whom he knew through a movie camera club. Gewertz and/or Hays would typically ask to see the film and then request an exchange of film clips. When they realized that they were gathering together a fair amount of footage, the group decided to try and splice all of the clips together and then make a copy for each contributor.[7]

Mrs. Gewertz also found in her process of telephoning people along the motorcade route that Phil Willis and his family had witnessed the assassination, and that Mr. Willis had taken photographs of the events in Dealey Plaza. Willis's slides were obtained shortly after the assassination by the FBI, who returned them to Willis in January 1964. It was not until June of 1964, however, that he was interviewed by the FBI, and by that time he had locally marketed twelve of his slides for retail sales. Mrs. Gewertz also learned that a Mrs. Ashmore had taken still photographs in the vicinity of the Trade Mart on November 22. In later investigating of these amateur film makers, the FBI learned through Mrs. Gewertz of Ashmore, and on June 17, 1964, Mrs. Ashmore was also interviewed.

In the FBI report, Mrs. Evelyn Ashmore, a housewife living on Hyer Street, related that she had taken her 35mm camera to a location opposite the Ramada Inn on Cedar Springs Road to view the motorcade. She took several pictures of the area and also two pictures of Air Force Two and Air Force One as they came low overhead in their landing pattern for nearby Love Air Field.

Mrs. Ashmore photographed the President's limousine earlier in the motorcade. Mrs. Kennedy was wearing sunglasses at the time.

Around noon the motorcade from Love Field approached her and, ". . . She took one snapshot of the President just as he raised his hand

Mrs. Ashmore captures a blurry view of the presidential limousine on its way to the hospital, a poignant contrast to her earlier photo.

to brush some hair from his face." Believing she had not obtained a good photo, Mrs. Ashmore traveled to the west side of Stemmons Freeway on the service road across from the Trade Mart, where she knew he was scheduled to arrive. At about 12:35 she saw the President's car approaching at a high rate of speed, and she took a picture as it sped by. Seeing the car traveling up a hill towards Parkland Hospital, she knew something was wrong, a fact which was confirmed when she got into her car and turned on the radio.[8]

Mrs. Ashmore's color slide of the President's limousine racing down the service road towards Harry Hines Boulevard and Parkland Hospital is a blurry image in which the Lincoln convertible with presidential and national flags straight out against the onrush of air can be discerned at the front hood of the vehicle, while Secret Service Agent Clint Hill sticks up half in and half out of the back seat, unable to do anything but hope the driver, William Geer, will get the huge, powerful vehicle quickly to its new destination. The Lincoln is passing an 18-wheel trailer-truck on its right. The driver in the elevated cab, if he had time to notice the car to his lower left, could probably not grasp that he was being passed by the assassinated chief executive of his country. At the left background of the slide one sees what appears to be a few white helmeted motorcycle cops, with at least one and possibly more three-wheeled cycles in the area of the Trade Mart.[9]

Mrs. Gewertz was not interested in still photos, however, as her expanding project was focusing only on film sequences. She was also not the only one who had located movie clips of the motorcade. Wyman Parr, owner of Glendale Camera Shop on South Marsalis, though not having seen the motorcade, did through his business know some four men who had taken movies, and was beginning to coordinate their film sequences, while at the same time attempting to locate other amateur photographers. By January both groups became aware of the existence of one another. Jules Spiegel had heard about Mrs. Gewertz's efforts in the middle of December, and at the end of the month was also called by Parr, while Richard Allen, who had turned over his film to Parr, was contacted by Gewertz in January. Allen suggested Mrs. Gewertz get in touch with Parr. German native Rudolph Brenk, a general supervisor at Exline-Lowdon Company and vice-president of the Camera Guild of Texas, an 8mm camera club, had also taken some five to six feet of film of the motorcade at Harwood and Ross Streets. In February Mrs. Gewertz had located him and asked if he would be interested in a film exchange. Following a viewing of the Gewertz collected films, Brenk told Mrs. Gewertz that due to the number of films shown to him and their quality, he was not interested at that time. Shortly thereafter Brenk was called by Parr, of whom he might have already been aware, who asked him to look at Parr's collection. According to Brenk, he told both Parr and Gewertz that he would agree to join the venture if the two groups could get together and combine all the film clips. Brenk appears to have been a catalyst in the project, as he had experience in editing and film processing. At some point between January and February, Mrs. Gewertz felt that from the reaction she was receiving about putting together the film clips, such a combined film might have popular public appeal to warrant its being marketed. Following some serious friction and disagreements between the two groups, by March 18 an agreement had been hammered out. Eighteen, including six who had not taken film themselves, formed a group called the "Dallas Cinema Associates, Inc." The 18 members would share equally in any profit made from the sale of copies of the film. Brenk was president, Boren vice-president, and Mrs. Hays secretary. The members turned over their original clips to Brenk for editing, and he combined what he believed to be the valuable portions of each. Adding several subtitles, he created a film of approximately 175 feet with a running time of 12 minutes 50 seconds. The film was then sent to Technicolor, Inc., in Burbank, California, for further processing to achieve more unified shading and coloring. The group made a contract with Sanger-Harris Department Stores, allowing their exclusive rights of sale in the Dallas area for a one-month trial period, and according to plan the film was to be ready for sale at $24.95 by the middle of June.[10]

Titled *DCA Presents/President John F. Kennedy's Final Hour/Dallas, Texas, Nov. 22, 1963. ©1964*, the film included coverage by three amateurs at Love Field, three along Lemon Avenue, one at Turtle Creek Boulevard, three on Cedar Springs Road, two on Harwood, four on Main Street, and two at Dealey Plaza, one taken after the shooting. Scenes were also included of part of the motorcade going to Parkland, an ambulance leaving Parkland carrying the President's body, scenes of the assassination site the following day, shots of newspaper headlines, and the garage entrance to the Dallas Police Station at the time of

A zoom film sequence, possibly taken by Richard Stewart, looking westerly down Main Street towards the Plaza. The two cycles in the background locate the President's car, while in the right foreground are three camera cars and a congressional car.

Oswald's shooting. A commentary was to be included with each film, partially attempting to justify the commercial production of it, partially defending Dallas's name, and partially explaining how the film came about. A portion of the text read:

> After the tragic numbing hours of November 22, 1963, and its fateful aftermath had settled into its place in history, a pall of self-recrimination, misconceptions, and unjust accusations still lingered in the minds and hearts of people in this country and abroad.
>
> Foremost amidst this background of suspicion was the besmirching of the city of Dallas and its citizens for the supposed hostility toward the person of the President and his entourage. Having witnessed the exact opposite of this in an unprecedented show of warmth and affection towards the President, his wife Jacqueline . . . a group of citizens endeavored to gather a photographic record of this particular event that would best illustrate what they saw and to show the world

the pleasant warmth and enjoyment that surrounded the President on this, his last hour on earth.

Upon investigation, it was found that the news media had no documentary film on the motorcade itself, . . . Thus it was that the only available filmed record of the Dallas motorcade was that taken by amateur movie-makers along the route of travel.

After an exhaustive search was made to locate people who had taken movie film of this particular event, enough film was found to tell a coherent, poignant story of November 22, 1963, when a President and a city had a rendezvous with history.[11]

Marketed in Dallas for a time, Wolper Productions, a subsidiary of Metromedia, Inc., bought rights to this film and edited and produced a 16mm version. Although it is unclear how many copies of the film sold, the local marketing of the film was not a huge success, and a number of the shareholders lost interest in the project, while others had disagreements concerning the whole business. By 1966 Brenk was no longer associated with DCA, or the business venture.[12]

So much is known about this group of amateur film makers, their cameras and what they filmed, primarily because the FBI contacted and interviewed most of them. The FBI's interest developed through two different sources, one a local TV representative, and the other from one of the amateur film makers.

On April 10, 1964, Eddie Barker, News Manager of KRLD-TV, informed the Dallas FBI that he had obtained a copy of the group's film, and that it was made up of film clips taken by Dallas citizens of the Kennedy visit and scenes outside the Dallas Police Station on November 24, 1963. According to the language of the FBI report concerning Barker, he told the agents that upon running the film he noted the group, "had failed to obtain film taken at the scene of the assassination on November 22, 1963." Barker obtained a black-and-white copy of the film for the FBI on April 13, and an agent field report states, "A review of same fails to reveal any pertinent film taken at the time of the assassination of President Kennedy. . . ."[13] One of the DCA film sequences, however, had been taken at Dealey Plaza just prior to and following the assassination. The photographer was Johnny Martin, a man whose identity had been previously known by the FBI.

John Martin, Jr., was a 58-year-old native of Minnesota who worked as Superintendent of Safety at the Post Office Terminal Annex at 207 South Houston Street on the south edge of Dealey Plaza. Like many of the annex employees, Martin had decided to view the President's motorcade, and took his 8mm DeJur movie camera with him to work that Friday. At about 12:10 Martin left his fifth floor office and walked the short distance to the west side of Houston Street, a few feet north of Main Street. When the motorcade arrived at the corner of Main and Houston, Martin began filming as the presidential limousine turned north on Houston Street. As the limousine passed his position, Martin then scurried up Houston to the northern end of the reflecting pool adjacent to Elm Street and opposite the front entry to the Texas School Book Depository Building. Martin took a fleeting view of the car going in front of the Depository on Elm Street, and after he had stopped filming, he heard a report. As he related to Canadian researcher David Hawkins in a 1979 interview, ". . . and the shot came over my head, and I looked around to see who was throwing a firecracker. Then a few seconds later there were two more shots." Martin recalls the spacing of the shots to have been, "One shot then a space of time, then two more rapidly."

Filming over the north reflecting pool, Martin picks up a fleeting glimpse of the President's limousine on Elm. Ten-year-old Rosemary Willis is running to the left.

Shortly thereafter Martin recalls, "A couple came running up near me and said, 'Duck, because they're shooting at us!'" Martin resumed his filming in time to take movies of the motorcade camera cars traveling down towards the underpass, some of the car occupants taking pictures of the activity in the direction of the grassy knoll.[14]

Martin's initial reaction was that the shots had originated from the Texas School Book Depository. Chaos broke out in the Plaza and some motorcade cameramen, as well as police, initially concentrated on the grassy area on the north side of Elm Street, where the Newman family had fallen to the ground at the sound of the shots. Martin, like scores of others, ran towards the knoll area; Martin, in the words of the FBI report, ". . . thinking that perhaps the person who fired the shots had left the building and was being pursued by the police." He related to researcher Hawkins, ". . . I ran over there then and asked a man I found later was a Treasury Department [man] — I said, 'Why are they all running up here?' He says it seems like someone was chasing someone up here. When I saw him, he was right on top of the hill behind the gang that was running up there. I walked up part way and then turned around and came back, and told a policeman that they ought to surround the building there [Texas School Book Depository] because I think whoever shot was still in the building. I know that definitely that first shot came from over my head, and I figured that's the one that got him. So I asked this officer, and said, 'You better surround this building and not let anyone get out of here.'"[15]

Martin remained near the Book Depository for some ten minutes taking film of activities in front of the building, including witness Charles Brehm being interviewed, cops holding shotguns, views of Houston and Elm Streets including the entrance to the Book Depository, and a clip showing 16-year-old Amos Lee Euins, who had seen a man fire from the building. Euins was driven away on the back of a police motorcycle for questioning. Martin then walked back to the annex and phoned his wife, telling her about what he had witnessed.[16]

Martin had mentioned, as recorded in his FBI interview, that while in the vicinity of the knoll area, ". . . He stopped and talked to a man who he presumes was a Secret Service agent. . . ." Martin was not alone in recounting the presence of a Secret Service agent, as several others mention that fact in their testimonies. Many critics have used these statements, coupled with the knowledge that no agents in the motorcade remained at the shooting scene, to strongly suggest than the agent encountered was a "phony" and possibly an assassin using fake ID to disguise his true purpose.

Most of these incidents can probably be explained as a mistaken or presumed identity on the part of the spectator. Everyone knew about the President's civilian-clothed Secret Service, who always shadowed his every step, and it was not uncommon for many people to presume that non-uniformed officials around the President might be these special protectors. Prior to the motorcade, Arnold Rowland had seen a man in a window of the Texas School Book Depository holding a rifle with a telescopic sight. When asked later by Secret Service Agent Forrest Sorrels why Rowland had not told an officer at the time what he had spotted, Rowland explained, "I just thought he was a Secret Service man."[17]

There were many civilian-dressed protective or investigative personnel around the motorcade route and after the shooting at Parkland Hospital and Dealey Plaza. Released estimates mention that on-duty personnel for the motorcade included 40 Dallas Police Department plainclothes personnel, 16 Texas Department of Public Safety plainclothesmen, and 14 from the Sheriff's Office. After the shooting, many others not specifically assigned to the motorcade protection streamed into the Plaza area from nearby buildings, as did at least one Army Intelligence Corps Special Agent. It is not too incredible, given the intense excitement at the time, that some people assumed many of these civilian officials were Secret Service. FBI agents, carrying their commission books as ID as well as at least one CIA agent, are known to have quickly gone to Parkland Hospital. Other FBI agents arrived at Dealey Plaza. For a civilian to assume plainclothes officers were Secret Service was thus possibly a very human assumption that day.[18]

The testimony of Dallas Police Officer Joe M. Smith, however, causes a wrinkle in this explanation. When questioned by Warren Commission staff attorney Wesley Liebeler, Smith testified that when he reached the parking lot behind the knoll where there were various people, ". . . I pulled my pistol from my holster, and I thought, this is silly, I don't know who I am looking for, and I put it back. Just as I did, he showed me that he was a Secret Service agent. . . . He saw me coming with my pistol and right away he showed me who he was."[19]

Although the White House and vice-presidential protective detail remained with the presidential party, S.A.I.C. Sorrels had six special agents in his Dallas office. Sorrels, who was riding in the lead car of the motorcade, returned to the School Book Depository after the President was stretchered into the hospital, arriving at the shooting scene within 20 minutes. Sorrels had six other agents assigned to the Dallas Field Office, some of whom might have been in the vicinity of the Plaza area shortly after the shooting. Their whereabouts are not identified in official released records, except for Special Agent Robert Stewart, who after the President's death returned to the office, ". . . to correlate activities of other agents."[20]

One final telling bit of information is that Deputy Constable Seymour Weitzman, upon hearing the shots while standing at the corner of Main and Houston Streets, ran over to the railroad yard behind the knoll and testified to having seen other officers and ". . . Secret Service as well. . . ." Shortly thereafter Weitzman was given a piece of red material found in the street, which he turned over, ". . . to one of the Secret Service men and I told them it should go to the lab because it looked to me like human bone. I later found out it was supposedly a portion of the President's skull." Weitzman's specimen had thus apparently been given to a verified official, whether or not he was a Secret Service agent.[21]

Thus, though the identity of the "Secret Service agent," mentioned and identified as such by some witnesses, cannot be identified as to a specific individual or individuals, enough in the way of alternative explanations are possible to show this incident as quite possibly of no major importance — just mistaken identity.

Meanwhile, after phoning his wife from his office, John Martin returned to the School Book Depository area at about 12:50. By this time he had used up the first 25 feet of his film roll. "I turned the film over and I tested it and it seemed all right, and I put it back together and I started taking more pictures, and I thought I had all 50 feet. . . ." Later when at home Martin, ". . . took it out of my camera and came to find out there was 20 to 25 feet left in there, and there was a crimp in the film. That's something I have never had an experience with before."[22]

Martin had remained in the Dealey Plaza area for about 2½ hours, roaming the vicinity and talking with people. He made note of what he described as a bullet mark on the concrete pad of a sewer cover on the Elm Street infield grass area and recalls, ". . . I told the officer you better get your boss down here to check this thing out, because that will show where the bullet came from." This is the site Officer Foster and others examined following the shooting. Photographers Jim Murray, William Allen and others had made pictures of the scene.

Some time after the shooting, while standing about 50 feet north of Commerce Street on the west side of Houston, Martin saw a black-and-white Checker Cab traveling south on Houston Street. In 1979 Martin recalled concerning the cab's passenger, "He was not very far from me when he got in the taxi cab. I took the picture, but that's the part that doesn't come out. He had a kind of a black sweater on, I remember that, and his hair-do, I specially remember how he combed his hair. What I saw was kind of bushy and combed up high. And [he] turned around and looked at me rather intently, wondering what I was doing, and I was taking the pictures." In his FBI report of late March, Martin described the man as a white male in his early 20s, bareheaded and wearing a dark shirt which appeared to have vertical broken pinstripes. Martin told the FBI that at the time, ". . . the thought raced through his mind that 'Wouldn't it be funny if he were the assassin?'" The report goes on further to state that Martin, ". . . believed from pictures that he saw subsequently in the newspapers and on television, that this male was Lee Harvey Oswald."[23]

While in the Plaza area Martin had spoken with a number of people, and this is probably how one of the local "stringer" representatives of LIFE Magazine, who had quickly begun to canvas for potential photographers to use in their pictorial magazine, heard of Martin's film. When Martin arrived home shortly before 5:00 p.m., his son told him that representatives of the magazine had called and were interested in contacting him.

In 1979 Martin recolleced that a man named Hershorne came out to his home. This is most likely Sheldon Hershorne, a free-lance photographer whose work was often circulated through Black Star Photo Agency, and who may also have been helping out the local LIFE stringers. Martin agreed to turn over his undeveloped film to Patsy Swank, LIFE's Dallas representative, who in turn gave it to Richard Billings, Bureau Chief from LIFE's Miami office, who arrived in Dallas late Friday afternoon and set up operations at the Adolphus Hotel. This undeveloped film was then sent to New York City for development and review.[24]

Although LIFE Magazine found out about and had acquired the Martin film, no law enforcement agency was aware of its existence. It remained the case until the first week in December, when Martin was discussing the events with a friend who also worked on the fifth floor of the Terminal Annex, Harry D. Holmes. Holmes was a postal inspector who had watched the assassination and chaotic aftermath from the bird's-eye view of a window in his office overlooking Dealey Plaza. Holmes, while using binoculars, had heard the three reports and watched the President slump in his car and Mrs. Kennedy climb out onto the trunk. He also had taken part in the post-assassination investigation, as Oswald had taken out Post Office Box #6225 in the Post Office Building on November 1, and had also purchased there a P.O. Money Order for $21.45 to buy a rifle. Holmes had his men locate the original P.O. stub for the money order. Then on the morning of November 24, Holmes had been invited by Police Captain Will Fritz to sit in on an interrogation of Lee Oswald prior to his being moved to the County Jail. It was after that interrogation, when Oswald was being led to a vehicle transferring him to the County Jail, that he was gunned down by Jack Ruby. Martin related that while discussing the events of that weekend with Holmes, Martin told him about his film. ". . . And I told him, 'They don't even know I've got this film. I wonder if I should tell them.' So he picked up the phone and told the FBI I had it."[25]

On December 3 Martin was contacted by the FBI. He told the agent on the phone that he possibly had obtained movies of the Texas School Book Depository Building, and that he had given the film over to LIFE. On December 9, two special agents reviewed the developed film in New York and reported, "A review of the film revealed no pertinent details which would aid Dallas investigation." On December 17 the film was forwarded to FBI Headquarters in Washington, where a copy was made, and the original film was sent back to LIFE on December 22. At that point the FBI lost interest in the film and except for a very cursory statement being recorded noting

Martin's being present at the scene of the assassination, the Bureau did no further follow-up.[26] *LIFE*, with its possession and publication of the graphic frames from the Abraham Zapruder film of the assassination, also had little interest in the Martin movie, and returned it to him around February.

Sometime in February Martin was contacted by Wyman Parr concerning putting together strips of film taken by amateur photographers of the events, and when the DCA was incorporated on March 18, 1964, Martin became a member. According to Martin, quite a bit of his film was not used in the DCA print.

Aware of the creation of the President's Commission on the Assassination and its field workers in Dallas, and not having had any contact with investigators since December, Martin contacted Dallas U.S. Attorney Barefoot Sanders about his having been on the scene and his being positive the shots had come from the Depository Building. Sanders notified Commission representatives who in turn indicated they would not interview Martin if the FBI desired to interview him.

Dallas A.S.A.C. Kyle Clark notified FBI Headquarters about this communication from the Commission. It is apparent that the local FBI was not enthusiastic concerning the call or what they perceived to be Martin's making it sound as if they had not followed through on him. In an internal FBI memo of late March, Assistant Director Al Rosen reported to Assistant to the Director Alan Belmont, "Martin alleged he had never been interviewed. . . . Martin was previously contacted on 12/3/63 by an agent of our Dallas office in connection with some movie film Martin took of the assassination scene. Martin stated he had already turned the film over to a representative of *LIFE* Magazine. At this time Martin furnished no additional information or gave any indication he had any additional information relating to the assassination. Subsequent inquiry made by us has established Martin's film was of absolutely no use to our investigation. . . . A.S.A.C. Clark stated that Martin, like many others, is apparently now 'recalling' pertinent facts in view of the presence of staff members of the Commission in Dallas. *ACTION: In view of the request Dallas was instructed to interview Martin for full details regarding his alleged pertinent data and to appraise him of the fact he had been previously contacted by our office.*"[27]

The memo, quite sarcastic in tone, is also self-serving in attempting to discredit the motives of a witness while making it sound like the FBI had done its investigation as thoroughly as possible in December. Available records indicate no real interview was made in December, only the "contact" by telephone made by an agent concerning the whereabouts of Martin's film.

On March 31 Martin was interviewed by Agents Petrakis and Raymond. The interview resulted in the typing of two separate reports, one dealing with Martin's recollections of the assassination itself, and the other with facts regarding the DCA film, in which Martin listed names, addresses, and phone numbers of shareholders in the corporation.[28]

An Airtel to Washington from the Dallas Field Office on April 2 enclosed the reports and a statement that ". . . The individuals mentioned as being members of the above referred to corporation will not be interviewed." This Airtel was soon followed by a directive on April 6 from "Director, FBI" that ". . . It is essential that these individuals, if not already interviewed, be interviewed, particularly if they have any knowledge whatsoever regarding the assassination of President Kennedy. It is pointed out any of these individuals who allegedly took photographs of the presidential motorcade would appear to be logical individuals for interview. . . . You should also make efforts to review the film allegedly being produced by this corporation to determine if it has any pertinence to the inquiry being conducted by the President's Commission."[29]

The instructions were clear and could not be ignored. With whatever work load the Dallas office was under, they now had to interview a large group of amateur film makers. One gets the distinct feeling when looking over these memos and communications, that the Dallas office resented Martin's going to others about his information, as it indirectly criticized the FBI's earlier performance. As a result of their new interviews, they now had to open the fact-gathering even wider. A note on one FBI document, though true enough, indicates a personal lashing out at these DCA people by stating, "This appears to be a business venture capitalizing on the fortuitous location of these individuals on fateful day."[30] It seems to this author that the only reason these people were being interviewed was the fact that this venture was going public and the Bureau wanted to cover itself against possible later criticism of not conducting a thorough investigation.

In any event, as a result of the directive, FBI agents collected a very thorough set of interviews outlining the witnesses' stories, locations, cameras and film data. These reports were generally more complete and rich in detail than what was done with the photographers who were actually at and filming the assassination scene in Dealey Plaza.

Following Martin's interview on March 31, Agents Petrakis and Switzer began a plodding process of locating, interviewing, and writing up their findings regarding the people associated with the DCA film. Twenty-three interviews were conducted between April 4 and May 21, 1964, during which information on 18 separate film sequences was gathered. Eight people who did not take any film, including parents, husbands or wives of film makers, or people who had secured rights of others who had actually made the film, were interviewed. Five of those interviewed who had made film were not partners in the DCA corporation, while three who had actually filmed were not interviewed, although information about them was gathered. Personal stories were sometimes also recorded, such as Joe C. Brown, who brought his son to Love Field in order to see and film the President. Brown reminisced that as a Marine in World War II during an assault on an enemy island in the Coral Sea, his 50-foot lighter landing craft was knocked out of commission. The 13 men aboard were at the mercy of the sea for three days when a Navy torpedo boat, PT-109, answered their distress signal. Within 30 minutes they were rescued by a destroyer. Brown and the other men aboard owed their lives to Lt. John Kennedy and his PT boat crew, and ". . . It was because of this that he kept his boy out of school and brought him to Love Field with him, so he would have the opportunity to see President John Fitzgerald Kennedy."[31] It was also noted among the various interviews that Wyman Parr, the owner of the Glendale Camera Shop, and one of the coordinators of the film group, knew Jack Ruby, ". . . as a speaking acquaintance from infrequent visits to Ruby's club." Charles Rhodes, another DCA partner and head of stock at Sanger-Harris camera department, had twice repaired Ruby's personal Polaroid camera.[32]

Besides Martin, the only other amateur film maker in the DCA group who had taken any films of the assassination scene on November 22, was Ernest Charles Mentesana. A 45-year-old owner of a local grocery, on that Friday Mentesana and an employee traveled to the intersection of Turtle Creek Road and Cedar Springs Road at about 11:40. Mentesana took about 10 feet of film of the motorcade with his Wollensak camera with 1.9 lens as the President's car went by at about 12:10. After dropping the employee back at the store, Mentesana drove to the Katy Railroad Freight Depot near the Texas School Book Depository in order to pick up some previously purchased salvaged foodstuffs. While there he learned of the assassination, and still having his camera with him, Mentesana took several feet of ". . . the turmoil in and around the Depository Building." Mentesana joined the group of spectators who were standing on the west side of the Dal-Tex Building. Facing Houston Street and the Book Depository Building across the street, Mentesana and the others watched the high profile police activity. Officers carrying shotguns stood in the street, many looking up at the Book Depository and most poising their weapons so that they faced up at an angle from their bodies. A short clip features two police officers on the seventh floor east side fire escape of the Book Depository.[33]

One of Mentesana's film clips has become embroiled in controversy. Sometime around 1:00 he filmed a group of three police officers and several others in civilian clothes huddled together, most with their backs to Mentesana. They are in the east side of Houston Street between two parked cars. Across the street another parked car and the bottom floor of the Book Depository can be seen, the southeast corner facing Houston Street just out of frame at the left. The men are in animated discussion. One of the uniformed officers holds a long gun with its butt resting on his left hip and the barrel projected in a 45° angle from his body.[34]

The center of attention in the film clip is directed towards the people within the circle and not at the weapon which is physically outside the circle. At the time the DCA film was spliced together, Rudolph Brenk, possibly not knowing that many cops had prominently displayed long-barreled weapons on Houston Street, apparently thought this to be the assassination weapon. Making the DCA film as complete a story as possible, Brenk added a white-lettered lay-over caption to this part of the film reading, "THE ASSASSIN'S RIFLE." At the time of the film release, no one gave the caption more than curious notice, assuming it to be pictures of the Oswald rifle. In 1967 photographic researcher Richard Sprague came to the realization that this could not have been the Mannlicher-Carcano rifle. It was found later and its travels outside the Book Depository were known. If the rifle was not the one discovered on the sixth floor, then many critics of the government investigation felt it must be a second assassination weapon which had

A frame from the sequence filmed by Ernest Mentesana on Houston
Street and later identified in the DCA film with an incorrect caption

been found. The discovery must have been hushed up and the weapon made to disappear as part of a masterful and wide-ranging conspiracy. If there were two possible explanations to a question relating to the case — one simple and logical and the other complicated and incredible — many critics would typically go with the latter explanation. Soon unsubstantiated stories from nebulous or second-hand sources spoke of a rifle having been found on the roof of the Book Depository.[35]

Though many people worked themselves up to imagine scenarios for revealing the fact of this second gun, there is a simpler explanation. The officers were questioning someone now unknown or discussing the situation at hand. This happened on numerous occasions, several of them filmed that day. One cop still carried a weapon as many of his fellow officers had at that time around 1:00. As critics have noted, the weapon has neither a telescopic sight nor a sling, and the thick barrel seems to protrude seven or so inches past the stock. Comparing these frames with an assortment of still photos made by photographers William Allen and Jim Murray, the pictures show the pump shotguns carried by officers to be carried in the same manner as the one seen in the Mentesana clip, which compare very obviously to these police weapons, even to the end nub seen on some of these shotguns.[36] (See photo, page 503.)

If any unusual activity had taken place around the confines of the Book Depository for the first two hours following the assassination, all the photographers, still and movie, would have made a bee-line to the locale to shoot it. Several of the photographers later recalled that if something practically moved, they photographed it. Such was the case with the detaining of Larry Florer and numerous other witnesses and the removal of evidence including the rifle from the sixth floor of the Depository Building.

This sequence does not show a mysterious second rifle, but rather incidentally pictures a cop holding a police-issue shotgun.

Mentesana's completed film was sent to Fox Film Company in Dallas for processing. In early January, Mentesana was contacted by a co-member of the Dallas 8mm Movie Club, Albert Bunnell, who told him of Mrs. Gewertz's interest in gathering together film sequences. Subsequently Mentesana joined with the forming DCA. He died from a heart attack in 1969.[37]

Except for the Martin film, none of the sequences would appear to aid in the investigation. A copy of the edited film sequences, however, should at least be evaluated in Washington. In early July Warren Commission General Counsel J. Lee Rankin wrote to the DCA Post Office box requesting the availability of the film and if in the preparation of the film, they discovered any film taken at the scene of the assassination, other than those taken by Zapruder, Nix, and Muchmore. Rudy Brenk responded to the letter through the U.S. Attorney's office in Dallas with a copy of the film and his statement that so far as he knew, there were no other persons who took film at the scene of the assassination. Brenk was not asked about the unedited strips of film from which he made the edited reel, and although probably only Martin's original film would include scenes of the Dealey Plaza area around the time of the assassination, apparently no one in the government picked up on this to attempt to review Martin's complete film at that time.

Rankin requested Hoover at the FBI to have the DCA as well as the Wolper Production version of the film, which was also requested and provided by Wolper, examined.[38] Hoover reported to Rankin that both films had been examined, ". . . And it was found that it showed very little of the President's motorcade during the firing of the assassination shots." If members of Rankin's staff desired to view the film, they could so advise the FBI. And thus ended the investigation into the DCA.[39]

The full Martin film sequence remained one of the most obscure of the films taken that day. In 1967 researcher Richard Sprague had a long conversation on the phone with Martin about his film and subsequently was able to view it in its entirety. Sprague's notes about the film indicate the first sequence was made by Martin some 50 feet from the south curb of Elm Street while he was on the Houston Street sidewalk. The second sequence shows the President's car traveling down Elm in front of the Book Depository prior to the first shot. Sequence three, taken after the shots and lasting some 1 to 2 seconds, pictures the first camera car, followed by Martin's resuming filming again a few seconds later with the second camera car in view. Sprague's notes indicate the scene shows, "three or four men, a puff of smoke clearly drifting from the grassy knoll. One man is in the pergola shelter, while three or four are running between the wall and fence towards the RR tracks and then along the base of a longer fence at the top of the slope. Three camera cars are seen with two men in the second camera car, taking pictures towards the running men." The final motorcade sequence shows the same three cars further down Elm Street, the grassy slope area closer to the underpass and a portion of the fence at the top of the slope.[40]

In his third book on the subject, prolific self-publishing researcher Harold Weisberg, who believed the entire government investigation to be a whitewash, goes on to quote Sprague's interpretation of the film content:

> Dick believes this suppressed film shows five men on the grassy knoll and in apparent flight after the fatal shot. He believes that it also shows men present and well hidden at points from which they could have fired without being seen by the naked eye. The "puff of smoke" about which witnesses testified, which the Commission depreciated, is quite apparent and can be seen floating away.
>
> Dick's examination of the suppressed film shows clearly that there were professional cameramen in three vehicles of the motorcade. Many of them continue to take pictures as the cars passed the assassination scene. These pictures, whose contents might well mean nothing to the men looking for news interest, can be of an estimable value in photographic intelligence, to those familiar with what happened and who know what to look for. They show large numbers of people in the area, many identifiable, and where they went. They show, among the many other important things, the man in the doorway in the Altgens film, from a different angle, and after the lapse of a short interval. He is then in a different relationship with other people and objects in the picture.[41]

No scientific study has been made of the film concerning the so-called "puff of smoke" and the activities and actions of those recorded in the film has only been the subject of less than objective visual examination by critics.

Except for the edited sequences in the DCA film, Martin's movie has seldom been seen or individual frames published. Kept in a safety deposit box, the film which Martin is not sure is his original or a copy, is seldom looked at by its owner, who has given his sons responsibility for it. Occasionally Martin was invited to participate in broadcast events concerning the assassination, but he had no interest. He was called to New Orleans during the Garrison investigation, but was never called to the stand as a witness. Concerning the shots he had heard back in 1963, by 1979 Martin, possibly being swayed by new and vocal theories, had re-examined his previous statements and told an interviewer, "I'm doubtful now that there were only the shots that came from the sixth floor. I think now — I'm beginning to wonder if there weren't some from up in the hill."[42]

## CHAPTER NOTES

1.    *Consumer Bulletin Annual*, 1963/64, 9/1963, v. 38, p. 59.
2.    Ibid., p. 70.
3.    *Consumer Reports Buying Guide*, 12/1963, v. 28, no. 12, p. 311-314.

4.   Ibid., p. 307-309.

5.   FBI interview of Mrs. Irving Gewertz, 5/22/1964, CR 1066, p. 56-57; FBI interview of Irving Gewertz, 5/22/1964, CR 1066, p.52-53.

6.   Ibid.; FBI interview of Mrs. Frances Hayes, 4/14/1964, CR 1066, p. 16-17; FBI interview of Clarence Hayes, 4/22/1964, CR 1066, p.18; FBI interview of Bryant Boren, 4/22/1964, CR 1066, p.28; FBI interview of Richard Stewart, 4/29/1964, CR 1066, p. 32.

7.   Gewertz, op. cit.; Hayes, op. cit.; FBI interview of Albert Bunnell, 5/18/1964, CR 1066, p.39-40; FBI interview of George Kincaid, 4/15/1964, CR 1066, p. 13.

8.   FBI interview of Mrs. O. B. Ashmore, 6/19/1964, CR 1245, p. 52; Letter, Stewart Yeakel to Trask, 5/7/1990.

9.   Evelyn Ashmore 35mm transparency, 11/22/1963.

10.  FBI interview of Rudolf Brenk, 5/21/1964, CR 1066, p. 49-51; FBI interview of Wyman Parr, 4/22/1964, CR 1066, p. 23-24; *Dallas Cinema Associates Presents John F. Kennedy's Final Hour*, c. 1964.

11.  *DCA . . . Final Hour*, ibid.; Irving Gewertz, op. cit. p. 54-55.

12.  Harold Weisberg, *Whitewash II* (Dell paperback), p. 242; Telephone interview of Johnny Martin Jr., by Dave Hawkins, tape no. 115, 2/27/1979.

13.  FBI interview of Eddie Barker, 4/14/1964, CR 1066, p. 10.

14.  Telephone interview of Martin, op. cit.; FBI interview of John Martin Jr., [interview A] 4/2/1964, CD 897, p. 51-53.

15.  Ibid.

16.  *DCA . . . Final Hour*, op. cit.; *Hearings Before the President's Commission on the Assassination of President Kennedy*, v. 2, p. 201, 205.

17.  *Hearings*, op. cit., v. 7, p.351.

18.  Ibid., v. 18, p. 794-795, 798-799; Philip Melanson, *Politics of Protection*, p. 166; FBI interview of James W. Powell, 1/13/1964.

19.  *Hearings* op. cit., v. 7, p. 535.

20.  Ibid., v. 7, p. 347; v. 18, p. 797.

21.  Ibid., v. 7, p.107.

22.  Telephone interview of Martin, op. cit.

23.  Ibid.; FBI interview of Martin [interview A] op cit.

24.  Documents obtained from FOIA request #274,211, 10/28/1986, including documents marked "DL 89-43 / CTB:mam" and " 1 / DL 100-10461 / WGB/gm."

25.  *Hearings*, op cit., v. 7, p. 290-298; Telephone interview of Martin, op. cit.

26.  Documents obtained from FOIA request, op. cit., including documents marked "DL 89-43 / NY 89-75 / NPO / RE: Movies taken by John Martin," "Memorandum /To Director, FBI / From: SAC, New York / 12/17/1963," "SAC, New York / Director, FBI / 12/27/1963."

27.  Documents obtained from FOIA request, op. cit., including documents marked "1 / DL 100-10461 / RPG/cms," "Memorandum / To Mr. Belmont / From A. Rosen / 3/25/1964."

28.  FBI interview of Martin [interview A] op cit.; FBI interview of Martin [interview B] 4/2/1964, CR 1066, p. 7-9.

29.  Documents obtained from FOIA request, op. cit., including documents marked "Airtel / To: Director / From: SAC, Dallas / 4/2/1964," "Airtel / To: SAC, Dallas / From: Director, FBI / 4/6/1964."

30.  Documents obtained from FOIA request, op. cit., including document marked "NOTE:," n.d.

31.  FBI interview of Joe Brown, 5/22/1964, CR 1066, p. 43-45.

32.  FBI interview of Parr, op.cit.; FBI interview of Charles Rhodes, 4/22/1964, CR 1066, p. 30-31.

33.  FBI interview of Charles Mentesana, 4/28/1964, CR 1066, p. 35-36.

34.  Mentesana film, 1/22/1963.

35.  Ibid.; Joseph Backes, "Rediscovering the DCA Film:  President Kennedy's Last Hour," *The Third Decade*, 5/1993, p. 7-8; Robert Sibley, "The Mysterious, Vanishing Rifle of the JFK

Assassination," *The Third Decade*, 9/1985, p. 16-18; Richard Sprague, "Letter to the Editor," *The Third Decade,* 11/1985, p. 21-22.

36.     See various Allen photos made of officers on Houston Street as well as Murray Roll 1, #32-33, 35, 36, Roll 2, #13-16, 23-24. The print in Roll 1 #36 even shows what could be members of this group including the shotgun toting police officer.

37.     FBI interview of Mentesana, op. cit.; Sibley, op. cit., p. 18.

38.     Letter, J. Lee Rankin to Dallas Cinema Associates, P.O. Box. 15521, 7/2/1964; Harold Weisberg, *Photographic Whitewash*, p. 252-254.

39.     Ibid., p. 250-251.

40.     Richard E. Sprague papers, Georgetown University Library, Washington, D.C., folder 16, "Phone conversation with Johnny Martin, 2/25/1967."

41.     *Photographic Whitewash*, op. cit., p. 106. Study of the man in the door utilizing the Martin film as well as the Bell and Hughes films by critic and photo expert Robert Groden helped end the controversy as to whether the man was Lee Oswald or another Book Depository employee, Billy Lovelady. The film analysis supported other evidence that it was in fact Lovelady. See *Appendix to Hearings Before the House Select Committee on Assassinations*, v. 6, p. 288-289, 310.

42.     Telephone interview of Martin, op. cit.

Officer Wise, with police-issue shotgun #202, confers
with a superior on the Book Depository front steps.

# PART FIVE

# PHOTOGRAPHY AND THE NON-WITNESSES

Upon the request of the authorities for assassination-related photos, a number of citizens turned in motorcade pictures, attempting to be of assistance. This is one such photo taken on Main Street. Note the bunching of the back of President Kennedy's suit jacket.

One of two Westfall pictures identified by the FBI to have been taken the morning of November 22, 1963

## CHAPTER 24

# Color Photo, Inc.

In December of 1963 the Federal Bureau of Investigation obtained two photographs which they identified as having been taken by a Mrs. E. H. Westfall of the area around and including the Texas School Book Depository on the morning of November 22, 1963, prior to the assassination of President Kennedy. Subsequently, these same photographs have been included in the body of material gathered by assassination researchers concerning the photographic documentation of Dealey Plaza the day of the shooting.

A photograph taken prior to the 12:30 p.m. assassination which revealed the conditions of the area of the Texas School Book Depository would, at the least, be a "before" photographic curiosity worthy of note and preservation. It would serve as a chance glimpse of normalcy prior to a momentous event, akin to a photograph of the Challenger Space Shuttle poised on its launch pad on the early morning of January 28, 1986, prior to the launch and horrific explosion. At best, such a "before" photograph might also aid investigators in discerning what persons were present prior to the commission of the crime of the century, and could reveal the status of the suspect sixth floor "sniper's nest" window as well as others within the Book Depository Building. The Hertz sign atop the Book Depository, if included in the picture, might indicate the time of morning, and if that were not visible, then a study of the shadow patterns could provide an approximate time indicator. Thus, these "before" pictures could prove to be of some investigative as well as historic interest.

The government's interest in these two photographs can be partially reconstructed by an examination of the released FBI files of the Kennedy assassination case. On December 5, 1963, the Dallas FBI office sent a memorandum to Director J. Edgar Hoover forwarding an 8mm film taken by amateur cameraman Orville O. Nix, as well as two color photographs showing the Texas School Book Depository. The memorandum states, concerning the two still photographs:

> These photographs were taken by Mrs. E. H. Westfall, of
> Dallas, and the exposed film have been turned in to Color Photo Inc.,
> 1507 Sullivan Street. On 12/2/63, Laboratory Technician Kurt Foley,
> of same company contacted Dallas Office and advised he had some
> photographs which might be of interest to the FBI in connection with

the assassination of President Kennedy.  Mr. Foley, at the request of the Dallas Office, produced prints taken from these color slides.  The original color slides show that one photograph was taken at 10:12 a.m., which was taken at an angle southwest from the Texas School Book Depository.  The time that the second photograph was taken is unknown, but appears to have been taken between 11:00 and 11:30 a.m., as it depicts the crowd gathering on Houston Street to watch the presidential motorcade.  This film was taken looking in a northerly direction looking at the Texas School Book Depository Building.  Both photographs show that the pertinent window on the sixth floor of this building was closed at the time these photographs were taken.[1]

Copies of the two pictures were duplicated and retained in Washington by the FBI Photographic Unit, and the originally submitted copies were sent back to Dallas.[2] On December 19, 1963, a listing of the photographs and movies of the assassination scenes known to the FBI was compiled. These two photographs, identified as having been taken by Mrs. Westfall, were described as, "two color photographs of Texas School Book Depository Building, both photographs showing the pertinent window on the sixth floor as being closed, the photograph taken on the morning of November 22, 1963."[3]

Except for an additional listing of these photographs included in an FBI log some years later, these are the only documents revealed concerning Mrs. Westfall's photographs, when such information was asked for through a Freedom-of-Information request made in 1985. Also on file were copies of the two pictures themselves.[4]

Thus two FBI documents identified the pictures as having been taken on the morning of November 22, with one identifying the time of their being taken as 10:12, and the other as between 11:00 and 11:30. It appears that if any government personnel did attempt to further analyze the photographs, it was decided that their investigative value was minimal, perhaps, since it became known during the investigation that workers were on the sixth floor of the Depository Building the morning of November 22, laying down a plywood floor near the southwest corner until about 11:45 a.m. Thus the pictures were probably taken too early to reveal any sinister activity by the southeast corner window, the alleged "sniper's nest."[5] Except for the Zapruder film, and to a lesser extent, the Nix and Muchmore films, government investigators appear to have done very little with photographic research and interpretation of the assassination events. They often ignored photographs if the Texas School Book Depository Building was not included in the view. Some known photographic materials, such as the Charles Bronson slides and movies, were given only cursory examination without copies even being retained for later possible re-examination. Thus it was somewhat by happenstance that these two pictures had in fact made it into the permanent files of the FBI. Yet an examination of the photographs themselves leaves one who possesses a little knowledge about the events of November 22 with a feeling that things just don't look quite right.

The first picture reveals itself as having been taken from the grass infield between Elm and Main Streets, looking northerly towards a full view of the Depository Building. Some seven spectators, including a police officer, are milling around the area, while traffic is traveling southwesterly down Elm Street. The second photograph, taken from Houston Street, looks northwards at another full view of the Texas School Book Depository Building. A large crowd of spectators are on the western sidewalk behind a rope line, and cars and a truck are parked at the curb. At least six uniformed police can be discerned lining up along Houston Street. In both pictures, all visible windows of the Texas School Book Depository Building are closed.[6]

The second FBI-retained Westfall picture, supposedly made the morning of November 22

The initial reaction of one familiar with Kennedy assassination pictures and films is that there seem to be too many spectators, cars, and police on Houston Street than is revealed when the presidential motorcade actually arrives! The Elsie Dorman film and portions of other films taken at about 12:30 do not depict a rope line, nor so many police, nor any vehicles at these locations. In both Westfall pictures, the focus of interest appears to be the Book Depository, and it seems contrary to observations of crowds at other political events and motorcades, that so many spectators would arrive so early to view such an event. It also seems strange that if these were of the pre-motorcade events, why there were no preserved pictures in the sequence of the motorcade itself. The chief impression one gets is that the reason the pictures were made was to get a shot of the Depository Building, and unless the photographer was a student of local commercial architecture, the reasoning for taking them prior to the assassination makes little sense.

The pictures didn't make sense. Were they taken during the days following the assassination? If so, why were no memorial floral displays in view, and why did the Houston Street picture look so much like a crowd awaiting a parade or procession? Why did the FBI identify these as having been taken on the morning of November 22 if they had not been taken at that time? Could they have been taken during another parade prior to December 1963? Had the photographer tried to pass off another photographed event as the notorious one on November 22? These were questions that this author could not clarify in his own mind until a chance examination of videotapes of Dallas television station WFAA revealed most of the answers.

Nearly everyone living at the time remembers the dramatic shooting of Lee Oswald in the Dallas Police Headquarters basement, many having viewed it live as it happened. On Sunday, November 24, 1963, Oswald was going to be transferred from Police Headquarters to the County Jail located on Houston Street about one mile away. The shooting of Oswald by Jack Ruby took place at approximately 11:20 Central Standard Time (CST), and as a result, few people ever became much aware of the location to which Oswald was being transferred. Yet many Dallasites had journeyed to the Dealey Plaza area hopeful to see the Oswald transfer to the County Jail located on Houston Street.

The American Broadcasting Company, through its Dallas affiliate WFAA, was broadcasting the scene in Dealey Plaza from a camera located on the eastern side of Houston Street at approximately 10:30 CST. ABC newsman Roger Sharp described the scene as the camera panned Houston Street left from Elm to Main Street, back to Elm and the Texas School Book Depository, then tilting up to view the building. Sharp narrated, "Crowds of several hundred Dallas citizens have gathered along the Houston Avenue side of the Dallas County Courthouse, the route of the presidential motorcade, the area where President Kennedy passed momentarily before the fatal shots rang out. This is a curious crowd . . . police stationed every 15 feet along the entire block. This crowd, by the way, is considerably larger than the crowd that lined this very same street more than 46 hours ago when the presidential motorcade moved by." The panning camera picked up the identical scene as recorded in the second Westfall picture, only from a different position. It showed the crowd behind the rope, the police officers in the street, and the unmistakably same two cars and truck parked on the west side of Houston Street between the crowd and the police.[7]

Thus the second picture, and possibly the first, was taken the morning of November 24, and not November 22. This discovery brought up the question of who had misidentified the photographs in the first place. The FBI documents indicated that they were taken on November 22, but did not state directly that the photographer, Mrs. E. H. Westfall, had so identified her photographs.

This author decided to try and contact Mrs. Westfall to see if she could or would shed light on the question. Unfortunately, Mrs. Olga Westfall passed away back in 1970, and her husband, Elmer Hayes Westfall, died in 1983. Sylvia J. Sara, daughter of the Westfalls, however, still resides in the area; and through correspondence and by telephone, she was very gracious in clearing up the confusion. Mrs. Sara recounts, "I am very familiar with the photographs they took. I am certain that the pictures were taken on Sunday morning, November 24, 1963. I can remember their talking about perhaps being able to get a picture of Lee Oswald. I don't know how the government came to the conclusion that they were taken on November 22."[8]

The Westfalls had resided in Dallas since 1931, and none of the family was on hand on Friday, November 22, to view the presidential motorcade. Mrs. Sara recalls that when she heard of the assassination, she called her mother who was at home. On Sunday, Mrs. Sara was unable to go with her parents to Dealey Plaza, but she knows that her father took a number of slides with his small Kodak Brownie 27 camera, including pictures of the Courthouse. Mrs. Sara, when shown a copy of the picture taken near Elm Street, identified her mother as the lady "in a light colored coat standing on the grass." Mrs. Westfall took the film to a nearby drugstore where she shopped and in her name had it sent to be developed. Mrs. Sara can't remember if any government officials ever contacted her parents about taking the pictures, but remembers that they didn't get the pictures returned for a long time.[9]

An examination of the original six 1½" x 1½" large format 120 color transparencies taken by Mr. Westfall when observed together as a set, clearly shows that the scenes depicted are of the post-assassination period. The original uncropped transparency of the first FBI retained Elm Street picture shows the Hertz sign on top of the Depository to read 10:12, while a bunch of yellow flowers at the base of a tree on the other side of Elm Street are also observable. An additional, almost identical scene taken in the same vicinity, except a little further down Elm Street towards the triple underpass shows Mrs.

Westfall looking down at a large number of floral tributes. A third transparency was made looking directly across Elm Street to the north pergola with various groupings of flowers on the grassy knoll area. The Houston Street transparency from which the second FBI print was made again shows the Hertz sign atop the Depository Building but which now is on the temperature cycle, the first number unclear, but the second one apparently a "7." Also very evident in the original slide are numerous hanging cables, undoubtedly part of the live television "shore line" hookups with cables wrapped around a light pole near the southwest corner of Elm and Houston Street. Seven of the spectators at the

An additional slide taken slightly further down Elm Street shows Mrs. Westfall looking at floral tributes on Sunday, November 24.

front of the Houston Street curb hold various cameras, and the parked vehicle closest to the Westfall camera is a telephone car having the bell symbol on the front passenger door. Two additional transparencies show the east side of Houston Street including parts of the Dallas County Records Building and the County Criminal Courts Building, the location to which Oswald was to be transferred. In front of these buildings are mobile units of television stations KTVT, KRLD, and WFAA with cameras and crew on top of each, including what could well be ABC commentator Roger Sharp on the WFAA mobile unit.[10]

Mobile TV units line up on Houston Street in anticipation of the Oswald jail transfer.

It would appear that Mrs. Westfall's local drug store sent in the unprocessed roll of film to Color Photo, Inc., of Dallas to be developed. Edward C. "Cort" Foley was plant manager of Color Photo, Inc., located on Sullivan Street, one of three photo finishing plants in Dallas at the time. Eastman Kodak, Fox Stanley, and Color Photo serviced the amateur photographic needs of the area surrounding Dallas for a radius of about 100 miles, though Color Photo did not handle movie film. On Friday afternoon, Color Photo was in full gear on a normal 14-hour-per-day production, and when news of the assassination reached the plant, Foley remembers everyone was stunned, but that he did not give any thought at the time that potential photographs of the assassination event might turn up at his plant.

The plant was closed Saturday and Sunday, and Foley, when contacted about the events some 23 years later, recalls that beginning on Monday "people were turning in film like crazy, but that much film of the events was of floral tributes" at Dealey Plaza. Not able now to recall specifics of the chronology of the events, Foley does recall that the "FBI came in with printed-up notices that we put in every package that went out. Plus they had a couple of men sitting at the end of the processor watching prints come off. And we just culled out anything that we thought would be the least bit applicable, and we would put a notice in the customer's package that we were holding their film for a day or so until they could look at it further."[11] Foley recalls that the FBI were there for a good two weeks, and because you could easily miss possibly important pictures as the film came through the dryer, these 3x5 cards printed with red ink were provided by the FBI to be inserted in each package of film sent back to customers. The card was titled, "AS-

> ASSASSINATION OF PRESIDENT KENNEDY
> If this film contains pictures depicting the scene <u>at the time of</u> the assassination of President Kennedy please call your local F B I office

Card inserted into all packages of processed film

SASSINATION OF PRESIDENT KENNEDY," and requested people to contact the FBI if the pictures included the assassination.[12] Foley does not now recall the Westfall pictures, nor does he have copies of them in his small collection of extra prints made from some photographs at the lab. The FBI memorandum of December

5, 1963, indicates that Foley contacted the Dallas Office on December 2 concerning these Westfall slides. It is now unclear if Foley made the FBI aware of all of the Westfall pictures, or only of these two. In any event, he was requested and made copy prints of two of the original slides, thereby also cropping some information areas from the slide view. It appears that the copy prints were sent to Washington for an additional, and by now third generation, copy made of them. Perhaps due to the absence of floral remembrances in the Elm Street picture, and the government examiner's unfamiliarity with the gathered crowd at Houston Street on Sunday, November 24, these two pictures struck the local FBI as being representations of the Friday morning events. In any event, the informational mistake traveled with the pictures to Washington, and the mistake thus became part of the official record.

Snapshot photo made of the presidential convertible and follow-up
car as they rushed past Burrus Mills towards Parkland Hospital

An additional photograph processed by Color Photo, Inc., and directly relating to the post-assassination events, was uncovered a number of years ago by Texas researcher Howard Upchurch. On November 22, 1963, a color picture was snapped on the west side of Stemmons Freeway, looking across the pavement in an easterly direction towards the Dallas skyline, with a large enclosed grain storage elevator prominent on the far side of the street. Taken close to the present-day Continental Avenue exit off Stemmons, the picture depicts a panel truck traveling south-bound on Stemmons, while in the opposite lane may be discerned the presidential Lincoln and the Cadillac follow-up car traveling towards Parkland Hospital following the assassination which had taken place only a few moments earlier. The grain elevator is today still a visible landmark near Stemmons, being located on

Alamo Street and operated by the flour milling division of Cargill, and in 1963 known as Burrus Mills.[13] The slightly blurred photograph appears to have been taken on the side of the freeway, perhaps from a car or by a pedestrian wanting to catch a view of the motorcade on its way to the Dallas Trade Mart.[14]

Upchurch says of the photo that he first saw it when a friend's father, who had at one time worked for Color Photo, showed it to him. The father explained that shortly after the assassination, the film lab was visited by the FBI, and they left a printed card requesting that any photos of the assassination received for developing be turned over to them. The father made extra prints of some of the negatives sent to be developed, including this particular shot. Later, Upchurch was offered the photographs that his friend's father had copied, and thus it came into his possession.[15] Cort Foley also has a print of this scene in his retained copy photographs, and believes that its original format was that of a transparency. Neither the original transparency or negative nor the particular circumstances concerning its having been taken has surfaced.[16]

The above two examples of photographs processed by Color Photo, Inc., reveal that the FBI at a fairly early date had initiated a search for assassination-related pictures. Unfortunately, their efforts were not fully focused, and lacked investigative follow-through in both the scope and in the interpretation of photographs that were found, and in determining their potential value to an investigation.

## CHAPTER NOTES

1.     FBI memorandum, To: Director, From: S.A.C. Dallas, 12/5/1963, p. 2.
2.     FBI memorandum, To: S.A.C. Dallas, From: Director, FBI file #62-109060-2063, 12/19/1963.
3.     FBI letterhead memorandum, "Individuals known to have taken photographs . . . relating to the assassination of President Kennedy," 12/19/1963, p. 2.
4.     Trask Freedom of Information, Privacy Acts Request #260,804 & #263,251, 8/29/1985.
5.     *Report of the President's Commission on the Assassination of President John F. Kennedy*, p.143.
6.     Copies of Westfall color photographs #1 and #2 obtained through FOIA request.
7.     WFAA *Kennedy Tapes*, a rebroadcasting by WFAA on November 19-21, 1983. Report of Roger Sharp near Houston Street Sunday morning, 11/24/1963.
8.     Letter, Sylvia J. Sara to Trask, 8/10/1986.
9.     Telephone interview of Sara, 9/2/1986; Letter, Sara to Trask, 10/9/1986.
10.     Elmer H. Westfall 120 color transparencies #1-6, 11/24/1963.
11.     Telephone interview of Edward C. Foley, 9/25/1986.
12.     Letter, Foley to Trask, 11/2/1986.
13.     Notation provided by W. J. Whitley, Flour Milling Division of Cargill on letter sent 11/28/1986.
14.     Photograph in collection of Howard Upchurch.
15.     Letter, Upchurch to Trask, 12/11/1984, 1/2/1985
16.     Telephone interview of Foley, 9/25/1986.

## CHAPTER 25

# The Canadian Frauds

Dramatic news events always attract interest and discussion among large numbers of the public. Often when one first learns startling facts concerning a major news story, individuals find personal satisfaction in revealing these tidbits of information to those not already "in the know."

It is not so uncommon for some individuals to claim to possess inside knowledge of an event and for some who perhaps were only on the periphery of the event to go so far as to claim to being at the actual scene of the action. From the time of the death of the philosopher Socrates in ancient Greece, to the death of General James Wolfe in 1764 on the Plains of Abraham at Quebec, as well as at the death bed of assassinated President Abraham Lincoln at the Peterson Boarding House on the morning of April 16, 1865, various persons have claimed to be where they actually were not when great men died. Though in close proximity at the time of the 1968 assassination of Dr. Martin Luther King, aide Jesse Jackson was not on the balcony of the Lorraine Motel beside the mortally wounded civil rights leader. Yet Jackson on more than one occasion would later describe to audiences of his cradling of the dying Nobel Peace Prize winner in his very arms.[1] In dramatic, emotion-packed situations, some seem to be drawn to stretch a story of their close association with the people or events out of an emotional or psychological desire to be part of it. Human nature, wishful thinking, and possible nearness to these events often weigh in to convince some people to claim what did not occur — their presence at significant events.

There are numerous examples of various fakers, publicity seekers, and mentally imbalanced individuals who unfortunately often present themselves after the fact as legitimate spectators or even participants to history. With the development of rapid transportation and speedy communications, individuals can be at a location soon after a breaking news event or can at least quickly learn information about such events. In extreme cases one could fabricate a story, enabling him to fool others with passable knowledge of what actual witnesses did see.

The Kennedy assassination took place in a public setting before the eye and ear witness of hundreds of spectators. Given the nature of the event, the resulting confusion and the speed with which the shooting was communicated to the public, anyone with a devious mind and the semblance of a veracious story could claim to have been an "Everyman" present at this critical moment of American history. It would be the somewhat difficult and unrewarding task for others to prove the negative that someone who claimed to have been at Dealey Plaza had actually not been there. The burden of proof would be on those attempting to debunk such stories. At least several of these suspected non-witnesses are briefly discussed in other chapters. Both Beverly Oliver and Gordon Arnold claimed their presence at the assassination scene, though only telling their tales many years after the event when proof of their not being there would be even harder to prove. Two other purported witnesses, each claiming to have made pictures of the assassination events, surfaced from our neighbor to the north — Canada. One of these Canadian claimants' stories was quickly investigated, while the others' claims are even today shrouded in obscurity.

Norman Mitchel Similas was born at Barrie, Ontario, Canada in 1929 of Swedish descent. In his teenage years during the 1940s he had several run-ins with the law including earning a one-year probation on a breaking and entering charge. Employed by a variety of different firms over a 15-year period, Similas seemed attracted to promotional, advertising and sales job opportunities. In 1963 he lived with his wife and three children in Willowdale, Ontario, a suburb of Toronto. In late 1963 Similas was employed by the *Canadian Beverage Review*, the trade publication of the Canadian beverage industry. In 1963 the American Bottlers' Carbonated Beverages annual convention was held in Dallas, Texas. The event ran from November 18 to 22 with the Dallas Trade Mart on Stemmons Freeway serving as headquarters. Similas was assigned to attend and photograph highlights of the convention and to obtain copy for his publication. Preparing for these activities, he brought some 15 twelve-exposure rolls of 120 size film for use in a Japanese Mamiyaflex type camera.[2]

More than half a year after his trip, Similas recounted his experiences in Dallas in a Canadian magazine article published in ghost-written form "as told to Ken Armstrong." The article began, "I am a Canadian who crammed enough memories into 72 hours to haunt me for the rest of my life." A first-time visitor to Dallas, Similas, from his post-assassination perspective, said he had found the Dallasites he met to be generous, warm-hearted and hospitable, but possessing a hardness, ". . . and a rightist political philosophy so alarmingly extremist that I soon learned to button my lips when politics were discussed."[3] While attending the bottlers' convention, Similas later claimed to have personally met and photographed Vice-President Lyndon Johnson, a keynote speaker at the convention. Boasting in the magazine article to having fooled two local photographers about in which car Johnson would be arriving, Similas told of his later being able to get exclusive pictures of Johnson. The Vice-President reportedly asked Similas, "Say, you're the young man who fooled the other photographers, aren't you?" Placing his hand on his chest, Johnson is supposed to have asked Similas, while posing for his camera, "Shall I look like Napoleon?"[4]

Similas also says that during his trip he also met Jack Ruby, who had freely given out a number of passes to his Carousel Club to convention goers. Using the free passes, Similas and several companions arrived at the club on Thursday night, November 21. They were personally ushered by Ruby into a front-row seat, Ruby's "bear-like arm" around the Canadian's shoulder. "He came to our table several times during the burlesque and comedy act." When asked by Similas if he could take pictures of the entertainers, Ruby reportedly told Similas, "Sure, but why don't you save your film for President Kennedy when he drives through the city tomorrow. The parade route is just down the street." Ruby was described by Similas as a ". . . fast-talking, emotional guy like Sgt. Bilko." Bilko was a popular TV comedy program in which the sergeant, played by Phil Silvers, was a rapid mouthed wheeler-dealer.[5]

On Friday Similas claims to have taken Ruby's advice and gone to the area of the motorcade route. In his various accounts of his activities around 12:30 that afternoon, Similas's positions in the Dealey Plaza area shift according to which account of his one reads. From the day of the shooting Similas claimed to be an eyewitness and a photographer of the assassination events, though when one looks over his various recollections, they just don't add up to a credible account. By September 1964 Similas would tell a Royal Canadian Mounted Police interviewer, "I took my first picture as the lead motorcycle passed in front of me. At the same time as I took the first picture I heard the first shot fired. I didn't take any more pictures until a bus carrying the presidential Press party came into view. I started with a fresh roll of film and there were three exposures left when it was all over." [Nine pictures taken?] Similas initially thought the shots came from the direction of the triple underpass. He also claimed to have taken a picture of the Texas School Book Depository Building after seeing an agent in the follow-up car looking in that direction. "The President's car veered towards me and then took off accelerating very quickly."[6] It is interesting to note that the first bus in the motorcade was just making the turn from Main Street onto Houston, an entire diagonal block away from Similas, at the time the President's car was speeding down Elm Street following the shots..

Sometime after 12:30 on the day of the shooting, Similas returned to his hotel and called both his employer and the *Toronto Star* newspaper, telling them he had been a close witness to the assassination. If as later evidence seems to indicate, Similas did not actually see the shooting scene, but perhaps had seen the motorcade earlier on, or as it rushed to Parkland, his possible boasting of first-hand knowledge of the shooting may have originated from his phone calls home. Shortly after his call to Canada, Similas received a call at the hotel for a taped interview by a Hamilton, Ontario, radio station. His notoriety as a witness had begun. The Toronto newspaper had also briefly interviewed Similas on the phone, and besides running the story itself in its own paper, the *Star* distributed it through the Canadian Press Syndication. A number of newspapers throughout Canada and the United States picked up the story, which appeared in print by the next day. The story recounted that Similas, a 34-year-old Willowdale resident, was taking pictures of the motorcade when he witnessed the shooting from only 10 feet away. It then quoted his story:

> I was in Dallas on a convention and I decided to snap a picture of the President as the motorcade rolled by.

The crowds had thinned out just past an overpass near the Trade Mart, so I had a good position when the motorcade came by at about 8 miles an hour.

Then I suddenly heard a sharp crack. The first thing that came to my mind was that someone was setting off firecrackers. I turned away from the President's car and looked back to where the noise seemed to come from.

Then somebody — I don't know who it was — yelled: "The President's been shot."

I swung back to look at the car. A Secret Service man ran up with his gun drawn. A policeman beside me drew his revolver and his eyes searched the crowd.

Then another shot rang out and a third almost immediately on top of it.

I was still staring at the car. The Secret Service man opened the car door and I saw the President slumped down to the floor and falling toward the pavement.

Jackie Kennedy was sitting on the left side of the car and Governor Connally on the President's right.

I could see a hole in the President's left temple and his head and hair were bathed in blood.

The agent looked in and gasped: "Oh, my God, he's dead."[7]

Although this account might sound authentic to someone who knew little about the assassination, to someone familiar with the film evidence and other eyewitness accounts, this Similas version is fraught with blatant inaccuracies of the most obvious kind. Clearly, many eyewitnesses did miss parts of the event or mistakenly interpreted some of the evidence. This account, however, is of events and positions that never were.

Desiring to return home to Canada, Similas was unable to make airline reservations. With baggage, camera and film in hand, he caught a Greyhound bus connection from Dallas to Chicago, so informing his office. At a rest stop in St. Louis he bought several newspapers which were filled with assassination news, and read them as the bus proceeded to Illinois. Arriving at Chicago at about 6:30 p.m. November 23, Similas contacted Trans-Canadian Airways about a reservation and was told he had a message to call a local number. The regional Associated Press bureau had learned of Similas's probable passing through Chicago and wanted to speak with him and inquire about possible newsworthy pictures for which AP would pay — if usable to them. Similas showed interest and a car was sent to pick him up and bring him to the AP office. He handed over all of his exposed but undeveloped film to AP's day news photo editor, Ray Jefferies. Also present at the time was night photo editor Waldo D. Butler. The rolls, several only partially exposed with merely 4 or 5 shots on them, were speedily developed and examined prior to their being fully dried.[8]  Jefferies later recalled that he carefully examined the negatives and by virtue of his 30 years' experience, he could "read negatives as well as prints." They showed nothing that AP did not already have.  Many of the negatives were of individuals and groups taken at the Bottlers' Convention, while some showed crowds lining a street, probably taken in anticipation of the presidential motorcade.  Jefferies believed he recognized on two negatives what he thought could be the rear end and the front end of the President's car.  No occupants were evident and, "There was a lot of movement in the pictures as if he [Similas] was being pushed around in the crowd."[9]

Jefferies had found nothing newsworthy in the batch.  At the time Similas, for his part, did not claim to the AP editor that he made any exceptional pictures.  Jefferies would later recall that he felt somewhat skeptical that any of the pictures had been taken during or after the shooting, as it appeared these pictures might have been taken from a location on the route other than at the Texas School Book Depository area.  No buildings were discernibly clear, and windows (much less objects behind windows) were just not visible. Skepticism concerning Similas grew when he was reluctant to describe his personal recollections.  Jefferies had to drag out responses from the Canadian.  Similas would only confirm to Jefferies that the President's car passed in front of him and people in the car were "Bending over as if they were folding up." When asked why he had not taken pictures of the shooting, Similas hesitatingly answered he thought that he had, but at the time all was confusion.  Jefferies was left with the clear impression that this reluctant witness probably had not witnessed the assassination at all. Of Similas' later claim to having taken revealing though now missing pictures, Jefferies would comment, "they probably cooked up the story to make a fast buck."[10]

As Similas was to catch an 8:30 flight to Toronto, Jefferies offered to drive him to the airport.  The negatives were not dry, however, and Jefferies promised to send them immediately by mail express to Similas at his home address.  Later that night Butler packaged all the negatives and delivered them to an air express office for next-day delivery.

When finally arriving back home, Similas was contacted by Colin Davies, a reporter/photographer for the *Toronto Telegram* who interviewed Similas and subsequently looked over his negatives when they arrived from Chicago. According to Similas, while examining the negatives the reporter exclaimed, "There looks like two people at this window."  Similas later claimed that this negative showed the southeast corner window of the Texas School Book Depository and there were two people in it. According to Similas, the reporter then stated he thought he saw what appeared to be a rifle barrel between them.  This negative strip containing three exposures was given over to the reporter so that he could show it to his editor.  The editor visited Similas the next evening and looked at the rest of the negatives, borrowing the strip of three containing shots of Ruby's Carousel night club.[11]

A newspaper photo
of Norman Similas

When later interviewed by investigators, Davies recalled the meeting with Similas quite differently. He stated it was Similas who excitedly drew the reporter's attention to a window asking if the reporter didn't see two people in it. Davies said he felt it was the power of suggestion and that Similas wanted to see the two people in the negative so badly that he actually believed he did. The reporter believed the negatives worthless from a news standpoint, but according to Davies, he did not have the heart to disappoint Similas. He offered to take the negatives to his photo editor who would decide what should be done. Davies believed that Similas had indeed witnessed the assassination and that this man ". . . was sure going to get a lot of mileage out of the story." A photo of Similas, coupled with a short article, appeared in the Monday edition of the *Telegram*, but without any of the pictures he had taken. Similas called the newspaper requesting his negatives be returned. On Wednesday he received a letter from the paper with an apology that the borrowed negatives had been lost. An enclosed check for $50 was given in lieu of them. The next day he received three 8 x 10 prints with their negatives, which had been the ones loaned to the photo editor. He never received back his original strip, and by the time the FBI investigated the circumstances concerning Similas in September 1964, the photo editor had died.[12]

Similas's game, whatever it was, might have developed no further and he simply relegated to a footnote in history as a witness to the assassination with a less-than-accurate recall of events. A few months following the assassination, his story, however, was mentioned to Kenneth G. Armstrong by a mutual friend. Armstrong was editor of a Toronto-based periodical called *Liberty Magazine* and published by Harold Cook of the Fengate Publishing Company. Armstrong, thinking the story might make an intriguing article, contacted Similas. A three-hour conversation ensued, during which Similas promised to produce pictures which he had taken prior to and during the assassination, including one which showed two faces and a gun barrel at a window. Armstrong was excited about the potential story and the promise of important and unpublished photos. He wrote up a two-part article for his magazine, allowing Similas editorial review of all material. In the first article, published in July 1964, Similas is quoted to say, "I witnessed from a distance of less than seven feet the assassination of President Kennedy, and unwittingly photographed his assassin or assassins as a rifle was leveled at him from a nearby building. . . . One of the pictures I took as the presidential car passed, showed two figures beside the gun barrel in the window." Unfortunately no such picture accompanied the story. Armstrong was aware of the essential need of the photos to prove the article, and was told by Similas that they had been mailed. But they did not arrive for the first article's publication. Armstrong, suckered into printing the story without the Similas pictures, hoped they would turn up for the second installment. They never arrived, and though galley proofs were made of the second article, *Liberty Magazine* ceased publication, folding for lack of financial backing.[13]

To one on the lookout for plots and conspiracies, the lost Similas negatives and prints and the non-publication of the second article installment are fodder for their theories. To a reasonable observer, however, Similas's story, even with fragments of truth within it, appears on the whole unreliable. The article's published quotes attributed to Similas about the two men and a rifle barrel in the Texas School Book Depository were soon drawn to the attention of the Warren Commission investigation. The Commission requested the FBI to learn the facts and, ". . . If possible obtain the photographs referred to." A flurry of paper activity followed with the setting up of interviews in the United States, Japan and Canada, and including investigative mutual assistance being offered by the Royal Canadian Mounted Police. Through Canadian contacts whose identities are still unavailable through the Freedom of Information Act, Similas was interviewed and an investigation conducted. One late September 1964 cablegram from the Ottawa Legate to the FBI states, " [deleted words] Similas's eyewitness account based on assumption and misinformation probably deliberately to further his reputation as reported and to make his story saleable."[14]

By the end of October 1964, no Similas assassination pictures had been located, and his account was seen to be flawed by most all investigators and interviewees. As the Warren Commission had presented its final report in late September 1964, the Similas matter was moot and just allowed to drop.

During the critical research community's flurry of activity in 1967 and 1968, verification of Similas's story and his photographs were pursued. Several determined researchers including Richard Sprague and Gary Murr personally contacted Similas and were turned off by his evasiveness and promise of producing the photographs which never materialized. Some researchers continued to find evidence of the conspiratorial hand of the FBI having manipulated the evidence to discredit Similas. Yet Similas's pronouncements and activities, the stories of his having sent photos which never arrived, and his less than upstanding reputation among friends and acquaintances brought the thoughtful researcher to a conclusion that Similas and his assassination related photographs were principally a fraud.[15]

~

It was the graveyard shift at Dallas police headquarters early on March 24, 1964, the day after a Tarrant County jury had found Jack Ruby guilty of the premeditated first-degree murder of Lee Oswald. City Hall night switchboard operator Patsy Pair received a call from Canada. On the other end of the line was Victoria, British Columbia telephone night supervisor Bernice Williamson with a man on her line who had requested her to make a collect call to the Dallas Police Department. The man said he had some films of the Kennedy assassination, and Williamson had spoken with him long enough to believe that he probably did have something. Pair advised the Canadian operator that she could not accept the call without authorization. Asking her to hold, Pair quickly contacted Duty Sergeant Patrick T. Dean about the call, telling him that she had heard the man talk to the other operator enough to believe him to be serious. Dean, picking up the line, also heard the man and believing him to sound rational, okayed the collect call.

The man identified himself as Ralph Simpson and he recognized the sergeant as connected with the case, Dean having recently received press coverage for his important testimony during the Ruby trial. A short four-minute conversation culminating at about 4:50 a.m. ensued with Simpson explaining that he had been vacationing in Dallas on November 22 and was standing on the southwestern part of Dealey Plaza toward the railroad tracks. He spoke of filming with a full wide scope movie camera at the time of the assassination. Simpson believed he had filmed the assassination and had captured in the camera's background the building from where the shots originated. Incredibly he had not had his film developed! Dean had the impression the caller was scared about whether or not to keep the film, and Simpson volunteered that he had talked to an attorney named Batter, who had advised him to call someone in Dallas, though not the Warren Commission. Simpson asked Dean what to do, and Dean replied that he should mail it to the Commission. Simpson then declared that he would send the roll via air mail to Dean commenting, "You can have them. I haven't developed them, and you don't have to send me any copies of them back." Meanwhile the two operators had remained on the line. The man's phone number was 384-3780, which the Canadian operator, on contacting the local police, found to belong to the residence of R. H. W. Smele at 1141 Caldonia in Victoria. Shortly after hanging up, Dean learned of this name and address and that the call had cost $3.45 plus tax.[16] As Dean was scheduled to testify before a Warren Commission staff attorney just some 16 hours after receiving the call, he thought it a good nugget of information to volunteer during his testimony.

Sergeant Patrick Treavor Dean was an 11-year veteran of the Dallas Police Department and in 1963 was assigned to the patrol division. On a week's vacation, Dean had not been involved in the police activities the day President Kennedy was shot. Reporting to police headquarters on Sunday morning, November 24, Dean was assigned the task of coordinating the search and securement of the garage area of the building's basement and to continue in that capacity until after the accused assassin, Lee Harvey Oswald, was taken from the building and transferred to the County Jail. At 11:21, while Oswald was being escorted through the basement past a gaggle of police officers and press representatives, Jack Ruby rushed up to Oswald and fired a single fatal shot into his abdomen. Ruby was a local strip-tease night club owner with past ties to the "Mob." He was a man described by many who knew him as a thrill junkie who cultivated familiarity with many members of the police force as a kind of "hanger-on," and he had now killed and effectively silenced forever the accused presidential assassin.

Sergeant Dean, who had known Ruby from about 1960, found himself in an embarrassing situation. The cops had terribly bungled what should have been a simple transfer. Police Chief Jesse Curry in trying to satisfy the demanding press had unwittingly staged a televised execution. Soon after the shooting Dean accompanied Secret Service District Chief Forrest Sorrels to the fifth floor jail where Ruby had been temporarily taken. Sorrels asked Ruby some fast, basic questions, and within ten minutes the agent departed. Dean later contended that Ruby told him in Sorrels's presence that he had entered the basement through the ramp entering from Main Street. Sorrels was emphatic in later statements that he had heard no such conversation or comment by Ruby. In still later testimony presented by three police detectives, though not included in their initial written reports, the detectives confirmed their brother cop's statement, though Sorrels remained convinced this did not happen in his presence. It was generally believed in many circles, however, that after Ruby's arrest Dean strongly suggested to Ruby that he so describe his means of access to the basement. Ruby, when he would later give a straight answer to this question, rather than saying that he wished not to say how he got there, as he had commented a number of previous times, would finally go on record with this Main Street ramp explanation. Fairly or not, much speculation circulated that Dean had, either as a favor to a harmless friend of the police or due to more sinister reasons, allowed Ruby into the area via a different route.

Warren Commission staff lawyer Burt W. Griffin was familiar with the controversy and interviewed Dean on March 24, 1964. During one of several "off-the-record" conversations interrupting the stenographic interview, Griffin had urged Dean to "tell the truth," as the matter was important to the national interest. In a March 30 memo concerning the Dean interview, Griffin wrote his superior of his suspicion that Ruby had used a different entrance, ". . . to a point where Dean could have stopped him and that Dean, having been directly responsible for all basement security, is trying to conceal his dereliction of duty."[17] Griffin, a former U.S. Attorney with a reputation as a hands-on and thorough investigator, would in an additional memo to Chief Counsel J. Lee Rankin, state that he had conducted the interview ". . . on a basis of respect and friendship while maintaining a certain distance. I said, however, that I did not believe his testimony in some respects. . . ." During the interview Griffin, after explaining why and how Dean should tell the truth rather than repeating his previous testimony, told the sergeant that he didn't believe that Ruby told him on November 24 that he had entered the garage by the Main Street ramp. Nor did Griffin believe that Ruby had told Dean he thought of killing Oswald on the night of November 22.[18]

The attorney's comments rankled Dean. During the Ruby trial Dean had been a key prosecution witness. His testimony had put on the record that Ruby had told him shortly after the shooting that Ruby had in essence premeditated the murder. Ruby denied this premeditation, stating vigorously that the opportunity to shoot Oswald was a fluke in timing and the murder itself an emotional reaction. Dean's testimony was a major factor in the jury's finding Ruby guilty of first degree murder.

Though the Warren Commission staff kept hands off during the trial, once the verdict had been handed in, they now had the opportunity to interview those involved with the shooting events and scenes. Dean's statement concerning how Ruby had gotten past one officer on the ramp, through that assigned officer's negligence, was not a major factor in the trial, as any other explanation would only have made Ruby's case worse. On the surface, such a possible lie on Dean's part only seemed to be a good alibi against criticism by Dean's superiors. Yet in the Commission's questioning Ruby's premeditation of the shooting and the reliability of a chief prosecution witness, such evidence could jeopardize the entire case when it went to appeal, a fact not lost to Texas officials.

After the evening interview with Griffin, Dean went to his superiors reporting the off-the-record accusations by Griffin. Soon thereafter contact and angry exchanges were made between Texas officials and the Commission in Washington. Commission Chief Counsel Rankin, wanting to maintain good relations with Texas authorities as well as not wanting to have his staff accused of perpetrating "witch hunt" methods, essentially backed down from supporting Griffin and Ruby co-staff investigator Leon Hubert. Griffin was recalled to Washington and though unlike Hubert, who essentially resigned, Griffin continued to work on this area of the case. He was now out of the loop, however, and not allowed to participate in the subsequent questioning of Ruby before the Commission. Sorrels's firm statement that Dean had not obtained the ramp access information from Ruby in his presence, was simply ignored. Along with Dallas D.A. Henry Wade and Texas Attorney-General Waggoner Carr, Sergeant Dean was allowed to testify before the Warren Commission in Washington on June 8, 1964, concerning the truthfulness of his former testimony, and the accusations made by Griffin.[19]

During part of the off-the-record conversation between Dean and Griffin back in March, while Griffin was accusing Dean of being less than forthright over his testimony, Dean apparently brought up the telephone conversation he had had earlier that same morning with the man from Canada. Dean also mentioned this incident to the Commission in Washington when explaining to Chief Justice Warren that he had not perjured himself and resented Griffin's accusations. Dean commented that "I said, [to Griffin] 'I have come over here with the idea of giving you all the information that I have.' In fact, I had some additional information that I had gotten the night before and it was a call I had received from some man in Victoria, Canada, who said he had a reel of movie film that he had taken of the assassination." Dean then briefly explained the incident. Warren thanked Dean for his frankness to come and talk to the Commission, and reiterated that Commission staff had no right to tell a witness he was lying, but rather it was the Commission's business to appraise the testimony of all the witnesses. Many subsequent researchers felt that the Commission definitely did not fulfill Warren's statement of fully appraising this witness's testimony as regards Ruby's statements.[20]

It is still unclear today if Dean's testimony about Ruby's premeditation statement and that he had come down into the police basement by means of the Main Street ramp, are any more truthful than the tale told Dean by the Canadian telephone caller. Though the matters were different, it may be the case that both stories were fabrications. But here we get ahead of our story.

The morning following his lengthy interview with Dean, Burt Griffin contacted the Dallas FBI about the Simpson call. Griffin requested that, ". . . if the Bureau does not have this film, immediate contact [should] be made with Simpson for interview and circumstances surrounding his taking the film."[21]

In Washington the Bureau contacted its Seattle office telling them to make arrangements to have Simpson "Immediately interviewed through your liaison contacts R.C.M.P. [Royal Canadian Mounted Police]. Determine circumstances surrounding his taking of film and whether film actually does exist. If film does exist and has not been forwarded to Dallas Police Department, attempt to make arrangements to obtain film. Handle expeditiously."[22]

A report was fast in coming. Through telephone contact with Canadian police, a source advised that he had previously interviewed Ralph Henry William Smele, whose name was associated with the phone number traced from the collect call. Though the previous interview was on an unrelated subject, the source indicated he did not consider Smele a "nut." Before March 26 was over, Corporal R.E.G. Blackmore of the Royal Canadian Mounted Police had interviewed Smele. According to the report forwarded to Washington: "On the evening of March 26, 1964, [deleted material] advised that he had just completed interviewing Ralph Henry William Smele, 1141 Caldonia Street, regarding the above matter. Smele admitted making the telephone call to the Dallas Police Department using the fictitious name of Ralph Simpson. He advised he had never been to Dallas and never had any film as referred to in the telephone call. The only reason he could give for calling was that he had been watching a television program and had been drinking and had decided to call. He expressed amazement that he was identified as the caller. He stated he now realizes the seriousness of such type call and the only other explanation he could give for it was that he is 'given to dreams.' He advised that he is not now working, but has previously been employed in demolition work on buildings. He expressed regret for having made the telephone call."[23]

No further follow-up was deemed necessary or warranted by the FBI. If the information was passed on to the Warren Commission staff, no record of it has surfaced. Dean in further testimony given in Dallas to Leon Hubert, Jr. on April 1, mentioned that as yet he has not received anything from Simpson by mail, and he again recounted the story of his June 8 testimony in Washington.[24] Although interest in Simpson/Smele was completely dropped by the FBI and Commission, references to his phone contact with Dean were included within the published volumes of the Warren Commission *Hearings*. This half-told story was occasionally noted by assassination authors and researchers as a loose end not followed through by the Commission. The internal FBI reports concerning Smele were not available until years later, and as recently as 1991 a Canadian researcher wrote how the incident ". . . remains a mysterious aspect of the JFK assassination investigation. . . ."

The researcher, Peter Whitmey, did learn through Smele's sister-in-law that his mother's maiden name was Simpson, that Smele had been in the Canadian navy for many years, was an alcoholic who died in 1982 and had been known for playing practical jokes. Neither the sister-in-law nor the nephew who had been contacted by Whitney were aware of Simpson/Smele's 1964 telephone call to Dallas.[25]

The probable alcohol-laced phone prank in March 1964 resulted in a waste of investigative time, effort, and money; and like so many aspects of the Kennedy case, even though the probable truth was discovered by investigation, the rumors continued to persist.[26]

## CHAPTER NOTES

1.      Ralph David Abernathy, *And The Walls Came Tumbling Down*, p. 449-450.
2.      Harold Weisberg, *Photographic Whitewash*, p. 215-217.
3.      Ken Armstrong, "The Dallas Puzzle," *Liberty*, 7/15/1964, p. 13, 20, 33.
4.      Ibid., p. 33.
5.      Ken Armstrong, "The Dallas Puzzle, part II," obtained by Trask through FOIA request #288,780, 12/1987; "Oswald Killer Like TV's Sgt. Bilko Says Willowdale Man Who Met Him," *Toronto Telegram*, 11/25/1963, p. 10.
6.      Weisberg, op. cit., p. 217-218.
7.      Ibid., p. 217; "10 Feet From President," *New York Times*, 11/23/1963, p. 5. Several other publications picked up Similas' account including *TV Radio Mirror* in which the story was quoted on page 20 of their February 1964 issue.
8.      Weisberg, op. cit., p. 218; FBI report on Waldo D. Butler, file #105-82555-5093, 10/9/1964 & FBI report on Ray Jefferies, file #105-82555-5179, 10/21/1964 from Trask FOIA request, op. cit.
9.      Ibid., Jefferies, p. 3-4.
10.     Ibid.; Memorandum, Stephen Merrill, 500th INTC Group, G-2, U.S. Army, Japan, file #105-82555-5179, 10/21/1964, from Trask FOIA request, op. cit.
11.     Weisberg, op. cit., p. 218-219.
12.     Ibid., p. 218-219, 221.
13.     Ibid., p. 221-222; Armstrong, op. cit., p.13.
14.     Airtel, To: Legate, Ottawa, From: Director, FBI, file #105-82555-4765, 9/4/1964, p. 2; Cablegram, To: Director, From: Legate, Ottawa, no. 113, file #105-82555-4856, 9/15/1964; Ibid., no. 114, file #105-82555-4940, 9/18/1964; Ibid., no 120, file #105-82555-5002, 9/23/1964; Airtel, To: Director FBI, From:Legate, Ottawa, file #105-82555-4940, 10/2/1964, all from Trask FOIA request. The author made an attempt, through an administrative appeal, for the disclosure of two paragraphs deleted from the October 2, 1964, airtel. In June 1988 the appeal was denied and the material remains classified. The deleted material possibly deals with names of a person or persons in Canada assisting in the investigation including the possible surreptitious obtaining of the galley proofs of the unpublished article, "The Dallas puzzle, part II."
15.     Letters from Gary Murr to Harold Weisberg, 11/18/1967 & 12/8/1967; Letter from Richard Sprague to Murr, 1/4/1968; Letter, Murr to Sprague, 1/16/1968; Letter, Weisberg to Murr, 12/23/1967, all from the Richard Sprague Papers, Special Division Collections at the Georgetown University Library, Washington, D.C. An examination of other photos and films taken on Elm Street at the time of the assassination shows no unaccounted man taking pictures of the scene as close as Similas claims to have been located to the President's vehicle.
16.     *Hearings Before the President's Commission on the Assassination of President Kennedy*, v. 5, p. 256; v.12, p. 443-445; v. 19, p. 445-447.
17.     Seth Kator, *Who Was Jack Ruby?*, p. 2.
18.     Ibid., p. 149-150.
19.     Ibid., p. 154-155,162-163; *Hearings*, op. cit., v. 5, p. 254-258.
20.     Ibid., v. 5, p. 256-258; v.12 p. 443-445.

21. Teletype, To: Director, From: Dallas, file #105-82555-2855, 3/26/1964, from Trask FOIA request #313,260, 3/1989.

22. Teletype, To: SAC Seattle, From: Director, file #105-82555-2750, 3/26/1964, from Trask FOIA request, op. cit.

23. Report of SA Alfred G.Gunn, Seattle, 4/3/1964, from Trask FOIA request, op. cit.

24. *Hearings*, op. cit., v. 5 p. 256; v. 12, p. 446.

25. Peter Whitmey, "The Long Distance Call," *The Third Decade*, 3/1991, p. 18.

26. In another telephone incident relating to nonexistent film, the *Detroit News* received a call on December 7 from a "Mrs. Beck" who claimed she had a 16mm color film of the assassination taken from the overpass. According to Richard Sprague, Mrs. Beck claimed she was a student at the University of Michigan at Ann Arbor who was visiting Dallas. Mrs. Beck never fully identified herself, the Detroit FBI was unable to locate her, and the film was never received at the paper. (Airtel, To: Director, From: SAC, Dallas, File #62-109060-6082, 1/15/1968, p. 7; Richard E. Sprague, "The Assassination of President John F. Kennedy: The Application of Computers to the Photographic Evidence," *Computers and Automation*, 5/1970, p. 50.)

# The "Babushka Lady"

Her presence was established in several films and photographs. Abraham Zapruder briefly and inadvertently captured the woman in 21 frames of his film as he panned right following the presidential car's progress down Elm Street. Marie Much-more also incidentally picked up the woman's form while she filmed the same scene, but in a position behind and 50 feet further back. What made this woman's presence no-ticeable and of interest to later researchers was that this woman appeared to be taking a movie film before and during the President's fatal head shot from a distance of only some 15 feet from the Elm Street curb. An examination of published photographs shows a number of other unidentified people in the crowd further up on Main and even on Houston Streets who were also taking pictures and films of the President. As interesting as many of these unpublished and still unknown pictures might be, this woman's actions on Elm Street and her close proximity to the assassination itself would make her film extremely important. There is also the distinct possibility that from her position, this mystery woman might have included on her film the Texas School Book Depository Building in her earlier filming of the car coming down on her right, and perhaps even

A frame from the Muchmore film showing the "Babushka Lady" possibly filming during the presidential assassination

scenes of the soon to be famous "grassy knoll" at the time of the fatal shot. She stood on Elm Street just behind Charles Brehm and his five-year-old son, whose bodies might have obscured part of her view of the President's limousine, as did perhaps briefly the two left-side motor-cycles when they passed between her and the limousine.

From at least the time when Charles Bronson took his picture of the Elm Street shooting scene at about Zapruder frame #Z220-Z225, through to the movements of Secret Service Agent Clint Hill grappling onto the back of the presidential Lincoln, as seen around Muchmore movie film frame #55, this woman is observed with both hands holding what seems to be a camera. Her body is always pointed in the direction of the limousine, and though she might have been holding a still camera (or even binoculars), her panning action and body English give the distinct impression that she is in fact filming the incident.  Wearing a buff-colored raincoat, the woman is most noticeable for the light-colored triangular scarf tied around her head.  To the assassination research community she quickly became known as the "Babushka Lady."

Following the shooting, when the Brehms and Mary Moorman and Jean Hill, the two couples closest to the "Babushka Lady," had fallen to the ground in protective reaction, this woman continued to stand.  In a 35mm slide made just after the shooting by Wilma Bond, the "Babushka Lady" continues to hold her camera close to her chest while watching the flurry of photojournalist activity centering around the Newman family also sprawled on the ground on the opposite side of Elm Street.  In subsequent pictures made several minutes later, when numerous other spectators streamed into the area and are milling around the north side of Elm Street around the concrete steps leading up to the Pergola area, this same "Babushka Lady" is seen in several photographs made by William Allen and Jim Murray within this crowd, her camera possibly still in her hands. She is also seen to have a strap with shoulder protector worn around her right shoulder and resting on her left hip. With a box attached, it looks very much like a camera case.

Who was she, and what became of her film?  Apparently no one grabbed her at the scene as was the case with many eyewitnesses and photographers who were questioned by the authorities or the press.  Her film did not get picked up in the FBI sweep of the three major local Dallas photo and film processing companies.  But neither did several other film sequences.  The press, including several on-the-scene free-lancers and stringers like Jim Murray and Patsy Swank, did not happen upon the woman in the several hours following the shooting.  Yet an FBI memo written on November 25 shows that agents were aware of her possible investigative value.  Writing of the Bronson transparency, which included her image in his picture, the memo states, "One of the 35mm color slides depicts a female wearing a brown coat taking pictures from an angle, which would have, undoubtedly, included the Texas School Book Depository Building in the background of her pictures.  Her pictures evidently were taken just as the President was shot."[1]

The woman may have left the Dealey Plaza scene soon after the shooting incident and possibly had her film developed elsewhere as was the case with Robert Croft.  Or perhaps the camera or film was defective, and she did not capture anything on film and was embarrassed to so admit.  Although we know many of the scores of eyewitnesses to the assassination, a goodly number have never been positively identified due to reluctance or fear on their part.  Once the Zapruder film was published in *LIFE* magazine, and its impact universally known, one would think any other such dramatic films would be brought to the media's or authorities' attention by other such film makers. Yet silence prevailed.  Did something dark and mysterious occur to this film, or is there a simple though unrevealed explanation?  The "Babushka Lady," her story, and the possible film failed to surface.

In this Jim Murray photo, the dark-haired "Babushka Lady" can be seen in profile
just below the license plate of the car furthest down Elm Street in the middle of the picture.

Wearing a raincoat with collar, and seen with a camera case on a
shoulder strap, the "Babushka Lady," with back to the camera, stands to the right
of another woman wearing a head scarf and a light sweater.

Then in 1970 Texas architect and committed assassination researcher J. Gary Shaw learned of the identity of a woman who claimed to have taken films of the assassination. Shaw interviewed her several times as did others of the research community in 1971, including Dallasite Mary Farrell, and Washington attorney Bernard Fensterwald, Jr. In early July, 1971, the woman was interviewed for some six hours by interested researchers. According to Fensterwald, "She said she took a color movie at about where the "Babushka Lady" was located but couldn't pick herself out with any definiteness in . . . photos. Next day she turned undeveloped film over to two agents who claimed to be federal, but who she said dressed like Texas Rangers. Didn't get names or receipts. Has never seen film since. Not much we can do with this in my view."[2]

The woman uncovered by researchers, was the former Beverly Oliver whose story and association with the assassination was quite fantastic, if indeed true. Seventeen years old in 1963, Oliver was from a conservative, bible-belt family who had been described by one investigator as "religious fanatics." Of uncommon beauty, Beverly had reacted to her upbringing by finding work at a strip club in Dallas known as the Colony Club, separated by a parking lot from Jack Ruby's Carousel Club. According to Beverly, on November 22, 1963, she took a new super 8 Yashica movie camera mounted with a zoom lens to the Plaza to film the motorcade.[3]

By 1988 Oliver's recollection of the shooting was firmly established. Though aware of noise and initially thinking it was caused by some kind of firecracker, it wasn't until the President was shot in the head that she understood what was occurring. She ". . . was looking in the viewfinder as the President passed and just as he got past me the whole back of his head blew off. And I was looking at it through a viewfinder on a zoom lens. There was never any question in my mind that somebody from behind the picket fence had shot and blown the back of the President's head off. It looked like a bucket of blood was literally thrown out the back of that limousine."[4]

According to Oliver, the Monday following the assassination she was met on the landing leading up to the Colony Club by two men who were plainclothes federal agents. They requested of her the film she had taken for use in the investigation. Not sure which agency they were with nor receiving a receipt for her film, she claims nonetheless to have handed the roll over to them, they promising to return it within ten days. At the time the undeveloped film was still in her camera. The camera was stored in her make-up kit and not in a camera case. Also in the kit was a Prince Albert tobacco can filled with marijuana. Not wanting them to discover this, she quickly complied with their request. The film was never returned and Oliver through to 1992 never made a query about her property. She later claimed not to have spoken up about this incident as "I didn't want to become a statistic. I didn't want to become one of those people that shot myself in the back of the head with a shotgun."[5]

It seemed that Oliver had another nugget of startling information that she did not tell any authorities, and only revealed it to researchers when she was "discovered" in the early 1970s. According to Oliver, several weeks prior to the assassination while on break from the Colony Club she, as was often the case, visited the Carousel Club to watch the strippers' show there. A stripper acquaintance, Janet Adams Conforto, known professionally as "Jada," was sitting at a table with Jack Ruby and another man. Beverly sat down with them to have a drink and Jack introduced Beverly to his friend as "Lee Oswald of the CIA." Following the televised shooting of Oswald by Ruby at the police department basement on November 24, Beverly suddenly realized this was the same man to whom Ruby had introduced her.[6]  Oliver also later claimed that Oswald was a frequent visitor to Ruby's club as was New Orleans figure David Ferrie, who would later be linked to the Kennedy case by New Orleans D.A. Jim Garrison during his 1967 investigation.  Oliver claimed Ferrie, a weird character who would later die under mysterious conditions during the early stage of Garrison's investigation, was such a frequent visitor in 1962 and 1963 to Ruby's Carousel Club, that she mistook him for the club's assistant manager.  According to Oliver, Ruby was engaged in all types of underworld activity. "Jack was a very precious friend of mine. I probably knew him as well as anyone on the face of this earth."[7]

Oliver married George McGann not long after the assassination. McGann was a well known north Texas organized crime figure described by her and others as a gangland killer.  In September 1970 McGann was himself gunned down in a mob hit in Big Spring, Texas.[8]

Following her husband's death, Beverly had a conversion of sorts. In the summer of 1971 researcher Mary Farrell, who got to know Oliver at that time, wrote a co-researcher that, "She became involved with a very bad element to the chagrin of her 'Preacher' father and all her relatives. I think now she thinks she may be killed and she wants to do all this 'testifying' and confessing to her bad past and her now changed life in order that if she is killed, her people will be able to say, 'She died in the hands of the Lord,' etc. . . ,  At present she is singing religious songs at revival meetings, but the quote 'bad element' are constantly letting her know that they are keeping their eyes on her."[9]

It was during this time following the death of her husband that Beverly revealed her story about the film and the meeting of Oswald at Ruby's club. She also revealed to researchers that in 1968 she and her husband had met and had a two-hour conversation with presidential candidate Richard M. Nixon in a Miami hotel![10]

Her story was indeed remarkable, but little solid substantiation of it could be made. No clear photo exists of the facial features of the "Babushka Lady," though one can tell she was dark-haired and not of a frail build.

Beverly initially could not pick herself out in photos which showed the woman and others around the Plaza infield area on November 22, and she could not exactly remember when she changed her hair color to its platinum blonde color, though it could well have been after November 22, 1963.[11] By the late 1980s she spoke of wearing a wig on that Friday in 1963 and of having on under her all-weather coat a green and white polka-dot silk dress. Shaw, Farrell, Penn Jones, and other Dallas area researchers eventually were won over to Beverly's story, though they appeared reluctant at first. Beverly never was able to show any conclusive evidence of her presence at Dealey Plaza on November 22, and as new or contrary evidence has been presented to her, her memory is refined and the story is readjusted. Her features are dissimilar to those displayed in one poor profile view of the post-assassination "Babushka Lady." Oliver now claims this person generally identified as the "Babushka Lady" is not her.[12]

A most obvious flaw in Oliver's original recounting of being in Dealey Plaza was her statement that she had taken her film of the assassination using a new super 8 Yashica movie camera. The super 8 movie film stock included a larger projected frame area on the film strip due to the change in location and the smaller size sprocket holes. This improvement upon the standard 8mm film stock was not in distribution in 1963 and as a matter of fact, the first super 8mm camera was not available to the U.S. market until November 1965! Oliver now contends that she was mixed up about the camera and that it was an 8mm foreign-made experimental model.[13]

Beverly's basic story seemed to become more set and sure as time passed. By 1988 when interviewed for a British documentary, her story was powerful, though some of the more fantastic aspects of it, including the Ferrie connection, Oswald's being introduced as "of the CIA," and the Nixon meeting, were not included. She states in her interview concerning the missing film, "And there would probably be a lot of unanswered questions answered if my film could be found." In 1990 the son of former Dallas Police Officer Roscoe White made a startling but unsubstantiated announcement that his father had participated in the assassination as a shooter. In a subsequent interview, Oliver then revealed of seeing White in uniform walking away from the knoll area after the shooting.[14]

During the House Select Committee on Assassinations investigation in 1977, Beverly's Ruby-Oswald link was touted as possibly new and important evidence. Meticulous California researcher Paul L. Hoch wrote to several Committee members pointing out some of the fantastic claims of Beverly, ". . . which give her claim very low inherent credibility." Though admitting he was not privy to information which the Committee might have, he wanted them to know these stories had been in circulation for quite some time.[15]

Nothing concerning the film or Beverly Oliver was included in the published House Select Committee report. Though some ambiguity arose over whether or not this mystery film had in fact surfaced, Select Committee Chief Counsel Robert Blakey was quoted in a *Dallas Times Herald* story in 1979 concerning questions as to this film's existence by stating that, ". . . There is no higher official than me on the staff of the Committee and I know nothing about the film."[16]

For a good portion of the 1970s into the 1980s Beverly and her new husband, Charles Massagee, traveled on the Christian evangelical circuit. Massagee, a preacher since age 18, traveled with his gospel singer wife in a mobile home 40 weeks of the year conducting revivals primarily at Southern Baptist churches. Never a shrinking violet, Oliver by the late 1980s was in an active stride. Following her appearance in the British documentary in 1988, her story was picked up by motion picture director Oliver Stone and included in a small but significant part of the conspiracy proof within the highly touted film *JFK*. An appearance on the *Geraldo* television show in March 1992 was followed by further appearances and an active presence at Dallas assassination conferences in 1992 and 1993. As of 1993 she was co-writing a book of her own. And well she should, as this 1963 master of disguise had seen it all. An eyewitness and photographer of the assassination, she had known all the principals except for the presidential limousine occupants. Her personal meetings could link Lee Oswald, David Ferry, Roscoe White, and Jack Ruby to what seemed a "dream team" of conspirators. This one person and her film, if located, seems to be the Rosetta Stone of the assassination conspiracy.

If we find it too incredible to believe Beverly Oliver's veracity, then the mystery of the "Babushka Lady" continues as one of the most intriguing aspects of the assassination. Was this woman actually filming, did the film survive, or did some mechanical or human error intervene? Why did she not come forward to tell her story? All these questions, which beg either fantastic or mundane interpretation, still remain unanswered.

## CHAPTER NOTES

1.      FBI Memorandum by S. A. Milton L. Newsom, 11/25/63.
2.      Letter, Bernard Fensterwald, Jr. to Richard Sprague, 7/9/1971, from Georgetown University Library, Sprague Collection, file 5, #138; J. Gray Shaw, *Cover-Up*, p. 51.
3.      Letter, Mary Ferrell to Richard Sprague, 7/22/1971, from Georgetown University Library, Sprague Collection, file 11; Penn Jones, *Forgive My Grief IV*, p. 155; Jim Marrs, *Crossfire*, p. 36; Talk by Oliver at Dallas ASK Conference, 10/23/1992.
4.      British Broadcasting Corporation, Central TV, *The Men Who Killed Kennedy*, part 3, 1988; Talk by Oliver, ASK Conference, op. cit.
5.      BBC, op. cit.; Marrs, op. cit., p. 36; *Geraldo*, 3/30/1992; Mark A. Oakes, *Eyewitness Video Tape: Real JFK Facts*, Beverly Oliver interview; Trask conversation with Beverly Oliver, 10/22/1992.
6.      Marrs, op. cit., p. 37; BBC, op. cit., part 2.
7.      Shaw, op. cit., p. 56: Jones, op. cit., p. 155; Talk by Oliver, ASK Conference, op. cit.
8.      Christopher Scally, "So Near . . . And Yet So Far," unpublished manuscript, 1980, p. 81; Jones, op. cit., p. 100; Seth Kantor, *Who Was Jack Ruby?*, p. 207-208; Oakes, op. cit.
9.      Letter, Ferrell, op. cit.
10.     Shaw, op. cit., p. 54; Jones, op. cit., p. 155.
11.     Letter, J. Gary Shaw to Richard Sprague, 10/27/1971, p. 1-2, from Georgetown University Library, Sprague Collection, folder 4; Oakes, op. cit.
12.     Beverly Oliver, "Beverly Oliver Responds: An Open Letter to the Research Community," *The Third Decade*, 7/1993, p. 11.
13.     Oakes, op. cit.; "Oliver Responds," op. cit., p. 11; Comments by John Storch at Dealey Plaza, 11/21/1993.
14.     BBC, op. cit., part 3; Oakes, op. cit.
15.     Letters, Paul L. Hoch to Rep. Christopher J. Dodd, 4/3/1977; to Rep. Richardson Preyer, 4/8/1977; to Rep. Louis Stokes, 4/25/1977; and to Rep. Yvonne B. Burke, 4/25/1977.
16.     Gary Mack, *Continuing Inquiry*, v. 4, no. 6, 1/22/1980, p. 14.

# Postscript

Several stories and fragments of information still circulate regarding other possible pictures relating to the assassination which were either ruined or have never been located. The most familiar of this genre is the film which a woman appears to have been taking on the south side of Elm Street at the time of the assassination. As discussed in the previous chapter, the possible film taken by the "Babushka Lady," if it indeed does now exist, would be one of the most important documentary pieces of evidence. Also as noted elsewhere, various surviving pictures and films taken at the time in Dealey Plaza show certain as yet unidentified people among the crowd who are seen carrying and in some cases pointing cameras. It will probably be the case that well into the 21st century a previously unknown Dealey Plaza photo will occasionally surface. There are a variety of reasons why some people would not necessarily want to make it known that they have such images. Fear of the unknown, a desire for privacy, and an incomprehension that such photos might be of historical interest could motivate some people not to have stepped forward with such potentially important primary source material. Such photographic items are undoubtedly still out there, awaiting discovery.

There are also cases of photos known to have been taken, but which didn't survive. *Dallas Morning News* reporter Hugh Aynesworth wrote of newspaper employee Sally Holt who had taken a photo of the President's limousine at the time it was making its turn onto Elm Street and including the School Book Depository in the background. Once it was realized shots had originated from that building, Holt rushed back to the *News*, and in her haste to unload the film from the camera, inadvertently exposed the roll to light.[1]

According to Jack Ruby's sister, Eva Grant, Dallas lawyer Tom Howard, who was one of Ruby's original defense team, was supposed to have had in his possession a photo showing the President at the time of his being assassinated. Probably only a rumor, no confirmation was ever made of this. Howard died in 1965.[2] So too, within the records of the FBI there is a listing of a North Texas State University Student, Gary Field, among a list of people who took assassination-related photos. Attempts to identify and locate him have proved fruitless.[3]

There are no known pictures of the President's vehicle arriving at Parkland Hospital or of interior photos of the hospital's emergency area during the President's being there. Representative Henry B. Gonzalez was rumored to have had a camera with him in the motorcade and to have taken photos at the hospital, which photos no longer exist. Researcher Todd Wayne Vaughan was able to get a definitive statement from the congressman in the 1990s. Gonzalez had three cameras with him while he accompanied the presidential tour of Texas. One of these cameras, a small one, was in his possession during the motorcade. Following the shooting Gonzalez arrived at the hospital in one of the trailing motorcade dignitary cars. He went into the hospital and while there took, ". . . general shots and not closeups or detailed in any way. I took the pictures after the President's death, and the photographs would not have shown anything other than a body with a sheet draped over it." Unfortunately, shortly thereafter Gonzalez's cameras, with unprocessed film still in them, were stolen from his car in San Antonio. "I never did see the small camera or its film again."[4]

Years after the assassination, motorcade cycle officer J. W. Courson recalled an incident at Parkland Hospital shortly after he had arrived with the presidential party. "A young boy came up from somewhere with a small, cheap-looking box camera. The limousine door was open and the kid stepped up and snapped a picture of that mess on the floor. An agent reached over and took the camera, peeled it and told him, 'That's all the pictures for today.'"[5]

The potential of finding previously undiscovered photographic sources is exciting and one can certainly bemoan the loss of pictures ruined or stolen. Yet there is a real potential that those original primary source artifacts which do survive, the original negatives, transparencies, and films themselves, are in danger of being lost to history. Unless they are handled properly, stored securely, and preserved in an environment where they can be protected from the ravages of time, neglect, and decomposition, they will not survive. Almost from the moment a photograph is created, a process of chemical self-destruction begins which, unless retarded, can make negatives and prints useless within several generations. By nature photographic images are ephemeral items designed for short-term enjoyment rather than long-term study. It has only been in the last several decades that historical photography has even been accepted as a legitimate and important tool of historical research. Most of the picture takers in Dealey Plaza on November 22, 1963, had no thoughts of preservation. Rather, the photographs and films were created as a souvenir of a procession in which the President of the United States was participating. The motion picture and still camera photo-journalists present were also thinking not of the historical record, but of the concerns of their producers and editors. They wanted to get images that could be quickly communicated to a consumer public through television or the newspaper, a process which would begin afresh the next day as new events occurred and were covered.

Today the original Mary Moorman Polaroid prints taken 30 years earlier have faded and are devoid of much of their original image. Original color film from 1963 has begun to shift in tones. With the exception of those materials stored in the humidity-controlled cold storage facilities of the Kennedy and Johnson Presidential Libraries and within the collections of the National Archives, most of the accumulation of pictures and films made of the assassination-related events remain in private hands or are still being used by private agencies. If it had not been for some of the early researchers of these photographic materials, most notably Richard E. Sprague, the presence of some material would have been all but unknown.

Large numbers of negatives and original prints are now misfiled or missing from among the collections of the various newspapers and photo agencies. Most of this is undoubtedly the result of unknowing carelessness or pilfering by others. One of the most serious, though unsubstantiated, cases of pilfering is the possible abuse by a well-known photographic researcher. Several critics and staff of the House Select Committee on Assassinations contend that while this man served as a photographic consultant, he copied for personal use all the assassination-related photographic materials that came into the Committee. Beyond that possibly unethical practice, however, is the accusation by some that the man, instead of keeping the copies of the films and photos he made, retained some of the originals and returned copies. If true, these actions are not only reprehensible and probably criminal, but also a horrendous affront to the historical record.[6]

It behooves the archival repositories not only to passively accept, but to actively solicit those photographic materials still in private hands, and to make arrangements with the various commercial photo agencies which still possess original negatives and/or prints to make prints or copy negatives and then to deposit the originals in an environment conducive to their long-term survival. Though they did not know it would be the case at the time, those photographers and camera people who in photographically covering a presidential visit to Dallas, incidentally recorded one of the most significant historical events of the 20th century. The importance of their documentation of that event transcends monetary or personal considerations. These images must be preserved as much as any images of the past or of any governmental records. We owe it to history.

## CHAPTER NOTES

1.      Hugh Aynesworth, "Assassination in Dallas," *D Magazine*, 11/1983.
2.      *Hearings Before the President's Commission on the Assassination of President Kennedy*, v. 14, p.479-480.
3.      Airtel, To: Director, From: SAC Dallas, "Individuals known to have taken photographs or films of the presidential motorcade," file #62-109060-2020, 12/19/1963; Letter, Admissions Office, North Texas State University to Trask, 2/27/1985.
4.      Letter, Rep. Henry B. Gonzalez to Todd Wayne Vaughan, 6/8/1992 & 6/20/1992.
5.      James C. Bowles, "The Kennedy Assassination Tapes," "Office 'F.'"
6.      Harrison Edward Livingstone, *Killing the Truth*, p. 420-421, 435-436.

# Appendix

## PRESIDENTIAL MOTORCADE

The following is a brief listing of the vehicular make-up of the motorcade procession as actually constituted on November 22, 1963. This information is taken from the author's research as well as from *Presidential Motorcade Schematic Listing* (© 1993) by Todd Wayne Vaughan.

| | |
|---|---|
| **Advance Car** | Dallas Police Dept. sedan driven by Captain of Traffic Division P.W. Lawrence 1/2 mile in front of motorcade. |
| **Pilot Car** | DPD white Ford sedan driven by Deputy Chief G.L. Lumpkin with two DPD detectives, a U.S. Army officer, and White House advance man. |
| **Advance Motorcycles** | Three DPD two-wheel motorcycles under the command of Sgt. S.Q. Bellah. |
| **Lead Motorcycles** | Five DPD two-wheel motorcycles under the command of Sgt. S. Ellis. |
| **Lead Car** | DPD white Ford sedan driven by DPD Chief J.E. Curry with SAIC F. Sorrels, SA W. Lawson, and Sheriff J.E. "Bill" Decker. |
| **Presidential Lincoln** | SA W. Greer & ASAIC R. Kellerman, Gov. & Mrs. Connally, President & Mrs. Kennedy. |
| **Escort Motorcycles** | Four DPD two-wheel motorcycles ridden by B.J. Martin, B.W. Hargis, J.M. Chaney & D.L. Jackson. |
| **S.S. Follow-Up Car** | Black Cadillac convertible with eight Secret Service agents and presidential aides K. O'Donnell and D. Powers. |
| **Vice-Presidential Car** | Steel gray Lincoln convertible (Lic.# P2 6524) carrying Vice-President & Mrs. Johnson, Sen. R. Yarborough, ASAIC R. Youngblood, and driver. |
| **V.P. S.S. Follow-Up Car** | Yellow Ford Mercury sedan carrying vice-presidential aide C. Carter, three Secret Service agents, and driver. |
| **Dignitary Car 1** | White Ford Mercury convertible carrying Cong. R. Roberts, Mayor & Mrs. E. Cabell, and driver. |
| **Press Pool Car** | Blue-gray Chevrolet sedan telephone car carrying representatives of UPI, AP, ABC, *Dallas Morning News,* and Assistant Press Sec. M. Kilduff. |
| **Camera Car 1** | Yellow Chevrolet Impala convertible carrying three cameramen, two technicians, and driver. |
| **Camera Car 2** | Silver Chevrolet Impala convertible carrying five photographers & driver. |
| **Motorcycles** | Two DPD two-wheel motorcycles ridden by H.B. McLain & M.L. Baker. |
| **Camera Car 3** | Gray Chevrolet Impala convertible carrying three local cameramen, two local photographers, and driver. |
| **Dignitary Car 2** | White Ford Mercury convertible carrying presidential aide L. O'Brien, three congressmen, and driver. |
| **Dignitary Car 3** | White Ford Mercury convertible carrying five congressmen and driver. |
| **Dignitary Car 4** | Gray Lincoln sedan carrying a state senator, three congressmen and driver. |
| **Staff Car** | Ford Mercury station wagon carrying a Governor's aide and President's Military and Air Force aides. |

| | |
|---|---|
| **Motorcycles** | Two DPD two-wheel motorcycles ridden by J.W. Courson & C.A. Haygood. |
| **Bus 1** | Continental Trailways White House Press bus. |
| **Local Press Car** | Chevrolet sedan with four Dallas Morning News reporters. |
| **Bus 2** | Continental Trailways White House Press bus. |
| **Motorcycles** | Two DPD two-wheel motorcycles ridden by R. Smart & R. Dale. |
| **Extra Car 1** | Chevrolet sedan. |
| **Western Union Car** | Black Ford sedan with two representatives of Western Union. |
| **Signal Corps Car** | White Chevrolet Impala sedan carrying Signal Corps officer A. Bales & Army "bagman" I. Gearhart. |
| **Extra Car 2** | White top, dark body Chevrolet Impala sedan. |
| **Bus 3** | Continental Trailways Staff and Official Party bus. |
| **Police Car** | Black & White Ford sedan DPD Accident Prevention Bureau car. |
| **Motorcycle** | Solo DPD 3-wheel motorcycle. |

~

The following are descriptions of film sequences taken by several amateurs at the time of the assassination.

### ROBERT HUGHES FILM SEQUENCE

| No. of frames | Scene |
|---|---|
| | [Hughes standing in street near the S.W. corner of Main & Houston Streets] |
| 44 | View of top floors of old Dallas County Courts Building. |
| 91 | View looking E. up Main Street tilting in the air with the skeletal frame of a tall building under construction visible in the distance, as well as the Texas Bank sign; tilt down to street and cop with white hat; pan left to N.E. corner of Main & Houston. |
| 42 | View up Main Street, cop on right, black man walking to right across street. |
| 45 | View of a young man wearing glasses and standing next to Hughes with a woman wearing a black scarf behind, man looks into camera, Courts Building in background. |
| 36 | Looking up Main St. as white motorcade lead car comes forward. |
| 267 | Close to same location and view but now of President's car coming down Main out of building shadows; (f 40) shoulder of person on right intrudes into frame; (f 65) pan left following President's car making turn onto Houston St., (f82) cop on left comes into view, he wearing white hat and with hands clasped behind his back; (f 120) motorcycle on Hughes side in view as President's car passes around corner; (f135) spectator takes picture; (f140) second motorcycle into view, cop now on right of frame as camera continues to pan left; (f142) President's follow-up car at frame right; (f232) Vice-President's car at frame right. |
| 88 | Looking N. down Houston St.as President's car continues down street away from camera, T.S.B.D. visible on left of frame up to the 6th floor corner window set and next set of windows on the left; slight pan left, Dig. Car 1 & Telephone Car come into view on right. Final frame in sequence shows 4 sets of TSBD windows on 6th floor visible , President's car has turned left on Elm St. in front of TSBD, cop on extreme left of frame near foreground standing on Houston St. |
| 72 | Same filming location, but having begun filming more towards the right so that Dal-Tex Building is at left of frame. Two, then three convertible camera cars in view; (f18) motorcycle appears at frame right next to Hughes' position and off frame at (f52); (f24) cop wearing glasses at frame right walking to left and disappears at (f52); camera has been slowly pan right; |

(f39) Dig. Car 2 appears at frame right, in Camera Car 2 Stoughton is seen facing buildings on E.; Camera Car 3 occupants are looking backwards towards Main St. as sequence ends.

------ [Assassination]

[Hughes appears to have changed location having moved slightly W. down Main street and training his camera W. towards Elm St.]

195    Blurry frames begin sequence looking towards grassy knoll, pan left to underpass,then right; (f 71) Camera Car 1 & 2 seen moving very slowly, motorcycle cop just getting off cycle on far side of Elm St. while man running for first Camera Car, first car has stopped as the second car overtakes it (ca. f 85) on the left, passes and goes on, followed by first car, and then (f 184) the third Camera Car; as sequence ends man is still running for first car which is now near underpass. Throughout sequence a group (3?) of men are in front of and near Hughes while others are crossing Main St. Others are on the other side of the street, and all are looking towards Elm Street.

93    Camera is now looking right of the last sequence. At first frame 3 wheel cycle appears at frame right traveling W. down Main Street; (f18) man in dark coat runs across street to frame right; (f33) second 3 wheel cycle also travels down Main and disappears frame left (f61); black boy wearing cap runs across street; several other cars are seen; (f73) Bus comes into view to (f93).

142    Hughes' attention and camera now drawn E. to corner of Main & Houston Streets. He shoots crowd of spectators hurrying W. down Main Street, except for one woman who is walking E. towards traffic light and a man (f40) wearing a hat who also walks E. towards corner; (f41) station wagon on frame right begins W. down Main St. and disappears (f75) at left; (f102) panel truck appears and leaves (f136); (f140) man on right runs across street to (f142).

[Hughes now has traveled to parking lot N.W. of grassy knoll]

84    Many people milling around in foreground, automobiles parked behind, and railroad passenger cars in background.

[Hughes at knoll pointing camera E.]

143    Camera pointed at buildings at corner of Houston & Elm Streets and pan right to Dallas Records Building, to Court Building, to N. peristyle and monument, to new Court Building under construction, to Annex Post Office and Elm Street in foreground with vehicles on it and people milling around, then showing Elm Street only and finally pan left back to pergola.

[Hughes back to parking lot scene]

61    Roof of car seen in frame foreground with people and last two parked railroad cars seen.

61    N.E. view of upper 3 floors of TSBD, tilt down slightly, building letters "ORY" seen at W. side, top of building, part of Hertz sign on roof also visible.

[Hughes has moved to Elm Street near front entry of TSBD]

169    Crowd of people seen near front doorway, group of blacks in the street and people walking left to right, Brennan in hardhat on steps.

81    Camera now looking towards the right, TSBD sign on first floor near corner of the building is seen, Dal-Tex Building and fire escape at frame right, people milling around; pan right to Elm St., some people looking up; (f70) holes in frames appear indicating film trailer. 1 frame shows back of man's head on left, and building (possible County Records Building) in background.

Total: 1714 frames of Dealey Plaza sequence. 685 frames prior to assassination. 1029 frames following assassination.

### F.M. BELL FILM SEQUENCE

**No. of frames**                       **Scene**

[Bell on pedestal at S. end of N. peristyle]

71    View easterly down Main Street.

| 248 | View down Main St. of President's car & motorcycle; spectators and police officer at left; pan left (f79) to County buildings; follow President's car on Houston to corner of Elm St. |
| 62 | View towards S.E. corner of TSBD and concrete reflecting pool wall; pan left as President's car passes in front of TSBD; (f38) front tire of President's car at left of wall post; (f56) tree obscures about everything. |
| ------ | [Assassination]<br>[Bell off pedestal and moved around peristyle facing Elm Street] |
| 2 | Dark frames. |
| 6 | 1 blurred frame; 1 frame showing motorcycle; 2 blurred frames pan left; frame of Presidential follow-up car on extreme left, motorcycle at right; blur frames pan left. |
| 86 | Blur frame showing underpass, 3 motorcycles on far side, white lead car entering underpass, pan left also shows Main St. underpass, President's car and other cars go under Elm St. underpass followed by motorcycle which had been on left of President's car; (f56) President's car begins to overtake lead car on left under underpass; (f66) Vice-President's car visible on right; (f79) Vice-President's follow-up car visible on right. |
| 74 | 4 frames blur as camera pans right, last blur reveals woman wearing scarf and standing, other person on ground, (f10) motorcycle visible on left of frame; (f28) standing woman discernible as "Babushka Lady," and man and boy (Brehm) on ground at right; (f33) pan slightly right, see woman in red coat and another (Hill & Moorman), Newman family seen on ground across street, also appears that Sitzman is getting off platform at Zapruder position; (f40) motorcycle cop (Hargis) running at right, pan right, (f65) he goes out of view on left as camera pan right to right end of pergola, see post and 2 figures on ground. |
| 44 | Action picks up looking at Elm St. left of knoll stairs with 4(?) people in foreground, and man on ground near curb (Bothun?); (f7) pan right past stairs; (f12) see cycle on right, continue pan right; (f28) running cop from right (Hargis) returning to cycle while motorcycle cop rides down Elm St. from right; (f34) cycle passes running cop; sequence stops with running cop near center of frame, last frame a blur. |
| 286 | Action picks up near sign to left of stairs (stairs not seen), people running towards Elm St. from infield, light color car on left of frame (Camera Car 1) stopping, motorcycle cop (Haygood) getting off cycle at right; (f7) man rushing for camera car, (f10) past sign; camera pan slightly left; (f28) man jumps into car; (f31) next car (Camera Car 2) seen coming from right as Camera Car 1 begins moving out and leaves (f58) at left; (f63) next car (Camera Car 3) appears at right with man standing in car filming; obscured (f81) on left, camera pan slightly right so stairs are in middle of frame; (f86) another car visible on right, (f112) car leaves view; (f116) sedan car on right; (f140) sedan leaves at left; people going across Elm St. up grassy knoll; camera pan left passed parked cycle; (f200) many stream across street; (f217) pan left to underpass, cars seen going; (f232) see Main St. underpass, pan left; (f254) cars on left traveling up Main St., people in foreground. |
| 80 | View of area near top of knoll stairs, pergola shelter on right of frame, pan left showing people running up stairs.<br>[Bell moves further back from Elm St.] |
| 48 | View taken of same scene looking towards Elm St., people standing, 2 cars; pan right. |
| 83 | Same location; (f29) cop comes from left; (f37)leaves at right, many people, parked cars.<br>[Bell at Postal Annex] |
| 119 | Looking at top of S.W. side of TSBD from a camera location of an upper floor of the Postal Annex Building; (f43) pan right to show whole TSBD, then pan left. |
| 90 | Looking down to traffic corner of Elm & Houston; pan to entrance of TSBD and monument. |
| 168 | Looking down at Houston St.; pan left and tilt up to corner of Elm St.; pan to TSBD, right to Dal-Tex building to Records Building and corner of Main & Houston St. |

Total: 1467 frames of Dealey Plaza sequence. 381 frames prior to assassination. 1086 frames following assassination.

## MARIE MUCHMORE FILM SEQUENCE

| No. of frames | Scene |
|---|---|

[Muchmore is on the W side of Houston at Main]

**60** Overexposed frames at corner of Houston and Main, (f11) color begins to emerge; people are at the corner, but not yet a crowd, traffic in street; (f43) station wagon begins to cross from right, traffic light facing camera is red.

**39** Same location, light now green.

**55** Camera has panned to right showing Court House and pickup truck, which is not yet moving; (f30) man begins to cross street from right.

**87** Time has passed, crowd now on corner, pedestrian walkway seen on Houston St., sequence shows 3 cycles in wedge formation turn onto Houston with two others behind coming up to make turn.

**185** President's car begins to make turn; (f44) man moves across camera frame at right and is gone by (f50); (f110) President's car directly in front of camera as camera pans left, Records Building in background; (f133) one cycle and then at (f137) another cycle appear in foreground; (f156) elbow of man is seen at left, camera pans left; man is taking picture (f165); he is out of view at (f179); follow-up car also in view in part of this sequence reappears at (f183) as camera shifts left.

**99** After a brief pause in filming, the follow-up car is seen having continued a few feet forward; (f55) camera no longer has a clear view of President's car and pans right picking up Vice-President's car; (f60) passengers are clearly seen; camera pans left (f76); camera again can see President's car and follow-up car in same view as Vice-President's car; (f85-87) are blurry frames; (f88) picks up Vice-President's follow-up car with its rear driver side door ajar; camera begins tilting to the right at (f88) approximately 30 degrees.

[Muchmore in new position at the peristyle looking over towards Elm St., where she records the last few seconds of the assassination scene]

**66** First frame is blurred, in second frame Mrs. Kennedy is seen on the extreme right, "Babushka Lady" on left with the President's car visible to the rear wheel; film is extremely jiggly; (f12) shows full vehicle,(f18) shows red coat of Jean Hill on left; at (f24) a motorcycle is at right, (f22) first frame showing men on stairs at north side of Elm St.; (f26) see Moorman with camera; splice at (f41) and (f43) with middle section missing; head shot at (f42-43); SS Agent Hill can be seen beginning at (f41), at (f45) he is off follow-up car, seems to reach President's car (f56); (f49) man on steps in red shirt begins to react to shot.

Total: 591 frames of Dealey Plaza sequence. 525 frames prior to assassination. 66 frames during assassination.

## ORVILLE NIX FILM SEQUENCE

| No. of frames | Scene |
|---|---|

[Nix near SW corner of Houston and Main Sts. with camera pointed towards Records Building]

**114** President's car has already passed, follow up car with SA Hill just into view, at right man's shoulder obscures lower right frame; and out of way (f20); Kennedy disappears (f21) at left, camera does not pan to follow; motorcycle cop on opposite outboard side appears at right (f40); Vice-President car seen (f69) at right, Yarborough visible (f81) and then Johnson (f86), camera has begun to pan slightly right; person on left blacks out more and more of frame up to 1/3 of area.

[Nix has moved 20 feet W of Houston corner and points camera NW towards Elm St. recording part of the assassination sequence]

122 Frame tilted slightly to right and looking towards grassy knoll; (f1) shows about half of the President's car with spectator Mrs. Newman on extreme right, a girl is running with back to Nix towards President's car, she stops (f29) dead in her tracks and thereafter leans back towards right in recoil motion; so called car with "shooter" visible behind the knoll in first 77 frames; impact to President's head at (f27); Bothun glimpsed (f35) at left, SA Hill seen (f37) running towards car; (58) outboard motorcycle closest to camera overtakes second cycle, which has stopped; Mrs. Kennedy begins rising from seat (f50), man in red shirt at knoll stairs first seen (f61); Altgens seen (f73) in picture-taking stance, Summers on ground (f65-66) clearly seen by (f83); SA Hill's feet on car (f88), light post between car and Nix first visible (f73) on left, disappears (f102), group of three spectators seen in infield (f122) as President's car speeds left.

[Nix has moved slightly further W on Main St. and into the street itself]

147 4 blurred frames of road; tilts (f12) up from road to people crossing street; (f17) pergola area behind Elm seen; Cancellare seen taking picture (f21), disappears from view (f55), and seen running to left (f100-128), car seen on road near left frame (f22), and Atkins (f58) running in street; panning left to see (f62) Summers on ground, at (f94) car passes by him, glimpse (f120 a man standing and filming in a second vehicle, last two frames are blurred.

Total: 383 frames of Dealey Plaza sequence. 114 frames prior to assassination. 122 frames during assassination. 147 frames after assassination.

## CHARLES BRONSON FILM SEQUENCE

| No. of frames | Scene |
|---|---|

[Bronson is standing on a concrete pedestal at the SW corner of Houston & Main Street]

108 First few frames are washed out, at (f7) the view looking towards Houston & Elm with the Plaza obelisk and the E corner of the TSBD behind it is visible; in foreground are several black men looking towards Elm, blinking light seen near corner [sequence taken as ambulance was picking up a man at that corner who suffered some type of seizure]; most of the crowd have their attention diverted to the ambulance, cars are traveling down Elm; at about (f69) the top of the obelisk and most of the upper SE corner windows of the TSBD are in view, though in approx. 101 frames most of the "assassin's window" is in view; clip reveals very little panning.

63 View of motorcade coming down Main Street to Houston, see crowd ringing intersection and in W Main Street roadway, as people move to street several motorcycles begin turn onto Houston.

87 Most of bottom of frame obscured by top of bus stopped on Main St., woman's head also takes up 1/5 of frame on left; view shows President's car and follow up car traveling down Houston in background near the Records Building.

26 Bronson has turned left to film Elm street as President's car is now parallel to Zapruder's position; follow up car close behind, SA Hill off follow up car, Mrs. Kennedy leaning over towards President, reacts (f22) to shot to head, "Umbrella Man's" umbrella still up, tree branches on left foreground obscure upper third of frame sequence.

Total: 284 frames of Dealey Plaza sequence. 108 frames prior to motorcade. 150 frames of motorcade prior to assassination. 26 frames during assassination.

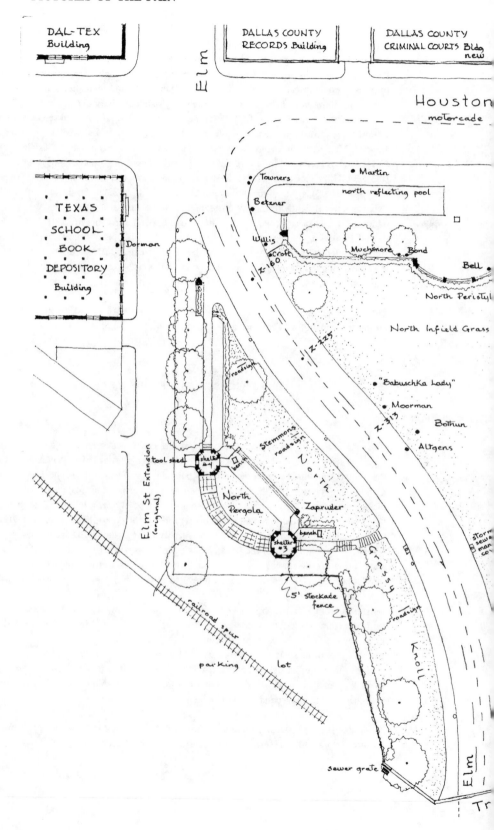

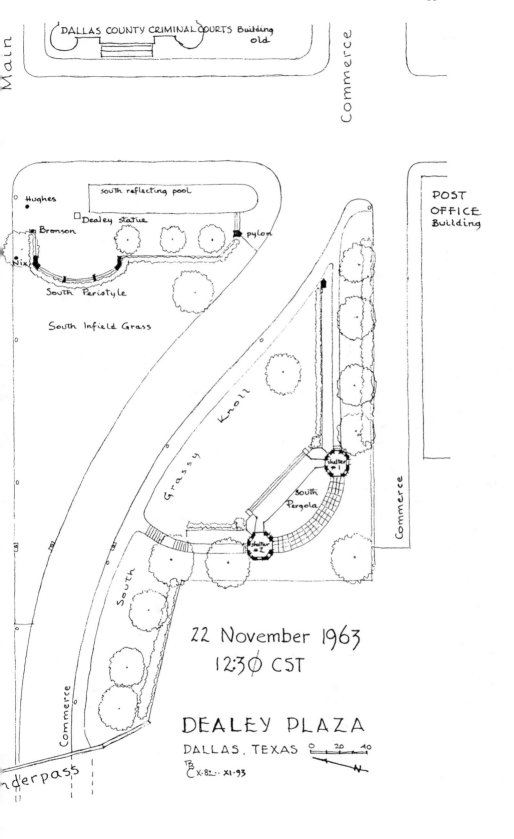

DALLAS COUNTY CRIMINAL COURTS Building
old

Main

Commerce

Commerce

POST
OFFICE
Building

south reflecting pool

Hughes

Dealey statue

Bronson

pylon

Nix

South Peristyle

South Infield Grass

Grassy Knoll

shelter #1

South Pergola

Commerce

shelter #2

South

Commerce

Underpass

22 November 1963
12:30 CST

DEALEY PLAZA

DALLAS, TEXAS    0  20  40

PB
C X·82 ·· X1·93

N

# Selected Bibliography

This selected bibliography lists major books, magazine articles and unpublished manuscripts utilized in the text. For references to interviews conducted by the author, documents obtained through the Freedom of Information Act, information found within correspondence, newspaper articles, audio, video, broadcast and film sources, assassination-related newsletters and journals including *The Third Decade: A Journal of Research on the John F. Kennedy Assassination, Echoes of Conspiracy, The Continuing Inquiry, Coverups!* and other sources, one should consult the Chapter Notes.

Alvarez, Luis W. "A Physicist Examines the Kennedy Assassination Film." *American Journal of Physics*, September 1976.

Alyea, Tom. "The JFK Conspiracy HOAX."

Anson, Robert Sam. *They've Killed the President.* New York: Bantam Books, 1975.

*Appendix To Hearings Before the Select Committee On Assassinations of the U. S. House of Representatives. . . .* Washington, D.C.: U.S Government Printing Office, 1979.

Armstrong, Ken. "The Dallas Puzzle." *Liberty*, July 15, 1964.

Associated Press, Editors. *The Torch Is Passed: The Associated Press Story of the Death of a President.* New York: Associated Press, 1963.

Aynesworth, Hugh. "Assassination in Dallas." *D Magazine*, November 1983.

Barber, Stephan. *Double Decker.* Self-published, 1989.

Belin, David W. *Final Disclosure: The Full Truth About the Assassination of President Kennedy.* New York: Charles Scribner's Sons, 1988.

Bloomgarden, Henry S. *The Gun: A Biography of the Gun that Killed John F. Kennedy.* New York: Grossman Publishers, 1975.

Bowles, James C. "The Kennedy Assassination Tapes: A Rebuttal to the Acoustical Evidence Theory." 1979.

Brennan, Howard L., with J. Edward Cherryholmes. *Eyewitness to History. The Kennedy Assassination: As Seen by Howard Brennan.* Waco, Texas: Texian Press, 1987.

Breo, Dennis L. "JFK's Death, Part II." *The Journal of the American Medical Association*, May 27, 1993.

*The Buying Guide Issue of Consumer Reports.* Mount Vernon, N.Y.: Consumers Union, 1963.

Caldwell, Shirley W. "The Dallas County Administration: 'The Texas School Book Depository.'"

Canfield, Michael, with Alan J. Webermann. *Coup d'Etat in America: The CIA and the Assassination of John F. Kennedy.* New York: Third Press, 1975; San Francisco: Quick American Archives, 1992.

Connally, John. "Why Kennedy Went to Texas." *LIFE*, November 24, 1967.

*Consumer Bulletin Annual.* 1961-62; 1962-63; 1963-64.

Corbett, Francis. "John F.Kennedy Assassination Film Analysis." *Optics in Law Enforcement*, April 1977.

Curry, Jesse. *JFK Assassination File.* Dallas: American Poster & Printing Co., 1969.

Cutler, R. B. *Seventy-Six Seconds In Dealey Plaza: Evidence of Conspiracy.* Beverly Farms, Mass.: Self-published, 1978.

Denson, R. B. *Destiny in Dallas: On-The-Scene Story In Pictures*. Dallas: Denco Corporation, 1964.

Epstein, Edward Jay. *Inquest: The Warren Commission and the Establishment of Truth*. New York: Viking Press, 1966.

Fielding, Raymond. *The American Newsreel, 1911-1967*. Norman, Okla.: University of Oklahoma Press, 1972.

Ford, Gerald R., with John R. Stiles. *Portrait of the Assassin*. New York: Simon & Schuster, 1965.

Garrison, Jim. *On the Trail of the Assassins*. New York: Sheridan Square Press, 1988.

Gates, Gary Paul. *Air Time: The Inside Story of CBS News*. New York: Harper & Row, 1978.

Graves, Florence. "The Mysterious Kennedy Out-Takes." *Washington Journalism Review*, Sept./Oct. 1978.

Groden, Robert J., and Harrison Edward Livingstone. *High Treason. The Assassination of President John F. Kennedy: What Really Happened*. Baltimore: The Conservatory Press, 1989.

Gun, Nerin E. *Red Roses from Texas*. London: Muller, 1964.

*Hearings Before the President's Commission on the Assassination of President Kennedy*. Washington, D.C.: Government Printing Office, 1964.

Heninger, Sim. "Conspiracy Exposed: The J.F.K. Assassination Films." 1984.

Hurt, Henry. *Reasonable Doubt. An Investigation Into the Assassination of John F. Kennedy*. New York: Holt, Rinehart and Winston, 1985.

Jackson, Bob. "Contact." *American Photographer*, December 1981.

*JFK Facts Update. Preview Edition*. Tulsa, Okla.: [1993].

*John Kennedy Assassination Film Analysis*. Lexington, Mass.: Itek Corp., 1976.

Johnson, Bob. "Too Busy For Tears." *The AP World*, August 1972.

Jones, Penn. *Forgive My Grief III*. Midlothian, Texas: The Midlothian Press, 1969.

———. *Forgive My Grief IV*. Midlothian, Texas: The Midlothian Press, 1974.

Kantor, Seth. *Who Was Jack Ruby?* New York: Everest House, 1978.

Kirkwood, James. *American Grotesque: An Account of the Clay Shaw—Jim Garrison Affair in New Orleans*. New York: Simon & Schuster, 1970.

Kunhardt, Philip B., Jr., ed. *Life in Camelot: The Kennedy Years*. Boston: Little, Brown and Co., 1988.

Lane, Mark. *A Citizen's Dissent: Mark Lane Replies*. New York: Holt, Rinehart and Winston, 1966.

———. *Rush to Judgment: A Critique of the Warren Commission's Inquiry into the Murder of President John F. Kennedy, Officer J. D. Tippit, and Lee Harvey Oswald*. New York: Holt, Rinehart and Winston, 1966.

"Last Seconds of the Motorcade." *LIFE*, November 24, 1967.

Lattimer, John K. *Kennedy and Lincoln: Medical and Ballistic Comparisons of Their Assassinations*. New York: Harcourt Brace Jovanovich, 1980.

———. "Additional Data on the Shooting of President Kennedy." *The Journal of the American Medical Association*, March 24/31, 1993.

Leekley, Sheryle and John. *Moments: The Pulitzer Prize Photographs*. New York: Crown, 1978.

Lewis, Richard Warren. *The Scavengers and Critics of the Warren Report: The Endless Paradox*. New York: Dell, 1967.

*LIFE-Itek Kennedy Assassination Film Analysis*. Lexington, Mass.: Itek Corp., 1967.

Lifton, David S. *Best Evidence: Disguise and Deception in the Assassination of John F. Kennedy*. New York: Macmillan, 1980.

Livingstone, Harrison Edward. *Killing the Truth: Deceit and Deception in the JFK Case*. New York: Carroll & Graf, 1993.

"Lone 'Pro' on Scene Where JFK Was Shot." *Editor and Publisher*, December 7, 1963.

Manchester, William. *The Death of a President: November 20-25, 1963*. New York: Harper & Row, 1967.

Marrs, Jim. *Crossfire: The Plot That Killed Kennedy*. New York: Carroll & Graf, 1989.

"A Matter of Reasonable Doubt." *LIFE*, November 25, 1966.

Mayo, John B. *Bulletin from Dallas: The President is Dead*. New York: Exposition Press, 1967.

Melanson, Philip H. *The Politics of Protection: The U.S. Secret Service in the Terrorist Age*. New York: Praeger, 1984.

"Murder of the President," *LIFE*, November 29, 1963.

"New Clues In J.F.K. Assassination Photos." *The Magnet*, July 1967.

*Nix Film Analysis*. Lexington, Mass.: Itek Corp., 1967.

Prendergast, Curtis. *The World of Time Inc.: The Intimate History of a Changing Enterprise*. New York: Atheneum, 1986.

Rather, Dan, with Mickey Herskowitz. *The Camera Never Blinks: Adventures of a TV Journalist*. New York: William Morrow, 1977.

*Report of the President's Commission on the Assassination of President John F. Kennedy*. Washington, D.C.: U.S. Government Printing Office, 1964.

*Report of the Select Committee on Assassinations, U.S. House of Representatives: Findings and Recommendations*. Washington, D.C.: U.S. Government Printing Office, 1979.

Roberts, Charles. *The Truth About the Assassination*. New York: Grosset & Dunlap, 1967.

Savage, Gary. *JFK First Day Evidence*. Monroe, LA: The Shoppe Press, 1993.

Scally, Christopher. "So Near . . . And Yet So Far. The House Select Committee on Assassinations' Investigation Into the Murder of President John F. Kennedy." 1980.

Schonfeld, Maurice W. "The Shadow of a Gunman." *Columbia Journalism Review*, July/August 1975.

Sharrett, Christopher. "Review of Itek Corporation's John Kennedy Assassination Film Analysis." 1971.

Shaw, J. Gary, and Larry R. Harris. *Cover-Up: The Governmental Conspiracy to Conceal the Facts About the Public Execution of John Kennedy*. Cleburne, Texas: Self-published, 1976.

Sidey, Hugh. *John F. Kennedy, President*. New York: Crest Books, 1964.

Slater, Robert. *This . . . Is CBS: A Chronicle of 60 Years*. Englewood Cliffs, N.J.: Prentice Hall, 1988.

Sloan, Bill, with Jean Hill. *JFK: The Last Dissenting Witness*. Gretna, LA: Pelican Publishing Co., 1992.

Smith, Merriman. "The Murder of the Young President." UPI [1964].

Sprague, Richard E. "The American News Media and the Kennedy Assassination." *Computers and Automation*, June and July 1973.

——. "The Assassination of President John F. Kennedy: The Application of Computers to the Photographic Evidence." *Computers and Automation*, May 1970.

——. "The Framing of Lee Harvey Oswald." *Computers and Automation and People*, October 1973.

——. "More Evidence of the Framing of Lee Harvey Oswald." 1982.

——. *The Taking of America 1-2-3*. Self-published, 1976.

——. "Twelve Sets of Important Photographs of the Assassination of President Kennedy." 1980.

Stolley, Richard B. "What Happened Next . . . ." *Esquire*, November 1973.

Stoughton, Cecil, et. al. *The Memories: JFK, 1961-1963*. New York: W. W. Norton, 1973.

Summers, Anthony. *Conspiracy*. New York: McGraw-Hill, 1980.

*There Was a President*. New York: Random House, 1966.

Thompson, Josiah. *Six Seconds in Dallas: A Microstudy of the Kennedy Assassination*. New York: Bernard Geis Associates, 1967; (rev.) Berkeley, 1976.

Towner, Tina. "View from the Corner." *Teen*, June 1968.

Tuchman, Mitch. "Kennedy Death Films." *Take One*, May 1978.

United Press International and *American Heritage* magazine. *Four Days, The Historical Record of the Death of President Kennedy*. New York: American Heritage Publishing Company, 1964.

Van Der Karr, Richard K. "Crisis in Dallas: An Historical Study of the Activities of Dallas Television Broadcasters During the Period of President Kennedy's Assassination." Master of Arts Thesis, Indiana University, 1965.

——. "How Dallas TV Stations Covered Kennedy Shooting." *Journalism Quarterly*, 1965.

Wainwright, Loudon. *The Great American Magazine: An Inside History of LIFE*. New York: Alfred A. Knopf, 1986.

"The Warren Report." *LIFE*, October 2, 1964.

Weisberg, Harold. *Photographic Whitewash: Suppressed Kennedy Assassination Pictures*. Frederick, Maryland: Self-published, 1967, 1976.

——. *Whitewash: The Report on the Warren Report*. Hyattstown, Maryland: Self-published, 1965.

——. *Whitewash II: The FBI-Secret Service Coverup*. New York: Dell, 1965.

Wensburg, Peter C. *Land's Polaroid: A Company and the Man Who Invented It*. Boston: Houghton Mifflin Company, 1987.

Winchester, James H. "TV's Four Days of History." *Reader's Digest*, April 1964.

Wolbarst, John. *Pictures in a Minute*. Baltimore, Md.: Photographic Book Pub. Co., 1956.

*Year 1964 Encyclopedia News Annual*. New York: Year, Inc., 1963.

Youngblood, Rufus W. *20 Years in the Secret Service: My Life With Five Presidents*. New York: Simon and Schuster, 1973.

An early view amateur photo of the motorcade taken from West Mockingbird Lane.
Camera Car 2 is emerging from the shadow at the lower edge of the photo.

# Photo Credits

The author is extremely grateful to the many individuals and organizations who have graciously allowed photographic and illustrative materials to be reproduced in this book. Whenever possible, the author has attempted to include full-frame images of first or early generation photographs for reproduction. In some instances poor quality prints are used when the visual image itself is important to the text and when no better image was located. Photographs are reproduced without any retouching. The photographic images created during the assassination events ran the gamut from amateur snapshots made with poor quality film through cheap cameras with poor optics to large format negatives made from high quality cameras by professional photojournalists. Thus the reproduction quality within this volume is mixed. Besides recording the visual history of the assassination, this book also reveals much about the state of photography in the early 1960s.

Where possible, all known photographic sources are named and acknowledged. In the case of photos created by news gathering organizations, when the original creator is not named, the author has attempted, through the reconstruction of negative sequences and contact sheets, to identify the photographer within the text. In those cases where a clear identification has been made, the photographer will be included in these credits within parentheses. The author has attempted to locate individual photographers or agencies which created or own rights to these images.

John F. Kennedy Library: [21] (Abbie Rowe), [22] (Rowe), 25, 30-36 (all Cecil Stoughton), 38-39 (Stoughton), 51 (Stoughton), 54 (Stoughton), 305 (Stoughton), 362 (Rowe), 366-367 (Thomas Atkins), 368 (Stoughton), 369 (Atkins), 371 (Atkins), 376 (Atkins), 378 (Atkins), 408 (Atkins); Cecil W. Stoughton: 27, 40, 43, 44; LBJ Library Collection: 46-48 (all Cecil Stoughton), 408 top, [583] 625 (J. Raymond Jones); John Shroeder: [55]; R.B. Cutler: [56] 220; National Archives: 58, 60, 64-67, 70-71, 103-105, 185-186, 190, 204, 207, 235 top, 352, 435, 457, 522 bottom, 526 bottom, 527, 530, 556, [606]; The Author's Collection: [63] 68, 72, 108, 168, 261, 280 bottom, 284, [306] 590; James W. Altgens: 73, 308-310, 311 top, 312, 317; *The Dallas Morning News*: 75(Johnny Flynn), 394 (Clint Grant), 396-397 (Grant), 402 (Grant), 406, 407 (Joe Laird), 409 (Laird), 436 (Tom Dillard), 437 top (Doris Jacoby), 438 (Dillard), 452-453 (Dillard), 455 (Dillard), 458 (Dillard), 541 (Jacoby), 549 (Jack Beers), 550 (Beers) 554 (Beers); WFAA-TV: 78, 521 (Tom Alyea), 522 top (Alyea), 531 (Alyea), 532 (Alyea), 534-535 (Alyea), 539, 478 (Bert Shipp), 479; KRLD-TV: 86; Itek: 124, 125 272 (Hughes), 273; House Select Committee on Assassinations: 134, 136, 173, 174, 196; John K. Lattimer: 143; Todd Wayne Vaughan and James Michael Vaughan, Jr.: 146; Richard O. Bothun: 155, 156, 158; Hugh Betzner, Jr.: 160; *LIFE* Magazine © Time Warner Inc.: 161 (Hugh Betzner, Jr.), 403 (Art Rickerby); Copyright © Jim Murray Film. All Rights Reserved: 163, 178, 428 bottom, 519, 523, [472] 493, 494, 495, 496, 497, 498, 499, 500, 501, 502, 503, 504, 505, 506, 507, 608 top; Copyright © 1964 Phil Willis, re-copyright to year 2039: 169, 170, 171, 175, 176, 177, 179; Wilma I. Bond: 202, 203, 208, 210, 211, 212, 213; Tina Towner: 217; Jim Towner: 218; Robert E. Croft: 223, 224, 225; JFK

A telephoto shot of the motorcade proceeding down Main Street.
Agent Hill squats on the rear step of the presidential Lincoln.

# Name Index

This index chiefly covers proper names found in the text itself. Generally, chapter notes referring to sources cited will not be included in this index. However, chapter notes which include new information and/or names of photographer witnesses will be included.

**PICTURES OF THE PAIN**

has been published in a sewn and cased limited first edition.

Jacket designed by A. L. Morris

End papers drawn by R. B. Cutler

Book design and layout by Ethel and Richard Trask

Text composed in Dutch 801 by Ethel B. Trask

The printing and binding was executed by Thomson-Shore, Inc., Dexter, Michigan, on 60# white text stock conforming to Permanent Page Standards.

~

Richard B. Trask is an archivist who lives with his wife Ethel and daughter Elizabeth in a circa 1681 house which they have restored in Danvers, Massachusetts. An authority on the Salem Village witchcraft delusion of 1692, Trask served as historical consultant to an American Playhouse docudrama on the subject. He is curator of the historic 30-acre Rebecca Nurse Homestead. Author of several books and dozens of magazine articles, Trask lectures extensively, has taught college courses on history and architecture and has appeared on numerous television and radio programs and documentaries. His research into the Kennedy assassination began at age 16.

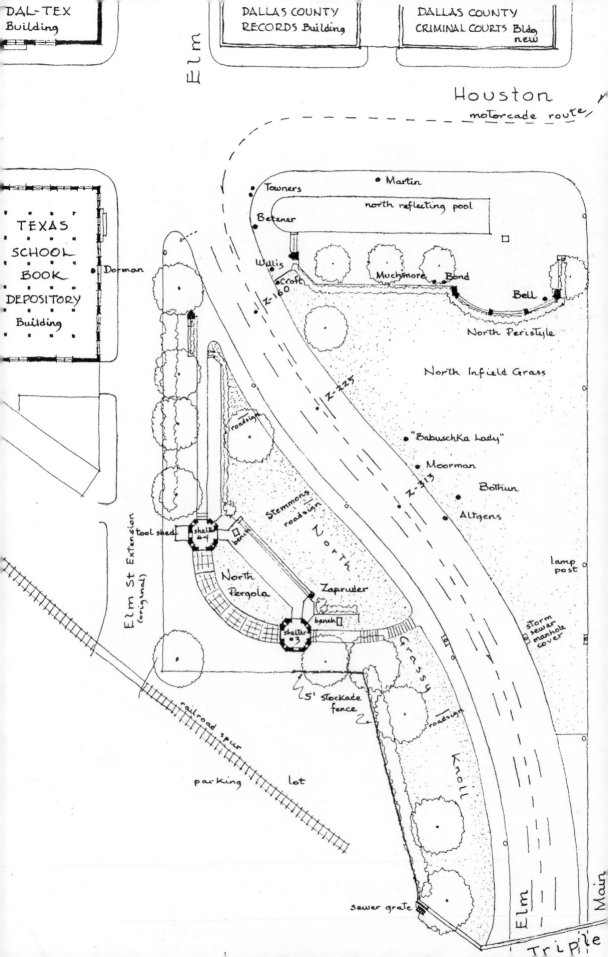